BUSINESS ECONOMICS
Principles and Cases

BUSINESS ECONOMICS
Principles and Cases

By MARSHALL R. COLBERG
Professor of Economics and Chairman,
Department of Economics
Florida State University

DASCOMB R. FORBUSH
Associate Professor of Business Economics
School of Business
Northwestern University

GILBERT R. WHITAKER, JR.
Associate Professor of Business Economics
School of Business
Northwestern University

ASSISTED BY THE CONTRIBUTION TO
PREVIOUS EDITIONS OF

WILLIAM C. BRADFORD
Professor of Business Economics and
Associate Dean of Faculties, Northwestern University

THIRD EDITION • 1964
RICHARD D. IRWIN, INC.
HOMEWOOD, ILLINOIS

THIRD EDITION

First Printing, January, 1964

Second Printing, February, 1965

Third Printing, January, 1966

Library of Congress Catalogue Card No. 64–11710

PRINTED IN THE UNITED STATES OF AMERICA

Preface

THIS BOOK combines text and case materials for use in courses where economic analysis is applied to the solution of business problems. These courses may have such titles as Business Economics, Managerial Economics, or Economics of the Firm. They are offered both by Schools of Business Administration and by Departments of Economics. Such courses may serve either as alternatives or as complements to traditional intermediate courses in microeconomic analysis. The cases serve to illuminate the content and applicability of such basic economic concepts as marginality, opportunity cost, and market structure that are developed in this text.

The authors have attempted to write the book for students at the junior or senior levels who have had a course in principles of economics and for first year graduate students in business administration. Some prior training in accounting, finance, and statistics is desirable but not essential to an understanding of this volume. Mathematical formulations, apart from geometrical figures, are not emphasized except where necessary for precision, as in the case of capitalization formulas.

Our emphasis is upon executive decisions that are concerned with the allocation of resources—decisions that can be made more rationally within the framework of economic analysis.

A substantial expansion of coverage over that of the 1957 edition has been effected, and many subjects previously covered have been brought up to date or otherwise improved upon. Capital budgeting is given fuller treatment; some elements of organization theory and administrative design theory are included; antitrust policy and law are described in more detail; principles of plant location are somewhat expanded; and tax law is updated by inclusion of such recent changes as the investment tax credit. A great many new cases are included, although a number of the better ones from the 1957 edition have been retained.

The broad coverage of the text and the diversity of the cases (this edition contains 30 per cent more material than the previous edition) allows considerable flexibility in laying out the course that best meets the needs of a particular situation. The instructor may choose to work entirely with this book and in a term work through all the chapters, probably using about two thirds of the cases. Alternatively, he may choose to omit certain topics and emphasize others or to stress quantitative techniques. The *Instructors Manual* contains additional problem material, suggested outside assignments, and alternative ways of using various cases that should prove helpful in meeting the varied needs of particular schools.

An undertaking of this sort owes much to the work of others. Eugene C. Holshouser has given us permission to use material from his statistical demand study of frozen orange concentrate. Excerpts from a statistical study of cost by Joel Dean have again been included. Charles B. Franklin made valuable suggestions pertaining to the appendix on the theory of games. Professor Melvin L. Greenhut was helpful in connection with the chapter on plant location, while Professor Homer Black sharpened our knowledge of the investment tax credit. The work of Professors Richard M. Cyert and James G. March provided the basis for one of the cases on organizational behavior. Professors Zarko Bilbija and George Macesich were among other academicians who made useful suggestions.

Among the members of the Northwestern University faculty who made contributions, we single out John A. Larson, Myron A. Umbreit, Cecil Gillespie, John B. Watkins, and William Dejon for work on particular cases. Businessmen who have made case contributions in their dual role as graduate students are John Mills, Bernard Forrest, William Gapp, T. F. Mogan, and L. Dean Scane. We wish also to express our thanks to Dean Richard Donham for the encouragement he has given to case development.

Special thanks are due to the many executives and corporations who were cooperative in supplying their experience and time in making this book possible. Grateful acknowledgment should also be made to the publications, trade associations, and government agencies, later cited in footnotes, from which statistical and background materials have been drawn.

We wish also to thank Mrs. Gennelle P. Jordan, Mr. Douglas Windham, Mrs. Janice J. Rowe, Mr. Harry Lavo, Mrs. Gretel K. Murphy, Mrs. Theresa Lein, and Mrs. Lee Kershner for their loyal assistance in moving the manuscript toward final publication.

January, 1964   MARSHALL R. COLBERG
                                             DASCOMB R. FORBUSH
                                             GILBERT R. WHITAKER, JR.

Table of Contents

CHAPTER 1

◆◆◆◆◆◆◆◆◆◆◆◆◆◆◆◆◆◆◆◆◆◆◆◆◆◆◆◆◆

Uncertainty, Risk, and Profit

ECONOMICS is the study of the optimal use of scarce resources to satisfy human wants. It consequently deals with both the extent to which labor and capital are employed and the way in which these factors are allocated among alternative goods and services. Economics is primarily a social science rather than one which has as its purpose the analysis of efficient behavior on the part of the individual business firm. Nevertheless, social economy requires that business enterprises be well located, be alert to the demands of consumers, be of efficient size, be operated efficiently, and be compelled by competition to pass on to buyers the advantages of their efficiency. A good deal of economic analysis is concerned, consequently, with principles of efficient action applicable to the firm. This book will discuss some of these principles and will present business cases the solution of which should be facilitated by the application of the associated analysis. A good businessman need not be an economist, but a knowledge of economics is likely to sharpen his thinking about his own firm's problems and sometimes will aid him in making wise decisions which would not otherwise be obvious. Certain types of business decisions are sufficiently difficult and important to justify use not only of all relevant theoretical analysis but also of expensive empirical investigation.

Only Uncertainty Is Certain

It is often said that nothing is certain except death and taxes. In an important sense, not even these qualifications need be made. The entire institution of life insurance is based on the uncertainty of the date of death of the individual in comparison with the calculability of mortality rates for large numbers of persons within various age groups. Also, the amount and nature of the taxes which will be assessed by governmental bodies are often important uncertainties of life.

If the future could be known with certainty, correct economic decisions could be made by everyone. The worker could know precisely where and how to earn the largest income, the business executive would know in advance the outcome of alternative ventures which he might undertake, and the investor would be fully cognizant of the relative desirability of the various investment opportunities open to him. Decision making would not be difficult, and professional decision makers (business executives) would not be highly paid. Investment in a newly formed uranium mining company would be as safe as investment in a well-established utility company.

In the actual world the existence of uncertainty causes future incomes to be imperfectly predictable. Often, it is possible for the individual to choose between receiving income which is definite in amount according to terms either of a contract or of an unwritten agreement, or receiving income which depends, instead, on the outcome of the economic activity in which he participates. In the first case the individual can be fairly sure as to what his income will be in the near future, while in the second case the degree of predictability is lower. A fisherman, for example, may work for a regular daily wage or, alternatively, may share in the proceeds of the sale of the catch. The latter arrangement is very common because of the unusually high degree of uncertainty regarding the production function (relation of output to input) in the fishing industry. Similarly, a manager may be employed at a specific salary rate by a chain grocery store or, alternatively, may operate his own store where the return for his labor and capital investment depend on the success of the operation. Similarly, a person wanting to invest funds in a particular corporation may become a bondholder, a preferred stockholder, or a common stockholder. In the first case, he would be a creditor of the firm, receiving interest in a fixed annual amount. His income would not depend on the success of the firm except that a sufficiently unprofitable situation might endanger both his receipt of interest and the safety of his principal. As a preferred stockholder the degree of uncertainty of his return would be somewhat lower, while as a common stockholder the investor faces the greatest degree of uncertainty, both as to return and as to safety of principal.[1]

Hired and Self-Employed Resources

Labor contracted at a specific wage or salary rate, a rented building or machine, and funds borrowed from bondholders or banks may con-

---

[1] Over a long period of time, however, common stock may offer the investor more nearly a guarantee of stability or gain in *real* income and real value of principal. This is traceable primarily to the propensity of governments to follow inflationary monetary and fiscal policies.

veniently be considered to be examples of "hired" resources from the point of view of the firm. Labor secured on an income-sharing basis, including that contributed by owners of the enterprise and capital contributed by stockholders, partners, or individual proprietors may be termed "unhired" or "self-employed" resources or factors of production. Persons who dislike uncertainty are likely to take steps to receive their income primarily as a contractual return, while those with less aversion to uncertainty are likely to prefer to receive a larger proportion of their income on a noncontractual basis.

In a competitive economic system the payments to hired factors of production are based on the estimated marginal revenue productivity of these resources—that is, on the additional revenue which firms expect to secure from the sale of the additional output attributable to a unit of a resource, other productive inputs remaining unchanged in amount. Since contractual payments must be arranged in advance, and since firms compete with one another in hiring factors of production, the payments to hired resources reflect businessmen's anticipations as to the worth of these resources. In business, as elsewhere in life, expected and realized situations frequently differ. If a favorable turn of events— a sudden increase in people's willingness to spend their money for goods and services, for example—causes firms' incomes to exceed expectations, increased residuals are left over after all costs have been deducted from gross income. An unfavorable turn of events, or overoptimism on the part of businessmen in bidding up the prices of factors of production, will reduce the size of the residuals which remain to firms after paying for all hired inputs. The "self-employed" or "unhired" resources receive their incomes out of these amounts which remain after hired resources are paid off at contractual rates.

Accounting and Economic Profit

The accountant designates as "profit" or "net income" (before taxes) the amount which is left over out of gross income after all payments to hired factors. The economist points out that further deductions must be made from this amount in order to get a somewhat less arbitrary picture of the success of the firm's operations in any period. The accountant's measurement, while suited to the purpose for which it is made, is greatly affected by the extent to which resources are remunerated on a contractual basis. Other things being equal, the greater the extent to which the needed resources are hired rather than self-employed, the lower will be the net income shown in the accounting records. In order to avoid this arbitrary element, the cost of self-employed resources, evaluated by determining what they could earn if employed on a contractual basis instead, must also be deducted. The alternative earnings of unhired factors are often called "implicit costs." Hence, deduction of implicit as well as explicit costs from gross income gives "economic profit." Deduction of explicit costs alone gives accounting profit.

The above distinction is of great practical importance because of the existence of a heavy federal tax on corporation "profits." Often, it is possible for a firm to raise additional capital funds by selling either bonds or common stock. If it sells bonds, the funds are "hired," and the interest paid is an explicit cost of doing business. If, instead, stocks are sold, the funds are owned, and there is no explicit interest cost which can be deducted in arriving at accounting profit. There is an implicit cost involved in that the funds raised by selling stock could instead have earned some contractual rate in an alternative employment. By selling stock instead of bonds, the corporation subjects itself to a larger corporate income tax. In recent years, many firms have raised additional capital funds by means of bonds rather than stock, in order to secure this tax advantage. In other cases, firms have converted preferred stock into bonds for the same reason.[2]

Accounting profits of corporations in the United States in recent years are shown graphically in Exhibit 1. Federal corporate income taxes have amounted to almost half of aggregate profits over the period covered by the chart. A little less than half of the corporate profits after taxes have been "plowed back" into the companies, chiefly as a means of financing plant expansion. The same data are shown in Exhibit 2. If similar data were compiled for economic profits of corporations, total profits would be lower by the amount of "normal return" on capital owned by stockholders and included in dividends in the chart and table. That is, dividends paid out are really a combination of interest on invested capital and profits earned by corporations. In individual cases (and sometimes in the aggregate) the actual profit share is negative rather than positive.

The distinction between economic and accounting profit is also of importance in either evaluating the worth of an enterprise which is

---

[2]In order not to affect the relative desirability of different types of securities from the corporation's point of view, a corporate income tax could theoretically be levied on economic profit rather than accounting profit. In practice, however, a knotty problem of calculating appropriate alternative contractual rates of return on securities would exist. A simpler alternative would be elimination of interest as a cost in computing net profit for income tax purposes.

for sale or deciding whether an enterprise should be continued. Typically, the individual enterpriser contributes his own labor and some capital to the operation of his firm. This involves an implicit cost, since his labor and capital could, alternatively, earn income elsewhere on a contractual basis. Since no explicit cost is involved, the enterpriser is unlikely to show any cost on his books for the use of his own resources. If the firm is offered for sale, it becomes important for a potential buyer to keep in mind the exclusion of these costs. Since the alternative earn-

Exhibit 1

CORPORATE PROFITS AND THEIR DISPOSITION

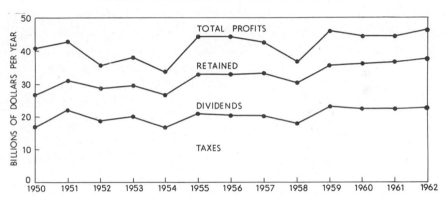

ing power of the buyer's labor may differ from that of the labor of the previous owner, the best appraisal of the desirability of making the purchase may involve the use of the buyer's alternative income-earning possibilities rather than those of the previous operator. Like all decisions of this sort, the decision regarding purchase of a business involves *anticipated* rather than past incomes, and these anticipations are fraught with uncertainty. In the absence of better information, however, anticipations may have to be based on past performance.

In order to decide whether a somewhat marginal enterprise is worth continuing, the businessman may do well to think in terms of an "economist's balance sheet." Such a balance sheet would value individual assets according to their income-earning potential in other uses, that is, according to their present market prices. Historical costs, which provide the basis for the accountant's balance sheet, would not enter into consideration. If the total market value of such individually evaluated assets exceeded their value as a whole to the enterprise, as calculated from future earnings prospects, the indicated decision is to liquidate the business by selling assets separately. The process of discounting anticipated future earnings of the business as a whole in order to find the present value of its net assets (assets minus liabilities) will be discussed in some detail in a later chapter.

Even if the decision is to remain in business, this way of thinking about the "opportunity cost" of retaining assets may lead to useful decisions. For example, the present market value of an asset may be so high that the firm in question should sell the asset and replace it with a cheaper one. This is especially likely to happen with land that is vacant or that supports a well-depreciated building. A periodic check of its value to other possible users might lead a firm to a more rational decision on whether this particular parcel of land should remain in the business.

Exhibit 2

CORPORATION PROFITS, TAXES, AND DIVIDENDS

(In Billions)

Year	Corporation Profits before Taxes	Corporate Tax Liability	Dividend Payments	Undistributed Profits
1950	$40.6	$17.9	$ 9.2	$13.6
1951	42.2	22.4	9.0	10.7
1952	36.7	19.5	9.0	8.3
1953	38.3	20.2	9.2	8.9
1954	34.1	17.2	9.8	7.0
1955	44.9	21.8	11.2	11.8
1956	44.7	21.2	12.1	11.3
1957	43.2	20.9	12.5	9.7
1958	37.4	18.6	12.4	6.4
1959	47.7	23.2	13.7	10.8
1960	44.3	22.3	14.5	7.5
1961	43.8	22.0	15.3	6.5
1962	46.8	22.2	16.6	8.0

Source: Council of Economic Advisers, *Economic Indicators*, December, 1962 (Washington, D.C.: U.S. Government Printing Office, 1962), p. 7, and U.S. Department of Commerce, *Survey of Current Business*, July, 1963.

Uncertainty Theory of Profit

If the future were always perfectly predictable, the income received by a factor of production would be the same whether it were remunerated on a contractual or on a residual basis. Persons paid on the former basis would not be willing to accept less than they could get as residual claimants; and similarly, those receiving residual incomes would not accept less than they could earn at contractual rates. In the actual, uncertain world, there is usually a difference between the income which resources earn on a contractual and self-employed basis—that is, economic profits (positive or negative) usually exist. In a year of especially good business, for example, economic profits generally are likely to be positive. Most stockholders will receive better rates of return than bondholders, while persons in business for themselves may do better, on the average, than if they had worked for someone else. In a year of depressed business activity the situation is likely to be just the opposite—that is, economic profits in most lines are apt to be negative.

Since there would be no economic profits in a perfectly predictable world, uncertainty is the basic reason for the existence of profits in the actual world. It is necessary, however, to distinguish between true uncertainties and those more manageable uncertainties which can be insured against. Examples of the latter are uncertainty as to the duration of life, uncertainty as to whether a particular house will burn, and uncertainty as to whether a car or truck will be involved in an accident. If statistical probabilities have been worked out with sufficient accuracy to make it possible for a company to sell insurance against occurrences of a particular contingency, a definite contractual payment by the firm to the insurance company will guard against financial loss on this account. Professor Frank Knight has termed such insurable uncertainties "risks," in order to distinguish them from the uninsurable uncertainties which must be faced by those who receive their incomes on a noncontractual basis. The two types of uncertainties can also be usefully distinguished as "transformable" and "nontransformable," the former being those which can be avoided at a definite cost by means of insurance or other types of hedging (to be described later in this chapter), and the latter being those which cannot be side-stepped by the businessman by means of transformation into a definite cost.[3] Shifts in tastes, inventions, discoveries of new natural resources, and interruptions in the state of peace or war are changes which can neither be anticipated nor be insured against. They are examples of the true uncertainties which cause economic profits—positive and negative—to exist.

Profits and Liquidity

Professor Boulding frames the uncertainty theory of profit in liquidity terms.[4] He emphasizes that the ownership of goods of any sort—fac-

---

[3]J. F. Weston, "A Generalized Uncertainty Theory of Profit," *American Economic Review,* March, 1950, p. 44, suggests this terminology.

[4]K. E. Boulding, *Economic Analysis* (New York: Harper & Bros., 1948), pp. 429–31.

tories, inventories of finished products, goods in process—involves the sacrifice of liquidity. That is, an alternative on the part of the owner would be the holding of cash instead of goods. Boulding points out that even holding cash involves risk of loss because the general price level may go up, thereby reducing the real value (purchasing power) of a stock of cash. He believes, however, that greater risk is involved in holding any particular good because the good may not only decline in value because of a fall in the general level of prices but it may also decline because of supply-demand conditions peculiar to that commodity.[5] Also, the holding of liquid purchasing power permits the snapping-up of bargains which may become available and quick entry into fields where innovations offer a favorable opportunity. Because of these advantages of liquidity, Professor Boulding has stated that profits can be considered to be the necessary reward to induce firms to hold goods, and he points out that this ownership of goods is indispensable to the existence of enterprise. It should be noted that this theory hinges on uncertainty regarding future prices; consequently, it is logically a part of the broader uncertainty theory of profit.

Innovation Profits

The innovation theory of profits is concerned with the impact of changes which occur with the passage of time. Perhaps the most widely known statement of the theory is that of the late Professor Schumpeter, who attributed economic profits to innovations made by businessmen.[6]

The innovation theory can be described as follows: A firm introduces a new product or a new idea, which results in yielding an existing product at a lower cost; or differentiates its product, which results in a wider acceptance by consumers; or promotes various combinations of these ideas, which gives the firm an advantage over its competitors. As a result, the firm enjoys an economic surplus from this advantage. Eventually, either new firms are attracted to the field by the profits of the successful firm, or competitors produce close substitutes and thus reduce the sales of the innovator. Or competitors may adopt the cost-reducing methods of the innovating firm, causing the latter to lose its temporary advantage. All this requires the passage of time; but when the adjustment has worked itself out, the advantageous position of the

---

[5] It should be noted, however, that the modern tendency of government to follow inflationary monetary and fiscal policies reduces the riskiness of holding goods and increases the chance of loss by holding cash.

[6] Joseph S. Schumpeter, *The Theory of Economic Development* (Cambridge: Harvard University Press, 1934), chap. v.

innovating firm has been lost, and its economic surplus has disappeared. As the number of firms adopting the innovation or producing a sufficiently close substitute increases, the profits of all firms tend to decline.

Such a theory implies the freedom of new firms to enter the field without restriction other than that imposed by time—a lag during which the profits of innovation can be received. So long as such a condition exists and all potential competitors possess complete knowledge of past events in the business world, no firm can enjoy innovation profits indefinitely.

The innovation theory is logically part of the broader uncertainty theory of profit. Innovations in methods and products are one of the great unpredictables which cause positive and negative economic profits to exist. If innovations could be fully foreseen, they would not have this effect. All firms would be ready to introduce a new production method, for example, as soon as it was available, and no special advantages would accrue from the method. Since such prediction is not possible, and since adjustments take time, innovations would occasion profits even if our economic system were highly competitive in all respects.

Monopoly Profits

While "negative profits" or "losses," in the sense of less than normal returns, are about as common as positive profits in fully competitive situations, monopoly is often a source of more persistent profits. Cartel agreements, whereby firms in a particular field set prices above the competitive level, are an important source of profit. Exclusive franchises are common in the utility and transportation fields; and these, of course, confer monopoly power on their owners. While public regulation of privately owned transportation and utility systems does much to prevent franchise holders from securing very large profits, such public regulation often is not sufficiently effective to prevent above-normal returns. Also, monopoly profits are frequently made by governments which sell such commodities as electric power and water in noncompetitive situations, such profits frequently being used as a partial substitute for taxes.

Patents give their holders exclusive monopoly power for a period of time. These powers and the associated profits have been considered to be appropriate as a reward for the creative effort of their holders. It should be noted, however, that patent monopoly is not always profitable. Many patents are never exploited commercially because, while they may be technologically unique, the demand-cost situation is not sufficiently favorable.

Copyrights also confer monopoly power for a limited period of time (28 years, with a right of extension for another 28 years by the author or his widow or children). The law protects not only the authors of books but also artists and composers of music. Under the common law a person is entitled to the exclusive ownership of his property until publication. If he obtains a statutory copyright, he secures the privilege of exclusive right to publish and sell the work and prevent others from doing so. In the case of the author of a drama, his rights are twofold. He is entitled to the profits from sale of the manuscript and also from performance.[7]

Securing a copyright is only a mechanical matter involving compliance with a statute pertaining to the filing of copies with the Copyright Office. Unlike the Patent Bureau, this office does not study other copyrights to see whether there has been literary piracy. It is up to the courts, in the event of litigation, to determine whether infringement of legal rights has occurred.

Product differentiation by such means as trade names, distinctive packaging, and highly publicized differences (real or fictitious) from rival commodities give some degree of monopoly power to a great many firms. This source of monopoly profits is often less dependable than that of a franchise or patent, and heavy advertising may be necessary to maintain the advantage over time. However, the importance of a well-known slogan, picture, or package should not be underestimated.

A particularly advantageous location can also bring monopoly profits to a firm. This is especially likely to be true if the site is owned by the enterprise itself, since otherwise the rental charged by the owner is apt to be so large as to make the location no more favorable than some poorer site which could be rented more cheaply. However, if the enterpriser in question—say, a clothing retailer—owns the store and the land, he could, alternatively, lease this property to another firm and secure a favorable rental income. Monopoly profits due to locational advantages are, consequently, difficult to distinguish from rental income.

Innovation and monopoly theories of profits are somewhat related. Temporary monopoly power often results from an innovation in product, production technique, marketing, location, or advertising. This sort of monopoly power tends to diminish unless further innovations by the firm outpace the efforts of competitors to take advantage of the same profitable new avenues.

---

[7] Milton C. Jacobs, *Outline of Theater Law* (New York, 1949), p. 2.

The Transforming of Uncertainties

As was pointed out earlier, it is useful to distinguish between "transformable" and "nontransformable" uncertainties. The latter provide the basic explanation for the existence of profits in an economy of private, competitive industry. Nevertheless, a good deal of knowledge and judgment are required by businessmen in order to successfully and economically transform the types of uncertainties which are avoidable at a certain cost. The time and effort which must be spent in this type of activity vary a great deal from business to business. The process of transforming uncertainties into definite costs can be called "hedging."

Hedging, in essence, involves the purposive holding of two opposite positions at the same time. Roughly, it can be described as betting in two opposite ways at the same time. The purchase of insurance is of this nature and hence is a variety of hedging. When a businessman buys fire insurance, he is, essentially, betting that a fire will occur on his premises; the insurance company is betting that this will not happen. Even if the fire does occur, the directors of the insurance company are unlikely to be dismayed because the company will undoubtedly win its bets with numerous other persons who bought fire insurance, and the successful wagers should at least offset the unsuccessful ones. As the owner of a building and its contents, the businessman is, of course, hoping that no fire will occur, since this would bring financial loss. In order to protect himself in this position, he must take an opposite stand —that is, he must bet that a fire will occur. Whatever the actual outcome, he should not fare too badly, since he will have converted an important uncertainty into a definite cost—the cost of the insurance premiums.[8]

Hedging is often possible even when insurance cannot be purchased against occurrence of an unfavorable event. Instead of betting with an insurance company, one can often place a bet with someone else. For example, suppose a young man attends a ball game in San Francisco with the president of his company, who is a Dodger fan. And suppose that at the start of the game the boss (illegally) places a bet of $100 on the Dodgers to beat the Giants with a wealthy individual in the next box. The young man can then improve his prospects with the

---

[8]Even apart from the consequences of the disruption of business, the insured person is apt not to recover his entire loss, since insurance companies normally do not sell policies to cover the whole value of inflammable property. To do so might place too much temptation in the way of some policyholders to win their bets with the company. Even beneficiaries of life insurance policies have been known to take steps to secure the proceeds prematurely.

company by boldly placing a similar bet with the stranger. While waiting at the refreshment stand to have the boss's order filled, however, he may bet $100 on the Giants. Assuming that the odds are even on both teams, he has avoided the risk of loss (and the possibility of gain) but has advanced a notch in the president's esteem (provided that the latter does not learn about the hedge).

Long and Short Positions

An important variety of hedging in the business world consists of taking offsetting "long" and "short" positions. Like the offsetting $100 bets on the Dodgers and Giants, this is not sensible unless the firm is forced into one position as an incident to doing business. If the position is a dangerously speculative one, it is conservative to hedge against it, thereby incurring a small, certain cost rather than risking a large, speculative loss.

An individual is in a "long" position whenever he owns any commodity, security, or other asset of value. His hope is then that the asset will increase in money value as a result of the operation of supply-demand forces.[9] His fear is that market forces will reduce the value of his asset. On the other hand, a person in a "short" position hopes that the market price will decline rather than rise, since he has made a contract to deliver a commodity, security, or other asset at a future date for a specific price. The more cheaply he can purchase the asset when the delivery date rolls around, or the more cheaply he can produce it in time to meet the delivery requirement, the larger his gain will be. A contractor, for example, who has agreed to construct a building, road, or other project for a specified sum may be considered to be in a "short" position with respect to that asset. One of his problems, once that contract has been signed, is that the cost of materials, labor, and other inputs may increase during the construction period, so as to make the job an unprofitable one. In order to hedge against this contingency, he must take a long position with respect to the needed inputs.

He may, for example, sign a lease to rent the needed equipment at a specified price for the period of construction; or alternatively, he may buy the equipment. He may attempt to secure a contract with the labor unions involved, which will make his labor costs more predict-

---

[9]It is also possible to be long on money itself. This occurs whenever a cash balance is held. The hope of the individual is then that the purchasing power of the cash will increase—i.e., that prices will fall. Conversely, one is "short" on money when in debt, since it is necessary to make future delivery of principal and interest to a creditor.

able. With respect to materials, he has two alternatives: (1) He may buy all of the necessary materials ahead of time, storing them until needed; or (2) he may contract to have them delivered to him at specified prices at specified future dates. Either way, he would have a hedge against an increase in their price. Once the contractor has assumed correct "long" positions on most of the inputs required for construction of the project, he would be fairly well hedged against unfavorable price changes. He would have transformed some uncertain costs into predictable ones.

Futures Markets

Hedging operations on the part of businessmen in many lines of activity are made possible by the existence of organized markets in which commodities are traded both at "spot" or "cash" prices for immediate delivery and at "futures" prices for deferred delivery.[10] Futures contracts are regularly made for some dozens of relatively homogeneous and storable commodities such as wheat, corn, oats, lard, cottonseed oil, cotton, cocoa, coffee, refrigerated eggs, Maine potatoes, lead, zinc, and copper. In the month of April, for example, Mr. A may contract to buy, and Mr. B to sell, a specified quantity of wheat during the month of December at a specified price. The seller has the option of making delivery on any day within the month of December, delivery actually taking the form of delivery of warehouse receipts for the commodity. Mr. B also has the option of delivering any of several grades of wheat rather than just a specified grade; and a discount or premium from the agreed price then is effective, since the agreed price relates to a standard grade.

The financial pages of certain newspapers regularly carry quotations of both spot and futures prices. In April, for example, prices of spot, May, July, September, and December wheat are quoted. Since quoted futures prices are based on anticipated demand-supply conditions in those future months, they may be thought of as traders' present expec-

---

[10]Holbrook Working, in an informative article entitled "Futures Trading and Hedging," *American Economic Review,* July, 1953, p. 315, points out that it is not accurate to state that a futures contract *always* involves deferred delivery because, for example, some sellers of September wheat futures in September may intend to make immediate delivery. It is safe to say, however, that most futures contracts do involve deferred rather than immediate delivery. Unfortunately, from a pedagogic point of view, much trading which is not in the futures markets also involves deferred rather than immediate delivery. International commodity trading and purchase and sale of many manufactured goods regularly involve deferred delivery. Also, commodities bought in the "cash" market are frequently sold on terms providing for 30-, 60-, and 90-day credit.

tations as to what spot prices will be for the same grade when those months roll around. In an uncertain world, these expectations are seldom entirely correct. The constant changes in futures prices reflect the buying and selling actions which are constantly taking place, the price movements generally being in the direction of more correctly reflecting the cash prices which will actually prevail in the future months, since later quotations are based on later information. Quoted futures prices are, therefore, likely to be a good forecast of price movements. If, for example, May coffee is selling at 55 cents, July coffee at 51 cents, September coffee at 47 cents, and December coffee at 45 cents a pound, a housewife can look forward with some confidence to a reduction in the cost of coffee in her budget.

Spot and Futures Prices

The "spot" or "cash" market for a commodity differs in important ways from the futures market. Whereas a futures contract can usually be satisfied by delivery of any of the grades of the commodity, a spot transaction pertains to the transfer of a specific lot of a specific grade, the transaction often being consummated in a face-to-face meeting of buyer and seller. When a spot transaction is made, the buyer actually wants to receive delivery of the commodity, and delivery will be made unless the contract is canceled by subsequent agreement between the two parties. On the other hand, most of the buyers of futures do not actually want to take delivery on these contracts, nor do sellers usually want to make actual delivery. Instead, the buyer of a futures contract usually "offsets" this contract by a similar futures sale prior to delivery time; if the price has gone up, he makes a gain equal to the difference in price (less commissions and taxes). Similarly, the seller of a futures contract usually offsets the contract with a purchase of futures prior to delivery time; he gains if the purchase can be made at a lower price than he has sold for, and he loses in the opposite case.

Speculation and Arbitrage

The futures market is a great convenience to both speculators and hedgers, since the actual commodity need not be handled, and since buyers and sellers normally do not have to be concerned about selection of the specific grade, place of delivery, and other details. A speculator who believes that a presently quoted futures price is too low— that is, that demand will be stronger in relation to supply than present quotations indicate—is likely to *buy* a futures contract. If his expectation is correct, he can later offset this purchase with a similar sale at a higher price. On the other hand, a speculator who believes that a presently quoted futures price is too high can *sell* futures, profiting by a later offsetting purchase if his "bearish" expectation turns out to be correct.

Instead of attempting to take advantage of a change in a single price over time, a speculator may, instead, attempt to turn to his advantage a difference between two prices when that difference appears to be out of line. Suppose that a study of market conditions suggests strongly that July oats futures are underpriced relative to September oats. This would suggest an arbitrage transaction in which July oats would be bought and September oats would be simultaneously sold. It would then not matter whether the more normal differential were established by a rise in the price of July oats, by a fall in September oats, or any other combination of change, so long as a smaller difference in price came to be established. The arbitrager would gain on either the long or the short transaction and lose or break even on the other one, but his gain would exceed his loss. Similarly, an improper differential between two markets—say, between the New York and New Orleans cotton markets—could be turned into an arbitrage profit by a simultaneous purchase in the relatively low market and a sale in the relatively high market.

The arbitrager can be considered to be "betting two ways at once." His action differs, however, from that of the hedger in that the latter is forced to assume one of his positions (make one of his bets) as an incident to carrying on his regular line of business activity. The arbitrager takes both of his positions as a speculative matter. In practice, it is often impossible to characterize an individual as purely a hedger or purely an arbitrager on a particular transaction, since a hedger is not averse, of course, to making an arbitrage profit, whenever possible, in the process of protecting himself against an adverse price change.

Hedging by Selling Futures

A wheat farmer, contemplating his growing crop in July, realizes that he is an involuntary speculator in wheat on the "long" side. He may decide to hedge by selling September wheat, perhaps in about the quantity he expects to harvest in that month. By taking this action, he has, roughly speaking, already sold his growing crop at a specific price for delivery at harvest time, and he is in no danger of suffering a speculative loss between July and September. Actually, he is unlikely to deliver his own wheat on the futures contract; he will probably off-set his short position in late August or September by buying September futures in the same amount he had previously sold. Then he will sell his own wheat in the cash market.

If we assume that the quantity of wheat involved was 10,000 bushels and make certain price assumptions, the transactions can be summarized as shown in Exhibit 3.

Exhibit 3

Date	Transaction	Farmer Receives	Farmer Pays
July 20............	Farmer has growing wheat which will yield an estimated 10,000 bushels when harvested. Cash price of wheat is $1.80 per bushel.		
July 20...........	Farmer sells 10,000 bushels of September wheat at $1.85 per bushel.	$18,500	
September 10.....	Farmer buys 10,000 bushels of September wheat at $1.70 per bushel.		$17,000
September 10.....	Farmer sells his own wheat in cash market (10,000 bushels at $1.70 per bushel).	17,000	
		$35,500	$17,000

In the situation pictured, the farmer would be glad that he hedged, since he has a net gain of $18,500 (from which, however, commissions and taxes must be deducted), whereas his crop would have brought him $17,000 if he had not hedged. The cash price of wheat declined 10 cents a bushel between July 20 and September 10, but this was more than offset by the 15-cent decline in September futures over the same period. The protection received from this sort of hedging is based on the fact that cash and futures prices generally move in the same direction. These two prices may, however, not move by the same amount; consequently, the hedger is apt to make either a speculative gain or a loss of moderate proportions.[11] If the price of cash

[11]Actually, the farmer did not engage in a pure hedging transaction, since he was short on mature wheat but long on immature wheat prior to harvest time. If he had held wheat in storage and had sold wheat futures in the same amount, the long and short positions would have been more definitely offsetting.

wheat had increased from, say, $1.80 per bushel on July 20 to $1.90, the farmer would have a larger net income by not hedging. The existence of government price supports at some designated percentage of "parity" may make hedging by farmers less necessary. (However, both spot and futures prices can fall below support levels.) The price-support program thus places part of the speculative risk of a price decline on the shoulders of the taxpayers.

Hedging is practiced extensively by certain types of processors. For example, the practice has expanded in recent years in the case of southern textile mills.[12] These mills buy spot cotton early in the season and sell cotton futures as a hedge. Offsetting futures purchases are made as orders are received for textiles. This gives them substantial protection against losses on their long position in cotton. If cotton has declined in price between the time it is purchased and a textile order is received, the mill may have to quote a price on textiles which reflects the lower price of cotton. In this case, however, a profit will be made on the futures transactions, and this may equal or even exceed the reduction in revenue occasioned by the need to cut the price of textiles.

Hedging by Buying Futures

Much of the hedging which occurs involves the initial purchase, instead of sale, of futures. This method is followed when the businessman has taken a short position in a raw material or finished good. Suppose a candy manufacturer receives large orders in September for delivery of his product in time for the Christmas season. He is obliged to quote a definite price on the future delivery of candy and is therefore in a short position. He can hedge against a rise in his production costs by adopting a long position in sugar, his principal raw material. If spot and futures prices for sugar move in a parallel fashion during the next few months, as they generally do, an increase in his production costs due to a rise in the price of cash sugar should be quite closely offset by his profit on the purchase and sale of sugar futures. If, on the other hand, spot sugar declines in price, the candy manufacturer would have been better off had he not hedged. An added inducement to hedging, however, is that banks may be willing to make loans for working capital purposes only when the borrower has hedged appropriately against unfavorable price changes.

---

[12]J. B. Bear and O. G. Saxon, *Commodity Exchanges and Futures Trading* (New York: Harper & Bros., 1949), p. 242.

The candy manufacturer's transaction might be summarized as shown in Exhibit 4.

In spite of the increase in the price of sugar, the candymaker should receive an adequate net return for his product. He has secured the needed sugar for $6,720 (the difference between his payments and receipts in the sugar transactions). This is a price of 6 cents a pound (plus commissions and taxes on the sugar transactions), which is the price he was able to anticipate in September when he fixed his candy prices. If November sugar had been selling at a price which appeared to be too high, he could have hedged instead by buying spot sugar in September and storing it until he needed it. It is usually more convenient, however, to hedge by means of futures transactions.

Exhibit 4

Date	Transaction	Manufacturer Receives	Manufacturer Pays
September 15.....	Candy manufacturer sells candy which will require 112,000 pounds of sugar, the candy to be delivered early in December.		
September 15.....	Candy manufacturer buys 112,000 pounds of November sugar at 6 cents a pound.		$ 6,720
November 15.....	Candy manufacturer sells 112,000 pounds of November sugar at 7 cents a pound.	$7,840	
November 15.....	Candy manufacturer buys 112,000 pounds of spot sugar at 7 cents a pound.		7,840
		$7,840	$14,560

Miscellaneous Hedges

Such businessmen as bakers, bottlers of soft drinks, coffee and cocoa importers, flour millers' cold-storers of eggs, cottonseed and soybean crushers, copper smelters, and many others make extensive use of hedging. Often, the choice of whether to hedge at all, and if so, what sort of hedge to use hinges on the relation between spot and futures prices. If futures prices appear to be abnormally low relative to spot prices, it may not be wise to hedge by selling futures; the chance of their declining further may be too poor. In this situation, it may be best to attempt to arrange short and long positions which call instead for purchasing the underpriced futures.

In a more general sense, a great many types of protective actions by individuals and business organizations can be considered to be "hedging." Diversification of an investment portfolio between the stocks of various corporations, between stocks and bonds, between long-term and short-term bonds, and between securities and cash holdings is a general type of hedge. The use of general-purpose machine tools rather than highly specialized tools or of convertible rather than nonconvertible equipment is a hedge against the uncertainties of demand. Similarly, the production of many commodities rather than of just one may be a useful hedge. The hiring of executives with several capabilities instead of highly specialized men is similar to the use of convertible rather than specialized equipment.

CASE 1–1: SUNBRITE PAINT CORPORATION

In 1924, John Watson entered the wholesale paint and varnish business. In addition to paints and varnishes, he carried the usual allied products such as brushes, thinners, sandpaper, etc. Prior to entering this business, he had for many years operated a retail hardware business; and when he had accumulated sufficient capital, he established Watson Brothers Wholesale Paint Company. He was joined in this business by his brother Walter. The company carried several brands of nationally advertised paints and varnishes, and by 1930 the firm was serving all of New England and a few of the upper Middle Atlantic states. The firm employed five salesmen, who traveled the territory and were compensated on a commission basis. The company enjoyed a period of growing and prosperous business until the sudden downturn of business activity in 1930.

As employment and income declined during the early part of the Great Depression, so did the sales and profits of Watson Brothers Wholesale Paint Company. Early in 1932, after several requests from many of his dealers for a line of paint which would sell below the price of the national brands, John Watson foresaw the opportunity to enter the paint-manufacturing business. He believed that because of the decline in prices generally, he could build a small plant to produce a line of outdoor paints which would give him a lower overhead per unit than many of the established firms whose plants were constructed in earlier years at higher prices. He therefore contracted for the construction of a building of 40,000 square feet at a location some four miles from the location of the wholesale business. A separate corporation, the Sunbrite Paint Corporation, was set up to manufacture and distribute Sunbrite paint.

Because of the experience of John Watson with paints over a period of years, he was able to produce a paint of slightly lower quality than some of the national brands, and it was priced about 20 per cent below the national brands. The Sunbrite paints were offered in eight colors and sold only in gallon and half-gallon cans. During the first full year of operations, 1933, the corporation produced the profit and loss statement shown in Exhibit 1.

Exhibit 1
SUNBRITE PAINT CORPORATION
Statement of Profit and Loss, January 1–December 31, 1933

Sales..........................		$119,411.52
Cost of goods sold..............		71,377.80
Gross profit.................		$ 48,033.72
Expenses:		
Salaries......................	$28,210.47	
Depreciation.................	6,316.19	
Telephone....................	382.38	
Insurance....................	1,245.49	
Advertising..................	1,937.67	
Bad debts....................	731.83	
Taxes........................	2,013.90	
Interest.....................	1,600.00	
Heat and light..............	2,655.06	
Total Expense.............		45,092.99
Net Profit.................		$ 2,940.73

It should be pointed out that in preparing the statement shown in Exhibit 1, no salary was drawn by either John or Walter Watson for their services to the Sunbrite Paint Corporation. Both were on salary with Watson Brothers Wholesale Paint Company at the rate of $7,500 each on an annual basis. During the first year of the Sunbrite Paint Corporation, both had spent the larger share of their time with the new firm. In addition, the Sunbrite Paint Corporation owned no trucks. All transportation of goods to and from rail and truck terminals was done by the trucks of the Watson Brothers Wholesale Paint Company, and no charge was made against the Sunbrite Paint Corporation. Furthermore, all the clerical, accounting, and billing operations of the Sunbrite Paint Corporation were handled by the regular office staff of the Watson Brothers Wholesale Paint Company. About two thirds of the finished goods of the Sunbrite Paint Corporation were stored in the warehouse of the Watson Brothers Wholesale Paint Company, and no charge was made for this.

John Watson, upon reviewing the statement in Exhibit 1, concluded that the investment had been a profitable one and that the operations would continue. As the depression continued, the national brands of paint were reduced in price but were still slightly above Sunbrite. The Sunbrite Paint Corporation showed profits of $3,117.22 in 1934, $2,993.22 in 1935, $5,251.74 in 1936, $9,108.14 in 1937, and $6,933.68 in 1938. The profits shown for these years were computed on identically the same basis as shown in Exhibit 1. Profits remained below $10,000 until the outbreak of World War II, when the company found itself called upon to produce to capacity to meet the increased demand resulting from a great deal of military construction in the New England area.

Walter Watson had a son, James, who had graduated from college as a chemistry major in the spring of 1941 and joined the Sunbrite Paint Corporation in the production operations but was soon called into military service in the chemical warfare division. After the war, James returned to the Sunbrite Paint Corporation and began experimentation upon the quality of the firm's paints. With the sharply increased demand for construction as a result of restrictions during the war, sales of paint for the company increased. However, James was concerned over the fact that the national brands were of superior quality; and with the rise in personal income, preference for quality appeared to overcome the price differential between Sunbrite and other well-known brands. He therefore improvised a laboratory in the Sunbrite plant and engaged in some experimentation.

In 1949, he was able to develop a paint which would retard dry rot in wooden construction. Since this was a problem in the New England area, especially in the construction of wooden boats and structures near the ocean, the company's sales soon reached the sum of $700,000; and net profits, again computed as in Exhibit 1, exceeded $57,000 in 1950.

While attempting to improve the qualities of the paint in respect to control of dry rot, James developed a paint which would inhibit rust when applied to metal and also tended to arrest rust when applied to the affected areas. He obtained a patent upon the formula for this paint and shrouded the manufacturing process in secrecy. For two years the Sunbrite Paint Corporation had difficulty in convincing paint users of the qualities of this rust-inhibiting paint, but once this resistance was overcome, sales began to soar.

In 1954, because of increasing sales, it was necessary to enlarge the Sunbrite plant. Rather than enlarge its present location because of relatively high-priced land, an entirely new plant was built about two miles from the center of the city, adjacent to a railroad and a major highway. In 1957, sales exceeded $4 million, and net profits amounted to $355,-136.35 after taxes.

When the new plant was completed, John and Walter Watson retired from the Sunbrite Paint Corporation, from which they had never drawn a salary, and devoted their time to their wholesale business. The Sunbrite Paint Corporation had in the meantime found itself serving a national market, and had set up a sales organization and sold to a large extent through manufacturers' representatives.

Sales for 1960 were $54,632,419.84. Net profit, as certified by a public accounting firm, was $5,118,227.21. None of the other major paint manufacturers had yet put a paint on the market which could compete with Sunbrite, and from what James Watson could determine, it appeared that none would be offered in the near future.

QUESTIONS

1. Would you accept the profit and loss statement as shown in Exhibit 1 to be correct? Why? What adjustments, if any, are necessary?
2. Is the net profit shown in Exhibit 1 the economic profit of this firm?
3. Do you agree that John Watson was wise to continue operations in 1934 on the basis of the company's performance in 1933?
4. What is the nature of the profits the company showed after 1950? To what extent are these profits a reward for uncertainty?

CASE 1-2:   THE KOWMAN CORPORATION

The Kowman Corporation, established in 1938, was a family-owned corporation engaged in the business of warehousing. At the time of incorporation the firm was authorized to issue 50,000 shares of common stock with a par value of $10 per share and 1,000 shares of preferred stock at $100 per share. The latter stock bore a dividend rate of 6 per cent on a cumulative basis. When the firm commenced operations, Mr. Kowman was named president of the corporation and was issued 500 shares of common stock. Mr. Kowman's two sons and two daughters were issued 100 shares each. No further issues of stock have been made since.

Late in 1937, Mr. Kowman had purchased at a bankrupt sale, for $89,000, an eight-story building which had been used as a factory. It contained 320,000 square feet of floor space, and was equipped with one large freight elevator and a smaller combination freight and passenger elevator. It was remodeled at a cost of $14,250 and turned over to the Kowman Corporation in exchange for the 1,000 shares of preferred stock. With this building the corporation entered the business of warehousing both commercial and household goods.

In 1946, Mr. Kowman acquired another building at a war-surplus sale at a price of $210,000. This building had 255,000 square feet of floor space, consisting of three stories and a large loading platform at the rear. It was equipped with one large freight elevator as well as a truck ramp to the second floor. In 1950 the corporation erected a third building, two stories high, with a freight elevator, containing 183,000 square feet of floor space, at a cost of $191,000. This building was located adjacent to that purchased by Mr. Kowman at the war-surplus sale. Both of these buildings were located at the edge of the city, while the original building was approximately four blocks from the main business section of the city. The second building was leased by Mr. Kowman to the Kowman Corporation for $15,000 per year for a twenty-year period, the corporation to pay all costs of remodeling, maintenance, insurance, and taxes. Remodeling costs were $23,000 and were charged off as current expenses in the 1947 fiscal year. The buildings were identified on the books of the corporation as buildings A, B, and C, in the order of their acquisition.

The business was operated by Mr. Kowman's two sons. Each had received, since 1952, a salary of $25,000 per year. One of Mr. Kowman's daughters was secretary of the corporation at a salary of $7,500 per year, while the other daughter served as treasurer at a similar salary. Neither of the two daughters performed actual service for the firm other than signing documents in their official capacities. Until 1950, Mr. Kowman himself had received no salary; but effective that fiscal year, he drew an annual salary of $10,000, although his services were chiefly advisory and of a perfunctory nature.

The initial capital of the company was supplied by the amounts paid in at par value for the common stock outstanding and by loans from Mr. Kowman as the need arose. The funds for building C were provided by Mr. Kowman without interest. These funds were being repaid out of profits. After the profit and loss statement was prepared each year, exclusive of dividends on the preferred stock, all profits above $1,000 were paid to Mr. Kowman on this note. At the end of 1954, $41,000 had been repaid to Mr. Kowman toward the cost of building C.

The company had shown a small profit each year since its beginning.

Dividends on the preferred stock were paid each year, and none were in arrears. The building for which this stock was issued was appraised at $250,000 when the company was approached by a prospective purchaser who desired the building for business use. As the profits remaining after dividend payments on the preferred stock had increased over the years, executive salaries had been adjusted upward.

In the spring of 1955 a national warehousing and van service com-

Exhibit 1

THE KOWMAN CORPORATION

Statement of Profit and Loss, January 1, 1954–December 31, 1954

Storage receipts	$232,492.57	
Miscellaneous receipts	1,352.39	
Total Receipts		$233,844.96
Expenses:		
Executive salaries	$ 75,000.00	
Operating salaries and wages	39,423.64	
Insurance	21,535.62	
Telephone	1,686.17	
Taxes*	14,319.26	
Heat, light, and power	6,231.75	
Maintenance†	21,472.05	
Miscellaneous expense	1,124.35	
Supplies	7,461.41	
Depreciation:		
Building A	5,000.00	
Building C	9,550.00	
Trucks and vans	3,000.00	
Rental expense, Building B	15,000.00	
Total Expense		220,804.25
Total Profit		$ 13,040.71
Less: Dividend on preferred stock		6,000.00
Net Profit		$ 7,040.71

*Includes social security, real estate, and transactions taxes, but not income taxes.
†Includes $7,335.50 for a new roof on building A.

pany approached Mr. Kowman with a proposal to purchase the Kowman Corporation. This national company had one warehouse in the same city as the Kowman Corporation, with approximately one third as much space as Kowman. This warehouse was supervised by a local manager at a salary of $12,000 per year. In the event the purchase was completed, the national company proposed to increase this manager's salary to $15,000 per year and to dispense with the various executives currently with the Kowman Corporation. In reply to a request from the national company for a profit and loss statement, together with some other nonstatistical information, the Kowman Corporation submitted its profit and loss statement, as shown in Exhibit 1.

After an analysis of this information the national company made an offer of $750,000. This price would include the purchase of building B and also the surrender of all outstanding capital stock to the purchaser.

QUESTIONS

1. Is the statement of profit and loss, as shown in Exhibit 1, acceptable to you? Why? If this statement is not acceptable, prepare one which is, and explain your corrections.

2. Would you, as the chief executive officer of the national company, have made an offer of $750,000? Why? Would you offer more or less?

3. Assume that the purchase offer valued building A at $300,000, building B at $250,000, and building C at $200,000. On the basis of the remaining data in Exhibit 1, prepare a profit and loss statement for the national company, and explain any differences in results. Compute depreciation on the three buildings on a twenty-year basis, using the straight-line method.

CASE 1-3: CALKINS-WALKER, INC.

Calkins-Walker, Inc., was a ladies' apparel and specialty store which carried a complete line of ladies' furnishings, notions, and cosmetics of high quality only. Prices ranged from the upper-medium lines to the high-priced luxury lines. More than 60 per cent of its business was on an open-account basis, and more than 25,000 accounts were currently active. The company was located in the main downtown business and shopping district of a large metropolitan area. The population of the city proper was approximately three million, with another two and a half million persons in the adjoining suburbs.

The firm had been in its present location for more than 35 years. It occupied the first four floors of a seven-story building, the remainder being used as office space from a separate entrance on the street fronting the building. The space occupied by Calkins-Walker was leased on a 30-year basis. The lease agreement provided for a basic rental of $85,000 per year when annual net sales were $750,000 or less, plus 2 per cent of net sales when net sales exceeded $750,000 but were less than $1.5 million, and plus 3 per cent of net sales in excess of $1.5 million. This lease had been renewed in 1949. The original lease contained lower rentals than the current one.

Within a five-block radius of Calkins-Walker, there were three department stores which carried similar merchandise in the same price range. These stores also carried less expensive lines. There were several smaller specialty shops in the same area which carried many of the same lines as Calkins-Walker, but none carried a complete line. There were also a few shops which carried higher priced lines than Calkins-Walker, but they were comparatively small and catered almost exclusively to the luxury trade.

The suburban areas surrounding the city had developed to a large extent according to income level. To the north, there were several communities with the highest income level of the metropolitan area. On the western side was another group with only slightly lower incomes, and to the south was a smaller number of areas with high incomes. Within the city itself the higher income groups lived in the north and northwest portions of the city. The southern and eastern portions of the city were inhabited primarily by an industrial population. In the higher income suburban areas were a few old and well-established shopping centers. In two of these areas, there were branches of two of the large downtown department stores. In addition, there were several of the smaller, higher priced ladies' specialty shops, among them several of the nationally better known ladies' ready-to-wear firms.

From 1932 to 1935 the company suffered losses on operations and showed only a small profit in the years which followed. No dividends were declared from 1932 to 1939. Although it was difficult to obtain adequate supplies of all lines of merchandise during the period of World War II, the company earned good profits in spite of price controls. From the end of the war until 1949 the company enjoyed a substantial increase in sales each year. Sales reached a new high in 1948, at $2,421,335.27. In 1949, there was a decline to $1,947,217.31. Recovery followed in 1950, with sales increasing to $2,003,112.53. Beginning with 1951, sales began to decline, in spite of the fact that incomes in the area were increasing.

The decline in sales prompted Mr. Frederick, the president and general manager of Calkins-Walker, to investigate. He observed that there had been a large growth of population but learned that it was concentrated in the suburbs. By 1948, there had been some net loss of population by the city to the suburbs, especially in the middle and upper-middle income groups. To the northwest, west, and south of the city, entire communities were being erected. The established suburbs were also growing and developing much of their vacant land. Mr. Frederick believed that the growth of the suburbs had only begun and was concerned by the effect of their growth upon downtown shopping areas.

The growth of the suburbs had far exceeded the development of public transportation, so that by early 1949 the private automobile was the primary means of suburban transport. The increase in the number of motorcars resulted in overcrowded traffic and parking conditions in the downtown areas. It was feared that this situation would discourage shoppers from the suburbs, and various studies had been made or were under consideration. To date (1955), nothing concrete had developed.

In the new communities, shopping centers were rising. In some cases, they were planned and included in the original blueprints of the community. In others, they had grown independently and unplanned. Mr. Frederick was of the opinion that the conventional, planned shopping center was not the proper location for a suburban store of Calkins-Walker. He felt that the clientele of his store was not attracted by a shopping center, but that better results could be obtained by a store separate from a center if a suburban location was decided upon. He felt that there was no place at all for a store in the newer communities, but that the greatest possibilities lay in the growing and older high-income suburbs.

In order to protect the company against possible loss of markets and declining sales and profits, Mr. Frederick proposed that the firm select now the best possible locations and secure them by option until such time as the future of the downtown shopping area became more discernible. His position was that with the options the company would be assured of three possible alternatives: (1) suburban expansion with eventual abandonment of the downtown location, (2) more intensive downtown development and abandonment of suburban expansion, and (3) an integration of both urban and suburban developments.

Three desirable parcels of land in three different suburbs were currently available by option. They could be optioned either for purchase or for long-term lease. The initial option period would run for one year at a fee of $2,000 per month, renewable in six-month periods, but with the renewal fee open at the end of each option. Mr. Frederick recommended that the company acquire these options at the stated fee. Three directors of the company objected on the grounds that it was "throwing money down the drain."

QUESTIONS

1. Would you acquire the options? Explain.

2. If the options are acquired, would you say Mr. Frederick has hedged? (Do you find him simultaneously taking long and short positions?)

3. Would you classify the taking-up of these options as "insurance"? Explain.

4. What sort of developments within the city proper might increase the value of the downtown location, making a move to the suburbs less desirable?

CASE 1-4:   BROADWAY ANGELS, INCORPORATED

Early in 1963 a business friend passed along to George Tompkins the prospectus for Broadway Angels, Incorporated. Tompkins' interest in the theater was well known to his friends, and as a bachelor he could afford a speculative investment of $1,000.

The prospectus gave the following information about objectives and the nature of the business:

Purpose

Broadway Angels, Incorporated, has been formed to give the small investor an opportunity to employ funds in diversified entertainment enterprises connected with the Broadway theater. Generally, this opportunity has been limited to persons with substantial capital or income.

Business

Broadway Angels, Incorporated, will produce and finance all types of legitimate theatrical productions, touring companies, television and radio shows.

Individual backers or "angels" who invest through limited partnership agreements in Broadway shows are rarely in a position to survey the field carefully or make judicious selections from the many possibilities that are available. They cannot easily diversify their investments over a series of shows because of limited capital, and they have little opportunity to participate in any of the profits which may accrue to producers and coproducers. We believe that the individual may solve these problems by becoming an investor in a properly operated corporate enterprise.

It is well recognized that producing and backing shows is highly speculative. Diversification should therefore prove advantageous. Since Broadway shows continue to find backers and producers, it is obvious that there are people who are successful, and some even highly so, in these ventures. It is reasonable to suppose that certain of these people possess, or have acquired, a degree of experience and ability which has been a considerable factor in their success. An amply financed corporation should be in a position to discriminately employ this professional talent.

Broadway Angels, Incorporated, will utilize professional advisers to assist the management of the company in selecting and producing shows in which stockholders' money will be placed. Advisers will receive stated fees for services performed, and will only be paid a salary when directly engaged to aid in the selection of desirable productions or to work in a particular production so selected.

Broadway Angels, Incorporated, will not admit any outside partners or utilize any partial backers for the shows which it produces, but will finance such shows exclusively with its own capital, unless a change is made in this policy....

It is well understood by the management, the advisers, and all those who have direct contact with these fields that even these proposed safeguards will not eliminate failures and losses in certain of the enterprises. This point should be thoroughly understood by the stockholder. However, this informed and intelligent approach, it is believed, will make Broadway Angels an improved medium through which the average person may place money in theatrical enterprises.

Objective

It is planned to work toward an eventual schedule of five to ten Broadway productions per annum, specializing in plays with budgets estimated to run from $40,000 to $75,000, until circumstances or profits warrant expansion into a small number of musical shows.

Opinion

It is the opinion of the directors, officers, and professional advisers that a professional selection and production of a series of shows by one company will result in a considerably higher ratio of successes to failures than is found in an analysis of any season's group of shows, and that a sound corporate and business administration will save money, cut costs, minimize taxes, and increase profits.

The present practice on Broadway of raising money for each production on a separate basis from an everchanging group of "angels" is expensive, and has become increasingly difficult during the past decade due to fundamental economic changes. An organization with permanent capital such as Broadway Angels, Incorporated, is a specific answer to this problem.

The losses in show business are apparent: One hundred per cent of the capital invested in one show may be lost. But perhaps it is not as generally known how large are the returns on certain successful shows. Items appearing in newspapers have reported the following: "Voice of the Turtle" showed a profit of 3,000 per cent on the initial investment; "Member of the Wedding" cost $75,000 to get started and has made a total of $210,000; "Mister Roberts," by its last performance on January 6, will have paid off five to one; "The Happy Time" has grossed over $1 million; those who have invested in "Detective Story" have to date been paid off with a profit of approximately 200 per cent; "Harvey" paid off $40 to $50 for every $1.00 invested.

Tompkins noted that of the 2.2 million authorized shares, the president of the company held 370,000, for which he had paid $21,000 (10 cents a share for 170,000 shares and 1 cent a share for 400,000, of which he had contributed 200,000 to the company to be used "for bonuses in connection with financing and other corporate purposes"). Now being offered to the public were 570,000 shares at 50 cents a share, of which 37.5 cents would be net to the company after underwriting discounts and commissions. If he bought 2,000 shares for $1,000, he would be entitled to become a member of the honorary "Front Row Club." As far as he could tell, the officers and advisers of the concern all had at least minor theatrical experience, and a few of the advisers were moderately well known as producers, directors, or advisers.

Before coming to a decision, Tompkins got out a survey paper he had prepared from theatrical papers a few years before on the profitability of the 1948–49 season on Broadway. He thought that theatrical operations had remained similar enough so that its findings were relevant to his present decision. That report read as follows:

Ever since the 1920's the theater on Broadway has been suffering a steady decline in the number of productions, number of theaters, and total gross. In spite of this over-all decline, individual shows such as "Oklahoma," "Mister Roberts," and "South Pacific" are scoring record-breaking successes. An increasingly sharp dichotomy between a few fabulous hits on one hand an a large group of total losses even on moderately well-received plays has become apparent.

The unheralded "Oklahoma," whose producer, the Theatre Guild, had to make the unusually generous 60–40 split of profits to get the necessary funds (usually the backers share 50–50 with the producer) had netted $7 million by June, 1950; $4,185,000 had been returned to investors on an investment of about $100,000, while the Theatre Guild took out $2,790,000. Authors Rodgers and Hammerstein felt future earning power to be great enough to refuse any sale of screen rights. Of the shows that were still running on Broadway, "Mister Roberts" had returned $1 million in profits on a $100,000 investment in less than two years, with the net from two companies continuing at a $14,000 a week rate.

To get both sides of the picture, it is necessary to take a look at an entire theatrical season. From June, 1948, to June 1949, 63 productions (excluding certain experimental productions and repertory efforts) were launched in New York, 48 productions were classified by *Variety* as failures, and the total loss on such productions estimated as $4,500,000. The 15 shows classified as hits cost $1,940,000 and had earned back $2,176,000 by the end of the theatrical year. Actually, two of the "hits" finally ended up slightly in the red because of the illness of the star in the case of "As the Girls Go" and a disappointing and curtailed road trip for "Anne of the 1,000 Days." Whether or not the 1948–49 theatrical productions can be thought of as profitable as a whole depends upon the eventual returns of three spectacular successes, "South Pacific," "Kiss Me, Kate," and "Death of a Salesman," which were still running on Broadway and on the road. The comfortable successes with profits up to 100 per cent on investment included "Edward, My Son"; "Goodbye, My Fancy"; "Howdy, Mr. Ice"; "Lend an Ear"; "Light Up the Sky"; "Madwoman of Chaillot"; and "The Silver Whistle," and may have accounted for as much as $600,000 in return on investment. Three more spectacular successes, "Detective Story," "Where's Charley?" and "Private Lives" (the latter cost an incredibly low $25,000) probably have returned a similar amount.

A summary of the successes and failures is shown in Exhibit 1.

One of the failures, "Life With Mother," demonstrates how uncertain the theater may be. The show was a sequel to the record long-run hit, "Life With Father"; received an excellent critical reception; started out with a large advance sale; and then faded with only $60,000 out of a $100,000 investment recovered. It later folded in its first week on the road when its backers hoped that a road tour might pull it out.

Variety (May 25, 1949) summed up the profitability of the season as follows: "It is figured possible that when the current hits are through paying off, even excluding the probable return from film sales, the profits may equal the losses on flops and thus balance the books for the season as a whole. Taking into consideration the return from screen rights to such hits as 'Death of a Salesman,' 'Detective Story,' 'Kiss Me, Kate,' etc., the season may show a moderate over-all profit. If the costly flops of occasional or come lately producers ('All for Love' lost $500,000) were excluded, the debit total for the season would be substantially reduced. In other words, if an investor bought more or less standard slices of all productions of all established managements he would probably be assured of a modest over-all profit."

[*Exhibit 1*]

	Number	Loss (Estimated)	Profit (Estimated)
Failures (48)			
Total..........................	44	$4,200,000	
Some capital recovered.........	4	300,000	
Hits (15):			
Break even....................	2		....
Moderate (up to 100 per cent return)....................	7		$ 600,000
Substantial (over 100 per cent return)....................	3		600,000
Smash (likely returns of $500,000 or more)....................	3		2,000,000 to January 1, 1950

Most theatrical productions are organized as limited partnerships with the backers' obligation limited to their investment plus a possible 20 per cent overcall. The breakdown of the gross of "South Pacific," the most successful of the 1948–49 shows, shows the renumeration received by various factors of production:

Weekly gross exclusive of federal taxes at capacity.......	$50,600
Theater rental—25% of first $40,000 and 25% of any gross over $50,000 (these are unusually favorable terms; the theater often receives as much as 35% with none of the gross exempted).....................	10,150
Authors' 10% of gross (Rodgers, 4½%; Hammerstein, 4½%; Michener, 1%)............................	5,060
Director (Logan), 2½%.............................	1,265
Stars' 14% of gross (7% to Ezio Pinza, 7% to Mary Martin, as against $2,000 weekly guarantee).................	7,085
Operating expenses—rest of cast, publicity, share of stage crew, musicians, ice, and advertising (the theater is responsible for some of these costs)...................	16,000
Net, of which 50% goes to the producers, 50% to the backers (investors)...............................	11,000 (approximate)

Of the producers' share, 60 per cent goes to Surrey Enterprises, owned equally by Rodgers and Hammerstein; 27 per cent to director and coauthor; 13 per cent to producer Hayward. Of the backers' share, 2 per cent goes to book author Michener, whose investment was paid out of profits, the rest to major backers Hayward and 20th Century–Fox and other investors.

One road company, financed out of profits, launched its tour in the spring of 1950 and will probably net much more a week, with grosses frequently over $80,000 in large auditoriums and smaller star guarantees. A second road company is being formed. The Broadway net is probably up by close to $2,000 since Pinza left the show in the spring of 1950.

"South Pacific" was financed at $225,000 with provision for an overcall of $45,000, but it was such a hit on the tryout that it was brought into Broadway for only $163,000.

QUESTIONS

1. Would you advise Tompkins to invest in Broadway Angels, Incorporated?
2. How should theatrical profits be classified, as compensation for risk bearing, innovation profits, monopoly profits, etc.?
3. Is there a clear-cut distinction between profits and returns to other factors of production in the theater? What factors of production share in the risk? (In connection with this, work out the break-even point for "South Pacific," and contrast the returns received by the various factors of production at the break-even point and at capacity.)

CASE 1–5: JAMES BARKLEY, GRAIN MERCHANT

In February, 1963, James Barkley, a member of the Chicago Board of Trade, headed his own firm and was one of a decreasing number of individual grain merchants in Chicago. While Chicago retained its leading position as a market for commodities futures, the volume of cash grain sent to Chicago for sale had greatly diminished in the postwar period.

Barkley specialized in oats. His customers used the grain for animal feeding, and he particularly concentrated on selling oats to feed dealers serving horse-racing stables. He depended upon his skill and knowledge of the grain to make favorable purchases. He then had the grain processed by a local elevator to upgrade it into types that would meet the preferences of his customers. A typical transaction would incur the following costs per bushel of oats:

1.50 cents—Elevation (paid for unloading car into elevator bin, weighing, subsequent reloading, etc.).
0.50 cents—Clipping (paid for shearing off oat beards from kernels; this process raises the weight per bushel several pounds).
0.75 cents—Cleaning.

0.25 cents—Inspection and weighing (paid to state and to the Board of Trade weighmaster).

1.00 cent —Shrinkage (actually, this could be as high as 3 per cent or as low as zero, depending on process used).

Four cents of the usual 6-cent margin Barkley sought thus had to be paid out. He estimated that one of the 2 cents remaining would be net for him after the payment of office, telephone, printing, and other expenses. Not all lots would require exactly the same processing. Some might be given a recleaning, others would be bleached (while the horses might not distinguish dark oats, certain owners valued lightness). While frequently Barkley was able to sell his oat purchases immediately, he found it desirable to carry an inventory of from four to ten carloads to meet sudden demands of customers. Full carrying charges, including storage and financing, typically were 1¾ cents per bushel per month, but Barkley had obtained storage from his elevator in return for the oat clips.

It was a real challenge to keep the firm going at an acceptable net; and for the last few years, Barkley had fallen short of his annual target of four hundred carloads (1,000,000 bushels of oats). Thus, he supplemented his main business by occasionally handling special lots of other feed grains, by occasionally speculating in other commodities, and by clearing futures transactions for other grain firms. He almost invariably, however, hedged his own purchases of oats by selling an equivalent amount in the futures market. He did not, however, customarily hedge his basic inventory requirement of four carloads or 10,000 bushels.

On February 19, he purchased two carloads of oats (a total of 5,000 bushels) at "two over" which he hoped to sell in a few days at "eight over" after the oats had been clipped and cleaned. If not hedged, this would bring his long position to six carloads. Cash grain was quoted in terms of the nearest futures (see Appendix); thus, "two over" meant a price of 73½ cents, since the March futures were then quoted at 71½. He could finance the purchase partly through a bank loan and partly from his own limited capital (the banks were willing to finance the whole purchase only if the transactions were hedged).

Barkley had been bullish about the commodity market in general. In his January 23 letter to his regular customers, he had stated that "there is not too much in the present picture to give much comfort to a bear." The short-run oats picture also was fairly tight, and cash grain deliveries in Chicago were slow. But March futures for oats had fallen from 73¾ on January 23 to the current 71½. The relative price of corn was still favorable, and it would be substituted for oats by some feeders. In terms of weight equivalent, corn at \$1.25 would be about equal to oats at 71½, but the March futures for corn were actually selling at \$1.17.[13]

Conflicting advice was being given by two leading market bulletins. One noted, as to oats: "A very slow local trade. A prominent local long was seen as a seller late in the week. Would stay on the sidelines." The other stated: "The oat market followed the lead of corn and allied feeds, showing a modest gain for the week. Oats appear to be a buy at current levels."

Barkley had no strong opinion about how the market for March futures would move, in view of the mixed evidence. Before following his usual practice of selling in the most current futures market, he did look over the chart of the range in which March futures had moved over the last five years on the relevant dates. These figures are shown in Exhibit 1.

Exhibit 1

CLOSING FUTURES PRICES FOR MARCH DELIVERY OF OATS:
FEBRUARY 19–MARCH 5, 1953–63
(Cents per Bushel)

	February 19*	High within Period	Low within Period	March 5*
1953	73¼	75⅛	73⅛	73¾
1954	76⅛	77⅞	74	77¾
1955	75¾	75¾	71⅞	72⅛
1956	64	64	59⅝	60½
1957	75⅞	76	74⅜	75¼
1958	65⅜	66⅜	63⅛	66⅜
1959	64½	66	64½	64½
1960	73½	75¾	73	75¼
1961	63	63¾	62⅜	62⅜
1962	62	65⅛	61⅞	65⅛
1963	71½			

*Or nearest date on which market was open.
Sources: Board of Trade of the City of Chicago and *Wall Street Journal.*

QUESTIONS

1. Do you think Barkley should hedge his two-carload purchase? Can you see why his basic inventory should not be hedged?
2. Outline the hedging transaction required now and when he sells. Under what circumstances would he achieve a perfect hedge?

---

[13]Actually, a bushel of oats is a weight measure, 32 pounds to a bushel. The grades Barkley sold after clipping weighed 40 pounds or more to a bushel and thus would be measured as 1.25 or more bushels. The standard for corn is 56 pounds per bushel.

3. Assume Barkley sells on March 1, 1963, at "eight over." Would he have realized his hedge? (Look up the futures price in the *Wall Street Journal*.)

APPENDIX TO CASE 1–5:   CASH MARKET OPERATION[14]

Grain that is on consignment illustrates the sales problem of the commission merchant. As the agent for the country grain elevator, he must sell it to the best possible advantage, and for this he earns a commission. The commission merchant phones the shipper to report the grade, acquaint him with market conditions, and to find out if he wishes to sell the car or hold it over until the following day in the hope of getting a better price.

Commission merchants, called cash grain receivers by the trade, have ready access to a wide range of buyers. At other tables in the cash market are Board of Trade members representing terminal warehouses, exporters and many of the grain processors. [Barkley acted primarily as one of these buyers.]

Buyers move from one table to another inspecting samples. They dip into the paper sample bags and carefully examine the grain. They make a quick appraisal of the foreign material and damage, then squeeze the grain in their hand in a rough attempt to confirm the moisture content notation on the outside of the bag. They sniff it for objectionable odors such as smut, kerosene, must and so on. In short, they assure themselves that the sample bears out all of the grade-making determinations noted by the sampling agency.

Practically every carlot of grain that is sold on the Chicago Board of Trade is priced in relationship to the current quotations in the nearest futures delivery month of that grain. Sellers solicit bids from potential buyers in terms of a premium over or discount under that futures price.

Supposing a cash grain commission merchant had a car of #2 yellow corn to sell. He shows the sample to buyers. Perhaps on that day, the run of corn into Chicago has been small, so bids are in terms of a premium over the near future. One buyer may bid 2 cents over, another 2¼, the best bid received may be 2½ cents.

If the commission man has his customer's instructions to sell at the best price possible, he'll take the 2½ cent premium offer. Or perhaps he feels the market may firm up, so he calls the country shipper to discuss the sales and receive a decision. If the decision is to sell now, the commission man goes to the high bidder, tells him he'll take the offer, and the 2½ cent premium is applied to the price of the near future showing on the blackboard at that moment.

Thus, the general price level is determined by the futures market, but the premium or discount in the cash market measures the demand for the grain by exporters, warehousemen or processors as of right now.

---

[14]Reprinted from Board of Trade of the City of Chicago, *The Market Place* (Chicago, 1962).

CHAPTER 2

•◆•◆•◆•◆•◆•◆•◆•◆•◆•◆•◆•◆•◆•◆•◆•

Economic and Business Forecasting

IN THE previous chapter, it was pointed out that many businessmen protect themselves from unfavorable price changes by means of hedging. If hedging is "pure"—that is, if it does not at the same time include an element of speculation—it does not require that a forecast be made, because the businessman is protected regardless of which way the relevant price moves. For most business decisions, however, no perfect hedge is available, and reasonably accurate forecasting is necessary for profitable operations. The typical businessman must constantly "stick out his neck," and careful forecasting may help him keep ahead.

Forecasting is not always carried out as an explicit function, but it is necessarily implicit in numerous decisions which must be made within the firm. If forecasting is not a centralized, explicit activity, there is danger that important forecasts will be made, in effect, by persons who are not in the best position to engage in this activity. For example, the sales forecast may be implicit in the decisions made by the order clerk who, upon investigation, would probably be found to be using rule-of-thumb methods rather than to be making use of all of the information which might be brought to bear on the problem.[1]

A *Fortune* magazine survey of 405 companies (accounting for one fourth of all United States industrial assets) revealed that 141 of these companies employ staff economists and that an additional 55 firms use outside consultants.[2] While these economists and consultants engage in many different kinds of analysis (plant location, pricing, financing, etc.), most of them are active to some degree in economic and business forecasting. The former consists of making forecasts of *general* business activity such as movements of national income, aggregate industrial production or employment, total exports or imports, or fluctu-

---

[1]This is suggested by Carl A. Dauten, *Business Fluctuations and Forecasting* (Cincinnati: South-Western Publishing Co., 1954), p. 6.

[2]Charles E. Silberman and Sanford S. Parker, "The Economy's Scouts," *Fortune*, December, 1955, p. 100.

ations in security price indexes. Business forecasting pertains more directly to the activity of the particular firm, consisting of short- and long-term forecasts of sales, price forecasts for important raw materials and equipment, availability of resources at plant sites under investigation, and a host of other matters of specific interest. The separation between economic and business forecasting is not always sharp, however. Actually, the two are frequently intertwined in the same forecasting process. Industry sales are projected on the basis of an economic forecast of general business conditions, and the business forecast of the firm's sales considers the industry projection as well as any special factors such as a promotional campaign or new product. While the firm's sales are likely to be highly correlated with the sales of the industry of which it is a member, this relation will not necessarily hold, especially over the longer run (during which new firms may enter or leave the field). In view of this difficulty of classification, no sharp dividing line will be drawn in this chapter between economic and business forecasting. Instead, the various popular methods of forecasting will be discussed separately. Most of these are applicable both to general and to specific prediction.

Uses of Forecasting

The value of economic forecasting to the federal government is quite obvious to the extent that the prevailing policy is to use fiscal and monetary measures to prevent depressions and severe price inflation. Substantial changes in federal spending and taxing may take many months to put into effect, especially if Congress is not in session at the right time, and this means that a serious downturn in business would have to be predicted far ahead of time if fiscal measures were to prevent its actual occurrence. Monetary policy can be changed more quickly and is consequently less dependent on effective forecasting.

The deliberate use of monetary and fiscal policy to prevent undesirable fluctuations in over-all economic activity and prices suggests an interesting problem in verification of the accuracy of forecasts. A correct forecast of a coming depression might appear to have been incorrect if prompt and adequate governmental efforts actually prevented its occurrence. Yet the forecast would actually have been instrumental in preventing the decline in economic activity.

The same caution in evaluating the accuracy of a forecast must be exercised when an individual firm is large enough to affect by its own actions the event which is predicted. A forecast of an insufficient capacity to meet demand in five years might itself be sufficient to cause a firm to build enough new capacity to meet the demand. (This self-defeating effect of the forecast would be amplified if rival firms were induced by the firm's actions also to expand their plant capacity.) Usually, however, the individual firm is not sufficiently important to affect the outcome by its own reactions to a forecast. If inflationary monetary policy on the part of the federal government caused a general rise in raw-material prices, for example, the power of the individual firm to prevent such a price rise would be negligible.

The uses of forecasting to the firm are many. As has already been suggested, plant expansion (or contraction) plans should be based on a long-term forecast of demand for output.[3] In order to be fully relevant for this purpose, a forecast should cover the period during which fixed capital equipment is normally amortized. Short-term price movements are of great importance to the businessman with respect to inventory holdings. Normally, an expected increase in price will make it advantageous to build up stocks in advance of the price rise (provided carrying costs are not too great). In general, the expectation of inflation will make it desirable for a firm to place itself in more of a debtor position by means of such actions as borrowing and reducing its holdings of cash and accounts receivable. A forecast of general deflation will make it desirable for the firm to attain more of a creditor position by means of building up cash, accounts and notes receivable, and other assets whose value is fixed in dollars, and to substitute common stock for bonds in its own capital structure.[4]

Forecasting the appropriate rate of production for a number of months into the future may be extremely important as an aid to procurement of materials and components which must be ordered far in advance of their use. The same is true of workers who require a period of training before they are useful to a company. On the other hand, ordinary supplies and unskilled labor may usually be purchased as the need arises, and forecasting is of little importance in relation to their acquisition.

---

[3]The term "output" should be considered to comprehend not only the product of a manufacturing firm but also the services furnished by a retailer or wholesaler, the transportation furnished by a truck or train, the housing services provided by apartment buildings, etc.

[4]An interesting empirical study of the effect of debtor and creditor positions on the firm is described by Reuben A. Kessel, "Inflation-Caused Wealth Redistribution: A Test of a Hypothesis," *American Economic Review*, March, 1956, p. 128. He found that the debtor-creditor hypothesis has predictive usefulness. Kessel's results are in keeping with the old idea that there is more "leverage" behind a stock when the company also has bonds outstanding; his analysis is, however, more thorough and more sophisticated.

Trend Projection

Probably the most common way of forecasting the future is simply to construct a chart depicting the actual movement of a series and then to project (extrapolate) the apparent trend of the data as far into the future as is desired for the purpose at hand. The projection is usually a straight line, but it may instead be curvilinear. This is sometimes classified as a "naïve" method of forecasting, since it is based on no particular theory as to what causes the variable to change but merely assumes that whatever forces contributed to change in the recent past will continue to have the same effect. Trend projectors are often able to show a high percentage of forecasts which are correct in direction, at least; but the method has the serious defect of missing all of the sudden downturns or upturns—and these are just the changes which it is most important to predict correctly.[5]

On the other hand, trend projection may be about the only available method when the variable under consideration is affected by a large number of factors the separate influence of which cannot readily be measured because of lack of data, lack of time, or other reasons. The analyst may, for example, have a feeling that a series is affected by the general growth of the economy as population increases, capital accumulates, and technology improves; and if he has confidence in this underlying growth, he may feel, quite rationally, that the observed upward trend in the series in which he is interested will continue. His simple extrapolation is then not entirely naïve, although he might be able to do better by using more complicated methods provided the necessary data are available—and on time. As in using any method of forecasting, it is important that the analyst be familiar with the field with which he is working. It would, for example, be ridiculous to measure the increase in retail toy sales in December over November and to project this increase in order to predict the January sales.

A simple example of forecasting by means of trend projection is given in Exhibit 1. Actual total consumer credit outstanding, as reported by the *Federal Reserve Bulletin* (June, 1960) is plotted as of the ends of the years 1953 through 1959. Over this period, there was a rapid increase in consumer credit, with the increases in 1955 and 1959 being especially rapid. The sharp increase in the use of credit cards was partly responsible for the 1959 jump. A straight-line projection of the apparent trend is made for the years 1960 through 1962.

---

[5]This is pointed out by Charles F. Roos in a useful article, "Survey of Economic Forecasting Techniques," *Econometrica*, October, 1955, p. 366.

This demonstrates the sort of problem which confronts the trend projector. It is an arbitrary matter whether one projects the trend as computed over the entire period (as has been done) or considers that the upward trend has accelerated, as indicated by the upsurge in 1959. If one were influenced strongly by the latter, he would tilt the extrapolation more sharply upward, perhaps using a curve concave on the upside. Trend projection is often naïve. At the same time, if a quick estimate is needed, projection of the trend does offer a way of getting some answers which at least reflect the current tendency of the Ameri-

Exhibit 1

TREND PROJECTION—QUICK BUT DANGEROUS

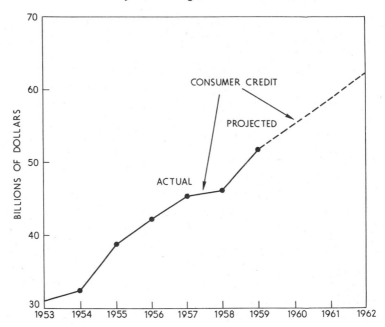

can people to live beyond their present incomes, and the general propensity of the federal government and banking system to go along with their desires and make the desired borrowing possible.

Leading Indexes

As has been suggested, a main shortcoming of trend projection as a forecasting technique is that it necessarily fails to foresee the vital turns, downward and upward, in the series under consideration. It is these turns which call for the most important changes in inventory policy, hiring policy, capital budgeting, debtor-creditor position adjustment, and other matters. A great deal of statistical research has been devoted to the problem of finding "leading indexes"—that is, sensitive series which tend to turn up or down in advance of other series. The value of such indicators (if reliable) is obvious. If one could discover a series which would reliably lead stock or commodity price indexes, it would not be difficult to become rich (that is, if this method of prediction did not come into general use; in that event, it would cease to lead these speculative prices). Actually, stock prices themselves have been found to be significant leading series for industrial production and for other important indicators of business health. For example, the stock market crash of 1929 preceded the calamitous depression of the 1930's. However, stock market price movements reflect the opinions and actions of speculators and investors; and the more basic question still remains as to what information affects, or should affect, the opinions of the most alert and best-informed speculators.

In 1950, Dr. Geoffrey Moore of the National Bureau of Economic Research tested the cyclical behavior of over 800 statistical series. He selected 18 monthly and three quarterly series which appeared to be outstanding business indicators. These are not all leading indexes, however; some are coincident with business fluctuations, and others lag behind general business activity. Earlier work along this line was done by Charles F. Roos, who in 1938 examined 248 monthly indexes in an effort to find which ones had lead characteristics.[6]

Data for representative leading indicators for the years 1959–63 are indicated in Case 2–4 (page 76). One difficulty is immediately apparent: The leading indexes often point in different directions at the same time, so that until their movements become substantial in magnitude and similar in direction, it is hard to know where they are leading. Nevertheless, a downturn of some of these indicators after a consistent rise might at least warn the businessman that a general turn is more likely than before. A downturn of a substantial number might well be a signal for action in anticipation of lower prices and reduced business activity. The indicators should not be utilized in a mechanical way but rather as one basis for judging coming business conditions. Their use requires alertness in watching for first publication of an index and for anticipating movements before they are published. For example, industrial stock averages are published daily as well as monthly.[7]

---

[6] Roos, op. cit., p. 369. Roos states that series which he found in 1938 to have lead characteristics still retained these characteristics in 1954.

[7] A recent appraisal of leading indexes has been made by Arthur M. Okun, "On the Appraisal of Cyclical Turning-Point Predictors," Journal of Business, April, 1960. He points out that premature signals may do more harm than good, and that there seems

Manufacturers' New Orders

New orders placed with manufacturers should clearly have lead characteristics.[8] Orders are an early reflection of the demand for a product; and a sizable change in the volume of orders is very likely to be followed by changes in purchases of raw materials, in employment, in rate of production, and perhaps in the demand for loans or equity capital. New orders for *durable goods* should be especially valuable to the forecaster of general economic conditions because they reflect investment decisions, and such decisions are of great importance in generating changes in national income. Also, if the information can be secured by industry totals, such new orders may be valuable to the firm which sells materials or equipment to a durable goods manufacturer. An increase in orders for merchant ships, for example, should eventually lead to increased orders for steel, wood, turbines, radio equipment, lifeboats, etc.; and the producers of such materials and equipment may find it desirable to take steps in anticipation of their receipt of orders from the shipbuilders.

The lead characteristics of new orders which are of importance to firms selling to capital goods producers should depend not on the durability of the good once it is produced but rather on its "period of production" (in the sense of the lag between receipt of an order and completion of shipment) and on the timing of the need for materials in the production process. For example, knowledge of the volume of new orders for merchant ships might not be very important to the producers of steel for the hulls, since these steel producers would quickly receive their orders from the shipbuilders, anyway. The knowledge might be more valuable to firms which build marine radio and radar equipment, because they might not so quickly receive orders from the shipbuilders.

Data for manufacturers' new orders and sales of all durable goods are given by months in Exhibit 2 for the years 1960, 1961, and 1962, and for the first three months of 1963. These series are plotted in Exhibit 3. The data have been adjusted by the Department of Com-

---

to be a difference in the value of leading indexes in predicting cyclical peaks and troughs. For predicting downturns, average hours worked per week, residential building contracts, and wholesale prices had the best record over the period tested. For predicting upturns, business failures (inverted), residential building contracts, and common stock prices had the best record.

[8]Roos, *op. cit.*, pp. 372–73, considers new orders to be the outstanding leading index. He points out that new orders for capital goods usually turn down before important declines occur in production and even in stock prices.

Exhibit 2

NEW ORDERS FOR AND SALES OF DURABLE GOODS, 1960–63
(In Billions, Adjusted for Seasonal Variation)

Month	New Orders	Sales
1960:		
January....................	$14.2	$15.5
February..................	14.8	15.7
March....................	14.6	15.2
April.....................	14.5	15.0
May......................	14.7	15.1
June.....................	14.3	14.9
July.....................	13.8	14.7
August...................	14.4	14.4
September................	14.6	14.4
October..................	13.7	14.1
November................	13.6	13.8
December................	13.2	13.6
1961:		
January..................	12.9	13.2
February..................	13.4	13.3
March....................	13.8	13.7
April.....................	14.4	14.1
May......................	14.8	14.6
June.....................	14.9	14.7
July.....................	15.0	14.8
August...................	15.7	15.1
September................	15.8	15.0
October..................	16.1	15.3
November................	16.1	15.6
December................	16.2	15.7
1962:		
January..................	16.4	15.5
February..................	16.2	16.0
March....................	16.0	16.3
April.....................	15.7	16.4
May......................	16.0	16.4
June.....................	15.4	15.9
July.....................	16.3	16.3
August...................	15.9	16.4
September................	15.9	16.3
October..................	16.6	16.3
November................	16.3	16.5
December................	16.0	16.2
1963:		
January..................	16.7	16.0
February..................	17.1	16.5
March....................	17.2	16.6

Source: U.S. Department of Commerce, Office of Business Economics, *Survey of Current Business.*

merce to eliminate the usual seasonal variations; this should make month-to-month changes more indicative of important changes in the economic climate. An examination of the data suggests that new orders are a useful leading index, but also warns the analyst not to pay too much attention to small fluctuations in orders; these need not affect future sales, since the backlog of unfilled orders furnishes the means for producers to keep up production and sales in the face of falling orders.

Exhibit 3

MANUFACTURERS' NEW ORDERS FOR DURABLE GOODS
TENDS TO LEAD SALES

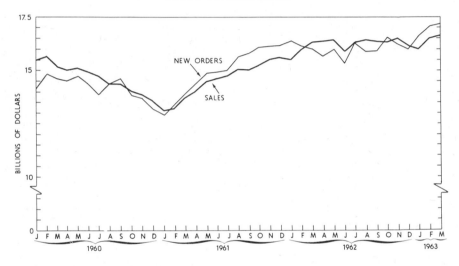

Econometric Methods

The most elegant (and sometimes the best) method of forecasting is by the use of econometrics. This term covers a variety of analytical techniques, most of them being a blending of economics, statistics, and mathematics. Econometric models of the entire economy are constantly being worked upon and improved. These models contain among their variables such factors as net investment, consumption, government expenditures, taxes, and net export or import balance, since these are key determinants of national income according to the prevailing theory of income determination. To the extent that some of the determining variables can be predicted, the econometric model may be useful in forecasting such over-all measures of economic activity as gross national product and national income. If, for example, it could be shown by statistical study of the past that investment in one year is largely determined by profits of the previous year and that consumption is heavily influenced by the amount of liquid savings accumulated before January 1 of the year in question, the econometrician could use these relationships in his forecasting model. If past relationships continued to hold true (which may be a big "if"), he could make a usefully accurate prediction.

One danger in the use of econometric models of the economy is that they appear to be so elegant and so esoteric that they may give a false impression of their reliability. During World War II, several influential economists used econometric models to predict that there would be mass unemployment after the war. Instead, the actual problem turned out to be one of excessively full employment in the sense that total demand was so great as to bring about not only full employment but also inflation. Both consumption expenditures and private investment expenditures for the immediate postwar period were seriously underestimated by the model builders, and this led to their erroneous forecasts.[9] Their error stemmed especially from the assumption that observed prewar relationships would persist after the war, whereas, in fact, such factors as accumulated shortages and large supplies of liquid savings brought about drastic upward shifts in consumption patterns.

Development of a relatively dependable econometric model for the United States economy is a difficult problem, and one which requires constant attention. In each period, as new observations are secured, the equations should be recomputed so that "structural change will manifest itself as it occurs."[10] It is desirable that monthly or quarterly data be incorporated in the model so that short-period forecasts may be made.[11]

Much simpler econometric techniques are frequently valuable, especially for forecasting which is of narrower scope than an economy-wide model. Suppose one is interested in forecasting total expenditures on recreation. One might theorize that of the variables which probably influence such expenditure, disposable personal income should be an outstanding candidate. From publications of the U.S. Department of Com-

---

[9]This situation is described in considerable detail by Frank D. Newbury, *Business Forecasting* (New York: McGraw-Hill Book Co., Inc., 1952), chap. vii.

[10]Lawrence R. Klein, *Econometrics* (Evanston, Ill.: Row, Peterson & Co., 1953), p. 264. Klein is one of the leading model builders.

[11]An eight-equation model utilizing quarterly data is given by George J. Malanos and Henry Thomassen, "An Econometric Model of the United States: 1947–1958," *Southern Economic Journal,* July, 1960. The authors concluded that the chief cyclical variation has originated with spending upon consumer durables. They predicted a continued economic upswing in 1960 (p. 27). (Actually, business activity declined, as the sales data plotted in Exhibit 3 illustrate.)

merce, one could secure the data shown in Exhibit 4. These can then usefully be plotted against one another, as in Exhibit 5.

It is apparent that there has been a close correlation between disposable personal income and consumer expenditures on recreation. The only point which is far off the freehand regression line is the one for 1945, when recreation was inhibited by wartime restrictions. This sort of simple correlation analysis may help a businessman understand the forces which affect his sales and, perhaps, help him in his planning for

Exhibit 4

RECREATION AND DISPOSABLE INCOME
(In Billions)

Year	Disposable Personal Income	Expenditures on Recreation
1929...................................	$ 83.1	$ 4.3
1933...................................	45.7	2.2
1940...................................	76.1	3.7
1945...................................	150.4	6.1
1950...................................	207.7	11.3
1955...................................	274.4	14.2
1956...................................	290.5	15.2
1957...................................	305.1	15.9

Source: *Statistical Abstract of the United States* (Washington, D.C.: U.S. Government Printing Office, 1959).

the future. To the extent that the statisticians who compile national income statistics make forecasts of disposable personal income, these could readily be translated into forecasts of recreation expenditures on an over-all basis. This would be done by locating the predicted disposable personal income on the horizontal scale and moving up to the straight line in Exhibit 5.

Other factors which might, in theory, affect expenditures on recreation should also be investigated. If, for example, the age distribution of the population and the average number of hours worked per week should also be found to be significant, the analyst might make a multiple correlation study (using familiar statistical techniques) in order to discover their past effect on recreation expenditures. If these relationships remained reasonably constant in the near future, and if some forecast of the independent variables could be secured,[12] the correlation study would make possible a forecast of recreation expenditures.

---

[12]It would not be difficult, for example, to forecast the age distribution of the population in the near future, since these people would already be living, and since death rates are quite predictable.

Or suppose it were important to forecast the consumption of gasoline by private automobiles for one year into the future. (This forecast might be required by the U.S. Treasury to help that agency estimate receipts from an actual or proposed gasoline excise tax.) One would immediately realize that gasoline consumption can be considered to be a function of the average number of cars in the hands of users during the coming year and the average gasoline consumption per car for the year. Each of these averages could be estimated separately and then multiplied.

Exhibit 5

EXPENDITURES ON RECREATION FOLLOW DISPOSABLE PERSONAL INCOME

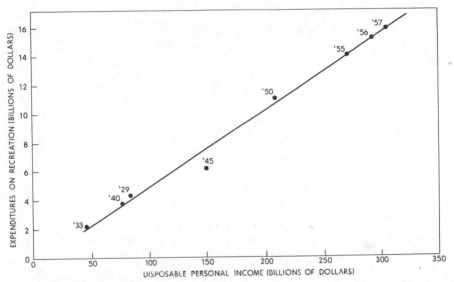

The average number of cars in the hands of users next might be considered to be a function of the inventory in owners' hands at the end of the current year, plus half of the estimated sales during the following year, minus half of the estimated number of cars to be scrapped during the coming year.[13] Inventory data could be secured accurately; scrappings could probably be estimated quite closely from past records. Sales of new cars would be most subject to error; but these are much less important, anyway, than the inventory of old cars. The analyst would probably rely on automobile sales as predicted by the automobile industry itself, since in this way he would be incorporating

---

[13]This assumes sales and scrappings to be evenly distributed between the first and second halves of the year. If this assumption did not appear to be justified from an examination of available data, it could be modified.

the results of analysis which is probably superior to that which he could turn out himself (and which procedure would, in any case, be time-saving).

In order to estimate gasoline consumption per car, it would be desirable to make a correlation study for the recent past, relating this variable to such independent variables as disposable personal income, price of gasoline, and the ratio of primary road mileage to number of vehicles. (This latter might be a rough measure of congestion which should affect gasoline consumption per car.) To the extent that the important factors were included, to the extent that past relationships continued to hold true, and to the extent that some of the independent variables are predictable, a suitable forecast of average yearly use of gasoline per car could be obtained. This prediction, plus that of the average number of cars in the hands of users, would permit a prediction of gasoline consumption and gasoline tax collections.

Survey Methods

It has been pointed out that the forecaster who wishes to make optimum use of econometric methods must constantly recompute his equations as later data become available. Also, he should often be willing to incorporate the work of others into his own system if he has reason to believe that their estimates are better than those which he could make or if this procedure will be worth while as a timesaver. Similarly, he should be willing to substitute the results of intentions surveys on such matters as planned investment and consumption if he feels that such data are more accurate than those which he can compute from past relationships. On the other hand, the analyst is free to use computed relationships if he does not have sufficient faith in the predictive value of a survey.

Intentions surveys seem to have increased in popularity in recent years as a basis for forecasting important economic variables. The Department of Commerce and the Securities and Exchange Commission conduct a joint quarterly survey in order to ascertain recent and anticipated expenditures for plant and equipment. More highly publicized surveys of planned investment are made by the McGraw-Hill Department of Economics. The more distant plans probably have less predictive value than near-term plans. McGraw-Hill surveys mainly the larger companies in the larger industries. These not only account for a very substantial part of total investment but also are likely to have more carefully formulated plans than smaller firms, plus greater ability actually to effectuate investment decisions. Data on actual and planned investment are published by the McGraw-Hill Department of Economics in separate pamphlets and in *Business Week* magazine.

One of the tables from a recent McGraw-Hill survey is shown in Exhibit 6. The survey indicated that a substantial increase in investment spending was planned for 1962 over 1961. However, preliminary plans for 1963, 1964, and 1965 did not suggest a further increase. This may have been a factor in Congressional concern for tax cuts and reforms to stimulate capital spending by private industry. It should be remembered, however, that consumers' expenditures are even more important in affecting the level of national income, according to some leading economists.

Exhibit 6

ACTUAL AND PLANNED CAPITAL SPENDING, 1961–65
(In Billions)

INDUSTRY	ACTUAL,* 1961	PLANNED, 1962	PRELIMINARY PLANS		
			1963	1964	1965
All manufacturing........	$13.67	$15.41	$14.89	$15.15	$15.03
Mining.................	0.98	1.09	1.00	0.99	0.98
Railroads..............	0.67	0.85	0.75	0.77	0.76
Other transportation and communications........	5.07	5.50	5.07	5.05	4.94
Electric and gas utilities...	5.52	5.74	5.68	6.11	6.19
Commercial.............	8.46	9.39	8.83	8.12	7.71
All Business..........	$34.37	$37.98	$36.22	$36.19	$35.61

*U.S. Department of Commerce, Securities and Exchange Commission.
Source: *Business' Plans for New Plants and Equipment,* 1962/1965, 15th Annual Survey by McGraw-Hill Department of Economics, (New York, 1962).

A well-known survey of consumers' spending intentions is conducted by the U.S. Bureau of the Census in collaboration with the Federal Reserve System. Findings are published in the *Federal Reserve Bulletin.* This survey is based on about 17,000 interviews. This is obviously a small sample of the entire consuming population of the United States and encounters the further difficulty that consumers often do not "plan" the purchase of a new car, for example, but buy on the spur of the moment. Also, many consumers do not have financial records in good enough shape even to know what they have bought in the recent past, much less what they plan to buy. Nevertheless, it has been observed that the survey results have proved reliable as predictors of the direction of movement of consumers' purchases of durable goods.[14]

A few of the figures from the October, 1962, Survey of Consumer Buying Intentions are shown in Exhibit 7. In general, the survey appears to have correctly indicated that 1963 would be an even better year than 1962 in the automobile industry. At the same time, the substantial extent to which consumers do not have firm plans is disclosed. Much more information than is shown in Exhibit 7 is regularly published. For example, buying intentions are shown for other durable goods, and are shown according to family income and age of the head of the household.

Exhibit 7

PLANS TO BUY AUTOMOBILES AND HOUSES
(Percentage of All Families)

	1961	1962			
BUYING PLAN	October	January	April	July	October
New or used car:					
Planning to buy within 12 months..	18.5	18.1	18.9	17.4	19.5
Doesn't know about 12-month plan.	8.0	7.7	7.9	7.6	8.0
House (new or existing):					
Planning to buy within 24 months..	10.6	9.8	10.0	10.1	10.4
Doesn't know about 24-month plan.	6.4	6.1	6.4	6.0	6.7

Source: *Federal Reserve Bulletin*, November, 1962.

Requirements Forecasting

An important and very common type of sales forecasting is quite obviously open to firms selling materials or components to other firms which set up production schedules for end items. Firms which regularly supply General Motors with components can clearly gauge their future sales prospects by securing the General Motors output schedules—assuming, of course, that these schedules are sufficiently "firm," that General Motors will not decide to make its own components, and that the company in question will continue to get the General Motors business.

In recent years an allied form of forecasting has become possible to the extent that the federal government establishes production programs and schedules. During World War II, for example, President Roose-

---

[14]James H. Lorie, "Forecasting the Demand for Consumer Durable Goods," *Journal of Business,* January, 1954, p. 66. This entire issue is devoted to forecasting in various areas of the economy.

velt called for the production of 60,000 military airplanes in 1942 and 125,000 in 1943. These goals were followed by detailed production schedules which were supposed to add up to these totals. (Actually, they did not, especially for 1942.) From the detailed schedules of airplane production the federal statisticians were able to compute requirements for aluminum, engines, propellers, radio equipment, and thousands of other components. To the extent that end-product schedules were realistic for airplanes and other munitions, the detailed requirement schedules gave firms producing materials and components an excellent forecast of their own sales possibilities.

A similar situation existed just after the war, when the veterans' emergency housing program was put into effect by Congress. Unlike the wartime munitions programs, this program did not call for government purchase of the end product. Rather, it was an attempt to use priority ratings, allocation orders, limitation orders applied to less essential construction, subsidies on building materials, and other unusual measures to secure the rapid construction of homes for purchase by veterans. To the extent that realistic housing schedules were set up by the government (and here, too, schedules tended to be overoptimistic), it was possible for industries supplying such materials as brick, tile, nails, wallboard, and clay sewer pipe to compute their probable sales to the housing industry.

Recently, the federal government has formulated a huge interstate highway program. This clearly makes it possible for the portland cement industry, asphalt industry, aggregates producers, pipe producers, steel industry, and others to make approximate calculations of their probable sales in support of this tremendous program. An advantage of this sort of program from the view of materials suppliers is its recession-proof nature. In fact, a business recession would probably increase their sales on this account, since the highway program would very likely be speeded up as an emergency public work.

The firm faces a number of problems in forecasting its sales as related to a government production program:

1. The end-item schedules usually reflect a combination of political, administrative, and economic considerations. They are likely to be placed deliberately too high in order to stimulate private firms to set their sights high. Often, the end-item schedules reflect more what government officials believe is required than what can actually be produced within the specified time period.

2. The firm may not get its share of the industry sales in support of a government program. (Or it may be able to get more than its share.)

3. There are usually some opportunities for substitution of one material for another. Computation of requirements is complicated by this possibility, since there is usually no set "bill of materials" which can be depended upon. Portland cement and asphalt are important examples of substitute materials.

4. "Pipeline" requirements create difficulties. It is necessary for producers not only to turn out the materials and components needed for incorporation in end items, but also to build up inventories at various stages in the transportation-production process. In part, these inventories are needed to "fill the pipeline," so that a steady input into end items can be secured. These inventory needs are often especially difficult to predict.

In general, as government activities have come to loom larger in our economy, it has become more and more important for firms in many lines to gear their activities to government procurement programs or to government scheduling of some private activities. This requires a sort of forecasting and suggests the importance of following not only federal governmental activities, but also those of state and local governments. States usually budget on a two-year basis; New York and California, however, budget annually. Also, about 115,000 local governments have budgets.[15] An examination of available pertinent budgets may give valuable hints to the businessman as to sales possibilities. Budget proposals are usually not supported fully by legislative bodies, of course, so actual appropriations details may give more accurate (but less early) information. Also, the businessman may do well to follow the progress of bond issues of state and local governments, since these are often made for specific capital purposes and therefore have some predictive significance.

Loaded-Dice Techniques

Numerous other ways of looking into the future—some of which are more ethical than others—are based on getting information which is not generally available or on securing information sooner than other people get it. Simply knowing the status of the present and of the immediate past can be of great help in planning operations instead of, as in many situations, having to depend on facts that are weeks or even months old. For example, one use of computers by automobile and appliance manufacturers is keeping continual track of dealers' in-

---

[15]George W. Mitchell, "Forecasting State and Local Expenditures," *Journal of Business,* January, 1954, p. 18.

ventories so that the current rate of retail sales is known. A naïve short-run forecast that next week's sales are going to be the same as this week's when current sales are known is probably usually superior to the most elaborate method of projection that depends on data that are several weeks old. An interesting historical example of the latter occurred in 1815. By using their own news service, the Rothschilds received advance news of the outcome of the Battle of Waterloo, which gave them their chance to make a fortune on the London Stock Exchange.[16] A similar situation in which advance news has value to speculators occurs when the U.S. Department of Agriculture compiles its crop estimates in Washington, D.C. If the estimates are larger than had been expected, futures prices will fall, and the speculator with advance news can profit by selling grain futures before the new estimates are publicly released. The opposite is true if the estimates are lower than had been expected. This situation has led some persons to attempt to communicate with cohorts outside the building as soon as the estimates have been assembled. It is said that a man was once caught passing a signal from a washroom by means of adjusting the height of the window shade. Strict security measures are employed by the Department of Agriculture to prevent the premature export of crop estimates from the building.

"Forecasting the forecast" obviously presents another possibility along these lines. If, for example, an individual were able to come up with a close approximation of his own to the federal crop estimate and were able to make the estimate soon enough, he might be in a position to make speculative profits. (Actually, the cost of gathering and analyzing the necessary data would, in this particular case, probably bring a net loss rather than a profit.)

Methods of securing advance information vary from those which merely require alertness to those which are downright dishonest. Alertness was displayed by Andrew Carnegie, who secured advance information on industrial production by counting the number of smoking chimneys.[17] A less clearly ethical way of forecasting land values is used in the oil industry, where men are regularly employed to watch the drill rigs of other companies through field glasses and to rush to the nearest phone to take up all available options on adjacent land if they see oil struck.[18]

---

[16]Cecil Roth, *The Magnificent Rothschilds* (London: Robert Hale, Ltd., 1939), p. 23, says that contrary to popular legend, Nathan Mayer Rothschild's news service was not based on pigeon post.

[17]"Business Forecasting," *Business Week*, September 24, 1955, p. 6.

[18]Richard Austin Smith, "Business Espionage," *Fortune*, May, 1956, p. 119.

At the bottom of the list ethically are a variety of sharp and often illegal practices which may be ways either of ascertaining what exists or of forecasting what is coming. Engineering employees of rival firms are sometimes asked in job interviews to answer questions designed to disclose products and processes rather than to ascertain fitness for employment. Telephone wires may be tapped or a tiny portable transmitter planted under an executive's desk. Or industrial secrets may be stolen in outright cases of breaking into and entering premises. It is strongly recommended, however, that only the legitimate means of forecasting be studied further by the student. Otherwise, he may end up wearing "pen" stripes instead of pin stripes.

CASE 2–1:   AVERY SCREEN WIRE PRODUCTS COMPANY

In 1949, Walter Avery obtained a sales job with a local firm which sold and installed aluminum storm sash and doors and metal weather-stripping. He was quite successful in this business and, in 1953, established his own sales firm in the same business.

His market at first consisted primarily of older residences and a few commercial buildings; but subsequently, he began to obtain contracts to provide metal doors and sash on new homes where the undertaking was not large. For the new homes and buildings, Mr. Avery purchased the standard-size doors and windows from a manufacturer of such items. On older homes, however, the window and door openings were often of variable sizes and seldom standard by modern dimensions. To provide metal sash and doors for the latter, he contracted with various small shops to make the items to order. This was rather expensive and allowed him only a small margin on his sales.

Mr. Avery observed that commercial and apartment buildings were also using more metal sash and doors as well as trim. He often lost bids on these jobs because of price and quantity involved. In order to obtain any of this business on a substantial scale, Mr. Avery was convinced he could only do so profitably if he produced his own doors and windows. He therefore set up a small shop to assemble his products. He purchased aluminum and steel extrusions and wire screen direct from metal fabricators, and glass from suppliers. This arrangement permitted him to bid on both residential and commercial buildings, since he could now supply not only in quantity but also to specification. Financing this operation presented some problems; but by pledging his construction awards with his bank, he was able to obtain sufficient working capital to handle the increased volume of sales.

The business prospered, and by 1957 the firm employed sixty per-

Exhibit 1

AVERY SCREEN WIRE PRODUCTS COMPANY
Monthly Sales, Sash and Doors—January, 1954–May, 1961

Month	1954	1955	1956	1957	1958	1959	1960	1961
January	$ 9,132	$ 22,891	$ 44,033	$ 72,004	$ 90,633	$ 100,344	$ 99,181	$ 96,555
February	7,911	25,614	41,929	69,199	87,521	96,597	97,664	91,492
March	8,204	24,572	39,051	68,044	84,319	93,885	94,118	89,532
April	10,512	27,447	42,540	71,552	88,525	90,357	92,337	88,117
May	19,327	31,551	45,880	78,439	93,995	93,433	93,889	88,913
June	27,114	37,119	51,364	89,507*	96,197	99,518	97,414	
July	31,215	40,336	57,002	94,962	99,562	103,655	102,937	
August	22,461	46,111	63,099	95,101	103,212	105,541	106,004	
September	18,314	51,210	68,553	97,210	105,527	107,555	108,954	
October	19,761	51,040	74,500	97,235	106,329	107,348	109,033	
November	20,411	51,115	74,266	96,404	107,374	106,591	108,181	
December	21,515	47,229	75,427	95,891	104,193	103,284	105,910	
	$215,877	$456,235	$677,644	$1,025,548	$1,167,387	$1,208,108	$1,215,622	$454,609

*Includes sales to mail-order house under private brand.

sons and occupied rented quarters of approximately 30,000 square feet. In this same year the name of the firm was changed from John H. Avery, Contractor, to Avery Screen Wire Products Company. Early in 1957, Mr. Avery obtained a contract with a large mail-order and retail firm to manufacture metal windows and doors for it under the private brand name of the mail-order firm. In order to meet the increased sales resulting from this contract, the Avery company constructed a building to its specifications and installed some new and laborsaving equipment to increase production. One half the cost of this expansion was financed by the mail-order firm.

Exhibit 2

AVERY SCREEN WIRE PRODUCTS COMPANY
Monthly Sales, "Metalfab" Buildings—April, 1958–May, 1961

Month	1958	1959	1960	1961
January..................		$ 78,545	$ 128,665	$134,144
February................		82,147	130,499	134,109
March...................		89,515	132,557	135,007
April....................	$ 39,200	92,338	135,851	135,617
May.....................	43,731	101,288	137,772	136,411
June....................	46,884	111,315	139,550	
July.....................	57,102	127,882	148,662	
August..................	59,137	131,471	146,889	
September...............	68,443	131,486	145,314	
October.................	73,877	132,007	145,110	
November...............	72,896	131,218	142,199	
December...............	73,459	130,449	139,322	
	$534,729	$1,339,661	$1,672,390	$675,288

The new plant offered many economies of production. Metal was now purchased directly from mills and fabricated by extruding machines in the plant. Also installed were two wire-weaving machines to produce several grades of wire screen. New-type cutting and forming machines were also installed. Although sales in 1957 exceeded $1 million, the new plant upon completion presented a problem of excess capacity. In an attempt to make use of this excess capacity, the company undertook to produce and market sash, doors, and trim under its own brand name of "Avery." These were sold through manufacturers' representatives and by 1959 were on sale in thirty-one states. In addition to doors, sash, and trim, the company in 1958 introduced prefabricated metal buildings ranging in size from 4 by 6 feet to 20 by 30 feet. The smaller buildings were used frequently by homeowners and small

Exhibit 3

VALUE OF CONSTRUCTION CONTRACTS AWARDED, NONRESIDENTIAL AND RESIDENTIAL, 1957–61

(In Millions)

Month	1957 Nonresidential	1957 Residential	1958 Nonresidential	1958 Residential	1959 Nonresidential	1959 Residential	1960 Nonresidential	1960 Residential	1961 Nonresidential	1961 Residential
January	$ 914	$ 817	$ 759	$ 777	$ 818	$1,022	$ 801	$ 927	$ 813	$ 974
February	820	875	751	727	704	1,073	698	988	804	870
March	1,092	1,107	967	1,071	913	1,541	1,067	1,294	1,027	1,371
April	838	1,232	958	1,240	1,187	1,831	1,048	1,480	1,050	1,454
May	1,120	1,297	1,124	1,346	1,072	1,677	1,110	1,453		
June	1,186	1,135	976	1,364	1,055	1,762	1,110	1,483		
July	961	1,287	1,076	1,557	1,191	1,690	1,152	1,329		
August	1,008	1,284	1,079	1,451	961	1,551	1,177	1,433		
September	866	1,151	892	1,460	1,006	1,466	1,124	1,277		
October	910	1,165	955	1,595	1,003	1,515	1,165	1,390		
November	878	930	775	1,206	801	1,092	916	1,253		
December	699	759	748	981	790	993	994	878		

Source: U.S. Department of Commerce.

firms for auxiliary storage, while the larger buildings were used by construction firms for storage and garage purposes. The largest size was often used by farms and industrial firms, since several units could be erected and fastened together to make a building 20 feet wide and any desired length in multiples of 30 feet. The largest unit had a ridge-type roof and could be had in heights ranging from 9 to 17 feet. As shown in Exhibit 2, sales of these buildings, sold under the trade name "Metalfab," exceeded the volume of sash, door, and trim.

Exhibit 1 shows monthly sales of sash, doors, and trim from 1954 through May, 1961. Exhibit 2 shows sales of "Metalfab" buildings of all sizes from April, 1958, through May, 1961. Exhibit 3 shows residential and nonresidential building contracts by months for all states from 1957 through 1960.

In June, 1960, Mr. Avery was preparing to place orders for steel and aluminum plate, aluminum wire, and miscellaneous nuts, bolts, and screws to meet his coming year's needs. By placing his order for an entire year with arrangement for advanced deliveries, the firm was able to obtain substantial price advantages. In studying his sales for several years, Mr. Avery noted with concern that sales for the first four months of 1960 were lagging slightly behind 1959, whereas in the past each year had shown successively increasing sales.

In discussing the problem with his sales manager, the question of prices for the following year was considered. The sales manager suggested that perhaps the company should reduce its prices in order to stimulate sales. Mr. Avery stated that he was doubtful if a price reduction would result in increased sales.

QUESTIONS

1. Would you say that the variations in sales are the result of an emerging seasonal variation? Why? If you think there is evidence of seasonal variation, why had it not appeared in earlier years?
2. Is there evidence of cyclical fluctuation? What?
3. Test the data for any lead-lag relationship between the "value of construction contracts awarded" series and Avery's sales that could be useful for forecasting.
4. What price policy would you recommend, in view of the leveling-off in sales?
5. What is the nature of demand for sash, doors, and trim?

CASE 2-2:   CONTINENTAL RADIO AND TELEVISION CORPORATION

In 1924 the Landle Electric Company was manufacturing a line of electric motors, condensers, switches, and transformers which it sold to other manufacturers and industrial users. In November of that year the company began to manufacture radio receiving sets and speakers. At the time, radio sets were a relatively recent invention, and it was the company's first venture into the consumer market. Distribution of these sets was made through wholesalers and jobbers.

The first models produced by Landle Electric were priced at $555, exclusive of aerial. Radio sets were well received by the public so that by 1928, there were several hundred companies producing more than a thousand different brands. The Landle company manufactured all the components for its sets except tubes, cabinets, and speakers. These were purchased from other manufacturers. The earliest sets were practically handmade, but by 1929 the company was using assembly-line operations. Sales in 1928 were more than nine thousand sets.

In July, 1927, largely because of its success in the consumer market with radios, the company began the manufacture and sale of electric refrigerators, another consumer item which had been introduced to the public within the preceding few years. Using its present facilities and some newly constructed ones, the company manufactured its own compressors and motors, but purchased the boxes from another manufacturer. Sales of refrigerators also expanded until the depression which began in 1929.

The Landle company suffered sharp declines in sales and profits immediately following the economic collapse in 1929. In addition, prices of all the items it produced declined approximately 50 per cent. Price declines in radios, however, had begun in 1925; but this was due in large measure to technological improvements in both design and methods of production. Early in 1930 the company found itself with a large inventory on its own account as well as in the hands of its dealers. About 20 per cent of the radio inventory was eventually junked because of obsolescence.

In 1934, Landle Electric Company merged with the Nadine Corporation, a producer of commercial refrigerators and milk coolers. In 1935, another merger was completed with a producer of home laundry equipment. Thereafter the company was known as the Continental Radio Corporation.

During World War II the company devoted almost all of its facilities to the production of military goods, manufacturing various types of

Exhibit 1

WHOLESALE PRICE INDEX OF TELEVISION RECEIVERS
(1947–49 = 100)

Month	1947*	1948*	1949*	1950*	1951*	1952*	1953†	1954†	1955†	1956	1957	1958	1959	1960	1961
January....	..	..	..	..	..	..	74.5	73.5	69.0	69.7	69.9	71.2	70.2	69.0	69.3
February....	..	..	..	..	..	..	75.6	73.8	68.8	69.9	69.9	70.7	70.2	69.1	68.7
March.......	..	..	..	..	..	..	74.9	73.8	68.8	69.9	69.5	70.7	69.6	69.1	..
April........	96.3‡	100.1‡	103.6‡	96.8‡	92.8‡	92.9‡	74.9	73.8	68.8	69.5	69.5	70.7	69.6	69.0	..
May........	..	..	..	..	..	..	74.9	73.8	69.0	69.3	69.5	70.7	69.6	69.0	..
June........	..	..	..	..	..	..	75.0	70.6	68.8	69.1	69.7	70.0	69.6	69.0	..
July.........	..	..	..	..	..	..	74.3	70.3	68.9	69.3	70.8	71.1	70.9	69.0	..
August......	..	..	..	..	..	..	74.0	68.5	68.9	69.6	71.4	71.2	70.1	68.9	..
September...	..	..	..	..	..	..	74.2	68.7	69.3	70.1	71.4	71.2	70.1	68.9	..
October......	..	..	..	..	..	..	74.2	68.7	69.5	69.9	71.4	71.2	69.5	68.9	..
November....	..	..	..	..	..	..	74.2	69.2	69.5	69.9	71.4	69.3	69.2	68.9	..
December....	..	..	..	..	..	..	74.0	69.2	69.7	69.7	71.6	69.3	69.2	69.3	..

*Not available on a monthly basis.
†Prices of television sets only.
‡Yearly average of radio, phonograph, and television sets.

electronic equipment. A limited quantity of repair parts was produced for its consumer line. In 1946, after reconversion to its line of industrial and consumer goods, the company was among the first to place television sets on the market. The name of the company was then changed to Continental Radio and Television Corporation. In 1947 the company added electric dryers, electric ranges, and home freezers to its line.

The initial stages of television production presented several problems. Whereas the company had originally made almost all of the component parts of its radio sets, it now made relatively few of them. Other than condensers, transformers, and switches, it purchased its parts from other producers and assembled the sets. Television parts were deeply involved in patent rights, so that it was decided to purchase as many components as possible and to assemble the sets. Furthermore, recalling its early experience in the production of radios, expensive research in electronics was necessary to develop and produce many parts in television sets. It was anticipated that, like radios, television sets would undergo considerable improvement in design and performance which would result in changes in methods of production. The company's 1947 sets were priced from $395 to $795, depending upon screen size and cabinet style. In 1950 the company's prices ranged from $209.95 to $495 for sets with much larger viewing screens and more efficient performance. By 1960, there had been further slight price reductions, the company's prices ranging from $199.95 for portable sets to $439.95 for console types. Some models were offered for as high as $795, but this was due to more luxurious cabinets and extras such as remote-control devices. As shown in Exhibit 1, prices had remained fairly stable since 1955, although quality of service and performance had improved considerably.

In March of 1961 the sales manager was requested to provide a forecast of the number of television sets to be produced for the 1962 model year, together with suggested prices. Because so many of the components of sets were purchased from other manufacturers, it was necessary to place orders for the year's requirements in April for July delivery. New-model sets were usually introduced in September of each year. About two months' production was necessary to provide dealers with sufficient inventory at the time the new line was announced.

Continental Radio and Television Corporation sold all of its products in the national market, except for approximately 4 per cent, which was exported. In the television market the company had accounted for about 7 to 12 per cent of the total market and in 1961 anticipated a

10 per cent share. Exhibit 2 shows shipment of television sets by the firm from 1947 through 1960. As indicated in Exhibit 3, production of television sets experienced a phenomenal growth from 1947 to 1950, and then grew more slowly until 1955. Since 1956 the industry has failed to produce seven million sets annually. The large reduction in output in 1951 reflects restriction upon materials due to the Korean War.

Exhibit 2

SHIPMENT OF TELEVISION RECEIVERS, 1947–60

1947	7,152
1948	43,902
1949	135,307
1950	447,840
1951	376,999
1952	426,748
1953	577,264
1954	551,002
1955	681,745
1956	673,936
1957	659,481
1958	499,314
1959	601,578
1960	626,117

Exhibit 3

MONTHLY PRODUCTION OF TELEVISION RECEIVERS, 1947–60

Month	1947*	1948*	1949*	1950*	1951	1952
January	..	..	..	..	650,700	404,
February	..	..	..	..	679,300	409,
March	..	..	..	..	870,000	510,
April	..	..	..	..	500,000	322,
May	..	..	..	..	406,000	309,
June	..	..	..	..	352,500	361,
July	..	..	..	..	148,900	198,
August	..	..	..	..	146,700	397,
September	..	..	..	..~	337,300	755,
October	..	..	..	..	411,900	724,
November	..	..	..	..	415,300	780,
December	..	..	..	..	467,100	921,
Total	178,800	975,600	3,000,000	7,464,000	5,385,700	6,096,

*Not available on a monthly basis.
Note: In March, 1961, Continental had trade information indicating that January and Febr production had been 367,900 and 444,400 receivers, respectively. Indications were that March produc would be slightly under 500,000 sets.

In preparing his forecast, the sales manager was aware of several developments in the market. The rapid growth from 1947 to 1950 was clearly the result of the introduction of a new medium of communication. The growth was not dampened by the Korean War alone, but was limited by the fact that relatively few new television broadcasting stations had been approved by the Federal Communications Commission since 1948. A large number of applications was still pending, but new stations were usually approved only in areas where there was no station. Many areas had only one station, so that the choice of programs was limited. After 1948 the Federal Communications Commission had approved a number of applications for ultrahigh-frequency stations; but in the sales manager's opinion, these had not been successful. Many of the ultrahigh-frequency stations shortly went out of business. It had been necessary to build sets which would receive high-frequency signals as well as ultrahigh-frequency signals, and also to produce adapters for sets which were manufactured prior to the establishment of ultrahigh-frequency stations. Very few of the adapters were sold.

Another factor in the market was that much of the replacement of sets sold from 1947 to 1955 had been fairly well completed. The earlier sets had small screens, required installation charges, and frequently demanded expensive service. Sets produced after 1954–55 had larger screens comparable in size to current models, required only

1953	1954	1955	1956	1957	1958	1959	1960
719,200	420,600	654,600	588,300	450,200	434,000	437,000	526,500
730,600	426,900	702,500	576,300	464,700	370,400	459,500	503,500
810,100	599,600	831,200	680,000	559,800	416,900	494,000	549,500
567,900	457,600	583,200	549,600	361,200	302,600	389,300	422,600
481,900	396,300	467,400	467,900	342,400	267,000	431,900	422,200
524,500	544,100	590,000	553,000	543,800	377,100	571,000	518,900
316,300	307,000	344,300	336,900	360,700	275,000	350,400	268,900
603,800	633,400	647,900	612,900	673,700	507,500	547,400	462,300
770,100	947,800	939,500	894,200	832,600	621,700	808,300	678,900
580,400	921,500	759,700	820,800	662,000	495,600	706,600	500,000
561,200	858,500	631,700	680,000	574,600	437,800	560,800	429,800
449,800	833,400	604,600	627,000	573,500	414,900	593,200	405,500
215,800	7,346,700	7,756,600	7,386,900	6,399,200	4,920,500	6,349,400	5,688,600

Source: U.S. Department of Commerce.

nominal or no installation charge, and called for more infrequent service. Since 1954 the company had offered portable sets in several models, and these had sold more than other models in the complete line. The relatively recent introduction of stereo reproduction of records and magnetic tape was considered a major factor of competition with the higher priced console and combination television sets.

In the mid-1950's, price cutting had broken out at the dealer level; and to some extent, it had been pushed back to the manufacturer's level. As indicated in Exhibit 3, sales had been lagging since 1955, which had stimulated price concessions by dealers. The growth of discount houses had, in effect, obliterated the significance of suggested retail price by the manufacturer. In spite of this situation, Continental Radio and Television Corporation continued to publish a suggested list price for each model. Evidence of continued deterioration in prices is shown in Exhibit 1.

In December, 1960, the company had an inventory on hand of 453 of the 1960 models, with 3,271 in dealer hands. This was not considered an undesirable level. The company had 67,449 of the 1961 models on hand, and there were 198,552 in dealer hands. The 1960 models would probably be cleared by price reductions. The problem of color television was not considered as serious as a few years ago but was still a factor. In 1960 the company had produced and sold 6,000 color sets and had no inventory on hand of that model year. Included in the 1961 inventory above are approximately 16,000 color sets. The number of color telecasts was increasing, and it was anticipated that all of the three major television networks would be telecasting some part of their programs in color by 1963. Prices on color television sets had remained fairly constant, but the quality of color reception had been sharply improved, and they required far less frequent service.

As far as price considerations were concerned, the company anticipated increased costs of production. Almost all of its factory employees were union members, many of whom would seek new contracts during the year as present contracts expired. It was a foregone conclusion that labor costs would rise whether it be in the form of higher wages, fringe benefits, or both. It was anticipated that some reduction in the unit cost of production could be made in 1961 because of improved methods of production. In view of the present economic situation, it was recommended that no price changes be made for the 1962 model year.

Exhibit 4

DISPOSABLE INCOME, CONSUMER EXPENDITURES, CONSUMER SAVING,
GROSS PRIVATE INVESTMENT ANNUALLY, 1946–60
(In Billions)

Year	Disposable Income	Consumer Expenditures	Consumer Savings	Gross Private Investment
1946...........	$160.6	$147.1	$13.5	$28.1
1947...........	170.1	165.4	4.7	31.5
1948...........	189.3	178.3	11.0	43.1
1949...........	189.7	181.2	8.5	33.0
1950...........	207.7	195.0	12.6	50.0
1951...........	227.5	209.8	17.7	56.3
1952...........	238.7	219.8	18.9	49.9
1953...........	252.5	232.6	19.8	50.3
1954...........	256.9	238.0	18.9	48.9
1955...........	274.4	256.9	17.5	63.8
1956...........	292.9	269.9	23.0	67.4
1957...........	308.8	285.2	23.6	66.1
1958...........	317.9	293.2	24.7	56.6
1959...........	337.3	314.0	23.4	72.4
1960...........	351.8	328.9	22.9	72.4

Source: U.S. Department of Commerce.

Exhibit 5

CONSUMER CREDIT OUTSTANDING, 1954–60
(In Millions)

Year	Total	Consumer Durables Other than Automobiles and Modernization
1954....................	$32,464	$ 6,751
1955....................	38,882	7,634
1956....................	42,511	8,580
1957....................	45,286	8,782
1958....................	45,544	8,923
1959....................	52,119	10,476
1960:		
January................	51,468	10,386
February...............	51,182	10,254
March.................	51,298	10,192
April..................	52,353	10,281
May...................	52,991	10,339
June...................	53,662	10,462
July...................	53,809	10,452
August................	54,092	10,477
September.............	54,265	10,543
October...............	54,344	10,625
November.............	54,626	10,715
December.............	56,049	11,215
1961:		
January................	54,726	11,365
February...............	53,843	11,136

Source: U.S. Department of Commerce.

The general business outlook itself was somewhat mixed. The index of industrial production had been declining since February, 1960, and the decline had continued into 1961. On the other hand, consumer disposable income had shown no such tendency. The consumer price index had, however, continued to rise slowly but steadily throughout this same period. In the same period, private housing starts had also declined, while interest rates on mortgages as well as commercial loans had risen. There were some feelings of optimism, however, in that many economists predicted that the decline would come to an end in the summer of 1961 and a definite upturn would appear in the fall.

Exhibit 6

ACTUAL COSTS, MODELS 110 AND 210, TELEVISION RECEIVERS,
1960 AND 1961

ITEM	1960		1961*	
	Model 110	Model 210	Model 110	Model 210
Materials......................	$ 40.25	$ 29.82	$ 40.19	$ 29.67
Direct labor...................	21.26	18.97	21.70	19.05
Depreciation..................	2.04	2.02	2.06	2.03
Indirect labor.................	7.51	5.21	7.61	5.39
Factory overhead..............	3.34	2.99	3.39	3.08
Administrative and selling expense.	2.39	2.10	2.40	2.20
Total Cost.................	$ 76.79	$ 61.11	$ 77.35	$ 61.42
Suggested retail price...........	$299.95	$199.95	$299.95	$199.95

*Estimated.

Exhibit 4 provides data on income, consumer spending, and saving. Exhibit 5 shows the amount of consumer instalment credit outstanding, as well as that pertaining to durables other than automobiles. Exhibit 6 shows the cost of production of the two basic models of sets manufactured by Continental, as well as suggested list prices for the respective models.

QUESTIONS

1. Appraise the difficulties faced by Continental in forecasting in comparison with those of other business firms—for example, a gasoline refiner and distributor, and a building materials producer. Outline possible approaches to short-run forecasting for Continental after analysis of the data given.

2. What implications does your answer to question 1 have for questions of business policy, such as the advanced ordering of set components?

CASE 2-3: PROCTER & GAMBLE[19]

Procter & Gamble produces a wide line of quality shortenings, of which the best-known retail brands are Crisco and Fluffo. Shortenings made for restaurant, bakers, and industrial use include such brand names as Primex, Sweetex, Pertex, Selex, Flakewhite, and Frymax.

For many years, Procter & Gamble's shortenings were made entirely from vegetable oils, such as soybean oil and cottonseed oil. Early in the 1950's, however, the company began to merchandise three brands that utilized lard as an ingredient. In the manufacture of these products, lard and soy bean oil can be interchanged without downgrading the product. Furthermore, the percentage of lard used in the manufacturing process can be varied over a fairly wide range. For example, let us assume that in early 1959 the company could use a maximum of twenty tank cars of lard per week (60,000 pounds per tank car) when the price was favorable. When the price of lard was unfavorable, the soybean oil usage could be increased and the usage of lard reduced to six or seven tank cars per week.

Purchases of lard are made from a large number of packing houses. Most of these suppliers merchandise some of their lard in their own products. These products include lard sold in retail packages and lard sold to bakers, hotels, etc. A few packers also make shortening from mixtures of lard and vegetable oil. The packers' surplus lard production is sold as "loose" lard in tank cars. Procter & Gamble purchases loose lard in tank car quantities, with delivery made 1 to 3 weeks after purchase. Contact with the sellers is maintained by telephone, plus an occasional visit. Some of the telephone contact is direct with sellers, but in other cases a broker acts as an intermediary. All of the sellers and brokers, of course, are in contact with other buyers. The price for each transaction is really a separate negotiation, and actual trading prices can fluctuate from day to day or even from transaction to transaction. The trading prices are determined by the supply and demand conditions effective in the market at a given time.

Because of the nature of trading, it is impossible to quote a precise "market" price at any time. However, the loose-lard quotation on the Chicago Board of Trade is widely used as a market indicator by both buyers and sellers. A brief summary of these quotations is shown in

---

[19]This is one of a series of marketing problems prepared by Procter & Gamble, and the authors express appreciation to the company for permission to use it. Brand names, raw-material names, market prices, freight rates, and lard production figures are actual. However, figures regarding the company's usage are hypothetical.

Exhibit 1
CHICAGO BOARD OF TRADE QUOTATIONS FOR LOOSE LARD
(Cents per Pound, Delivered Chicago Basis, on Tank-Car Lots)

Date	High	Low	Average of Daily Closes
1951–52:			
October...	b 17⅝	a 13¾	16.40
November.	n 15	b 12⅞	13.95
December.	n 14⅞	a 12⅝	13.73
January..	n 13⅞	12½	13.00
February..	n 12⅜	10	11.46
March....	n 11⅜	10	10.58
April......	10¼	9¼	9.62
May......	11½	9⅛	10.32
June......	10⅞	9⅝	10.19
July......	11½	b 9	9.89
August....	10¼	n 8⅝	9.38
September.	b 10	8¼	9.14
1952–53:			
October...	n 8⅞	n 8⅛	8.48
November.	b 8¾	8⅛	8.37
December.	n 8¼	7¼	7.68
January...	7¾	6⅞	7.23
February..	8½	n 7	7.90
March....	9½	n 8¼	9.07
April......	9¾	n 8¾	9.26
May......	10½	9⅞	10.32
June......	10¼	8	9.13
July......	12⅞	n 10	11.62
August....	17¼	12¼	14.88
September.	n 20	13	17.11
1953–54:			
October...	n 17¼	14	15.79
November.	15	n 13½	14.11
December.	b 17	b 15½	15.98
January...	a 16¼	14½	15.22
February..	b 16⅜	b 15½	16.04
March....	18⅛	15¾	16.91
April......	n 20½	a 17⅝	18.86
May......	n 18	16¼	17.11
June......	n 17¼	n 14⅛	15.40
July......	a 17	n 15½	16.19
August....	n 18⅞	a 16	17.10
September.	16⅝	n 14⅜	15.52
1954–55:			
October...	b 15½	n 13¾	14.24
November.	b 15¼	n 12⅜	13.76
December.	12⅞	a 11¾	12.16
January...	11⅞	11¼	11.51
February..	n 11⅜	10⅝	10.99
March....	b 11⅝	a 10⅝	10.87
April......	n 12¼	n 11⅜	11.88
May......	11¾	b 10½	11.18
June......	n 11¼	n 10½	10.82
July......	n 11¼	n 9¾	10.52
August....	b 10⅝	b 9¼	9.91
September.	n 11¼	n 9⅞	10.29
1955–56:			
October...	n 12¼	n 9⅝	10.71
November.	10⅜	n 9	9.89
December.	9¼	8½	8.90
January...	b 9¾	n 8½	9.01
February..	n 10	n 9⅜	9.70
March....	n 10⅛	n 9⅜	9.71
April......	n 12	n 10	10.93
May......	n 12¼	10¾	11.29
June......	10¾	9⅞	10.18
July......	n 11⅞	9¾	10.41
August....	12¼	n 10½	11.42
September.	n 12⅜	n 11⅛	11.87
1956–57:			
October...	n 13	n 11½	12.20
November.	13⅞	a 11⅜	12.66
December.	n 14	n 12¾	13.45
January...	n 14¼	n 13¼	13.97
February..	n 14¼	13⅛	13.55
March....	a 13¼	a 12¾	13.02
April......	n 13¼	12½	12.87
May......	12½	n 10¾	11.44
June......	n 13	n 11¼	12.26
July......	b 13	n 12⅝	12.86
August....	n 13	n 11½	12.34
September.	n 13⅛	n 11¼	12.38
1957–58:			
October...	n 12 5/16	n 11½	11.94
November.	n 11¾	11	11.22
December.	n 11⅛	n 10¾	10.91
January...	10⅞	10⅜	10.62
February..	12⅞	10½	11.54
March....	12	11⅜	11.65
April......	11¾	11⅛	11.55
May......	12	11½	11.67
June......	12	11	11.51
July......	12¾	11⅜	12.03
August....	13⅜	12¼	13.01
September.	12	11	11.47
1958–59:			
October...	12½	11	11.65
November.	11	10	10.46
December.	10	8⅝	9.28
January...	8⅞	8½	8.62
February..	8⅝	8¼	8.49
March....	8⅝	8¼	8.39

Note: The letter *a* means asked; *b*, bid; and *n*, nominal.

Sources: Data for 1951–57 highs and lows from annual reports of Board of Trade of the City of Chicago; 1958 highs and lows from *Procter & Gamble Chart Book;* monthly averages from *Procter & Gamble Chart Book.*

Exhibit 1. The term "delivered Chicago basis" means that the seller allows freight from the origin to Chicago, and the buyer pays the balance of the freight (see Exhibit 2 for actual freight rates for typical points). For example, lard purchased from Davenport, Iowa, at 9 cents per pound, delivered Chicago basis, would actually be delivered to

Exhibit 2

CRUDE RENDERED LARD FREIGHT RATES, EFFECTIVE MARCH 4, 1959

(In Cents per Hundredweight)

ORIGINS	– DESTINATIONS				
	Chicago	Cincinnati	New York	Dallas	Long Beach
Illinois:					
Chicago..........		64	130	118½	272
Indiana:					
Indianapolis........	30	34	121		
Muncie...........	60	34	118		
Iowa:					
Davenport.........	29	88	143	130	260
Dubuque..........	29	90	144	134	260
Fort Dodge........	52	115	170	130	260
Mason City........	47	110	162	133	260
Storm Lake........	61	124	178	134	260
Waterloo..........	41	104	157	132	260
Minnesota:					
Austin............	47	110	162	134	260
Missouri:					
St. Joseph.........	63	122	174		236
Nebraska:					
Fremont...........	70	133	186	104½	244
Ohio:					
Columbus..........	76	46	106		
Troy.............	70	39	114		
Wisconsin:					
Madison...........	29	88	136	139	267

Cincinnati, Ohio, at 9.59 cents per pound. (It should be noted that loose lard is hardly ever sold for future delivery, and speculation in the raw material is more likely to be accomplished by outright purchase. Physical possession of lard results in a carrying charge of about 5 cents per hundredweight per month.)

Procter & Gamble uses lard in Cincinnati, Ohio, and Dallas, Texas. Approximately two thirds of the usage is at Cincinnati, which is supplied from two areas. The first area includes most of western Ohio, Indiana, southern Illinois, and Kentucky. Lard from this area can normally be purchased, "delivered Cincinnati," at the Chicago loose-lard price, plus ¼ cent per pound. This area will normally supply the company with six or eight cars of lard per week during the heavy slaughter season, but only two or three cars per week during the late spring, summer, and early fall. The second supply area for Cincinnati includes Iowa, Minnesota, Wisconsin, and Nebraska. Normally, good quantities of lard can be purchased from points in this territory on a Chicago basis. Lard for Dallas comes from the Iowa-Nebraska area, with a little coming from local producers. Purchases of lard for Dallas from Iowa-Nebraska are normally on a Chicago basis. There is little lard produced west of Omaha and Kansas City.

Competitive manufacturers of shortenings are also able to use lard as an alternative for soybean oil. Chicago is an important production point for shortenings of this type, and buyers at this location can usually purchase lard delivered to their plants at the Chicago loose-lard quotation. Other manufacturers of shortening throughout the country use some lard, and it is believed that the majority of their purchases are made on a Chicago basis.

In order to convert crude fats into shortening, a series of processing operations is required. From a cost standpoint, there is little difference between the cost to convert soybean oil to shortening compared with the cost of processing lard, except for the loss of weight during the refining operation. The weight loss for lard is slightly over 2 per cent, while the effective loss of weight for soybean oil is 7 per cent. About half of the value lost is recovered in by-product form.

Procter & Gamble cannot be considered a speculative buyer of material, since the company normally does not take extreme positions, either long or short. Generally, the company is willing to buy material fairly steadily as required and make its profit through manufacturing and mechandising. At times, however, the company will think that a market trend is fairly evident and under these circumstances will make some change in its owning position. In past years, Procter & Gamble has been quite successful in accumulating large supplies of lard during periods of low price.

On April 1, 1959, the price for soybean oil was 9¼ cents f.o.b. Decatur, Illinois (see Exhibit 3). This converted to delivered prices of approximately 9½ cents Chicago, 9¾ Cincinnati, and 10 cents

Dallas. On the same day, Chicago lard was 8⅝ cents. Using Iowa freight rates, this made delivered prices about 9¼ cents Cincinnati and 9½ cents Dallas, which was a relatively attractive pricing situation for lard.

Lard prices had moved quite widely since World War II, creating a number of speculative possibilities (see chart, Exhibit 4). The April 1,

Exhibit 3

CHICAGO SOYBEAN OIL FUTURES, MARCH, 1959

(Cents per Pound)

		FUTURES				
DATE	CASH SPOT	May	July	September	October	December
March 2.....	9.375	9.27	9.17	8.92	8.82	8.82
3.....	9.375	9.27	9.18	8.94	8.83	8.83
4.....	9.50	9.40	9.34	9.08	8.96	8.95
5.....	9.50	9.31	9.24	8.99	8.85	8.85
6.....	9.375	9.29	9.24	9.00	8.87	8.85
9.....	9.375	9.28	9.23	8.99	8.84	8.82
10.....	9.375	9.30	9.27	9.00	8.84	8.81
11.....	9.50	9.39	9.34	9.04	8.88	8.85
12.....	9.50	9.37	9.34	9.04	8.89	8.85
13.....	9.375	9.30	9.26	9.00	8.90	8.86
16.....	9.375	9.29	9.26	9.03	8.97	8.92
17.....	9.375	9.28	9.25	9.03	8.96	8.92
18.....	9.375	9.31	9.27	9.03	8.93	8.91
19.....	9.25	9.23	9.20	8.94	8.83	8.82
20.....	9.25	9.26	9.21	8.98	8.91	8.87
23.....	9.25	9.22	9.17	8.96	8.89	8.85
24.....	9.25	9.20	9.15	8.92	8.87	8.84
25.....	9.25	9.19	9.14	8.91	8.86	8.84
26.....	9.375	9.27	9.21	8.99	8.94	8.92
30.....	9.375	9.29	9.25	9.07	9.02	8.98
31.....	9.25	9.24	9.21	9.01	8.95	8.92
April 1.....	9.25	9.19	9.16	8.94	8.88	8.85

Note: Cash spot basis: prompt or ten-day shipment.

1959, price was near the low of a two-year decline from 14 cents. There were some indications that the market was "bottoming out," and buying was fairly aggressive in late March. On the other hand, the Commodity Research Section of the Buying Department prepared a report (Exhibit 5) showing that hog slaughter for the rest of 1959 would exceed that of the same months in 1958. Hog slaughter follows fairly regular cycles, with production upswings lasting from 14 to 30 months. The estimates of lard production, stocks, and domestic consumption for the period February-September, 1959 (in Exhibit 6) were also prepared by the Commodity Research Section. These were based on the slaughter figures and on past consumption data. The lard export estimates were based on a USDA survey of foreign demand and were believed to be accurate.

Exhibit 4

AVERAGE MONTHLY PRICE—CRUDE SOYBEAN OIL
AND LOOSE LARD (CHICAGO)

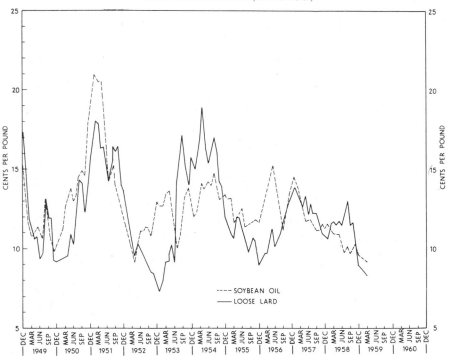

Soybean oil prices had also declined from the 14-cent level in early 1957 to the 9¼-cent level. This price had shown some signs of stability during March, and the company expected little price change until new crop prospects became known. The "intent to plant" report issued by the USDA on March 10 indicated a slightly higher acreage of soybeans more or less in line with a rising trend which began before the war. The summer growing weather would be the most important crop determinant. A poor yield would mean higher oil prices, while an excellent yield could reduce prices. The market effect of the weather would probably not be felt until August or September.

Exhibit 5

COMMERCIAL HOG SLAUGHTER*
(Thousands of Head)

Month	1951–52	1952–53	1953–54	1954–55	1955–56	1956–57	1957–58	1958–59	1959–60
October	6,950	6,878	6,094	6,223	7,226	7,507	7,224	6,979	(7,700)†
November	7,856	7,099	6,649	6,969	8,100	7,705	6,536	6,227	(7,300)
December	8,285	8,777	6,452	7,409	8,672	6,790	6,603	6,955	(7,500)
January	8,415	7,764	5,874	6,810	8,038	6,880	6,714	7,030	
February	7,164	5,812	4,887	5,761	7,102	5,996	5,421	(6,728)	
March	7,140	6,232	5,648	6,714	7,514	6,381	5,793	(7,071)	
April	6,563	5,450	4,724	5,449	6,260	5,977	5,920	(6,700)	
May	5,622	4,548	4,205	5,098	5,865	5,866	5,301	(6,155)	
June	5,256	4,448	4,272	4,608	5,177	4,792	5,010	(5,550)	
July	4,657	4,106	4,123	4,197	5,064	5,032	5,162	(5,710)	
August	4,642	4,279	4,723	5,423	5,524	5,310	5,348	(5,780)	
September	5,479	5,078	5,769	6,158	5,967	5,997	6,165	(6,790)	
Total	78,029	70,471	63,420	70,819	80,509	74,233	71,197	(77,675)	(85,000)

*Commercial hog slaughter = all slaughter of hogs except slaughter on farms.
†Parentheses indicate estimate.

Exhibit 6

COMMERCIAL LARD SITUATION IN THE UNITED STATES

(In Millions of Pounds)

Date	Beginning Stocks	Production	Exports	Domestic Usage	Used in Shortening
1955–56:					
October............	75	214	56	158	31
November..........	75	264	67	174	34
December..........	98	292	70	173	27
January............	147	273	65	171	30
February..........	184	232	48	158	38
March.............	210	254	62	169	36
April..............	233	207	59	155	39
May...............	226	199	69	145	43
June..............	211	180	45	143	29
July...............	203	170	42	153	25
August............	178	172	41	168	40
September.........	141	177	38	157	30
1956–57:					
October............	123	228	47	198	46
November..........	106	247	47	203	56
December..........	103	226	48	169	44
January............	112	226	38	199	47
February..........	101	198	36	151	37
March.............	112	216	62	147	30
April..............	119	207	44	155	26
May...............	127	211	66	152	34
June..............	120	174	51	136	31
July...............	107	166	35	136	24
August............	102	159	24	160	27
September.........	77	173	31	150	22
1957–58:					
October............	69	216	43	174	28
November..........	68	207	37	159	38
December..........	79	216	33	161	34
January............	101	221	33	188	36
February..........	101	170	36	144	36
March.............	91	177	36	147	32
April..............	85	188	22	164	30
May...............	87	178	36	142	30
June..............	87	167	31	157	28
July...............	66	167	34	144	19
August............	55	158	27	136	17
September.........	50	182	25	161	17
1958–59:					
October............	48	217	39	170	21
November..........	56	201	40	147	25
December..........	70	228	26	177	27
January............	95	228	42	172	
February..........	109	211	38	159	
March.............	123	231	40	175	
April..............	139	224	45	170	
May...............	148	210	45	155	
June..............	158	196	40	160	

Exhibit 6 (Continued)

Date	Beginning Stocks	Production	Exports	Domestic Usage	Used in Shortening
1958–59:					
July...............	154	190	40	170	
August.............	134	182	40	170	
September..........	106	203	40	165	

Notes:

1. Commercial lard is all lard produced in the country except for lard from farm slaughter. The commercial lard production is reported by the USDA.

2. The figures on beginning stocks, exports, and used in shortening are collected by the Bureau of the Census from monthly questionnaires.

3. Beginning stocks include stocks of lard in all positions except lard in the hands of retailers and consumers.

4. The historical figures for domestic usage are determined by deduction, using the production, export, and stock figures.

5. The figures reported as used in shortening include only lard that is mixed with other fats to form a compound shortening and do not include lard that is used as lard. The quantity used in shortening is also included as a part of domestic usage.

6. All data are estimated for the period February-September, 1959.

On April 1, 1959, the company owned about ten weeks' supply of lard (two hundred carloads), all purchased after December, 1958. In order to insure uninterrupted factory schedules and be able to buy on an orderly basis, the company felt that a minimum of 6 weeks' ownership was necessary. The vice president for purchases and the manager of fats and oils purchasing met on April 1 to develop a position with respect to lard purchases. One alternative considered was to extend the coverage of lard beyond the present position. The second alternative was to buy additional lard but to "hedge" this lard in the soybean oil futures market by selling futures contracts. Each purchase of lard would be offset by an equivalent "short" sale of July or September soybean oil futures on the Chicago Board of Trade. This would be profitable if soybean oil declined more rapidly than lard, since the profit on the short sale of soybean oil would be larger than the loss on lard. It would also be profitable if lard moved up more rapidly than soybean oil. A loss would occur, of course, if the spread between the two prices widened. The third and fourth possibilities would be to maintain the present lard position or to reduce it below the present level.

There was another alternative which was not seriously considered. This was the purchase of lard with hedge sales made on the Chicago Board of Trade drum-lard futures market. The manager of fats and oils purchasing did not like to be short on this market because of the difficult problem of making delivery if it were necessary. Deliveries are not usual on futures markets, but trading of drum lard is so limited that a "short" might find it preferable to deliver drummed lard instead of closing out his contract by a purchase. Delivery requires that drummed lard be put into cold storage at Chicago, and the company has no drumming or cold-storage facilities in Chicago and normally owns no lard in that city. Another reason was the lack of any normal or fixed relationship between loose-lard prices and drum-lard prices. For the purposes of this case, you may assume that the company was correct in not considering this alternative.

QUESTIONS

1. What decision should be made concerning lard ownership?
2. What forecast was required for your answer to question 1? How did you make it? What alternative methods could be used with the data available? With other data that the company might have secured?

Date	(1) Average Work Week of Production Workers, Manufacturing (Hours per Employee)	(9) Construction Contracts Awarded for Commercial and Industrial Buildings (Millions of Square Feet of Floor Space)	(13) Number of New Business Incorporations	(17) Price per Unit of Labor Cost Index (1957–59 = 100*)	(19) Index of Stock Prices, 500 Stocks (1941–43 = 10)
1959:					
January......	40.0	31.93	15,831	103.0	55.62
February.....	40.2	32.16	16,622	103.8	54.77
March.......	40.4	35.11	16,229	103.4	56.15
April........	40.6	41.92	16,463	105.1	57.10
May.........	40.7	38.55	16,72.	106.2	57.96
June........	40.6	34.19	15,291	105.4	57.46
July........	40.3	37.64	16,650	104.4	59.74
August......	40.4	34.14	16,007	103.9	59.40
September....	40.0	38.38	15,768	103.0	57.05
October......	40.1	41.44	14,822	102.4	57.00
November....	39.7	36.03	15,134	101.4	57.23
December.....	40.2	39.44	15,525	104.3	59.06
1960:					
January......	40.4	37.32	16,561	103.6*	58.03
February.....	40.1	36.93	15,274	102.9	55.78
March.......	39.9	36.73	15,233	102.7	55.02
April........	39.8	38.73	15,280	102.1	55.73
May.........	40.1	39.25	15,176	101.5	55.22
June........	39.9	40.31	15,630	101.1	57.26
July........	39.9	38.87	15,828	101.5	55.84
August......	39.6	39.38	15,114	100.7	56.51
September....	39.4	38.96	15,112	100.8	54.81

CASE 2-4: LEADING INDICATORS AND CYCLICAL TURNING POINTS

Such has the interest been in the use of leading indicators to predict upturns and downturns in general business conditions that the U.S. Department of Commerce through its Bureau of the Census has published for several years *Business Cycle Developments,* a monthly available about the twentieth of the month following that of the data. It includes about seventy principal indicators—leading, coincident, and lagging—and draws heavily upon the pioneering work of the National Bureau of Economic Research in its selection of the indicators and in its presentation of analytical measures utilizing the indicators. Any business economist engaged in forecasting where general business con-

Exhibit 1

BASIC DATA FOR BUSINESS CYCLE SERIES, EIGHT LEADING
INDICATORS AND FOUR ROUGHLY COINCIDENT INDICATORS
January, 1959, through April, 1963

(23)	(24)	(29)	(43)	(47)	(49)	(52)
Index of Industrial Material Prices 1957–59 = 100*)	Value of Manufacturers' New Orders, Machinery and Equipment Industries (Billions of Dollars)	Index of New Private Housing Units Authorized by Local Building Permits (1957–59 = 100*)	Unemployment Rate, Total (Invert for Cyclical Indicator) (Per Cent)	Index of Industrial Production (1957–59 = 100*)	Gross National Product in Current Dollars, Quarterly Series (Annual Rate, Billions of Dollars)	Personal Income (Annual Rate, Billions of Dollars)
89.0	4.46	1,243	5.97	100.3		371.7
88.9	4.73	1,293	5.82	101.9	472.2	373.9
90.4	4.97	1,337	5.66	103.6		378.4
91.2	4.80	1,258	5.18	106.6		381.9
91.9	4.85	1,230	5.04	109.2	488.5	384.9
92.2	5.11	1,234	5.04	109.6		386.9
92.2	5.16	1,186	5.16	107.6		387.1
92.6	4.85	1,190	5.37	103.6	482.3	383.7
93.9	5.02	1,154	5.55	103.2		384.5
94.5	5.12	1,088	5.79	102.0		384.2
94.6	4.99	1,083	5.76	102.6	488.3	388.7
93.7	5.37	1,147	5.46	108.8		393.7
105.7*	5.04	98.3*	5.29	111.7*		395.7
104.3	5.14	97.9	4.96	111.0	501.7	395.2
102.4	5.06	88.1	5.45	110.5		395.3
103.8	5.12	95.1	5.21	109.7		400.2
104.1	5.17	95.9	5.18	109.9	504.8	401.6
102.7	5.01	88.5	5.46	109.6		402.5
101.6	4.78	91.6	5.48	109.1		402.4
102.1	4.96	87.3	5.66	108.7	503.7	403.2
101.2	4.87	87.4	5.60	107.8		403.8

Exhibit 1 (Continued)

Date	(1) Average Work Week of Production Workers, Manufacturing (Hours per Employee)	(9) Construction Contracts Awarded for Commercial and Industrial Buildings (Millions of Square Feet of Floor Space)	(13) Number of New Business Incorpora- tions	(17) Price per Unit of Labor Cost Index (1957–59 = 100*)	(19) Index of Stock Prices, 500 Stocks (1941-43 = 10)
1960:					
October	39.5	39.44	15,035	101.0	53.73
November	39.3	39.44	14,264	101.2	55.47
December	38.5	38.15	14,097	100.1	56.80
1961:					
January	39.0	36.21	13,607	99.6	59.72
February	39.3	36.49	14,570	99.9	62.17
March	39.3	37.49	14,658	99.8	64.12
April	39.7	35.62	15,327	100.9	65.83
May	39.8	35.16	15,298	101.1	66.50
June	39.9	36.73	15,431	101.7	65.62
July	40.0	36.57	15,492	102.3	65.44
August	40.0	39.32	15,277	103.4	67.79
September	39.6	38.73	15,402	103.6	67.29
October	40.2	33.88	16,035	103.2	68.00
November	40.6	41.61	16,149	102.9	71.08
December	40.4	41.69	15,711	103.2	71.74
1962:					
January	39.8	38.99	15,279	102.2	69.07
February	40.3	44.10	15,775	102.4	70.22
March	40.5	45.19	15,727	102.8	70.29
April	40.8	40.87	15,372	101.9	68.05
May	40.6	45.39	15,363	102.2	62.99
June	40.5	42.99	14,990	102.3	55.63
July	40.5	39.86	15,171	103.4'	56.97
August	40.2	42.65	15,216	102.1	58.52
September	40.5	39.90	15,232	105.0	58.00
October	40.1	41.62	15,121	103.4	56.17
November	40.4	41.68	14,892	104.4	60.04
December	40.3	42.48	14,767	103.2	62.64
1963:					
January	40.2	44.94	14,457	102.9	65.06
February	40.3	46.98	15,398	102.3	65.92
March	r 40.4	38.92	15,474	r 102.9	65.67
April	p 40.3	n.a.	15,255	p 103.1	68.75
					(70.43)

Notes: Numbers at heads of columns denote the numbers given to the series in the source. Numbers 1–29 are NBER leading indicators, and numbers 43–52 are NBER roughly coincident series. All series are seasonally adjusted except 19, which displays no consistent seasonal.

Asterisks (*) denote series in which a major change in method or base of reporting is made between 1959 and 1960 data. For 1959 series, 17 was given on a 1947–49 equals 100 base. On this base, January 1960, rose to 105. Similarly, series 23 rose to 94.4 on the 1947–49 base used for 1959 figures. For 1959 series 29 is reported on an annual rate in thousands of housing authorizations. January, 1960, fell to 1,070 on th

(23) Index of Industrial Material Prices (1957-59 = 100*)	(24) Value of Manufacturers' New Orders, Machinery and Equipment Industries (Billions of Dollars)	(29) Index of New Private Housing Units Authorized by Local Building Permits (1957-59 = 100*)	(43) Unemployment Rate, Total (Invert for Cyclical Indicator) (Per Cent)	(47) Index of Industrial Production (1957-59 = 100*)	(49) Gross National Product in Current Dollars, Quarterly Series (Annual Rate, Billions of Dollars)	(52) Personal Income (Annual Rate, Billions of Dollars)
99.7	4.65	89.9	5.98	107.0	503.3	404.7
98.5	4.81	91.4	6.20	105.4		403.8
96.8	4.66	87.1	6.60	103.6		402.6
97.3	4.79	89.3	6.68	103.3		403.4
99.3	4.80	89.4	7.03	103.4	500.8	404.2
103.1	5.10	92.3	6.82	103.8		408.5
104.1	4.99	92.5	7.01	106.6		410.6
104.4	5.17	93.0	7.11	108.8	513.1	413.3
101.0	5.30	97.6	6.91	110.9		416.4
101.7	5.28	98.4	6.96	112.0		420.1
102.9	5.55	101.2	6.67	113.4	522.3	418.3
102.9	5.45	97.4	6.69	112.0		419.7
102.3	5.59	103.1	6.42	113.5		423.6
98.9	5.74	102.7	6.07	114.8	538.6	427.8
101.0	5.48	111.6	5.98	115.6		430.5
102.9	5.78	103.9	5.84	114.3		428.8
100.6	5.71	113.1	5.69	116.0	545.0	431.9
100.4	5.59	105.3	5.49	117.0		435.2
98.3	5.47	112.4	5.58	117.7		438.3
97.8	5.60	103.2	5.52	118.4	552.0	439.7
95.4	5.62	104.0	5.50	118.6		440.7
94.2	5.71	106.1	5.13	119.3		441.9
94.5	5.60	102.8	5.67	119.7	555.3	443.0
94.0	5.69	107.3	5.63	119.8		443.5
94.9	5.62	107.4	5.34	119.2		445.6
96.4	5.85	115.8	5.76	119.6	563.5	448.2
95.8	5.74	120.6	5.54	119.1		450.4
95.5	5.75	117.3	5.77	118.9		452.4
95.1	r 5.89	112.8	6.09	r 119.5	r 571.8	451.1
94.4	r 5.79	r 112.9	5.59	r 120.6		r 453.2
94.5	p 6.06	p 110.6	5.65	p 122.4		p 455.8
(95.3)						

sis. For series 47 the 1959 figures are expressed on a 1957 equals 100 base. On this base the index rose 111.1 in January, 1960. These different bases have been left in the table as a reminder of the occasional ajor and many minor revisions that are made in statistical indicators as better information becomes railable.

The letter r means revised; p preliminary; n.a., not available.

Sources: The 1959 data are from *Business Cycle Developments*, October, 1961; and the 1960-63 data e from *ibid.*, May, 1963.

Exhibit 2

DATES OF PEAKS AND TROUGHS OF BUSINESS CYCLES AND
SELECTED LEADING AND COINCIDENT INDICATORS

Business cycles—dates and
  duration:
  Dates of peaks............... November, 1948   July, 1953
  Months of expansion at peak...   37   45
  Dates of troughs.............   October, 1949
  Months of contraction at trough.   8

Corresponding peak and trough
  dates for special business indicators:
  1. Average work week.......   n.s.c.   April, 1949   April, 1953
  9. Construction contracts..... March, 1946 August, 1949   n.s.c.
  13. New business incorpora-
        tions................. July, 1946   February, 1949   n.s.c.
  17. Price per unit of labor..... January, 1948 May, 1949   February, 195
  19. Index of stock prices...... June, 1948   June, 1949   January, 1953
  24. Value of manufacturers' new
        orders................. April, 1948   April, 1949   February, 195
  29. Index of new private
        housing   n.a.   n.a.   n.a.
  43. Unemployment rate
        (inverted)............. January, 1948   October, 1949   June, 1953
  47. Index of industrial produc-
        tion................... July, 1948   October, 1949   July, 1953
  49. Gross national product in
        current dollars......... Fourth quarter, Second quarter, Second quarte
                                   1948   1949   1953
  52. Personal income......... October, 1948   October, 1949   October, 1953

Note: The letters *n.s.c.* mean no specific cycle related to reference dates. The reference dates a
those denoting the peaks and troughs of the general business cycle, and those selected by the Nation
Bureau of Economic Research have come to have at least semiofficial standing. The letters *n.a.* mea
not available.

ditions are important would find this publication a valuable source and
would wish to be familiar with the National Bureau's work, summed
up in the two volumes of *Business Cycle Indicators.*[20]

This case is designed to familiarize the student with both the possibilities and the pitfalls in using the leading indicators in forecasting.
No one of the eight leading indicators for which data are presented in
Exhibits 1 and 2 fully satisfies the following four criteria for the ideal
indicator that forecasters would like to have: logical reasons for supposing the indicator will lead general business conditions, a long statistical record of leadership (both of these increase one's confidence that
there should be a high probability of the lead relationship continuing),
consistent periods of precedence by highs of the indicator before cyclical
peaks and lows of the indicator before cyclical troughs, and substantial

[20]Geoffrey H. Moore (ed.) (Princeton: Princeton University Press, 1961).

	July, 1957 35		April, 1958 9	May, 1960 25	February, 1961 9
ıgust, 1954 13					
ɔril, 1954 n.s.c.	November, 1955 March, 1956	April, 1958 June, 1958		May, 1959 n.s.c.	December, 1960 n.s.c.
n.s.c. ecember, 1953 ·ptember, 1953	February, 1956 March, 1957 July, 1956	November, 1957 April, 1958 December, 1957	April, 1959 May, 1959 July, 1959	January, 1961 January, 1961 October, 1960	
nuary, 1954	March, 1957	February, 1958	May, 1959	October, 1960	
n.a.	February, 1955	February, 1958	November, 1958	December, 1960	
·ptember, 1954	March, 1957	July, 1958	February, 1960	May, 1961	
ɔril, 1954	February, 1957	April, 1958	January, 1960	January, 1961	
cond quarter, 1954	Third quarter, 1957	First quarter, 1958	Second quarter, 1960	First quarter, 1961	
arch, 1954	August, 1957	February, 1958	n.s.c.	n.s.c.	

Source: Appendixes A and B, *Business Cycle Developments*, May, 1963.

cyclical variation as compared with irregular variation in the leading series so that irregular movements will not be misinterpreted as harbingers of cyclical upturns and downturns.

The only one of the eight leading indicators in Exhibits 1 and 2 which has on the average displayed a greater cyclical component than irregular component in monthly changes is the index of industrial materials prices. Even for it, the irregular component has been 0.91 of the cyclical, while for construction contracts awarded the ratio has been 4.34, the highest for the eight series.[21] This problem of substantial irregular movements plus the great variation in lead time for individual series from cycle to cycle has led forecasters to seek various ways of systematically combining consideration of several of the leading indicators. One simple method of combination is a so-called "diffusion

---

[21]See Appendix C, *Business Cycle Developments,* May, 1963.

index,"[22] in which 100 indicates that all of the series have risen, zero that all have fallen, and in general the index represents the percentage of the group of indicators that have risen during the period of consideration. Interpretation of such an index remains somewhat of an art. A low index number in an expansionary period that is sustained for a number of months should foreshadow a downward turning point, i.e., a cyclical peak, while a high index number in a period of contraction should anticipate the upturn from a recession. How low or high, and how many months, remain matters of judgment. The forecaster is unlikely to rely solely on such an index which weighs all rises and falls equally regardless of the amplitude and duration of change or the significance he may attach to particular indicators. The data given in Exhibit 2 cover the May, 1960, downward turning point and the February, 1961, upwarding turning point, as well as the difficult period for forecasters in the latter part of 1962; working with these data should permit the student to see some of the possibilities and difficulties in using a simple type of "diffusion index."

QUESTIONS

1. Consider each of the eight leading and four coincident indicators in Exhibits 1 and 2 as to whether there are logical economic reasons for expecting each to lead or coincide with the movements of general business.

2. Construct a "diffusion index" for the eight leading indicators from the data in Exhibit 1 for February, 1959, through April, 1963. Would such an index have helped you forecast the May, 1960, and the February, 1961, turning points? Do you find the index more reliable than the indicators individually? Note: In computing the percentage of the eight series which have risen, count an unchanged series as half rise and half fall. The February, 1959, index will be 75, since six of the eight series rose.

3. As a business economist in the latter half of 1962, would you have found evidence for a cyclical downturn in these leading indicators?

4. At the time you are preparing this case, would you, on the basis of leading indicators, forecast a turning point? As a minimum, update the eight indicators of the exhibits. You may wish to go beyond the preparation of a diffusion index of these and consider other techniques of smoothing and averaging and other series, particularly those presented in *Business Cycle Developments*.

---

[22]The diffusion indexes presented in *Business Cycle Developments* are prepared from breakdowns of individual indicators into components rather than combinations of series. For example, stock prices are broken down into series for eighty-two industries, and the diffusion index shows what percentage of these have risen in a particular month. Therefore, we place quotation marks around "diffusion index" as used above.

CASE 2–5: QUARTERLY FORECASTS OF
GROSS NATIONAL PRODUCT

The new business economist for the Omega Corporation had discovered a strong and significant relationship between quarterly changes in gross national product (seasonally adjusted, constant 1954 dollars) and the company's unit sales. Each 1 per cent change in the GNP seemed to be associated with a roughly 3 per cent change in unit sales when other factors were allowed for. Quarterly figures corresponded with the company's production planning period, and thus a quarter in advance represented the appropriate forecast period. In the spring of 1963 the economist was investigating the variations in real GNP preparatory to the recommendation of forecasting procedures. He decided first to work with various simple methods of forecasting (often termed "naïve" or "agnostic") to see which could produce the greatest improvement over a random guess. He expected to use the best of the simple methods as a standard of comparison in order to evaluate whether the costs of a more elaborate approach (including the possible hiring of an outside economic consultant) would justify the expense. As a rough index to the costs of errors in forecasting GNP, he used the squares of the deviations of the quarterly percentage change "predicted" by each method from the actual percentage changes. The squares seemed more appropriate than the simple deviations because as a matter of business operations, Omega had the flexibility to adjust easily to small discrepancies in plans, so that the cost of errors of increasing size would increase far more than proportionally. No distinction was made between plus or minus deviations. (See Exhibit 1.)

QUESTIONS

1. Approximate the "level of costs" of errors in forecasting by a random prediction. For this purpose a tolerable predicting process would be to number the universe of 64 quarterly predictions from 00 to 64 and use a table of two-digit random numbers to make a "prediction" for each quarter. Alternatively, slips with the changes could be made out, shuffled, and drawn, replacing the slip after each draw. Compute the squares of the deviations of the predicted percentage changes from the actual percentage changes.

2. Evaluate the following three "agnostic" methods of forecasting over the 64 quarters (second quarter of 1947 through first quarter of 1963) by calculating the squares of the deviations of predicted from actual: (*a*) the assumption of no change (0 per cent); (*b*) projection of a long-run trend (use a 0.7 per cent quarterly change which is fractionally above the mean per cent change and slightly less than the median change of 0.8 per cent);

Exhibit 1

QUARTERLY GROSS NATIONAL PRODUCT, 1947–63

(Seasonally Adjusted—Constant 1954 Dollars)

Year	Gross National Product (Billions)	Per Cent Change from Previous Quarter
1947:		
First quarter....................	$278.4	
Second quarter..................	280.4	0.7%
Third quarter...................	282.9	0.8
Fourth quarter..................	287.2	1.5
1948:		
First quarter....................	286.4	−0.3
Second quarter..................	293.3	2.4
Third quarter...................	295.6	0.8
Fourth quarter..................	297.3	0.6
1949:		
First quarter....................	291.5	−2.0
Second quarter..................	290.3	−0.4
Third quarter...................	295.6	1.8
Fourth quarter..................	293.0	−0.9
1950:		
First quarter....................	302.7	3.3
Second quarter..................	312.0	3.1
Third quarter...................	325.6	4.4
Fourth quarter..................	331.6	1.8
1951:		
First quarter....................	334.0	0.7
Second quarter..................	340.0	1.8
Third quarter...................	346.3	1.9
Fourth quarter..................	346.9	0.2
1952:		
First quarter....................	349.6	0.8
Second quarter..................	349.3	−0.1
Third quarter...................	352.6	0.9
Fourth quarter..................	362.3	2.7
1953:		
First quarter....................	368.9	1.8
Second quarter..................	373.2	1.2
Third quarter...................	370.0	−0.9
Fourth quarter..................	363.9	−1.6
1954:		
First quarter....................	360.4	−1.0
Second quarter..................	359.5	−0.2
Third quarter...................	362.1	0.7
Fourth quarter..................	370.1	2.2
1955:		
First quarter....................	382.2	3.3
Second quarter..................	389.5	1.9
Third quarter...................	397.5	2.1
Fourth quarter..................	401.1	0.9
1956:		
First quarter....................	399.6	−0.4
Second quarter..................	400.4	0.2
Third quarter...................	401.4	0.2
Fourth quarter..................	407.1	1.4

Exhibit 1 (Continued)

Year	Gross National Product (Billions)	Per Cent Change from Previous Quarter
1957:		
First quarter..................	407.9	0.2
Second quarter................	409.3	0.4
Third quarter.................	409.1	2.0
Fourth quarter................	401.2	−1.9
1958:		
First quarter..................	391.6	−2.4
Second quarter................	394.6	0.8
Third quarter.................	403.1	2.2
Fourth quarter................	414.3	2.8
1959:		
First quarter..................	422.9	2.1
Second quarter................	434.2	2.7
Third quarter.................	426.3	−1.8
Fourth quarter................	429.1	0.7
1960:		
First quarter..................	440.5	2.7
Second quarter................	442.2	0.4
Third quarter.................	438.0	−0.9
Fourth quarter................	437.3	−0.2
1961:		
First quarter..................	433.9	−0.8
Second quarter................	443.9	2.3
Third quarter.................	450.4	1.4
Fourth quarter................	463.4	2.9
1962:		
First quarter..................	467.4	0.9
Second quarter................	470.8	0.7
Third quarter.................	471.6	0.2
Fourth quarter................	477.7	1.3
1963:		
First quarter..................	482.7	1.0

(*c*) the assumption that the change from this quarter to the next quarter will be the same as the change from that last quarter to this quarter. On the basis of this evaluation and any other pertinent considerations, which of these simple approaches would you recommend for future periods? Check your selection against data subsequent to that given in Exhibit 1.

3. To get an idea of the possible savings of more sophisticated methods, the business economist assumed that the cyclical turning points could be predicted within the proper quarter. (These turning points are listed in Exhibit 2 of Case 2–4 [pages 80–81].) He used method (*c*) above, except that he substituted a forecast of 0 per cent in the quarter of the turning point and forecast either a plus or a minus 2 per cent change for the quarter following, depending upon the direction of the turn. Would a significant saving in "cost" result? (Again, use the criterion of the squares of the deviations of "predicted" from actual.)

CHAPTER 3

•••••••••••••••••••••••

The Demand for Business Output

ONE GREAT advantage of an economic system based on private enterprise is the importance of the role which it allows consumers to play in guiding production. Businessmen can continue to produce only those items for which consumers are willing and able to pay enough at least to cover all of the necessary costs. The modern institution of advertising, however, frequently makes it unnecessary for the firm merely to accept demand as it is; rather, consumer expenditures can be influenced to a greater or lesser degree by advertising outlays and other selling efforts.

A businessman who attempts to estimate how many units of a product he will be able to sell during a certain period of time is aware that the amount will depend on the price at which he offers the good. At a higher price, it is almost invariably possible to sell fewer units than can be sold at a lower price. This is traceable to the basic economic situation that human wants are without limit while resources to satisfy these wants are limited. Consequently, at a higher price, people are willing and able to buy less of a good than at a lower one.

The businessman is also aware that many factors other than price affect his sales of a given product. Some of these factors are prices of close substitutes; consumers' buying power based on their current income, wealth, and the availability and cost of credit; consumers' tastes based on past experience; their desire to emulate or surpass neighbors; advertising; consumers' expectations as to future prices, income, and wealth; current and expected tax rates; and ancillary inducements such as trading stamps or detractions such as lack of parking space. While such factors particularly affect purchases of consumers' goods, they indirectly affect the sale of all materials, machines, etc. which are utilized in making these goods.

In words of the mathematically oriented economist, sales of a given commodity per time period are "a function of" the price of that commodity, prices of closely related goods, consumers' incomes and their distribution, population, tastes, and other factors. A statistical economist may use several variables in addition to the price of the good in question in an attempt to "explain" variations in sales. (Such a study may then be useful in predicting future sales fluctuations.) However, for a great many analytical purposes, price of the commodity under consideration can be considered to be *the* independent variable upon which the physical volume of sales depends. Other pertinent variables are then held constant for purposes of defining the demand function. (The student who has studied calculus may recognize that this is the process of finding the partial derivative of sales with respect to price of the same good, other variables being held constant.) The usual demand curve of economic analysis can be considered to be a special case in which all variables except price of the commodity under consideration are placed in *ceteris paribus*—that is, where other things that have an effect on sales are equal.

Exhibit 1
MARKET DEMAND SCHEDULE

Row	Price of Wheat (per Bushel)	Quantity Demanded (Millions of Bushels per Month)	Value (Millions of Dollars)
A.	$4.00	50	$200
B.	3.50	60	210
C.	3.00	70	210
D.	2.50	80	200
E.	2.00	90	180
F.	1.50	100	150
G.	1.00	110	110

The inverse relationship between quantity demanded and the price of a commodity is, consequently, one that holds with great certainty *if* other things, such as those enumerated above, remain unchanged. A firm which raises the price of a good may actually sell more than in an equal time period before the increase, but this will be because some factors other than price changed demand in a favorable direction. In this case an even greater gain in physical sales volume would have been made if price had not been raised.

A hypothetical demand schedule for wheat is shown in Exhibit 1. Since a great many farmers sell this commodity, the schedule pertains to the entire market rather than reflecting what any individual farmer could sell at the various alternative prices. As will be emphasized in Chapter 5, the individual seller has no control over price in a highly competitive market. However, the state of market demand has a great influence upon the price which he will be able to command for his product. It should be noted that the demand schedule shown in Exhibit 1 is greatly simplified, showing price only at 50-cent intervals. Also, "wheat" is not a strictly homogeneous commodity (there being several grades), nor is it sold only in a single market. Further, "price" must relate to an average price per month; or alternatively, the quantity demanded must be interpreted as the monthly rate of purchase which would take place at a particular price at a moment of time.

Exhibit 2

HYPOTHETICAL DEMAND CURVE FOR WHEAT—
PURCHASES DEPEND ON PRICE

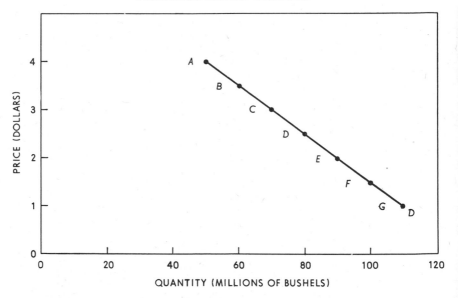

The market demand schedule of Exhibit 1 is plotted as a demand curve in Exhibit 2. For analytical purposes, this is usually a more convenient form than a demand schedule. Since the demand curve connects the various price-quantity combinations, it is drawn on the assumption that no irregularities occur in the relationship between the plotted points. The hypothetical data used in this example provide a straight-line relationship between price and quantity purchased. An actual demand curve for wheat may well exhibit some curvature; however, a straight-line relationship is more convenient to use, and most statistical demand studies for agricultural products have disclosed that a straight line fits the data about as well as more complex curves.

Slope and Elasticity

An examination of the demand schedule shows that a decrease in price of 50 cents per bushel is associated with an increase of 10 million bushels per month in quantity demanded. This relationship is unchanging throughout the demand schedule, giving the demand curve a slope of — 5 (— 50 ÷ 10).[1] This may be interpreted as meaning that a decrease of 5 cents a bushel will occasion an increase of one million bushels in the quantity purchased monthly.

Although the physical volume of sales is related linearly to price, the same is not true of the value of sales. This is evident from an inspection of the Value column of Exhibit 1 (this column being the product of price and quantity). Except at the top of the table, smaller quantities are worth more to the sellers than larger quantities. This is because the *percentage* decrease from 100 million to 90 million bushels, for example, is smaller than the *percentage* increase in price from $1.50 to $2.00 per bushel; that is, a 10 per cent decrease in quantity is associated with a 33⅓ per cent increase in price, and this causes the smaller quantity to bring a higher monetary return to sellers.

The dependence of total value on the relative percentage change of quantity and price often makes the measure of "elasticity" of demand a more useful one than the measure of slope. Elasticity of demand can be defined as the ratio of the percentage change in quantity demanded to the corresponding percentage change in price. It is mathematically necessary, however, to take the ratios of very small (strictly, infinitesimally small) percentage changes in order to measure elasticity at a particular price.[2] Along a downsloping straight-line demand curve, elasticity of demand differs at every point and is negative in sign. For convenience, however, the negative sign will be disregarded in the rest of the discussion.

---

[1] If this demand curve is considered to extend along the same straight line until it touches both axes, its equation becomes $P = 650 - 5q$, where P (price) is measured in cents per bushel and Q (quantity) is in millions of bushels. The slope (-5) appears as the coefficient of Q.

[2] If $\dfrac{dq}{q}$ denotes a very small percentage change in quantity demanded and $\dfrac{dp}{p}$ denotes a very small percentage change in price, elasticity of demand $(E) = \dfrac{dq}{q} \div \dfrac{dp}{p}$. This is usually written $E = \dfrac{dq}{dp} \cdot \dfrac{p}{q}$.

Elasticity and Revenue

The easiest way to compute elasticity of demand at a particular price involves use of a chart. The method can be demonstrated by reference to Exhibit 3. Curve D is a repetition of the demand curve drawn in Exhibit 2, except that it has been extended (by a broken line) until it crosses the vertical axis (at the price of $6.50).[3] Once this intersection has been ascertained, it is easy to find the elasticity at any price along the demand curve: Simply divide the price by the difference between that price and the price at the intersection. At a price of $4.00,

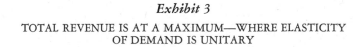

Exhibit 3

TOTAL REVENUE IS AT A MAXIMUM—WHERE ELASTICITY
OF DEMAND IS UNITARY

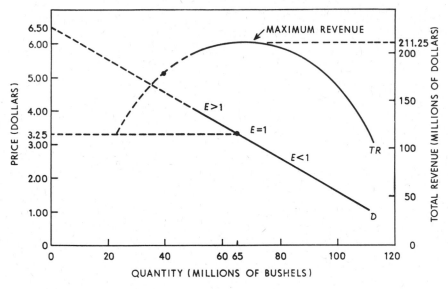

for example, the elasticity of demand is $4.00 \div 2.50 = 1.6$. Since this coefficient exceeds one, demand is said to be "elastic." At a price of $1.00 the elasticity of demand is $1.00 \div 5.50$, or a little less than 0.2. This is denoted as "inelastic" demand. "Unitary" elasticity of demand comes at a price of $3.25, since $3.25 \div 3.25 = 1$.

Sellers of wheat could maximize their income by setting a price of $3.25 per bushel, under the demand assumptions which we are using. Alternatively, it can be said that they can maximize their income by

---

[3]If the demand curve is not a straight line, the pertinent intersection with the vertical axis can be found by drawing a tangent to the demand curve at the price at which elasticity is to be measured and extending this tangent up to the Y axis.

marketing 65 million bushels per month. This can easily be seen in Exhibit 3, since the total revenue curve (which is plotted against the bottom and right-hand scales) reaches a maximum at a quantity of 65 million bushels. It is also apparent from this chart that a reduction in sales from 100 million to 80 million bushels, for example, will increase the total revenue received by sellers. This is because demand is inelastic in this region. On the other hand, a reduction in sales from 60 million to 40 million bushels would reduce total revenue, because demand is elastic in this region. It should be realized that sellers who are in competition with one another cannot choose the price or quantity which will bring the greatest total revenue to the group. Competitive wheat producers normally produce and market a greater quantity than the profit-maximizing amount, and society benefits from this greater output. However, from the point of view of the producers alone, it is advantageous to restrict output to the quantity at which elasticity of demand is unitary, or to a quantity which is less than this amount.[4] Such restriction of output to maximize sellers' incomes is only possible when control is exercised by means of private or governmental action which is cartel-like in nature.

Other Elasticity Concepts

The concept of "elasticity" can be used for purposes other than describing the degree of responsiveness of physical volume of sales to a change in price of the same good. Another rather popular measure is "cross elasticity of demand," in which the sales of one good are related to changes in the price of a closely related good. Price of the good itself and other independent variables are held constant. Cross elasticity is negative for goods that are complements. For example, a decrease in the price of camera film will increase the demand for developing of film even when the price of this service is unchanged. On the other hand, cross elasticity is positive for close substitutes; for example, a decrease in the price of oleomargarine will tend to decrease the consumption of butter. In either case, cross elasticity can be measured (when proper data are available) by dividing the percentage change in the quantity of good X sold by the percentage change in the price of closely related good Y, *ceteris paribus*.

---

[4] When cost of production is a consideration, the most profitable quantity to sell is less than the quantity which brings greatest total revenue. Optimum sales volume can normally be found only by considering cost as well as revenue, as will be noted in a later chapter.

Another rather widely used elasticity concept is "income elasticity of demand." For a given commodity, this may be defined as the ratio of the relative change in quantity demanded to the relative change in income of consumers. Again, price of the commodity in question and other variables which may affect sales are held constant for purposes of this measurement. The businessman is interested in this relationship (whether or not he speaks in terms of "elasticity") because it is important to changes in the level of demand for his products during a "business cycle" or over a longer period. A high income elasticity of demand tends to be a desirable factor in a growing economy, since demand responds strongly and favorably to an increase in income. This situation exists in many phases of the "recreation industry," for example. The boom in sales of pleasure boats may be noted here. At the other end of the scale, income elasticity may actually be negative for such "inferior" goods as lard, pork liver, and tripe. In general, the businessman in a progressive economy should be wary of entering such fields, and perhaps of entering fields where income elasticity is low even though positive.

It is possible also to measure elasticity of demand with respect to such variables as population and advertising, again holding "other things equal." The student should realize, however, that there is nothing magic about an "elasticity" measurement. To a large degree, it is only a matter of terminology. For example, we are really interested in the whole functional relationship between quantity demanded and price, between quantity demanded and income, etc. "Elasticity" measurements are a handy way of expressing an outstanding attribute of such relationships.

Demand Facing a Monopolist

It should be kept in mind that the demand which has been discussed so far is *market* demand rather than the demand for the product of an individual company. Where the entire output of the commodity is accounted for by a single firm, however, it is clear that demand facing such a monopolistic seller is identical with the market demand. Monopoly demand curves consequently slope downward to the right.

It is useful, in analyzing the monopolist's economic behavior, to employ the concept of "marginal revenue" as well as that of the demand schedule. Marginal revenue is simply the *additional* revenue secured by a seller from the sale of an additional unit of product. (Strictly, the unit should again be infinitesimally small.) If there were only one producer of wheat—an unrealistic assumption but one which is no longer unimportant, since farmers act somewhat in concert through the federal farm program and by means of private marketing agreements—the market demand schedule which we have been using would be the demand curve facing that firm. Marginal revenue from the sale of additional output would be found by taking the difference between successive total revenues and dividing these by the differences between successive quantities demanded. These calculations are shown in Exhibit 4.

Exhibit 4

COMPUTATION OF MARGINAL REVENUE

Row	(1) Change in Quantity (Millions of Bushels)	(2) Change in Total Revenue (Millions of Dollars)	(Col. 2 ÷ Col. 1) Marginal Revenue per Bushel
A....................	10	$20	$2
B....................	10	10	1
C....................	10	0	0
D....................	10	− 10	− 1
E....................	10	− 20	− 2
F....................	10	− 30	− 3
G....................	10	− 40	− 4

In order to get the change in quantity and in total revenue for row A, it is necessary to assume that a quantity of 40 million bushels would have been demanded at a price of $4.50 per bushel. This would have yielded a total revenue of $180 million, and the difference between this amount and $200 million is $20 million. Division of $20 million by the quantity increase of 10 million bushels means that each additional bushel sold added an average of $2.00 to the sellers' aggregate revenue. In row D through row G, marginal revenue is negative, showing that additional units sold actually reduce the total income of sellers (make negative additions to income).

It is clear that a monopolist seeking to maximize his profits would not sell any units which, through their depressing influence on price, would reduce his total revenue. That is, the monopolist will not operate in the region of negative marginal revenue. His price will be set at $3.25 per bushel or higher, and his sales will be 65 million bushels per month or less. (The exact optimum cannot be defined until cost is brought into the picture. This will be done in Chapter 7). Reference to Exhibit 3 suggests that he should operate in the region where demand is of unitary elasticity or higher, rather than where demand is inelastic. Although total revenue would be the same at quantities of 50 million and 80 million bushels, for example, the cost of producing the smaller amount would obviously be less.

Demand and marginal revenue for the hypothetical wheat monopolist are shown in Exhibit 5. The dotted portions indicate the course of the curves at quantities below 50 million bushels, assuming that the same linear relationship holds true. It can be seen that marginal revenue is zero at a quantity of 65 million bushels. It was noted earlier that elasticity of demand is unitary at this quantity. Consequently, it is clear that unitary elasticity and a marginal revenue of zero exist at the

Exhibit 5

PRICE EXCEEDS MARGINAL REVENUE FOR MONOPOLISTIC SELLER

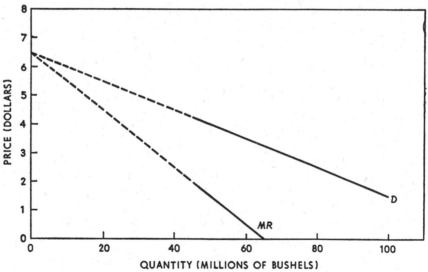

same output. When demand is elastic, marginal revenue is greater than zero; while in the region of inelastic demand, marginal revenue is negative. The logic of this last relationship is not difficult to understand: When demand is inelastic, it is necessary to cut price sharply on all units in order to sell a little more; hence the additional sale will decrease the total value of sales—i.e., bring in negative marginal revenue.

Some Qualifications

The demand curves which have been used so far show highly simplified "static" relationships which are especially useful in the economic theory of price determination. While they may also be useful to the businessman, it is likely to be important for him to keep in mind some complicating qualifications.

First, a reduction in price may temporarily reduce sales rather than increase them, since buyers may be led to expect further price cuts. This is a "dynamic" consideration which is neglected in the static theory of demand. Similarly, a price cut may "spoil the market," so that return to a higher price previously charged may not be feasible. Buyers are frequently more sensitive to changes in price than to the absolute level of price.

Second, even when some buyers immediately begin to buy more in response to a price cut, other buyers may be slower in changing their buying habits, so that a considerable period of time may elapse before the full effect of the price change works itself out.

Third, the demand and marginal revenue curves which have been drawn assume that all buyers are charged the same price. Actually, it may be possible to sell additional units by reducing price only to a new group of buyers, or only on additional sales to existing customers. Block rates used by public utility firms are a good example of quantity discounts. The practice of price discrimination will be examined in some detail in a separate chapter.

Fourth, although it is theoretically irrational for a monopolist to sell in the region of inelastic demand—since he can gain revenue by raising price—he may still find it expedient to do so. By charging a less than optimum price, he may be able to discourage would-be competitors, build up consumer good will for the long run, and perhaps reduce the likelihood of prosecution under the federal antitrust laws if he is selling in interstate commerce. (There are seldom laws against intrastate monopoly.)

Demand Facing Pure Competitor

Economists define "perfect" or "pure" competition as a situation in which there are so many sellers of a particular commodity that none can individually affect the price. In the absence of governmental interference, many agriculture commodities are produced under such conditions. Even today, truck-garden vegetables, poultry, eggs, and fish, for example, are often turned out by perfectly competitive firms.

Under pure competition the demand curve for the product of the individual firm is simply a horizontal line drawn at the price determined in the market. That is to say, market price is determined by over-all supply and demand, and the individual firm can sell as much as it wishes at this price. It cannot charge more than the market price without losing all of its customers (who are assumed to be both rational and mobile) and need not, of course, accept less than the prevailing price.

The demand for the product of a purely competitive firm is represented in Exhibit 6. Such a horizontal curve is infinitely elastic along its entire range.[5] The firm that has no control over price and can be designated as a "price taker" rather than as a "price maker." (The latter term is appropriate for a monopolistic firm.)

Exhibit 6

INFINITELY ELASTIC DEMAND FACES PERFECTLY COMPETITIVE FIRM

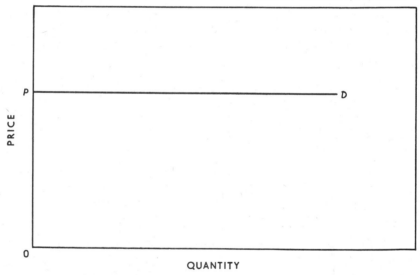

Pure Competition Is Uncommon

The case of pure competition is, in practice, much less common than that of monopoly, when the latter term is used to cover all situations in which the demand facing the individual firm is downsloping rather than horizontal. Most firms have some power to fix price, within limits, and hence are not fully competitive with others. The amount of this price-making power may be great—for example, in the case of a city-owned electric utility system, where the rates set by the municipal

---

[5]This can easily be verified by reference to the geometrical test described earlier. Since the horizontal demand curve intersects the vertical axis at the market price, the divisor is zero. Consequently, OP divided by zero gives and infinite elasticity.

authorities may be subject to no check by a regulatory commission. Or the amount of price-making power may be severely limited by the existence of close substitutes, as in the case of a seller of a particular breakfast cereal or sardines.

Some writers use the term "monopolistic competition" to denote the situation of a firm which has some monopoly power—due, perhaps, to selling under a brand name which no one else can use—but which faces the competition of more or less similar products. No clear line can be drawn between monopoly and monopolistic competition, however, since every monopolist faces some competition. The prewar Aluminum Company of America had great monopoly power in the production of this metal but nevertheless encountered a measure of competition from other metals produced both domestically and abroad.

In order to operate under conditions of perfect competition, a firm must sell an unbranded commodity (such as sweet corn) and must not be significantly separated spatially from other sellers of the same good. Many firms have a degree of locational monopoly due to their greater convenience to buyers. Vendors of refreshments at a football game, for example, have a separateness from other sellers which permits them to charge higher prices than those on the outside. Much advertising is designed simply to imprint brand names on the public mind, in order to lessen the severity of competition from similar or even identical goods.

Demand under Oligopoly

The demand curves which have been drawn so far were necessarily based on the assumption of *ceterus paribus*—i.e., all other factors which would affect the quantity demanded were held constant. These include prices of competing products, incomes and their distribution, and consumers' tastes. Where there are only a few sellers of a particular commodity, however, this assumption is not useful. Instead, it must be recognized that each seller will carefully watch the actions of his close competitors and frequently will react to any change which they make in price, quality, or selling effort. This is called an "oligopolistic" situation—the case of a few sellers. It is an extremely common real-world situation. Oligopolistic firms may turn out identical homogeneous products (e.g., brass tubing, aluminum sheets, or copper wire); or they may sell closely related but somewhat dissimilar goods (e.g., trucks, airplanes, typewriters, or soap powder).

A single demand curve cannot depict the price-quantity relationship for a commodity sold oligopolistically. If price is changed, the response of sales depends heavily on the actions which close rivals are induced to take. If, for example, price is lowered by one firm but rivals choose to maintain their prices and quality unchanged, the amount which buyers will purchase from the price cutter is likely to expand quite sharply. If rivals match a price cut, sales of the first price cutter are likely to increase only moderately, since others will share in the larger total sales volume. If rivals more than meet a price cut, the physical volume sold by the first price cutter may even fall off.

Exhibit 7

OLIGOPOLY DEMAND CURVES—SALES DEPEND ON RIVALS' REACTIONS

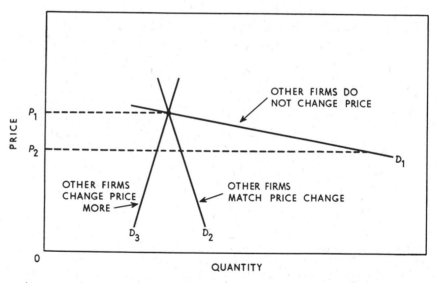

A general picture of the demand situation under oligopoly can be shown graphically. Such a chart is suggestive only, since it cannot show the results of all of the possible combinations of action and reaction on the part of oligopolistic rivals. Exhibit 7 pertains to an individual firm which is assumed, first, to be charging price OP_1. If the firm then lowers its price to OP_2 and its rivals do not change their prices, the physical sales of the price cutter may expand sharply, as indicated by curve D_1. (Since this curve is elastic between prices OP_1 and OP_2, total revenue received by the firm will rise.) If, instead, rival firms match the price cut, the volume of sales may expand only moderately, as indicated by D_2. (Since this curve, as drawn, is inelastic between prices OP_1 and OP_2, the dollar volume of sales would be down, despite the rise in physical volume.) It is even possible that the firm under consideration will encounter a positive sloping demand curve such as D_3. This is only likely if rivals more than match the first firm's price cut.

Above the original price OP the demand curves can be interpreted in a similar way. If our firm raises its price and its close rivals do not do so, sales may fall off quite sharply, as suggested by curve D_1. If the other sellers match the price increase, sales may fall off only moderately, as along D_2. If rivals should decide to raise their prices more than the first firm, that firm may enjoy higher physical and dollar sales, as indicated by D_3.

It is clear that there are so many possible combinations of oligopolistic price behavior (to say nothing of changes in such variables as quality, amount of advertising, premiums, credit terms, etc.) that demand curves for the individual firm are of limited usefulness. The same is not true of *market* demand curves for oligopolistic industries, however, and considerable effort has been expended in deriving statistical demand curves for such commodities as steel and cigarettes, where the number of producers is relatively small.

The consequences of the complex nature of demand under oligopoly will be examined in some detail in subsequent chapters. It is readily apparent, though, that a great many different results may ensue from a price change. The uncertainties inherent in the situation are conducive to the maintenance of stable prices through overt or tacit agreements between sellers. When such agreements break down, however, price wars may follow, especially when excess capacity exists.

Changes in Demand

For purposes of clear thinking, it is important to distinguish between movement along a particular demand curve and a shift in the entire curve. If, in Exhibit 8, market demand is represented by curve D_1 and price is at the level OP, an increase in price to OP' will reduce sales from OX to OX'. This can best be designated as a "decrease in amount demanded." On the other hand, a movement of the entire curve downward and to the left constitutes a "decrease in demand." This sort of change is represented by a movement of the curve from D_1 to D_2. When demand decreases, consumers are willing to buy less at *all prices* than they were previously ready to buy. An increase in demand is reflected in a shift of the entire curve upward and to the right.

A great many factors affect the demand for every commodity. Where a company carries a number of lines, as in the case of a department store, even internal competition may be important. This is sometimes a problem also between major divisions of a large manufacturing corporation, where the desire of managers of the several divisions to make a good showing may lead, if unchecked, to policies which are not optimal from the point of view of the firm as a whole.[6]

Most commodities are virtually independent of one another in demand except as general competitors for purchasing power. Other commodities—such as butter and oleomargarine, Fords and Chevrolets, and television and motion pictures—are close substitutes for one another. In this situation a decline in the price of one commodity tends to reduce the demand for the other. Other goods are complementary

Exhibit 8

CHANGE IN DEMAND MEANS SHIFT OF DEMAND CURVE

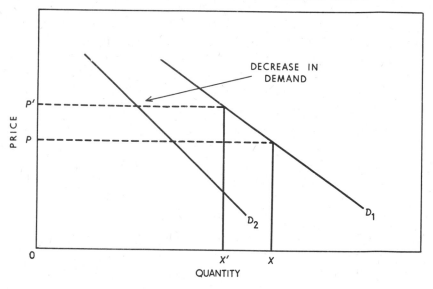

in nature, in that increased sales of one tend to increase the demand for the other. Examples are coffee and cream, tires and gasoline, electric power and appliances, and seed and fertilizer. In recent years, it has become apparent that television and certain types of motion pictures are complementary rather than substitutive, since the films are shown on TV. A difficult and important problem for promoters of professional sporting events is whether the televised event is a substitute for the

---

[6]Costly competition between the various divisions of a particular government agency is also common, especially because the check of declining profits is not present. A limited amount of intra-agency competition is sometimes useful, however, since each office may provide a check on ill-considered actions of the others.

performance itself. Careful statistical study may shed light on this sort of problem.

Many consumer and capital goods are complementary in a very important way. An increase in the demand for shoes increases the demand for shoe machinery. A change in the demand for housing affects the demand for a host of building materials and equipment, as well as construction labor. A decline in the demand for bread or cigarettes reduces the demand for wheat, tobacco, paper, etc. Further, a given percentage change in the demand for a consumers' good often causes a greater percentage change in the demand for a closely related capital good. This is known as the "acceleration principle." When demand for a consumers' good has been stable for a considerable period of time, annual demand for related machines—bottling machines, vending machines, ovens, etc.—may derive chiefly from replacement needs. If an increase in demand for the consumers' good then occurs, and existing machines are already being fully utilized, there will be a demand for new machines as well as for replacements. This may sharply increase the total demand for machines. On the other hand, a reduction in demand for a consumers' good, or even a slowing-down in the rate of expansion of demand, can cause a decline in the demand for related machines. Builders of railroad locomotives virtually halted production for a period during the deep depression of the 1930's.

Timing of Shifts

Changes in demand sometimes follow more or less regular patterns over time. Some of these patterns recur annually and are called "seasonal variations." A peak of sales just before Christmas in the department store trade represents a positive seasonal shift of demand, while a slackening of sales after the first of the year represents a negative shift of demand. Marked seasonal patterns of demand exist for such commodities as candy, portland cement, skis, automobiles, and firecrackers.

Companies engaged in the manufacture of electronics, drugs, certain chemicals, and certain new fabrics, to name only a few, have experienced a growing demand in recent years which has persisted even in periods when sales of most other goods have marked time or fallen off. These are examples of a long-term or *secular* increase in demand. The bituminous coal and silk hosiery industries present instances of secular declines in demand.

During World War II, there was a dramatic increase in the demand for many products. Aircraft producers, mining firms, textile mills, and building contractors were among those who experienced booms which, in some cases, reversed long-run secular declines in demand. Other products experienced strong postwar demand under the stimulus of the rearmament program. Such shifts can be called "erratic movements" of demand because they follow no regular pattern of recurrence or growth.

Of particular analytical importance because it affects the demand for *all* commodities is the level of economic activity within the nation. This relation exists because production of all sorts of goods and services is the source of the income with which the goods and services may be purchased. The most widely used measures of general economic activity are the national income estimates compiled by the Department of Commerce. These are the end product of a system of national economic accounting which has been developed only in recent decades and which is steadily being refined. There are still serious shortcomings, however, such as poor information on construction activity. Also, important segments of economic activity (such as the value added by "do it yourself" activities) escape measurement.

APPENDIX TO CHAPTER 3: STATISTICAL MEASUREMENT OF DEMAND

PART A: SOME THEORETICAL CONSIDERATIONS

A French mathematician, Augustin Cournot, writing in 1838,[7] is generally credited with having first clearly expressed the "law of demand" (sales as a function of price), both mathematically and graphically. More than half a century later, Alfred Marshall,[8] a famous British economist, greatly extended the application of the concept and popularized its use. Economists did not, however, seriously attempt to derive demand curves from actual statistical information until about 1910.[9] Most of the published results have been for commodities analyzed at the producer-manufacturer level or at the wholesale level. A smaller number of published studies pertain to demand at the retail level, although a great many more or less successful attempts have undoubtedly been made privately by businessmen and economists for all levels of

---

[7]*Researches into the Mathematical Principles of the Theory of Wealth,* translated by Nathaniel T. Bacon (New York: Macmillan Co., 1929), chap. iv.

[8]*Principles of Economics* (8th ed.; London: Macmillan & Co., Ltd., 1930), Book III.

[9]A history of statistical measurement of demand is given by Henry Schultz, *The Theory and Measurement of Demand* (Chicago: University of Chicago Press, 1938), chap. ii. This book is itself a classic in the field.

selling activity.[10] Agricultural products have proved to be especially adaptable to this type of empirical analysis; but such items as automobiles, tin plate, wool, fish, and railroad travel have also been treated in this way. Some federal agencies, such as the Department of Agriculture, are regularly involved in statistical studies of demand. Trade associations, marketing co-operatives, and large individual firms are also frequently interested in measurement of market demand. It should be kept in mind, however, that a statistical demand curve for an entire commodity may have little importance for the individual firm in a competitive situation where it supplies only a small fraction of the total output and where its control over price is negligible.

The benefits of accurate measurement of demand to the individual sellers or associations which are able to exercise control over price are quite obvious. As noted in Chapter 3, total revenue from sales can be derived readily from a demand schedule or curve. If these have been measured, the seller can determine whether his price is too high or too low to bring maximum monetary returns. (As already mentioned, maximum revenue does not, however, necessarily mean maximum profit, since cost of production is also a factor.)

Because of the key role attributed by economists to price as the determinant of sales of any commodity, it is customary to consider the price-quantity relationship as the end product of a statistical demand study. Other important factors such as population, income, advertising, and prices of substitutes are treated as causes of shifts in the demand curve. This procedure has the merit of being closely related to economic theorizing and of facilitating comparisons between commodities by placing them on similar bases. It is possible, however, to place price on the same basis as other variables in a statistical study of sales determination and perhaps even to leave it out of consideration as being relatively unimportant in some cases.

Shifts in Demand and Supply

The most common method of deriving statistical demand curves involves the use of time series data on prices, sales, and other relevant variables.[11] The first step is usually to plot all of the price-sales data

---

[10]Werner Z. Hirsch, "On the Phenomenon of Inelastic Demand," *Southern Economic Journal,* July, 1951, pp. 30–45, sets forth the results of 34 demand studies at the producer-manufacturer level, 16 studies at the wholesale level, and 14 at the retail level. Hirsch made a comprehensive survey of the field.

[11]Family budget data have been used by statisticians to derive demand curves for some consumer goods. This method will not be considered in the present Appendix.

on a chart where price is measured vertically and quantity sold is measured horizontally. (This has become conventional although theoretically, it would be preferable to plot price, the independent variable,
against the horizontal scale [X axis] and sales against the Y axis.)
If the investigator is unusually fortunate, he can immediately draw
the statistical demand curve merely by fitting a "regression" line to the
price-sales data.[12] Usually, however, it is necessary to consider additional
factors.

Exhibit 1

SUPPLY-DEMAND INTERSECTIONS DETERMINE PRICE QUANTITY DATA

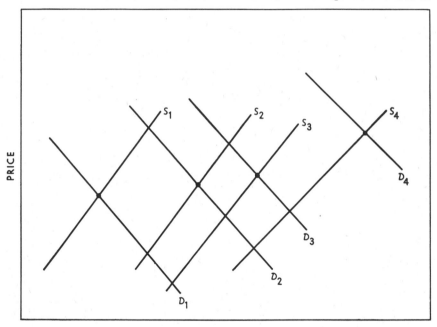

QUANTITY

In the case of a competitively produced commodity, each price-sales
point can be considered to have been determined by the intersection
of a supply and a demand curve. This is illustrated in Exhibit 1 for a
hypothetical situation in which both the demand and the supply curves
have shifted over a period of time. Each of the intersections (D_1 and
S_1 D_2 and S_2, etc.) indicates a short-run equilibrium price which existed

[12]Such a line of "best" fit may simply be drawn freehand in such a way as to minimize,
approximately, the sum of the deviations of the plotted points from the regression line.
Or mathematical methods such as the "least-squares" method may be employed. The
least-squares method may minimize the sum of the squared vertical distances, squared
horizontal distances, or squared perpendicular distances from the regression line.

at one time during the period studied. It is clear that if the demand and supply curves have both shifted rapidly to the right, as suggested by Exhibit 1, the price-quantity data plotted by the statistician would not trace out a demand curve, a supply curve, or any other of the curves of economic theory.

On the other hand, if the situation has been that of Exhibit 2, in which the demand curve was stable over the period while the supply curve shifted to several different positions (due, for example, to different crop yields in successive years), the price-sales data would trace

Exhibit 2

SHIFTING SUPPLY AND STEADY DEMAND—INTERSECTIONS TRACE
DEMAND CURVE

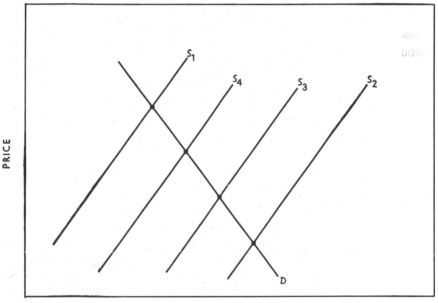

QUANTITY

out the demand curve which the statistician was seeking.[13] If the demand curve shifted only slightly while the supply curve shifted substantially, the intersections would come close to showing the path of an "average" demand curve for the period. It is not difficult, similarly, to see that if the supply curve were unchanged while the demand curve shifted, the price-sales data would trace out a supply curve.

In practice, unfortunately, the demand curve usually shifts a good deal over the period for which the statistician has price-sales data. Nu-

[13]The various possibilities are shown by E. J. Working, "What Do Statistical Demand Curves Show?" *Quarterly Journal of Economics,* February, 1927, pp. 212–35.

merous statistical devices are available for removing the shift and coming out with an approximation to the static demand curve of economic theory. A simple graphical method for accomplishing this end may be illustrated by its application to the hypothetical price-sales data of Exhibit 3. The "period" referred to is usually a year, but may be a shorter span of time. Price must refer to a weighted average for the period unless, of course, a single price persisted throughout the time interval.

Exhibit 3

HYPOTHETICAL PRICE SALES DATA

Period	Quantity Sold	Price per Unit
1............................	50	$ 9
2............................	75	8
3............................	65	15
4............................	110	10
5............................	150	7
6............................	150	14
7............................	200	9

As a first step in finding the influence of price on quantity sold, the analyst would probably plot these data as in Exhibit 4. At this point, he might be discouraged, because the plotted points do not even come close to falling along a negatively declining demand curve such as would be expected from a knowledge of the economist's "law of demand." An examination of the original data reveals clearly, however, that there has been an upward trend in sales over the seven periods. This is easily seen by reference to the fact that in period 1 a price of $9.00 was associated with sales of 50 units, while in period 7 the same price was coupled with sales of 200 units. One way of eliminating the trend in order to isolate the influence of price is to fit a trend line to the time series of sales.[14] Such a line has been fitted to the data in Exhibit 5. The next step is to measure the vertical deviations of the observations from the trend line. These deviations, which are both positive (above the line) and negative (below the line), are shown in Exhibit 6.[15] Since the trend has been eliminated from the sales, the

---

[14]This trend may be fitted freehand or by the method of least squares. In order to save time, it is often advisable to use freehand methods as a means of discovering the basic relationships and later, if it appears worth while, to rework the problem, using the more complex techniques.

[15]Instead of using deviations from the trend line, it is also feasible to compute "trend ratios" by dividing each observation by the value of the trend line for the same date. The trend-ratio method is used extensively by Schultz, *op. cit.*

Exhibit 4
PRICE-SALES DATA MAY FOLLOW NO PATTERN

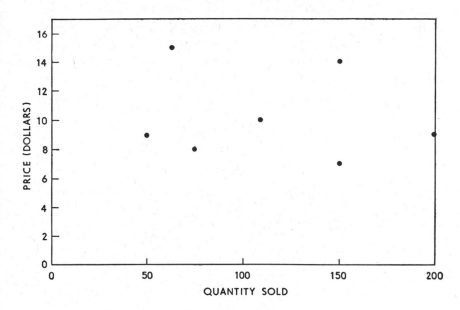

Exhibit 5
QUANTITY SOLD SHOWS SHARP UPWARD TREND

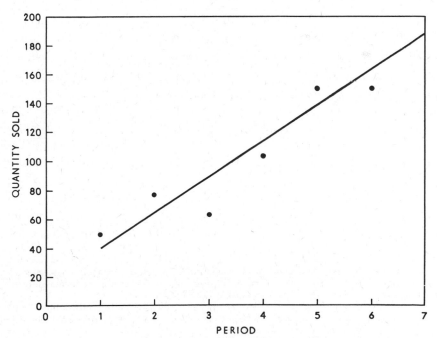

remaining fluctuations should be closely related to price if, in fact, price is an important determinant of the quantity sold. In order to test the latter hypothesis, the statistician can plot deviations of sales from trend against price for the corresponding time period. This step is shown in Exhibit 7. A rather close correlation of sales and price is apparent in Exhibit 7, and a freehand regression line has been drawn to fit the points. In order to convert this line into an "average" demand curve for the period, it is only necessary to add to the quantity measurements along this line the quantity read off the trend line of Exhibit 5 for the mid-period (No. 4). (This value is about 115.) And to get a picture of the demand curve as it was at the end of the period studied, it

Exhibit 6

DEVIATIONS OF SALES FROM
TREND

Period	*Deviations*
1	+ 9
2	+ 10
3	− 25
4	− 5
5	+ 11
6	− 13
7	+ 12

is only necessary to add instead a quantity of 188, taken from the trend line for period 7. A demand curve as of period 1 can be derived in a similar manner. This process yields the three demand curves of Exhibit 8. The upward shifting of demand is clearly apparent, and the analyst would have to take this shift into account in any attempt to use the demand curve for purposes of sales forecasting.

PART B: DEMAND FOR FROZEN ORANGE CONCENTRATE[16]

The problem of deriving a statistical demand curve for frozen orange concentrate is much like that which has been treated for a hypothetical situation. Demand for this good has increased rapidly as consumers have become acquainted with it and as grocery stores in all parts of the country have installed the necessary refrigerated cabinets.[17] At the same time,

---

[16]This part is based largely on a master's thesis written by Eugene C. Holshouser, *The Frozen Orange Concentrate Industry: An Analysis of Consumer Demand,* deposited in the library of Florida State University, August, 1953.

[17]In 1946 and 1947, however, when the industry was just getting started, the producers had serious financial difficulties, especially because concentrate moved very slowly at the grocery stores.

Exhibit 7

EFFECT OF PRICE APPEARS WHEN TREND IS REMOVED

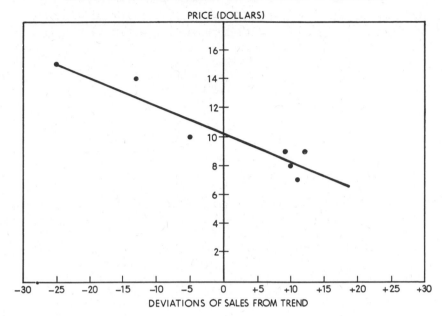

Exhibit 8

SHIFTING DEMAND CURVE APPEARS AS END PRODUCT

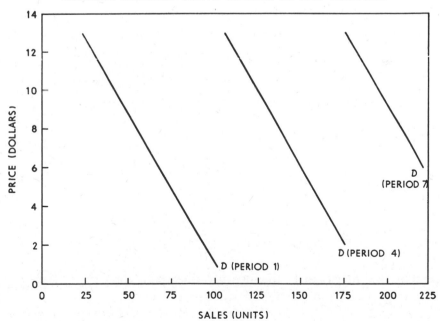

prices have fluctuated quite sharply with changes in supply, which in turn are traceable to changes in the orange crop; and there has been a general downward trend of price for the period studied. Exhibit 9 gives retail price and sales data for the six-ounce can of frozen orange con-

Exhibit 9

FROZEN ORANGE CONCENTRATE—PRICES
AND SALES

Month	Retail Price (Cents per Can)	Retail Sales (Thousands of Gallons)
1950:		
September	25.5	1,470
October	22.1	1,865
November	21.7	1,762
December	21.6	1,638
1951:		
January	21.6	1,716
February	21.5	1,917
March	22.1	1,872
April	21.9	1,892
May	21.9	1,768
June	21.6	1,775
July	21.8	1,756
August	21.3	2,022
September	20.7	2,470
October	20.4	2,608
November	19.7	2,600
December	19.1	2,619
1952:		
January	18.2	3,060
February	16.7	3,358
March	16.3	3,314
April	16.5	3,350
May	14.8	3,812
June	15.3	3,811
July	15.6	3,970
August	16.1	3,859
September	16.2	3,904
October	16.1	3,871
November	16.3	3,929
December	16.1	3,836

Source: Market Research Corporation of America, as shown in Eugene C. Holshouser, *The Frozen Orange Concentrate Industry: An Analysis of Consumer Demand*, master's thesis deposited in the library of Florida State University, August, 1953, p. 75.

centrate. In order to make the monthly sales totals comparable, a period of four weeks only in each month was used.

An examination of the price-sales data shows that the rapid increase in month-to-month sales was associated with a substantial decline in price. If quantity were plotted against price, the apparent influence of price would be great, and the demand would appear highly elastic. This would be an improper analysis of the effect of price, however, since much of the increase in purchases would have occurred even if price had not declined; that is, demand shifted rapidly to the right during the

Exhibit 10

LINK RELATIVES OF PRICES AND SALES

Month	Price Relatives	Sales Relatives
1950:		
October....................	86.7%	126.9%
November..................	98.2	94.5
December..................	99.5	93.0
1951:		
January....................	100.0	104.8
February...................	99.5	111.7
March.....................	102.8	97.7
April......................	99.1	101.1
May.......................	100.0	93.4
June......................	98.6	100.4
July.......................	100.9	98.9
August....................	97.7	115.1
September.................	97.2	122.2
October...................	98.6	105.6
November.................	96.6	99.7
December..................	97.0	100.7
1952:		
January....................	95.3	116.8
February...................	91.8	109.7
March.....................	97.6	98.7
April......................	101.2	101.1
May.......................	89.7	113.8
June......................	103.4	100.0
July.......................	102.0	104.2
August....................	103.2	97.2
September.................	100.6	101.2
October...................	99.4	99.2
November.................	101.2	101.5
December..................	98.8	97.6

period under consideration. It would be equally misleading, however, to conclude that price changes had no effect on sales of frozen orange concentrate.

One way to isolate the effect of price changes would be to fit a trend line to the sales data and correlate price with deviations from trend. This is the procedure illustrated earlier for a hypothetical situation. When the number of observations is large, this technique is rather time-consuming, however, and a general picture may be secured more speedily through the use of "first differences." This involves finding the month-to-month changes in price and in sales, and examining the relation between these changes. This method eliminates most of the trend in both series, permitting the analyst to see whether a decrease in price actually stimulated sales to go up more than they were already increasing. A closely related method is that of "link relatives." In this procedure, each sales figure is expressed as a percentage of the sales for the preceding month, and each price is similarly related to the previous

Exhibit 11

FROZEN ORANGE CONCENTRATE SALES RELATIVES ARE CORRELATED
WITH PRICE RELATIVES

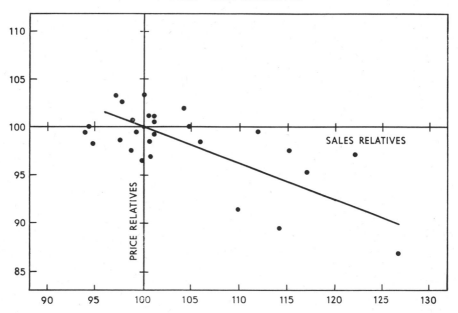

month's price. This method eliminates much of the trend and may be somewhat more accurate than the first-difference method if consumers react more strongly, for example, to a 1-cent cut from a 15-cent level than to a 1-cent cut from a 25-cent level. The former cut would produce a larger change in the series of link relatives than would the latter cut.

Link relatives for the monthly data on frozen orange concentrate prices and sales are shown in Exhibit 10. These are plotted against one another in Exhibit 11. While the scatter of points about the free-hand regression line is considerable, it is apparent that the large gains in sales were achieved in the months when price cuts were sharp. It is not clear how great a dampening effect on sales would have been exerted by sharp price increases, since there were no large price increases in the period studied. It appears probable that there would be a strong effect of this sort, however, since no large sales gains were made in the nine months during which moderate price increases took place.

Least-Square Analysis

The advantage of using graphic methods to discover price-sales relationships lies in the speed with which results may be obtained. And frequently, the statistician feels that it is irrational to spend very much time in finding a precise fit to the very imprecise data with which he may have to work. (It is *not* true that "anything worth doing is worth doing well.") However, where the graphical analysis indicates that a satisfactory demand curve can be obtained, and where the results may affect a managerial decision, it is often desirable to use the more accurate method of least squares in order to find a regression equation from which sales can be estimated.

One useful way of handling a situation in which demand has been shifting steadily upward is to use "time" as one of the variables which is considered to affect sales. The time variable will then take care of such factors as population growth, income changes, and changes in tastes, so far as these cause demand to shift in a regular fashion.[18] If this procedure is adopted, the quantity sold will appear in the final equation as a function of price and of time—that is, a larger quantity can be sold at the same price at later dates than at earlier dates; and at any date the lower the price, the larger the quantity which can be sold. Mathematically, this can be written:

1. $\quad q = f(p,t)$

where q is quantity demanded, p is price, and t is time.

In order to secure the regression line showing consumer purchases as a function of price and time, it is necessary to assign values to t—e.g., October, 1950, as 1; November, 1950, as 2; and so on, through December, 1952, as 27. Assuming a straight-line relationship to exist between the dependent variable (q) and the independent variables (p and t), the problem can readily be worked by means of the least-squares method

---

[18]Schultz, *op. cit.,* chap. IV, discusses this use of time as a variable in least-squares analysis. Schultz found this to be the most useful method of dealing with the demand for many agricultural commodities.

(which is explained in most statistics textbooks). The regression equation which appears as an end product of this statistical process[19] is:

$$2. \quad q = -217.1p + 40.0t + 6,320$$

To turn this equation into a relationship between price and quantity as of any particular month, it is only necessary to substitute the t value for that month in the equation. To get an "average" demand curve for the period, one should use a t value of 14 (which is the average of the t values). This gives the following equation:

$$3. \quad q = -217.1p + 6,880$$

In order to estimate sales for this central month at 15 cents per can, for example, one substitutes this value for p and solves for q (which turns out to be 3,623,000 gallons). This would be interpreted as follows: *If* the price had been 15 cents per can in November, 1951, sales of frozen orange concentrate would have been about 3,623,000 gallons. (Actually, the price was nearly 20 cents per can, and sales were 2,600,000 gallons.) The relation between price and quantity can similarly be measured for any other month of the period by substituting the appropriate value for t.

The coefficient of p (—217.1) indicates that a 1-cent change in the retail price per can of frozen orange concentrate was associated with a change in the opposite direction of about 217,000 gallons per month in consumer purchases. The coefficient of t (+40.0) indicates that purchases increased at a rate of 40,000 gallons a month due to changes in such factors as tastes, availability, population, and income. If study of the industry indicated no sudden change in these factors, the regression equation could be used for forecasting the volume of sales. This would be done by inserting the anticipated price and the numerical value of the month, counting from October, 1950, as 1. It should be emphasized that a close correlation for the period studied does not guarantee a close correlation for the future. However, analysis of the sort described is more likely to lead to a useful forecast of sales than would be obtained by a mere extrapolation of the trend of sales, because of the explicit recognition and measurement of the force exerted by changes in price.

A demand equation for frozen orange concentrate as of the end of

---

[19] As computed by Holshouser, *op. cit.*, p. 78. He found a coefficient of multiple correlation of —0.978.

the period studied (December, 1952) can easily be obtained by substituting 27 for t in equation 2. This gives:

$$4. \quad q = -217.p + 7,400$$

Equation 4 can easily be turned into a demand curve. If p is zero, q
will be 7,400; therefore the line will intersect the quantity axis as
7,400,000 gallons. If q is zero, p will be 34.1 cents per can. These points
determine the location of the demand curve, which is plotted in Exhibit
12.

Exhibit 12

STATISTICAL DEMAND CURVE FOR FROZEN ORANGE CONCENTRATE AS
OF DECEMBER, 1952

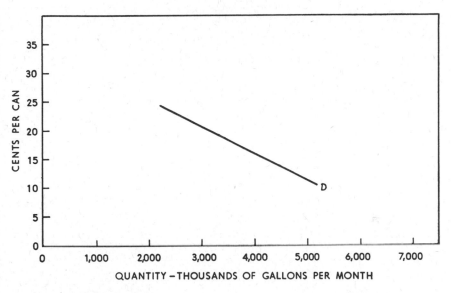

Elasticity of Demand

The simple geometrical technique described in Chapter 3 for measuring elasticity of demand can be applied to the demand curve of
Exhibit 12 to determine the elasticity of demand at any chosen price.
It may be of particular importance to a businessman to make this calculation at the price actually prevailing. A finding of elastic demand
would indicate that a price cut would bring in more revenue to the industry; a finding of inelastic demand would indicate that a price cut
would reduce industry revenue. If price is taken as 16.1 cents per can,
this price is divided by the difference between this price and the intersection of the extended demand curve with the vertical axis. The inter-

section is at 34.1 cents.[20] Consequently, the elasticity is 16.1 ÷ (34.1 — 16.1), which is equal approximately to 0.9, an inelastic demand. In addition to suggesting that a further price reduction would decrease total revenue, this measurement indicates that the frozen orange concentrate industry is a competitive one. A monopolistically controlled industry is not likely to sell in the region of inelastic demand, since total revenue could be increased by an increase in price and, in addition, the smaller quantity produced would have a lower total cost. It should not be inferred, of course, that monopoly is desirable from a social point of view, since consumers gain from the superior allocation of resources and productive efficiency which are engendered by competition.

CASE 3–1: CENTRAL PETROLEUM PRODUCTS, INC.

Central Petroleum Products, Inc., is a small integrated oil company operating in the states of Arkansas, Alabama, Louisiana, Mississippi, Tennessee, and Texas. The company purchases crude oil from independent producers, but owns its own refineries, distribution system, storage facilities, and more than 65 per cent of its retail outlets. Through these outlets the company offers for sale both regular and ethyl gasoline and a line of oils and lubricants under the brand name "Central." Included in the line of oils are three grades of furnace and heating oils. These latter oils are sold by salesmen, and delivery is made through and directly from bulk storage plants.

The company has been in business since 1936 and since that time has built up a rather profitable business. In 1959, it owned and operated 211 stations and sold its products through 187 dealers throughout its territory. The volume of business produced by the independent dealers was relatively small. In 1957, they accounted for only 14 per cent of the total gasoline and motor oil sales. While the company began its operations in El Dorado, Arkansas, where the home office is still located, its largest markets are Little Rock and Fort Smith, Arkansas; Memphis and Nashville, Tennessee; Birmingham, Alabama; Jackson, Mississippi; and Alexandria, Baton Rouge, and New Orleans, Louisiana. Approximately 60 per cent of its retail sales is to customers in these cities. The balance of sales is in smaller cities and rural communities in the territory.

---

[20]This intersection is found only for convenience in measuring elasticity of demand and should not be thought of as actually lying on the demand curve. It is not true, of course, that a price of 34.1 cents a can would completely eliminate the sale of frozen orange concentrate. A statistical demand curve should not be drawn to cover points outside the range of experience.

Since the company was primarily concerned with the marketing of gasoline, motor and fuel oils, and lubricants, the refining operations were somewhat, though not entirely, subordinated to the retail operations. In the refining process, several by-products were yielded as residuals which the company was not in a position to market. These by-products, such as asphalt, bunker oil, heavy lubricants, and similar products were sold to other refiners or processors. The output of these products, therefore, depended primarily upon the company's need for gasoline and oil to meet customer demand. The company owned three refineries, all of which were modern and well maintained. From a barrel of crude oil, there was, within limits, a certain proportion which could be refined into gasoline, lubricating oils and greases, fuel oil of various grades, and other residual products. This meant that in the face of a strong demand for gasoline, there would be a certain output of the other products in the production of gasoline. The liquid by-products of the refining process, such as motor and fuel oils, required storage in tanks which had to meet certain safety requirements and be located in areas approved by public authorities. It was not possible, for example, to refine the correct proportions of gasoline and fuel oil in a continuous refining process. More gasoline was consumed in the spring, summer, and fall months than during the winter, while fuel oil of the lighter weights was consumed more heavily during the winter, with lighter demands during the summer season. This meant that the company had to provide storage facilities for gasoline during the winter and fuel oil storage during the summer. In almost all cases, separate facilities were necessary for the two products.

The market in which the company sold the by-products it did not use was one in which the company had no control over price. Prices of these products varied over a limited range, depending upon the demand and supply situation of the moment. The company sold these products immediately upon refining rather than face additional costs of storage. The revenues received for these by-products affected, to some extent, the revenues which were anticipated from gasoline and motor and fuel oils which the company hoped to receive in order to show a profit.

The retail market in which the company competed was dominated by the major oil companies, such as Shell, Standard Oil, Gulf, and others. Central sold about 8 per cent of the gasoline and motor oil marketed in Memphis and New Orleans; about 6 per cent in Jackson, Mississippi; 5 per cent in Nashville, Tennessee; about 9 per cent in Baton Rouge, Louisiana; and 14 per cent in Little Rock, Arkansas.

Central had always sold its gasoline at the prevailing market price, although there were several independent cut-rate gasoline outlets in almost all of the territory. The company had maintained the quality of its products on a level comparable to that of the major companies and had priced its products accordingly.

Whenever a price change was made in any of the urban areas, it was almost always initiated by one or more of the major oil companies. Central had always followed these price changes both upward and downward. Such changes usually involved a difference of only 1 or 2 cents per gallon. Occasionally, a new independent company would attempt to invade the cut-rate market and offer unbranded gasoline at 5 or 6 cents below the price of the major brands. Usually, the cut-rate prices were about 2 cents per gallon below the major brands. If the new company attempted to hold its price more than two cents below the major brands, there would usually be a price cut by the major companies to within at least 2 cents per gallon of the invading company. This situation would prevail until the invading company raised its prices to the prior level of cut-rate companies or until it left the market. Prices would then quite often return to the former prevailing level for major brands.

Occasionally, there would be a price cut by a major company; this usually did not precipitate a price war but often reflected the demand and supply situation in gasoline. Since the consumption of gasoline declined in the winter months but production continued during that season, gasoline stocks were usually pressing upon storage facilities in early spring unless it had been a mild winter, so that fuel oil production had been light, resulting in lower refinery runs. If gasoline supplies were pressing upon storage facilities, there might be a price reduction by a major company which was usually followed by all other companies, including Central. If storage facilities were adequate, there might be an upward adjustment of prices, since gasoline consumption would begin to rise in the spring and demand was met by current refining plus gasoline in storage. Central had never initiated a price change either upward or downward.

In February, 1958, Central found itself with a large carry-over of gasoline stocks in its Memphis and Little Rock markets. Not only were the storage tanks at the refineries practically filled, but the bulk stations were carrying more than normal supplies of gasoline. Asphalt, bunker oil, and a by-product used in the manufacture of synthetic rubber were in demand, and prices were slightly higher than usual. The company had an ample supply of crude oil but was unable to carry on refining operations on a large scale because of the storage problem.

The retail price of ethyl gasoline in Memphis at the time was 38.6 cents per gallon, and regular sold at 35.6 cents, including state and federal taxes. The same prices prevailed in Little Rock. In order to move the gasoline out of storage and into the market, the president of Central suggested to the sales manager that the company reduce the price of gasoline in Memphis and Little Rock by 5 cents per gallon. To this the sales manager objected, stating that a cut of this size would immediately bring about similar reductions by the major companies, with the result that little, if any, more gasoline would be sold, and the com-

Exhibit 1

CENTRAL PETROLEUM PRODUCTS, INC.
Sales of Gasoline—Memphis Market Area
Monthly, 1957

	REGULAR		ETHYL	
MONTH	Gallons	Retail Price* per Gallon	Gallons	Retail Price* per Gallon
January	687,000	33.6¢	297,000	36.6¢
February	681,000	33.6	295,000	36.6
March	701,000	33.6	300,000	36.6
April	752,000	35.6	427,000	38.6
May	955,000	35.6	469,000	38.6
June	1,001,000	35.6	501,000	38.6
July	1,021,000	35.6	500,000	38.6
August	1,152,000	35.6	519,000	38.6
September	1,099,000	30.6†	553,000	33.6†
October	1,101,000	30.6†	574,000	33.6†
November	921,000	35.6	497,000	38.6
December	700,000	33.6	345,000	36.6

*Includes state and federal gasoline taxes.
†Price war lasting fifty-seven days.

pany would receive less for it. The president, on the other hand, believed that a reduction in the price would increase the sale of gasoline even if the major companies did meet the reduction. He argued that all the companies would sell more gasoline because of the lower price and that therefore Central would gain by a price reduction of the amount he suggested. The sales manager suggested that if there were to be a price reduction, it be no more than 1 cent per gallon, since he did not believe the major companies would follow such a small cut and the company would then have a price advantage over the major companies.

The president of Central was dubious about this policy, since he thought a reduction of only 1 cent would not stimulate the sale of gasoline sufficiently to help the company reduce its gasoline stock so that it could resume refining operations and again enter the market for the by-products.

Exhibit 1 shows the company sales in the Memphis market area by months for the year 1957, together with prevailing prices for both regular and ethyl grades. The same prices prevailed in Little Rock.

QUESTIONS

1. Would you recommend that Central initiate a price reduction at this time? If so, would you recommend the 5-cent or the 1-cent reduction?
2. Did the president think the demand for gasoline was elastic or inelastic? Why? The sales manager? Why? What is your opinion of the elasticity of the gasoline market?
3. Did the sales manager think the gasoline market for Central was elastic or inelastic? Why?
4. What is the nature of demand for gasoline? On the basis of your answer, would you say that the demand for gasoline is elastic or inelastic?
5. Would you say that the elasticity of demand for Central is greater or less than the elasticity of the total gasoline market? Why?

CASE 3–2:   UNIVERSITY OF THE MID-WEST

University of the Mid-West was established in 1902 as a private non-profit educational institution to provide instruction in the arts and sciences. From an initial enrolment of 127 students, it has grown to its present enrolment of 5,400 students, of whom 611 are enrolled in the graduate school. The university is located near the center of a mid-western state in a small city of approximately 69,000 population.

The operations of the university include the provision and maintenance of living accommodations for 3,000 students in dormitories, 1,900 for men and 1,100 for women. Upper-class male students, married students, and graduate students are permitted to live in private homes in the city. Instruction is carried on in eleven buildings, which include classrooms, laboratories, and offices for faculty and administration. All of the buildings have been constructed from the proceeds of gifts and grants from individuals and foundations.

The university is governed by a self-perpetuating board of trustees consisting of twenty-one members. The administrative staff consists of the president, two vice presidents, and seven deans. The board is the policy-making body of the university, usually acting upon recommendations submitted to it by the faculty and administration through the president. All financial matters, including budget and fees, are subject to approval of the board.

The budget for the operation of the university is $12 million for the current academic year. Tuition is currently $900 per year, payable at the beginning of each semester. Less than 1 per cent of the student body are part-time students; the remainder carry a full academic load. Tuition for graduate students is the same as for undergraduates. In the current year, student fees account for $4.86 million of income, dormitory receipts amount to $2 million, endowment income is anticipated to be $4 million, and gifts and miscellaneous receipts are expected to reach about $950,000. Out of this income are expenditures for faculty salaries, which comprise almost one half of the total budget, dormitory and dining hall maintenance and expense, purchases of current supplies and equipment, scholarship funds, and general maintenance of buildings and grounds.

The size of the incoming freshman class each year depends upon available dormitory facilities, since the university does not permit freshmen and sophomores to live in other than university housing or in the few fraternity and sorority houses. These latter houses accommodate approximately 400 students. Thus the size of the freshman class varies from 1,200 to 1,400 students, depending upon space available. In addition to incoming freshmen, the university admits about 250 transfer students each year from other colleges and universities or junior colleges. The incoming freshman class is selected from among approximately 4,000 applicants. About 2,000 to 2,200 applicants are offered admission, which results in a net class of approximately 1,200 to 1,400. About 20 per cent of the incoming freshman class are usually awarded scholarships to make it possible for them to meet the expenses of education. The university is fairly selective in its admissions policy, requiring better than average scholastic aptitude test scores as well as preference for high school seniors in the upper 25 per cent of their class. This policy is generally known by high school counselors, and the admissions office advises in all of its publicity that students who do not meet these minimum requirements should not apply.

In spite of such admission requirements, about 10 per cent of the freshman class do not return for their sophomore year, although this has not been due to academic reasons alone. Some have left for financial reasons, health, and other miscellaneous causes. Enrolment in the spring term has almost always been approximately 200 students less than in the fall term. Again, while academic reasons have been the chief cause, the other reasons cited above are also a factor.

The current tuition rate has been in effect since September, 1956. Within a radius of 175 miles, there are two large state universities. Within a larger' radius of 300 miles, there are two other state universities. The highest tuition for state residents at any of these universities is $225 per year. The lowest rate is $150. The highest tuition for out-of-state students is $550 and the lowest $375 per year. Enrolment at University of the Mid-West in the 1956–57 academic year was 4,950 students, including graduate students. While enrolment has increased since that time to the present 5,400, an increase of slightly less than 10 per cent, enrolment at the four state universities has risen by more than 30 per cent. The last dormitory on the campus of University of the Mid-West was opened in September, 1956, at the beginning of that school year. This was a building providing housing for 425 students, and there were eighty-one vacancies in the building during the first year. The university could have accommodated more students until the academic year 1959–60, but it was unable to select additional students without seriously lowering its admission requirements. Since 1959–60, there have been no vacancies in the dormitories, and the available rooms and apartments in the city were practically fully occupied.

For the academic year beginning in September, 1962, the president, in the preparation of his budget, felt that a substantial increase in faculty salaries was long overdue. The salary scale was somewhat below that of other private schools of comparable size and, in some instances, substantially below that of the state universities. He estimated that a minimum increase of 10 per cent was necessary to retain the present faculty as well as to attract new faculty members. In addition, there was need to provide additional fringe benefits in the way of additional retirement annuity, group life insurance, and improved health insurance. It was estimated that this would add $800,000 to the budget. There was also need to make upward adjustments in the compensation of the staff, which consisted of secretaries, clerks, and maintenance and service personnel. This would require an additional $150,000. In order to keep the library not only current in its book purchases but to expand its services, an additional $105,000 was required to finance additional book and periodical purchases, which had been somewhat restricted in the last two years. Increases in the costs of supplies and miscellaneous expenses were estimated at $95,000. There was also a need to increase the scholarship funds in order to attract better students who were unable to finance an education at Mid-West without assistance.

The long-term outlook for enrolment was optimistic. It was estimated that the number of students in college by 1970 would be approximately twice that of 1960. It was the immediate problem which was more serious. No substantial increase in enrolment at Mid-West was anticipated until the bulge of high school students to be enrolled in the colleges in 1964 to 1966. In order to permit an increase in enrolment, it would be necessary to construct additional dormitory space. It was hoped that a donor could be found who would provide the funds for such a building; but at present, none was at hand. The president intended to propose to the board of trustees that if no donor could be found by the summer of 1963, the university make application to the College Housing Loan Fund, a government agency, for a loan to construct a dormitory which would house at least 450 students. It was estimated that the university could accommodate an additional 400 to 500 students without materially adding to its instructional and operating costs. In the meantime, it was necessary to obtain more funds to meet the need outlined above for the coming year.

Since the president foresaw no substantial additions to annual gifts from friends and alumni, he proposed an increase in tuition fees for the coming year. Together with his proposed budget, he submitted a proposal to the board of trustees for a tuition increase based upon the estimates shown in Exhibit 1.

Exhibit 1

PRESENT AND PROPOSED TUITION FEES AND ENROLMENTS

Present and Proposed Rates	*Current and Estimated Enrolment*
$ 900	5,400
1,000*	5,300†
1,100*	5,150†
1,200*	5,050†

*Proposed.
†Estimated.

Exhibit 2 shows tuition rates in effect at a selected number of private colleges and universities in the United States for the academic year 1961–62.

The president supported his proposal to the board with an observation that approximately 35 per cent of the students at Mid-West came from the midwestern states, 25 per cent came from the northeastern and middle states along the Atlantic seaboard, 20 per cent from the far West and Northwest, and the remainder from the Southeast and Southwest, as well as twenty-three foreign countries. He recommended that a tuition increase of $300 per academic year be approved by the board.

Exhibit 2

TUITION AND FEES OF SELECTED PRIVATE COLLEGES AND
UNIVERSITIES IN THE UNITED STATES

Institution	Tuition	Fees	Total
Beloit College	$1,275	....	$1,275
Brown University	1,600	....	1,600
Carleton College	1,150	$ 48	1,198
Cornell University	1,340	260	1,600
Dartmouth College	1,550	....	1,550
Denison University	1,100	150	1,250
Harvard University	1,446	74	1,520
Knox College	1,300	75	1,375
Lawrence College	1,275	20	1,295
Middlebury College	1,300	56	1,356
Mount Holyoke College	1,500	20	1,520
Pomona College	1,250	55	1,305
Princeton University	1,550	50	1,600
Stanford University	1,260	....	1,260
Swarthmore College	1,300	150	1,450
Syracuse University	1,370	100	1,470
Wellesley College	1,500	....	1,500
Yale University	1,550	....	1,550

QUESTIONS

1. Do you agree with the president's recommendations? Why?
2. Should short- or long-term considerations prevail in adjusting the tuition rates at this time? Explain.
3. Comment upon the elasticity of demand for enrolment at Mid-West.
4. Should the fact that Mid-West is a nonprofit educational institution have any effect upon the determination of tuition rates? Can you reconcile your answer with the anticipated large increases in enrolment by 1970?

CASE 3–3: CONTINENTAL AIRLINES

In early November of 1961, Continental Airlines startled the air industry by proposing a cut-rate fare plan at a time when air-line losses were shaping into a colossal $34.7 million. The plan called for a third, "no frills" jet class with fares 25 per cent under conventional jet coach fares. The proposal came after four years of slow growth in air-line traffic and at a time of jet overcapacity in the industry.

Air-line traffic had grown at an average rate of 18 per cent a year between 1950 and 1957, but slowed thereafter to 6 per cent and had virtually stopped by 1961. The big question before the Civil Aeronautics Board, whose job it is to regulate the air lines in the public interest, was whether the lower fare would lure enough new passengers to increase air profits, or whether it would result in heavier losses for a number of air carriers. United Air Lines, the largest air carrier in the nation, led the fight against the proposed "economy class."

Continental's President, Robert Six, outlined the basic conflict as he saw it. "Underlying the multiple attacks on this plan to stimulate new air travel is the apparently common belief . . . that air transportation has lost its potential for further penetration of the competitive travel market." However, said Six, "there is substantial evidence that growth has been retarded to a marked degree by the considerable increases in the level of fares that have occurred in the past several years. . . . Fare levels today are 16.4% higher in first-class and 34.8% higher in coach than they were in 1957, coincidently the last year in which the industry realized a substantial growth in traffic!"[21] (See Exhibit 4 for trends in revenue passenger-miles and fare yield per passenger-mile.)

Continental rested its case upon the demonstration that its proposal would require only 2.4 per cent of the intercity surface travel market (projected in passenger-miles) in its total market area to switch to air travel for the "economy plan" to break even.[22] Continental's position was stated to the Civil Aeronautics Board as follows:

At the present time, over 75% of our jet revenue passenger miles are in Club Coach service. We know that a portion of this traffic is business traffic that has been diverted from First Class. We do not believe very much of this business traffic will be diverted to the new "economy service," since it will be "Spartan" in nature. . . . In the Club Coach section of the aircraft, we will be providing 42 seats at a load factor of 50–55%, or approximately 40% of the traffic we are now carrying in this section with capacity reduced 50%. In the economy section, we anticipate a load factor of 60%, comprised of 25 to 30 passengers diverted from existing Club Coach service and 15 to 20 new passengers in the markets, attracted by new low fares. This new traffic will consist of the following:

1. Newly created traffic among the people now unwilling or unable to spend the time required to travel by surface means and unable to afford air travel at existing price levels.

---

[21]*Forbes Magazine,* December 15, 1961, p. 16.

[22]Continental's area consisted of a rough triangle between Chicago, Los Angeles, and Houston, Texas, including (in addition to these cities) Kansas City, Denver, Dallas, Fort Worth, Oklahoma City, Albuquerque, Phoenix, and El Paso.

2. More frequent travel among present air travelers due to reduced prices.

3. Travel diverted from surface transportation.

These load factors would result in a requirement for Continental Airlines to develop approximately 550,000 additional revenue passenger miles per day. Even assuming that no new travel is created, this represents a diversion from existing surface travel of only 2.4% of the [22.5 million daily estimated surface passenger miles in Continental's market area]. There is no question but that this modest diversion from surface transportation media will be realized with the planned reduction of fares.[23]

Exhibit 1 contains additional calculations by Continental as to needed traffic generation, assuming that the entire industry followed its lead.

A few days after Continental submitted its proposal, United and other companies issued formal protests before the CAB. United averred

Exhibit 1

ADDITIONAL TRAFFIC NECESSARY TO MAINTAIN REVENUES UNDER
VARYING ASSUMPTIONS IF ENTIRE AIR-LINE INDUSTRY
ESTABLISHED ECONOMY FARES

	Assuming All Coach Traffic Diverted	Retention of 40% of Coach Traffic
Coach RPM's, 1961 (billions)...............	15.4	15.4
Yield (based on Los Angeles–Chicago)........	0.05668	0.05668
Coach revenue (millions)...................	$872.9	$872.9
Per cent coach revenue....................	0	40%
RPM's retained...........................	0	6.2
Amount of coach revenue retained...........	0	$349.2
Amount of economy revenue needed.........	$872.9	$523.7
Economy yield (75 per cent of coach)........	0.04251	0.04251
Economy RPM's needed...................	20.5	12.3
Total RPM's.............................	20.5	18.5
Additional RPM's needed (billions)..........	5.1	3.1

Source: *Brief of Continental Airlines* (CAB Docket Nos. 13163 *et al.*).

that demand for air travel now followed the general level of the economy and that the levels of consumers' incomes more nearly determined their willingness to travel. Continental replied: "Certainly the business recessions of 1958 and 1960 have played their part. How major a part they played is open to question as evidenced by the fact that air travel in 1954 and 1957 grew a healthy 13.6% and 13.2% respectively, in years also considered recession periods. . . . Why then are today's [November, 1961] levels of air travel not substantially greater since consumer income, after taxes, is at a record rate of $367.8 billions versus a level of $354.4 billions in 1960?"

---

[23]*Brief of Continental Airlines* (CAB Docket Nos. 13163 *et al.*).

United also suggested that "for longer haul business travel, the distinguishing characteristics of air transportation such as speed and comfort provide a value so great, price is not, in United's opinion, a serious consideration." Continental replied: "The . . . table [shown in Exhibit 2] . . . clearly illustrates that as the total dollar savings become larger, the more attraction it has for the traveling public."

Exhibit 2

RPM'S IN BILLIONS

Length of Passenger Trip (Miles)	Per Cent Coach of Total Air Travel*
0–299	11.4%
300–499	25.0
500–749	31.0
750–999	48.5
1,000–1,499	65.6
1,500–1,999	66.3
2,000–2,849	67.1

*CAB figures for 1960.

In addition, Continental utilized *Fortune* magazine's 1959 air-line study as a "demonstration that price consciousness when related to income plays heavily on demand for air travel, and that to induce these people to travel, a substantial reduction in existing levels of air fares must be made." The *Fortune* study indicated that air trips were taken by:

1. One out of every two adults with a family income of $15,000 and over
2. One out of five adults with a family income of $10,000–$14,999
3. One out of 10 adults with a family income of $7,500–$9,999
4. One out of 14 adults with a family income of $6,000–$7,499
5. One out of 20 adults with a family income of $5,000–$5,999

However, United Vice President A. M. de Voursney, referring to Continental's position, later stated in a speech: "Proponents of the idea . . . that this huge automobile travel volume represents the future market for air travel . . . point out that . . . only 28% of the adult population have ever flown. But it is also true that . . . only 71% have ever taken a train trip, 48% have taken a bus trip, and only about 40% have ever stayed in a hotel room overnight."

De Voursney continued: "If the airlines could capture a fraction of this market, it is reasoned, our traffic increase would be tremendous. Of course, you must realize that most of the market [intercity travel] is short haul; next, that it is highly seasonal; and that it is also a market in which the traveler takes along a lot of luggage. . . ."

Both sides claimed that they had evidence from past statistics to support their position concerning the importance of price in stimulating air travel. One of United's past arguments had been that when a 17 per cent increase in fares was granted in February, 1958, the height of the recession, the increase had no appreciable effect on its passengers. Stated United:

As of February 5, there were 85,750 passengers holding advanced reservations . . . scheduled for departure after February 10, the effective date of the fare increases. . . . In an effort to advise each of these passengers, United . . . made 55,300 calls. In many instances it was possible to contact several passengers with one call and there were only a very limited number of passengers whom we were unable to reach. Only three passengers canceled reservations and only twelve . . changed from first class to coach service . . . . It is unnecessary for me to discuss [CAB] Bureau Counsel's theories of what might happen in event of fare increase when we now have concrete evidence of what does happen . . . .[24]

United also introduced figures from which it concluded that "an analysis of traffic in the top 100 pairs of cities shows that in those markets in which coach service was introduced between March-September, 1953, and March-September, 1957, the growth in passenger traffic between these two periods was only 6.6% greater than in all other markets." Continental did not deny this, but replied that "by 1953 more than half of the top 100 passenger markets already had coach service." Continental therefore proceeded to analyze traffic in the leading markets prior to any introduction of coach service (see Exhibit 3).

Exhibit 3

PASSENGERS

	Number of Markets	September, 1948	September, 1952	Per Cent Increase
Markets in which coach service was provided in 1952 but not 1948....................	50	245,162	429,394	75.1
Markets in which no coach service was provided in either 1952 or 1948..............	41	203,139	250,204	23.2

Continental also submitted that "total traffic to and from Miami, for the first quarter of 1961, was 12.7% below levels of 1957 . . . while the three markets provided with Air-Bus service by Eastern . . .

---

[24]*Brief of United Air Lines* (CAB Docket No. 8008).

reflected an increase of 11.2%. . . . Fare levels for this Air-Bus service are approximately 17% below piston coach levels and more than 25% below jet coach levels."

President W. A. Patterson of United called Continental's plan "unjust and unreasonable," "a device to give a temporary advantage," and "a move of desperation," and expressed fear that it "may make it impossible for a large section of the industry to meet its fixed obligations." Continental's President Robert Six charged that United was "satisfied with the *status quo,*" and said that in "resisting" the introduction of widespread coach service in the past, it had been shortsighted.

After considering the arguments, the CAB, by a three-to-two vote, suspended Continental's plan because, in the words of the majority, "there is substantial question as to the economic validity of the proposed fares if applied to the industry as a whole."

In August, 1962, Continental submitted a revised proposal for economy fares to the CAB. The new proposal was widely interpreted as an attempt to appease those who objected that the original plan would result in lower total profits for the air lines. The revised plan would establish economy fares 20 per cent below conventional coach fares, instead of 25 per cent as originally proposed, and it would in effect raise conventional coach fares by establishing a nearly identical "business class" with fares about 10 per cent higher than the older coach fares. This was a step United had long advocated in the belief that the spread between first-class and coach fares was too wide and not commensurate with the difference in comfort and service. United had argued that higher coach fares would stop the shift from first-class to coach travel. Moreover, the revised plan called for the fares only on the Chicago–Kansas City–Denver–Los Angeles routes, and some flights would still provide the former first-class and coach service at the old rates. In revised form the CAB permitted a six-month "experiment" proposed by President Six, but carefully hedged its approval. According to the *Wall Street Journal,* "the CAB said it's 'uncertain' what 'appeal' the reduced fares would have to the public and we cannot, therefore, forecast accurately the impact of the proposal on the net revenue of the carriers." However, the board added, "a controlled experiment such as has been suggested may provide answers to problems confronting the industry."

Among the lines in direct competition with Continental, United and American immediately filed and were granted similar petitions for the Chicago–Denver–Los Angeles routes. United billed its classes as "New Economy First Class" and "New Economy Coach," with fares identical to Continental's. TWA, however, chose not to match the other lines.

Instead, it inaugurated "a new Briefcase Commuter Service" featuring bar service and better meals at regular coach fares.

Shortly after the "experiment" started, the *Wall Street Journal* reported: "Several carriers protested [to the CAB] that the experiment would undercut fares far beyond those on the Chicago–West Coast routes and destroy the test by tempting travelers to go out of their way via the cheaper flights." The CAB noted that "restrictions on connecting traffic are more likely to impair than enhance the validity of the experiment," since 36 per cent of Continental's traffic normally was connecting traffic.

Continental's experiment was generally acknowledged to be the most important up to that time in attempting to broaden the market for air travel. Other air lines had experimented with reduced fares; but generally, they had dealt with special travel markets. Eastern's Air-Bus, already mentioned, serves as low-cost air transportation to Florida for vacation travelers. Eastern also inaugurated piston-engine "no-reservation shuttle service" between Boston, New York, and Washington in an attempt to be competitive in a heavy travel market. M. A. MacIntyre, President of Eastern, reported in June, 1962, that "since the shuttle service began, total Boston–New York–Washington air traffic has increased 41% . . . [while] Eastern's share . . . has jumped to 60% from 30%." Mr. MacIntyre also reported shuttle service earnings of $700,000 before taxes for the first quarter, while total earnings of the company were $173,000 after taxes.

Allegheny Airlines and TWA also operated a no-reservation shuttle service between Philadelphia and Pittsburgh at a fare of about $15 (in 1960). Regular first-class passengers had priority on the seats, while vacant seats were sold to those who walked on at the low fare. Both air lines in 1960 reported high passenger load factors, with a 60–40 split between first-class and walk-on passengers.

Pacific Southwest Airlines, a local California carrier, operated an extremely low-fare service between San Diego, Los Angeles, and San Francisco. It boasted fares of only 3.8 cents per mile (as opposed to Eastern's 6.5 cents on its shuttle service) and large, fast Electra planes. As a result, the 1½-hour trip between Los Angeles and San Francisco cost only $13.50, compared with $12.65 for train and $9.61 for bus, both of which took 10 hours. According to an article in the June 30, 1962, issue of *Business Week:*

> Pacific Southwest insists it has attracted new air travelers .... About 30% of its weekend passengers are Navy personnel, most of whom used to ride the bus or else hitch-hike. . . .

On holidays, when business travel is lightest, PSA has been jammed with customers. Last Easter Sunday, it . . . carried an average of 90 per flight (capacity 98) and on the Thanksgiving weekend, it carried . . . 94 per flight.

Exhibit 4

REVENUE PASSENGER-MILES AND FARE YIELD PER REVENUE PASSENGER-MILE, DOMESTIC AIR TRAFFIC, 1946–61

| | REVENUE PASSENGER-MILES (IN MILLIONS) | | | AVERAGE FARE YIELD PER PASSENGER-MILE* |
YEAR	First Class	Coach	Total	
1946........				4.63¢
1947.......				5.06
1948.......				5.76
1949........		Coach service introduced		5.76
1950........	6,710	1,056	7,766	5.55
1951........	8,939	1,272	10,211	5.60
1952........	9,775	2,346	12,121	5.55
1953........	10,580	3,717	14,247	5.45
1954........	10,925	5,321	16,246	5.40
1955........	12,501	6,716	19,217	5.35
1956........	13,577	8,066	21,643	5.32
1957........	15,012	9,487	24,449	5.30
1958........	14,391	10,045	24,436 Jet service introduced	5.63
1959........	15,853	12,274	28,127	5.87
1960........	14,846	14,387	29,233	6.08
1961†......	13,700	15,400	29,100	n.a.‡

*Weighted average of fares and miles flown at each fare. Yield can decline either from a price decrease or from a shift of passengers from first-class to coach service.
†Estimated by Continental in early 1961. The total was later revised to 29.3 billion. Actual total was 29.5, according to *Forbes* magazine, May, 1962, p. 20.
‡Not available.

Exhibit 5

COMPARISON OF ECONOMY FARES WITH OTHER AIR FARES AND SURFACE TRANSPORTATION FARES

	Chicago–Los Angeles	Chicago–Denver
Air first class....................	$131.40	$68.00
Air coach......................	102.30	53.75
Original economy proposal........	77.00	39.00
Accepted "business class".........	116.00	61.00
Accepted "economy".............	85.00	44.00
Rail first class..................	85.56	39.95
Rail coach.....................	67.39	31.46
Bus...........................	54.30	24.60

Source: "Business class" and accepted "economy" fares obtained from official Continental Airlines schedule, effective October 28, 1962. All other fares supplied by Continental documents as of 1961.

. . . At the same time it is undoubtedly true that regular air travelers are flying PSA to save money. It gives them a ride almost as fast as the more expensive pure jet, makes a point of being on time and doesn't charge for costly frills. . . . United admits its load factor . . . has dropped about 10% this year.

A survey of reasons given for travel in 1954 led one student of the industry to draw the following three conclusions, which he felt indicated the extent of the problem of finding a mass market for air travel:[25]

1. All reasons can be assigned to either a business requirement, a personal desire, or a genuine emergency.

Exhibit 6

SOME SELECTED COMPARISONS OF AIR TRAVEL TO OTHER MODES OF TRANSPORTATION

INTERCITY REVENUE PASSENGER-MILES, AIR VERSUS TOTAL COMMON CARRIER*

Year	Per Cent of Total Common Carrier Passenger-Miles
1940	3%
1950	14
1960	49

AUTOMOBILE AND COMMON CARRIERS, 1960*

Mode of Transportation	Per Cent of Total Intercity Revenue Passenger-Miles
Air	4.2%
Rail	2.4
Bus	2.0
Automobile	91.4

REVENUE PASSENGER-MILES (MILLIONS)†

Year	First-Class Parlor and Sleeping Cars	Air Lines	Air Lines as Per Cent of Total
1949	9,349	6,753	41.9
1953	7,950	14,760	65.0
1959	3,773	29,269	88.6

*Source: United Air Lines.
†Source: Federal Aviation Administration, *FAA Statistical Handbook of Aviation* (Washington, D.C.: U.S. Government Printing Office, 1960).

---

[25]Graham H. Aldrich in "Market Analysis of Air Traffic Potential," a paper presented in 1954, as cited by John H. Frederick in *Commercial Air Transportation* (5th ed.; Homewood, Ill.: Richard D. Irwin, Inc., 1961), p. 371.

2. Rarely has a form of common carrier transportation, in and by itself, constituted a bona fide "reason" for travel.
3. The discovery of a "new reason" to motivate passenger travel is rare to the point of nonexistence.

Exhibits 4, 5, and 6 present additional information and data pertinent to the air-line industry.

QUESTIONS

1. Is the market for air travel elastic or inelastic? What factors should be considered?
2. Suppose you were a board member of the CAB who felt that the "economy fare" proposed should be allowed a trial. How would you design an "experiment" to test the theory that the demand for air travel is elastic? That is, what results would you look for, and what controls or limitations, if any, would you put on the test?
3. What has happened to commercial air fares since the time of this report?

CASE 3-4: THE DEMAND FOR CHICKENS AND BROILERS

The domestic sale of broilers has grown from 883,855,000 pounds in 1946 at an average price of 32.7 cents per pound to 6,020,417,000 pounds in 1960 at an average price of 16.9 cents per pound. On the

Exhibit 1

DOMESTIC SALES OF BROILERS AND CHICKENS, 1945–60

Year	Broilers* (1,000 Pounds)	Price per Pound	Chickens (1,000 Pounds)	Price per Pound
1946	883,855	32.7¢	2,317,984	27.6¢
1947	936,442	32.3	2,144,133	26.5
1948	1,126,643	36.0	1,803,759	30.1
1949	1,570,197	28.2	1,954,034	25.4
1950	1,944,524	27.4	1,858,998	22.2
1951	2,414,767	28.5	1,791,376	25.0
1952	2,623,934	28.8	1,637,026	22.1
1953	2,904,174	27.1	1,581,950	22.1
1954	3,236,248	23.1	1,508,118	16.8
1955	3,349,555	25.2	1,228,777	18.6
1956	4,269,502	19.6	1,187,543	15.9
1957	4,682,738	18.9	1,013,856	13.6
1958	5,430,674	18.5	1,046,870	13.9
1959	5,762,951	16.1	1,061,580	10.9
1960	6,020,417	16.9	903,084	12.2

*Commercial broilers are young chickens of heavy breeds to be marketed at two to five pounds live weight and from which no pullets are kept for egg production.
Source: U.S. Department of Agriculture, *Agricultural Statistics, 1961* (Washington, D.C.: U.S. Government Printing Office, 1962), and earlier editions.

other hand, the domestic sale of chickens has declined from 2,317,-984,000 pounds in 1946 at an average price of 27.6 cents per pound to 903,084,000 pounds in 1960 at an average price of 12.2 cents per pound. Exhibit 1 presents price-quantity data for broilers and chickens from 1945 to 1960, inclusive.

QUESTIONS

1. Can you construct a statistical demand curve for chickens? For broilers?
2. Explain why the quantity of chickens consumed declined as the price fell.
3. What is your expectation about the cross elasticity of demand between broilers and chickens? Can it change over time? Why?

CHAPTER 4

•✦•✦•✦•✦•✦•✦•✦•✦•✦•✦•✦•✦•✦•✦•✦•

Cost in the Short and Long Run

IT IS common in economic analysis of price to distinguish between the "short run" and the "long run." The former is defined as a period which is long enough to permit changes to be made in the rate of use of existing capacity but not long enough to permit a change in the amount of productive capacity itself. When a change is made in amount of capacity, the action is termed a "long-run" adjustment. While useful, the distinction is quite arbitrary, and the businessman may often have trouble in deciding whether a particular action is of a short-run or long-run nature. This is because a great many changes in the rate of production involve some modification of, and some addition to, the existing capital equipment, so that while the principal action may be of a short-run nature, certain long-run adjustments are apt to be involved.

Measurement of cost plays several different roles in a business firm: (1) It is a necessary measurement in the determination of net income; (2) it is an instrument of control of efficiency of operation within the firm; (3) it is an important factor affecting the pricing of products; and (4) it is related to certain types of governmental regulation of business activity. These roles will be briefly surveyed in turn.

From the viewpoint of the individual company, costs derive from the need to purchase inputs at market prices. Usually, the firm is not a sufficiently large buyer of a particular input to affect its price significantly. Rather, the various employment opportunities open to a resource determine total demand; and together with the supply of the resource, this determines the market (going) price. If a given firm is to be successful in its bid to use scarce resources, it must pay the owners at least as much as they could earn in the best alternative employments. A block of land in the center of a thriving city cannot be used as a junk yard, since the junk dealer would have to bid for the land against banks, retail stores, and similar establishments that could offer high prices due to the high value productivity of the land. Even if the junk dealer already owned such property, he would find it desirable to sell or rent out the centrally located land and acquire space for his business in the cheaper periphery of the city.

As a consequence of this process, the cost of producing any product can be regarded broadly as the "opportunity" lost to society because an alternative output must be sacrificed. If labor, portland cement, machines, and other resources are used to build a new highway, the "real" cost consists of the sidewalks, buildings, stadia, or other structures that could alternatively have been built by the use of the same resources. It should be kept in mind, however, that the "opportunity cost" to society is small or nonexistent when a resource that would otherwise have been unemployed (during a depression, for example) is put to work on a particular product. (The lost "opportunity" for a previously unemployed man may have been only unwanted leisure—or perhaps some "do it yourself" projects.) If a resource is capable only of one type of employment, the sacrificed opportunity when it is employed in that use will be zero. However, if a firm has to bid against other firms in the same industry for the use of that factor, the price will reflect this intraindustry competition even though competition from outside the industry does not exist.

Income Determination

As it bears on the determination of income, cost is a necessary basis for numerous actions of management. Some of these, such as tax payments, bonuses, and dividend declarations, rely largely on income results of the current period. Other actions, such as wage increases and plant expansion, are usually based on the sustained results of several accounting periods. Costs, as used in determining income, appear as part of the accounting statement of profit and loss. They are the aggregate of accounting charges pertaining to a given period for the entire operations of the firm. Some costs, such as direct labor and materials, offer no difficulty of allocation to the current period. Others, such as outlays on machinery and on research and development, are undertaken not only with a view to present benefits in the current accounting period but for benefits in subsequent periods. There arises the problem of allocation of these expenses over several time periods—that is, the determination of depreciation and other charges attributable to given fiscal periods. The accountant's distinction between current and capital expenditures is as arbitrary as the economist's parallel distinction between the short and the long run. This is well illustrated by the following quotation: "If the accounting period were increased from the customary year to a decade, most of what is now treated as capital expenditure would become chargeable to income; while if the period

were reduced to a day, much of what is now treated as current maintenance would become capital expenditure."[1]

It should be recognized that many accounting measurements are
merely estimates rather than "firm" figures. Depreciation charges are
an outstanding example. For tax calculations, depreciation may be
charged off at a maximum permissible rate, in order to reduce taxable
income. For general financial reporting a slower rate of depreciation
may be appropriate. Thus, even in the well-defined area of income
accounting, the meaning of costs depends somewhat on the uses to
which they are to be put.

Control

A different type of cost information is required for purposes of control of the firm's operations. Here, the problem is that of isolating
the particular costs bearing on that segment of the firm's operations in
which the controller's interest centers. This may be a department, a
process, a product, or other cost "center." How to reduce costs of certain
operations, whether to adopt a new technique, what sales channels to
use—these are decisions in which cost information of a specific sort
can be useful. In dealing with these issues, the focus of the businessman's interest is frequently the cost of producing or selling a *unit* of
product. Cost accounting, as distinguished from financial accounting,
develops cost information related to the production and distribution of
each unit of product. To the direct costs, such as labor and materials,
associated with each unit of product are added prorated amounts of
overhead burden—representing the general charges for indirect labor,
depreciation, taxes, maintenance, and such other items as are not directly traceable to the unit of product. This gives the "actual" unit
costs of making and selling the product. However, since a fluctuation
in the volume of production would result in greater or less *per unit*
charge for overhead, a rise or fall in unit cost under this scheme is
not necessarily attributable to greater or less efficiency of plant management. To impound the effect of changing volume of production on
unit costs, accountants have devised *standard cost* systems, which establish normal or standard amounts of overhead to be charged against

---

[1]George O. May, "Improvements in Financial Accounts," lecture on the G. Lowes Dick-
inson Foundation, Graduate School of Business Administration, Harvard University, April
12–14, 1937, p. 4; quoted in Conference on Price Research, *Cost Behavior and Price
Policy* (New York: National Bureau of Economic Research, 1943), p. 23.

each unit of product.[2] If actual production exceeds or falls short of this standard volume, the resulting difference between actual and standard costs is carried directly to a "Variance" account (which is closed periodically to the Profit and Loss account). But the standard unit cost remains unchanged by variation in output. In constitutes a yardstick by which management measures the internal efficiency of performance.

Pricing

A third use of cost analysis relates to pricing. Obviously, the aggregate costs shown on the statement of profit and loss afford little direct assistance in setting prices for a company's products. This is especially true where numerous lines and conditions of sales are involved. Unit costs determined by cost accountants come closer to the mark. There are many situations, however, in which businessmen are forced to abandon accounting costs and to determine prices by other methods. In general, the cost information needed for pricing is distinctly different from that required for income determination or for internal management control. "Sunk" costs, while affecting net income, should be disregarded by the businessman when he determines price and current output policy. This has led accountants to modify formal cost accounting information in the direction of determining the additional or incremental costs involved in changing output. These methods, while they have to do with the accounting records of the company, embody some of the concepts of cost employed by economists, especially the marginal cost concept.[3] It is in the field of cost determination and pricing that economic analysis can make one of the greatest contributions to business practice. The economic analysis of cost will be discussed further.

Government Regulation

Finally, the growth of government activity in economic life has led to an increased use of cost information to justify prices. Business firms have found it necessary and desirable to justify their action on the basis of cost under such laws as the "unfair practices" acts (which are in

---

[2]Standard cost systems also establish standard charges for variable costs, such as labor and materials. Departures of actual unit variable cost from standards are usually attributable to causes other than variation in volume of production.

[3]An interesting article which shows the importance of the economist's cost concepts to recent developments in cost accounting is J. S. Earley, "Recent Developments in Cost Accounting and the 'Marginal Analysis,'" *Journal of Political Economy,* June, 1955, pp. 227–42.

effect in many states and which prohibit certain sales "below cost"), and the federal Robinson-Patman Act (which permits price discrimination only to the extent that "costs differ"). Public utility firms, railroads, truckers, taxicab operators, and others whose rates are subject to regulation frequently appeal to cost in seeking to justify rate increases. And in periods of emergency government control over a great many prices, petitions for increases in ceiling prices are usually based on showings of increased cost.

Fixed and Variable Costs

In short-run analysis, it is extremely useful to distinguish between fixed ("constant," "sunk") costs and variable costs. The former are those which can be considered to be unaffected in their total by variations in the rate of use of existing plant capacity. The latter are those which vary with the rate of output from the fixed plant. In the former classification fall such items as depreciation on buildings which the firm owns, taxes and insurance on these buildings, and the minimum amount of maintenance expenditure which is necessary to keep them from deteriorating unduly. Machinery normally outlasts a single accounting period, and its life may not be greatly affected by short-term fluctuations in the rate at which it is used. Under these conditions, depreciation on machinery would be classified as a fixed cost. And this would be true for purposes of correct business decisions, even though cost accounting conventions might cause depreciation to be associated with each unit of output. Salaries, especially those paid to company officials, are unlikely to vary—in the short run, at least—with the rate of production; hence, they can be considered as fixed costs. Interest on invested capital, license fees, and rental charges on land are other examples of fixed costs.

On the other hand, direct labor costs, social security taxes, material costs, depreciation which is closely related to use, and cost of gas, coal, and electric power are examples of variable costs. Interest paid on working capital needed to finance current production would probably fall in this category also, since its amount would vary with output, even though the relation might be less precise than it would be for other variable costs.

Union activity in recent years has been directed quite heavily toward stabilizing the incomes of nonsalaried workers through securing guaranteed wage plans—the employer guaranteeing two thirds of regular pay for a half-year period, for example, regardless of the amount of time actually worked. This has the effect of converting direct labor costs into semifixed costs. Although wage payments will still be related to the rate of production, the relation between the two may be much less close than in the situation where the firm pays only for hours spent in productive activity. Other costs, such as advertising and salesmen's compensation, may be difficult to classify as either wholly fixed or wholly variable in nature.

The analytical importance of the distinction between fixed and variable costs is related to a general philosophical principle of rational behavior suggested by such sayings as "Don't cry over spilled milk" and "That's water over the dam." That is, rational behavior in general requires neglect of past actions about which nothing can be done and concentration on making the most of future opportunities. If, for example, one has unwisely wasted ten minutes by standing in a line at the bank and has made little progress, this investment of time should not deter one from switching to any other line where the *additional* time required promises to be less. Similarly, a man who has bought a security at 100 and has watched it fall to 60 should not buy an equal amount at the lower price in order to bring his "average" to 80 unless he finds after careful study that no better investment opportunity is then open to him. That is to say, the money previously sunk into the stock at a high price is irrelevant to further investment decisions.

The principle just illustrated is of great importance to the businessman in making rational short-run decisions as to output and price. It indicates that *marginal* cost rather than *average* cost should guide such decisions. Average cost is affected by the amount of investment which has been made in capital equipment, and by insurance, interest, and other fixed expenses. Marginal cost, however, is *additional* variable cost and, as such, can either be incurred or be avoided in the short run. Consequently, it is comparable to the additional time in the bank line and constitutes the proper cost to be regarded in making output decisions.

A hypothetical short-run cost schedule for a small factory is shown in Exhibit 1. Output is assumed to be capable of variation between zero and twenty units per day.

Attention will first be directed to the "total" columns of the table—i.e., columns 2, 4, and 6—and to the Marginal Cost column (8). Total fixed costs remain at $32, regardless of output. Total variable costs rise continually as output increases, rising at first by decreasing increments and later by increasing additions as output is stepped up. These increments are shown in column 8 as "marginal cost"—the cost added by one more unit of output. (Marginal cost can be measured either as additional total variable costs or as additional total costs, since the only changes in total costs are those caused by changes in variable costs.) This pattern of total variable costs and, consequently, of marginal cost is traceable to operation of the famous law of diminishing returns. In the low-output range (one to six units) the efficiency of organization of production increases as more labor, materials, and other

Exhibit 1

DAILY COST SCHEDULE FOR A SMALL FACTORY

(1) Output (No. of Units)	(2) Total Fixed Costs	(3) Average Fixed Costs	(4) Total Variable Costs	(5) Average Variable Costs	(6) Total of All Costs	(7) Average Total Cost	(8) Marginal Cost
1........	$32.00	$32.00	$ 7.20	$ 7.20	$ 39.20	$39.20	$ 7.20
2........	32.00	16.00	12.90	6.45	44.90	22.45	5.70
3........	32.00	10.67	17.40	5.80	49.40	16.47	4.50
4........	32.00	8.00	21.00	5.25	53.00	13.25	3.60
5........	32.00	6.40	24.00	4.80	56.00	11.20	3.00
6........	32.00	5.33	26.70	4.45	58.70	9.78	2.70
7........	32.00	4.57	29.40	4.20	61.40	8.77	2.70
8........	32.00	4.00	32.40	4.05	64.40	8.05	3.00
9........	32.00	3.55	36.00	4.00	68.00	7.55	3.60
10........	32.00	3.20	40.50	4.05	72.50	7.25	4.50
11........	32.00	2.91	46.20	4.20	78.20	7.11	5.70
12........	32.00	2.67	53.40	4.45	85.40	7.12	7.20
13........	32.00	2.46	62.40	4.80	94.40	7.26	9.00
14........	32.00	2.28	73.50	5.25	105.50	7.53	11.10
15........	32.00	2.13	87.00	5.80	119.00	7.93	13.50
16........	32.00	2.00	103.20	6.45	135.20	8.45	16.20
17........	32.00	1.88	122.40	7.20	154.40	9.08	19.20
18........	32.00	1.78	144.90	8.05	176.90	9.83	22.50
19........	32.00	1.68	171.00	9.00	203.00	10.68	26.10
20........	32.00	1.60	201.00	10.05	233.00	11.65	30.00

Source: Albert L. Meyers, *Elements of Modern Economics* (3d ed.; New York: Prentice-Hall, Inc., 1948), p. 158. Reproduced by permission.

variable inputs are used in conjunction with the fixed plant. That is, a better proportion is attained between fixed and variable inputs, and this shows up the declining rate of increase in total variable costs. Above a daily output of seven units the factory is operating in the stage of diminishing marginal returns, which causes marginal cost to rise or, in other words, causes total variable costs and total costs to increase at an increasing rate. This is because each additional input (e.g., each additional worker) adds less to output but must be paid the same amount (e.g., the same wage rate). Each output unit is consequently producible only at a higher additional expense.

While marginal or incremental cost is rising, however, average variable costs (column 5) may be declining. This is apparent at outputs of eight and nine units. Also, average total cost per unit continues to decline even after average variable costs rise. This is apparent at outputs of 10 and 11. Average total cost is the sum of average fixed cost and average variable cost; it is possible, therefore, for an increase in the latter to be more than offset by a decrease in the former in its effect on average total cost. The effect of "spreading the overhead" is directly observable in column 3, where average fixed costs decline continuously as the rate of output is stepped up.

It should be kept in mind that price and output decisions are made by the management of the company (firm) rather than by the officials in charge of a factory (plant). A single firm may own dozens or even hundreds of plants; and many costs, such as advertising, research, and selling costs which are borne by the firm might not appear in the simplified sort of cost table which has been examined. To keep the problem manageable, however, and to bring basic principles into sharp relief, it will be assumed that the cost table used is for a firm rather than for a plant. (If the firm has only a single plant, the costs of the firm will probably not differ greatly from those of the plant.)

Break-Even Analysis

Businessmen often prefer to think in terms of total costs and total revenues rather than in terms of average and marginal cost and revenue. As a consequence, "break-even" charts are common in the business world. The name is something of a misnomer, however, since interest centers on the maximization of profits rather than merely breaking even. A break-even chart which utilizes the cost data of Exhibit 1 is shown in Exhibit 2. These data are assumed to pertain to a perfectly competitive firm which can sell any quantity it wishes at $10 per unit. Total cost starts at $32 (the fixed cost) and rises at a decreasing rate, and then at an increasing rate. The first break-even point comes at an output of just under six units per day. If fewer than this number of units are produced, total cost will exceed total revenue; if more than 18 units are produced daily, total cost will again exceed total revenue. A net profit can be made at outputs between these break-even points, the greatest profit coming at an output a little above 13 units, where the excess of revenue above cost is at a maximum.[4] This is the output which the firm will normally attempt to attain.

Break-even analysis is also useful to a firm which possesses some price-making power. Management is then forced to consider different prices as well as different outputs. The total revenue curve becomes a parabola similar to that of Exhibit 3 of Chapter 3 (page 90), its shape depending on the nature of the demand curve. Break-even points and maximum profit are found in a similar way. Frequently, break-even charts are drawn up *before* an article is put into production. From engi-

Exhibit 2

BREAK-EVEN CHART—COMPARES TOTAL REVENUE AND TOTAL COST

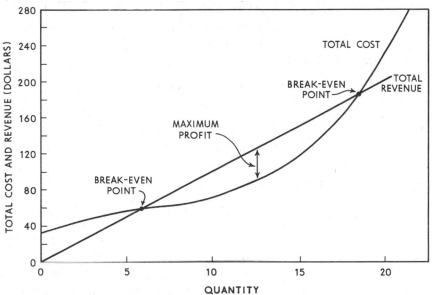

neers' and accountants' estimates a total cost curve can be drawn for an item which is being considered, while statistical study or executive experience can be drawn upon to arrive at an estimate of revenue possibilities. These calculations may help the firm to decide whether or not to produce the article. If the item is not yet in production, the estimated costs and revenues may, however, be so subject to error that the top executive will instead decide the issue on the basis of his general

---

[4]In drawing a break-even chart of this form, one implicitly assumes that output units are completely divisible—that the firm could turn out 13.45 units, for example, if it wished. This may or may not be the case. If it is not the case, the best output is simply the attainable output at which the positive difference between total revenue and total cost is maximized—thirteen units in Exhibit 1. It should also be kept in mind that it is implicitly assumed that all output is sold currently.

experience with similar situations, a general belief in the desirability of innovation and growth, or other grounds.

Average and Marginal Cost Curves

Economists usually prefer to work with average and marginal costs and revenues rather than with total costs and revenues. Cost accountants usually have average cost per unit as their principal and measurement although, to an increasing extent, they are interested in measuring marginal cost.[5] One reason for this preference lies in the fact that the break-even point of view may be misleading. A break-even chart seems to imply that the firm should not produce in the short run unless it can at least break even. Actually, this is only correct from a long-run point of view—that is, when management is considering whether or not to invest in plant. ("Breaking even" from a long-run point of view means the recovering of all costs, including a normal interest return.) In the short run the firm should produce if it can at least break even on its variable costs rather than its total costs.

The four principal short-run cost curves of economic theory are shown in Exhibit 3, the data being plotted from the figures in Exhibit 1. Average fixed cost (AFC) is of little importance except as a reminder of the source of high cost per unit when fixed capacity is lightly utilized. Average variable cost (AVC) is of limited use, being important chiefly as a means of identifying the "shutdown" price— the lowest price at which it is worth operating rather than suspending operations. This shutdown price is found at the lowest point on the average variable cost curve and is equal to a little less than $4.00 per unit.[6] At any lower price, it would pay to close shop, since variable costs (which are avoidable costs) could not be covered. Minimum average total cost is much higher—slightly above $7.00 per unit. This means that there exists a substantial range of prices (about $4.00 to $7.00) where it is better to produce at a loss than to shut down. The average total cost (ATC) curve is a handy one if used in conjunction with price, since profit per unit is the difference between price and average total cost. For purposes of making short-run operational decisions, however, it is the marginal cost (MC) curve which is impor-

---

[5]Earley, *op. cit.*, p. 239, points out that accountants are increasingly finding the measurement of marginal cost important in the pricing of multiple products. Most firms are actually multiple- rather than single-product firms.

[6]If total variable cost were plotted in a break-even chart (Exhibit 2) and price were set below the shutdown price, the two curves would not intersect—i.e., the firm could not find any output at which it could break even on its variable costs.

tant. If price cannot be changed—as is true for the perfectly competitive seller—output should be expanded to the point of equality between marginal cost and price.

The logic of using marginal cost as a guide to short-run output
decisions is not difficult to follow if it is kept clearly in mind that marginal cost is *additional* cost per unit. As long as price (the additional
income per unit) exceeds marginal cost, output is too low, because

Exhibit 3

AVERAGE AND MARGINAL COST CURVES FOR SMALL FACTORY

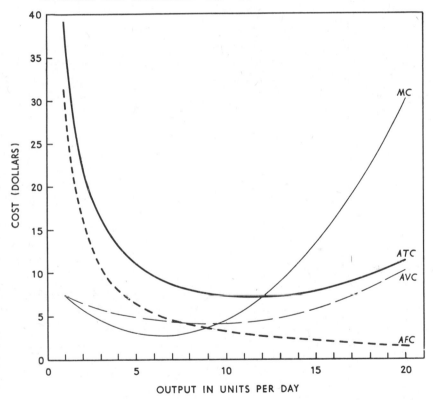

further units will add more to revenue than they add to cost. But if
marginal cost exceeds price, output is too large—some units are adding more to cost than to income. Consequently, optimum output occurs
when marginal cost is equal to price.[7] This rule, however, implies perfect divisibility of output units. If such divisibility does not exist, the

[7]Marginal cost must be rising, rather than declining. If marginal cost were declining
but equal to price, an equilibrium would not exist, because additional units could be
turned out which would add more to income than to cost.

rule of profit-maximizing, short-run behavior must be slightly modified as follows: Produce all units for which price exceeds marginal cost, but none for which marginal cost exceeds price. If price is $10.00 per unit, for example, this rule would require production by the small factory of Exhibit 1 at a daily rate of 13 units. The thirteenth unit would be worth producing because it would add $10.00 to income and would add $9.00 to cost. The fourteenth unit would not be worth producing, since its sale would add $10.00 to income, but its production would add $11.10 to cost. An optimum output of 13 units is, of course, the same as that arrived at by means of the break-even chart, except for the problem of divisibility of units.

A somewhat more confusing question of divisibility is involved when the manager of the firm must make an "all or nothing" decision rather than being able to choose the particular rate of output he wants. Suppose that our same small factory must accept or reject an order for 12 units at a price of $5.00 per unit, and that no other sales opportunities are presently open to the firm due, for example, to its being the slack season of the year. The marginal cost relevant to this decision is not $7.20, but $4.45 (which is the average variable cost). This is because the choice must be between either zero or 12 units of output. The entire variable cost of $53.40 is the additional cost which taking the order would involve. This amounts to $4.45 per unit. It would therefore be better to accept the order than to turn it down. Even though the order would not yield a profit over *total* costs, the income would more than cover total *variable* costs. Examination of Exhibit 1 shows that the loss on the order would be $25.40. However, if the order were turned down, the loss would be $32.00, the entire amount of the fixed costs. Even though filling the order would not yield enough income to cover all costs, it would cover all variable costs and contribute *something* toward meeting the "overhead." When a profit cannot be made, it is of course, wise to minimize the loss.

Adaptability and Divisibility of Plant

As a matter of convenience in drawing, average variable, average total, and marginal cost curves are usually made quite markedly U-shaped.[8] While this does occur in actual practice, many other shapes are possible. It is frequently claimed, for example, that marginal costs

---

[8]This also helps emphasize the mathematical rule that the marginal cost curve must intersect both the average variable cost and the average total cost curves at their lowest points.

are approximately constant over a wide range of output. This would clearly be the case for a firm which purchases and resells commodities instead of manufacturing them. If all additional quantities of a good (say, TV sets) could be bought at the same price from the manufacturer, the retailer's marginal costs would be nearly the same, regardless of the volume which he bought and resold. The added cost of handling each additional set would consist chiefly of the manufacturer's price.

If attention is concentrated on the producers of goods, it is useful to examine the concepts of "adaptability" and "divisibility" as they apply to plant capacity.[9] A plant may be said to be "adaptable" to the extent that it is capable of being used with changing amounts of variable inputs. A piece of farm land, for example, is quite adaptable to different amounts of fertilizer and labor, while a steam shovel is highly unadaptable in the sense that it can be used with only one operator at a time. Plant capacity is highly "divisible" when it contains a large number of identical machines—for example, 20 identical machines for producing concrete blocks, 50 nail-making machines, or 10 printing presses within a single manufacturing establishment. Complete indivisibility exists when the plant consists of one long assembly line, each station of which is wholly dependent on the previous ones.

Divisible but unadaptable plants are common in manufacturing, since many machines are built to operate at only one rate, and require a fixed number of operators and specific amounts of material per time period. In this case, marginal costs are horizontal over a wide range of output. In order to secure more output, a greater number of machines is utilized, and each requires a fixed complement of labor, power, and materials; consequently, each one adds the same amount to cost as the previous ones. Reduced output in this case is attained by the shutting-down of a number of machines, and each one which is shut down reduces total variable cost by the same amount.

If plant capacity is indivisible but highly adaptable, a U-shaped marginal cost curve will result. Marginal costs will at first fall, as a better proportion is attained between the indivisible fixed plant and the variable inputs; but eventually, the proportions will become less compatible, and marginal costs will rise. The high degree of adaptability of the plant would cause both the decline and the increase of marginal costs to be gradual.[10]

---

[9]See George J. Stigler, "Production and Distribution in the Short Run," *Journal of Political Economy,* June, 1939, pp. 305–27.

[10]Several other combinations of adaptability and divisibility are described by Stigler, *op. cit.*

Long- and Short-Run Changes

Most firms are regularly confronted with the problem of whether to change the short-run rate of output of the commodities they handle. For the manufacturing firm the meaning of "changing the rate of output" is quite clear. In the case of wholesalers and retailers the concept is less obvious, especially because such firms are almost invariably multiple-product firms, and because the notion of "output" is somewhat vague. If a retailer adds clerks to his staff within a given store, it is clear that he has made a short-run adjustment. If he adds a new line of canned goods or drops an item previously carried, he is similarly making a short-run change if the adjustment does not require an addition to, or subtraction from the amount of fixed capital he has invested in his store. If, however, he is forced to increase this investment in order to accommodate added personnel or merchandise, his action is "long run" in nature. While an aggressive enterpriser is likely to give thought quite often to the profit possibilities which might be open through expansion of his scale of activity, actual implementation of long-run plans is more difficult than that of short-run desires because such matters as additional financing, construction, product alterations, and new advertising are usually involved.

Economic theory considers long-run changes to consist primarily of changes in the amount of plant capacity. Such adjustments are then considered to carry along with them the necessary increases or decreases in such variable inputs as labor, materials, fuel, and supplies. In practice, it is often necessary that additional executive talent be hired when plant capacity is expanded. And occasionally, it is necessary to replace most of the top executives of a corporation in order to make a substantial change in the nature of the operations.

The Long-Run Cost Curve

It is useful to think of long-run cost curves as "planning curves" for plant and firm size. That is, they are useful as planning devices rather than in an operating sense, since output which is actually produced is turned out with some particular scale of plant (operated at some short-run rate). The long-run cost curve, to the extent that its form is known to the businessman, is useful in helping him plan the best scale of plant, or the best size of firm, for his purposes. If he anticipates that sales will be sufficient to justify that amount of investment, and if he is able to raise the necessary capital, the entrepreneur will want to build plants of a size which will minimize average production costs. If he cannot secure the needed capital or does not anticipate sufficient demand, he will settle for smaller scale operations.

The relation between short-run average cost curves for plants of various sizes and long-run average cost can be seen in Exhibit 4. Only five alternative sizes of plant are assumed to be technically possible due, for example, to the need to use some type of machine which is available only in one (large) size. The five possible plants may be assumed to utilize one to five of these indivisible units of equipment. If the anticipated rate of output during the life of the plant is less than OM, it will be most economical to have the smallest size plant (for which

Exhibit 4

SHORT-RUN AVERAGE COST FROM A PLANNING VIEWPOINT—COST DEPENDS ON SCALE OF OPERATIONS

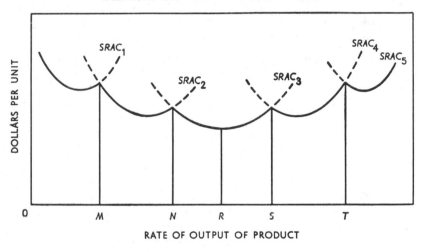

$SRAC_1$ is the expected short-run average cost curve). If the expected output rate is just a little more than OM, it would be possible to use the smallest size plant; but the next larger size plant, utilized at a relatively low rate, would give lower average cost. If anticipated output is between ON and OS, it will be desirable to build a plant of "optimum" size, associated with curve $SRAC_3$. A larger plant may encounter problems of co-ordination which will increase average costs. It is easy to conceive of a food-retailing store, for example, which is so large that clerks and customers would have to spend an undue amount of time in stocking shelves and finding items. A manufacturing plant may be so large as to create unusually severe automobile, truck, and railroad congestion. Curves $SRAC_4$ and $SRAC_5$ reflect the diseconomy of having excessively large plants. The problem of high costs due to undersized plants which are unable to make sufficient use of some types of specialized machinery, skilled management, and optimal organization of processes is in practice, however, much more common than that of the plant which is oversized. This is true especially because of a shortage of capital funds frequently compels enterprisers to build smaller plants than they would otherwise build.

In drawing Exhibit 4, it was assumed that some sort of indivisibility of equipment permitted the plant to be built in only five alternative sizes. As a consequence, long-run average cost is shown by the wavy

Exhibit 5

LONG-RUN AVERAGE COST—WITH COMPLETE DIVISIBILITY

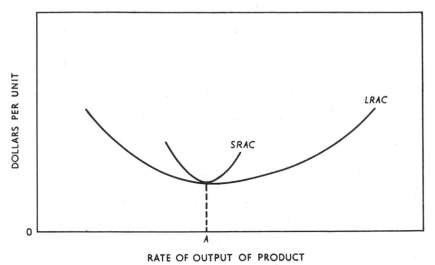

RATE OF OUTPUT OF PRODUCT

solid line in that diagram. However, it may instead be possible to build a plant of any desired size; and the long-run average cost curve then becomes a smooth, saucer-shaped curve, such as *LRAC* of Exhibit 5. This curve can be conceived of as being the one which is tangent to all of the possible alternative short-run average cost curves when an unlimited number of sizes of plant is technically possible. It touches the *minimum* point of only one of these curves—*SRAC* in Exhibit 5.

Typically, in manufacturing and trade, anticipated sales per period are much greater than *OA*, the rate at which output can be produced at the lowest average cost by building plant to an optimal scale. In this situation a large number of plants, each of the best size, will be built if the situation is properly anticipated. Usually, many firms will participate in the ownership of these plants, but any or all firms may control many plants. If, however, the advantages of large-scale production are such that the output of one plant of efficient size is a large fraction of the sales of the product in the entire market, it is clear that there will be room for only a small number of plants, and consequently, only a small number of companies. A small city usually has only a few brickyards and a few "ten-cent" stores, for example.

An Empirical Study of Scale

This situation is illustrated by an interesting statistical study carried out by a well-known economist.[11] From engineering data the percentage of the national capacity in various industries accounted for by one plant of the most efficient size was estimated. These percentages are shown in Exhibit 6.

Exhibit 6

SCALE OF EFFICIENT PRODUCTION IN VARIOUS INDUSTRIES

Industry	Percentage of National Industry Capacity Provided by One Efficient Plant, circa 1951
Category 1:	
Flour milling	$\frac{1}{10}-\frac{1}{2}$
Shoes	$\frac{1}{7}-\frac{1}{2}$
Canned fruits and vegetables	$\frac{1}{4}-\frac{1}{2}$
Cement	$\frac{4}{5}-1$
Distilled liquor	$1\frac{1}{4}-1\frac{3}{4}$
Petroleum refining	$1\frac{3}{4}$
Meat packing, fresh	$\frac{1}{50}-\frac{1}{5}$
Tires and tubes	3
Category 2:	
Steel	$1-2\frac{1}{2}$
Metal containers	$\frac{1}{2}-3$
Rayon	4–6
Soap	4–6
Farm machines, except tractors	4–6
Cigarettes	5–6
Category 3:	
Gypsum products	$2\frac{1}{2}-3$
Automobiles	5–10
Fountain pens	5–10
Copper	10
Tractors	10–15
Typewriters	10–30

Source: Joe S. Bain, "Economics of Scale, Concentration, and the Condition of Entry in Twenty Manufacturing Industries," *American Economic Review*, March, 1954, p. 36.

---

[11] Joe S. Bain, "Economics of Scale, Concentration, and the Condition of Entry in Twenty Manufacturing Industries," *American Economic Review*, March, 1954, pp. 15–39.

It can be seen in Exhibit 6 that an efficient typewriter factory has to include from 10 to 30 per cent of the national capacity for this commodity, while an efficient tractor plant must include 10 to 15 per cent of the total, according to these estimates.[12] This would leave room for approximately three to 10 efficient typewriter plants and seven to 10 tractor plants in the country. Somewhat smaller scale production in relation to total demand is possible in the industries listed in category 2. Around 20 efficient plants could exist in each of the following fields: cigarettes, farm machines apart from tractors, soap, and rayon. In flour milling, shoe manufacturing, and canning of fruits and vegetables, the advantages of scale in relation to market are such that 200 to 1,000 plants of efficient size can exist.

The same statistical study gives estimated capital requirements for one efficient plant. An automobile plant requires an outlay of between $250 million and $500 million; a tractor plant, about $125 million. A steel plant costs $265 million to $665 million, while a fountain pen factory runs about $6 million. Shoe factories are relatively cheap—$0.5 million to $2.0 million each. These figures show forcibly why it is so much easier to set up such businesses as filling stations, plants for production of concrete blocks, repair shops, and haberdasheries than to enter the industries covered by the survey. An exception among the listed industries was meat packing, where capital requirements for an efficient plant were reported as "very small."

Flexibility of Plant

From a planning viewpoint the plant associated with curve $SRAC$ in Exhibit 5 is the one which is constructed to such a size as to take full advantage of the "economies of scale" without being so large as to encounter diseconomies. Exhibit 2 is drawn on the assumption that the planner can anticipate with complete certainty the output rate at which he will want to operate the plant over its useful life. Actually, there may be considerable uncertainty in the planner's mind as to the rate at which he will subsequently find it desirable to operate. As a type of hedge against this uncertainty, he may decide to build a plant which incorporates more "flexibility," in the sense that it can be operated at nonoptimum rates of output without greatly increasing the short-run

---

[12]The difficulty of getting unbiased information on this subject should not, however, be underestimated. Personnel connected with industries featuring high concentration of production would be inclined to attempt to justify such concentration as technically necessary.

average cost. Hedging usually involves cost, however, and in this case
the building of a more flexible plant is likely to mean that minimum
average cost will be higher than if the output rate could be perfectly
foreseen and the plant designed specifically for that rate.

The meaning of building flexibility into a plant is illustrated graphically in Exhibit 7. $SRAC_1$ is the short-run cost curve applicable to a
plant of optimum size built specifically to operate at the least-cost output rate OA. The other curve, $SRAC_2$, is associated with a plant of
about the same size which has been built to give more flexibility of operation, in the sense that nonoptimum outputs can be turned out without greatly increasing the average cost. At outputs below OX and above

Exhibit 7

BUILT-IN FLEXIBILITY—A HEDGE AGAINST UNCERTAINTY

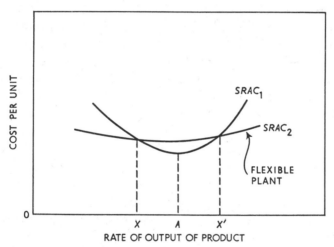

OX' the more flexible plant can be operated more cheaply. At outputs
between X and X', however, the less flexible plant operates more economically. If the planner expects with sufficient confidence that it will
usually be desirable to operate between X and X', he will prefer the
plant associated with $SRAC_1$. If he believes output will fluctuate
sharply from period to period, or if he is highly uncertain as to what
output rates will prove consistent with demand, he may decide in favor
of the more flexible setup.

Flexibility of operation may be attained by making the plant highly
divisible. As pointed out earlier, a divisible plant may contain a large
number of identical machines. In order to reduce output, a smaller
number of machines is used, but each of these can be operated effi-

ciently. If the plant had only one or a few machines, a reduction in the rate of output would probably raise unit cost more sharply, as in $SRAC_1$. Flexibility can also be obtained by some substitution of labor for capital equipment. If the ratio of labor to capital is kept relatively high, a reduction in output can be effected without much increase in average cost by laying off workers or reducing hours of employment. (A machine which is owned or rented by the firm on a long-term contract cannot be "laid off" in order to reduce fixed costs.) To the extent that guaranteed wage plans are put into effect, however, the achievement of flexibility through the maintenance of a high ratio of labor to equipment is less feasible.

Size of Firm and Cost

The "planning curves" shown in Exhibit 4 pertain to the variation in average costs as the scale of plant is altered. If the firm has only one plant, and if most of its costs are production costs, the best size of firm will be governed almost entirely by the optimum size of plant. If the firm is a multiplant organization, its optimum size may have little relation to the optimum scale of plant. (Large food-retailing companies, for example, are probably somewhat more efficient than smaller firms in this field, although individual plants [stores] are of moderate size.)

It may be necessary for a firm to be large in order to secure the efficient operation of its plants when the efficiency of each plant is related to the operation of the others. This seems to be the situation in the interstate bus business, for example, where plants (buses and terminals) are small, but where a large number of buses is needed in order to maintain regular schedules and where the terminals must be numerous if adequate common carrier service is to be furnished. Up to a point, at least, a larger firm enjoys advantages in raising capital, in purchasing, in carrying on research, and in selling. These activities require for their most efficient performance certain specialized personnel, equipment, or procedures which a small firm may be unable to afford. (The possibility of hiring the services of experts who also serve other firms somewhat reduces the diseconomy of small size, however.) A large integrated firm—one which owns plants at different stages in the production process—will probably have lower costs than a nonintegrated company if there is an important degree of monopoly power at some of the earlier stages, since integration will make it possible to avoid paying monopolistic prices for materials. Unless the firm uses enough materials to make possible their production on an optimum scale, however, integration may be unprofitable. Use of part of the output and sale of the rest may afford the integrated firm a chance both to avoid high-priced materials and components, and to secure an adequate scale of output at all levels.

An advantage of large size from a private—but not from a social —point of view may consist in the monopoly power thereby secured by the firm. This power may make it possible for the firm both to charge prices for output in excess of those that could be charged under competitive conditions and to pay lower prices for certain inputs than could be obtained with thoroughgoing competition in effect. Monopoly in the purchase of inputs is frequently called "monopsony" by econ-omists. A firm may have monopsony power while it lacks monopoly power. In general, however, large size is conducive to both. The effect of the exercise of monopsony power is a lowering of costs, while mo-nopoly is profitable because it permits the establishment of a more favorable relation between price and cost.

APPENDIX TO CHAPTER 4:   STATISTICAL STUDY OF COST

The following excerpts are derived from a case study of a retail shoe chain by Joel Dean and R. Warren James.[13] They illustrate an inter-esting attempt to determine the nature of long-run costs by means of statistical investigation of a group of retail shoe stores. This sort of analysis parallels the statistical measurement of demand as an attempt to give empirical content to economic theories.

A.   *Nature of the Sample*

From the several hundred stores operated by the parent shoe corporation, a sample of 55 stores was selected for the purposes of this analysis. Annual data on the retail operations of each store were made available for the two years 1937 and 1938.[14] The sample of stores was selected in such a way as to provide a fairly uniform coverage of various operating conditions. An attempt was made, therefore, to choose a group of stores selling different proportions of the various types of shoes which were, at the same time, representative of the sales volume of the stores in the chain as a whole.

In order to secure as high a degree of comparability as possible, the sample was further restricted on the basis of the following considerations. First, only those stores situated in the metropolitan area of a large city were included. It was thus possible to minimize regional variations in wages, rentals, and public-utility rates. Moreover, since this area is under the control of one supervisor, differences

---

[13]*The Long-Run Behavior of Costs in a Chain of Shoe Stores: A Statistical Analysis,* University of Chicago Studies in Business Administration, Vol. XII, No. 3 (Chicago: Uni-versity of Chicago Press, 1942).

[14]These two years were selected both because of their recency and because of their oc-currence in markedly different phases of the business cycle.

in managerial efficiency attributable to supervisory skill were eliminated. Second, although the parent shoe corporation operates several shoe chains, each of a different price class, stores from only one of these chains were included in this sample, in order to obtain the homogeneity of sales service associated with uniformity of selling price. Third, the sample was restricted to those stores selling men's, boys', and girls' shoes only, stores selling women's shoes being excluded. Fourth, stores recently opened were excluded from the sample, on the grounds that they might exhibit marked peculiarities because of immaturity. "Immaturity" in this case signifies not only that systematic underutilization may exist but also that sufficient time has not elapsed to allow the store to adapt its merchandise to the special characteristics of its market. Fifth, some attempt was made to select the sample on the basis of a uniform time distribution of sales, but it cannot be claimed that this was rewarded with any success.

. . . .

As far as the factor market which confronts the firm is concerned, it appears that the demand of the individual stores is such a small proportion of the total that the prices of input factors are independent of the action of the individual store. Even though there is centralized purchasing by the shoe corporation of some supplies, and some centralized hiring, which may affect factor prices, the influence of any one store can be neglected.

B. *The Measurement of Size*

The concept of the size of the individual firm is not a simple one. Size, however measured, cannot be dissociated from capacity in some sense. It is necessary to make a primary distinction between "technical" and "economic" capacity. Technical capacity refers to a maximum rate of operations, an upper limit set by the technical character of the plant and equipment. Economic capacity, on the other hand, refers to some rate of operations which is optimal from the point of view of cost—i.e., the rate at which average cost is a minimum. "Normal" capacity, in addition, may refer to some average or modal rate of operations which is not associated with either technical or economic capacity.[15]

Of the many size concepts possible, it is necessary to select one which is practically measurable, which is relevant to cost, and which at the same time permits comparisons of the sizes of different firms. There are available several concepts of size which can be measured and which are not without significance for cost. The choice can be narrowed to the following three types of measure: (1) physical size of plant and equipment, (2) input capacity, and (3) output capacity.

1. *The Amount of Fixed Equipment.* Size may refer to the aggregate of productive resources that are not alterable in the "short run." The amount of fixed equipment, however, is difficult to measure in terms that permit interfirm comparison, unless the equipment is highly standardized and in homogeneous units. If equipment is standardized, significant aspects of size for comparative purposes could be obtained—for example, by counting the number of spindles

---

[15]E.g., in E. H. Chamberlin's treatment of the individual firm under monopolistic competition, output is established at some level less than the "economic" capacity.

in a cotton mill, the number of beds in a hospital, the number of knitting machines in a hosiery mill, or some such similar units.[16] In the case of shoestores, one can obtain physical measures of plant size from the number of seats in a store, the area of floor space, or the number of standard lighting units (if electrical fixtures are sufficiently standardized). All these measures are subject to such a high degree of accidental variation, however, that none of them gives a trustworthy measure of size which permits interstore comparability.

2. *Input Capacity.* It may be possible in some instances to devise a measure of size based on input capacity. A commonly used index of size is the number of employees in an enterprise (in census classifications, for example). Raw-material inputs may also serve this purpose—for example, the crude-oil input of a refinery, the size of the charge of a blast furnace, or the number of tons of ore per day a crushing machine can handle. It may, however, often be extremely difficult to select from the complex of inputs that aspect which is most relevant. Especially when human services are involved, the concept of input capacity lacks the precision which is desirable when measurement is required. In the case of retailing, where the dominant input is labor service, measurement presents special difficulties, so that input measures were rejected as a possible index of size.

3. *Output Capacity.* Another alternative is to look on the size of a firm as defined by its output. Here again, however, some important difficulties are encountered. First, when output consists of variegated products, a complex measurement problem is introduced.[17] It may, therefore, be necessary to employ index numbers to deal with cases of multiple products. Second, it is necessary in this case, as well as in the case of input capacity, to distinguish whether output represents the maximum possible rate of production, the optimum rate (for a given body of fixed plant), or some modal rate. In one of these cases the measure of size by output is clearly superior to any other. This occurs under the circumstances in which each output is produced at the minimum total cost for that output. Here, there is a one-to-one correspondence between output and size, although it is true that this case may represent idealized behavior. Despite the fact that firms rarely operate under these minimum-cost conditions, the use of actual output as representative of size is the most satisfactory measurement device obtainable.

The next question to be considered is the information which is available concerning the output of the shoestores. The total sales of each retail outlet in the sample are composed of the following types of merchandise: *(a)* men's shoes; *(b)* boys' shoes; *(c)* girls' shoes; *(d)* hosiery (men's, boys', and girls'); *(e)* rubbers; and *(f)* sundries. These categories are self-explanatory except for sundries, which include bedroom slippers, shoelaces, shoe polish, and other small accessories. The dollar volume of sales of each category was available for 1937 and 1938, and information concerning the physical volume of sales of men's

---

[16]The use of value measures, while it has the advantage of comparing heterogeneous physical units, raises complex problems of valuation which need not be considered here.

[17]The superiority of an input measure arises when the degree of input homogeneity is greater than the degree of output homogeneity—e.g., in oil refining, it is simpler to use the input of crude oil rather than the complex of end products.

and children's shoes was also provided.[18] The assortment of shoe styles stocked differed somewhat from store to store, but information concerning the composition of shoe sales with respect to the various types and styles was not available.[19]

With this information at hand, the next step was to derive from it some satisfactory index of output. Retail selling output is best considered as the production of sales service. Sales service is the contribution of the shoe salesman to the prospective purchaser in the form of help, advice, and expert knowledge. Without too much violence to the facts, this sales service can be treated as a homogeneous product. Although the quantity and quality of sales service per transaction may differ somewhat from type to type, from style to style, from store to store, and from time to time in the same store, the variability of sales service is nevertheless limited. There are several influences making for uniformity of service standards. For example, all the stores in the sample are in one city, are under the same supervisor, and have standardized recruiting and training policies. Moreover, the employment of extra salesmen drawn from a trained reserve force tends to prevent serious impairment of service standards during rush periods. Since marked deterioration of service would result in loss of customer goodwill and patronage, it may be presumed that, with good management, efforts will be made to confine variations in service quality within narrow limits. The assumption is probably correct that the intangible output of sales service is highly correlated with some aspect of retail transactions which is capable of measurement. The immediate problem is to select some one composite measure of the volume of shoe sales, in either physical or value terms, which will most reliably reflect output in terms of sales service.

· · · · · · ·

Despite the omission of sundry sales, it was decided to employ number of pairs of shoes sold, including both men's and children's shoes, as the best available index of output. This choice was made on grounds of convenience and because a more satisfactory measure was lacking.

C. *The Measurement of Cost*

The primary cost data made available by the shoe corporation show the details of the annual expenditures of each store in the sample. The total operating cost is broken down into 23 accounts, for each of which the annual total is known for the two years 1937 and 1938.

Two of the elements of cost listed deserve special mention, however. These are general indirect expense (which is an allocation to each store of its share of the expenses of the chain as a whole which cannot be accurately charged to one account) and administrative expense (which is the share of the corporation's central administrative expenses charged to each store). In view of the arbitrary method of allocation, it was considered that the inclusion of these two elements

---

[18]The lack of data concerning the physical volume of sales of hosiery, rubbers, and sundries constituted an important gap in the data, which prevented examination of the effect on cost behavior of varying the proportion of total *physical* sales composed of these miscellaneous items.

[19]Since the styles and sizes stocked were adapted to the peculiarities of the individual store's clientele within the limits of the standard styles carried by the chain, it appeared unlikely that important heterogeneity in the sales-service unit resulted from the relatively minor store-to-store variations in assortment of styles.

might obscure the relations which it was desired to investigate. Consequently, in the calculation of operating cost, these two elements were omitted.

In order to obtain an insight into the behavior of broader categories of cost, the elements of cost were classified into the following groups:

1. Selling expense
   - a) Salaries
   - b) Reserve salaries
   - c) Employees' discount
   - d) Hosiery award
   - e) Shoe bonus
   - f) Advertising
   - g) Taxes
2. Handling expense
   - h) Delivery (including inbound, outbound, and interstore)
   - i) Insurance
   - j) Postage
   - k) Supplies
   - l) Miscellaneous
3. Building expense
   - m) Rent
   - n) Light
   - o) Heat
   - p) Window display[20]
   - q) Repairs
   - r) Depreciation
   - s) Water, ice

. . . .

D. *Statistical Findings*

As pointed out already, a separate analysis of the relation of cost to input in the 55 shoestores was undertaken for each of the years 1937 and 1938. This was advisable not only because of the lack of precise comparability in the data for the two years but also because of the additional confirmation that would be afforded by agreement in the two sets of results. Preliminary examination of the relation between cost and output indicated that the pattern of cost behavior was essentially the same in both years.

This preliminary analysis of the data by means of scatter diagrams showed the observations to be distributed in a fashion which indicated logarithmic dispersion. This was substantiated by the appearance of the scatter diagrams when plotted on double logarithmic paper. Consequently, except in the analysis of average cost behavior, the logarithms of the cost and output variables were employed in the calculations throughout the investigation.

Correlation analysis was used as the basic statistical technique, either linear or curvilinear functions being fitted to the data by the method of least squares. The fitting procedure was carried through, first, for total cost, which is the aggregate of reported expenditures of the store excluding allocated administrative

---

[20]The inclusion of window display under building expense rather than under selling expense may be questioned. It is classed as it is mainly because of its similiarity to interior display. On the other hand, almost the whole of a store is devoted to display and advertising, so that if the window display were classified as advertising, so should much of the other building expense. Its inclusion in one or the other category is, however, not an important matter.

Exhibit 1

SHOE STORE CHAIN

Simple Regressions of Total Cost on Output Measured by Shoe Sales in Paris

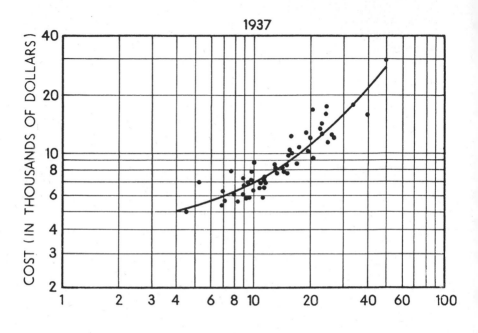

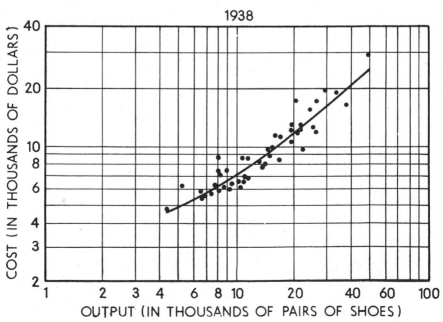

expense and general indirect expense. Second, the behavior of average cost, derived directly from the data, was examined by means of correlation analysis.

. . . .

1. *Total Cost.* The relation of total cost to physical volume of shoe sales
for 1937 and for 1938 is shown in the scatter diagrams in the upper and lower
panels of Exhibit 1. A detailed examination of the position of the individual
stores indicated that the relation between cost and output remains fairly stable
during these two years. The principal virtue of logarithmic analysis is that
changes in the magnitude of the logarithms of the variables in which interest lies
represent relative changes in the variables. Consequently, the slope of a function
which is in logarithmic terms gives the elasticity of the function of the variables
themselves. From a knowledge of the behavior of the elasticities, it is immediately possible to deduce the shape of the cost-output functions. The parabolic
shape of the fitted regression lines shows that the relative change in cost is
increasing, compared to the relative change in output. In other words, since the
slope of the regression line is always becoming steeper, the elasticity of total
cost is increasing over the whole range of output. On the basis of this knowledge of the behavior of total cost elasticity, it is easily possible to translate the
relations portrayed on the double logarithmic scatter diagram into arithmetic
terms.

For example, in order to analyze the behavior of average cost, it is necessary
only to make use of the proposition that average cost elasticity is equal to total
cost elasticity minus one. It is, therefore, apparent that unitary elasticity of total
cost corresponds to zero elasticity of average cost. If total cost elasticity moves
from values less than unity to values greater than unity, it is seen that the
corresponding elasticity of average cost is at first negative, then zero, and finally
positive. This means that the average cost curve displays the familiar U-shape
with a minimum point where average cost elasticity is zero. An inspection of
Exhibit 1 indicates that for both 1937 and 1938 the minimum point of the
average cost curve is reached at an output of approximately 33,000 pairs, since
it is at this level of output that total cost elasticity (the slope of the regression
curve) is unity.

It is unfortunate that only three stores in the sample have outputs in excess
of this critical level of operations, for one can, therefore, have little confidence
in the precise magnitude of the optimum rate of operations. This does not mean,
however, that the significant change in the elasticity of total cost is attributable
only to the influence of the large stores. Even if they are excluded from the
analysis, an upward bend occurs in the regression line—in fact, it becomes more
marked, and the parabolic shape of the average cost curve is even more clearly
defined.

There are, indeed, some grounds for the exclusion of the three largest stores
from the sample. Those stores which sell more than 30,000 pairs of shoes
annually may have special characteristics which set them apart from the smaller
stores in the sample. The three large stores are located in the downtown area and
therefore are faced with selling conditions which are different from those of the
stores in the outlying regions. While downtown stores generally have marked
daily peak loads at noon and in the late afternoon, peripheral stores are more
likely to be subject to heavy peak loads on different days of the week—e.g.,

Saturdays. This influence, which depends on location, may be sufficient to explain the atypical behavior of these stores. If one could be sure that these stores are not homogeneous, they could be omitted from the analysis altogether. If this were done, there would be stronger confirmation of the existence of an optimum-size shoestore for outlying metropolitan markets. However, since even without the retention of these large stores the existence of an optimum size is clearly shown, it was decided to retain the large stores in the statistical analysis.

· · · · · · ·

2. *Average Cost.* Apart from the information concerning average cost derived from the regression functions fitted to the logarithms of the cost and output data, supplementary confirmation was obtained directly by the analysis of average cost behavior. Scatter diagrams were made of average cost per 100 pairs of shoes sold for the two years, the pictorial representation of this being shown in Exhibit 2. Regression functions were also fitted to the average cost data. The scatter of the extreme observations is so wide that the behavior of average cost is not well defined in that region where the optimum output was found to be by other methods. Consequently, the upward trend of average cost is not apparent when the three large stores are excluded.

E.   *The Nature and Measurement of Retail Output*

A primary difficulty is encountered in attempting to define precisely the character of the output of a retail enterprise. The traditional theory of the individual firm considers the output produced by the firm to be units of physical commodities—gallons, bushels, tons, etc.

· · · · · · ·

Physically, retail commodities as a rule undergo no change in being placed in the hands of consumers. Therefore, the treatment of production as a physical process of transformation is not appropriate to retail selling. Nevertheless, the retail store makes an essential contribution to the completion of this transformation.

· · · · · · ·

The assumption upon which this study is based is that the output of a retail enterprise consists of the services which it renders to purchasers. These services place the physical commodities conveniently at the disposal of the consumer, widen his range of choice, and add to his knowledge of quality, grades, and prices.

· · · · · · ·

It is necessary now to consider the assumptions underlying the measurement of size by rate of output and to investigate the bearing of the special features of the type of retail enterprise under discussion on this identification. The simplest case is the representation of size by "normal" or planned output, where the technical equipment of the enterprise is adjusted ideally to the originally planned output. The rate of output is assumed to be uniform and synchronized to a repetitive demand situation for each future period or "week." Moreover, equipment is assumed to be at all times utilized at its planned capacity. This is, however, an idealized case; and some account must be taken of the fact that all firms subject to daily, seasonal, and cyclical fluctuations in demand and using,

Exhibit 2

SHOE STORE CHAIN
Simple Regression of Average Cost on Output Measured by Shoe Sales in Paris

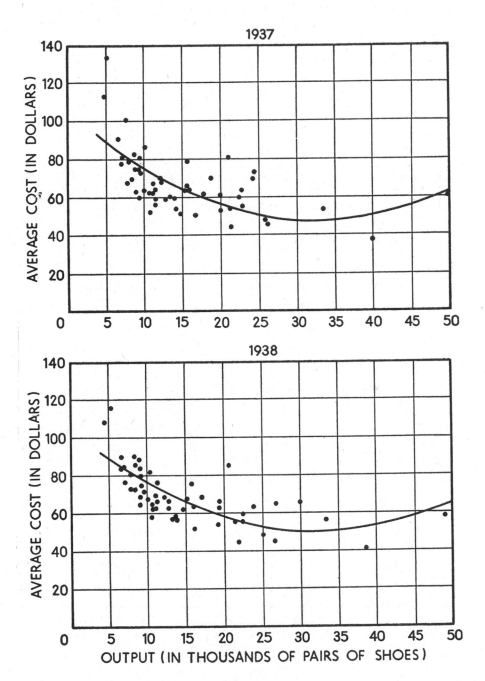

none the less, equipment which outlasts successive waves of high and low demand, face a recurrent problem of unused capacity. It is not a question of errors of planning in many cases; rather, it is foreseen by the entrepreneur that the existing demand situation gives rise to marked peaks and troughs. It will be essential for the entrepreneur to secure some degree of flexibility in operations.

.   .   .   .   .   .

When the extreme variability of output which characterizes retail selling is introduced, there is no longer any clear-cut relation between output and size. Plants will be constructed so that peak loads can be handled in some manner, but it may well be true that under such circumstances the minimum-cost combination cannot be achieved for any output. Rather, the fixed plant may be designed to achieve sufficient flexibility so that it is possible to produce for demand in both the peaks and the troughs. As a result of such an uneven time distribution of demand, therefore, the precise correspondence of output and size which is relevant in the case of uniform and repetitive demand does not exist.

CASE 4–1:   AIR-FREIGHT RATES

On October 15, 1944, American Airlines inaugurated an air-freight service in addition to its carriage of passengers, mail, and express. By January, 1946, several other air lines engaged in the transportation of passengers, mail, and express had also entered the field. These carriers were licensed by the Civil Aeronautics Board to fly regularly scheduled trips between designated points and were known as "certificated carriers." Initially, they carried freight only in the same aircraft as passengers, mail, and express, but subsequently, the larger lines, such as American Airlines, United Air Lines, TWA, and Pennsylvania Central Airlines, instituted the use of all-cargo planes in which no passengers were carried. These aircraft made regularly scheduled flights, as permitted in the certificate of the carrier, and frequently carried mail and express as well as freight cargo.

After July, 1945, a number of noncertificated carriers was organized and began to compete with the certificated carriers for air-freight traffic.[21] On August 1, 1947, the Civil Aeronautics Board set up a classification of noncertificated cargo carriers which permitted these new air-freight companies to operate on a scheduled basis as common carriers. The CAB also required them to file tariffs and reports. Slick Airways, Inc., California Eastern Airways, Air Cargo Transport, Inc., and the Flying Tiger Line transported the largest share of the total volume of traffic carried by this group.

----

[21]Prior to August 1, 1947, noncertificated carriers were not required to file tariffs with the Civil Aeronautics Board. They were not certificated to fly on a scheduled basis, but made irregular flights at rates negotiated with each individual shipper.

The rates set up by American Airlines on October 15, 1944, established a system of class and specific commodity rates, and applied these rates on a mileage block basis. For the four classes of commodities, A, B, C, and D, the distance charges were 50.0, 43.0, 36.5, and 30.0 cents per ton-mile, respectively, all rates including pickup and delivery service. With minor variations, the other certificated carriers followed the same system of tariffs, except that some tariffs were lower than that of American Airlines. Upon the entry of United Air Lines into the airfreight business on February 1, 1946, its tariff eliminated the four

Exhibit 1

GRADUATED RATES QUOTED BY UNITED AIR
LINES EFFECTIVE FEBRUARY 1, 1946

Weight Group (Pounds)	Rate Basis per Ton-Mile (Cents)	Percentage of 100-Lb. Rate
100–499	26.5	100.0
500–999	25.6	96.6
1,000–1,999	24.7	93.2
2,000–2,999	23.0	86.8
3,000 and over	21.2	80.0

Source: H. W. Torgerson, "History of Air Freight Tariffs," *Journal of Air Law and Commerce*, Winter, 1948, p. 50. All rates are on an airport-to-airport basis.

classes of commodities and set up instead a single general commodity class with graduated rates according to weight classification, to which the rates shown in Exhibit 1 applied. Other carriers soon made adjustments to meet the rates and terms of United Air Lines. Effective July 15, 1946, Pennsylvania Central Airlines filed a tariff quoting lower rates than competitors except on quantity shipments. TWA followed shortly in a partial rate adjustment to meet the competition of Pennsylvania Central Airlines.

The noncertificated carriers soon began to compete vigorously in the air-freight market. In February, 1946, Air Cargo Transport announced a schedule of rates which varied with the weight of shipments. The ton-mile rates, as advertised, were 22 cents for shipments of 1,000 pounds, 21 cents for 4,000 pounds, and 20 cents for 5,000 pounds. As the number of companies in the noncertificated group increased, rates were gradually reduced. The average revenue per ton-mile flown by

Slick Airways in the months of March, April, May, and June, 1946, was 20.1, 16.1, 17.5, and 13.6 cents, respectively.[22]

The certificated carriers made adjustments to meet the competition of the noncertificated carriers; and on August 1, 1947, a consolidated tariff was filed on behalf of all the certificated trunk-line carriers.[23] In this tariff the basic ton-mile rate was again lowered, the 100-pound rates being constructed on a basis of 20.0 cents per ton-mile, as compared to 26.5 cents per ton-mile in earlier tariffs. This tariff, with minor exceptions, brought about lower rates on all commodities. On the same date, Slick Airways, a noncertificated carrier, filed a tariff with rates between New York and other principal cities served by it from 12 to 39 per cent lower, according to weight, than rates shown in the consolidated tariff of the certificated carriers. Other noncertificated carriers filed tariffs early in August similar to that of Slick Airways. On October 5, 1947, American Airlines, PCA and United Air Lines, which competed actively with the noncertificated carriers, filed specific commodity tariffs which were not on a uniform basis but approximated 13.8 cents per ton-mile on shipments from New York to Chicago and 12.8 cents per ton-mile from New York to Los Angeles. These rates were lower than those of the noncertificated carriers on shipments weighing between 100 and 999 pounds. TWA met this reduction of rates in part. United also filed a new tariff, effective October 25, 1947, giving substantial reductions; in this, it was joined by some of its competitors among the certificated carriers.

Upon petition of Slick Airways and the Independent Air Freight Association, Inc., the CAB halted these rate reductions by suspending the supplemental tariffs of United, Inland, Southwest, Western, and TWA, and also the specific commodity rates of PCA, TWA, and American, with some qualifications. The CAB then ordered an investigation of these tariffs and the tariffs filed by ten noncertificated cargo carriers. The board stated that the purpose of this investigation was "to attempt to develop some national principles for tariff-making in air transportation as well as to inquire into the validity of the tariffs that have been filed."[24] To carry out its inquiry, the board required all carriers of both types to submit briefs and exhibits supporting their tariffs.

Although the arguments presented in these briefs indicated a sharp

---

[22]H. W. Torgerson, "History of Air Freight Tariffs," *Journal of Air Law and Commerce,* Winter, 1948, p. 52.

[23]This tariff consisted of three parts: (1) a rules tariff, (2) a pickup and delivery tariff, and (3) a rate tariff. This tariff had the effect of making the tariffs of the various participating certificated carriers more uniform.

[24]Torgerson, *op. cit.,* p. 61.

difference of opinion over the question of costs for the purpose of rate making, the revenue aspects of the problem were not neglected. Exhibits 2 and 3 show estimates of the relationship between rates and volume of traffic as air-freight rates approach the level of surface rates. "Expert economic witnesses who appeared for the various parties generally agreed that in transportation history, each new form of trans-

Exhibit 2

ESTIMATED ANNUAL TRAFFIC VOLUME (NOW
PRIMARILY SURFACE-BORNE) WHICH WOULD
BECOME AVAILABLE AT RATES INDICATED

Rate per Ton-Mile (Cents)	Ton-Miles (Millions)	Rate per Ton-Mile (Cents)	Ton-Miles (Millions)
35	30	15	800
30	60	12	3,550
25	100	10	5,000
20	200	8	7,400

Source: *Exhibit SA–4B, Exhibits of Slick Airways, Inc.* (CAB Docket No. 1705 *et al.*), p. 13.

Exhibit 3

ESTIMATES OF FRESH FRUITS AND VEGETABLES
WHICH WOULD BE MOVED BY AIR FREIGHT
AT RATES INDICATED

Rate per Ton-Mile (Cents)	Ton-Miles	Rate per Ton-Mile (Cents)	Ton-Miles
15	24,419,000	5	967,711,000
10	63,714,000	3	4,018,743,000
7	333,127,000		

Source: Spencer O. Larsen, *Wayne University Studies in Air Transport*, No. 1 (Detroit, 1944), p. 5; based on historical movements of 1941.

portation which has persisted offered services and rates which were able to (1) divert some traffic from older transportation systems, and (2) create new traffic. Air freight, in its genesis, has shown such propensities."[25] In addition, representatives of several carriers pointed out that it might be necessary at times to quote rates below cost in order to develop traffic.

The certificated carriers tended to treat the transportation of freight as a by-product of their main operations in the transport of passengers,

---

[25]*Examiner's Report* (CAB Docket No. 810 *et al.*), p. 236.

Exhibit 4

BRANIFF AIRWAYS, INC., REVENUES AND EXPENSES FOR QUARTER-YEAR ENDED SEPTEMBER 30, 1947
Showing Direct Distribution to Services Affected and to Proration "Pools"

Description	Total	Passenger	Mail	Express	Freight	Allocable to All Cargo	Balance Allocable to All Services
Operating revenues:							
Passenger............................	$2,779,168	$2,779,168	....	....	....	....	....
Mail...............................	112,832	....	$112,832	....	....	....	....
Express............................	78,495	....	....	$78,495	....	.....	....
Freight............................	26,299	....	....	....	$26,299	.....	....
Excess baggage.....................	25,875	25,875	....	....	....	....	....
Other (including charter)...........	40,739	24,661			8,673	....	$ 7,405
Totals.........................	$3,063,408	$2,829,704	$112,832	$78,495	$34,972	....	$ 7,405
Operating expenses:							
Flying operations..................	$ 746,259	$ 4,648	....	....	$ 2,426	....	$ 739,185
Flying maintenance.................	366,911	2,400	....	....	1,453	....	363,058
Flying depreciation................	370,432	3,301	....	....	1,483	....	365,648
Total Direct Flying.............	$1,483,602	$ 10,349	....	....	$ 5,362	.....	$1,467,891
Ground operations.................	$ 464,601	$ 2,017	$ 933	....	$ 523	$66,631	$ 394,497
Ground indirect maintenance........	245,502	....	....	....	....	....	245,502
Passenger service.................	246,030	246,030	....	....	....	....	....
Traffic and sales.................	357,463	307,361	684	....	1,102	....	48,316
Advertising and publicity..........	73,442	....	....	....	....	....	73,442
General and administrative.........	218,469	15,826	852	....	1,436	1,178	199,177
Ground equipment, depreciation.....	42,615	14,038	305	....	622	657	26,993
Total Operating Expense.........	$3,131,724	$ 595,621	$ 2,774	....	$ 9,045	$68,466	$2,455,818
Net Operating Profit or Loss........	$ 68,316*	$2,234,083	$110,058	$78,495	$25,927	$68,466*	$2,448,413 *

* Loss.
Source: *Exhibit No. B-4*, p. 1, *Exhibits of Braniff Airways, Inc.* (C.A.B. Docket No. 1705 *et al.*).

mail, and express. The noncertificated carriers, on the other hand, transported freight as their main and only product. Although all certified carriers were requested to present an exhibit showing both revenues and expenditures pertaining individually to passenger mail, express, and freight service, only one carrier, Braniff Airways, submitted such an exhibit. The remaining companies stated that lack of information and time prevented them from presenting an accurate statement. The statement of Braniff Airways is shown in Exhibit 4.

Exhibit 5

AVERAGE WEIGHT, AVERAGE LENGTH OF HOP, AND
AVERAGE LENGTH OF SHIPMENT FOR SELECTED
CERTIFICATED AND NONCERTIFICATED
CARRIERS

Carrier	Average Weight per Shipment (Tons), Week of September 7, 1947	Average Length of Hop in Miles, Week of September 7, 1947	Average Length of Shipment in Miles, Third Quarter, 1947
Certificated:			
American	0.0736	n.a.*	900†
United	0.0776	291.9	1,030†
PCA	0.1179	140.5	345
Braniff	0.0443	161.2	557
TWA	0.0820	265.4	1,178
Noncertificated:			
Slick	0.1361	740.2	2,069.1
Flying Tiger	0.4431	1,341.8	1,837.7
California Eastern	0.1767	742.9	2,101.0
Air Cargo	1,5284	n.a.*	564.2

*Not available.
†Estimates.
Source: *Average Weight per Shipment, Exhibit PC 226A* (CAB Docket No. 1705 *et al.*, January 20, 1948). *Average Length of Hop, Exhibit PC 235* (CAB Docket No. 1705 *et al.*, February 20, 1948). *Average Length of Shipment, Exhibit PC 227A* (CAB Docket No. 1705 *et al.*, January 20, 1948).

The noncertificated carriers served primarily a few large cities on the East and West coasts. Slick Airways served regularly 11 principal points; California Eastern, seven; and the Flying Tigers, eight. The certificated carriers, on the other hand, served a substantially larger number of cities; American Airlines, for example, provided all four of its services to 65 cities broadly distributed over the United States. United Air Lines, similarly, covered a wide geographic area. PCA and TWA served a smaller number of cities over a somewhat more restricted geographical area. The distance factor was greater for the noncertificated than for the certificated carriers. Average load was also greater in the noncertificated carriers than in the certificated. Both distance and weight factors are shown in Exhibit 5. These factors, which affected the costs of carrying freight, became one of the principal points of dispute between the two groups of carriers as to the nature of certain costs.

The certificated carriers based their main argument upon the principle of "out-of-pocket" costs directly attributable to the provision of air-freight service. In their arguments before the CAB, they pointed out that because their aircraft provided regularly scheduled flights for the carriage of passengers, mail, and express, and because there was adequate unused capacity in these carriers, it was not necessary to include as costs of freight service any expenses for flying operations, depreciation of flying equipment, and ground operations, which would

Exhibit 6

AVAILABLE FREIGHT SPACE AND PERCENTAGE UTILIZA-
TION ON COMBINATION AIRCRAFT FOR AMERICAN
AIRLINES, UNITED AIR LINES, AND TWA FOR
THE FIRST TEN MONTHS OF 1947

Carrier	Available Space (Ton-Miles)	Ton-Miles of Freight Carried	Percentage Utilized
American....................	76,692,230	6,870,096	8.95
United.....................	60,828,015	3,351,723	5.51
TWA......................	40,374,432	2,009,152	4.97
Average................			6.87

Source: *Brief of Public Counsel to C.A.B.* (CAB Docket No. 1705 *et al.*, March 22, 1948), p. 30.

be carried on even if there were no freight service. Exhibit 6 shows the average monthly utilization of this space by American, United, and TWA for the ten-month period ended October 31, 1947.

Several factors were emphasized which affected the percentage utilization of this space.

Since [freight] cargo moves primarily between 9 P.M. and 9 A.M., most available space on combination planes during the period 9 A.M. to 9 P.M. is not commercially usable. . . . During the period between 9 P.M. and 9 A.M. United originated 65 per cent of its freight from its major stations. . . . Since cargo moves primarily on week days, a large proportion of the space flown on week ends is not commercially usable. The testimony of PCA shows that 70 per cent of its cargo is carried Tuesday through Friday. . . . United's calculations do not relate the available space to the place where the cargo demand exists. If there is a cargo demand at Chicago, tonnage available on combination planes at Reno is not commercially usable space. . . . When the directional flow of cargo is considered, a large proportion of cargo space on combination planes is not commercially usable. Exhibits of United show that 82 per cent of United's cargo is westbound and only 18 per cent eastbound. . . . For the certificated carriers as a whole the eastbound traffic was only 37.6 per cent of the westbound.[26]

There are shown in Exhibit 7 comparative costs of freight service for selected certificated and noncertificated carriers. The column headed "Carriers' Estimate" is the approximate out-of-pocket cost to the cer-

Exhibit 7

COMPARATIVE COSTS OF FREIGHT SERVICE IN CENTS PER AVAILABLE
TON-MILE AND PER ADJUSTED REVENUE TON-MILE FOR SELECTED
CERTIFICATED AND NONCERTIFICATED CARRIERS

| | AVAILABLE TON-MILES | | | ADJUSTED REVENUE TON-MILES | | | CARRIERS' ESTIMATE: |
CARRIER	Air Operating Expense	Ground and Indirect Maintenance Expense	Other Ground and Indirect Expense	Air Operating Expense	Ground and Indirect Maintenance Expense	Other Ground and Indirect Expense	OTHER GROUND AND INDIRECT EXPENSE APPLICABLE TO FREIGHT
Certificated:							
American........	11.98	2.50	9.40	19.30	4.03	15.15	5.44
Braniff..........	14.91	2.47	9.47	24.40	4.04	15.50	2.46
PCA............	13.26	2.12	10.00	25.41	4.06	19.14	5.67
TWA...........	13.14	3.07	9.82	20.71	4.83	15.48	5.91
United..........	11.56	1.85	9.61	18.26	2.93	18.27	9.80
Average.......	12.74	2.35	9.29	21.72	4.01	15.83	
Noncertificated:							
Air Cargo........	10.67	0.79	5.75	15.65	1.16	8.43	
California Eastern.	5.89	0.13	3.66	10.71	0.24	6.65	
Flying Tiger......	9.30	0.40	3.85	12.78	0.56	5.29	
Slick............	5.81	0.74	4.86	7.26	0.92	6.06	
Willis...........	6.82	1.30	2.69	16.95	3.24	6.69	
Average.......	6.67	0.55	4.21	9.92	0.82	6.27	

Sources: *Exhibits PC 433A, 433B, Public Counsel's Exhibits* (CAB Docket No. 1705 *et al.*, January 20, 1948).

tificated carriers for the transportation of air freight. These estimates do not include an allocation of expenditures for personnel, facilities, and equipment at stations where passenger, mail, express, and freight traffic are handled jointly. It was noted in the hearings:

These added cost arguments appear valid with respect to station personnel, facilities and equipment at any point where traffic volume is low, that is, where

[26]*Brief of United Airlines, Inc., before the Civil Aeronautics Board*, March 22, 1948, pp. 33–36, *passim.*

all traffic can be handled by the minimum staff, and even where greater volume would require additional clerks and handlers, some economy might conceivably be realized by having the station manager take on the added supervisory work. But when the larger traffic points are considered, the argument loses force— as freight traffic grows in volume the relative amount that can move in combination as opposed to all-cargo equipment will become less. A considerable all-cargo operation at any point will make necessary separate freight terminal handling and loading facilities, perhaps at a different airport than is used for passenger flights. Rather than acquire additional space for freight reservation employees at the relatively expensive locations used for passenger sales, they will doubtless be located in less costly space, probably at the freight terminal. As traffic grows, a fairly complete segregation of passenger and freight operations will follow. Any appreciable physical separation of passenger and freight loading points would tend to reduce the practicability of using passenger-plane space for air freight. Thus, while there is found some merit in the added cost presentation of the carriers, as traffic increases it is foreseen that the operations at major points will closely resemble those of an independent all-cargo operator. As to station costs at relatively small traffic points the argument will probably remain valid as against a conventional operation serving property only.[27]

In one instance, American Airlines estimated the cost of carrying freight in combination planes at 2.1 cents per ton-mile,[28] while National Airlines estimated its total cost of freight transportation at $6.54, the cost of printing waybills.[29] It was the use of these costs at the lower limit to air-freight rates to which the noncertificated carriers objected.[30] They claimed that the certificated carriers, on the basis of out-of-pocket costs, were charging rates below the cost of service and were engaging in unfair competition. The noncertificated carriers contended that some of the flying depreciation, and maintenance costs should be charged to the carriage of freight. They further claimed that, because of air-mail

---

[27]*Examiner's Report* (CAB Docket No. 810 *et al.*), pp. 245–46.

[28]*Examiner's Report* (CAB Docket No. 1705 *et al.*), p. 252.

[29]Note 66, p. 48, *Brief of Public Counsel to C.A.B.* (CAB Docket No. 1705), pp. 32–48.

[30]For the quarter ended September 30, 1947, Capital Airlines reported that the total revenues per ton-mile for its all-cargo operations was 65.19 cents. For this same quarter, direct flying costs were 68.38 cents per ton-mile, and indirect costs were 6.30 cents per ton-mile, making a total of 75.49 cents total cost per ton-mile. The total loss on operations of all-cargo equipment amounted to $10,958, based on the 106,393 miles flown. Capital Airlines had operating revenues of $110,503 from carrying freight on its combination airplanes, on the basis of 437,840 ton-miles of freight on combination planes at a cost of 6.30 cents per mile; total cost of freight on combination aircraft amounted to $27,585, leaving a profit of $82,918 from freight operations on combination planes. Subtracting the loss on all-cargo freight operations leaves a net profit of $71,960 for all freight operations of Capital Airlines. Owing to a substantial increase in volume, attributed to lower rates, Capital Airlines showed a net profit on its all-cargo operations as well as its combination operations of freight service for the months of October and November, 1947.

payments, the certificated carriers could fly freight at lower rates and compensate themselves for any deficits by petitioning for an increase in mail payments.[31] The certificated carriers denied this and in their defense argued that any such revenue from air-freight service over and above their out-of-pocket costs *reduced* their need for air-mail subsidy.

Public counsel of the CAB raised the question of the future of the air-freight business. It was pointed out that in the first nine months of 1947, 70 per cent of all revenue ton-miles of freight was carried in all-cargo planes. Only 31.7 per cent of the revenue ton-miles of freight carried by certificated carriers was, however, carried in all-cargo planes.[32] Witnesses for both certificated and noncertificated carriers were confident that the air-freight industry was at the beginning of a

Exhibit 8

AIR FREIGHT CARRIED, 1945–47, AND ESTI-
MATES FOR 1948, ALL CARRIERS

Year	Freight Carried, Revenue Ton-Miles	Percentage Increase over Previous Year
1945	3,189,106	. . . . .
1946	41,451,956	1,200
1947	82,739,186	100
1948 (estimated)	208,705,703	152

long period of great growth. All parties concerned were asked to estimate their 1948 freight ton-miles. The total of these estimates, compared to the actual experience of previous years, is shown in Exhibit 8. In determining the future relative importance of the all-cargo plane and the combination plane, it was recognized that the important element was not the growth of freight traffic per se but its growth relative to passenger traffic. If the freight traffic in the future were to grow much more than the passenger business, then the trend would

---

[31]"In determining the [air-mail] rate in each case, the Authority shall take into consideration among other factors . . . the need of each such carrier for compensation for the transportation of mail sufficient to insure the performance of such service, and together with all other revenue of the air carrier, to enable such carrier under honest, economical and efficient management, to maintain and continue the development of air transportation to the extent and of the character and quality required for the commerce of the United States, the Postal Service, and the National Defense" (Civil Aeronautics Act of 1938, Sec. 406 [*b*]).

[32]*Brief of Public Counsel to C.A.B.* (CAB Docket No. 1705 *et al.*, March 22, 1948), pp. 22–23.

be toward a proportionately greater use of all-cargo planes.[33] Exhibit 9 shows the growth of property traffic compared to passenger traffic from 1938 to 1947, at the time of the CAB investigation.

Public counsel of the CAB, however, stated that . . . the combination plane has a definite place in the freight field. It enables combination carriers to provide an expedited around-the-clock service which benefits some shippers. It also enables the carriers to serve small towns where the operation of all-cargo planes would not be economically feasible. . . . But a complete acceptance of the by-product theory really means that costs would have no bearing on rates charged.

Exhibit 9

GROWTH OF PROPERTY TRAFFIC* COMPARED
TO PASSENGER TRAFFIC, 1938–47†

YEAR	COMPARISON BY REVENUE TON-MILES		COMPARISON BY PERCENTAGE (1938 = 100)	
	Property‡	Passengers§	Property	Passengers
1938.........	2,173,134	47,560,000	100.00	100.00
1939.........	2,704,837	67,975,600	124.47	142.93
1940.........	3,464,684	104,713,100	159.43	220.17
1941.........	5,240,867	137,715,200	241.17	289.56
1942.........	11,728,747	140,583,500	539.72	295.59
1943.........	15,139,359	161,713,000	696.66	340.02
1944.........	16,411,299	216,713,000	755.19	454.38
1945.........	22,104,306	333,627,800	1,017.16	701.49
1946.........	65,103,622	572,963,194	2,995.84	1,204.72
1947.........	111,209,749	579,621,516	5,117.48	1,218.72

*Includes both freight and express. Prior to July, 1945, freight and express statistics were reported together. Although reported separately since then, they have been combined to make the data comparable.

†Includes sixteen certificated carriers from 1938 to date, plus nine all-freight carriers from the time of their entrance into service during 1945–46.

‡Converted from pound-miles to ton-miles for period 1938 to June, 1945.

§Converted from passenger-miles to ton-miles on basis of 200 pounds per passenger for years 1938–45.

Sources: *Annual Airline Statistics, Domestic Carriers, and Recurrent Reports,* Appendix D, p. 2 (*Brief of Public Counsel to C.A.B.* [CAB Docket No. 1705 *et al.,* March 22, 1948]).

---

[33]Testimony of Mr. C. R. Smith, Chairman of the Board, American Airlines, Inc.:

"*Question:* Mr. Smith, in American's future thinking about air freight, do you anticipate that most of the freight in the future will be carried in combination aircraft or in all-cargo type?

"*Answer:* I think the trend will be toward carrying a higher proportion than now in all-freight planes. In other words, we are definitely proposing to add additional all-freight planes to our service . . . and the bulk of the tonnage will be carried in all-freight planes."

Testimony of Mr. Moore of United Air Lines:

"*Question:* In view of this trend [toward all-cargo planes] on United's system, would it be fair to say that the all-cargo plane will assume an increasing importance in the carriage of freight by United?

"*Answer:* If you are looking into the ultimate future, I think yes." (*Brief of Public Counsel to C.A.B.* [CAB Docket No. 1705 *et al.,* March 22, 1948], p. 28.)

Combination carriers would therefore have a free hand to destroy competition from companies operating all-cargo planes. If the future of freight were primarily related to its carriage on combination aircraft this outcome would be not only proper but desirable. But that is not the case. The future lies more and more with the all-cargo planes.[34] [Exhibit 10 shows the comparative growth of property and passenger traffic since 1947.]

Exhibit 10

DOMESTIC PROPERTY VERSUS PASSENGER AIR-TRAFFIC GROWTH,
1948–60

FISCAL YEAR ENDED JUNE 30	REVENUE TON-MILES (IN THOUSANDS)		PERCENTAGE GROWTH (BASE 1947–48)	
	Property Traffic*	Passenger Traffic	Property Traffic	Passenger Traffic
1947...............	97,764†	588,015	82%	101%
1948...............	139,302	571,173	118	98
1949...............	164,420	648,808	139	111
1950...............	198,360	769,725	167	132
1951...............	207,473	1,015,781	175	174
1952...............	230,163	1,205,283	194	206
1953...............	250,832	1,420,299	212	243
1954...............	269,870	1,616,754	228	277
1955...............	315,517	1,912,395	266	328
1956...............	338,382	2,158,521	286	369
1957...............	365,358	2,405,984	308	412
1958...............	397,901	2,406,472	336	412
1959...............	461,359	2,779,186	390	475
1960...............	518,315	2,897,029	437	496

*Mail, express, and freight ton-miles.
†Does not include regular mail carried under special contract and foreign mail, so base is average of 1947–48.
  Source: Federal Aviation Administration, *FAA Statistical Handbook of Aviation* (Washington, D.C.: U.S. Government Printing Office, 1961).

The board's investigation revealed that a number of air lines, both certified and all-cargo, were transporting cargo at rates less than their costs. The large all-cargo carriers in the first nine months of 1947 had average revenue per ton-mile of 13.29 cents, while cost averaged 17.52 cents. Even United admitted that it was not covering its out-of-pocket costs of 15.59 cents.[35]

The board, therefore, established minimum rates, based on the operating costs of a DC-4 all-cargo plane. These rates were 16 cents per ton-mile for distances under 1,000 miles, and 13 cents per ton-mile for distances over 1,000 miles.[36] The CAB desired to prevent rates from

[34]*Aviation Week,* April 5, 1949, p. 40.
[35]*Ibid.,* April 5, 1948, p. 39.
[36]*Ibid.,* June 21, 1948, p. 49.

falling below direct costs. The air lines were expected to set rates high enough to cover their other fixed expenses.

At the same time that the board issued its minimum rate order, it began an investigation of the possibility of allowing discounts on "back-haul" commodities carried by the freight air lines. The freight air lines desired such discounts in order to promote more shipments by air in west-to-east and south-to-north directions, directions which traditionally had been low in volume. Slick Airways reported that for 1947, it had a 95 per cent load factor on its east-west flights, but only 65 per cent on the return trips.[37]

The back-haul discounts were of varying amounts, but ranged to as much as 60 per cent off the previously established minimums, or to below 8 cents per ton-mile. This was far below the full cost of operation, but proponents of the discounts pointed out that the costs of a scheduled flight were fixed—that any extra cargo on the return trip was "gravy." Before the discounts were allowed, some freight air lines complained that the low back-haul load factors had prevented them from scheduling as many east-to-west flights as they felt they needed. Comparisons of direct and total costs for various aircraft are shown in Exhibit 11.

Exhibit 11

CARGO PLANE COSTS PER AVAILABLE TON-MILE
(Averages of Air Lines Flying the Planes)

Plane Type	Direct Flight Cost Only (Cents per Ton-Mile)	Total Cost (Cents per Ton-Mile)
Curtiss C–46	8.71	13.83
Douglas DC–4	11.33	n.a.*
Douglas DC–6A	10.72†	17.52†

*Not available.
†Somewhat high due to the expense of inaugurating this new equipment.
Source: *Aviation Week*, October 5, 1953, p. 79.

After the minimum rates were approved, competition forced actual rates to conform closely to the minimum rates. However, rising operating costs resulted in a slow rise in freight rates, so that by 1953, rates were about 10 per cent above the minimums. In 1953, Slick Airways and Flying Tiger petitioned the CAB to raise the minimum rates 25 per cent since, the all-cargo lines were barely breaking even, or worse. Such a rise in the minimum rate was calculated to increase

---

[37]*Ibid.*

actual rates by about 12 per cent. The CAB raised the minimums over the strenuous objections of American Airlines. American argued that "since, in 1952, it was able to maintain a 68.3 per cent load factor on its all-cargo operations, yet carry 68.5 per cent of its cargo traffic in aircraft along with its passengers, mail, and express, it could in using such aircraft, carry freight cheaper than the all-cargo carriers." American argued that the board should use its average costs to fix rates, not those of the all-cargo carriers.[38]

However, the board's order reiterated that at the time it set minimum rates, it had "determined that the proper development of air freight required that minimum rates be based on attainable costs in all-cargo planes."[39] American's objections were overruled, and the minimum rates were raised to 20 and 16¼ cents, respectively, from the previous rates of 16 and 13 cents.

In 1956, American Airlines and the Flying Tiger Line persuaded the board to grant a new class of service called "deferred air freight." As defined by the CAB, deferred air-freight shipments were "shipments moving on a space-available basis subject to release at destination airport not prior to the third day after receipt where movement is under 2,100 miles and not prior to the fourth day after receipt where movement is over 2,100 miles."[40] Rates were set 55 to 65 per cent under the established minimums, and ranged from 9 to 15 cents per ton-mile.[41]

American claimed the service was needed and justified because:

1. Aircraft carrying passengers, mail, express, and regular freight still had a considerable amount of unused capacity.
2. The handling of freight on a deferred basis would involve no additional operating expenses or ground-handling costs, since movement and storage would take place during slack periods.

The delayed delivery date was a device to discourage any but a selective use of deferred freight by regular air-freight customers. The air lines thought they would pick up additional traffic from those using Railway Express, since the rates and delivery times were quite similar.

A similar "fill" service was provided by the Post Office Department, in 1959 when it provided a plan whereby regular first-class mail (not air mail) could be carried on a "space available" basis by the air lines

---

[38]John H. Frederick, *Commercial Air Transportation* (5th ed.; Homewood, Ill.: Richard D. Irwin, Inc., 1961), p. 246.
[39]*Aviation Week,* October 5, 1953, p. 80.
[40]*Ibid.,* March 5, 1956, p. 39.
[41]*Ibid.*

at a ton-mile rate somewhat less than that yielded by freight. At that time the CAB which set the rates, maintained that the lower rates were valid, in part, because "to assign a full share of costs to a service designated and offered to reduce the cost burden imposed upon the primary services would be to ignore entirely the essential differences between a priority and a space-available service . . . where, within the range below allocated costs but above added costs, the rates should fall is largely a matter of judgment."[42]

Since the direct costs of handling the mail were even lower than those of handling freight, the CAB set the mail rate lower.

QUESTIONS

1. Do you agree with the position of the certificated carriers concerning costs of carrying air freight in combination planes?

2. Exhibit 4 shows that only a small share of total expenses is attributable directly to passenger traffic. Would the reasoning of the certified carriers with regard to air freight apply with equal force to passenger traffic?

3. Does the cost structure of the noncertificated carriers make them more sensitive than certificated carriers to rate changes?

4. Why did the CAB approve the base of "added costs" for setting up "backhaul," "deferred freight," and "first-class mail" rates when it would not accept the base of "added costs" proposed by the certificated carriers such as American? Was the board inconsistent?

5. Assuming that rates for all types of service (passengers, air mail, air express, freight) are not to go below the direct costs attributed to each service, how would the concept of elasticity help in the determination of the rate for each service? In 1947 the average cost for shipping by rail freight was about 5 cents per ton-mile. In view of other facts in the case, what does this suggest about the future of air-freight rates?

CASE 4-2: NORDON MANUFACTURING COMPANY

Nordon Manufacturing Company calculated the following manufacturing costs for one of its two major products:

```
Materials (8 pounds "BC" at $1.50)...................$12.00
Labor (6 hours at $2.50, 2 hours at $2.00).............. 19.00
Manufacturing expense (8 hours at $0.50).............. 4.00
                                                      _____
                                                       $35.00
```

The standard for manufacturing expense (overhead) was calculated at a rate of 80 per cent of practical capacity from the flexible budget

[42]*Ibid.,* October 26, 1959, p. 39.

Exhibit 1

MANUFACTURING EXPENSE BUDGETS BY LEVEL PERIOD (ONE MONTH)

	PERCENTAGE OF PRACTICAL CAPACITY				
	60%	70%	80%	90%	100%
Standard hours................................	11,250	13,125	15,000	16,875	18,750
Variables and semivariables:					
Assistant foremen (semivariable)...............	$ 600.00	$ 600.00	$ 900.00	$ 900.00	$ 900.00
Materials-handling labor (variable).............	900.00	1,050.00	1,200.00	1,350.00	1,500.00
Repairmen (semivariable)......................	400.00	400.00	600.00	800.00	800.00
Old-age benefit tax (semivariable)..............	39.00	41.25	51.00	56.25	58.50
Oil (semivariable).............................	180.00	180.00	224.74	224.74	224.74
Miscellaneous factory supplies (variable)........	210.00	245.00	280.00	315.00	350.00
Repairs and replacement parts (semivariable).....	400.00	400.00	490.00	550.00	550.00
Power and light (variable).....................	270.00	315.00	360.00	405.00	450.00
Total Variables and Semivariables.............	$2,999.00	$3,231.25	$4,105.74	$4,600.99	$4,833.24
Fixed:					
Rent...	$1,950.00	$1,950.00	$1,950.00	$1,950.00	$1,950.00
Foreman.....................................	400.00	400.00	400.00	400.00	400.00
Materials storekeeper.........................	300.00	300.00	300.00	300.00	300.00
Depreciation on machinery.....................	416.66	416.66	416.66	416.66	416.66
Insurance on machinery and inventory..........	163.80	163.80	163.80	163.80	163.80
Taxes on machinery and inventory.............	163.80	163.80	163.80	163.80	163.80
Total Fixed..................................	$3,394.26	$3,394.26	$3,394.26	$3,394.26	$3,394.26
Total Manufacturing Expense.................	$6,393.26	$6,625.51	$7,500.00	$7,995.25	$8,227.50

for manufacturing expense shown in Exhibit 1. Expenses other than manufacturing are $8.00 a unit at the 80 per cent rate ($6.00 fixed, $2.00 variable).

QUESTIONS

1. What will be the over- or underabsorbed manufacturing expense (volume variance) if operations are at 60 per cent of practical capacity? At all other levels of operation? Illustrate graphically on an average cost chart and on a total cost chart.

2. Will a $44 price always result in profits?

3. Will a $42 price always result in losses?

4. Compute the marginal cost curve for output from 60 to 100 per cent of capacity.

5. Nordon, which has been operating at 70 per cent of capacity (1,640 units per month), with little prospect of a better rate in the next six months, has an opportunity to take a private-brand order for 3,000 units to be delivered at the rate of 500 per month at a price of $36.75 a unit. Assume no effect on other sales, and estimate the effect of accepting this order on Nordon's profits.

6. What advantage are there in working out expense figures at several levels of output for pricing decisions? For operating control?

CASE 4-3:   AUTO SPECIALTY PRODUCTS, INC.

Auto Specialty Products, Inc., of Kansas City, Kansas, manufactured a wide line of automobile accessories such as spotlights, rear-view mirrors, hubcaps, wheel covers, continental tire kits, bumper guards, gasoline-tank and radiator caps, automobile trim, and floor mats. In addition to its main plant in Kansas City, the company owned and operated a plant in Birmingham, Michigan. Hubcaps, wheel covers, continental tire kits, and bumper guards were produced in the Michigan plant. All other products were produced in Kansas City.

The firm served a national market. A large share of the hubcaps, trim, wheel covers, and bumper guards were produced for two automobile manufacturers. All items produced by the company were sold in the replacement market through garages, service stations, and automobile parts chain stores, and, in some areas, through department stores. The company maintained five warehouses in various parts of the United States and one in Toronto, Ontario. Company salesmen, employed on a salary and commission basis, served jobbers, wholesalers, and department stores. Sales to automobile manufacturers and chain stores were usually handled by the president or vice president of the firm. Several of the items, such as hubcaps, wheel covers, trim, and bumper guards, required a new design each year as automobile models changed. Other items in the line were not modified so frequently.

In the decade following the close of World War II the company had expanded with the growth of automobile production. In the period immediately following the war, replacement demand had been rather heavy; but as new cars became more available, replacement demand declined noticeably. To a large extent, this was offset by increasing demand for those items sold to automobile manufacturers. The Korean War restricted supply on some items, such as trim, hubcaps, and wheel covers. In 1955 the automobile industry had its largest year since 1950.

With the decline in replacement demand, price competition among the items in these lines increased. Further decline in demand was anticipated in this market. Furthermore, the forecast for new-car production in 1956 was about one million units less than in 1955. The greatest competition in the replacement market was appearing in hubcaps and wheel covers. The automobile parts chain stores were the largest single customers for these items other than the automobile manufacturers. The items were sold in case lots, consisting of five dozen to the case. Each was marked with the brand name of the make of car or bore a design with no name.

Hubcaps, until 1955, had sold at $28.75 per case, while wheel covers were priced at $67.50 per case. In May, 1955, to meet competition, prices were reduced to $25.50 and $61.50 per case, respectively. In October, 1955, the president of the company, Mr. Wallace, began negotiations with one of the larger automobile parts chain stores on several items. On one item, wheel covers, he learned that a competitor had offered a price of $49.75 per case. Mr. Wallace met the price and obtained the order for 1,125 cases of wheel covers. Upon his return to Kansas City, he learned from other sources that some competitors were offering even lower prices. He called a meeting with Mr. Kemp, the sales manager, Mr. Waxman, the production manager, and Mr. Ollen, the controller, to discuss price policy on wheel covers.

Exhibit 1 shows the cost of producing wheel covers per case. This item passed through six departments in process of manufacture: stamping, welding, buffing, painting, polishing, and packing. Total sales in 1954 were 14,176 cases, of which 6,731 were in the replacement market. In view of the competitive situation, Mr. Kemp believed that in order to maintain sales in the replacement market, the company would have to offer a price of $47.50 per case. If the price were kept at $61.50, he estimated 1956 replacement sales would be approximately 5,000 cases. If the price were lowered to $47.50, he estimated replacement sales at 17,500 cases. Mr. Waxman said that he could not produce the covers at costs any lower than shown in Exhibit 1. Mr. Ollen recommended that the line be discontinued if the price were less than $61.50, since it would involve the company in further losses. He pointed out that on the basis of the costs shown in Exhibit 1, the price Mr. Wallace quoted to the chain would result in a loss. He suggested that the line of wheel covers be dropped immediately and that efforts be devoted toward the development of a product which would be more profitable. Mr. Wallace pointed out that the development of a new product which could be produced with the same equipment would probably require many months. He further stated that the decline in sales of new cars would result in an improvement in replacement sales within a year or two.

Exhibit 1

STANDARD COSTS, CHROME-PLATE WHEEL COVERS, PER CASE

Material*	$16.61
Direct labor	19.52
Packaging and crating	1.14
Equipment repairs	0.71
Depreciation	1.37
Indirect labor†	6.26
Factory overhead‡	4.89
Administrative and selling costs§	2.93
	$53.43

*Steel prices were expected to rise 5–10 per cent as a result of a new wage agreement in the steel industry.

†Allocated on the basis of 30 per cent of direct labor.

‡Allocated on the basis of 25 per cent of direct labor.

§Allocated on the basis of 15 per cent of direct labor.

QUESTIONS

1. Was Mr. Wallace wise in meeting the competitive price of $49.75 per case? Explain.

2. In view of Mr. Kemp's sales estimates, which price would you find more profitable? Why?

3. Do you agree with Mr. Ollen that the line should be dropped immediately? Why?

4. What effect will the anticipated rise in the price of steel have upon prices in the short run? In the long run?

CASE 4-4: L. E. MASON COMPANY

In the spring of 1962 the officers of the L. E. Mason Company of Boston, Massachusetts, were concerned about the inventory position of the company's Red Dot line of electrical conduit fittings. The Red Dot line consisted of approximately 180 different fittings made of die-cast aluminum.[43] The fittings were sold throughout the United States by manufacturers' representatives, who took the goods on consignment in twenty warehouses. The company also maintained a factory warehouse in Brockton, Massachusetts, from which shipments were made to the field warehouses and also directly to some customers.

Prior to World War II the L. E. Mason Company was primarily engaged in the bronzing of baby shoes. This activity had led the company to the production by permanent molding of the bases upon which the baby shoes were mounted. With the advent of the war, supplies were no longer available for the bronzing of baby shoes, and the company used its facilities for the production of magnesium castings for incendiary bombs. During the war period the company acquired die-casting equipment. After the war the L. E. Mason Company converted to a proprietary line of gifts and housewares based on the die-casting process, did job-order die casting and resumed the bronzing of baby shoes; in 1958, it decided upon producing the Red Dot line of electrical conduit fittings to make fuller use of its die-casting facilities. In 1962, its business was in three major categories: (1) the Red Dot line, (2) a line of die-cast gift items such as coasters and book ends (some bronzing of baby shoes), and (3) job-order die casting using customer-purchased dies.

Production and Inventory Control

Mr. Kenneth Sullo, Chief Engineer, stated that his methods of production planning, production scheduling, and inventory control for the Red Dot line were based upon four major criteria: (1) the annual sales

---

[43]Die casting is a manufacturing process in which molten metal is forced into a metal mold or die under pressure. A high-quality casting with excellent surface finish and dimensional accuracy may be produced. Castings are typically made of the lower melting point alloys of zinc, tin, lead, brass, aluminum, and magnesium. Dies are placed into a die-casting machine, which holds them in place with hydraulic pressure. The molten metal is forced into the cavity of the die under pressure. The machine releases the pressure on the die, and the casting is removed. The rate at which castings may be produced depends upon the size of the casting and the pressure required. Small items may be produced very rapidly in large volume through the use of multiple-cavity dies. The castings typically require only simple trimming, tapping, and inspection before packing. Dies may range in cost from a few hundred to several thousand dollars. Scrap may be re-melted and used again.

forecast for the Red Dot line, (2) the necessary minimum inventory, (3) the desire to make economic production runs on the die-casting machines, and (4) the desire to maintain stable levels of production and employment to avoid the costs inherent in fluctuating production.[44]

The first step in production and inventory planning after receiving the annual sales forecast for the Red Dot line from the sales department was to divide the forecast by twelve to obtain the expected average monthly sales in dollars. This dollar figure was converted into pieces by dividing average monthly dollar sales by the weighted average sales value of a single item to obtain the desired monthly production rate in pieces.

From past sales records, it was possible for Mr. Sullo to determine average monthly sales of each item in the line. These sales varied from almost zero for some items to many thousands of pieces for others. Sales patterns varied somewhat among the twenty warehouses; but the billing clerk, under the supervision of Mr. Sullo, was generally able to allocate the consigned merchandise to the field warehouses in a reasonably satisfactory manner. That is, localized shortages were relatively infrequent.

Inventory records of the field warehouses were maintained at the factory from daily sales reports by the manufacturers' representatives and from shipping records; these records, together with the main warehouse inventory records, were reported in total to Mr. Sullo on about the tenth of each month, accurate as of the first of the month. With this report, Mr. Sullo was able to see quickly which items were in short supply. Those items below a four-month supply were recorded on his production scheduling sheet for further consideration.

In general, Mr. Sullo allowed two weeks' time for trimming, tapping, other intermediate operations, and inspection. Therefore, items were scheduled for casting at least two weeks before their inventory was expected to reach the two-month minimum supply limit which is explained below. An item with two and one-half months' supply or less on hand at scheduling time was scheduled immediately. Others were scheduled so that production began two weeks before the inventory was expected to be at a two-month supply. Using a four-month supply as the cutoff for scheduling enabled Mr. Sullo to schedule monthly production in accordance with his two-month supply rule.

---

[44]The recession of 1960–61 had forced layoffs in order to keep inventory levels from becoming too high. When it became necessary to expand production again, it was difficult to get workers, and it took the company approximately six months to regain the former peak level of output.

Minimum inventory levels were determined by Mr. Sullo on the assumptions that one week's supply was necessary in each of the field warehouses, that it took up to one week to receive sales information from the warehouses, and that shipping time was often as long as a week. An extra week's supply was added for safety, giving a one-month inventory in each of the field warehouses as an order point. An additional month's nationwide supply was desired in the factory warehouse to back up the field warehouses and for direct shipments to customers. Thus the total minimum acceptable level of inventory was a two-month supply.

Through experience, Mr. Sullo found that high-volume items could get as low as one and one-half months' supply without causing great difficulty and that, paradoxically, slow-moving items could be troublesome when the total supply available was at a six-month or greater level. This he attributed to more difficult forecasting for the slow-moving items and to problems of distribution among the warehouses.

In Exhibit 1 several items were taken from a typical monthly production scheduling form. Column 1 gives average monthly sales in pieces for the forecast period; column 2, the description or name of the item; column 3, the quantity in inventory in months' supply as of the first of the month; and column 4, the amount to be run (economic run) in pieces and months. Column 5 gives the number already available (cast and in process since the first of the month); column 6 gives the date to begin casting; column 7 gives the amount packed since the first of the month; and column 8, the date to begin packing. .

From the items placed on the production schedule, Mr. Sullo scheduled an assortment that enabled monthly production to equal approximately one twelfth of expected annual sales, taking into account the current inventory levels of the items, the quantities already cast or in process, and any other information available.

An outage in the main warehouse could also cause alterations in the production schedule, depending upon the nationwide supply of the item and its distribution.

If the nationwide supply of the item was sufficient, Mr. Sullo might suggest that shipments be made among the warehouses instead of scheduling immediate production. In some cases, shifting among the warehouses was more costly than scheduling additional production; however, Mr. Sullo believed that this had educational value for the sales department and that employees would become more adept at estimating sales and distribution if they were unable to interrupt production schedules at will.

Exhibit 1

L. E. MASON COMPANY

Production Schedule (Selected Items)

(1) AVERAGE MONTHLY SALES	(2) ITEM	(3) ON HAND, JULY 1 (Months)	(4) AMOUNT TO RUN		(5) IN PROCESS, JULY 12	(6) START CASTING DATE	(7) ALREADY PACKED	(8) START PACKING DATE
			Pieces	Months				
800	A	3.6	2,400	3		August 2		August 18
400	B	2.7	1,600	4		At once		July 21*
1,800	C	1.4	7,200	4	2,000	At once		At once
15,000	D	1.9	30,000	2	8,000	Running		At once
50	E	5.0	500	10		July 18		August 1

*Behind schedule, i.e., less than two weeks allowed between packing and casting.

Economic production-run sizes on the die-casting machines were determined by Mr. Sullo on the primary criterion that it was desirable to run any setup on the machines for at least one three-shift day. Setting up the machines could take up to fifteen man-hours in order to get proper temperatures and to obtain quality castings.

Current Situation

In the spring of 1962 the total inventory dollar value in the twenty field warehouses and in the main warehouse was three-month supply of finished castings at current and expected sales volumes expressed in dollars. Estimated economic order quantities for approximately sixty slow-moving items revealed that these items alone accounted for about two thirds of the value of the three-month supply on hand. Mr. Sullo felt that he really should have a four-month supply on hand in order to service sales properly.

QUESTIONS

1. Does Mr. Sullo's production control and inventory planning system lead to optimal decisions? If not, what modifications would you suggest?

2. Using the hypothetical information below concerning items X, Y, and Z in the line, how many units would you schedule for production in the production period October 10–November 10?

	X	Y	Z
1961 average monthly sales (units) .	1,000	25,000	100
Range of monthly sales (1961)	200–2,500	0–50,000	50–150
Hourly wage rate.	$2.00	$2.00	$2.00
Inventory on hand (October 10). . .	2,200	15,000	100
Production rate.	150/hr.	500/hr.	250/hr.
Material cost per unit.	$0.25	$0.50	$0.15
Estimated annual cost of holding one unit in inventory.	0.03	0.10	0.02

3. What information should Mr. Sullo call for in order to decide whether or not to increase the total value of his inventory to a four-month supply?

CASE 4–5:   ROBBINS MANUFACTURING COMPANY

Many products can be made either in factories which use automatic machines or in plants using hand assembly by semiskilled workers. Robbins Manufacturing Company, after considerable study, found that it could build any one of three plants: the largest, an almost completely automatic factory; an intermediate one, utilizing an assembly line with some automatic machinery; or the smallest, relying heavily on hand assembly. Estimated costs of producing one type of electronic circuit under these three assumed plant conditions were as shown in Exhibit 1.

Exhibit 1

	Plant A, Automatic	Plant B, Assembly Line	Plant C, Hand-Operating
Unit costs:			
Materials....................	$ 2.00	$ 2.00	$ 2.00
Direct labor................	0.30	0.60	1.00
Equipment cost*..............	1,000,000.00	300,000.00	125,000.00
Maintenance and overhead:			
Fixed portion...............	300,000.00	125,000.00	100,000.00
Variable costs per unit........	0.20	0.25	0.60
Annual output capacity (units)† ..	1,000,000.00	500,000.00	250,000.00

*Assume straight-line depreciation over ten years to zero value for each plant and an interest rate on initial investment of 10 per cent.

†For outputs greater than the annual capacity of any plant, these plants and their costs would simply be duplicated.

QUESTIONS

1. What is the lowest cost plant arrangement for outputs of 100,000, 500,000, and 1,000,000 units? A diagram would be helpful.

2. Your firm has already built plant C, and annual sales for the item have been and are expected to be 100,000 units, at a price of $4.00 per unit. Should the company continue to produce this item? If your answer is yes, should it use plant C or build another plant?

3. In the light of your analysis in question 1, explain briefly why a company whose competitors are turning to automation may refuse to take the same step.

CHAPTER 5

◆◆◆◆◆◆◆◆◆◆◆◆◆◆◆◆◆◆◆◆◆◆◆◆

Prices and Output
Under Competition

THE THEORY of price determination under conditions of perfect competition is one of the most important parts of the science of economics. Like all fruitful theory, it is based on assumptions which are not entirely descriptive of the real world. The "unreality" of the assumptions has lead a good many economists to consider competitive price theory to be of little value. This is a mistake because the force of competition is a basic one in most lines of business activity, and the model of pure or perfect competition reveals the nature of the adjustments which this force brings about. Real-world adjustments by firms faced with a great deal of competition are not so precise and pat as those of the perfectly competitive firm of economic theory, but they are similar in nature.

Assumptions of Perfect Competition

Four assumptions are fundamental to the theory of price determination in perfectly competitive markets:

1. There must be a large number of sellers of the same product—so many that no one seller can affect the market price by his own actions.
2. There must also be many buyers of the good, so that no one buyer can affect the market price.
3. There must be full knowledge on the part of all buyers and sellers of the market price and other essential factors.
4. Firms must be able freely to enter and leave a competitive industry. No government approval or license to enter must be required; no approval must be needed to abandon an activity (as is required, for example, before railroads can abandon a passenger-train run).

Further assumptions must be made in order to describe competitive price determination most simply in a "static" framework where enough key variables are held constant (placed in *ceteris paribus*) to make meaningful statements possible. The principal variables which are assumed constant in static price theory are consumers' wants, total resources of the economy, and the state of technological development.

189

Actually, these variables are always changing, but it is necessary for a basic understanding to study competitive price determination under the simplifying assumption that they are constant. Subsequently, these variables can be allowed to change (one at a time) and the consequences of such change observed.

Demand and Supply Determine Price

Under pure competition, price is determined by demand and supply, both of the latter being understood to be schedules showing a functional relationship between quantity and price. The demand schedule shows the quantities which buyers are able and willing to purchase per unit of time at various alternative prices. Under static assumptions, this schedule will "stay put" because tastes and resources are assumed to be unchanged during the period under consideration. Supply is a schedule of quantities which sellers are able and willing to sell per unit of time at various alternative prices. Demand and supply together determine competitive price, since there will be only one price at which buyers and sellers will both be satisfied, in the sense that no buyer who is willing to pay that price will be deprived of a purchase and no seller who is willing to accept that price will be deprived of a sale. Under the assumption of full knowledge on the part of participants in the market, the price will not settle at the equilibrium after a series of oscillations but will immediately "snap" to the equilibrium.

Views of Supply

The supply schedule, or its geometric representation as a supply curve, is apt to be more troublesome to the student than the demand curve. This is because the supply curve differs according to the problem under consideration even within the static analytical framework. (This is not true of the demand curve facing the industry; it stays the same.) The principal problems referred to are (1) the price at which the existing stock of a commodity will sell, (2) the rate at which new output will be forthcoming from existing productive capacity and the effect of this production rate on price, and (3) the price and output which will tend eventually to be established if demand remains the same but firms have had sufficient time to enter an unusually profitable field or exit from a relatively unprofitable one. These problems are designated as "market" or "very short run," "short run," and "long run," respectively.

Very Short Run

The very-short-run problem of disposing of existing inventory can be most easily demonstrated by considering a "perishable" commodity. In an economic sense, perishability may mean that the commodity will be without value in the next time period because of the collapse of demand rather than from physical deterioration. Calendars, novelties such as hula hoops, style goods, and low-priced seasonal goods should often be treated as strictly perishable in nature. Certain fruits and vegetables, especially when the market is soon to be closed for Sunday or

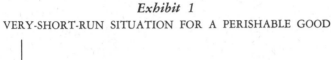

Exhibit 1

VERY-SHORT-RUN SITUATION FOR A PERISHABLE GOOD

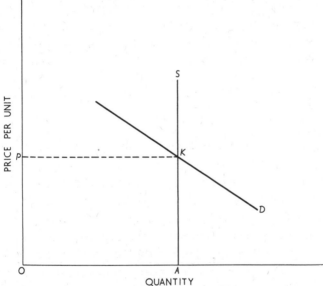

for a holiday, are traditional examples of perishable goods which should be sold for whatever they will bring, regardless of their original cost to the seller. Similarly, the housing services which will be provided by hotel or motel rooms are perishable in the sense that a particular night's services will be completely lost if occupancy is not secured that night.

If a good or service is perishable in nature, its very-short-run supply curve is vertical, reflecting the willingness of sellers to take any price they can get (but hoping, of course, for a high one). Price may be said to be determined by demand as far as present actions are concerned, although previous actions which created the present inventory will influence the present price.

In Exhibit 1 the demand and very-short-run supply curves for a perishable good are shown. Except in the sense noted above, the price is determined entirely by the strength of demand, making immediate customers especially precious to the owner of a perishable good. Price OP will clear the market of the good. The total income to all sellers will be OPKA. This may be lower than the total which could be secured by the sellers acting in concert and maintaining price (at the point of unitary elasticity), throwing away any unsold units. If competition exists, however, no seller can hold out for a price above OP, since others will offer the good more cheaply. Inasmuch as full knowledge on the part of sellers and buyers is assumed, no seller will even try to sell above price OP, and no buyer will even bid less than OP. Price will "snap into place" at OP. (Other results can be obtained under different assumptions, but it should be remembered that we are first examining the economist's model of pure competition under static assumptions—a model which is instructive in real-world situations where competition and knowledge are substantial even though not complete.)

Very-Short-Run Supply for Durable Goods

The very-short-run supply curve of goods which are durable in nature is not vertical. Sellers will have "reservation prices" below which they will not offer the good, since it will be salable in the next time period if not disposed of in the time period under consideration. The situation on the supply side is especially complicated when buyers and sellers are not distinct groups. In the case of houses and automobiles, for example, the largest part of the potential supply in any short period is in the hands of families rather than in those of producers or distributors of these important consumer durable goods. The distinction between buyers and sellers is further blurred by the "trade-in" practice, which is common for cars and of increasing importance for housing. The seller of a newly produced item may have to buy an older model from a customer in order to make a sale. Exhibit 2 illustrates a very-short-run supply and demand situation for a durable good such as residential housing (assuming that homogeneous housing units can be defined).

The price at which owners of housing may be willing to sell bears little relation to the price which they actually paid. Many houses sell for several times their original cost or, when neighborhoods deteriorate or population moves away, for much less than original price minus normal depreciation. The cost of *reproduction,* however, in the sense of the present cost of constructing competitive dwellings, has a great deal to do with the prices at which old housing will be offered on the market. It should be noted that for such commodities the competitive assumption of a great many sellers is quite realistic, even if only a few firms produce the commodity. But in a market such as that for automobiles, where many consumers do not consider a used item to be a close substitute for a new one, the observation has less force.

Exhibit 2
VERY SHORT RUN FOR DURABLE GOOD

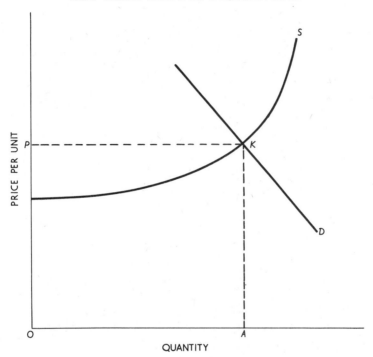

Partial Equilibrium: Short Run

The second view of supply under competitive conditions focuses on the rate of output of commodities from existing plant facilities. This analysis can be handled most readily in a "partial equilibrium" framework in which attention is paid to a single competitive industry and its firms. The view is also "static," in that population, wants, resources, and technology are assumed to be unchanged during a period long enough to permit the economic forces to bring about their full results.

In calculating the best rate at which to operate his plant, the manager of a firm should disregard sunk costs and should consider only additional or marginal costs. This is in accord with the general principle of rational action explained in Chapter 4. Consequently, the marginal cost curve is the short-run supply curve except that any portion which lies below minimum average variable cost does not influence supply. This is true because the rational entrepreneur will not produce at all if the price of a unit of output will not cover its variable (avoidable) cost. (This automatic shutdown might not occur in practice if such factors as the desire to keep the organization together happened to be of importance.)

Exhibit 3

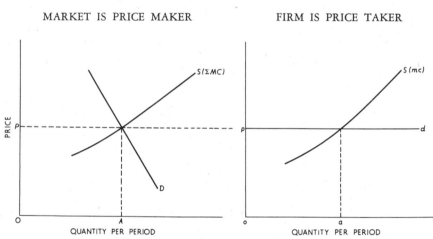

Summation of the supply curves of all firms yields the industry short-run supply curve, reflecting amounts that the industry is willing to supply per period at different prices which might conceivably prevail. Interaction of demand and supply forces determines what this price will actually be, and what rate of output will be generated. This is illustrated for a hypothetical competitive industry on the left side of Exhibit 3. A single firm in the same industry is represented on the right side of the same chart. The firm is a "price taker," in that consumers are assumed to be aware of the market price and unwilling to pay more, while the manager of the firm is unwilling to accept less. The latter has the power to determine his own output and will produce at a rate *oa,* where his marginal cost is equated to price.

Partial Equilibrium: Long Run

The industry and firm in Exhibit 3 are adjusted to the short-run demand and cost situation in which they must operate. In order to secure a picture of the forces at work in a fully competitive industry, it is necessary to assume that there is also complete adjustment in a long-run sense. This requires that the correct number of firms be in the industry and that each firm be of the best (lowest cost) size. Optimum-sized firms must be assumed to be operating optimum-sized plants and to have the best number of such plants. Full "economies of scale" are assumed to have been realized from both a firm and a plant viewpoint (since otherwise survival would not be possible in a fully competitive market).

Exhibit 4

INDUSTRY LONG-RUN EQUILIBRIUM   FIRM LONG-RUN EQUILIBRIUM

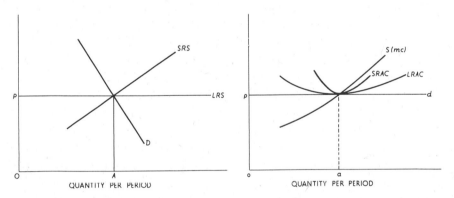

Exhibit 4 includes the same demand and short-run supply curves as Exhibit 3, but adds the curves needed to show that long-run equilibrium also has been reached. On the industry side, this is shown by the intersection of demand, short-run supply, and long-run supply curves at the same point. The long-run supply curve, LRS, shows the minimum cost of production per unit, as the industry is assumed to be of different sizes (i.e., as it is assumed to be comprised of different numbers of firms, each of the most efficient size). Since the LRS curve is shown as horizontal, a "constant cost" industry is being examined. The intersection of the LRS, SRS, and D curves at a single point indicates that the number of firms has been correctly adjusted to meet the existing demand at minimum unit cost.

On the firm side of Exhibit 4 the minimum point on the short-run average cost curve touches the minimum point on the long-run average cost curve. This shows that the firm in full competitive equilibrium is forced to be of the most efficient size. Also, it is operated at the most efficient rate, since the marginal cost curve also touches the demand curve at this point. The firm is just covering its full cost of production, including a competitive (alternative) return on all capital utilized, whether furnished by outsiders or insiders.

When an industry is in full equilibrium, short-run and long-run price are identical. Very-short-run price is also at this same level, since inventories will be "normal" in size. Price cannot be raised or lowered if inventories are to be kept in balance. Inventory theory is complex for nonequilibrium situations and will not be considered in this book.

Comparative Statics

Description of full static equilibrium is useful in suggesting the nature of the adjustments which will occur if there is a change in an important variable affecting a competitive industry. Suppose demand for the product suddenly declines. Price will decline, and output will quickly be cut back by each firm, and consequently by the industry as a whole. Firms will then earn less than normal profits, or will incur losses, since price will be below average cost. Under the assumptions used in comparative statics, the lower demand is not just temporary, but will persist until a new equilibrium has been established.

Re-establishment of long-run equilibrium requires that a sufficient number of firms leave the industry to move the SRS curve of Exhibit 4 sufficiently far to the left to cause it to intersect the new, lower demand curve and the LRS curve at a common point. This means that productive capacity will have been reduced enough to make possible least-cost production of an appropriately reduced amount per time period. Price will be back to the level which existed prior to the decline in demand. Fewer firms will now be able to operate in this industry, but those which remain will secure a normal return on capital and will be able to operate at a normal, least-cost rate. Similarly, an increase in demand will attract new firms, since abnormally high profits will at first be enjoyed. The entrepreneurs who are quickest to detect the favorable situation will reap greater profits than those who enter tardily. Eventually, price will be driven down again to its long-run equilibrium level by the entry of new firms into the field.

General Equilibrium Effects

Although partial equilibrium analysis which concentrates on a particular industry and its firms is an indispensable tool of economics, care must be taken not to overlook important repercussions on other industries if these are significant to the problem at hand. That is, the only complete analysis is "general equilibrium" analysis where a great number of economic variables are treated simultaneously and their interrelations fully accounted for. No analysis can be completely general in nature, since many variables of extremely limited significance must be, and should be, omitted from consideration. Partial equilibrium analysis runs the risk of stopping too soon, however.

If the demand facing a particular competitive industry declines, for example, causing price to decline, there must be offsetting increases in other prices if the money supply and its velocity remain unchanged. As resources leave the industry in question, they will become available to other industries. As use of these resources increases the rate of output of other goods, their prices will decline, while price in the first industry moves back toward its long-run supply price.

The foregoing is not meant to be a complete analysis of the general equilibrium effects of a decline in demand in a particular industry, but rather is designed to bring out the desirability of a sufficiently broad "way of thinking" about economic problems. This can be illustrated more practically by an observation on the economics of plant location. States and communities often cite "low taxes" as a factor which should induce new plants to come in. The observer who understands the danger of an unnecessarily "partial" way of thinking will immediately inquire whether taxes are low because education and other publicly provided services are inadequate. If this is the case, low taxes are not properly considered as an inducement to industry. This is especially clear if firms will have to incur costs themselves (e.g., for fire protection) which are ordinarily provided by government.

Skill in tracing through some of the more important general, as contrasted with partial, consequences of a change in a variable is frequently valuable but should not be carried too far. Time may be wasted by attempting to trace remote and uncertain effects, and incorrect predictions become more likely. The skill of a successful analyst depends heavily on his being able to select the most important variables in a problem while disregarding others, and in tracing through their repercussions just far enough.

General View of Competition

Most firms have some degree of control over the price which can be secured from their output. Often, this control is very limited, however, because the demand curve facing the firm is so nearly horizontal. The company is then virtually a price taker, and the decisions which management must make do not differ greatly from those of the purely competitive firm. Many industries in which pure competition does not exist can best be analyzed as if they were competitive. That is, the most significant predictions of the consequences of such factors as a change in demand or cost, the imposition of an excise tax, the appearance of a substitute product, or the growth of foreign competition can usually be made by disregarding minor degrees of monopoly power. In part, this is because the available statistical information regarding the industry is unlikely to be in a form which will fit a more complex model more closely than it does the relatively simple competitive model.[1]

CASE 5–1: PRICES IN PHILATELY[2]

Millions of collectors and many stamp dealers in the United States rely heavily on *Scott's Standard Postage Stamp Catalogue,* which describes and gives prices for over 200,000 stamps in its recent annual editions. After stating that "Condition is the all important factor of price. Prices are quoted for stamps in fine condition," the Scott catalogue goes on to explain its prices as follows:

The prices appearing in this Catalogue were estimated after careful study of available wholesale and retail offerings together with recommendations and information submitted by many of the leading philatelic societies. These and other factors were considered in determining the figures which the editor considers represent the proper or present price basis for a fine specimen when offered by an informed dealer to an informed buyer. Sales are frequently made at lower figures occasioned by individual bargaining, changes in popularity, temporary over-supply, local custom, the "vest pocket dealer," or the many other reasons which cause deviations from any accepted standard. Sales at higher prices are usually because of exceptionally fine condition, unusual postal markings, unexpected political changes or newly discovered information. While the minimum price of a stamp is fixed at 2 cents to cover the dealer's labor and service cost of assorting, cataloguing and filling orders individually, the sum of these list prices does not properly represent the "value" of a packet of unsorted or un-

---

[1]The reader is referred to Milton Friedman, "The Methodology of Positive Economics," *Essays in Positive Economics* (Chicago: University of Chicago Press, 1953), for a discussion of the interesting question whether realistic assumptions lead to realistic predictions.

[2]Philately is defined as the "collection and study of postage stamps . . . usually as a hobby" (*Webster's New World Dictionary* [Cleveland: World Publishing Co., 1957]).

mounted stamps sold in bulk which generally consists of only the cheaper stamps. Prices in italics indicate infrequent sales or lack of adequate pricing information.[3]

The Post Office Department at periodic intervals issues *Postage Stamps of the United States,* which gives fuller details on each United States stamp and gives the quantity issued for all commemoratives and air-mail stamps. Exhibits 1, 2, and 3 give the quantities issued and cata-

Exhibit 1

QUANTITY ISSUED AND CATALOGUE PRICES OF THE UNITED STATES
COLUMBIAN EXPOSITION ISSUE—1893

Denomination	Quantity Issued (in Thousands)	Scott Catalogue Price, 1962*	Scott Catalogue Price, 1949*
$0.01................	449,196	$ 0.10	$ 0.03
0.02................	1,464,589	0.05	0.02
0.03................	11,501	2.50	1.10
0.04................	19,182	0.85	0.35
0.05................	35,248	1.00	0.40
0.06................	4,708	3.25	1.85
0.08................	10,657	1.00	0.50
0.10................	16,517	0.85	0.45
0.15................	1,577	7.50	5.00
0.30................	617	13.00	8.00
0.50................	244	17.50	11.00
1.00................	55	50.00	36.00
2.00................	46	50.00	30.00
3.00................	28	90.00	57.50
4.00................	26	110.00	70.00
5.00................	27	220.00	77.50

*For canceled stamps.
    Sources: *Scott's Standard Postage Stamp Catalogue* (New York: Scott Publications, 1949 and 1962); and *U.S. Postage Stamps, 1847–1957* (Washington, D.C.: U.S. Government Printing Office, 1957).

logue prices of canceled stamps for three groups of stamps that could be considered "blue chips" because of the wide popularity of United States commemoratives and air mails. More recent United States commemoratives probably have limited chances of appreciation because of the large quantities issued, usually 120 million, and the very substantial purchases by collectors. Mint commemoratives have been made freely available to all who desired them for a year or two after issue at the U.S. Philatelic Agency. This comparative abundance may have influenced

[3]*Scott's Standard Postage Stamp Catalogue* (New York: Scott Publications, 1962), p. v.

Exhibit 2
QUANTITY ISSUED AND CATALOGUE PRICES OF UNITED STATES
COMMEMORATIVE STAMPS OF THE 1920'S

Date	Issue	Denomi-nation	Quantity Issued	Scott Catalogue Price, 1962*	Scott Catalogue Price, 1949*
1920...	Pilgrim Tercentenary	$0.01	137,978	$ 0.50	$0.20
1920...	Pilgrim Tercentenary	0.02	196,037	0.35	0.12
1920...	Pilgrim Tercentenary	0.05	11,321	4.50	2.50
1921...	Harding Memorial	0.02	1,459,487	0.06	0.03
1921...	Harding Memorial (imperforate)	0.02	770	1.50	1.10
1921...	Harding Memorial (rotary press)	0.02	99,950	0.20	0.10
1924...	Huguenot-Walloon Tercentenary	0.01	51,387	0.55	0.25
1924...	Huguenot-Walloon Tercentenary	0.02	77,753	0.50	0.20
1924...	Huguenot-Walloon Tercentenary	0.05	5,659	4.50	2.75
1925...	Lexington-Concord	0.01	15,615	0.60	0.30
1925...	Lexington-Concord	0.02	26,596	1.15	0.45
1925...	Lexington-Concord	0.05	5,349	3.00	2.00
1925...	Norse-American	0.02	9,105	1.10	0.60
1925...	Norse-American	0.05	1,901	5.50	3.00
1926...	Sesquicentennial Exposition	0.02	307,732	0.20	0.08
1926...	Ericsson Memorial	0.05	20,281	1.40	0.60
1926...	Battle of White Plains	0.02	40,639	0.40	0.20
1927...	Vermont Sesquicentennial	0.02	39,975	0.35	0.18
1927...	Burgoyne Campaign	0.02	25,628	0.80	0.45
1928...	Valley Forge Issue	0.02	101,330	0.20	0.08
1928...	Aeronautics Conference	0.02	51,342	0.30	0.12
1928...	Aeronautics Conference	0.05	10,320	1.00	0.50
1929...	George Rogers Clark	0.02	16,685	0.30	0.18
1929...	Electric Light Golden Jubilee	0.02	31,679	0.25	0.12
1929...	Electric Light Golden Jubilee (rotary)	0.02	210,119	0:09	0.03
1929...	Electric Light Golden Jubilee (coil)	0.02	133,530	0.20	0.06
1929...	Sullivan Expedition	0.02	51,452	0.18	0.10
1929...	Battle of Fallen Timbers	0.02	29,338	0.35	0.18
1929...	Ohio River Canalization	0.02	32,681	0.20	0.08
1928...	Battle of Monmouth†	0.02	9,780	0.35	0.18
1928...	Hawaii Sesquicentennial†	0.02	5,520	0.80	0.30
1928...	Hawaii Sesquicentennial†	0.02	1,460	2.75	1.20
1929...	Kansas Issue†	0.01	13,390	0.22	0.10
1929...	Kansas Issue	0.015	8,240	0.50	0.20
1929...	Kansas Issue	0.02	87,410	0.10	0.05
1929...	Kansas Issue	0.03	2,540	2.50	1.75
1929...	Kansas Issue	0.04	2,290	1.35	0.80
1929...	Kansas Issue	0.05	2,700	1.20	0.80
1929...	Kansas Issue	0.06	1,450	3.25	2.50
1929...	Kansas Issue	0.07	1,320	3.75	1.35
1929...	Kansas Issue	0.08	1,530	11.50	5.50
1929...	Kansas Issue	0.09	1,130	1.40	0.90
1929...	Kansas Issue	0.10	2,860	1.25	0.90

Exhibit 2 (Continued)

Date	Issue	Denomination	Quantity Issued	Scott Catalogue Price, 1962*	Scott Catalogue Price, 1949*
1929...	Nebraska Issue†	$0.01	8,220	$ 0.22	$0.12
1929...	Nebraska Issue	0.015	8,990	0.20	0.10
1929...	Nebraska Issue	0.02	73,220	0.15	0.05
1929...	Nebraska Issue	0.03	2,110	1.10	0.50
1929...	Nebraska Issue	0.04	1,600	1.60	0.75
1929...	Nebraska Issue	0.05	1,860	1.60	0.80
1929...	Nebraska Issue	0.06	980	4.00	2.75
1929...	Nebraska Issue	0.07	850	3.00	1.50
1929...	Nebraska Issue	0.08	1,480	4.50	1.50
1929...	Nebraska Issue	0.09	530	5.25	3.75
1929...	Nebraska Issue	0.10	1,890	4.00	2.50

*For canceled stamps.

†These issues are listed separately since they were regular issues that were overprinted.

Sources: *Scott's Standard Postage Stamp Catalogue* (New York: Scott Publications, 1949 and 1962); and *U.S. Postage Stamps, 1847–1957* (Washington, D.C.: U.S. Government Printing Office, 1957).

people into collecting first-day covers; a mere 350,000 to 500,000 of these were mailed for each issue in the late 1950's. Government policy in 1962 was also indicated to be against allowing the great enhancement of value through the discovery of important errors. When faulty sheets of the Dag Hammarskjold issue were discovered in 1962, the Post Office Department reissued the error for purchase by all who desired it. Thus the spectacular price appreciation of the best-known U.S. error, the inverted airplane in the tricolored 24-cent issue of 1918, seemed unlikely to be repeated.

QUESTIONS

1. What is the general relationship between price and the quantity issued? What are possible explanations for the price not varying proportionally (though inversely) with the quantity issued?

2. In what respects does the model for price determination in the very short run fit American postage stamps? In what respects does it differ?

3. Are the changes in prices between 1949 and 1962 best explained by shifts in supply or demand, or both? Show diagrammatically.

4. Is there any evidence that demand is stronger for one group of these stamps than another? (Consider the overprinted stamps as a separate group.) Is it reasonably conclusive?

5. Assess United States used air-mail and commemorative stamps as an investment. Assume that you purchased the complete sets of "fine stamps" de-

Exhibit 3

QUANTITY ISSUED AND CATALOGUE PRICES, UNITED STATES AIR-MAIL STAMPS, 1918–30

Date	Issue	Denomination	Quantity Issued (in Thousands)	Scott Catalogue Price, 1962*	Scott Catalogue Price, 1949*
1918..............	Definitive first issue	$0.06	3,396	$ 5.00	$ 2.00
1918..............	Definitive first issue	0.16	3,794	9.50	4.50
1918..............	Definitive first issue	0.24	2,135	8.00	4.00
1918..............	Definitive first issue (center inverted)	0.24	0.1	10,000.00	3,500.00
1923..............	Definitive	0.08	6,415	2.75	1.40
1923..............	Definitive	0.16	5,309	8.50	4.00
1923..............	Definitive	0.24	5,286	4.75	2.25
1926–27..........	Definitive	0.10	42,093	0.15	0.04
1926–27..........	Definitive	0.15	15,597	0.50	0.20
1926–27..........	Definitive	0.20	17,616	0.40	0.12
1927..............	Definitive (Lindbergh)	0.10	20,379	1.00	0.15
1928..............	Definitive	0.05	106,888	0.20	0.05
1930..............	Definitive	0.05	97,641	0.15	0.04
1930..............	Definitive (rotary 1931)	0.05	57,340	0.15	0.04
1930..............	Century of Progress	0.65	94	35.00	18.00
1930..............	Century of Progress	1.30	72	50.00	35.00
1930..............	Century of Progress	2.60	61	95.00	57.50

*For canceled stamps except center-inverted 24-cent stamp, which exists only uncanceled and whose price is quoted in italics in the Scott catalogue.

Sources: *Scott's Standard Postage Stamp Catalogue* (Scott Publications, 1949 and 1962); *U.S. Postage Stamps, 1847—1957* (Washington, D.C.: U.S. Government Printing Office, 1957).

scribed in the exhibits in 1949 at 90 per cent catalogue[4] and were able to sell in 1962 at 65 per cent catalogue. Do not include 24-cent "error" in your portfolio.

A second popular way that some collectors have sought to invest in stamps is to buy sheets of fifty of current commemoratives at face value. For example, one could have purchased 100 sheets of a 1949 3-cent commemorative for $150. In 1962 the stamps catalogued at 8 cents apiece and might have been sold to a dealer for 3½ cents. Would either of these investments have been good ones?[5]

CASE 5–2:   BADGER AND SIEGEL

Badger and Siegel were two very small producers of a standardized product in a very competitive market. Both priced at the prevailing market price, and both desired to maximize profits. Both plants were about the same size and had a potential capacity of producing 10,000 units per year. Normally, however, both tended to operate at not over 80 per cent of capacity, for unit variable costs increased rapidly for any extra production. This increase was caused by the fact that one stage of production required very skilled workmanship. These highly paid workers in consequence worked overtime when production exceeded 80 per cent of capacity. Any production between 80 and 85 per cent of capacity increased variable costs on this extra output by 10 per cent. If production went above 85 per cent and not over 90 per cent, the *additional* units cost an *additional* 15 per cent over the unit variable costs for outputs up to 80 per cent. Any units produced over 90 per cent of capacity cost 20 per cent more than the basic variable costs. At 80 per cent of capacity, Badger's unit fixed costs were $3.00. These costs in total did not change within the range of his production. For outputs through 80 per cent capacity, his variable costs were $9.00 per unit. Siegel did not use quite as much machinery, and his costs at 80 per cent capacity were as follows: unit fixed, $2.00; unit variable, $10.50. In 1959 the price dropped from $12.60 to $12.40. At this price, Siegel was operating at a loss in 1963 when he was working at 80 per cent of capacity.

Since Badger and Siegel were friends, Siegel asked Badger what to do under these circumstances. Badger told him that in such a case, he

---

[4]Actually, for stamps to have been sold and resold at these ratios to catalogue values would probably have required their being exceptionally fine.

[5]It was quite possible that the seller might get only face value. The dealer probably would sell such stamps at 6 cents and would require a wide margin on such low unit transactions. While United States stamps are always good for the face value, wholesalers have been frequently able to purchase them in bulk at 6 per cent below face.

should forget fixed costs and watch variable costs only. Badger said that he watched his variable costs and continued production just so long as his additional costs did not exceed the selling price. Thus, if the price in the market was $12.40, Badger continued to increase output until his additional variable (marginal) costs approximated $12.40.

Siegel, however, insisted that since his costs at normal capacity were $12.50 per unit, he could not possibly reduce his losses by forgetting his fixed costs. He insisted that average costs were the more significant.

In order to settle the argument, Badger and Siegel agreed that they would estimate their costs at various levels of production. They decided to start at 5,000, then estimate them at 7,000, 8,000, 8,500, 9,000, 10,000, and 11,000 units. For production between 10,-000 and 11,000 units additional variable costs were estimated at double the level at 8,000 units.

QUESTIONS

1. Make this cost-output study for both Badger and Siegel, and indicate how many units each should produce.

2. Assume that there are 50 firms in the industry with Badger's costs and 50 with Siegel's costs. Plot the industry supply schedule.

3. What long-run changes of price and composition of this industry would you predict under the assumptions of pure competition?

CASE 5–3: THE BITUMINOUS COAL INDUSTRY IN THE EARLY 1960'S

By 1961 the consumption of bituminous coal in the United States was at approximately 1939 levels, about 375 million tons. As a source of energy, however, it furnished only 21 per cent of United States consumption of energy fuels and water power, as against over 45 per cent in 1939. Production, which had reached a postwar peak of more than 600 million tons in 1947, had dwindled to just over 400 million tons. Two of the five major categories of use in 1947 had been almost eliminated by oil and gas competition—the railroads were almost entirely converted to diesel power, and retail deliveries for home and commercial heating were a small fraction of even the 1947 figure, which in itself reflected many years of decline because of the increasing use of oil and natural gas. Two other categories of use had dwindled badly—coking coal because of increased efficiencies in its utilization by the steel industry, and uses in other manufacturing because of the inroads of competitive fuels.

Only sales to electric power utilities, fifth in 1947, were on the increase and amounted to almost half the use of coal in 1961. Several favorable and potentially favorable factors were behind this growth and bright prospects for the future. Most prominent was the phenomenal growth potential of the output of electricity, which had doubled about every seven years since the start of the century and, while the rate of expansion had slackened off, was still forecast to rise by 5–6 per cent a year. In providing this additional output, steam-electric capacity rose more rapidly than the total (which includes hydro, internal-combustion, and nuclear power). The increase in steam-electric capacity, and thus the potential market for coal, was over 137 per cent in the ten years ended in 1961, while the increase in all other types was but 70 per cent, and there were no immediate prospects that expansion of nuclear power would shift a growing dependence on conventional steam-electric power. In the two regions that had relied most heavily on hydropower, the East South Central and the Pacific, steam-electric production had increased over 300 per cent, since the remaining unexploited water resources were small relative to the increase of demand for electricity.

The potential growth in the need for fuel by utilities would fall somewhat short of the growth in demand for electricity if past trends in efficiency of the use of converting the BTU content of fuels into kilowatt-hours of electricity continued. For coal, the pounds used per net kilowatt-hour dropped from 1.096 in 1952 to 0.863 in 1961 (or from 13,286 BTU's to 10,355 BTU's), but the average annual decrease in unit coal requirements had dropped from over 3 per cent to less than 2 per cent. Similar increases in efficiency were being secured by oil and gas users, although their average BTU requirements were higher— 11,429 and 11,318, respectively.[6]

The other favorable factors were those that improved the competitive position of coal as against residual oil and natural gas in obtaining steam-utility business. Technological improvements in mining techniques, best symbolized by the continuous mining machine, had more than doubled the output per man-day in bituminous mines from 1951 to 1961, to 14.38 tons as shown in Exhibit 1. Such an average figure understated the productivity potential of the best new mines. Operating on a scale of over a million tons a year, a few had achieved productivities in the range of 60 tons per man-day. In 1962, at least one midwestern coal company signed a long-run contract which depended for its profit-

---

[6]See National Coal Association, *Steam-Electric Plant Factors* (Washington, 1961), Table 7.

Exhibit 1

UNITED STATES PRODUCTION AND PRICE OF BITUMINOUS COAL AND OF NATURAL GAS, 1939–61

Year	Number of Mines	Average Value per Ton of Coal, F.O.B. Mine	Production of Bituminous Coal*	Tons of Output per Man-Day	Production of Natural Gas*	Price Index, Natural Gas†
1939	5,820	$1.84	394.9	5.25	105.5	n.a.§
1947	8,700	4.16	630.6	6.42	191.3	n.a.
1952‡	7,275	4.90	466.8	7.47	332.3	n.a.
1953	6,671	4.92	457.3	8.17	347.9	n.a.
1954	6,130	4.51	391.7	9.47	362.1	n.a.
1955	7,856	4.50	464.6	9.84	389.5	n.a.
1956	8,520	4.82	500.9	10.28	417.2	n.a.
1957	8,539	5.08	492.7	10.59	441.6	n.a.
1958	8,264	4.86	410.4	11.33	455.8	101.7
1959	7,719	4.77	412.0	12.22	497.6	110.9
1960‡	7,865	4.69	415.5	12.83	527.6	116.6
1961‡	7,800	4.65	400.0	14.38	530.7	118.6

*In millions of tons; natural gas production is shown as equivalent tons of bituminous coal.
†Wholesale price index from Bureau of Labor Statistics.
‡The average "as consumed" cost at utility plants was $6.61, $6.26, and $6.20, respectively, per ton of coal in 1952, 1960, and 1961; $2.09, $2.18, and $2.24 per barrel of oil and 15.1 cents, 24.9 cents, and 26.2 cents per thousand cubic feet of gas in the same three years.
§Not available.
Sources: U.S. Bureau of Mines, cited in National Coal Association; *Bituminous Coal Facts* (Washington, 1962); *Statistical Abstract of the United States* (Washington, D.C.: U.S. Government Printing Office, 1962).

ability on achievement of even greater outputs per man-day. The combination of increased capital requirements, increased scale of operations, and long-term contracts with large customers instead of sales of spot coal represented further departures from the purely competitive model, though evidence suggested in 1962 that the fundamental characteristic of such a model—very little discretion over price for the coal producer—was still largely satisfied.

A second recent development in lowering the effective costs of coal to utilities was the reduction and potential reduction of transportation costs. As a commodity low in value per weight unit, the costs of transportation had traditionally broken the market for coal into many regional and local markets. New technological possibilities in the transportation of coal as a slurry through pipe lines and in the cheaper transmission of electricity at higher voltages (which would allow generating stations to be located close to the mines rather than the markets), combined with a new aggressiveness by the railroads in trying to hold their traditional business through price concessions and special service, such as the shuttle train which would operate between mine and generating station as a unit, had begun to reduce the freight-rate obstacle to coal sales. In March, 1963, the Baltimore & Ohio Railroad put into effect a 25 per cent reduction in rail rates, which could reduce the utility cost by as much as 10 per cent, in parts of the Middle Atlantic region. The New York Central reduced rates from a Peabody Coal Company mine in Lynneville, Indiana, to the Commonwealth Edison Company plant in Hammond from $3.07 to $1.45, accompanying the use of a unitized train.[7]

The very virtues of natural gas for other uses such as residental and home heating probably limited the further inroads it could make in the utility market and were reflected in rising prices for natural gas. Residual fuel oil, which was a redoubtable competitor on the Atlantic Coast, although somewhat hampered by rather flexible quotas—the 1963 quota of 575,000 barrels per day represented a 70 per cent increase over the original limit imposed in 1959—might increase its market share if quotas were completely removed. As a waste product from Venezuela which could be shipped to seaboard plants at low water-transportation rates, residual oil could be priced just below the equivalent coal prices.

Exhibit 2 presents data on the changes between 1952 and 1961 in the relative market shares, the average cost per million BTU's, and

---

[7]Both of these rate developments are referred to in *Forbes* magazine, May 15, 1963, pp. 23–27.

Exhibit 2

STEAM-ELECTRIC UTILITIES' FUEL CONSUMPTION AND COST EXPERIENCE—TOTAL UNITED STATES AND BY REGIONS[1]
1961 Compared with 1952

	New England	Middle Atlantic	East North Central	West North Central	South Atlantic	East South Central	West South Central	Mountain	Pacific	United States Total	Coal-Consuming States[2]
Total per cent of BTU's supplied by:											
1. Coal in 1952	51.0	84.0	91.0	47.0	77.0	70.0	1.0	29.0	..	67.0	81.0
2. Coal in 1961	63.0	78.0	96.0	45.0	78.0	92.0	..	30.0	..	65.0	84.0
3. Oil in 1952	49.0	11.0	..	2.0	13.0	..	..	11.0	55.0	10.0	7.0
4. Oil in 1961	34.0	14.0	..	..	9.0	..	..	7.0	29.0	8.0	5.0
5. Gas in 1952	..	5.0	9.0	51.0	10.0	30.0	99.0	60.0	45.0	23.0	12.0
6. Gas in 1961	3.0	8.0	4.0	55.0	13.0	8.0	100.0	63.0	71.0	27.0	11.0
Cost per million BTU's (Lewis):											
1. Coal in 1961	36.2	29.9	25.0	26.2	25.8	19.7	..	19.6	..	25.8	25.8
2. 1961 as per cent of 1952	97.3	102.7	96.1	90.3	95.5	98.0	.	86.0	..	94.5	94.5
3. Oil in 1961	37.7	36.2	..	..	35.2	..	..	25.6	32.6	35.5	36.4
4. 1961 as per cent of 1952	104.7	102.5	..	..	105.4	..	..	107.1	114.8	107.3	103.1
5. Gas in 1961	..	37.7	26.4	22.8	32.5	25.4	19.0	28.5	35.2	25.1	27.1
6. 1961 as per cent of 1952	..	142.3	136.1	112.9	174.7	174.1	204.3	178.1	175.1	173.1	136.9
Total consumption in coal equivalent, 1961 (millions of tons)	11.3	44.0	72.3	21.1	40.2	29.7	28.8	9.5	24.1	281.0	215.1
Total consumption, 1961, as per cent of 1952	147.6	129.1	155.1	182.8	179.6	366.6	180.6	342.0	323.7	179.5	167.3

[1]The regions above consist of the following states: *New England*—Connecticut,* Maine,† Massachusetts, New Hampshire, Rhode Island, Vermont.* *Middle Atlantic*—New Jersey, New York, Pennsylvania* (62.3).‡ *East North Central*—Illinois* (45.3), Indiana* (15.0), Michigan,* Ohio* (31.0), Wisconsin.* *West North Central*—Iowa (1.0), Kansas† (0.7), Minnesota, Missouri (2.7), Nebraska, North Dakota* (2.7), South Dakota. *South Atlantic*—Delaware, District of Columbia,* Florida, Georgia, Maryland* (0.8), North Carolina,* South Carolina, Virginia* (27.4), West Virginia* (113.6). *East South Central*—Alabama* (12.1), Kentucky* (64.5), Mississippi,† Tennessee* (6.3). *West South Central*—Arkansas† (0.3), Louisiana,† Oklahoma† (1.0), Texas.† *Mountain*—Arizona,† Colorado (3.7), Montana (0.4), Nevada,† New Mexico† (0.5), Utah (5.3), Wyoming* (2.4). *Pacific*—California,† Oregon,† Washington† (0.2).

[2]Coal-consuming states exclude the West South Central and Pacific regions and Arizona, Mississippi, and Florida (the last exclusion for comparability with previous years).

*Over 90 per cent of steam-electric consumption is coal.
†Under 10 per cent of steam-electric consumption is coal.
‡Figure in bracket represents coal production in 1961 for states producing at least 200,000 tons (in millions of tons).
Source: Adapted from National Coal Association, *Steam-Electric Plant Factors* (Washington, 1961), Table A.

the total consumption in tons of coal equivalent for the three competitive fuels. Caution must be used in interpreting these aggregate figures, particularly the cost figures, which were not reported for all plants. It also should be kept in mind in interpreting these figures that the natural gas industry is subject to extensive price and service regulation, that the quantities of oil offered are substantially influenced by the operational limitations of leading oil-producing states and by import quotas, and that coal was being sold without important price and quantity regulation. Year-to-year fluctuations are concealed in this trend comparison between two years that are nine years apart, but it may be noted that in 1961, over-all market shares were virtually unchanged from 1960, while coal costs dropped an estimated 1.0 per cent, oil costs rose 2.9 per cent, and gas costs rose 5.5 per cent on a BTU basis.[8]

QUESTIONS

1. Is there evidence (particularly in Exhibit 2) that changes in relative costs of fuels to utility customers have aided the sales of coal? Explain carefully, suggesting hypotheses for some of the seeming anomalies in the data.

2. Consider in what ways the coal industry approaches the criteria for pure competition. What are the important departures? Would you predict a greater or lesser resemblance to the purely competitive model in the future?[9]

3. Individual mines differ greatly in their cost characteristics—thickness of the seams of coal and other desirable physical characteristics, degree of mechanization, location in regard to important markets, etc. Assume no control over price, and explain as well as you can the survival of such a variety of cost functions for different types of mines.

---

[8]The drop in the cost of coal per ton, "as consumed" by steam-electric utilities, was from $5.26 to $5.19 (National Coal Association, *op. cit.*).

[9]The student may wish to consult a more comprehensive industry analysis as in W. Adams, *Structure of American Industry* (3rd ed.; New York: Macmillan Co., 1961); or periodical coverage such as that in *Forbes* magazine, May 15, 1963, pp. 23–27.

CHAPTER 6

❖❖❖❖❖❖❖❖❖❖❖❖❖❖❖❖❖❖❖❖❖

Price Policy when Sellers Are Few

A VERY common situation in manufacturing, wholesaling, retailing, and other fields is that of "oligopoly," where the number of sellers of a particular item is so small that each seller must consider his rivals' reactions to his own actions. It was pointed out in Chapter 3 that the oligopolist is not faced by a single demand curve but rather that the curve can assume a great variety of shapes (and even a positive slope), depending on the nature and extent of rivals' reactions. Oligopoly thus differs sharply from both monopoly and pure competition, in both of which situations demand can be considered to "stay put" while the firm adjusts itself to the demand-cost situation.

Oligopoly is common in local markets throughout the country. Many towns and cities are large enough to support only a few drugstores, variety stores, department stores, theaters, building materials producers, etc. Especially where there is considerable geographic separation between cities, each such seller serves a substantial percentage of the local market and is usually highly sensitive to attempts of competitors to capture larger shares of the market by price cuts or other means.

The larger the market in which a product is sold, the more opportunity there is for a large number of firms (of efficient size) to participate. Nevertheless, oligopoly is common also in industries which serve national and international markets. Here, the situation is usually not literally one of only a "few" sellers; but frequently, there are only a few large firms plus a number of small firms, with the dominant companies accounting for a large percentage of total sales. An oligopolistic situation then exists between the large firms, each being highly sensitive to the actions of the others. Usually, the small firms in the field are reluctant to follow price policies which put them in sharp conflict with the industry leaders. (Many interesting exceptions occur, however, where small companies with aggressive management consistently follow policies of their own choosing.)

211

Concentration of American Industry

A popular statistical device for showing the existence of oligopolistic situations on a national basis is the "concentration ratio." This measure is the percentage of total output, shipments, sales, or employment accounted for by the largest firms in a given industry. Such ratios are published from time to time by the Bureau of the Census and the Federal Trade Commission. The ratios are greatly affected by the broadness or narrowness of industry classification—e.g., the "food and kindred products" industry covers such a wide range of activities that it can scarcely show up as concentrated.

Exhibit 1

PER CENT OF TOTAL VALUE OF SHIPMENTS MADE BY FOUR LARGEST COMPANIES, 1958

Industry	Concentration Ratio
Tin cans and other tinware	80%
Cigarettes*	79
Motor vehicles and parts	75
Tires and inner tubes	74
Tractors	69
Aircraft†	59
Aircraft engines	56
Organic chemicals	55
Blast furnaces and steel mills†	53

*Value of production used instead of shipments.
†Value added by manufacture used.
Source: *Statistical Abstract of the United States* (Washington, D.C.: U.S. Government Printing Office, 1962), pp. 786–87.

Exhibit 1 shows industry concentration ratios compiled by the Bureau of the Census on the basis of per cent of the value of total shipments accounted for by the four largest firms in 1958. The Standard Industrial Classification of industries was used, and only the largest forty-five industries as determined by value of shipments were considered. According to these ratios, highest concentration was in the manufacture of tin cans and tinware. American Can and Continental Can have long been the dominant firms. Cigarette production is highly concentrated, and television viewers are likely to be well aware of the importance of the American Tobacco Company, Liggett & Myers, R. J. Reynolds, and Brown & Williamson in the industry. The "Big Four" in automobiles—General Motors, Ford, Chrysler, and American Motors —are even more widely known.

On the other end of the scale, concentration ratios of 10 per cent or less were reported for dresses, ready-mixed concrete, machine shops, sawmills and planing mills, plastic products, lithographing, and commercial printing. These industries tend to be more competitive than those of Exhibit 1. However, local monopoly power does not show up in the ratios—e.g., there might be only one ready-mixed-concrete dealer in a town that is well separated from other urban areas. Also, competition from imported products does not show up in the ratios. As is well known to students (who seem usually to be most familiar with the automobile and brewing industries), the importation of foreign cars is often a worry to Detroit. In considering the concentration ratios of Exhibit 1, it is also important to remember that many highly concentrated industries (such as the small-arms ammunition industry) do not show up because of their relatively small size in terms of value of output. The broadness or narrowness of industry classification may determine whether an industry is considered a "large" one as well as affecting concentration measurements. Concentration ratios should not be considered to be measures of monopoly power for the reasons given and also because they are computed "horizontally." Vertical integration, which can be a source of monopoly power, does not affect the ratios.

A multiproduct firm may turn out a large part of the output in one or more industries but only a small portion of output in others. It has been pointed out in a recently published book that in a market characterized by high concentration, a leading firm may have to diversify in order to achieve a rapid growth rate. This is apt to be more effective than strenuous efforts to secure a larger share of the market in which it is already a major factor.[1]

Price Policy of Big Business

Companies that are in the top four among the concentrated industries shown in Exhibit 1, and many others in manufacturing, transportation, mining, communications, electric power, banking, and other fields, are often characterized as "big business." Officials of such firms inevitably emphasize the competitiveness of the activities in which they are engaged, and it is true that few are so well insulated from competition, actual and potential, that they can continue to prosper unless management is alert and ready to adapt to changing conditions. At the same time, large firms are in a position to take a longer run view of profit making, in part because their financial strength nearly guarantees that they will be in business for a long time. A short-term opportunity to

---

[1]Michael Gort, *Diversification and Integration in American Industry* (Princeton: Princeton University Press, 1962), p. 137.

make unusual profits is more likely to be passed up by a very large company if it involves a possibility of damaging its "public image." The long waiting lists for some popular makes of cars following resumption of automobile production after World II were an indication that sellers were not attempting to maximize immediate profits. (A queue of buyers can always be broken up by a sufficiently high price.)

It is sometimes said that many large firms set price to cover all costs and provide a "target rate of return" on capital. However, it is difficult to believe that such target rates are much different from maximum rates of return except that they may incorporate a longer run view of the effect of current prices on demand, entry of new rivals, union wage demands, and government action in such matters as antitrust, tariffs, and award of contracts. Examination of the pricing policy of large companies is especially difficult because many products are usually turned out by a single firm. Different degrees of control over supply, and consequently of price, are likely to prevail for various products. General principles regarding pricing policy of large firms, as far as they differ from the theory of price determination in general, cannot be stated with confidence. Perhaps the most revealing information is obtained by intensive study of particular firms. Some case studies of pricing by large companies are included in this book.[2]

Plant Concentration and Company Concentration

The Federal Trade Commission studied the matter of plant concentration in relation to company concentration for 1947. Plant concentration measures the percentage of industry output turned out by a designated number of plants. Thus an industry in which both plant concentration and company concentration are high is one which has both a small number of plants and a small number of firms. It is also possible for plant concentration to be low while company concentration is high. This situation would mean ownership of a large number of plants per firm. It is also common, of course, for both plant concentration and firm concentration to be low.

Exhibit 2 lists industries in two groups: (1) On the left are those with the greatest difference between plant and company concentration; (2) on the right are those in which company concentration is only slightly above plant concentration. In general, it can be said that the number of firms existing in the industries on the right is based in large

---

[2]Also see A. D. H. Kaplan, J. B. Dirlam, and R. F. Lanzillotti, *Pricing in Big Business* (Washington, D.C.: Brookings Institution, 1958).

measure on economics of scale in the manufacturing process. Most of the firms in these fields have only one plant, so that firm size is closely correlated with plant size. Firms within the industries shown on the left are mainly multiplant organizations, so that there is little relation between firm size and plant size. The size of the larger firms in this left-hand list must be explained in terms of economics of large firms (in financing, buying, advertising, research, etc.) or else large size is due to mergers or other actions which may have been designed to increase monopoly power.

Exhibit 2

INDUSTRIES WITH LARGEST AND SMALLEST DIVERGENCIES BETWEEN COMPANY AND PLANT CONCENTRATION

Largest Divergence	*Smallest Divergence*
Petroleum and coal products	Electrical motors
Transportation equipment	Fabricated metal products
Primary metals	Apparel and related products
Leather and leather products	Printing and publishing
Food and kindred products	Instruments and related products
Paper and allied products	Machinery, except electrical
Chemicals and allied products	Lumber, except furniture
Stone, glass, and clay products	Miscellaneous manufactures
Textile mill products	Furniture and fixtures

Source: *Study of Monopoly Power*, Hearings before the Subcommittee of the Judiciary, House of Representatives, 82d Congress, First Session (Washington, D.C.: U.S. Government Printing Office, 1955), Serial 1, Part 2, p. 3.

The compressed and liquefied gas industry constitutes a striking example of low plant concentration and high company concentration, even though it did not make the left-hand list in Exhibit 2. The 20 largest plants accounted for only about 20 per cent of the industry's value of product, whereas the 20 largest companies accounted for 94 per cent of the industry total.[3] Another example of the same sort of situation is the distilling industry. The four large distillers—National Distillers, Schenley Distillers, Seagram Distillers, and Hiram Walker —operated a total of 54 plants, according to the same Congressional hearings.

If company concentration is high and plant concentration is also high, antitrust action is unlikely, because there is a presumption that large firms are needed to secure low production costs. If, however, company concentration ratios are high while plant concentration is low, there is more likelihood that unnecessary monopoly power exists. (The concentration ratios alone do not *prove* this, of course.) As men-

---

[3]*Study of Monopoly Power,* Hearings before the Subcommittee of the Judiciary, House of Representatives, 82d Congress, First Session (Washington, D.C.: U.S. Government Printing Office, 1955), Serial 1, Part 2, p. 13.

tioned earlier, concentration ratios do not measure the important matter of the degree of vertical integration (control of successive stages of production) which exists, and this must be kept in mind when the possible antitrust implications of such ratios are assessed. And even where company concentration is low, price conspiracy and monopolistic mergers are watched by the Federal Trade Commission.

Pure and Differentiated Oligopoly

Pure oligopoly may be said to exist when sellers of a homogeneous commodity are few in number. This situation is more common among producers of industrial materials than in the consumer goods fields. Most consumer goods are differentiated from one another by means of brand names, trade-marks, and packaging, and usually by some differences in physical characteristics. Materials and components turned out by different companies for use as inputs into production processes are more frequently identical. Even if the name of the producer is stamped on the good, this is not apt to influence an experienced industrial buyer if the product is, in fact, identical with that of another firm. Consumers of finished products, on the other hand, are often influenced by brand names and advertising, even where no substantial difference in the commodity actually exists. (Aspirin is a famous example.) As a consequence, "pure oligopoly" may be said to be present in such fields as the manufacture of primary aluminum, primary copper, aluminum rolling and drawing, and certain gypsum products, whereas "differentiated oligopoly" exists for automobiles, cigarettes, hard-surface floor coverings, typewriters, sewing machines, and a great many other commodities.

When oligopolistic firms are few in number and have identical products, their demands are highly interdependent. As concentration of production diminishes, and as products are more differentiated, demands are less closely interdependent. If the number of firms selling in a market becomes large enough so that each can disregard the reactions of his rivals to his own price-output actions, the market situation is often designated by economists as "monopolistic competition" or "pure competition," depending on whether differentiated or nondifferentiated products are sold. In each case a single demand curve confronts the firm; in the former case, this is a downsloping monopoly demand curve; while in the latter case, it is a horizontal line. If there are *no* rivals selling the same commodity in the same market, the situation is designated as monopoly. The distinction between "monopoly" and "monopolistic competition" is not a clear one, however, since it encounters the same difficulty of classifying industries as is involved in compiling statistics on concentration. If "industry" is defined very narrowly and products are differentiated, there is only one firm in each industry (e.g., the "Campbell soup industry"). If the industry is defined more broadly, the Campbell Soup Company becomes instead one firm of a number in the "canned soup industry." On a still broader basis, it is one of a very large number of firms in the "food and food products industry." Whether the company is "oligopolistic" or not depends on whether, in fact, its price adjustments will cause speedy reactions on the part of the other companies. If such reactions would occur, the company can be classified as a "differentiated oligopolist."

Graphic Comparison of Oligopoly Positions

The distinction between an oligopolistic and a monopolistic firm can be made clearer by the use of a chart. The firm for which demand is represented on the left side of Exhibit 3 is in a position where its

Exhibit 3

INTERDEPENDENT DEMANDS— RIVALS' REACTIONS IMPORTANT	INDEPENDENT DEMAND—RIVALS' REACTIONS NOT SIGNIFICANT

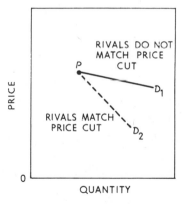
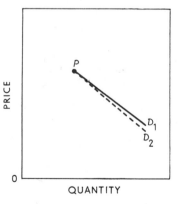

sales depend strongly on the reactions of its close rivals to a price cut from the prevailing level indicated by point P. If rivals do not match a price cut, sales will expand along the highly elastic curve D_1. This may be called its *ceteris paribus* demand curve,[4] since it is drawn on the assumption that other things (especially the prices charged by rival

---

[4] This terminology is used by J. S. Bain, *Pricing, Distribution, and Employment* (New York: Henry Holt & Co., 1953). This work contains an excellent discussion of price and output decisions under oligopoly.

sellers) remain constant. If, however, rivals match the price cut, sales will expand less substantially along the less elastic curve D_2. In the right-hand diagram the *ceteris paribus* and "rivals match" demand curves are very close together. Consequently, the firm is nearly in a position to disregard the reactions of other sellers to its own price adjustments; the firm is almost in a monopoly position, where there is a single demand curve to which it can adjust. If the two demand curves were entirely coincident, rather than just close together, the firm would be monopolistic rather than oligopolistic and could be independent in its policies. Monopoly can thus be considered to be a limiting case of oligopoly in which rivals' reactions are of negligible importance.

The Incentive for Making and Breaking Agreements

The demand situation portrayed on the left side of Exhibit 3 is an underlying cause of conservative pricing practices and outright collusive action on the part of sellers in oligopolistic markets. If price is at the level indicated by point *P,* the firm in question may be reluctant to "rock the boat" by lowering price, because the sales result of the cut will depend so greatly on what competitors do in response. The uncertainties inherent in the situation are conducive to "letting well enough alone" or making outright price agreements to which all sellers promise to adhere. At the same time, the sharp gain in sales which any one oligopolist can make by lowering price while others hew to the line offers a constant temptation to cut price openly or in a less overt manner. Small firms are often troublesome to the larger ones in this regard, since they may be able to cut price a bit without making it worth while for the larger firms to retaliate in any way. A small firm accounts for such a small percentage of total sales that it may get away with a price cut even when the industry practice is to agree on price. Should the manager of the small firm miscalculate, however, he may precipitate a price war in the industry—a war in which he may well be a casualty.

Price-fixing agreements for commodities sold in interstate commerce are illegal under the federal antitrust laws. (These laws will be examined in Chapter 16.) The federal government, through the Federal Trade Commission and the Department of Justice, has brought a substantial number of such agreements to light.[5] Collusion on price

---

[5] From 1920 to 1940 the Federal Trade Commission issued "cease and desist" orders involving price agreements in the following industries: viscose rayon yarn, pin tickets, flannel shirts, turbine generators and condensers, liquid chlorine, medical cotton goods,

is always difficult to prove, however. In part, this difficulty springs from the fact that under perfect competition the prices charged for a particular commodity are identical. It is not always clear whether identical prices are the result of competition or monopoly. The antitrust job of the federal authorities is made more difficult when products are differentiated rather than homogeneous, since prices are then unlikely to be identical even where a price agreement has been entered into. Costlier varieties of the product are apt to be priced somewhat higher, even when all prices are arrived at collusively. It should also be kept in mind that price agreements are not illegal in intrastate commerce. In fact, they are often actively encouraged by state and local governments. Also, while the right hand of the federal government is attempting to discourage price fixing, the left hand is encouraging it and supplying the machinery for enforcing the agreements.

A striking example of governmentally induced price fixing was found under the National Recovery Administration (NRA) codes of the New Deal era. "Soon after he took office in 1933 the Administrator announced that, although conduct in accordance with approved codes was exempted from prosecution under the antitrust acts, it was not intended to authorize price agreements. Nevertheless, 560 of the first 677 codes contained some provision relating to minimum prices or costs."[6] The most important codes permitting direct setting of prices were those in the bituminous coal, lumber, and petroleum industries. The immediate result was an abrupt rise in prices in these industries. Because of the difficulties of enforcement and lack of general agreement as to the desirability of prices set by the code authority, there was widespread evasion. In the case of the coal industry, subsequent legislation attempted to carry on industry-wide price making after the NRA had been declared unconstitutional by the Supreme Court.

Similarly, price agreements between firms, as well as individual price fixing, have been fostered by the federal and state "fair-trade" laws and by the state "unfair practices" acts. Marketing co-operatives, with their power over sales and prices, have been encouraged by legislation; and extensive governmental and private price determination is involved in the federal farm programs. Governmental encouragement of labor

---

calcium chloride, corn cribs and silos, certain types of waterworks and gas-system fittings, fire-fighting equipment, pulverized iron, rubber heels, music rolls, lithographed labels, plumbing supplies, fertilizer, metal lath, gasoline, and brushes (Clair Wilcox, *Competition and Monopoly*, TNEC Monograph No. 21 [Washington, D.C.: U.S. Government Printing Office, 1940], p. 132).

[6]Arthur R. Burns, *Decline of Competition* (New York: McGraw-Hill Book Co., Inc., 1936), pp. 471–72.

unions has tended to cause wage rates to be determined by collective agreements rather than through competitive market forces. In addition, interest rates are subject to a good deal of government control. Some of these matters will be examined in more detail at a later point. Their inclusion here is to remind the reader that industrial, labor, and financial price determination is frequently removed from the arena of open competition by means of deliberate legislative action. Once sellers have been brought together by government action, as occurred under the NRA, they are apt to continue to act in collusion even after the legislation has ceased to be in effect.

When sellers decide to collude rather than to compete in price and other matters, their action can take various forms, some of which are much more rigid than others. The principal forms may be classified as (1) a cartel arrangement, (2) overt price agreement without cartelization, (3) tacit agreement on price, and (4) "follow the leader" pricing. These will be discussed in turn.

Cartels

Although the word "cartel" attained popularity (or notoriety) in reference to associations of firms trading internationally in such commodities as sulfur, explosives, magnesium, and rubber, its use is appropriate for any combination of sellers who turn over to a central authority their power to determine price. Frequently, the authority also is given power to allot exclusive sales territories, to control entry into the industry, and to control production. Cartels are common in such fields of intrastate commerce as dry cleaning and haircutting, where antitrust laws do not apply. Fluid-milk prices in most parts of the country are controlled by commissions established under either state or federal law, thus cartelizing the sale of this important commodity. Cartels may operate either in oligopolistic industries or in fields where the number of competing sellers would otherwise be large. International cartel arrangements in which American firms participate very often take the form of patent-licensing agreements.[7]

When price is determined centrally for all sellers in an industry, an attempt may be made to maximize profit for the group as a whole. In this case, price-output policy would be the same as that of a single-firm monopoly, the demand curve to which adjustment is made being the demand facing the industry as a whole. A difficulty involved in such

---

[7]See Dudley F. Pegrum, *The Regulation of Industry* (Homewood, Ill.: Richard D. Irwin, Inc., 1950), p. 396, for a discussion of this matter.

central price determination is the unlike cost situation for different firms. This may make the price which is optimal for the group as a whole differ from that which some firm or firms would like to have in force. A solution may be the establishment of two or more different prices to be charged by two or more subgroups of firms. For example, downtown cleaners may charge one uniform price per garment, while cleaners in outlying areas are permitted to charge a somewhat lower price. Where the central policy is clearly detrimental to the interests of a particular seller, there is always a chance that he will leave the association. If he then lowers the price and the cartel decides not to retaliate, his own sales are likely to increase sharply. Similarly, if the cartel makes sales territory, output, or other assignments which are not to the liking of a particular firm, there may be a possibility of its withdrawal from the association. Some of these possibilities will be analyzed in the next chapter.

Price Agreements without Cartelization

Frequently, businessmen enter into definite price agreements without the mechanism of a formal cartel arrangement. Trade associations, chambers of commerce, and other organizations often afford the necessary opportunities for sellers to meet and agree on price. Unlike cartel-determined price agreements, these are usually of a *sub rosa* nature; and frequently, great care is taken to destroy any written evidence of such agreements.

Interlocking directorates may also provide a useful instrument for preventing genuine price competition. The Federal Trade Commission, which looks with suspicion at such multicompany use of a single official, compiled a table dealing with this matter for the 200 largest nonfinancial and 50 largest financial corporations in 1935. Exhibit 4 summarizes this information. It can be seen that most of the large corporations had at least one director who did not devote his time entirely to the corporation. More often than not, directors of the large corporations also helped to direct three or more other companies. Opportunity for collusive action of many kinds is suggested by the data.

Noncartel price agreements are less likely than cartel agreements to have as their goal the approximate maximization of profits for the group as a whole. Stronger companies are likely to have especially great influence in determining price. As a consequence, agreements are more likely to be quite unsatisfactory to some firms and are more apt to be broken by disgruntled sellers than where the association is a more formal one. A decline in business activity is especially likely to strain a price agreement, since excess capacity will then appear and this will provide firms with a special incentive to cut price in order to gain volume. Similarly, the establishment of an excessive number of firms in a particular field, even in a period of general prosperity and expansion, may lead to the breaking of price agreements and to price wars. Price wars frequently occur in the retailing of gasoline, for example, due to the erection of too many filling stations in an area.

Exhibit 4

INTERLOCKING OF CORPORATE DIRECTORSHIPS

TYPE OF CORPORATION	ALL CORPORA- TIONS	CORPORATIONS INTERLOCKING WITH:		
		One or More Other Companies	Two or More Other Companies	Three or More Other Companies
Industrial..............	107	91	71	60
Utilities................	54	46	34	26
Railroads..............	39	38	36	31
Banks.................	30	30	28	22
Other financial.........	20	20	18	12
	250	225	187	151

Source: *Study of Monopoly Power*, Hearings before the Subcommittee of the Judiciary, House of Representatives, 82d Congress, First Session (Washington, D.C.: U.S. Government Printing Office, 1955), Serial 1, Part 2, p. 76.

Often, agreements to charge identical prices, to charge "manufacturers' suggested prices," or to avoid head-on price competition are tacit (unspoken) rather than overt. There may simply be a general understanding among sellers that the welfare of each is promoted by non-aggressive price policies. This form of agreement is the most tenuous of all and the most likely to be broken when it appears advantageous to a seller to do so.

Price Leadership

An effective method of avoiding price competition in oligopolistic industries is often found in the practice of price leadership. (This practice may, however, run afoul of the antitrust laws; and it has done so in recent years, as will be described in Chapter 16.) Under this system of tacitly collusive pricing an important firm is usually the one to decide upon and initiate a price change, which is then automatically followed by the other companies. It is, of course, difficult to generalize with respect to how much consultation takes place between industry officials prior to the initiation of a price change by the leader. If a great deal of interchange occurs, the system may not differ basically from that of overt agreement on price. If, however, the leader initiates the change after little or no advice from others in the industry, the form of collusion is quite different in nature. It is then primarily an "agreement to agree" on price rather than an agreement as to what the actual price should be.

Exhibit 5

RIVALS' REACTIONS HAVE
GREAT IMPORTANCE

RIVALS' REACTIONS NOT HIGHLY
IMPORTANT

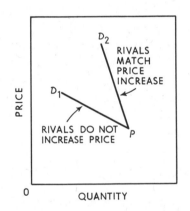
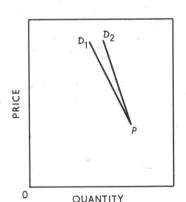

Frequently, the largest firm in the industry acts as price leader. If the product is sold in interstate commerce, there is danger in this practice, however, since the pattern may be too obvious to any interested antitrust investigator. For this reason, it may be safer to have other firms initiate the price change from time to time, with the "leader" a temporary follower. To carry out this sort of rotation of leadership, however, may require so much co-operation that the tacit collusion approaches overt price agreement rather than simple price agreement.

Some light can be cast on the phenomenon of oligopolistic price leadership by means of a chart similar to Exhibit 3 of this chapter. In Exhibit 5, both sides of the diagram show the demand curve which would obtain if rivals match a price increase or do not match a price increase.[8] On the left-hand side, sales by the price-raising firm will fall off sharply if rivals do not increase their prices. On the right side, however, it does not make a great deal of difference to the price-raising firm whether or not rivals go along with the change. This may be the situation because the firm represented on the right accounts for a large percentage of the sale of the commodity. This firm is in a better position to be the industry price leader than the firm on the left, because in the event of a rebellion on the part of the other companies, with respect to following its lead, it will not lose heavily in sales. The more vulnerable firm on the left would find its volume badly reduced if it attempted to lead a price increase and others did not follow. If there is an understanding that the large firms will let a smaller one lead, this danger is of course diminished.

Possession of the power of price leadership makes it easier for a firm to calculate the probable effect on sales, since there is assurance that others will follow a price change. The "rivals match" demand curve becomes the one which the leader can count on in its attempt to set price and output in such a way as to maximize its own profits; that is, it can attempt to equate marginal cost with marginal revenue computed from this demand. A price leader which is anxious to insure industry co-operation on a long-run basis may, however, set a price which it does not consider optimal for itself if its own optimum price would be quite unsatisfactory to other companies.

Price Stability and the Kinked Demand Curve

In the absence of price leadership, a rather likely situation facing an oligopolistic firm is that rivals will match a price cut (which is a threat to their sales) but will not follow a price increase (which poses no threat). A combination of segment D_1 of Exhibit 5 and D_2 of Exhibit 3, with the segments meeting at an angle at point P, constitutes a famous construction—the "kinked oligopoly demand curve." As described in Chapter 3, this construction has been used to explain why there is frequently a good deal of price stability in oligopolistic markets. An individual firm which raises price will find its sales reduced sharply if rivals do not follow. But if price is cut, the gain in physical volume may be moderate as rivals follow the cut, and dollar volume of

---

[8]Exhibit 3 was based on reactions following a price cut rather than an increase in price. For purposes of analyzing price leadership, it is more convenient to assume an increase in price.

the firm's sales may even decline. This can be a "heads you win, tails I lose" proposition in which it is better not to chance a price change at all.

Nonprice Competition

Even where it is the industry practice not to compete in price, firms are usually in vigorous competition for sales—"nonprice competition" then exists. There are three principal forms of nonprice competition: (1) variation in quality and style, (2) sales promotion, and (3) extension of services and other terms of trade. These methods of competition are sometimes alternatives; frequently, they supplement one another.

Quality and Style Competition

In relatively few markets today are firms engaged in selling competing standardized products. This is especially true of final consumer goods, as was pointed out earlier. Competition in quality, style, and design is the most common form of nonprice competition.

The concept of "quality" is by no means simple. It involves numerous variables, some of which can be measured; others are incapable of measurement. Any one product can involve several quality variables. An automobile, for example, can be appraised as to horsepower, durability, gasoline consumption, probable frequency and cost of repairs, comfort, riding qualities, safety, and ease of handling.

Competition in some industries has served to give the consumer substantial improvements over the years, with part of the gain reflected in lower prices and the rest in better quality. For example, since World War I, automobile tires have been both improved greatly in quality and lowered in price. Economy of operation is another aspect of quality competition which can be measured approximately. According to tests made by the Procurement Division of the United States Treasury in 1931, the average consumption of five makes of 6-cubic-foot refrigerators was 44 kilowatt-hours per month. A test based on 14 makes in 1938 showed average electricity consumption to have declined to 35 kilowatt-hours per month.[9] By 1954, this amount of current was sufficient to operate the average 8.3- to 9.6-cubic-foot refrigerators for a

---

[9] *Price Behavior and Business Policy,* TNEC Monograph No. 1, 76th Congress, Third Session (Washington, D.C.: U.S. Government Printing Office, 1940), p. 64.

month, according to tests by Consumers Union.[10] Improvements such as these afford successive occasions for firms to engage in nonprice competition.

Although many quality changes are physically measurable in terms of performance, as a rule it is impossible to translate these changes into price equivalents.[11] Where quality changes are of the intangible sort involving design, taste, and style, not even measures of physical performance are available. Yet these intangible elements are often the chief determinants of consumer choice. In women's clothing, for example, the indefinable element of style is far more important than are thread count, tensile strength of the cloth, or quality of workmanship. The success of a new model of automobile is determined more by the design of the hood than by the efficiency of the motor.

The degree to which quality competition emphasizes measurable elements of the product varies with commodities. Where industrial buyers constitute the chief market, there is a tendency to stress such features as operating economy, tensile strength, and durability. In consumer goods markets, sellers find it desirable to emphasize the intangible elements of quality, style, and design because these are less easily copied. Sellers of food products seldom mention their conformity with government standards of quality; sellers of dresses do not usually emphasize fiber content; and distributors of cosmetics do not ordinarily refer to the quality of ingredients of their products. Flavor, style, and attractive containers are more important selling features.

Sales Promotion

As an alternative to varying the product, many business companies compete by incurring selling expenses which are directed primarily at creating demand. Collectively, these expenditures can be called "sales promotion." Among the most spectacular is advertising, which involves outlays for newspaper and magazine publicity, direct mail, catalogues, television and radio programs, window displays, and packaging. The basic characteristic of these expenditures is that they are undertaken with a view to influencing the buyer, though some changes of the physical form of the product, as in packaging, may also be involved. Obviously, in some cases, it is difficult to distinguish changes in the

---

[10]Calculated from data given in *Consumer Reports,* September, 1954, p. 403.

[11]Andrew T. Court made an interesting attempt to develop a price index for automobiles which would reflect changes not only in price but also in weight, wheel base, and horsepower, expressed in terms of price (cf. A. T. Court, *Dynamics of Automobile Demand* [New York: General Motors Corp., 1939], pp. 99–117).

product expressly designed for their effect on the consumer from those which have substantive utility. Who is to say whether a catsup bottle which is conveniently designed for table use may not also be the one whose contours catch the consumer's eye on the supermarket shelf?

Related to advertising is the use of trade-marks and brand names. The purpose of these is to furnish an easy means of identifying a particular seller's product. It is conceivable that brands might be employed merely to enable the buyer to identify products embodying certain measurable quality differences. But usually, sellers combine the use of brands with advertising which attempts to persuade buyers that the product has certain desirable intangible characteristics which are unique or which it possesses in greater degree than competing goods. The brand is built into a limited monopoly, with a regular following created by advertising.

The effectiveness with which trade-marks and brands can protect a product against price competition varies with different lines of goods. In fields in which comparisons are relatively simple, or in markets where buyers are well equipped technically (as in many industrial goods markets), there is a strong tendency for buyers to switch to competing brands as soon as substantial price differences appear. On the other hand, where the consumer is unable to compare rival brands intelligently, the effective use of brands and trade-marks frequently permits wide price differentials to be maintained between virtually identical products. A lack of correspondence between price and United States Department of Agriculture grade for particular food products often exists. In the case of grocery products the element of taste is so subjective that comparisons among brands are very difficult; as a result, sellers are presented with an opportunity to create demand through nonprice competition. Similar situations exist in many other lines. A Federal Trade Commission investigation revealed that the Goodyear Tire and Rubber Company sold tires to Sears Roebuck under the brand name "Allstate" which were of the same quality as those marketed by Goodyear under its own "All Weather" brand. The difference in wholesale prices between these two brands ranged from 29 to 40 per cent in the period 1927–33. At retail, Allstate tires were sold at prices 20 to 25 per cent below those of All Weather tires.[12] The most striking illustrations of the insulation from price competition afforded by brand names are in the drug and cosmetic field. The consumer is almost completely uninformed as to the merits of rival products; few are aware of

---

[12]Federal Trade Commission, Docket No. 2116.

the significance of specifications of the United States Pharmacopoeia. Here, patent-medicine advertising has free rein.

Other devices of sales promotion include personal selling, free distribution of samples of the product, give-away contests (which have gained such great popularity in recent years, especially on nationally televised programs), and other methods, such as the use of coupons exchangeable for other products. With regard to personal selling, it should be noted that some use of salesmen's time is for "production," such as making estimates, giving instruction in the use of the product, handling complaints, and making collections. But it cannot be doubted that the chief use of salesmen is for promotion of demand for the product. As such, personal selling is an alternative or a supplement to other means of sales promotion.

Competition in Services and Other Terms of Trade

Such concessions as freight allowances, discounts, trading stamps, and coupons with definite cash value can be translated in terms of price. There are many terms of trade and collateral services, however, which cannot easily be commuted into price differences. The increased resort to nonprice competition has led many sellers to use "escape devices" in order to attract trade.

The inability of businessmen to compete in price because of legal barriers or because of private price agreements or cartel arrangements has frequently led to ingenious methods of nonprice competition. Under the NRA, when prices were controlled by code provisions, a retail druggist in California, unable to cut prices, employed a medium to give free psychic readings to his customers! An automobile dealer was accused of price cutting because he bought six suits of clothes from a tailor to whom he sold a car.[13] In many cases, of course, the services form an integral and necessary part of the sales transaction. The purchaser of an automobile or household appliance reasonably looks to the manufacturer to maintain adequate facilities for repair and replacement of parts. The conscientious effort made by many sellers of technical goods to supply continuing service for their products bespeaks the importance of this form of nonprice competition. It is to be clearly distinguished from the proliferation of unwanted services which exists in some fields.

---

[13]*Price Behavior and Business Policy,* p. 56.

APPENDIX TO CHAPTER 6: NONPRICE CONCESSIONS

Under the NRA codes, businessmen were frequently forbidden to cut prices. As a result, numerous forms of evasion sprang up. The following list of concessions designed to influence sales was prepared by the Division of Industrial Economics of the National Recovery Administration:

1. Concessions primarily related to the time of buyer's payment:
   Discounts.
   "Terms" and "conditions" of sale or payment.
   Credit practices.
   Credit terms.
   Cash discounts.
   Periods of free credit.
   Interest rate beyond free credit period.
   Datings.
   Seasonal datings.
   Instalment sales.
   Deferred payment.
   Anticipation of bills.
   Sales to delinquent accounts.
   Sales not contingent upon buyer's credit standing.
   Payment due when money received from other sources.
   Retained percentages.

2. Concessions primarily related to risks of buyer:
   Guarantees.
   Price guarantees.
   Contracts for deferred delivery not subject to price change.
   Price offer not subject to change.
   Advance notification of price change.
   Delaying acceptance of order.
   Options.
   Agreements indefinite as to time or quantity.
   Offers without time limit.
   Offers not expiring within specified period of time.
   Offers without withdrawal provisions.
   Guarantees against defective goods.
   Product guarantees.
   Product guarantees against other than defective merchandise.
   Uniform product guarantees specified in code.
   Guarantees in excess of manufacturer's warranty (distributing and fabricating codes).
   Maintenance guarantees.
   Adjusting incorrect shipments.
   Accepting return of merchandise.
   Accepting return of obsolete, discontinued, or "unsalable" merchandise.
   Exchanging merchandise.

Accepting return of other than defective merchandise.
Repurchase agreements.
"Money-back" agreements.
Sales subject to trial.
Sales on approval.
Shipments without order.
Sales on consignment or memorandum.
Storing goods with customer.
Display for direct sale in customer's store.
Renting or leasing industry products.
Resale guarantees.
Agreeing that payment be governed by sales of secondary product.
Accepting orders for specific jobs before customer secures award.
Guaranteeing accounts due customer.
"Compensation of customer for business losses."
Unilateral agreements (buyer not bound).
Contracts containing penalty clauses.
Contracts not subject to adjustment necessitated by noncontrollable factors.
Assuming liability for nonperformance caused by noncontrollable factors.
Assuming liability for damage to buyer's drawings or equipment caused by noncontrollable factors.
Assuming liability for errors in plans or specifications furnished or approved by buyer.
Assuming liability for consequential damages.
Assuming liability for patent infringement.
Failure to give advance notice of discontinued lines.

3. Concessions primarily related to supplying additional goods:[14]
Any gratuities.
Free deals.
Premiums.
Sales of other or additional goods at reduced prices.
Combination sales.
Combination offers.
Coupons.
Samples.
Scrip books.
Prices.
Sales promotion awards.
Containers.
Special containers.
Labels.
Special labels.
Special equipment.

---

[14]To modernize this list, it is important to add trading stamps!

Accessories.

Certain advertising material.

Display materials.

Printed matter (other than advertising material).

4. Concessions rendered buyer through use of seller's employees or property:

Any unusual service.

Providing sales help.

Demonstrating.

Estimating.

Furnishing drawings.

Furnishing plans and specifications.

Furnishing surveys and formulas.

Installation and erection.

Inspections.

Furnishing unusual processing services specified in codes.

Stamping or markings.

Repair and maintenance.

Reconditioning.

Engineering services.

Handling.

Crating or packing.

Repacking.

Delivery service by seller's trucks.

Warehousing and storage.

Lending of equipment.

Permitting retention of trade-in equipment.

5. Concessions rendered buyer through financial assistance or favors:

Favors.

Entertaining.

Patronizing publications in which buyer is interested.

Participating in group showing.

Gifts.

Gifts to organizations (in which buyer is interested).

Paying buyer's personal expenses.

Paying permit or inspection fees of buyers.

Paying customer's insurance.

Paying customer's advertising expenses for products other than member's.

Assuming reversed telephone or telegraph charges.

Assisting customer to obtain used products for trade-ins.

Assisting customer to find purchaser for used products.

Subsidizing or financing buyer.

Employing customers, employees, relatives, associates.

Purchase of buyer's capital stock.

Financing payments due customers.

6. Concessions related to manner and/or time of shipment:

Split shipments.

Shipments smaller than specified minimum.
Tolerance in time of shipment.
Deferred delivery.

7. Concessions through payment or diversion of commissions or fees to customer:

Payment of commissions or fees by members to buyers.
Payment of commissions or fees by members to other than bona fide or controlled sales representatives.
Payment of commissions or fees by members to purchasing agents compensated by buyers.
Payments of commissions or fees by agents of members to buyers.
Splitting of commissions or fees by agents of members with agents of buyers without buyer's knowledge.
Splitting of commissions or fees by members or their agents with buyers or their agents.
Payment of brokerage to other than bona fide brokers.

8. Concessions through allowances or payments for value rendered by buyer:

Allowances.
Trade-in allowances.
Advertising allowances.
Catalogue allowances.
Distribution service allowances.
Container allowances.
Installation allowances.
Allowance for further processing.
Maintenance or repair allowance.
Rental allowances for space hired.
Allowances on supplies furnished by purchaser for production of product ordered.
Cartage allowances when buyer receives goods at factory.
Allowance for special service.
Label allowances.
Purchasing from buyer.
Renting from buyer.

9. Concessions through acceptance of competitor's materials from buyers:

Exchange of own for competitor's products.
Purchase of competitor's products from customer.

10. Concessions through sale of substandard or obsolete goods:

Sale of seconds.
Sale of used goods.
Sale of damaged goods.
Sale of rebuilt or overhauled goods.
Sale of demonstrators.
Sale of obsolete goods.
Sale of discontinued lines.
Willful manufacture of substandard products.
Sale of returns.
Sale of scrap.

Sale of chaff.
Sale of culled goods.
Sale of surplus stock.

11. Concessions granted during performance contrary to provisions of agreement:
    Rebates.
    Departure from credit of contract.
    Settlement of old accounts at less than full value.
    Permitting improper deductions when buyer remits.
    Permitting buyer's cancellation or repudiation.
    Substitution of higher quality or greater quantity of goods.
    Substitution of new contract at lower price.
    Receipting bills before payment.
    Extending or exceeding contract.
    Collateral agreement not to enforce part of contract.
    Departure from delivery date of contract.
    Retroactive settlement or adjustments.

12. Acceptance of forms of payment in which concessions may be concealed:
    Accepting securities.
    Accepting buyer's capital stock.
    Accepting goods from buyer.
    Accepting real or personal property.
    Accepting negotiable instruments.
    Accepting other than lawful money.
    Accepting credit transferred from one buyer to another.
    Selling for customer account and accepting proceeds for credit.
    Accepting form of payment other than specified in code.
    Accepting rental payments as part payment on purchases.
    Accepting deposit made to another manufacturer
    Assignments (of receivables, etc.).

13. Types of agreements, offers, invoicing, etc., by means of which concessions may be concealed:
    Oral agreements.
    Oral offers.
    Oral appraisals.
    Oral orders.
    False billing.
    False orders.
    False receipts.
    False agreements.
    False offers.
    Delayed billing.
    Misdated invoices.
    Misdated contracts.
    Misdated orders.
    Misdated offers.
    Misdated receipts.
    Invoices omitting terms of sale.

Invoices omitting date of shipment.
Invoices omitting specifications.
Invoices omitting other specified detail.
Agreements omitting terms of sale.
Agreements omitting date of shipment.
Agreements omitting specifications.
Agreements omitting other specified detail.
Offers omitting terms of sale.
Offers omitting date of shipment.
Offers omitting specifications.
Offers omitting other specified detail.
Orders omitting terms of sale.
Orders omitting date of shipment.
Orders omitting specifications.
Orders omitting other specified detail.
Split billing.
Lump-sum offers.
Unitemized billing.
Orders not subject to member's acceptance.
Auction sales.

14. Types of agreements, offers, invoicing, etc., primarily designed to prevent the concealing of concessions:
Uniform contract form.
Uniform order form.
Uniform bid or quotation form.
Standard invoice form.
Standard leasing form.
Form of contract.

CASE 6–1:   THE RIVERSIDE METAL COMPANY[15]

On May 9, 1939, Mr. H. L. Randall, president of the Riverside Metal Company of Riverside, New Jersey, submitted the following statement of price policies to the Temporary National Economic Committee: "The price schedules issued by the Riverside Metal Company are contingent upon the prices published by the larger units of the industry. From time to time these larger units publish their scale of prices, and our company has no alternative except to meet such published prices in order to compete."

Beryllium is an element which can be combined with copper, nickel, and certain other metals to produce alloys which possess great qualities of hardness, lightness, and strength. The principal industrial form in which this metal is used is in the alloy, beryllium copper, which consists of about 2 per cent beryllium and 98 per cent copper. The chief

---

[15]Material for this case was derived largely from *T.N.E.C. Hearings,* Part 5, 76th Congress, First Session (Washington, D.C.: U.S. Government Printing Office, 1939.)

advantages of beryllium copper are the combination of extraordinary high-fatigue properties with good electrical conductivity. Beryllium alloys have many industrial uses, such as parts for electric motors, telephone instruments, diamond drills, and airplanes. Altimeters used in airplanes have beryllium copper diaphragms because these are more sensitive than other materials. Beryllium alloys are also used in bushings on machine parts.

Exhibit 1

BERYLLIUM COPPER BASE PRICES, 1935–39

	RIVERSIDE METAL CO.				AMERICAN BRASS CO.		
Date	Sheet	Wire	Rods	Date	Sheet	Wire	Rods
February 25, 1935.....	0.97	1.25	0.97	February 6, 1935....	0.97	1.25	0.97
June 28, 1935.....	0.96	1.24	0.96	June 27, 1935....	0.96	1.24	0.96
August 22, 1935.....	0.96½	1.24½	0.96½	August 20, 1935....	0.96½	1.24½	0.96½
September 19, 1935.....	0.97	1.25	0.97	September 17, 1935....	0.97	1.25	0.97
October 27, 1936.....	0.98	1.26	0.98	October 27, 1936....	0.98	1.26	0.98
November 7, 1936.....	0.98½	1.26½	0.98½	November 7, 1936....	0.98½	1.26½	0.98½
December 15, 1936.....	0.99	1.27	0.99	December 15, 1936....	0.99	1.27	0.99
December 31, 1936.....	1.00	1.28	1.00	December 31, 1936....	1.00	1.28	1.00
January 14, 1937.....	1.01	1.29	1.00	January 14, 1937....	1.01	1.29	1.01
February 16, 1937.....	1.02	1.30	1.02	February 16, 1937....	1.02	1.30	1.02
February 22, 1937.....	1.03	1.31	1.03	February 22, 1937....	1.03	1.31	1.03
March 8, 1937.....	1.05	1.33	1.05	March 8, 1937....	1.05	1.33	1.05
March 31, 1937.....	1.06	1.34	1.06	March 31, 1937....	1.06	1.34	1.06
April 6, 1937.....	1.05	1.33	1.05	April 6, 1937....	1.05	1.33	1.05
April 20, 1937.....	1.04	1.32	1.04	April 20, 1937....	1.04	1.32	1.04
October 26, 1937.....	1.03	1.31	1.03	October 26, 1937....	1.03	1.31	1.03
November 23, 1937.....	1.02	1.30	1.02	November 23, 1937....	1.02	1.30	1.02
January 20, 1938.....	1.12	1.30	1.12	January 20, 1938....	1.12	1.30	1.12
January 28, 1938.....	1.11½	1.29½	1.11½	January 28, 1938....	1.11½	1.29½	1.11½
May 20, 1938.....	1.10½	1.28½	1.10½	May 20, 1938....	1.10½	1.28½	1.10½
July 5, 1938.....	1.11	1.29	1.11	July 5, 1938....	1.11	1.29	1.11
July 25, 1938.....	1.11¼	1.29¼	1.11¼	July 25, 1938....	1.11¼	1.29¼	1.11¼
September 19, 1938.....	1.11½	1.29½	1.11½	September 19, 1938....	1.11½	1.29½	1.11½
October 10, 1938.....	1.11¾	1.29¾	1.11¾	October 10, 1938....	1.11⅞	1.29⅞	1.11⅞
October 13, 1938.....	1.12	1.30	1.12	October 13, 1938....	1.12	1.30	1.12
April 20, 1939.....	1.11	1.29	1.11	April 20, 1939....	1.11	1.29	1.11

Source: *T.N.E.C.*, *Hearings*, Part 5, 76th Congress, First Session (Washington, D.C.: U.S. Government Printing Office, 1939), pp. 2284, 2287–88.

Beryllium metal is derived from beryl oxide-bearing ores, which are refined by a relatively simple process. For technical reasons, refiners sell beryllium in the form of a master alloy, which contains 3.5–5 per cent beryllium, with the remainder copper. Fabricators melt the master alloy and add copper to bring the final beryllium copper alloy to the desired weight, frequently 2 per cent in beryllium content.

In 1939, beryllium master alloy was being produced from ore by two principal companies, the Beryllium Corporation of Reading, Pennsylvania, and the Brush Beryllium Company of Cleveland, Ohio. These companies also fabricated the master alloy into sheets, strips, castings, and other products. Both companies sold master alloy to fabricators of beryllium alloy products. The largest of these fabricators was the American Brass Company of Waterbury, Connecticut. The Riverside Metal Company was one of the smallest fabricating firms in the beryllium alloy industry.

The following testimony from the hearings of the Temporary National Economic Committee[16] describes some aspects of price policies used in the industry (see also Exhibit 1).

MR. COX: You are the president of the Riverside Brass Co.?
MR. RANDALL: Riverside Metal Co.
MR. COX: What is the business of that company?
MR. RANDALL: The business of the Riverside Metal Co. is the fabrication of nonferrous alloys into rod, wire, sheet, and strip. We supply the manufacturer with a raw product.
MR. COX: You buy the master alloy and fabricate the material?
MR. RANDALL: That is correct.

· · · · · · ·

We make nickel silvers, phosphor bronzes, some brass; I think altogether we have an alloy list of over 80 different alloys.
MR. COX: Are all of the alloys which your company makes alloys which are also made and sold by the American Brass Co.?
MR. RANDALL: I think that would be true.
MR. COX: How large a company is your company? Will you give us your capitalization?
MR. RANDALL: Our capitalization is one and a half million dollars, and we are almost the smallest unit in the industry; there may be one or two smaller, but I think we are almost the smallest.
MR. COX: Can you give us any approximate figure to indicate what percentage of the industry your company controls?
MR. RANDALL: Less than one and a half per cent.

· · · · · · ·

MR. COX: From whom do you buy the master alloys?
MR. RANDALL: We buy the master alloys from the Beryllium Products Corporation.
MR. COX: That is Mr. Gahagan?
MR. RANDALL: Mr. Gahagan.
MR. COX: Have you always bought all of your master alloy from that company?
MR. RANDALL: Practically all; yes.

· · · · · · ·

MR. COX: Mr. Randall, would it be correct to say that there is a well crystallized practice of price leadership in the industry in which you are engaged?

[16]*Ibid.*, pp. 2084 ff.

MR. RANDALL: I would say so.

MR. COX: And what company is the price leader?

MR. RANDALL: I would say the American Brass Co. holds that position.

MR. COX: And your company follows the prices which are announced by American Brass?

MR. RANDALL: That is correct.

MR. COX: So that when they reduce the price you have to reduce it too. Is that correct?

MR. RANDALL: Well, we don't have to, but we do.

MR. COX: And when they raise the price you raise the price.

MR. RANDALL: That is correct.

MR. COX: Do you remember that in February 1937, Mr. Gahagan's company reduced the price of the master alloy from $30 to $23 a pound?

MR. RANDALL: I didn't know it at that time.

MR. COX: You did know there was a price decrease.

MR. RANDALL: I do now.

MR. COX: Weren't you buying from Mr. Gahagan?

MR. RANDALL: I think we were buying from them but it was quite some time after that I got the information that the price had gone down.

MR. COX: After that decrease in the price of the master alloy, it is a fact, isn't it, that there was no decrease in price of the fabricated product which you made?

MR. RANDALL: I don't remember about that, I don't know, because I don't know when that decrease took place.

MR. COX: Looking at your sheet prices for the year 1937, you started at $1.01 a pound on January 14, 1937, and rose progressively until you reached $1.06 on March 31, and then on April 6, 1937, they dropped to $1.05. You remember those.

MR. RANDALL: Yes; I remember those. That was copper.

.　.　.　.　.　.　.

MR. COX: But you do know there was about that time a decrease of $7 a pound in the price which you were paying to Mr. Gahagan.

MR. RANDALL: Yes; I do know that.

MR. COX: I will put this question to you, Mr. Randall. Why didn't you reduce the price of the fabricated product following that decrease in the price of the master alloy?

MR. RANDALL: Well, of course I would not make a reduction in the base price of beryllium copper unless the American Brass made a price reduction in beryllium copper.

MR. COX: And the American Brass Co. made no reduction at that time?

MR. RANDALL: If they did, we did, as indicated on that sheet.

MR. COX: Assuming you didn't make a price change then, the reason you didn't was because the American Brass Co. didn't.

MR. RANDALL: That is correct.

MR. ARNOLD: You exercise no individual judgment as to the price you charged for your product, then, in a situation?

MR. RANDALL: Well, I think that is about what it amounts to; yes, sir

MR. ARNOLD: When you say you have to follow, you don't mean anybody told you you had to follow?

MR. RANDALL: No sir; I don't mean that at all.

MR. ARNOLD: But you have a feeling something might happen if you didn't?

MR. RANDALL: I don't know what would happen.

MR. COX: You don't want to find out, do you?

THE CHAIRMAN: Well, as a matter of fact, Mr. Randall, if the American Brass Co. raised the price would the Brass Co. consult you about raising it?

MR. RANDALL: No, sir; not at all.

THE CHAIRMAN: You would, however, follow them without exercising any independent judgment as to whether or not it was desirable.

MR. RANDALL: That is correct.

THE CHAIRMAN: Suppose the American Brass Co. raises its price, but you are satisfied with your output and with the profit that you are making at the old price. Why is it necessary for you to increase your price to your customers, who are already paying you a price sufficient to give you a profit that is satisfactory to you?

MR. RANDALL: I don't know that it is necessary; as a practical matter, if we didn't raise our prices the American Brass Co. or other companies, whoever they might be, would put their price back to where it was.

MR. CHAIRMAN: That wouldn't bother you, because you were making a profit at the old price.

MR. RANDALL: Not on beryllium copper.

THE CHAIRMAN: Why do you do it?

MR. RANDALL: It is the custom of the industry, at least of the smaller companies, to do that.

THE CHAIRMAN: And other small companies do the same thing?

MR. RANDALL: Yes, sir.

THE CHAIRMAN: Is there any reason outside of custom for it?

MR. RANDALL: No, sir.

THE CHAIRMAN: Isn't it likely to reduce the amount of business that you can obtain?

MR. RANDALL: I don't think so.

THE CHAIRMAN: Well, if a competitor raises the price for an identical product, isn't it likely to believe that the producer who does not raise the price would get more business?

MR. RANDALL: I imagine it would, if the other price stayed where it had been raised to. I think that might work out over a period of time.

THE CHAIRMAN: You see, I am trying to get some understanding of the exact reasons why this price policy is followed, and it is not an answer—understand me, I am not criticizing your answer—that carries conviction merely to say it is the custom of the industry. There is a reason for customs. What, in your opinion, is the reason for this custom to follow the leader?

MR. RANDALL: Well, of course, that is a custom which has been prevalent, I think, in the industry for many, many years prior to my entry into it.

THE CHAIRMAN: Oh, yes; we hear a lot about price leadership, but I am trying to get the picture of this practice as you see it, and why you follow it.

MR. RANDALL: Well, I don't think I have ever given the matter very much consideration. We simply, when the new prices come out, print them just as they are. We don't give the matter any consideration. The prices are published and we print those prices.

THE CHAIRMAN: Is there any sort of compulsion, moral or otherwise?

MR. RANDALL: Absolutely none.

THE CHAIRMAN: Do you think it is a good practice?

MR. RANDALL: Well, I have never given the subject very much consideration.

THE CHAIRMAN: Now, of course, it is one of the most important subjects in your business.

MR. RANDALL: Yes; it is, of course.

THE CHAIRMAN: The price that you get for your product.

MR. RANDALL: I can't answer that question. I don't know whether it is a good practice or whether it isn't a good practice. I know that it has been the custom of the industry for years on end, and I know that it is what we do, that's all.

THE CHAIRMAN: A moment ago, in response to either Mr. Cox's question or my question, you answered that if you did not follow the price up, then the American Brass Co. or some other company would come down again.

MR. RANDALL: I don't think I said they would. I said they probably would or they might. I don't know what they would do.

THE CHAIRMAN: Then I made the comment that that would not be a disturbing result, because it would mean merely the restoration of the old price. I could imagine, however, that you might start a price war, and that the other companies might go below you. Is there a possibility that that is what you have in mind??

MR. RANDALL: I didn't have it in mind until this moment. That is a possibility; yes.

THE CHAIRMAN: So you want the committee to understand that so far as you and your company are concerned, this price-leadership question is one to which you have never given any real consideration, and you have boosted your prices along with the American Brass Co. just as a matter of custom?

MR. RANDALL: Yes.

. . . .

MR. ARNOLD: . . . but if this policy is continued, you will continue to follow the American Brass regardless of what your costs are, won't you, so that won't be an element in the picture?

MR. RANDALL: Of course, to be perfectly frank, on that subject we don't know what our costs are on beryllium.

MR. ARNOLD: It wouldn't make any difference if you did, so far as the present prices are concerned, would it?

MR. RANDALL: No, sir; I don't think it would.

MR. ARNOLD: In other words, there is a situation here where there is a lot of competitors and no competition.

MR. RANDALL: Well, we simply, as I said before, follow the prices that are published, and that is what we have been doing for a good many years.

. . . .

At the conclusion of Mr. Randall's testimony, Mr. John A. Coe, Jr., general sales manager of the American Brass Company, was called to the stand. His testimony follows:

MR. COX: What is the nature of the business of the American Brass Co.?

MR. COE: The American Brass Co. is engaged in the production of copper, brass, bronze, and nickel silver in wrought forms, including sheet, wire, rods and tubes and other fabricated forms.

MR. COX: What is the capitalization of the company?

MR. COE: The American Brass Co. is a wholly owned fabricating subsidiary. of the Anaconda Copper Mining Co.

MR. COX: Can you tell us what the capitalization of the company is?

MR. COE: I do not know what it is.

MR. COX: You heard Mr. Randall testify that his company did less than 1½ per cent of the business in which he was engaged. Can you give us any approximate figure as to the percentage of the business which your company does?

MR. COE: Approximately 25 per cent.

·   ·   ·   ·   ·   ·   ·

MR. COX: You heard Mr. Randall's testimony with respect to the system of price leadership which prevails.

MR. COE: Yes.

MR. COX: Would you agree with his description of that system insofar as it denoted your company as the price leader?

MR. COE: I wouldn't agree with that statement.

MR. COX: You wouldn't agree with the statement?

MR. COE: No.

MR. COX: In other words, it is your position that your company is not the price leader in the industry?

MR. COE: We are not the price leader of the industry.

MR. COX: It is a fact, is it not, that your prices for beryllium copper have been substantially the same as those of Mr. Randall for a period between 1934 and the present time?

MR. COE: So far as I know, they have been practically the same.

MR. COX: Practically the same prices. Now, you say you are not the price leader. Is there any price leader in the industry?

MR. COE: There is none.

MR. COX: Then how do you explain the fact that the prices are the same?

MR. COE: We publish our prices; they are public information; anybody who wishes to, may follow those prices at his own discretion.

MR. ARNOLD: They all wish to apparently, don't they?

MR. COE: They do not, sir.

MR. ARNOLD: You mean they have not been following those prices?

MR. COE: On our product they have not, sir.

MR. ARNOLD: I got the impression, I may be wrong, that the prices of competitors and your prices have been substantially identical.

MR. COE: To some extent they have been identical. There are always variations in many prices.

MR. ARNOLD: You said that anyone who wish to might follow. Some of them certainly wish to.

MR. COE: Some of them do wish to.

MR. ARNOLD: And some of them did follow.

MR. COE: That is correct.

MR. ARNOLD: And therefore to that extent you have been the leader.

MR. COE: To some extent we have been the leader in that we have put out our prices. However, others have put out prices and we have followed them at times.

MR. ARNOLD: What other companies would you put in the position of price leadership aside from your own?

MR. COE: Practically any member of the industry.

MR. COX: Including Mr. Randall?

MR. COE: Including Mr. Randall.

. . . .

MR. ARNOLD: I take it that the prices are fixed generally by someone following someone else, and that sometimes they follow you and other times you follow others.

MR. COE: May I ask what you mean by "fixed"? We publish our prices; they become our prices; they are public information. In that way the prices of the American Brass Co. are fixed by us.

MR. ARNOLD: Then you understand what we mean by "fixed" and I repeat my question: Is it true that prices are fixed in this industry either by someone following you or by your following others?

MR. COE: Not in all respects. Many times we do not follow others in all respects; many times they do not follow us in all respects.

MR. ARNOLD: But there is a following on the part of the various companies in the industry?

MR. COE: A general following; yes, sir.

THE CHAIRMAN: Not that you impose your ideas as to what the price should be upon anybody else, or that anybody else imposes it upon you, but when any company makes a change in price, the tendency is for all to follow that change?

MR. COE: That is the tendency.

THE CHAIRMAN: And how long has that been the system?

MR. COE: As far back as I have been with the company that has been in vogue; water seeking its own level.

. . . .

THE CHAIRMAN: What factors go into the determination of the price?

MR. COE: The cost of our raw metals going into the alloys, plus our manufacturing differentials. The latter is determined by our price committee.

THE CHAIRMAN: And if the price of the raw material should go down, then one would naturally expect the price of the finished product to go down, unless there was some countervailing change in some other factor?

MR. COE: There are other factors to be taken into consideration; yes, sir.

THE CHAIRMAN: Well, now, would you say that the price fluctuates in the same degree that the price of these countervailing or these other factors fluctuate?

MR. COE: That is a difficult question to answer. I don't quite know what you mean by that.

THE CHAIRMAN: Well, I tried to make it simple. The price of the finished product would naturally, one would suppose, depend upon the cost of the various factors which go into making the finished product?

MR. COE: That is correct.

THE CHAIRMAN: Well, now, do you want the committee to understand that always the price of the finished product is determined by these other factors and by no other consideration?

MR. COE: The price is determined by the price of raw materials going into those products, plus our cost of manufacturing.

THE CHAIRMAN: Yes; those are the other factors?

MR. COE: Those are the other factors.

THE CHAIRMAN: And there is no other consideration that goes into the determination of the price?

MR. COE: That is correct.

THE CHAIRMAN: And how about this leadership, why do you follow somebody else's lead sometimes?

MR. COE: We can get no more for our product than other people can get for theirs; will charge for theirs.

THE CHAIRMAN: Here is another outfit which is supposedly competing with you, which is not as efficient as you are, and therefore which finds for example that there is a much heavier plant charge, let us say; therefore, it is not able to produce this finished product at as low a price as you, and because it doesn't produce it at as low a price as you, it has to raise the price, but according to your testimony when such a company raises the price, then you follow and raise your price, although your costs have not changed.

MR. COE: We have not necessarily raised our price.

THE CHAIRMAN: Oh, now, let's drop the world "necessarily." You have just said that you have done that and that other companies follow you occasionally. Now, Mr. Coe, we are merely trying to get the facts here; we are not laying the basis for a case against the American Brass Co. I am trying to get through my mind this picture of price leadership in industry.

Now, you have told us as explicitly as it can be told that in some cases other companies in the same business as you follow the price that you fix, and you have told us how you determine that price, and then you say in other instances you followed the price of other companies, and when you do that necessarily you do it upon factors that are not reflected in your business, but on factors that are reflected in the business of the company which raises the price. Now why do you do it?

MR. COE: We can get as much for our product as any competitor can get for his product.

THE CHAIRMAN: Now we are getting somewhere. If some other company raises the price and is getting that price, then you think you had better come up and equalize it?

MR. COE: I feel that our product is as good as any made by the industry.

THE CHAIRMAN: It may be better.

MR. COE: I hope it is.

THE CHAIRMAN: But the point in determining the price thing is that you base it not upon the actual costs of manufacture in your plants, but upon the highest charge that anybody in the industry makes by and large, isn't that the effect of this price leadership policy?

MR. COE: It is usually predicated on the lowest price that anybody makes.

THE CHAIRMAN: Well, of course, there was an old familiar saying that the price the companies charge is what the traffic will bear. Now isn't that the motto which guides those who follow the practice of price leadership?

MR. COE: It depends on what you mean by "traffic." Of course we have to compete with many other things besides brass and copper.

THE CHAIRMAN: Well, would you say the American Brass Co. puts its product out at the lowest possible price, bearing in mind all of these factors of cost?

MR. COE: It is necessary when we get our products to the ultimate consumer as low as we reasonably can, and still at a fair margin of profit, in order that we will not be—that our products will not be supplanted by substitutes.

THE CHAIRMAN: But under this plan of price leadership, is it not inevitable that the tendency would be to raise the price so as to cover the cost of the less efficient member of the industry?

MR. COE: The tendency has been just the opposite. The tendency has been to lower the price.

QUESTIONS

1. Was the price policy of the Riverside Metal Company based on sound economic reasoning? What assumptions about retaliation had Mr. Randall made—to a price set above that posted by American Brass? To a price set below that of American Brass?

2. Can you suggest an alternative price policy that might prove more profitable for the Riverside Metal Company?

CASE 6-2:   BILLINGS BAKERY SUPPLY COMPANY

The Billings Bakery Supply Company was a wholesaler of several thousand items which it distributed to about two thousand bakeries and meat packers throughout the nation. In addition to the thousands of items the company jobbed, it also owned and operated its own manufacturing facilities where it made bakers' and butchers' garments, etc., which it also distributed.

The company distributed its products (and the products it wholesaled) through approximately forty full-time salesmen. The salesmen were paid straight commission based on a percentage of the gross profit.

Competition was intense. Most of the items that Billings did not manufacture were also sold by competitive wholesalers. It was not unusual for five or more wholesalers to be calling on the same bakery selling the identical item. Therefore the three major factors determining what company received the order were the salesman's personality, service, and price. In the garment line, different product features constituted a basis for securing sales.

In early 1963 the sales manager of the Billings Company reviewed the results of two significant price cuts that had been made on July 1, 1962. A stainless steel 10-inch pan had been cut in price from $2.40 to $1.80 a unit, while the entire garment line had been reduced in price by 6 per cent. This meant that the price for the 48-inch, 8-ounce drill apron, a particular item whose sales figures he was examining, went down from $16.00 to $15.04 a dozen.

10-Inch Stainless Steel Baking Pan

For the past twenty years, Billings had sold a well-known and highly respected line of stainless steel ware manufactured by the Simpson Company, which was also carried by the majority of Billings' competitors. In January of 1962 a competitor of the Simpson Company (the Turner Company) had approached Billings and had asked the firm if it would be interested in a 10-inch stainless steel pan that it could sell for 25 per cent less than Simpson's (with an equal or greater profit). The Billings management was pessimistic that Turner could duplicate Simpson's pan, but gave Turner a sample of the 10-inch pan, which Turner did duplicate. On July 1, 1962, the Billings salesmen started selling the new 10-inch pan, stressing the fact that it was "identical with Simpson's, for 25 per cent less." Competition, for the six-month period that Billings had the new 10-inch pan, continued as before, with no price change in the company's stainless steel lines. Exhibit 1 shows the unit sales of the 10-inch pan (both Simpson's and Turner's) from July 1, 1961, to December 31, 1962.

Sales in July and August, 1962, were probably abnormally high because of heavy promotional activities along with the price reduction.

48-Inch, 8-Ounce Drill Apron

It had been felt that the garments manufactured by Billings were relatively price-elastic, and that a price reduction would greatly increase sales as well as over-all net earnings. Therefore, on July 1, 1962, the entire garment line was reduced approximately 6 per cent. One major competitor made an equivalent price cut, and another introduced a modified line at about the same time.

Exhibit 1

UNIT SALES OF 10-INCH STAINLESS STEEL PAN

From July 1, 1961, to December 31, 1962

SIMPSON PAN AT $2.40		TURNER PAN AT $1.80	
Date	Unit Sales	Date	Unit Sales
1961:		1962:	
July	54	July	1,100
August	59	August	1,008
September	49	September	950
October	66	October	595
November	60	November	550
December	47	December	577
1962:			
January	61		
February	80		
March	51		
April	58		
May	72		
June	42		

Exhibit 2

1962 SALES FOR 48-INCH, 8-OUNCE DRILL APRON

PRICE AT $16.00		PRICE AT $15.04	
Month	Sales (in Dozens)	Month	Sales (in Dozens)
January	116	July	54
February	76	August	68
March	90	September	84
April	75	October	51
May	53	November	69
June	52	December	103

Exhibit 2 shows the year's sales for the 48-inch apron—the six months before the price reduction and the six months after. No seasonal had been observed in past years' sales, other than that both January and December sales ran about 35 per cent above those of other months.

QUESTIONS

1. What are the indicated price elasticities for the pans and for the aprons? What factors might explain the great difference?

2. What working hypotheses might the sales manager formulate from this experience to guide future price experimentation?

CASE 6–3:   UNITED STATES STEEL AND THE 1957 AND 1962 STEEL PRICE INCREASES

In the seventeen years following the Second World War, public concern over the price of steel was virtually an annual event. There were six industry-wide strikes; and even in the years in which wage settlements were reached without a strike, a steel price rise almost invariably following an upward wage adjustment made the headlines. The brunt of much of the criticism fell upon the United States Steel Corporation. Although, by the 1960's, it controlled little over a quarter of the industry's capacity, far below the three-quarter share shortly after its formation in 1903 and the approximately 50 per cent it held in 1920, it remained "Big Steel," the giant of the industry, the only truly national steel manufacturer, and the traditional price leader. It bore the brunt of both inaugurating and defending the price increase in 1957 and the abortive increase in 1962, which are discussed below. Before examining these two periods, it is important to look at the situation in the early postwar period, when the adequacy of steel capacity was at least as pressing a question as the increases in steel price.

The Capacity Question (1947–50)

Controversy between the steel industry and the government regarding the former's productive capacity was not new; nor had either party maintained, through the years, a consistent view of the situation. In 1940, for example, the Federal Trade Commission reported: "There appears to be a tendency for obsolete mills to survive after new and more efficient plants have entered the field, resulting in excess capacity. . . ."[17]

As things turned out, steel capacity was expanded by approximately 14 million tons, or 17 per cent, during the period 1940–45. Nevertheless, following World War II, shortages of steel existed and provoked

---

[17]*The Basing Point Problem*, TNEC Monograph No. 42, 77th Congress, First Session (Washington, D.C.: U.S. Government Printing Office, 1941), p. 3.

further debate. In May, 1947, Walter S. Tower, President of the American Iron and Steel Institute, expressed a cautious attitude and claimed that existing capacity was adequate for both the domestic and the export markets. He recalled that in 1921 the industry had operated at about 35 per cent of capacity and implied that the future might hold a cutback almost as severe.

Wilfred Sykes, then President of Inland Steel Company, asserted in June, 1947, that current steel capacity would be adequate for all potential demands. He supported his statement by the use of estimates based on per capita steel consumption during the peak year 1929, census estimates by the Bureau of the Census, and allowance for export purposes.

Conversely, Louis H. Bean, a government economist, recommended that steel production be increased from the indicated 85 million ton production for 1947 to between 100 and 110 million tons in order to bring about prosperity and full employment through the period 1947–50.

Representatives of labor likewise expressed their views that additional steel capacity was needed. Walter P. Reuther, President of the United Automobile Workers, CIO, and Otis Brubaker, Director of Research, United Steelworkers of America, condemned the pessimistic attitude of the steel industry toward increasing production. Mr. Reuther declared that it was "a program of planned scarcity plainly calculated to enhance profits and to fortify their monopoly hold over this basic industry."[18] Both Mr. Reuther and Mr. Brubaker endorsed the findings of Mr. Bean and presented other data which indicated steel requirements to be between 100 and 110 million tons in order to maintain full employment between 1947 and 1950. Moreover, Mr. Reuther recommended that if the steel industry could not or would not equip itself to produce the steel required for full employment, the government should see that the steel was produced.

On October 13, 1950, shortly after the intervention in Korea, C. Girard Davidson, Assistant Secretary of the Interior, claimed that a 10 per cent expansion planned by the steel industry, to be completed by the end of 1952, would not be enough to meet normal civilian and military requirements and that the steel industry should increase capacity 25 to 30 per cent. Mr. Davidson stated that the "timidity of the

---

[18]Special Committee to Study Problems of American Small Business, *Steel Supply and Distribution Problems,* Interim Report, 80th Congress, Second Session, Senate Report No. 825 (Washington, D.C.: U.S. Government Printing Office, 1948), p. 29.

steel men could drive us into the kind of economic bust which continued inadequacy of steel inevitably brings. . . . Their shortsightedness could limit our economic power to meet military needs."[19]

On October 26, Edward L. Ryerson, Chairman of the Board of Inland Steel Company, gave an address at the business forum of the American Society of Metals at the 1950 Metal Congress and Exposition. He termed Mr. Davidson's proposals "sheer nonsense."[20] Mr. Ryerson went on to state that such proposals are establishing the pattern for the drive to nationalize the steel industry and that Mr. Davidson showed a complete lack of knowledge of steel industry operations in making such a proposal. Mr. Ryerson pointed out some of the difficulties in obtaining manpower, material, and capital for expansion and stated that it would take five years for shipbuilding facilities on the Great Lakes to build ore boats to transport the ore for a 20 million ton expansion in steel.

Following Mr. Ryerson's address, and in the same forum program, Mr. Charles Wilson, of General Motors, paused at the end of his formal address and stated that he could not resist the temptation to answer the challenge presented by Mr. Ryerson. Mr. Wilson said that the current shortage of steel resulted from failure of the industry to appraise the true growth of America. He claimed that the steel industry had made two basic mistakes: failure to consider (1) the postwar expansion in employment to 60 million persons and the market for goods thus created and (2) the growth in other industries. Mr. Wilson stated that steel capacity is now about eight times what it was in 1900. Meanwhile, he said, the oil industry has expanded from a 65 million barrel to a two billion barrel industry; the electrical industries expanded twenty times; and automobile output this year would be two thousand times larger. Mr. Wilson urged steel executives to "get the dust out of their eyes and go ahead with the rest of us."[21]

Mr. Ryerson answered Mr. Wilson's charge by pointing to the current expansion program of the steel industry for increasing capacity to 110 million tons by the end of 1952. This expansion program was planned so as to have a minimum impact on normal production. A major increase in capacity required substantial amounts of steel for ore

[19]"Boost Steel Capacity 25%—Davidson," *Chicago Journal of Commerce,* October 14, 1950, p. 1.
[20]"Ryerson Labels Davidson's Steel Proposal Sheer Nonsense," *Iron Age,* November 2, 1950, p. 108.
[21]"Wilson Steel Criticism Draws Fire," *Chicago Journal of Commerce,* October 30, 1950, p. 1.

Exhibit 1

STEEL INGOT CAPACITY AND PRODUCTION

Summary, 1921–45

Years	Capacity, January 1* (Millions of Tons)	Production for Period (Millions of Tons)	Per Cent of Capacity Operated for Period†	Low and High Years
1921–30................	64–73	478	70.6	34.5 (1921)—88.5 (1929)
1931–40................	77–82	399	50.5	19.5 (1932)—82.1 (1940)
1941–45................	85–96	427	94.3	63.5 (1945)—98.1 (1943)

*Given for first and last year of period.
†Calculated as ratio of sum of annual productions over sum of annual capacities.

By Years, 1946–58

Years	Capacity, January 1 (Millions of Tons)	Production (Millions of Tons)	Per Cent Capacity Operated	Years	Capacity, January 1 (Millions of Tons)	Production (Millions of Tons)	Per Cent Capacity Operated
1946................	92	66.6	72.5	1953................	117	111.6	94.9
1947................	91	88.9	93.0	1954................	124	88.3	71.0
1948................	94	88.6	94.1	1955................	126	117.0	93.0
1949................	96	77.9	81.0	1956................	128	115.2	89.8
1950................	99	96.8	96.9	1957................	133	112.7	84.4
1951................	104	105.2	100.9	1958................	141	85.3	60.5
1952................	108	93.2	85.8				

Source: Computed from annual statistical reports of the American Iron and Steel Institute.

boats and plant facilities. To rush the program would result in immediate shortages of some types of steel.

In November, 1950, the government passed a bill which permitted a sixty-month amortization for tax purposes of the cost of defense facilities. The steel companies were able to qualify for much of their expansion under these provisions. As may be noted in Exhibit 1, the expansion of capacity in the five years following January 1, 1951, of 24 million tons doubled that of the preceding five years, and an even higher rate continued in 1956 and 1957.

UNITED STATES STEEL AND THE 1957 PRICE INCREASE

In the spring of 1957 the issue of the prospective change in steel prices was a matter of widespread interest. It was generally conceded that the key decision would be made by U.S. Steel, whose price lists usually were accepted by the rest of the industry. Under a three-year contract with the steelworkers, signed after the strike in 1956, U.S. Steel (and most of the firms) faced wage increases and fringe benefits estimated by the union at 16.4 cents an hour and by the company at 20–21 cents an hour, to go into effect on July 1, 1957.

Both in steel and in the economy the over-all picture had been one of price rises and at the same time a leveling-off of production. The rate of steel operations had already tapered off somewhat, and the outlook was for a further drop. Nevertheless, steel profits were running at record levels. The consumer price index had broken out of the narrow range between 113 and 115, where it had remained from late 1951 through early 1956, and risen steadily for a year, causing considerable public concern.

Among the groups appealing to U.S. Steel to hold the price line were labor unions, customers, the administration, and Congress. On the other side, competing steel companies expressed hopes for a price rise much larger than the one U.S. Steel announced on July 1 (the rise represented a $6.00 per ton average increase in steel base prices, or about 4 per cent).

Customers' Criticism.   The reaction of some customers to a steel price rise in early 1957 is indicated in the following quotation:

The National Assn. of Furniture Manufacturers chided the steel industry for raising prices. It demanded that steel leaders and other top executives "exhibit a higher degree of statesmanship."

In a strongly worded telegram signed by John M. Snow, executive vice-president, the organization said it felt "grave concern" over announced and proposed price hikes on basic wire, spring wire and other steel used in furniture making.

The telegram reminded the steelmen that President Eisenhower wants prices held down.

The additional costs will have to be passed on to consumers, "thereby preventing an important segment of our population from sharing fully in America's steadily improving standard of living," the telegram said.

It was sent to United States Steel Corp. . . .[22]

The Position of the Administration.   The administration had urged restraint in the *Economic Report of the President for 1957:*

Specifically, business and labor leadership have the responsibility to reach agreements on wages and other labor benefits that are fair to the rest of the community as well as to those persons immediately involved. Negotiated wage increases and benefits should be consistent with productivity prospects and with the maintenance of a stable dollar. And businesses must recognize the broad public interest in the prices set on their products and services.

On June 27, 1957, the American public read the reports of a press conference held by the President of the United States on the preceding day. The President expressed the view that control of inflation cannot be solely a governmental function:

The only point I make is this: Government, no matter what its policies, cannot, of itself, make certain of the soundness of the dollar, that is, the stability of the purchasing power of the dollar in this country. There must be statesmanlike action, both by business and labor.

Frankly, I believe that boards of directors of business, of business organizations, should take under the most serious consideration any thought of a price rise and should approve it only when they can see that it is absolutely necessary in order to continue to get the kind of money they need for the expansion demanded in this country.[23]

The Congressional Hearings

Congress had threatened an investigation of the steel price-profit pictures after steel had raised its prices in 1956, and it was a dead certainty that it would investigate this time. The only question was what committee, and Senator Kefauver's Antitrust and Monopoly Committee took on the job in August, 1957. The top management of United States Steel journeyed to Washington en masse. Other steel firms, union leaders, and economists also testified. Excerpts from the testimony follow.

---

[22]*Chicago Sun-Times,* March 4, 1957.
[23]*New York Times,* June 27, 1957.

Opening Statement of Roger M. Blough, Chairman of United States Steel

[*Learning Three Important Truths from a "Noble Experiment."*] Possibly some of you gentlemen may recall that several years ago—on May 1, 1948, to be exact—United States Steel tried to lend what weight it could toward slowing down the inflation that was then running riot. And possibly you recall, too, the result of that experiment. If not, let me refresh your memory.

In the previous year, 1947, the Cost of Living Index had jumped 14½ per cent above the level of the year before. That was the largest annual increase ever recorded since the First World War period; and it is interesting to note, in passing, that this 14½ per cent rise in that one year was more than 3½ times as great as the total increase that has occurred in the past three years put together. We were deeply concerned about inflation—as we still are—for among the industrial population of America, the steel industry has been one of the principal victims of inflation. It was a major problem for our company and we decided to do something about it if we could.

Fortunately, we had a unique opportunity to do so, for under the terms of our contract with the union that year, our workers could seek a wage increase; but they could not strike to obtain it.

So instead of granting the union's demand for higher wages, we determined to reduce the price of our products by $25 millions—or an average of about $1.25 per ton. Reductions on individual products ranged from $1 to $5 per ton and applied particularly to those steel products which we hoped would bear most directly upon the cost of living—the kinds of steel, in short, that go into automobiles, household appliances, tin cans, roofing and siding for buildings and various wire products such as nails, wire netting and fencing.

Now remember, please, that at this time steel prices were already lagging far behind other prices generally. From 1940 to May of 1948, they had advanced only 40 per cent; while the price index of all commodities had gone up 2½ times as much; food products, 3½ times as much, and farm products more than four times as much as steel.

But still, we cut our prices, and in announcing this price reduction, Benjamin Fairless—then President of the Corporation—made a statement which sounded very much like some of those we hear today. He said:

"We in United States Steel believe that costs and prices in general are too high today for the good of the nation. We are firmly of the conviction that American industry and labor should cooperatively do everything in their power to avoid further increases in costs, which—if permitted to occur—must result in higher prices for almost everything we buy. Certainly the best interests of all of our people will not be served by a further lowering in the purchasing power of the dollar."

Mr. Fairless went on to express the hope that our action would have a "beneficial effect throughout the nation," and that it might help to bring "an early stabilization or reduction in the cost of living." But he also made it clear that if costs and wages continued to move forward elsewhere on a broad front, we would have to rescind our price cut and grant wage increases in fairness to our employees.

I'm sure you all know what happened. Other unions demanded another big round of wage increases—and got them. Other companies had to raise prices to pay for them. Our costs kept soaring skyward. We might as well have tried to stop an express train with a peashooter. So three months later, we had to rescind our price action, increase the pay of our workers, and try to catch up with the parade that we had fallen so far behind.

This "noble experiment," however, was not a total loss for it taught us three important truths that I hope may someday be widely understood: First that no one company, no one industry, and no one union can alone stop the march of inflation. Second that neither the steel industry or any other industry ever sets the wage pattern in America; for the post-war wage pattern has been a never-ending spiral in which each industry, in its turn, is called on to pay a little more than the preceding industry did, and the next industry must then pay a little more than that. And third, we learned from the stark statistical evidence, that a cut in steel prices produces no discernible or identifiable effect upon the cost of living. The actual mathematical facts may interest you. . . .

And so, Mr. Chairman, if we are going to investigate steel prices at this hearing, by all means let us investigate steel prices; but in so doing let us not delude ourselves or anyone else into the notion that we are thereby striking at the roots of inflation!

[*Five Costly Strikes in Last Eleven Years.*] I am aware, of course, that U.S. Steel is often blamed for wage inflation. It is said that we do not really fight against uneconomic wage increases, because we can easily pass them along to our customers. And it has been suggested to this committee that we be barred by law from raising prices following a wage increase—the supposition being, presumably, that we will thus be forced to resist the union more strongly.

The real point is this: To enforce what we regard as inflationary wage demands, the union has struck our plants five times in the past eleven years; and we have taken these costly strikes in an effort to hold the line against inflation. But hardly has one of these strikes begun before there is a nationwide demand that we settle it. Our customers must have steel or close their plants. Their employees face layoffs and loss of pay. The Government, too, must have steel; and daily the pressures upon us keep building up. And ultimately—if we do not settle—we may face the threat of government intervention, as happened five years ago when the then President of the United States seized our plants illegally and sought to grant the union demands in full.

In our most recent negotiation last year—after a five-week strike—we signed a labor agreement. It was that labor agreement which foreordained our recent price increase.

Under that three-year labor agreement, we hoped to narrow at least slightly the inflationary gap between our rapidly-mounting wage costs and our slowly-rising output per man hour. Only time can tell if what we did represented progress.

On July 1 of this year we faced what our recent total wage-cost history demonstrates was about a 6½ per cent increase in our total costs per man hour; and to cover these costs in part, we raised our steel prices by an average of 4 per cent.

This action of ours was promptly denounced on the floors of Congress and elsewhere as being "irresponsible" and contrary to the "public interest."

[*Meeting Responsibilities Depends upon Extent of Profits.*] Now if the popular thing to do were always the responsible thing to do, a businessman's lot would be a much happier one—and so, I suspect, would a Senator's. There is no doubt that the *popular* thing for U.S. Steel to have done would have been to permit its mounting costs to rise, uncompensated, and thus to endanger not only the financial strength of the company, but also the jobs of its employees, and even, perhaps, the security of the nation. But would that have been the *responsible* thing to do; and would it have been in the public interest?

You see, United States Steel, like any other enterprise, has many responsibilities which must be weighed not only in the light of present day pressures, but also in the light of long-range necessities. One of these is our obligation to our shareowners, who are widely assumed to be people of great wealth—people who do not really need their dividends anyway.

But a survey which we took among them four years ago showed that more than half of these stockholders had incomes of less than $4,500 a year, and many of them had less than $2,000.

But entirely apart from its obligations to its owners, United States Steel has grave, long-range responsibilities to the nation as a whole—responsibilities which are continuously taxing its financial resources—and the extent of United States Steel's ability to meet these responsibilities is directly dependent on the extent of its profits.

In the face of inadequate depreciation allowances, it is reinvesting a substantial part of its profits in the replacement of obsolete and worn out equipment in order to remain efficient and productive, and to hold costs and prices down. No one will doubt that that is a part of our responsibility.

As an important industrial unit, research—regardless of how costly it is— is also a part of our responsibility. And we believe our new research center at Monroeville, Pennsylvania, is further evidence of our efforts to carry out that responsibility. In our laboratories there, we are seeking to develop new steels that will withstand—as no other metal can—the terrific heats that will be generated by atmospheric friction in the supersonic planes of the future. There, too, we are engaged in a program of fundamental research designed to extend man's knowledge of the iron atom, and to discover—as scientists believe they may—a metal twice as strong as any now existing in the world.

Beyond all that there is the ever-present need for new steelmaking capacity so that the economic growth and security of this nation may never be jeopardized by the lack of steel. To play our full part in maintaining an adequate steel supply is—we believe—a compelling responsibility. That is our business, and there is no better reason for our existence.

But no one of these responsibilities is possible of fulfillment by a profit-starved industry, or by a company suffering from financial malnutrition.

Questioning of Mr. Blough by Senator Kefauver[24]

The most difficult question for Mr. Blough to answer in the administered prices hearings came in an exchange covering six pages, of which the following is an excerpt. Senator Kefauver had just finished mentioning that "President Eisenhower publicly expressed the hope that industry and labor would hold back on wage and price increases. . . ."

SENATOR KEFAUVER: Let us examine that a little further, Mr. Blough. Why did you not raise your prices $10? There were such rumors.

MR. BLOUGH: A moment ago, Senator, you permitted me to proceed with a further examination of your statement. Now I would like very much to do that. I am trying to do this in an orderly fashion, and I will be very happy to go into the question which you are now asking at a later time.

SENATOR KEFAUVER: Mr. Blough, just one question I asked you: It was rumored that you might raise your price $10 a ton, or $12, or some other price, and I said on the radio and television I thought you had taken some heed of President Eisenhower and his public statements. Why did you not raise your price $10 or some other figure?

MR. BLOUGH: I suppose that we will either have to do one thing or another. We will either have to explain the whole story about our price increase or we will have to go on with the further examination of your statement. I will try to give you an adequate answer.

SENATOR KEFAUVER: I won't go into details, but you could have raised it to $7 or $8 or $9 or $10 or some other figure.

MR. BLOUGH: Last week there was an editorial in the—

SENATOR KEFAUVER: Mr. Blough, just answer that question and then we will pass on to whatever else you want to.

MR. BLOUGH: I was answering it, Senator, in my way. The editorial said that the Kefauver committee was laying a trap for us, and that was the trap that they were laying for us, that very question.

SENATOR KEFAUVER: What editorial, Mr. Blough?

MR. BLOUGH: It was an editorial in one of the New York newspapers. I'll be glad to furnish it for the record.

. . . .

SENATOR KEFAUVER: Mr. Blough, I want to say to you and whoever wrote the article we are not laying a trap for anybody.

. . . .

SENATOR KEFAUVER: We have tried to give you a chance to be heard fully yesterday, to read your statement, and we want to give you a chance to be heard fully, but we want to ask some questions. My question, that you have

---

[24]*Administered Prices,* Hearings before Senate Subcommittee on Antitrust and Monopoly, 85th Congress, First Session (Washington, D.C.: U.S. Government Printing Office, 1957), Part 2, pp. 227–29. The statements of the steel company and union executives were submitted in the same hearings and are reproduced from U.S. Steel and United Steelworkers releases.

not answered yet, was about raising of price. You raised the price $6 a ton and you could have raised it $8, $9, $7, or $10. Last year you raised it $8.50.

MR. BLOUGH: In the light of all the factors it was our judgment that the price that we raised steel on July 1 was approximately the price at which it could have been properly raised at that time, and I want to make it clear that what I am now indicating to you will be fully explained in our future testimony.

. . . . . .

SENATOR KEFAUVER: We will get it before us later on, but I am asking you a simple question. We have it here and I will read it over. If in your judgment of the facts, you decided $7, $8, $9 or—

MR. BLOUGH: I think my answer to that is that I don't know.

SENATOR KEFAUVER: You don't know whether you could have raised it $8 or $9.

MR. BLOUGH: I think that is the only proper answer to that question.

SENATOR KEFAUVER: Suppose, in your judgment, you thought that $7.50 was the right price, do you have the power or could you have raised the price of steel of your company $7.50?

MR. BLOUGH: I will have to answer that the same way, that I am not sure that I can give you a categorical answer to that question.

The Cost Facts of United States Steel—Statement of Robert C. Tyson, Chairman of Finance Committee, United States Steel (Excerpts)

Besides Mr. Blough, many other U.S. Steel executives testified: President Hood on "Closing the New Inflationary Gap," Vice President Austin on "The Role of Research," Vice President Cooper on "Productivity in U.S. Steel," etc. Mr. Tyson's major conclusion, that absorbing costs would be disastrous, follows.

According to the Bureau of Labor Statistics, steel prices in 1955 averaged 7.8 per cent less than they did in 1956. Taking that percentage off of our 1956 sales would reduce them and the tax base by $330 million. This would cause a drop in our income taxes from $331 million to $159 million, thus more than cutting them in half. There would also be a drop in our dividends, in our income reinvested, or in both from a total of $348 million to $190 million, that is, from 8.2 per cent of sales to 4.9 per cent. If profits were to continue to shrink at this pace it would be little more than another year before they were entirely wiped out, and all income taxes with them. After that the Treasury would have to look elsewhere for taxes, stockholders would be entirely without dividends, industries supplying us with tools of production would have to look elsewhere for orders to replace those lost from us, deterioration in the tools of production would supersede the modernization and expansion out of which comes increased productivity, the jobs of our own employes would become endangered, no one would lend money to the industry, and certainly no one would buy new stock in it—and, finally and ironically, the price of steel, after this brief interruption, would again have to march upward at the cost inflation rate just to keep on breaking even. So the technical answer to whether rising costs can be absorbed without a price increase is, "Yes—for some companies for a brief and disastrous period." But I submit that there is no good purpose served in so doing. The evil in this matter is the basic cost inflation; once it has happened the alternatives are to try to keep productive America functioning with cost-covering price increases, or to head it towards the insolvency that no one really wants. . . .

In conclusion, gentlemen, the big basic cost fact affecting U.S. Steel's financial affairs is the unremitting and rapid rise in employment costs— far beyond the rates of increase in productivity. This appears to be a common denominator of all manufacturing activities with the result that there is a very close and inevitable rise in all our costs per employe hour. Historically this cost rise got way ahead of prices during World War II. Following that war steel prices have ever since been experiencing the effects of the continuing cost-push. Steel prices have not, however, during the entire period, ever sufficiently restored the prewar cost-price relationships to result in a profit margin, conventionally stated, equal to that of 1940. This is despite the fact that operating rates in many subsequent years have been substantially higher than they were in 1940. Moreover, depreciation as conventionally stated and permissible for tax purposes is, as a by-product of the inflation, far from realistic—whether we like it or not, it costs a great deal more to replace plant and equipment than is yielded from depreciation and accelerated amortization, when the depreciation is based on prices paid long ago for similar plant and equipment. This means that additional functions of just keeping the company "even with the board" fall upon what is called income, with the result that only a portion of such income can be regarded as available for the purposes formerly served by income in prewage inflation days. The records of U.S. Steel cumulatively and convincingly show that as long as nation-wide wage inflation continues at rates exceeding the increases in productivity a price inflation will be compelled. By squeezing out profits there could be a brief lull, but prices thereafter would have to reflect directly the rising costs. In the meantime such squeezing out of profits, if adopted and enforced as a national policy for industry in general, would obviously bring about great unemployment. It brings to mind the 1930's, the last time when the American economy had to operate without profits and a period the like of which we all hope will never be repeated. [See Exhibits 2, 3, and 4.]

Opening Statement by David J. MacDonald, President, United Steelworkers of America

The United Steelworkers of America is a proud Union, proud because we have served our 1,250,000 members and their families well, proud because we have brought new dignity and well-being to these men, women and children; proud because we have helped to give new vigor and spirit to whole communities and areas.

Exhibit 2

UNITED STATES STEEL'S FINANCIAL STORY, 1910–56

(Dollars in Millions)

Year of Operation	Products and Services Sold	Employ- ment Costs	Products and Services Bought	Wear and Exhaustion	Interest and Other Costs on Debt	Income and Other Taxes	Income or Loss	Preferred Stock Dividend	Common Stock Dividend	Reinvested in the Business	Per Cent Income of Sales
1910..........	491.8	175.0	157.1	32.5	30.6	9.2	87.4	25.2	25.4	36.8	17.8
1911..........	431.7	161.6	146.3	27.8	31.1	9.6	55.3	25.2	25.4	4.7	12.8
1912..........	533.9	189.6	214.3	33.4	32.6	9.8	54.2	25.2	25.4	3.6	10.2
1913..........	560.8	207.5	191.6	34.0	33.3	13.2	81.2	25.2	25.4	30.6	14.5
1914..........	412.2	162.7	153.7	26.6	33.2	12.6	23.4	25.2	15.2	17.0*	5.7
1915..........	523.7	177.3	189.8	34.3	32.8	13.6	75.9	25.2	6.4	44.3	14.5
1916..........	902.3	263.9	265.3	43.0	32.0	26.6	271.5	25.2	44.5	201.8	30.1
1917..........	1,284.6	347.9	345.9	83.3	31.0	252.3	224.2	25.2	91.5	107.5	17.5
1918..........	1,344.6	453.0	339.2	98.8	30.7	297.6	125.3	25.2	71.2	28.9	9.3
1919..........	1,122.6	479.7	364.5	89.9	30.1	81.6	76.8	25.2	25.4	26.2	6.8
1920..........	1,290.6	581.8	413.6	80.0	29.3	76.2	109.7	25.2	25.4	59.1	8.5
1921..........	726.0	333.2	249.9	40.1	28.5	37.7	36.6	25.2	25.4	14.0*	5.0
1922..........	809.0	323.4	334.7	47.1	28.4	35.8	39.6	25.2	25.4	11.0*	4.9
1923..........	1,096.5	470.4	377.4	56.9	28.0	55.1	108.7	25.2	29.2	54.3	9.9
1924..........	921.4	443.6	266.9	53.2	27.3	45.3	85.1	25.2	35.6	24.3	9.2
1925..........	1,022.0	458.2	333.6	61.6	27.1	50.9	90.6	25.2	35.6	29.8	8.9
1926..........	1,082.3	469.3	346.7	70.4	26.8	52.4	116.7	25.2	35.6	55.9	10.8
1927..........	960.5	412.7	323.1	64.4	26.1	46.3	87.9	25.2	49.8	12.9	9.2
1928..........	1,005.3	402.9	338.4	73.2	25.7	51.0	114.1	25.2	49.8	39.1	11.4
1929..........	1,097.4	410.2	350.0	69.8	14.9	55.0	197.5	25.2	63.8	108.5	18.0
1930..........	828.4	371.7	234.8	63.8	5.6	48.1	104.4	25.2	60.4	18.8	12.6
1931..........	548.7	258.4	187.2	50.4	5.5	34.2	13.0	25.2	37.0	49.2*	2.4
1932..........	287.7	138.5	141.8	41.6	5.3	31.7	71.2*	20.7		91.9*	24.7*

Year											
1935	539.4	253.9	191.2	49.8	5.0	38.4	1.1	7.2	....	6.1*	0.2
1936	790.5	339.0	287.5	59.0	4.9	49.6	50.5	50.4	....	.1	6.4
1937	1,028.4	447.1	342.6	64.1	5.1	74.6	94.9	58.5	8.7	27.7	9.2
1938	611.1	294.4	228.3	50.3	8.3	37.5	7.7*	25.2	....	32.9*	1.3*
1939	846.0	386.5	293.5	63.4	9.3	52.2	41.1	25.2	....	15.9	4.9
1940	1,089.1	464.3	358.3	72.6	13.6	68.1	102.2	25.2	34.8	42.2	9.5
1941	1,622.3	628.3	604.6	98.6	6.0	168.6	116.2	25.2	34.8	56.2	7.2
1942	1,863.0	782.7	673.4	128.2	6.2	201.3	71.2	25.2	34.8	11.2	3.8
1943	1,972.3	912.9	730.6	134.0	6.3	125.9	62.6	25.2	34.8	2.6	3.2
1944	2,082.2	957.2	814.4	139.0	5.0	105.8	60.8	25.2	34.8	0.8	2.9
1945	1,747.3	825.5	670.1	123.4	3.5	66.8	58.0	25.2	34.8	2.0*	3.3
1946	1,496.1	704.5	560.4	68.7	4.8	69.1	88.6	25.2	34.8	28.6	5.9
1947	2,122.8	903.6	839.4	114.0	2.5	136.2	127.1	25.2	45.7	56.2	6.0
1948	2,481.5	1,035.7	1,008.9	146.0	2.4	158.9	129.6	25.2	52.2	52.2	5.2
1949	2,301.7	945.9	885.7	119.7	2.3	182.2	165.9	25.2	56.1	84.6	7.2
1950	2,956.4	1,179.4	1,118.8	143.9	2.2	296.6	215.5	25.2	92.7	97.6	7.3
1951	3,524.1	1,374.5	1,327.9	162.1	2.0	473.3	184.3	25.2	78.3	80.8	5.2
1952	3,137.4	1,322.1	1,307.6	176.9	1.9	185.3	143.6	25.2	78.3	40.1	4.6
1953	3,861.0	1,569.2	1,418.7	236.6	2.1	412.3	222.1	25.2	78.3	118.6	5.8
1954	3,250.4	1,387.0	1,134.3	261.8	5.2	266.7	195.4	25.2	85.5	84.7	6.0
1955	4,097.7	1,614.9	1,355.2	285.2	9.1	463.2	370.1	25.2	122.9	222.0	9.0
1956	4,228.9	1,681.0	1,487.5	277.6	7.7	427.0	348.1	25.2	144.9	178.0	8.2

Note: The data are in some respects necessarily approximate and are based on the yearly earnings reported annually to stockholders, without adjustment for surplus charges and credits, except that the years 1942 and 1943 reflect renegotiation settlements made in the succeeding years. For example, taxes are as accrued before adjustments. Employment costs include pensions and social security taxes and, beginning with 1949, also include payments for insurance and other employee benefits. Asterisk (*) denotes deficit.

Source: *Administered Prices*, Hearings before Senate Subcommittee on Antitrust and Monopoly, 85th Congress, First Session (Washington, D.C.: U.S. Government Printing Office, 1957), U.S. Steel exhibit.

Our Union's accomplishments go further, however. We have served the steel, aluminum, metal fabricating and other industries through the development of responsible collective bargaining, adherence to agreements, and cooperation with Management's efforts to produce in ever greater quantity products which have helped make our Country strong and prosperous and a great force for peace.

Exhibit 3

EMPLOYMENT COSTS PER HOUR, PRICES, AND PROFITS, 1940–56
Index—1940 = 100

YEAR	U.S. STEEL		WHOLESALE PRICE INDEX*	FINISHED STEEL MILL PRODUCT PRICES†	U.S. STEEL INCOME AS A PER CENT OF SALES
	Employment Costs per Employee Hour	Total Costs per Employee Hour			
1940	100.0	100.0	100.0	100.0	9.5
1941	109.1	124.3	111.2	100.4	7.2
1942	121.0	131.6	125.6	100.6	3.8
1943	128.1	127.3	131.1	100.7	3.2
1944	138.4	138.9	132.3	100.7	2.9
1945	142.1	138.1	134.6	103.1	3.3
1946	152.2	144.5	154.0	112.2	5.9
1947	165.4	173.6	188.6	130.8	6.0
1948	183.7	198.2	204.3	148.8	5.2
1949	190.9	204.8	194.1	161.1	7.2
1950	218.3	241.1	201.8	169.2	7.3
1951	237.5	274.3	224.7	182.8	5.2
1952	260.7	280.5	218.4	186.8	4.6
1953	277.1	305.4	215.5	201.0	5.8
1954	293.4	307.0	215.9	209.7	6.0
1955	318.2	349.1	216.6	219.5	9.0
1956	350.0	384.1	223.7	238.0	8.2
Average annual rate of change compounded:					
1940–46	7.3%	6.3%	7.5%	1.9%	
1946–56	8.7	10.3	3.8	7.8	
1940–56	8.1	8.8	5.2	5.6	

*All commodities—U.S. Bureau of Labor Statistics.
†U.S. Bureau of Labor Statistics.
Source: *Administered Prices*, Hearings before Senate Subcommittee on Antitrust and Monopoly, 85th Congress, First Session (Washington, D.C.: U.S. Government Printing Office, 1957), U.S. Steel exhibit.

Our interest extends to the welfare of the entire Nation and the whole Economy. We have conducted ourselves in collective bargaining mindful of our manifold responsibilities. We have sought progress based on facts. We have sought benefits which are justified by comparative studies, by the needs of our members and by the financial ability of the employers with whom we deal.

We resent the repeated charges made in recent years by certain industrial leaders that our Union has fostered inflation and has disregarded the welfare of the Nation. We do not like inflation. It is our members and the other millions of AFL-CIO members as well as other consumers who are forced to pay the higher prices. We carry on our collective bargaining activities mindful of the facts—

1. The steel worker is producing more and more per hour of work.
2. The steel companies are amassing ever greater profits.
3. The progress of the industry results in less people producing more steel.

No amount of talk and argument can overcome these plain facts. We are guided in our collective bargaining policies by the certainty that increased productivity—that is, steel produced per hour worked by each man—justifies higher wages and greater benefits for the employees and exerts no inflationary pressure. Economic disaster would result if labor did not strive to keep up with this increased productivity.

Exhibit 4

STEEL INDUSTRY CAPITAL EXPENDITURES VERSUS FINANCING, 1946–56

Eighteen Companies Representing 88 Per Cent of Steel Capacity in 1957
(Dollars in Millions)

	EIGHTEEN COMPANIES		U.S. STEEL	
	Capital Expenditures	Per Cent of Property Expenditures Met by New Money	Capital Expenditures	Per Cent of Property Expenditures Met by New Money
Property expenditures...........	$8,395.5		$3,003.2	
Met by wear and exhaustion......	4,628.7		1,992.5	
Met by new money.............	$3,766.8		$1,010.7	
Borrowing.....................	$2,441.6		$ 362.1	
Sale of stock..................	462.0		29.7	
	$2,903.6		$ 391.8	
Less: Refinancing..............	545.3		37.0	
Outside financing..............	$2,358.3	62.6%	$ 354.8	35.1%
Property expenditures met by reinvestment.................	1,408.5	37.4	655.9	64.9
Property expenditures met by new money..................	$3,766.8	100.0%	$1,010.7	100.0%

Source: Annual reports of companies; Moody's Investors' Service; Standard & Poor's *Standard Corporation Descriptions; Administered Prices*, Hearings before Senate Subcommittee on Antitrust and Monopoly, 85th Congress, First Session (Washington, D.C.: U.S. Government Printing Office, 1957), U.S. Steel exhibit.

If the Steel Industry chooses to boost prices despite the increases in productivity, it owes the Nation an explanation. To charge the Union with being responsible for this situation is not consistent with the facts and figures. We are here to provide to the Congress such facts and understanding as we have to

throw complete light on the situation and to demonstrate the utter falsehood of
the charges directed against our Union by certain Steel Industry leaders.[25]

Statement of Otto Brubaker, Director of Research, United Steelworkers of America
Why a Steel Price Increase in 1957?

[*Question of Public Interest.*] There is a grave question of public interest
raised by the Industry's July 1957 price increase, namely, "Is it proper to
raise prices when the operating rate is falling and demand, though still relatively good, has softened significantly?" Apparently the Industry believes that
any time—whether demand is high or low, whether it is rising or falling—is
a good time to raise prices. It has just raised its prices at a time when demand
is far below that of 1956 and early 1957. This may well mean even less production and less employment. In a truly competitive operation, which Steel
insists it is, it is customary for competitors to cut prices when demand falls. This
is done to stimulate consumption and, consequently, production and employment. The Steel Industry's employment (production and maintenance) fell
from a level of 566,000 in the ten strike-free months of 1956 to 547,400 in
April 1957 as the operating rate declined from 98.6% for these ten months
to 89.5% in April—a loss of 18,600 jobs. As the operating rate dropped
further to about 80% recently, the number of unemployed rose further—
probably to about 25,000. Yet the Industry not only has not cut prices, but it
has raised them. This may well suggest the question, "Has the Industry chosen
a course of restricted, though still fairly high, output at higher prices and more
unemployment as against the other alternative of lower prices, more production
and more employment?" Certainly it is the ability of the Steel Industry to
make such choices, the action of its leaders in making them, and the Industry's
apparent freedom to raise prices at will despite the level of demand, that has
earned it the name of an "administered price" industry.

Among our Conclusions—
1. Steel price increases in the post World War II period have been ex-
   orbitant in relation to increased costs.
2. Steel price increases have been the most important medium for increasing steel profits—"administered profits" achieved through "administered
   prices."
3. Steel price increases have been unrelated to wage increases—except for
   purposeful coincidence in timing so that many major Steel price increases
   occur simultaneously with wage adjustments. This serves the purpose of
   providing a scapegoat—the Union and its wage increases.
4. As has been true of a whole series of Steel price increases, the 1957
   Steel price increase of $6 per ton was not "necessitated" by wage in-
   creases or other cost increases. It was designed to produce a further
   enlargement of Steel profits and to widen already excessive profit margins.
   It brought the price increases within the past year to *$19.50* per ton.

---

[25]*Ibid.* MacDonald's and Brubaker's testimony was offered on August 20, 1957.

Exhibit 5

COST AND PRICE CHANGES, 1939–57, U.S. STEEL CORPORATION
(Data Submitted by United Steelworkers of America)

Year	Total Employment Costs (per Ton)*		Total Purchased Materials and Services Costs (per Ton)*		Steel Prices (BLS.) (Index—1939 = 100)
	Amount	Index—1939 = 100	Amount	Index—1939 = 100	
1957 (first half)†	$71.58	216.8	$56.89	226.9	259.0
1956	70.30	213.0	62.21	248.1	241.8
1955	63.31	191.8	53.13	211.9	223.3
1954	68.53	207.6	56.05	223.6	213.0
1953	62.54	189.5	56.54	217.6	203.9
1952	62.56	189.5	61.87	246.8	188.9
1951	55.81	169.1	53.92	215.1	184.9
1950	52.11	157.9	49.43	197.2	171.4
1949	51.94	157.3	48.63	194.0	162.8
1948	50.14	151.9	48.85	195.0	150.2
1947	44.64	135.2	41.47	165.4	131.6
1946	46.40	140.6	36.91	147.2	112.3
1945	44.84	135.8	36.40	145.2	103.3
1944	45.47	137.7	38.69	154.3	100.9
1943	45.31	137.3	36.26	144.6	100.9
1942	37.97	115.0	32.67	130.3	100.7
1941	30.77	93.2	29.61	118.1	100.6
1940	30.92	93.7	23.86	95.2	100.1
1939	33.01	100.0	25.07	100.0	100.0
Change, 1939–57	$38.57	116.8%	$31.82	126.9%	159.0%
Change, 1947–57	$26.94	60.3%	$15.42	37.2%	96.8%

*The costs (employment and materials) are not precisely comparable to the steel price changes, since the costs include items other than steelmaking costs alone and are therefore *overstated* in dollar amounts. The trend over the years, however, can be appropriately compared. Per ton costs are computed by dividing total costs by steel shipments as shown in U.S. Steel's annual reports.

†These figures do not reflect the July, 1957, increases in employment costs or steel prices. These increases will widen further the lead of steel price increases over costs per ton.

Source: *Administered Prices*, Hearings before Senate Subcommittee on Antitrust and Monopoly, 85th Congress, First Session (Washington, D.C.: Government Printing Office, 1957), United Steelworkers of America exhibit.

The *$6* increase will add about *$545 million* a year in increased revenues to the entire Industry and nearly *$160 million* to U.S. Steel Corporation. In making this price increase the Industry's price administrators, as usual, completely ignored the sharp productivity growth. . . .

The July 1957 wage increase (15.5¢ per hour or 5.9%) could have been *absorbed entirely* out of the 1957 productivity increase of 5% to date; because total employment costs are only approximately 35% of sales and the impact of a 5.9% wage increase is therefore only *2.1%;* and because with this sizable

Exhibit 6

STEEL SHIPMENTS AND PROFIT CHANGES FOR 1939 AND 1946–57, U.S. STEEL CORPORATION (ANNUAL RATE)

(Data Submitted by United Steelworkers of America)

Year	Profits before Taxes per Ton of Steel Products Shipped*	Profits before Taxes (in Millions)	Tons of Steel Products Shipped (in Millions)
1957 (first half)†	$35.65	$926.8	26.0
1956	28.41	679.1	23.9
1955	28.87	736.1	25.5
1954	19.08	385.4	20.2
1953	21.72	545.1	25.1
1952	13.28	282.3	21.1
1951	25.31	622.7	24.6
1950	21.46	485.0	22.6
1949	17.25	314.0	18.2
1948	14.20	294.0	20.7
1947	12.10	244.4	20.2
1946	7.93	120.6	15.2
1939	4.62	54.1	11.7

*The profits before taxes per ton of steel products shipped are reflective of the trend in profits per ton rather than the actual figures, since profits, as reported by the corporation, include profits on items other than steel products and are therefore *overstated.*

†These figures do not reflect the July, 1957, increases in costs or steel prices. These increases will widen further the profits before taxes per ton of steel products shipped.

Source: *Administered Prices,* Hearings before Senate Subcommittee on Antitrust and Monopoly, 85th Congress, First Session (Washington, D.C.: U.S. Government Printing Office, 1957), United Steelworkers of America exhibit.

productivity increase, unit costs show *no* increase at all, but instead a decline. Even if added wage "costs" were to be met only out of that *share* of the increased product represented by employment "costs," it would require only a fractional further productivity increase (*9/10 of one* per cent) in 1957 to permit *full absorption* of the 1957 wage increase just out of the *share* which employment costs represent in this increased productivity. . . .

. . . between 1947 and 1956 the Industry expanded its net profits from $394 million to more than a *billion dollars* ($1,031.5 million). Its rate of return on Net Worth climbed from 10.5% in 1947 to 12.8% in 1956. In the last quarter of 1957 Net Profits increased further to an annual rate of *$1,252.4 million,* and its rate of Return on Net Worth to *14.1%.* . . .

... In this same period between 1947 and 1956, when the rate of Return on Net Worth in Steel *increased* from 10.% to 12.8% (and to *14.1%* in the first quarter of 1957), Net Profits in relation to Net Worth *declined* in all manufacturing industries from *15.1%* in 1947 to 12.8% in 1956 and to 11.9% in first quarter of 1957. (F.T.C.-S.E.C. Quarterly Industrial Financial Report Series for All Manufacturing Corporations.) Likewise, Net Profits per Dollar of Sales, which were 5.7¢ in 1947 in all manufacturing corporations *declined* to 4.0¢ in 1955 and to 3.6¢ in 1956 (U.S. Departments of Commerce), at the same time they were *increasing* in Steel. ... [See Exhibits 5, 6, and 7.]

Exhibit 7

(Data Submitted by United Steelworkers of America)

HOURLY WAGE AND "FRINGE" COST FOR U.S. STEEL CORPORATION

Union estimate...16.4¢
Comparable U.S. Steel estimate...................................19.4¢

MAN-HOURS REQUIRED PER TON OF FINISHED STEEL SHIPPED

	1957	*1956*	*1955*	*1954*
Steel industry*........	15.2 (first half)	15.9	16.0	18.6
U.S. Steel†	15.5–15.8 (second quarter)	n.a.‡	16.5	19.0

INCREASED WAGE AND "FRINGE" COST PER TON IN JULY, 1957

Steel industry, using:
    Union wage estimate..................$2.49 (15.2 man-hours × 16.4¢)
    U.S. Steel wage estimate............... 2.95 (15.2 man-hours × 19.4¢)
U.S. Steel, using:
    Union wage estimate.......2.54–2.59 (15.5 and 15.8 man-hours × 16.4¢)
    U.S. Steel wage estimate....3.01–3.07 (15.5 and 15.8 man-hours × 19.4¢)

*Calculated by dividing adjusted total man-hours worked by all employees, as reported by AISI for the steel industry, by total shipments of finished steel in the years indicated.
†Man-hours worked per ton of finished steel by all employees in integrated steel operations of U.S. Steel Corporation as reported by Bradford Smith, U.S. Steel economist, for 1954 and 1955. For 1957 the figures are derived from employment figures (integrated steel operations) for the second quarter of 1957, as submitted to the subcommittee by U.S. Steel, the shipments of finished steel for U.S. Steel in the second quarter, and estimated average of 475–85 hours worked per quarter by each employee.
‡Not available.
Source: *Administered Prices*, Hearings before Senate Subcommittee on Antitrust and Monopoly, 85th Congress, First Session (Washington, D.C.: U.S. Government Printing Office, 1957), United Steelworkers of America exhibit.

Reactions of Competitors

Some of U.S. Steel's competitors were unhappy too, but for other reasons:

Competitors are unhappy because the Corporation doesn't boost prices enough. Avery Adams of Jones & Laughlin stated: "The announced price is grossly inadequate to cover total anticipated cost increases." U.S. Steel insists that it is only recovering costs—that its earnings improvements result from heavy capital expenditures and meticulous attention to efficiency. The industry, in seeking higher general increases, is arguing this year—as it did more quietly in last year's increase—that by holding prices lower than what the traffic would bear, U.S. Steel makes it progressively harder for the rest of the trade to finance modernization and expansion.[26]

This disappointment, however, did not delay the industry's speedy conformance to U.S. Steel's actions.

Republic Steel, Youngstown Sheet & Tube, and Lukens Steel published new price schedules on June 29, effective July 1. Bethlehem Steel Company, the second largest producer in the country, increased prices on July 1 "in line with the general trend." Within a week after the U.S. Steel announcement, every other major producer in the industry had followed the steel corporation's lead.

The Conclusion of the Senate Committee

Outside of natural monopolies which are regulated in the public interest, the political philosophy which governs this economy rests upon the concept of competition. The theory is that the free play of competitive forces provides the best method of making prices properly responsive to changes in market conditions and is thus the best way of assuring a proper allocation and use of resources.

It is apparent that, in a number of important respects, the characteristics of the steel industry are quite different from those associated with the economic models on which competitive theory was originally based. Notable among these differences are the high levels of concentration in the market, the long-established practice of price leadership which appears to operate just as effectively when prices are increased as when they are reduced, the relative absence of newcomers, the historical use of elaborate pricing systems which have produced complete identity of delivered prices at any given point of destination, etc.

Of even greater importance is the insensitivity of the industry's prices to changes in market conditions. Indeed, it is more than just insensitivity. Since World War II, prices have moved on a number of occasions in the opposite direction to that which would have been indicated by the changes in demand. Thus, the steel-price index continued its virtually unbroken rise even when demand and production declined (as they did in 1949, 1954, and 1957). It also continued its climb even when unit labor costs declined (as they did in 1950 and 1955). No matter what the change in cost or in demand, steel prices since 1947 have moved steadily and regularly in only one direction, upward. From the material presented in this report, it is clear that the price increase substantially exceeded the cost increase in 1957, and apparently also in 1956. It is also reasonably clear that, at the time the 1957 price increase was made, there was nothing in the information then available to suggest a forthcoming increase in demand which would support the higher prices. That the price increase was made and has been held in the face of these underlying conditions

---

[26]As reported in *Business Week,* July 6, 1957.

is a tribute to the perfection with which price leadership in the steel industry maintains price rigidity. . . .

. . . The subcommittee is seeking to ascertain whether present laws are sufficient to cope with the problem, or whether new laws are required. To answer this question, a great deal more must be learned about the nature and behavior of administered-price industries. If it is determined that new laws are required,

Exhibit 8

UNITED STATES STEEL CORPORATION: RELATIONSHIP BETWEEN PER CENT OF CAPACITY OPERATED AND RATE OF RETURN ON STOCKHOLDERS' INVESTMENT, AFTER TAXES, 1920–56

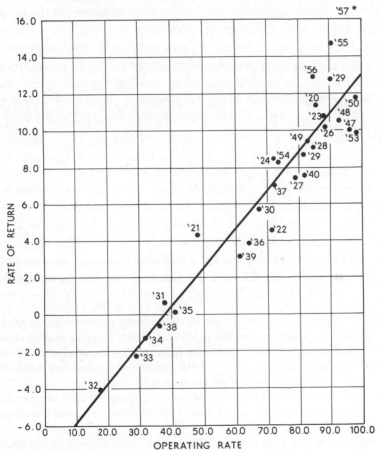

*First six months of 1957.
Notes:
1. A similar diagram was drawn for the steel industry showing profit for the first six months of 1957 of 16 per cent and zero profit at a 40 per cent operating rate.
2. After U.S. Steel's third-quarter report was out, the break-even point was estimated by business consultants Fred V. Gardner and Associates at 32 per cent—the lowest, Mr. Gardner said, that he had ever encountered.
Sources: *Administered Prices,* Hearings before Senate Subcommittee on Antitrust and Monopoly, 85th Congress, First Session (Washington, D.C.: U.S. Government Printing Office, 1957),

it is the subcommittee's belief and hope that they will be of such a nature as not to repeal or set aside the antitrust laws, but to make of the antitrust statutes a more effective instrument in dealing with present-day realities.

The time might have very well arrived when the 1890 Sherman Act and the 1914 Federal Trade Commission Act should be strengthened to meet the demands of a dynamic economy.[27] [See Exhibit 8.]

U.S. STEEL AND THE ABORTIVE 1962 PRICE INCREASE

After the price increase in 1957, there was a much smaller general increase in 1958 and only selective price adjustments from 1959 through 1961, with the over-all change in the last two years being slightly downward. It can be noted from Exhibits 9–13 that production, employment, profits, and exports were all substantially down from the levels of the middle 1950's. Man-hour productivity had risen substantially in 1959 and 1961 while employment costs were rising more slowly than before. Most of the industry had been subjected to a prolonged strike running from the early summer of 1959 to January, 1960.

On March 31, 1962, congratulations were extended to the steelworkers and to the steel industry for their "early and responsible settlement," well in advance of the June 30 deadline, and the earliest settlement in the quarter-century relationship between the industry and the union. This early settlement contrasted with the 1959 negotiations, which included a 116-day strike. President Kennedy, in a telephone message to David J. MacDonald, President of the United Steelworkers, said:

When I appealed to the Union and to the industry to commence negotiations early in order to avert an inventory buildup—with consequences detrimental to the nation at large as well as to the industry and its employees—I did so with firm confidence that the steelworkers' union and the industry would measure up to their responsibility to serve the national interest.

You have done so through free collective bargaining, without the pressure of a deadline or under the threat of a strike. This is indeed industrial statesmanship of the highest order.

The settlement you have announced is both forward looking and responsible. It is obviously noninflationary and should provide a solid base for continued price stability.

---

[27]Committee on the Judiciary, U.S. Senate, Subcommittee on Antitrust and Monopoly, *Administered Prices: Steel,* Senate Report 1387, 85th Congress, Second Session (Washington, D.C.: U.S. Government Printing Office, March, 1958), pp. 129–30.

Exhibit 9

PRODUCTIVITY, EMPLOYMENT COSTS, AND PRICES IN STEEL INDUSTRY, 1940–61

Year	(1) Ingot Production (Millions of Tons)	(2) Total Wage-Hours Worked (Millions)	(3) Ingot Tons ÷ Hours Worked (1 ÷ 2)	(4) Annual Percentage Change in (3)	(5) Average Total Employment Cost per Hour	(6) Annual Percentage Change in (5)	(7) Steel Products Price Index	(8) Annual Percentage Change in (7)
1940............	67.0	858	0.0781	....	0.905	....	100.0	....
1945............	79.7	1,009	0.0790	0.2*	1.307	7.0*	103.1	0.6*
1946............	66.6	837	0.0792	0.3	1.404	7.4	112.2	8.8
1947............	84.9	984	0.0863	8.9	1.563	11.3	130.8	16.6
1948............	88.6	1,029	0.0861	0.0	1.679	7.4	198.8	13.8
1949............	78.0	885	0.0881	2.3	1.753	4.4	161.1	8.3
1950............	96.8	1,023	0.0947	7.5	1.908	8.8	169.2	5.0
1951............	105.2	1,133	0.0946	0.0	2.114	10.8	182.8	8.0
1952............	93.2	971	0.0960	1.5	2.315	9.5	186.8	2.2
1953............	111.6	1,119	0.0997	3.9	2.440	5.4	201.0	7.6
1954............	88.3	901	0.0980	(1.7)†	2.512	3.0	209.7	4.3
1955............	117.0	1,062	0.1102	12.5	2.722	8.3	219.5	4.7
1956............	115.2	1,027	0.1122	1.9	2.954	8.5	238.0	8.4
1957............	112.7	990	0.1139	1.5	3.216	8.9	260.7	9.5
1958............	85.3	756	0.1128	(1.0)	3.513	9.2	269.8	3.5
1959............	93.4	769	0.1215	7.7	3.798	8.1	274.3	1.7
1960............	99.3	840	0.1182	(2.7)	3.820	0.6	273.9	(0.2)
1961............	98.0	775	0.1267	7.2	3.989	4.4	272.8	(0.4)

*Annual average over five years.
†Parentheses indicate negative changes.
Notes: Column 2 was obtained by dividing aggregate payroll of wage employees by hourly total payroll cost. Column 3, as a measure of man-hour productivity, could overstate the increase if the proportion of salary to wage workers increased and understate it if more processing was given to steel shipments. Column 5 includes payroll costs plus pension, insurance, S.U.B., and social security.
Source: American Iron and and Steel Institute, particularly *The Competitive Challenge to Steel* (Pittsburgh, 1963), p. 82.

Exhibit 10

COMPARISON OF STEEL INDUSTRY RETURN ON NET ASSETS WITH AVERAGE RATE OF RETURN FOR LEADING MANUFACTURING INDUSTRIES

Year	Average Return on Net Assets		Per Cent by Which Steel Industry Return was ABOVE (+) or BELOW (−) Average Rate of Return for Leading Mfg. Industries	Steel Industry Ranking Among Leading Manufacturing Industries	Number of Leading Industrial Categories Covered
	Steel Industry	Leading Manufacturing Industries			
1940	8.5%	10.3%	−18%	32nd	45
1941	9.6	12.4	−23	40th	44
1942	6.5	10.1	−36	45th	45
1943	5.6	9.9	−43	43rd	44
1944	5.2	9.8	−47	44th	45
1945	5.0	9.1	−45	44th	45
1946	7.5	12.1	−38	41st	45
1947	11.3	17.0	−33	42nd	45
1948	14.0	18.9	−26	38th	45
1949	11.5	13.8	−17	24th	45
1950	15.3	17.1	−10	28th	45
1951	12.3	14.4	−15	25th	46
1952	8.8	12.3	−28	35th	46
1953	11.6	12.5	− 7	21st	46
1954	9.4	12.4	−24	32nd	46
1955	15.2	15.0	+ 1	14th	46
1956	13.9	13.9	0	17th	41
1957	13.2	12.8	+ 3	17th	41
1958	8.2	9.8	−16	27th	41
1959	8.4	11.7	−28	35th	41
1960	7.8	10.6	−26	29th	41
1961	6.4	10.1	−37	33rd	41

Source: Computed from First National City Bank, *Monthly Letter*, April issues. See Exhibit 9.

An industry statement said the new benefits would increase employment costs by about 2½ per cent during the first year. This compares with an average annual increase of 3½ to 3¾ per cent under the contract negotiated in 1960, and with 8 per cent a year in the period between 1940 and 1960. R. Conrad Cooper of U.S. Steel, chief industry negotiator, said that the settlement cost did not fall wholly "within the limits of anticipated gains in productive efficiency." The industry statement estimated the cost of the settlement exceeded by about 50 per cent its productivity gain. Cooper added that the accord represented real progress in the development of voluntary collective bargaining in the steel industry.

Exhibit 11

UNITED STATES IMPORTS AND EXPORTS OF STEEL
MILL PRODUCTS

(Net Tons)

Year	Imports	Exports
1950	1,013,600	2,638,634
1951	2,176,996	3,136,639
1952	1,201,435	4,005,248
1953	1,702,991	2,990,751
1954	770,822	2,791,886
1955	973,155	4,060,998
1956	1,340,746	4,347,903
1957	1,154,831	5,347,678
1958	1,707,130	2,822,910
1959	4,396,354	1,676,652
1960	3,358,752	2,977,278
1961	3,164,256	1,989,179

Note: In ingot equivalent, each ton of steel mill products represented about 1.35 tons of ingots (figure varied from 1.32 to 1.37 in last five years).
Source: American Iron and Steel Institute, *Foreign Trade Trends* (1962).
See Exhibit 9.

Steps in the Negotiation

The 1960 steel contract provided for several wage increases, the last of which was scheduled for October 1, 1961. Prior to that date, executives of major steel companies were hinting at a general rise in steel prices to coincide with that wage increase. On September 6, 1961, President Kennedy wrote the heads of twelve steel companies, expressing his concern with stability of steel prices. Mr. Kennedy wrote:

. . . the steel industry, by absorbing increases in employment costs since 1958 has demonstrated a will to halt the price-wage spiral in steel. If the industry were now to forego a price increase, it would enter collective bargaining negotiations next spring with a record of three-and-a-half years of price stability. It would clearly then be the turn of the labor representatives to limit wage demands to a level consistent with continued price stability. The moral position of the steel industry next spring and its claim to the support of public opinion will be strengthened by the exercise of price restraint now.

Exhibit 12

STEEL INDUSTRY CAPITAL EXPENDITURES, DEPRECIATION,
DEPLETION, AND AMORTIZATION

1946–61

Year	Capital Expenditures for Additions, Improvements & Replacements	Depreciation, Depletion and Amortization
	Millions	
1946	$ 365	$169
1947	554	239
1948	642	302
1949	483	278
1950	505	327
1951	1,051	374
1952	1,298	450
1953	988	614
1954	609	670
1955	714	737
1956	1,311	748
1957	1,723	766
1958	1,137	673
1959	934	665
1960	1,521	698
1961	978	729

Source: Annual statistical reports of the American Iron and Steel Institute.
See Exhibit 9.

He eventually received replies from all twelve companies. The reply from Roger Blough for U.S. Steel denied that the cause of inflation would be found in the levels of steel prices and profits. Blough's letter noted that the President's letter "does raise questions of such serious import, including the future of freedom of marketing, that I feel impelled to include a word on that score also, for whatever value it may be." He wrote of "the admittedly hazardous task which your economic advisers have undertaken in forecasting steel industry profits at varying rates of operation. . . . Moreover, it might reasonably appear to some— as, frankly, it does to me—that they seem to be assuming the role of informal price setters for steel—psychological or otherwise."

Exhibit 13

AVERAGE HOURLY EARNINGS PER HOUR PAID FOR (BLS)
Steel versus Other Industries

Year	Steel Industry	All Manufacturing	Auto Industry
		Dollars per Hour Paid for	
1940	$ .84	$ .66	$ .94
1941	.94	.73	1.04
1942	1.02	.85	1.17
1943	1.12	.96	1.24
1944	1.16	1.01	1.27
1945	1.18	1.02	1.27
1946	1.28	1.08	1.35
1947	1.44	1.22	1.47
1948	1.58	1.33	1.61
1949	1.65	1.38	1.70
1950	1.69	1.44	1.78
1951	1.92	1.56	1.91
1952	2.02	1.65	2.05
1953	2.19	1.74	2.14
1954	2.23	1.78	2.20
1955	2.41	1.86	2.29
1956	2.57	1.95	2.35
1957	2.73	2.05	2.46
1958	2.91	2.11	2.55
1959	3.10	2.19	2.71
1960	3.08	2.26	2.81
1961	3.20	2.32	2.87

Source: U.S. Bureau of Labor Statistics. See Exhibit 9.

In January, 1962, President Kennedy urged an early agreement to avoid the upsetting uncertainty of a possible strike, and especially the speculation which precedes a strike deadline, such as heavy buying by steel users. At his news conference on January 15, Mr. Kennedy said that Secretary of Labor Arthur J. Goldberg, would be available "for what ever good offices he may perform." In reply to a question at the conference the President stressed his desire for a settlement which would not force an increase in steel prices, i.e., the cost of the wage increase should not exceed the savings resulting from increased productivity. The President's economic report to the Congress, released the following week, went so far as to urge that average productivity gains for the general economy be used as guidelines for wage settlements. The report of the Council of Economic Advisers recommended that the over-all increase in output per man-hour of $2\frac{1}{2}$ to 3 per cent a year be taken as the measuring rod for higher wages and fringe benefits in any industry. If efficiency of a specific industry was going up faster, this would call for price reductions.

One of the strongest statements about the role of government in collective bargaining was Secretary Goldberg's "definitive" statement of the Kennedy administration's labor-management philosophy to the Executive Club of Chicago, on February 23. Goldberg said that in the past when government officials assisted in collective bargaining, their only aim had been to achieve a settlement. But today, in the light of the nation's commitments at home and abroad, government and private mediators must increasingly provide guidelines to the parties in labor disputes. Such guidelines should insure "right settlements" that take into account the public interest as well as the interests of the parties. Goldberg said he did not mean that government should impose the terms of a settlement, but he claimed that "everyone expects the government to assert and define the national interest."

Anonymous steel industry sources took exception to the Goldberg position:

The moment the government goes beyond being a policeman or offering its service as mediator, it has an impact on the outcome of collective bargaining and converts it from an economic to a political process. From a broad philosophical standpoint, most businessmen feel that in a competitive system you serve the national interest in pursuing your private interest. Government exertion of its influence prevents the system from operating as it should. From a practical standpoint, labor represents more votes than business men, so business men feel that any settlement that is a political settlement is likely to be more pro-labor than pro-management.

George Meany, President of the American Federation of Labor and Congress of Industrial Organizations, also brusquely rejected Secretary Goldberg's "definitive" statement. Mr. Meany said:

I don't agree with it. The government's role is mediation, conciliation or anything else it can do to help industrial peace. When he says the role of the government is to assert the national interest, he is infringing on the rights of free people and free society, and I don't agree with him whatsoever. This is a step in the direction of saying the federal government should tell either or both sides what to do, and I don't agree with that.

Support for Secretary Goldberg came from Joseph L. Block, Chairman of Inland Steel, who was at the speaker's table when Goldberg spoke (Block was a member of President Kennedy's twenty-one-man Advisory Committee on Labor-Management Policy):

I heartily endorse Mr. Goldberg's concept. It is the government's function to elucidate the national objectives, to point out what the national needs are. Those guidelines should be taken into account in collective bargaining. A contest of strength where the stronger side wins doesn't prove a thing. Each side has to represent its own interest, but neither side must be unmindful of the needs of the nation. Who else can point out those needs but the government?

A. A. Berle, Jr., also supported the Goldberg view and the work of the Council of Economic Advisors, contending that there is an unwritten "social contract" holding both sides to certain responsibilities as well as granting both the privileges that make this power possible, and that under this social contract the government can—and perhaps must—intervene when economic power in private hands threatens the economic community of the United States. Berle sees the "emerging relationship" as this: "When the wage and price levels markedly affect, or threaten to upset, the economy of the country, the government claims power to step in on behalf of the 'public interest.'" The difficulty is in telling what the words "public interest" mean. Berle sees the Council of Economic Advisors as the future key agency here, for "its views on acceptable wage and price levels are, and should be, extremely important":

The council can advise the President—and through his authority advise both big labor and big corporations—about where the peril points are. It can advise the President when the government should intervene to modify private decisions based on power, either of labor to tie up plants by strike, or of management to set prices by administration. It can and indeed does keep a close check on these allegedly private decisions, taken in company offices or union headquarters. It could communicate to either or both when it sees a peril point approaching. And it can advise the President when intervention is needed in the "public interest"—that is, when employment, production and purchasing power under free competitive enterprise are likely to be weakened, when inflation becomes a danger, when economic stability generally is likely to be threatened.[28]

---

[28]A. A. Berle, J., "Unwritten Constitution for Our Economy," *New York Times Magazine,* April 29, 1962.

U.S. Steel's annual report, released on March 20, 1962, pointed to its holding of the price line in 1961. Mr. Blough's statement to stockholders said that in 1961 "the inexorable influences of the market place in our competitive free enterprise system continued to dictate the course of U.S. Steel's pricing actions." No reference to pricing plans for 1962 appeared in the report, but Blough indicated deep concern about competition and slack demand. Robert C. Tyson, chairman of U.S. Steel's Finance Committee, called "unsatisfactory" the idea that productivity is a criterion for setting wages. "The notion appears to be that if an enterprise or industry learns how to produce more efficiently, then it can pay more to its employees without raising its product's prices. If we can do this, it is proper to force us to do so." Mr. Tyson said this theory is unsatisfactory because if more money is paid to those with jobs, there is less available for rehiring those workers without jobs. Unemployment becomes chronic, and the incentives for creating new jobs are stultified. Productivity, he went on, is useful as a method of describing economic facts, rather than as a measure for determining wage rates. It indicates only that a price increase or widespread unemployment must result if the average wage level rises faster than productivity. "No increase in employment costs in excess of the nation's long-term rate of productivity increase can be regarded as noninflationary." (At this stage in negotiations the industry was holding out for employment cost increases not exceeding 2 per cent annually, coinciding with the annual productivity increase as figured by the companies for recent years.)

Steel Prices Go Up—and Come Down Again

U.S. Steel signed the labor contract agreed upon at the end of March on April 5. This contract provided for costs (not in direct wages but in other benefits) which were subsequently estimated at 10.6 cents an hour, or a total of $159 million a year for the industry, with some 520,000 workers. On April 10 the company announced an average increase of $6.00 a ton in the price of steel, accompanying the announcement with a statement signed by Leslie B. Worthington, President, explaining this increase:

Since our last over-all adjustment in the summer of 1958, the level of steel prices has not been increased but, if anything, has declined somewhat. This situation, in the face of steadily mounting production costs which have included four increases in steel-worker wages and benefits prior to the end of last year, has been due to the competitive pressures from domestic producers and from imports of foreign-made steel as well as from other materials which are used as substitutes for steel.

· · · · · · ·

In the three years since the end of 1958, United States Steel has spent $1,185,-000,000 for modernization and replacement of facilities and for the development of new sources of raw materials. Internally, there were only two sources from which this money could come: depreciation and reinvested profit. Depreciation in these years amounted to $610,000,000; and reinvested profit, $187,000,-000—or, together, only about two-thirds of the total sum required. So after using all the income available from operations, we had to make up the difference of $388,000,000 out of borrowings from the public. In fact, during the period 1958–1961, we have actually borrowed a total of $800,000,000 to provide for present and future needs. And this must be repaid out of profits that have not yet been earned, and will not be earned for some years to come.

During these three years, moreover, United States Steel's profits have dropped to the lowest levels since 1952; while reinvested profit—which is all the profit there is to be plowed back in the business after payment of dividends—has declined from $115,000,000 in 1958 to less than $3,000,000 last year. Yet the dividend rate has not been increased in more than five years, although there have been seven general increases in employment costs during this interval.

· · · · · · ·

In all, we have experienced a net increase of about 6 per cent in our costs over this period despite cost reductions which have been effected through the use of new, more efficient facilities, improved techniques and better raw materials. Compared with this net increase of 6 per cent, the price increase of 3½ per cent announced today clearly falls considerably short of the amount needed to restore even the cost-price relationship in the low production year of 1958.

In reaching this conclusion, we have given full consideration, of course, to the fact that any price increase which comes, as this does, at a time when foreign-made steels are already underselling ours in a number of product lines, will add —temporarily, at least—to the competitive difficulties which we are now experiencing. But the present price level cannot be maintained any longer when our problems are viewed in long-range perspective. For the long pull a strong, profitable company is the only insurance that formidable competition can be met and that the necessary lower costs to meet that competition will be assured.[29]

President Kennedy was informed of U.S. Steel's price increase at a meeting requested by Roger Blough at 5:45 P.M. on April 10. Mr. Kennedy spoke at his news conference the next day in "a tone of cold anger" in reading a long indictment of the steel companies' actions:

The simultaneous and identical actions of United States Steel and other leading steel corporations increasing steel prices by some $6 a ton constitute a wholly unjustifiable and irresponsible defiance of the public interest.

[29]*New York Times,* April 11, 1962.

In this serious hour in our nation's history when we are confronted with grave crises in Berlin and Southeast Asia, when we are devoting our energies to economic recovery and stability, when we are asking Reservists to leave their homes and families months on end and servicemen to risk their lives—and four were killed in the last two days in Vietnam—and asking union members to hold down their wage requests at a time when restraint and sacrifice are being asked of every citizen, the American people will find it hard, as I do, to accept a situation in which a tiny handful of steel executives whose pursuit of private power and profit exceeds their sense of public responsibility, can show such utter contempt for the interest of 185,000,000 Americans.

If this rise in the cost of steel is imitated by the rest of the industry, instead of rescinded, it would increase the cost of homes, autos, appliances and most other items for every American family. It would increase the cost of machinery and tools to every American businessman and farmer. It would seriously handicap our efforts to prevent an inflationary spiral, from eating up the pensions of our older citizens and our new gains in purchasing power. It would add, Defense Secretary Robert S. McNamara informed me this morning, an estimated $1,000,000,000 to the cost of our defenses at a time when every dollar is needed for national security and other purposes.

It will make it more difficult for American goods to compete in foreign markets, more difficult to withstand competition from foreign imports and thus more difficult to improve our balance-of-payment position and stem the flow of gold. And it is necessary to stem it for our national security if we're going to pay for our security commitments abroad.

And it would surely handicap our efforts to induce other industries and unions to adopt responsible price and wage policies.

The facts of the matter are that there is no justification for an increase in steel prices.

The recent settlement between the industry and the union, which does not even take place until July 1, was widely acknowledged to be non-inflationary, and the whole purpose and effect of this Administration's role, which both parties understood, was to achieve an agreement which would make unnecessary any increases in prices.

Steel output per man is rising so fast that labor costs per ton of steel can actually be expected to decline in the next twelve months. And, in fact, the Acting Commissioner of the Bureau of Labor Statistics informed me this morning that, and I quote, "employment costs per unit of steel output in 1961 were essentially the same as they were in 1958." The cost of major raw materials— steel scrap and coal—has also been declining.

And for an industry which has been generally operating at less than two-thirds of capacity, its profit rate has been normal and can be expected to rise sharply this year in view of the reduction in idle capacity. Their lot has been easier than that of 100,000 steelworkers thrown out of work in the last three years.

The industry's cash dividends have exceeded $600,000,000 in each of the last five years; and earnings in the first quarter of this year were estimated in the Feb. 28 *Wall Street Journal* to be among the highest in history.

In short, at a time when they could be exploring how more efficiency and better prices could be obtained, reducing prices in this industry in recognition of lower costs, their unusually good labor contract, their foreign competition and their increase in production and profits which are coming this year, a few gigantic corporations have decided to increase prices in ruthless disregard of their public responsibility.

Price and wage decisions in this country, except for a very limited restriction in the case of monopolies and national emergency strikes, are and ought to be freely and privately made. But the American people have a right to expect, in return for that freedom, a higher sense of business responsibility for the welfare of their country than has been shown in the last two days.

Sometime ago I asked each American to consider what he would do for his country, and I asked the steel companies. In the last twenty-four hours we had their answer.[30]

By the time President Kennedy had issued the above statement at his news conference on April 11, the majority of the larger steel producers had followed U.S. Steel's lead: Bethlehem, Republic, Jones & Laughlin, Youngstown, and Wheeling. A major administrative strategy was to attempt to persuade other important companies to hold the line.[31] By the end of April, only Inland Steel, Kaiser Steel, and Armco were in this category of holdouts, and firms with an estimated 16 per cent of capacity had not increased prices. On Friday morning, April 13, Joseph Block, Chairman of Inland's board, announced from Kyoto, Japan: "We do not feel that an advance in steel prices at this time would be in the national interest," and the official company announcement followed shortly thereafter:

Inland Steel Co. today announced that it will not make any adjustment in existing prices of its steel mill products at this time. The company has long recognized the need for improvements in steel industry profits in relation to capital invested. It believes this condition, which does not exist today, will ultimately have to be corrected. Nevertheless, in full recognition of the national interest and competitive factors, the company feels that it is untimely to make an upward adjustment.

Shortly after noon, Kaiser announced it would maintain prices, and at about the same time the Defense Department announced an award of $5 million of armor plate to Lukens Steel Company, one of the smaller holdouts. At 3:20 P.M., Bethlehem unexpectedly rescinded

---

[30] As reported in the *New York Times,* April 11, 1962.

[31] Wallace Carroll in "Steel: A 72-Hour Drama with an All-Star Cast," *New York Times,* April 23, 1962, states: "According to one official who was deeply involved in all this effort, the over-all objective was to line up companies representing 18 per cent of the nation's capacity. If this could be done, according to friendly sources in the steel industry, these companies with their lower prices soon would be doing 25 per cent of the business. Then Big Steel would have to yield."

its price increase; and at 5:28 P.M., United States Steel withdrew its price increases just seventy-one hours and fifty-eight minutes after its original announcement.

The following week, after the prices had come back down, the joint Senate-House Republican leadership issued a statement summarizing nine governmental actions used by the White House, and deploring their use:

1. The Federal Trade Commission publicly suggested the possibility of collusion, announced an immediate investigation, and talked of $2,000 a day penalties.

2. The Justice Department spoke threateningly of antitrust violations and ordered an immediate investigation.

3. Treasury Department officials indicated they were at once reconsidering the planned increase in depreciation rates for steel.

4. The Internal Revenue Service was reported making a menacing move toward U.S. Steel's incentive benefits plan for its executives.

5. The Senate Antitrust and Monopoly subcommittee began subpoenaing records from twelve steel companies, returnable May 14.

6. The House Antitrust subcommittee announced an immediate investigation, with hearings opening May 2.

7. The Justice Department announced it was ordering a grand jury investigation.

8. The Department of Defense, seemingly ignoring laws requiring competitive bidding, publicly announced it was shifting steel purchases to companies that had not increased prices, and other Government agencies were directed to do likewise.

9. The F.B.I. began routing newspaper men out of bed at 3:00 A.M. on Thursday, April 12, in line with President Kennedy's press conference assertion that "we are investigating" a statement attributed to a steel company official in the newspapers.

Taken cumulatively these nine actions amount to a display of naked political power never seen before in this nation.

Taken singly these nine actions are punitive, heavy-handed and frightening.

• • • • • • •

We condone nothing in the actions of the steel companies except their right to make an economic judgment without massive retaliation by the Federal Government.

Aftermath

Whether or not the steel executives who wore buttons bearing the words "I miss Ike" and in smaller letters, "I even miss Harry," had removed them by the spring of 1963 could not be scientifically determined. In any case the administration did not quarrel with a price rise covering about 20 per cent of the industry's products and resulting in about a 1 per cent increase in the over-all steel products price index. It was led by such smaller producers as Lukens, who later modified some of the rises to take into account lesser increases by U.S. Steel. Kennedy stated that the steel producers "have acted with some restraint in this case."

QUESTIONS

1. How did the steel industry's attempts to meet the capacity problem contribute to criticism of their pricing policies, as in 1957?

2. What economic facts allowed the steelworkers to present a reasonably strong argument that the price rise in 1957 was not necessitated by the wage increase? How did both U.S. Steel and the union select the statistics that strengthened their particular positions?

3. Why did Mr. Blough feel that Senator Kefauver was trying to "trap" him in the hearings in 1957?

4. Explain Mr. Kennedy's strong reaction to the price increase in 1962. Would you agree or disagree with his position?

5. Do you think the failure of U.S. Steel's price increase in 1962 was primarily because of political considerations, economic considerations, or a combination of both?

CASE 6–4: PRICE-LEVEL DETERMINATION BY GENERAL MOTORS

For many years, General Motors seems to have been following the same pricing procedures.[32]

The major steps in the pricing processes have been given as follows:

1. The preliminary product planning, so that a car such as Chevrolet may be sold within a general price range.
2. The establishing of standard prices on the basis of standard costs and a standard return at a standard volume.
3. The setting of the prevailing or list price. (Actually, this price has been set at a retail level, with the price to the dealer allowing a 25 per cent margin.)

The following material is from the *Hearings before the Senate Subcommittee on Antitrust and Monopoly of December, 1955*.[33] Mr. Burns was counsel for the committee, and Mr. Bradley and Mr. Donner were vice presidents and directors of General Motors.

---

[32]The most detailed exposition of the method is probably in Homer Vanderblue's article, "Pricing Policies in the Automobile Industry," *Harvard Business Review,* Summer, 1939 (see pp. 1–17). Other references are Kaplan, Dirlam, and Lanzillotti, *Pricing in Big Business* (Washington: Brookings Institution, 1958), pp. 48–55, 131–35; and Joel Dean, *Managerial Economics* (Englewood Cliffs, N.J.: Prentice-Hall, 1951), pp. 448–49.

[33]Washington, D.C.: U.S. Government Printing Office, 1956.

MR. BURNS: I would like to ask you some questions with respect to those principles, and the source of my information is the articles by Donaldson Brown, which I believe were published in 1924, entitled "Pricing Policy in Relation to Financial Return."

You are familiar with those articles?

MR. BRADLEY: Yes.

MR. BURNS: And do they express in broad terms the pricing policies which have been used by the corporation since that time?

MR. BRADLEY: That is correct.

MR. BURNS: Mr. Brown also made this statement with respect to attainable annual return and the pricing formula:

> The formulation of the pricing policy must be with regard to the p⸱rticular circumstances pertaining to each individual business. When formulated, it is expressed simply in the conception of what have been defined as standard volume and the economic return available.

Now, would you explain for the benefit of our record what is meant by the term "standard volume"?

MR. BRADLEY: Yes; I think I might illustrate the standard volume.

We endeavor in planning for capacity to—we take the number of days there are in the year, and then take out the Sundays and holidays, and then we take out the minimum number of days we produce this over a period of time to turn around—I mean, to bring out new models.

From that, we find there are 225, taking out all the Sundays, holidays, and Saturdays, and 15 full days, or 30 half days, for turning around, giving 225 days which we would like to run the plants, year in and year out.

But we don't use 225, we use 80 per cent of that as a standard volume, because ours is a business that you might call cyclical, and while it has been on the upswing for a number of years, there have been times when we had downswings—in fact, for a number of years we averaged below standard volume.

So, to allow for that cyclical factor and other conditions beyond our control, we take 80 per cent of that 225 days, times the rated capacity per hour. So that gives us 180 days. And that, multiplied by our daily capacity, gives us a standard volume, which we work up by divisions, and which we hope to average.

Well, we have had years below it, and years above it.

MR. BURNS: How long a planning period do you use in your consideration of standard volume?

MR. BRADLEY: Well, except for the number of days for the turnaround, we haven't changed our standard volume. The 80 per cent of the rated daily capacity times 225 days, that has remained constant over the years.

MR. BURNS: When you are planning—

MR. BRADLEY: Excuse me. We use that in planning capacity.

MR. BURN: Now, when you are making your projections for either new models or plant expansion, do you use any particular length of time as a planning period?

MR. BRADLEY: Well, of course, we make our economic studies for several years ahead, but they are not firm. They are subject to revision at any time. I mean, for example, we did not plan for as big volume as we have had in the last 2 or 3 years. With the national income, which has grown faster—the gross national product—with the movement out to the suburbs, and so on, so the big market has been bigger than we anticipated, but we try to look ahead a number of years and plan accordingly. We have to plan at least 2 years ahead or we would not have the capacity.

MR. BURNS: Well, now, what profit margin or attainable return have you used in pricing policy in recent years?

MR. BRADLEY: Well, actually in the back of our minds we have a standard, but one of the factors referred to there was competition. And the net profit may be below standard, or what we hope to have—the economic return attainable may be bigger in one business—one activity or one division than another. But we can always compare with what we expected.

We have not changed our general sights in a period of over 20 years.

MR. BURNS: What have been the general sights?

MR. BRADLEY: Ours is a fairly rapid turnover business, and our operations will yield between 15 or 20 per cent on the net capital employed over the years. . . .

· · · · · · ·

SENATOR O'MAHONEY: . . . What is this general overall percentage which is added to the cost of the car for overhead for the general staff?

MR. DONNER: The figure I haven't got in my mind. Maybe I can get it in a minute. It isn't a high percentage at all. I don't think it would be 1 per cent.

SENATOR O'MAHONEY: Let me ask you this way, then:

What are the basic elements of cost that enter into fixing the price of the car that is sold to the average automobile purchaser in the United States?

MR. DONNER: Sixty per cent of the cost is materials that we buy. Some thirty-odd per cent is payroll.

SENATOR O'MAHONEY: That includes all payrolls, the mechanics and the—

MR. DONNERS: Right up to the president.

SENATOR O'MAHONEY: Right up to the president?

MR. DONNER: There is a couple of per cent depreciation—

SENATOR O'MAHONEY: Yes, sir.

MR. DONNER (continuing): And I think a couple of per cent for taxes other than Federal income taxes.

Now, that roughly adds up to a hundred per cent of the cost.

· · · · · · ·

(After putting in the record S.E.C. figures for 1954 that showed profits after taxes as 9.9% of stockholder equity for all industry and 14.1% for motor vehicles and parts, Mr. Burns continued:)

I also would like to place in the record some figures from Moody's of the percentage of net income to net worth:

General Motors, 1948, 24.47; 1949, 31.37; 1950, 34.94; 1951, 20 per cent 1952, 20.59; 1953, 20.05; and their figure for 1954 is 24.43 percent. (1955 showed a 31% return. 1961 and 1962 results are given in Exhibit 1.)

QUESTIONS

1. Assuming that General Motors was using the pricing approach discussed, analyze the difference in operating results for 1961 and 1962. (Draw hypothetical demand, average variable cost, and average total cost curves to illustrate your analysis.)

2. General Motors' approach has been termed "sophisticated cost-plus pricing." How does GM break the circle that prices determine volume and volume determines cost and cost determines price? How can GM bring demand considerations into its pricing approach?

Exhibit 1

OPERATING RESULTS FOR GENERAL MOTORS, 1961–62

	1961	1962	Percentage Increase
Sales............................	$11,037,000,000	$14,159,000,000	+28%
Net income......................	893,000,000	1,459,000,000	+63
Shareholders' investment.........	6,026,000,000	6,650,000,000	+10
Unit sales, cars and trucks........	3,150,000	4,223,000	+35
Profits as percentage of investment.	14.8%	21.9%	+48

Note: Prices of cars remain basically unchanged from those of previous years, marking the fifth year of no basic change.
Source: *Annual Report for 1962, General Motors Corp.*

3. Could the other automobile manufacturers successfully use a similar approach to pricing? What modifications might be necessary? (The student will find it helpful to examine the operating results of at least one other car manufacturer to see if a target return of 15–20 per cent on investment would have been practical.)

CASE 6–5: ADVERTISING, PRICE, AND PRODUCT COMPETITION IN THE CIGARETTE INDUSTRY

Note: The first part of this industry case is an almost exact reproduction of the case called "Cigarette Advertising" in earlier editions which was based on materials in the early 1940's. The second part is a brief summary of postwar developments to early 1963 and may usefully be supplemented by more current material. It is worth while to recognize the great contrasts in the problems faced by the cigarette firms in the two periods and at the same time to note certain similarities. Particularly succinct summaries of current market developments should be found in the annual reviews published in December issues of *Printer's Ink* and *Business Week*. A comprehensive report on the medical problem and the industry's and the government's reactions may be found in *The Consumers Union Report on Smoking and the Public Interest.*[34]

PART I[35]

Advertising expenditures by manufacturers of tobacco products have for many years been among the highest of any industry. Much of the total has been devoted to the advertising of cigarettes. In 1939, cigarettes accounted for three fourths of the estimated total advertising expenditure of $60 million on tobacco products. In 1931 the Association of National Advertisers reported the expenditures of four large tobacco companies as averaging 8.23 per cent of sales. In the late 1930's, advertising expense of individual companies ranged from 6 to 30 per cent.

Approximately three quarters of all advertising expenditures on cigarettes and about the same share of total sales were made by these companies: the American Tobacco Company, with its Lucky Strike brand; the Liggett & Myers Company, with the Chesterfield brand; and the R. J. Reynolds Company, with the Camel brand (see Exhibit 1). The dominance of the cigarette market by these three companies, combined with their heavy advertising outlays, led certain critics to charge that other companies had been prevented from getting a large share of the market because they could not match these expenditures.

The R. J. Reynolds Company began the practice of concentrating advertising on one brand of cigarette with the introduction of Camels in 1913. Reynolds' share of the cigarette market rose from 0.2 per cent in 1913 to 40 per cent in 1917 and 45 per cent in 1925. Noting the success of Camels, the Liggett & Myers Company similarly concentrated advertising on its brand, Chesterfield, which had been launched in 1912. American Tobacco company followed with the Lucky Strike brand in 1917. In 1926 the P. Lorillard Company attempted to enter the field with its Old Gold brand. It embarked on an ambitious advertising campaign, financed by the flotation of a $15 million issue of debenture bonds in 1927. Despite large advertising expenditures, which exceeded $1.5 million by 1938, the Old Gold brand failed to increase its share of the market, as is indicated in Exhibit 2. In January, 1933, the Philip Morris Company launched a new blend of 15-cent cigarettes under the

---

[34]Mount Vernon, 1963.

[35]This part is based on materials contained in Professor Neil H. Borden's volume, *The Economic Effects of Advertising* (Chicago: Richard D. Irwin, Inc., 1942), chap. viii.

Exhibit 1

CIGARETTE CONSUMPTION BY BRAND AND TRACEABLE ADVERTISING EXPENDITURE IN NEWSPAPERS, MAGAZINES, FARM PUBLICATIONS, AND CHAIN RADIO, 1929–39

YEAR	CAMEL		CHESTERFIELD		LUCKY STRIKE		TEN-CENT BRANDS		ALL OTHER		GRAND TOTAL	
	Consumption (Billions of Cigarettes)	Traceable Advertising Expenditure (Thousands of Dollars)	Consumption (Billions of Cigarettes)	Traceable Advertising Expenditure (Thousands of Dollars)	Consumption (Billions of Cigarettes)	Traceable Advertising Expenditure (Thousands of Dollars)	Consumption (Billions of Cigarettes)	Traceable Advertising Expenditure (Thousands of Dollars)	Consumption (Billions of Cigarettes)	Traceable Advertising Expenditure (Thousands of Dollars)	Consumption (Billions of Cigarettes)	Traceable Advertising Expenditure (Thousands of Dollars)
1929	40.0	$ 1,942	26.0	$ 5,254	36.4	$ 6,589	....	.....	16.6	$7,022	119.0	$20,806
1930	38.0	4,813	25.0	5,968	42.6	10,095	....	.....	14.0	5,142	119.6	26,018
1931	33.0	10,006	24.6	9,130	44.6	13,649	....	.....	11.2	5,210	113.4	37,996
1932	·24.6	2,389	21.0	11,138	37.0	10,850	12.0	$ 26	9.0	4,058	103.6	28,461
1933	26.5	10,248	29.0	7,590	37.5	7,192	8.5	100	10.3	2,340	111.8	27,471
1934	32.0	10,382	33.5	9,575	33.5	8,120	13.0	143	13.6	3,441	125.6	31,661
1935	37.0	9,265	36.0	9,443	32.5	5,588	13.1	68	16.0	4,852	134.6	29,216
1936	43.0	9,042	38.0	8,909	37.0	6,846	16.0	827	19.2	6,848	153.2	32,472
1937	45.0	8,529	38.0	8,949	38.5	5,617	19.0	470	22.1	7,191	162.6	30,755
1938	41.0	8,362	37.4	9,279	38.3	4,095	24.0	483	23.0	4,866	163.7	27,085
1939	40.0	7,367	36.5	7,776	39.5	4,214	30.0	1,157	26.4	4,442	172.4	24,956
Average	36.4	$ 7,486	31.4	$ 8,455	37.9	$ 7,532	17.0	$ 409	16.5	$5,037	134.5	$28,809

Source: Neil H. Borden, *The Economic Effects of Advertising* (Chicago: Richard D. Irwin, Inc., 1942), p. 229.

brand name Philip Morris. The new brand was first tried experimentally in certain large cities, where it met with such success that the company began an extensive advertising campaign financed out of earnings. By 1939, expenditures for advertising exceeded $1.5 million, and the company was firmly intrenched in fourth place.

Exhibit 2

ESTIMATED DOMESTIC CONSUMPTION OF LEADING BRANDS IN BILLIONS OF CIGARETTES AND PERCENTAGE OF TOTAL CONSUMPTION BY BRANDS, 1929–39

YEAR	CAMEL		CHESTERFIELD		LUCKY STRIKE		OLD GOLD	
	Cigarettes (Billions)	% of Total	Cigarettes (Billions)	% of Total	Cigarettes (Billions)	% of Total	Cigarettes (Billions)	% of Total
1929...	40.0	33.6	26.0	21.8	36.4	30.6	8.0	6.7
1930...	38.0	31.8	25.0	20.9	42.6	35.6	8.0	6.7
1931...	33.0	29.1	24.6	21.7	44.6	39.3	7.6	6.7
1932...	24.6	23.7	21.0	20.7	37.0	35.7	5.7	5.5
1933...	26.5	23.7	29.0	25.9	37.5	33.1	5.5	4.9
1934...	32.0	25.5	33.5	26.7	33.5	26.7	5.0	4.0
1935...	37.0	27.4	36.0	26.7	32.5	24.1	5.3	3.9
1936...	43.0	28.1	38.0	24.8	37.0	24.2	6.8	4.4
1937...	45.0	27.7	38.0	23.4	38.5	23.7	7.9	5.0
1938...	41.0	25.0	37.4	22.8	38.3	23.4	6.3	3.8
1939...	40.0	23.2	36.5	21.2	39.5	22.9	5.3	3.1

YEAR	PHILIP MORRIS		MENTHOLATED BRANDS		COMBINED TEN-CENT BRANDS		ALL OTHER BRANDS		TOTAL BILLIONS	% OF TOTAL REPRESENTED BY THREE LEADING BRANDS
	Cigarettes (Billions)	% of Total	Cigarettes (Billions)	% of Total	Cigarettes (Billions)	% of Total	Cigarettes (Billions)	% of Total		
1929......	...	...	...	...	....	....	8.6	7.2	119.0	86.0
1930......	...	...	...	...	....	....	6.0	5.0	119.6	88.3
1931......	...	...	*	...	*	....	3.6	3.2	113.4	90.1
1932......	*	...	*	...	12.0	11.6	3.3	3.2	103.6	80.1
1933......	*	...	*	...	8.5	7.6	4.8	4.3	111.8	82.7
1934......	2.8	2.2	3.3	2.6	13.0	10.4	2.5	2.0	125.6	78.9
1935......	3.8	2.8	4.1	3.0	13.1	9.7	2.8	2.1	134.6	78.2
1936......	5.0	3.3	3.7	2.4	16.0	10.4	3.7	2.4	153.2	77.1
1937......	7.5	4.9	2.6	1.6	19.0	11.7	4.1	2.5	162.6	74.8
1938......	9.2	5.6	1.9	1.2	24.0	14.7	5.6	3.4	163.7	71.2
1939......	11.0	6.4	2.0	1.2	30.0	17.4	8.1	4.7	172.4	67.3

* Included in "All Other Brands."
Source: "Basic Survey—Tobacco," *Standard Trade and Securities*, Vol. XCVI, No. 20 (June 7, 1940), Sec. 3.

Relying on an inelastic demand for the product, the leading tobacco companies raised the wholesale price of cigarettes from $6.00 per thousand to $6.40 in October, 1929, and to $6.85 in June, 1931. These wholesale prices resulted in retail prices on the more popular brands of

14 and '15 cents per package. The maintained high prices of the leading brands encouraged transference of demand, particularly after June, 1931, to 10-cent cigarettes, as indicated by Exhibit 3. Prior to 1931, there were only two 10-cent brands of significance—Coupon, sold by Liggett & Myers, and Paul Jones, sold by Continental Tobacco Company. After June, 1931, several other companies entered the field: in September, Larus & Brothers, Inc.; in March, 1932, Brown & Williamson Tobacco Company reduced the price on its Wings brand to put it in the 10-cent class; in May, 1932, Sunshines, manufactured by the Pinkerton Tobacco Company, were put in the 10-cent class; in June, 1932, Axton-Fisher entered its new brand, Twenty Grand; during the same

Exhibit 3

PERCENTAGE OF TOTAL CIGARETTE SALES SECURED BY THE
10-CENT BRANDS BY MONTHS FROM JANUARY, 1931, TO
FEBRUARY, 1936, INCLUSIVE

Month	1931	1932	1933	1934	1935	1936
January	0.26	2.33	16.76	10.00	10.85	10.59
February	0.27	3.30	11.60	9.96	11.71	10.51
March	0.28	3.26	7.07	10.43	11.25	.....
April	0.27	6.13	8.55	11.11	11.70	.....
May	0.23	6.59	6.43	10.37	11.72	.....
June	0.28	9.12	7.03	10.01	11.36	.....
July	0.57	12.46	9.58	12.09	11.87	.....
August	1.82	17.76	8.67	12.38	13.72	.....
September	2.00	19.57	9.78	11.62	13.53	.....
October	2.41	19.00	9.54	12.46	11.01	.....
November	2.39	22.78	11.21	13.13	12.15	.....
December	2.88	21.31	9.26	12.28	12.54	.....

Source: *Report of the Federal Trade Commission on Agricultural Income Inquiry*, Part I: "Principal Farm Products" (Washington, D.C.: U.S. Government Printing Office, 1938). p. 462.

month, Scott & Dill came into the scramble; and in September, Stephano Brothers bought out Marvels. The rise in sales of the 10-cent brands during the depression was phenomenal. Starting almost from nothing in 1931 they accounted for over 20% of the domestic cigarette market for a few months during the fall of 1932."[36] On January 3, 1933, the Big Three reduced wholesale prices to $6.00 per thousand, and a month later to $5.50. Retail prices fell to 12.5 cents, then to 10 and 11 cents. With the price differential for the leading brands practically removed, sales of 10-cent cigarettes fell from 21.3 per cent of total sales in December, 1932, to 6.4 per cent in May, 1933. During all of this period, retail prices of Philip Morris cigarettes were main-

[36]*Ibid.*, p. 234.

tained at 15 cents. In January, 1934, the Big Three increased wholesale prices to $6.10 per thousand and in January, 1936, to $6.25, with resulting increases in retail prices to 12.5 and then 13.5 cents a package. The 10-cent brands responded by increasing to a share of the total market which ranged from 10 to 12 per cent. By 1939, however, this share had increased to over 17 per cent.

In 1936, most of the companies producing 10-cent cigarettes swung over to advertising, as indicated in Exhibit 1. Although it was clear that their margins could not permit the extensive advertising employed by the standard brands, they thought that a limited amount was desirable to build volume.

A survey by *Fortune* magazine in 1935 indicated that cigarette smokers did not frequently shift brands. In response to the question, "How many years have you been smoking this brand?" the survey reported the following replies:

Years	Per Cent	Years	Per Cent
1	12.6	5	10.1
2	12.9	Over 5	44.3
3	10.0	Don't know	4.2
4	5.9		

Managements of tobacco companies believed, however, that the stability of demand for their respective products was based largely on subjective valuations created by continued advertising outlays. Blindfold tests carried on experimentally among fifty-one subjects, all of whom smoked regularly and generally stuck to one brand, indicated the difficulty which consumers experienced in identifying brands. Each subject was tested with four cigarettes, three leading brands and one other. Each was told that his own brand would be among the four, which were presented in random order. Adequate time was allowed between smokes to compensate for taste confusion and fatigue. Although chance alone would have resulted in a 20 per cent identification, only 31 per cent of the smokers guessed their own brand. The results are shown in Exhibit 4.

Although consumers found it difficult to identify brands, there were some indications that they discriminated among different brands of cigarettes as to blending and flavor. When the R. J. Reynolds Company introduced Camel cigarettes in 1913, the product was based on a domestic blend of bright-leaf tobacco. This proved so popular that

Camels quickly rose to first place. Competition thereupon followed with the promotion of domestic blends. In the opinion of executives of the major companies the success of any cigarette was determined to a considerable extent by the flavor or blend of the product. The failure

Exhibit 4

IDENTIFICATION OF DIFFERENT CIGARETTE BRANDS IN BLINDFOLD TEST, 51 SUBJECTS

BRAND	PER CENT OF SUBJECTS IDENTIFYING BRAND IN COLUMN 1 AS:					
	Camel	Lucky Strike	Chester-field	Twenty Grand	Spud	Miscel-laneous
Camel................	31	14	38	6	2	10
Lucky Strike........	19	41	21	4	0	14
Chesterfield........	27	23	33	2	0	15
Twenty Grand.......	38	26	3	17	0	15
Spud..............	0	6	6	0	76	11

Source: R. W. Husband and Jane Godfrey, "An Experimental Study of Cigarette Identification," *Journal of Applied Psychology*, April, 1934, p. 222.

Exhibit 5

BILLIONS OF CIGARETTES SOLD AND TRACEABLE ADVERTISING EXPENDITURE IN NEWSPAPERS, MAGAZINES, FARM JOURNALS, AND CHAIN RADIO OF CIGARETTE BRANDS, IN THOUSANDS OF DOLLARS FOR EACH BILLION OF CIGARETTES SOLD, 1929–39

YEAR	CAMEL		CHESTERFIELD		LUCKY STRIKE		TEN-CENT BRANDS		ALL OTHERS	
	Advertising, Thousands of Dollars per Billion Cigarettes	Billions of Cigarettes Sold	Advertising, Thousands of Dollars per Billion Cigarettes	Billions of Cigarettes Sold	Advertising, Thousands of Dollars per Billion Cigarettes	Billions of Cigarettes Sold	Advertising, Thousands of Dollars per Billion Cigarettes	Billions of Cigarettes Sold	Advertising, Thousands of Dollars per Billion Cigarettes	Billions of Cigarettes Sold
1929...............	48.5	40.0	202.1	26.0	180.2	36.4	....	....	413.0	16.6
1930...............	126.7	38.0	238.7	25.0	237.0	42.6	....	....	367.3	14.0
1931...............	303.2	33.0	371.1	24.6	306.0	44.6	....	....	473.7	11.2
1932...............	97.1	24.6	530.4	21.0	293.3	37.0	2.4	12.0	450.9	9.0
1933...............	386.7	26.5	261.7	29.0	191.8	37.5	11.8	8.5	227.2	10.3
1934...............	324.4	32.0	285.8	33.5	242.4	33.5	11.0	13.0	253.0	13.6
1935...............	250.4	37.0	262.3	36.0	171.9	32.5	5.2	13.1	303.3	16.0
1936...............	210.3	43.0	234.4	38.0	185.0	37.0	51.6	16.0	230.3	19.2
1937...............	189.5	45.0	235.5	38.0	145.9	38.5	24.7	19.0	309.8	22.1
1938...............	203.9	41.0	248.1	37.4	106.9	38.3	20.1	24.0	211.6	23.0
1939...............	184.2	40.0	213.1	36.5	106.7	39.5	38.6	30.0	168.3	26.4
Average........	211.4	36.4	280.3	31.4	199.0	37.9	20.7	17.0	309.8	16.5

Source: Neil H. Borden, *The Economic Effects of Advertising* (Chicago: Richard D. Irwin, Inc., 1942), p. 243.

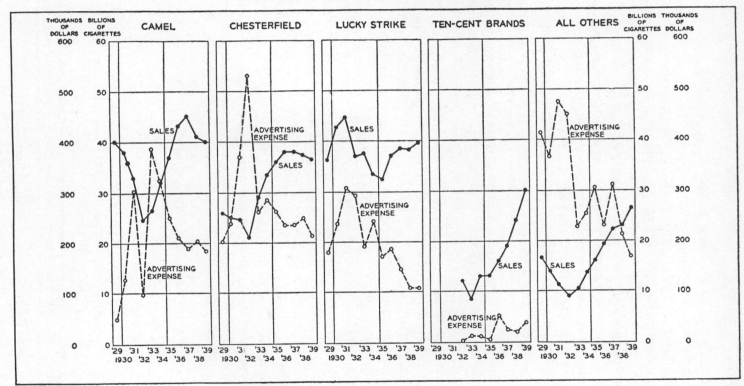

Exhibit 6

TRACEABLE ADVERTISING EXPENDITURES PER BILLION CIGARETTES,
AND SALES IN BILLIONS, BY BRANDS, 1929–39

Source: Neil H. Borden, *The Economic Effects of Advertising* (Chicago: Richard D. Irwin, Inc., 1942), p. 244.

of one brand of cigarettes, which was supported by large advertising expenditures, was attributed to the lack of success in finding an acceptable blend. In the first three months that the cigarette was on the market, it enjoyed a large sales volume, but soon it became evident to company executives that it had failed to win lasting consumer acceptance. Sales dropped. Investigation showed that many consumers, after once trying the new cigarette, did not repurchase. Executives believed that although the blend approximated those of the leading brands, it had failed basically because consumers did not like it. The importance of blend led the Philip Morris Company, before placing the cigarette of that name on the market in 1933, to work out a large number of blends. The blenders then chose what they regarded as the twenty best blends from this group and forwarded them to company executives for final selection. The executives, after careful consideration, finally selected the blend which later met with great consumer favor. Another illustration of the importance of blend was the tranference of demand from the inferior tobaccos of the 10-cent cigarettes to the standard brands in 1933 when differentials between these two groups were virtually eliminated. Consumers were evidently sensitive to quality differences where price differentials were not great.

Although advertising expenditures of each of the Big Three were vastly in excess of those of other companies in the field in the period 1930–39, the three leaders did not hold the same relative positions throughout the period. Moreover, as is indicated in Exhibits 5 and 6, the advertising outlays of these companies varied in effectiveness. Over this ten-year period, Chesterfield spent an average of $280,000 in advertising for each billion cigarettes sold; Camel spent $211,000; and Lucky Strike, $199,000. By contrast, the 10-cent brands spend less than $30,000 per billion cigarettes sold.

QUESTIONS

1. Was the over-all demand for cigarettes elastic or inelastic in the relevant price range during the depression of the 1930's?

2. What could you say about the demand for the product of any one of the large cigarette companies if it had cut price while the other large companies held the line on price?

3. What happened to demand in 1932?

4. Were the makers of 10-cent cigarettes well advised to use advertising?

5. Were the Big Three wise in raising prices in 1931?

6. Is cigarette advertising socially wasteful?

PART II

The Cigarette Industry in the Postwar Period

In January, 1963, *Fortune* magazine surveyed the cigarette industry under the title *"Embattled Tobacco's New Strategy."* The financial record of the industry had been much improved from 1957 through 1961, with returns on net worth ranging from a low of 8.95 per cent for Liggett & Myers in 1961 to a high of 21.36 per cent for P. Lorillard in 1958. The common stocks of the five major cigarette companies had risen from a low of 15 in 1957 to over 58 at the end of 1961, while the Standard & Poor's composite index rose only from 52 to 72. In 1961 the dollar sales of four of the five domestic producers hit all-time highs, and unit sales rose by 3.8 per cent, the seventh consecutive year of rises, ranging from 3.1 per cent to 6.5 per cent. The pessimistic sales and financial symptoms were modest enough, an increase of only 1.8 per cent in the number of cigarettes sold and an estimated decline in profits of 1 per cent for the five concerns from 1961 to 1962. Overshadowing these symptoms, however, were the accumulating evidence of the health hazards of cigarette smoking and the probability of the Advisory Committee on Smoking and Health of the U.S. Surgeon-General's office taking a strong official position against smoking. Much of the basic medical evidence had been public knowledge since the early 1950's, and substantial changes had already taken place in the product offerings of the industry. It is appropriate to review the important postwar developments in assessing industry problems in 1963.

Despite the antitrust conviction of the major cigarette producers[37] in 1946, the postwar period started brightly for them. Per capita cigarette consumption had almost doubled from the 1935–39 average of 1,641. Both habits formed during the war and higher incomes were probably helpful. The low-priced "10-cent" brands, which had maintained a persistent position throughout the 1930's despite retaliation efforts by the "Big Three" (these played a part in the antitrust conviction), were largely out of the market. Both prosperity and higher tax levels (since taxes were on a unit rather than value basis, the percentage price spread between regular and low-priced brands was less) limited the appeal of lower priced brands.

Perhaps because of the antitrust conviction, the major producers showed considerable restraint in raising cigarette prices, and profits were fairly modest in the early postwar years. There was some indication

---

[37]*American Tobacco Co.* v. *United States*, 328 U.S. 781 (1946).

of the product competition to come in the success of king-sized Pall Mall, which had 3.4 per cent of the market in 1947, but the traditional "Big Three" brands had over 80 per cent of the market (92 per cent with Old Gold and Philip Morris added in).

In the late 1930's, long before the publicity on lung cancer and cigarettes, the cigarette companies had started to use health appeals to promote their brands, and these themes continued in the postwar period. For example, in 1939, Philip Morris was claiming "that Philip Morris cigarettes are much better for the nose and throat, a superiority recognized by eminent medical authorities." This advertising emphasis may well have eased the way for the king-sized cigarettes, whose greater length was tangible evidence of further screening for the throat. Pall Mall was utilizing this appeal in 1949 with "Guard against throat scratch . . . enjoy smoother smoking. Pall Mall's greater length of fine tobacco travels the smoke further, filters the smoke and makes it mild."

In 1950 the Federal Trade Commission was finally able to issue cease and desist orders against three of the companies against the use of various health claims. Litigation had begun in 1942 and 1943. P. Lorillard tried to turn the FTC decisions against it barring claims of less nicotine or less irritation than other brands in this way:

"Okay mother, if you want a treat instead of a treatment, treat yourself to Old Golds.

"If you've been confused by medical claims for cigarettes, remember this: no other leading cigarette is less irritating, or easier on the throat, or contains less nicotine than Old Gold. This conclusion was established on evidence by the United States Government."

The years 1953 and 1954 brought fairly conclusive evidence that medical findings on the relationship between cigarette smoking and lung cancer could affect the market. Per capita consumption of cigarettes in the United States dropped from an estimated 3,509 cigarettes in 1952 to 3,413 in 1953 and 3,216 in 1954, after an almost continuous rise for several decades. The medical evidence had been building up for many years and would continue to be strengthened in subsequent years, but the basic outlines of the case were well established in 1953 and 1954:

1. Correlation studies indicated that the rapid rise in lung cancer in the various countries of the world followed the establishment of strong cigarette habits.
2. Retrospective studies of lung cancer victims indicated that the vast majority were regular cigarette smokers. These studies had become more persuasive as better control groups were set up to show that these vic-

tims differed from the rest of the population primarily in their smoking habits.

3. Human pathological findings found significant changes in the lungs of smokers that indicated precancerous conditions.

4. Experiments indicated that cancer could be induced in laboratory animals by components of the cigarette smoke.

5. Prospective studies, in which large samples of middle-aged men were classified as to smoking and other characteristics and were followed through several years to observe the time and cause of death, indicated death rates from lung cancer for heavy cigarette smokers of approximately twenty times that of nonsmokers. These prospective studies broadened the health issue from simply lung cancer to generally excessive mortality rates, particularly from coronary artery diseases, and confronted the public with such findings as the fact that heavy cigarette smokers die at rates of men who are seven or eight years older among nonsmokers.

Presumably influenced by the public health agitation and declining sales, fourteen tobacco companies, including all of the majors, formed the Tobacco Industry Research Committee to study all phases of to-

Exhibit 7

SHARES OF DOMESTIC MARKET FOR LEADING CIGARETTES

(All Brands with Over 2½ Per Cent of Market in Selected Years Are Listed)

		PERCENTAGES OF DOMESTIC SALES				
CIGARETTE (TYPE)	COMPANY	1931	1947	1953	1959	1962
Camel (R)	R. J. Reynolds	28.4	30.4	25.6	11.0	13.2
Lucky Strike (R). . .	American Tobacco	39.5	29.5	16.8	9.5	7.8
Chesterfields (R) . . .	Liggett & Myers	22.7	20.8	12.5*	3.6*	(2.0)*
Old Gold (R)	P. Lorillard	6.5	4.3	5.0*	2.5*	(0.2)*
Philip Morris (R)...	Philip Morris		6.9	7.2*	2.5*	(0.8)*
Kool (M-R)	Brown & Williamson			3.0	3.0*	(0.7)*
Pall Mall (K).	American Tobacco		3.4	12.4	14.1	14.4
Tareyton (K).	American Tobacco			3.6	2.5*	(0.6)*
Chesterfield (K). . . .	Liggett & Myers			3.5	2.5*	(2.4)*
Winston (F)	R. J. Reynolds				9.5	12.1
Viceroy (F)	Brown & Williamson				4.7	3.8
L & M (F)	Liggett & Myers				5.5	4.9
Marlboro (F)	Philip Morris				4.6	5.1
Kent (F)	P. Lorillard				8.0	7.0
Salem (M-F)	R. J. Reynolds				7.0	9.1
Parliament (F)	Philip Morris				2.5	(2.0)

*Excludes sales of other types.
Note: The letter R = regular; K = king size; M = mentholated; F = filtertip. Parentheses indicate shares below 2½ per cent.
Sources: Data for 1947–62 based on estimates from various December issues of *Business Week;* 1931 data from *American Tobacco Co.* v. *United States,* 328 U.S. 781.

bacco use, and from 1954 through 1962 contributed $6.25 million for about four hundred grants to research men. The public position taken by both it and the Tobacco Institute formed by the same companies in 1958 to advance public relations has been that the causative role of cigarettes in disease has not been proved and that more experimental research is needed. It was possible to maintain this position up to 1963 because the origins of cancer remained obscure, the causes seemed to be multiple, only long-continued cigarette smoking was the culprit pointed to by the studies, and the bulk of the evidence continued to be observational.[38]

Judging from the product revolution that took place between 1952 and 1960, substantial proportions of the smoking public felt that tangible reassurance was important. In 1953, as shown in Exhibit 7, no filter brand qualified with 2½ per cent of the market; as a matter of fact, the handful of then existing brands taken together constituted less than 2 per cent of the market. The greater length to "travel the smoke" of the king-sized cigarette seemed to be supplying whatever soothing effects cigarette smokers needed in face of the disagreeable statistics. The continuing growth of king-sized brands had cut the share of the five "regular" leaders from 92 per cent to 67 per cent since 1947; and Old Gold, Philip Morris, and Chesterfield had come out with the larger versions. As it turned out, the nonfilter king-sized category had almost reached its apex, and no brand but Pall Mall was to do well (as can be noted in Exhibit 8, Pall Mall had a 73 per cent share of the category in 1961).

By 1959, almost 50 per cent of consumption was of filter cigarettes, and the brand structure of the industry had been drastically transformed —no less than sixteen brands had approximately 2½ per cent of the market or more, as against four in 1931, six in 1947, and nine in 1959. The seven additions were all filter cigarettes, representing all of the six major companies except American Tobacco, which, however, possessed the new-brand leader, Pall Mall. No one brand had as much as one seventh of the market. Apparent cigarette consumption was up for the fifth year in a row; and in both 1958 and 1959, new per capita highs in consumption were reached.

It is worth giving some attention to the advertising and product strategies and tactics, and to the external pressures under which they were used during this period of rapid change. Exhibit 9 indicates that after being relatively stable in 1954 and 1955, advertising expendi-

---

[38]See Appendix to this case (pp. 309-12).

Exhibit 8

BRAND, SHARE, AND ADVERTISING EXPENDITURES OF CIGARETTE MANUFACTURERS BY MARKET SEGMENTS
Brand Name/Share of Market Segment
Cigarettes Sold, 1962 (Billions)/Advertising Expenditure per Million Cigarettes, 1961

	Filter (Plain)	Filter (Mentholated)	Regular	King Size
Cigarettes sold (billions)...................	202	72	125	99
Approximate share of market of each type.....	(41%)	(14%)	(25%)	(20%)
R. J. Reynolds.............................	Winston/30%	Salem/62%	Camel/52%	Brandon/new
	60.5/$249	45.4/$342	66.0/$138	
American Tobacco.........................	Tareyton/5%	Montclair/new	Lucky Strike/33%	Pall Mall/73%
	11.7/$517		39.0/$139	72.1/$180
				Tareyton/3%
				3.0/$517
Liggett & Myers...........................	L & M/12%	Oasis/1%	Chesterfield/8%	Chesterfield/12%
	24.5/$452	0.8/$2,292	10.5/$312	11.9/$312
P. Lorillard..............................	Kent/18%	Newport/11%	Old Gold/1%	York/2%
	35.4/$377	8.2/$774	1.2/$456	1.5/n.a.*
	Old Gold/2%	Spring/1%		Old Gold/1%
	4.5/$456	0.7/n.a.		1.0/$456
Brown & Williamson.......................	Viceroy/9%	Kool/17%	Kool (menth.) 3%	Raleigh/3%
	19.0/$387	12.2/$283	3.6/$283	3.4/$267
	Raleigh/4%	Belair/3%		Coronet/new
	7.6/$267	2.3/$3,343		
Philip Morris.............................	Marlboro/13%	Alpine/4%	Philip Morris/3%	Philip Morris/5%
	25.7/$360	2.6/$1,036	3.8/$316	5.1/$316
	Parliament/5%	Spud/0%		Commander/0%
	10.2/$651	n.a.		n.a.
	Benson & Hedges/1%			
	1.0/n.a.			

*Not available.
Sources: *Business Week*, December 1, 1962 (sales); *Advertising Age*, June 25, 1962 (advertising expenditures per million cigarettes, 1961, including advertising expenditures in magazines, newspapers, and television, but not radio, point of sale etc.).

tures literally exploded in 1956, with an increase in seven major media of about 40 per cent, and did not again stabilize until a 1959 level of more than double that of 1953 were reached. While profits as a percentage of sales were occasionally reduced during the period (four of the five American-owned major companies had reduced margins in 1956); for all but Philip Morris, the ratios were substantially higher in 1959 than in 1953; and all of the companies had increases in net

Exhibit 9

CIGARETTE ADVERTISING EXPENDITURES IN SEVEN MEDIA (1955–58)
(In Thousands)

Company	1958	1957	1956	1955
American Tobacco...............	$ 32,025	$ 24,888	$ 21,912	$ 21,283
R. J. Reynolds..............	28,492	25,748	23,608	20,123
P. Lorillard.................	23,730	12,537	9,873	12,274
Brown & Williamson........	21,415	23,360	17,595	5,824
Philip Morris..............	19,148	18,262	17,054	10,069
Liggett & Myers............	17,609	17,362	16,116	13,000
	$142,419	$122,157	$106,158	$ 82,573

Notes: For comparison, "in each of the years 1937, 1938 and 1939, American, Liggett and Reynolds expended a total of over $40,000,000 a year for advertising" (*American Tobacco Co.* v. *United States*, 328 U.S. 781).

Advertising Age, with less comprehensive figures, gave the following estimates of advertising expenditures (in millions): 1953, $68.2; 1954, $67.9; 1955, $71.9; 1956, $101.4; 1957, $111.4; 1958, $127.6; 1959, $141.5; 1960, $141.6; and 1961, $144.2.

Sources: *Printer's Ink*, October 30, 1959; *Advertising Age*, June 4 and 25, 1962.

Exhibit 10

NET INCOME OF FIVE MAJOR AMERICAN TOBACCO COMPANIES
1947–49 = 100

Year	American Tobacco	Liggett & Myers	Lorillard	Philip Morris	Reynolds
1961.....................	167	98	474	190	328
1960.....................	152	106	457	186	295
1959.....................	154	110	472	173	253
1958.....................	143	115	451	151	219
1957.....................	139	104	192	139	180
1956.....................	126	97	75	128	173
1955.....................	126	98	110	102	149
1954.....................	105	82	106	81	126
1953.....................	100	84	120	110	96
1952.....................	83	79	95	100	89
1951.....................	81	80	86	112	90
Average net income in 1947–49 base period.	41.1	27.2	5.99	11.3	35.7

Source: *Standard & Poor's Industry Surveys.*

income, with Lorillard and Reynolds having the greatest relative increases and Liggett & Myers the least (see Exhibit 10).

As far as the qualitative side of advertising efforts was concerned, the Federal Trade Commission and the industry had little difficulty in getting together. In September, 1954, the director of the commission's new Bureau of Consultation sent out the following letter:

Recent scientific developments with regard to the effects of cigarette smoking have increased the Commission's interest in advertising claims made for such products and have increased its responsibility under the law to prevent the use of false or misleading claims.

In our opinion, the scientific developments referred to above have likewise increased the responsibility of the industry to eliminate voluntarily from its advertising all claims and implications which are questionable in light of present scientific knowledge.

The spirit in which the industry has entered into the effort to resolve the scientific questions currently presented leads us to the belief that the industry also is appreciative of its added responsibility in the matter of advertising under the circumstances and for that reason will consider this an especially propitious time to effect voluntary cessation of every questionable claim and implication in its advertising, providing appropriate means to that end are available to it.

With these thoughts and that end result in mind, we have prepared suggested standards for cigarette advertising and enclose a copy thereof with the request that your company give them serious consideration.

It would be our thought, if acceptable standards for advertising can be developed, that the individual members of the industry could advise us of their intention of complying with them. We could then arrange a date by which the members will be expected to have effected a discontinuance of any claim not inconformity with the standards. The purpose of this suggestion is, of course, to enable all industry members to effect discontinuance of claims not in harmony with the standards reasonably simultaneously.

The letter went on to ask for comments, suggestions, and some indication as to whether compliance could be expected.

The list of standards recommended that:

1. No claims be made that cigarettes are beneficial to health in any respect, or that they are not harmful or irritating; and no reference to the presence or absence of any physical effect should be made.
2. No claims be made that length of cigarette or filter causes less nicotine, tars, resin, etc., unless scientifically and conclusively supported by an impartial party.
3. No reference be made to lungs, larynx, or any part of the body, or to digestion, nerves, energy, or doctors.
4. No implication be made of medical approval of a brand or of smoking in general.

5. Advertising be limited to discussion of taste, quality, flavor, enjoyment, and matters of opinion.
6. No unsubstantiated claims of comparative volume be made.
7. Only testimonials which are current, genuine, and do not violate other rules be used.
8. No false disparagement of another cigarette be made.

Within a week, Paul Hahn, president of American Tobacco Company, wrote the commission that he believed that advertisements of his brands—Lucky Strike, Pall Mall, and Tareyton—were devoid of questionable claims and implications. He went on to state that the company would look with favor on a process that would provide an effective means of bringing about general adherence to such a policy throughout the cigarette industry. He said feasibility of the commission's proposal would depend on whether such standards as might be developed would be binding on all cigarette advertisers and whether the commission could develop adequate sanctions.

E. A. Dan, president of R. J. Reynolds, commented that the industry could live under such standards if they were not straight-jacket rules. He said that a ban on mentioning parts of the body should not be so interpreted as to bar a mention of drawing smoke through the nose.

One year later, on September 22, 1955, The FTC published guides for evaluating cigarette advertising. The guides were the result of one year of conferences with the cigarette manufacturers and embodied substantially those rules which were proposed by the FTC in 1954. The "rule" stated in 1954 that advertising themes be limited to discussion of taste, quality, flavor, enjoyment, and matters of opinion was dropped; and in its place was put a statement that the guides were not intended to prohibit representations relating solely to taste, flavor, aroma, or enjoyment and would be amended "when and if the facts and circumstances warrant." Two notes were added explicitly recognizing filters. For example, "words, including those relating to filters or filtration, which imply the presence or absence of any physical effort or effects are considered subject to this guide."

Advertising Themes in 1956

The commission seemed to feel in 1956 that substantial strides had been made in eliminating questionable claims from cigarette advertising.

On July 26, 1956, David R. Reel, an attorney for the Bureau of Consultation of the FTC stated in a letter that "the Guides represent the Commission's effort to alleviate, so far as possible, in the public interest time consuming and expensive formal litigation involved in cigarette advertising such as it has experienced in the last 25 years. The cigarette producers, for the most part, are voluntarily abiding by the Guides and we believe that cigarette advertising has become, by virtue of the adoption of these Guides, more compatible with the laws enforced by the Commission."

The following are some of the advertisements which were used in mid-1956:

Loved for gentleness. Some people are known—and loved—for being gentle. So is this new cigarette. New Philip Morris, made gentle for modern taste, is winning new friends everywhere—especially among younger smokers. Enjoy the gentle pleasure, the fresh unfiltered flavor, of new Philip Morris. Now in the new smart package.

Sergeant Bilko serves his men. You get more pure pleasure from a Camel. For good rich taste and smooth mildness, Camel is by far the best liked cigarette today. Only Camels taste so rich yet smoke so mild.

Light up a Lucky, it's light up time! Men, this is it! No cigarette in the world ever tasted so good. You see, Lucky Strike means fine tobacco—mild good tasting tobacco that's TOASTED to taste even better. Outdoors or indoors, Luckies are the best cigarette you ever smoked! Cleaner, fresher, smoother.

Like your pleasure big? Smoke for real—smoke Chesterfields.

Only Viceroy has 20,000 filters for the smoothest taste in smoke. Twice as many filters as the other two largest selling filter brands.

You get a lot to like—the easy drawing filter feels right in your mouth. It works but doesn't get in the way. (Marlboros.)

Winstons taste good! Like a cigarette should! Get your flavor and filter too— this finer filter works so effectively.

Say, have you tried new Salems? A new idea in smoking—take a puff . . . it's springtime.

The Facts behind Filter Tip Cigarettes (1957)

While the FTC seemed tolerably satisfied with the compliance with the new advertising guides, serious questions were developing about what function the filter in a filter cigarette was serving. What miracle, for example, was the "miracle tip" of the L & M cigarette performing? What were "all the benefits of a filter" claimed by Kool? What did the "real filtration" of the Tareyton signify? And why should Viceroy have "twice as many filters"?

The Consumers Union Reports. In March, 1957, CU reported that its tests showed little difference in nicotine content of the smoke between filter cigarettes and those with no filters and only "somewhat less tar" from the filter cigarettes. They also found that the average nicotine and tar levels of filtertip cigarettes had risen over the 1955 level. As an extreme example, though its advertising still claimed the "micronite filter," Kent cigarettes showed eight times as much tar as the original 1952 Kent and one third more than the Kent of 1955.

The American Cancer Society Study. In June the conclusions of the elaborate Hammond and Horn study on the relation between smoking and death rates among men from 50 to 70 years of age were announced to the American Medical Association. A major conclusion was that the death rate of the cigarette smokers (in their sample of 190,000 men traced for forty-four months) was 68 per cent higher than the death rate of a comparable group of men who never smoked, age being taken into consideration.[39] The death rate from lung cancer ran from 3.4 per 100,000 per year for men who never smoked to 217.3 for men who smoked over two packs a day.

The Reader's Digest Articles. *Reader's Digest* had an independent consulting chemist run tests similar to those of CU. The magazine wrote up the results in somewhat more dramatic fashion. It pointed out that smokers switching from the regular cigarettes of the "Big Four" to the filter cigarettes rated lowest in tar and nicotine would gain tar reductions of only 7 to 17 per cent. But a switch to such leading sellers among filters as Marlboro, Winston, and L & M might actually lead to an increase in tars and nicotine. The article concluded: "It's entirely possible to manufacture filter tips much more efficient than any now on the market" and asked: "Why aren't these improved filter tips available?"[40]

In a second article in August the magazine gave Kent cigarettes a tremendous sales boost in an article entitled "Wanted—and Available—Filter Tips That Really Filter." The re-engineered Kent had been tested and found to deliver about 40 per cent less tar than the regular nonfilter cigarettes, and P. Lorillard's successful exploitation of this finding was widely copied by other companies with similar claims.

The Congressional Hearings. Congressman Blatnik of Minnesota, the Chairman of the Legal and Monetary Affairs Subcommittee of the House Government Operations Committee opened the July hearings by announcing that "our hearings today are concerned with the advertising of cigarettes—particularly filter tip cigarettes." The hearings opened

---

[39]*False and Misleading Advertising (Filter-Tip Cigarettes),* Hearings before a Subcommittee of the Committee on Government Operations, House of Representatives, 85th Congress, First Session (Washington, D.C.: U.S. Government Printing Office, 1957), p. 312.

[40]*Ibid.,* pp. 609, 612.

with Dr. E. C. Hammond testifying about the American Cancer Society report. Plans were to call later upon representatives of the tobacco industry; but none appeared, with the exception of Dr. Clarence C. Little, the Scientific Director of the Tobacco Industry Research Committee.

Dr. Little's basic position was that "I would like to get more facts before I am able to say whether there is any relationship between smoking and cancer. . . ."[41] He reported that his committee had appropriated $1.8 million since 1954 to individuals and institutions for cancer research and that he had no concern with or knowledge of cigarette filters. Dr. Little stated: "Fortunately we have been left absolutely clear of the commercial impact of a single blessed thing we are studying, they are letting us study anything we want and you would be surprised if you saw some of the things that are being studied. They are about as far removed from tobacco and its possible effect on cancer as you can possibly go."[42]

Dr. Wynder of the Sloane-Kettering Institute for Cancer Research recommended regulations that would encourage or perhaps even require the filter cigarette manufacturers to reduce their tar and nicotine content to 40 per cent below that of the standard regular-size cigarette. He admitted that at the present state of knowledge the filter could not selectively eliminate cancer-causing agents but simply could quantitatively reduce the intake of all tobacco smoke. He also summed up the result of a survey of five hundred patients who had switched to filters: "We found that more than 70 per cent of them had switched because they thought they were getting health protection or because of advertising which indicated they got health protection."[43]

Mr. Secrest, Acting Chairman of the FTC, testified as to the superiority of the new voluntary compliance system over the old time-consuming system of formal complaints. He noted that seventy-five changes had been made in advertising to meet the new guides and stated: "The Commission believes its industry-wide approach to cigarette advertising and its adoption of advertising guides has served to eliminate completely all health implications from cigarette advertising, thus achieving a marked and prompt improvement in the advertising of cigarettes."[44] He noted that the Surgeon-General, as Chief Health Officer of the United States, had announced on July 12, 1957: "In the light of these

[41]*Ibid.*, p. 48.
[42]*Ibid.*, p. 58.
[43]*Ibid.*, p. 99.
[44]*Ibid.*, p. 279.

studies, it is clear there is an increasing body of evidence that excessive cigarette smoking is one of the causative effects in lung cancer and while there are naturally differences of opinions in interpreting the data on lung cancer and cigarette smoking the Public Health Service feels the weight of the evidence is increasingly pointing in one direction: that excessive smoking is one of the causative factors in lung cancer."[45] In view of this announcement, Mr. Secrest announced that the commission has given a high priority to a consumer survey that "would reveal the public's current understanding of the meaning of the terminology used for filter tip cigarettes." He concluded: "Every day we are trying to get more and more compliance with those guides. When we get consumer testimony we will have some idea what a man thinks when he buys a filter cigarette or when he says the word 'filter' and if this committee has any advertising which they deem to be false or misleading, just let us have it and it will be corrected. Maybe it will be found false and misleading and maybe it don't, that depends upon the facts in the case."[46]

The Committee wound up its testimony with a note of appreciation for Mr. Secrest. Mr. Blatnik expressed regret that the tobacco industry "for some reason won't voluntarily come before us—a free, responsible public body in a public forum—and tell us what is superior about their filter, or justify at least in some measure the claims they are making before the entire American audience at great expense to themselves in promotion of the filter tips. . . ."[47] "Although we are closing the hearings, we would be glad to hear from the cigarette people upon further consultation amongst themselves or within their own industry, if they feel that in all fairness and to make the record complete they should be heard."[48]

The "Safer" Cigarette (1957–59). The changes toward reduced tars and nicotine in the smoke that took place from 1957 through 1959 were substantial. The major physical changes were in greater porosity and in venting of the cigarette paper and in the use of more resistant filters. Associated with these was the increased use of flavoring agents, including menthol, to make the reduced smoke intake more palatable. Regular Old Golds were shifted to a blend of low-nicotine and tar tobaccos, a move opposite to the use of stronger tobaccos which probably accounted for some of the increase of tars in filter cigarettes noted in 1957.

---

[45]*Ibid.,* p. 280.
[46]*Ibid.,* p. 305.
[47]*Ibid.,* p. 277.
[48]*Ibid.,* p. 306.

One manifestation of the change was the influx of new high-filtration brands, including Duke, Life, Spring, and Alpine. Duke, with a long filter and a paper overwrap which made it look even longer, produced only half the tars of the regular Kents, which were low in 1958. Even more important in terms of the 1959 market was the decline in tars and nicotine of the leading sellers among the filters: L & M, Marlboro, Viceroy, and Salem. Even Winston, the leader of them all, whose filter had been reported to have a practically indiscernible effect on tars and nicotine, showed a decrease of 15 per cent. Its slogan of "Its what's up front that counts" had been ironically valid.[49]

Cigarette smoking rose to a new over-all peak of 453 billion cigarettes, up almost 4 per cent from 1958,[50] when per capita consumption had hit the new high of 3,625 per year. The health scare seemed to have abated; and the Surgeon-General's opinion in November, 1959, that it has not been proved that reducing tars and nicotine in the smoke will provide a secure health safety factor caused scarcely a ripple in the stock prices of the major tobacco companies. While a study indicated that the percentage of Massachusetts doctors smoking cigarettes dropped from 52 per cent in 1954 to 38½ per cent in 1959, their reactions were not those of most Americans. Perhaps the greatest threat to the industry was in educational campaigns to apprise teenagers of the possible risks involved in cigarette smoking. A campaign in Portland, Oregon, had reduced the annual recruitment rate of new smokers from 13.0 to 7.7 per cent among high school boys and from 6.4 to 2.1 per cent among the girls. Other cities, including New York, were considering such programs.[51]

While filtertips gained slightly in market share, *Business Week* observed that they "seem to have peaked out at just under 50% of the total market."[52] Neither of the two publications conducting the best-known tests on cigarettes predicted the end of the swing toward "safer" products. *Consumer Reports* noted difficulty in providing "the latest results in the low-tar, low-nicotine race," since "with solid rewards of gold waiting, many cigarette companies are juggling and working over their products in the frantic manner associated with style changes in the garment industry."[53]

The *Reader's Digest* commented: "The tobacco industry will not admit publicly that it is seeking safer cigarettes. Indeed it continues

[49]As reported by Consumers Union in *Consumer Reports,* January, 1960.
[50]*Business Week,* December 26, 1959, p. 69.
[51]"Is It Safe to Smoke Now?" *Consumer Reports,* January, 1960, p. 17.
[52]*Business Week,* December 26, 1959, p. 68.
[53]*Consumer Reports,* January, 1960, p. 18.

to deny that any tobacco-health problem exists. . . . The men of the tobacco industry are not being fooled. They know that their task now is to get the gun unloaded before a new generation of customers decides that the game is silly, the stakes too high."[54]

Cigarette Advertising Themes (1959).   The advertising themes chosen by the ten leading brands seemed quite consistent with their filtration performances. The four nonfilter cigarettes chose variations on the theme of rich, honest taste:

> Nothing satisfies like rich, clean taste of top tobacco. (Chesterfield.)
> Get satisfying flavor . . . so friendly to your taste. (Pall Mall.)
> Remember how great cigarettes used to taste? Luckies still do.
> Have a real smoke. Have a Camel.

It was interesting to note that the themes chosen by filter cigarettes corresponded rather closely to the amount of tars left in the smoke: The brands are arranged in ascending order of tar content, with no significant difference between Viceroy, Marlboro, and Salem.[55]

> Kent filters best for the flavor you like. . . . Kent has reduced tars and nicotine to the lowest level among all leading brands.
> More taste by far . . . yet low in tar . . . and they said it couldn't be done. (L & M.)
> A thinking man's filter . . . a smoking man's taste. (Viceroy.)
> The better the makings, the better the smoke . . . exclusive Filter-Flavor formula . . . the improved Marlboro filter does what it's there for.
> Now even the paper adds to Salem's springtime freshness. Smoke refreshed.
> Winston's Filter-Blend up front is packed with pleasure . . . both a modern filter and Filter-Blend.

In December the FTC brought its first complaint since setting up standards and seeking voluntary compliance. It charged that the advertising claim that Life cigarettes are "proved to give you least tar and nicotine of all cigarettes" was not true, that representations of United States government endorsement were false (advertisements stated the figures were "on file with an agency of the United States Government"), and that a television commercial showing liquid being poured into Life's "millicel super filter" and that of another cigarette did not give "proof how Life gives least tar and nicotine."

The manufacturer, Brown & Williamson; the advertising agency, Ted Bates & Company; and the account executive were all charged

---

[54]"The Search for 'Safer' Cigarettes," *Reader's Digest,* November, 1959, pp. 44–45.
[55]As reported in *Consumer Reports,* January, 1960.

with misrepresentation in violation of the Federal Trade Commission
Act. Brown & Williamson, in its reply to the FTC, said:

New Life cigarettes are the lowest in tar of any cigarettes now produced
and we stand by this statement. We think it is totally unfair of the Federal Trade
Commission to ask us to file nicotine and tar test data as a service to the commission and then object to our informing the public we have done so.

The Federal Trade Commission claims that our advertising implies Government sanction. This is not true. Our figures on the tar and nicotine delivery of
the new Life cigarettes were submitted to the Federal Trade Commission at the
commission's own request and our advertising simply states that such figures
were filed.

It is our position that the demonstration cited by the Federal Trade Commission is in all respects truthful and is a proper and acceptable advertising
technique. We claim, and believe we have the right to claim that the Life millicel filter has greater absorptive capacity than other filters and the demonstration
illustrates that fact.[56]

Mr. Reeves, the account executive, in an interview with *Advertising
Age,* was asked whether he believed that an advertising agency should
take its client "as close to the line" as legally possible. His reply was
that the agency sought "the strongest possible claims for our client's
product—within the truthful limits of the product's performance." He
went on to observe the need for advertising to be policed, and not
by itself, stating: "It is the dream of an industry to have no outside
disturbing hand. But in building the fifth largest agency in the world,
we have come to the conclusion that self-regulation will not work."[57]

Brown & Williamson did not choose to fight. Instead, after consul-
tations with the industry the Chairman of the FTC announced that in
the absence of a satisfactory uniform test and proof of advantage to the
smoker, there be no more tar and nicotine claims in advertising.[58] Duke
and Life, the truly high-filtration cigarettes, left without the weapon of
advertising their only significant advantage, dwindled into obscurity.

What has been called the "tar derby," when widespread and frequently conflicting claims about the tar and nicotine elimination were
made, particularly in 1958 and 1959, had ended. No longer was the
consumer faced with claims like "up to 43% higher filtration," "now
lower in tars and nicotine than any leading cigarette," and "Life filters
best by far." A real improvement seems to have occurred in the filtra-

---

[56]*New York Times,* December 14, 1959. According to the Consumers Union ratings
previous cited, Life was significantly below all brands but Duke in tar content, but was
second to it.

[57]*New York Times,* December 27, 1959.

[58]In January, 1960.

tion quality of most filter cigarettes. According to the periodic studies of Consumers Union, the average tars in smoke per cigarette had dropped from 35 milligrams to 21 and from 40 to 27 for regular filter and king-sized filter cigarettes between March, 1957, and January, 1960.

The years 1960 through 1962 were relatively uneventful ones commercially for the cigarette companies. The market was more clearly segmented than ever, with 55 per cent of the consumption in filter cigarettes and the mentholated filters growing enough in importance to constitute a separate segment. The sales of king-sized cigarettes were again rising slightly, and Pall Mall continued its amazing dominance of that sector and strengthened its hold on first place. Since all other firms except Liggett & Myers were weak in that segment, it was not surprising to see new-product activity there—Philip Morris was introducing Coronet, Reynolds was launching Brandon in a new plastic pack, and Lorillard had inaugurated York in the longer "imperial" length. There were new filter brands, too, again aimed at weaknesses. American Tobacco, with nothing in mentholated filters since the failure of Riviera, launched Montclair, with menthol in the tip; and Liggett & Myers, with only L & M selling well, had come up with Larks, with a three-part filter. The advertising themes seemed generally compatible with the FTC standards and duly emphasized pleasure; and while the newness and intricateness of filters might receive attention, no definite claims of their performance in reducing tars or nicotine were made.

It might well be argued in early 1963 that no new strategy was called for. The cigarette firms had grown and prospered in the face of a great and increasing preponderance of scientific findings and opinion that the prolonged use of their product was closely associated with a particularly fearsome and increasingly common disease, and with significantly higher death rates in general. The firms had transformed themselves from essentially single-product producers to multiproduct producers, with over half their sales in lines that were almost exotic specialties scarcely ten years before. Yet there were anomalies in the situation that raised questions as to whether new approaches were not needed. Three quarters of cigarette sales were in the filter and king categories, products that at least in some minimal way were associated with the reduction of a health problem whose existence was denied by industry spokesmen. Partly because of industry policy and partly by government ruling, no informative advertising was permitted on a product quality of considerable interest and importance to many of the public, judging from their readiness to accept filter cigarettes.

Developments abroad, particularly in England, suggested that new pressures on the companies for changes in policy may well develop here. After the Royal College of Physicians issued a report on smoking and health, which said in its summary that "cigarette smoking is a cause of lung cancer, and bronchitis, and probably contributes to the development of coronary heart disease and various other less common diseases," the British ministeries of health and education followed up with an intensive educational campaign against smoking that had substantial short-run effects on cigarette sales.

Any possible government move in this country seemed likely to wait upon the report of the Advisory Committee on Smoking and Health appointed by the U.S. Surgeon-General with the approval of the President. The FTC, for example, has promised reconsideration of its strictures against tar and nicotine claims after this report.

In July, 1963, the industry, through the Tobacco Institute, made at least a start toward strengthening one of its most vulnerable points, that is, advertising directed at youthful audiences. It made the following general suggestions, disappointing some industry officials who wished more specific limitations, such as no athletes, or no romantic scenes. George V. Allen, President, reaffirmed the institute's belief that "smoking is a custom for adults," and suggested that cigarette advertisements should not give a contrary impression, that cigarette companies avoid sponsorship of programs whose content is directed particularly to children, and that models used in cigarette advertisements should be and should appear to be adults.

APPENDIX TO CASE 6-5: THE CONTROVERSY ON THE ASSOCIATION BETWEEN CIGARETTE SMOKING AND LUNG CANCER

Deaths in the United States reported to be caused by lung cancer (mostly among men) increased from less than 3,000 in 1930 to 23,000 in 1953. Many investigators, both in the United States and abroad, found high correlations between cigarette smoking and the incidence of cancer. These studies were summed up in the *Journal of the American Statistical Association* as follows:

Leading investigators generally agree that a significant part of the observed increase in lung cancer mortality represents a real increase in the rate at which lung cancer is developing in the population. This increase cannot reasonably be attributed to genetic change in the human population and therefore must be due to environmental factors. Available evidence linking tobacco smoking to lung cancer is fairly extensive and impressive: (1) The increase in lung cancer mortality has been generally parallel to an increase in cigarette consumption.

(2) In each of 14 case history studies there was a smaller percentage of non-smokers and a higher percentage of heavy smokers among lung cancer patients than among comparable controls. (3) Preliminary results of two population studies indicate higher mortality from lung cancer among smokers than among non-smokers and a still higher mortality among heavy smokers. (4) At least one team of investigators has produced skin cancer in animals with condensates of tobacco smoke.

There is disagreement whether the evidence at hand warrants a conclusion that smoking and lung cancer are causally related. The relative importance of smoking, air pollution, and occupational exposure to cancerigenic materials remains to be established.[59]

The Public Health Service Report (1957). In July, 1957, after the publication of the Horn and Hammond study, the Surgeon-General, Leroy E. Burney, as head of the Public Health Service, took a much stronger position than had before on the cause-and-effect relationship between smoking and lung cancer.

In June 1956, units of the Public Health Service joined with two private voluntary health organizations to establish a scientific study group to appraise the available data on smoking and health. We have now reviewed the report of this study group and other recent data, including the report of Dr. E. C. Hammond and Dr. Daniel Horn on June 5, to the American Medical Association in New York.

In the light of these studies, it is clear that there is an increasing and consistent body of evidence that excessive cigarette smoking is one of the causative factors in lung cancer.

The study group, appraising 18 independent studies, reported that lung cancer occurs much more frequently among cigarette smokers than among non-smokers, and there is a direct relationship between the incidence of lung cancer and the amount smoked. This finding was reinforced by the more recent report to the AMA by Drs. Hammond and Horn.

Many independent studies thus have confirmed beyond reasonable doubt that there is a high degree of statistical association between lung cancer and heavy and prolonged cigarette smoking.

Such evidence, of course, is largely epidemiological in nature. It should be noted, however, that many important public health advances in the past have been developed upon the basis of statistical or epidemiological information. The study group also reported that in laboratory studies on animals at least five independent investigators have produced malignancies by tobacco smoke condensates. It also reported that biological changes similar to those which take place in the genesis of cancer have been observed in the lungs of heavy smokers. Thus, some laboratory and biological data provide contributory evidence

---

[59]Sidney J. Cutler, "A Review of the Statistical Evidence on the Association between Smoking and Lung Cancer," *Journal of the American Statistical Association,* June, 1956, p. 267.

to support the concept that excessive smoking is one of the causative factors in the increasing incidence of lung cancer.

At the same time, it is clear that heavy and prolonged cigarette smoking is not the only cause of lung cancer. Lung cancer occurs among nonsmokers, and the incidence of lung cancer among various population groups does not always coincide with the amount of cigarette smoking. . . .

The service notes that the study group found that more study is needed to determine the meaning and significance of any statistical association between smoking and heart disease. . . .[60]

The Answer of the Industry Committee.   On the same day a release from the public relations firm, Hill and Knowlton, for the Tobacco Industry Research Committee took the agnostic position it had maintained in the light of previous studies: "The Surgeon General, in his statement today, places full reliance on the recent study group report which failed to acknowledge the considerable work in the field of lung cancer which does not coincide with the study group position. Actually, in recent years many doctors and scientists have publicly expressed their doubts or disbelief in the theory that smoking causes lung cancer. . . ."[61]

It cited the statistical reservations of Dr. Berkson, head of the section of biometry and medical statistics for the Mayo Clinic; the views of Dr. Harry S. N. Greene, Chairman of the Department of Pathology at Yale University, who held that "the case against tobacco is derived mostly from statistical associations and some experimental work with animals"; the point made by Drs. Milton Rosenblatt and James Lisa that "the reports on lung cancer and smoking are concerned with only two variables, whereas a great many are undoubtedly involved."[62]

Later, in July, 1957, Dr. Berkson reported in the research publication of the Mayo Clinic that the statistical sample used by Horn and Hammond was statistically biased in the high proportion of both non-smokers and of healthy men. He was also concerned about the high correlation of cigarette smoking with a wide range of diseases related with age other than lung cancer. "We might say speculatively that smoking accelerates the rate of living and age causes cancer."[63] He concluded that "I do not believe that from the statistical studies so far accomplished one can conclude definitely that smoking causes cancer, or even that it is necessarily 'associated' with it. On the other hand, at the very least these studies pose a strong presumption that smoking may

---

[60]*False and Misleading Advertising (Filter-Tip Cigarettes), op. cit.*, p. 555.
[61]*Ibid.*, p. 558.
[62]*Ibid.*, p. 557.
[63]*Ibid.*, pp. 776–85; direct quotations from pp. 777, 780.

cause cancer and/or may be otherwise deleterious to health and longevity." He called for more than "the sporadic efforts of individuals" and for a study "in experimental epidemiology" (involving adequate animal populations with "several intensities of smoking exposure and possibly stratified by age and weight").[64]

---

[64]*Ibid.*

CHAPTER 7

✦✦✦✦✦✦✦✦✦✦✦✦✦✦✦✦✦✦✦✦✦✦✦✦✦

Price Policy of Monopolies and Cartels

CLASSIFICATION of a firm for purposes of predicting its price-output policy is best accomplished by considering the demand curve facing the firm. As has been pointed out, this curve is horizontal under pure competition, downsloping from left to right under monopoly, and indeterminate under noncollusive oligopoly. When sellers in a particular market are few, the response of sales to a price change depends heavily on the reactions of close rivals to this change. Monopoly can be considered to be one limit of the oligopoly case—the limit at which rivals' reactions are of negligible importance because there are no sufficiently close rivals. (This does not mean that consumers' reactions are not important: These responses cause a smaller quantity to be taken at a higher price, and vice versa.) Unlike the perfectly competitive firm, a monopoly can have a price policy because it has some choice in this regard.

Sources of Monopoly Power

Monopoly analysis is clearly appropriate when a firm has an exclusive franchise to provide electric power, telephone services, or some other important public utility service. Utility rates charged by a privately owned company are almost always controlled by publicly appointed commissions, but unless the commissioners are extremely honest and efficient, there usually remain substantial opportunities for monopoly gains. Under even the best of conditions, there is much room for dispute as to what constitutes a "fair price" for a utility service. Such a price should yield a rate of return on capital equal to that which is received in unregulated enterprises were risk is "comparable." Actually no such situations may be available for comparison. Also, innumerable problems are involved in giving weight both to actual investment and to cost of reproduction in determining the value of utility property. Even after the value of capital and a rate of return at which to aim have been decided upon, serious error can be made in judging the effect of a rate change on profit. The demand function will not be known precisely. Also costs can get out of line, especially since there is a tendency for a firm which is limited by regulation in its pecuniary profit to move toward more nonpecuniary rewards. Some examples of these rewards are luxurious offices, pretty secretaries, and increased leisure time on the part of officials.

Monopoly privileges secured by the ownership of patents and copyrights can lead to very large profits if the item is an important one such as nylon, a new type of office equipment, or a best-selling novel. These have the advantage over utility services of being unregulated, but profits usually are easier for rival sellers to cut in on through partial imitation. The privilege of operating an exclusive concession at a baseball stadium or at a railroad station confers a considerable degree of monopoly power which may be highly profitable unless too high a charge is made by the owner for the privilege. Similarly, the sale of liquor in an urban area tends to be very profitable if the number of licenses is sufficiently limited by public authorities, unless license fees are so stiff as to take over most of the profit.

Frequently, government intervention is sought by sellers as a means of limiting competition. The farm program and interstate trucking are examples on a large scale. In most cities the number of barbershops and taxicabs is limited by public authority. Similarly, the milk business is usually regulated either by the state or by the federal government (through "marketing agreements"), with minimum retail and whole-sale prices being fixed.

Regional monopoly power is common even in fields which have a large number of firms when viewed nationally or internationally. This situation may arise when high transportation costs per unit limit the competition from distant sellers. Sellers of such heavy building materials as bricks and concrete blocks often possess monopoly power from this source although the total number of American producers is very large. Often, it is more profitable to sell in a relatively small region where the firm is the only one of its kind than to compete in a much larger market with a large number of other sellers. If the former type of business is highly profitable, it may be wise not to advertise the fact, since new entrants can quickly reduce the sales volume of the first seller. This problem is common in the sale of gasoline where new stations can spring up quickly.

Well-known trade-marks, brand names, and slogans give a measure of monopoly power to their possessors. Like locational monopoly, this advantage can fade rapidly as other names become known. A basic function of advertising is to keep brand names in the consumers' consciousness. Many stock market advisers consider it to be an advantage if a company sells its products directly to final consumers rather than to other firms. To the extent that this idea is valid, it is traceable in part to the greater vulnerability of consumers to large price markups based on irrational attachments to brand names and the effectiveness of advertising in building and keeping such affiliations.

Technical complexity often creates monopoly power. The bewildering array of different types of life insurance policies, each involving complex interest calculations, makes differentiation between a reasonable and an unreasonable price difficult. Automobile and television repairs have the same attribute. Many games of chance involve a sort of monopoly power on the part of the operator, since their complexity makes it possible to keep the price of participation unduly high without losing too many customers. The slot machine is ideal in this respect, since the price of attempting to secure a given pay-off with some particular probability is not even known to the gambler. Also, the actual price can be changed secretly by the operator.

Use of Marginal Revenue Concept

As was indicated briefly in Chapter 3, the idea of marginal revenue is important to an understanding of optimum price and output behavior under monopoly. If a single price is charged for all units sold in a given market, the firm with monopoly power must consider that, in charging a lower price in order to sell more units, it must accept a lower price on *all* units—not just on the added sales. This means that marginal (additional) revenue will not be as high as the price received per unit. This causes the marginal revenue curve to lie below the monopolist's demand curve, as illustrated in Exhibit 1.

Suppose that the chart pertains to a parking lot, football field, or theater with a definite capacity and where the variable costs are negligible. The monopolist's pricing decision can then be made by reference to the demand situation alone. If the capacity of the facility happens to be perfectly adjusted to the demand, this capacity will be OA (cars or persons), and optimum price will be at P_1. At this price, elasticity of demand is unitary, and the revenue is the greatest which can be secured at any price, given the existing demand. If capacity is only OC, optimum price will be at the higher level P_2, since all available spaces can be sold at this price. While total revenue will be less than in the previous case, it will be the greatest obtainable with the capacity. A third possibility is that capacity will be *OS*, which exceeds *OA*. In this case the optimum single price is not P_3, which would fully utilize the facility, but P_1. It is profitable from a private point of view to waste the capacity *AS*.[1] This may result not from any error in estimating demand but from fluctuations in demand through time.

Exhibit 1

MONOPOLY DEMAND AND PRICE—WHEN MARGINAL
COST IS ZERO

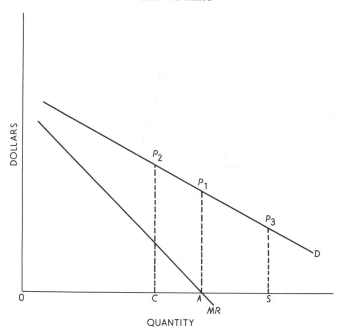

Effect of Positive Marginal Cost

The above case of monopolistic pricing is comparable to the "very short run" in competitive price theory when the good is perishable. (The services of a parking lot or football stadium are perishable even though the capital goods which yield these services are durable.) In order to understand short-run price-output policy under monopoly, it is necessary to add a marginal cost curve, as is done in Exhibit 2.

---

[1] It is interesting to consider the pricing of football tickets in a stadium belonging to a publicly supported educational institution. The price policy is usually geared approximately to the maximization of profits rather than to permitting as many taxpayers as possible to see the game. This does not "maximize profits" in a social sense.

The best rate of output from the point of view of the owners of the firm is *OX* because the marginal (additional) cost of turning out product at this rate is equal to the marginal revenue from the sale of this output. If the production rate exceeded *OX*, the units above this amount would add less to revenue than to cost, and profits would not be maximized. This is true even though the price at which such added units

Exhibit 2

MONOPOLY PRICE AND OUTPUT—WHEN MARGINAL
COSTS ARE POSITIVE

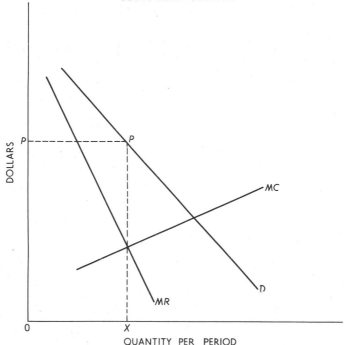

could be sold would exceed their addition to cost. If the firm sets price above *OP*, it will unduly restrict sales and output; it would be charging more than "the traffic can bear."

If errors are made in estimating either demand or cost, monopoly price can easily be set either too high or too low, of course. Under conditions of uncertainty, there is probably a tendency to set prices too high, especially since it may "spoil the market" (cause demand to shift downward) if price is set too low at first and then increased. If the business is one which attracts public attention, a price increase will bring unfavorable publicity.

Long-Run Adjustments

The relationship of price to average cost (not shown in Exhibit 2) determines whether the firm is making more than a competitive return on capital, is getting just a competitive return, or is incurring losses. If the firm's profit is above normal, and this is known, other companies will attempt to produce the same or similar commodities or to locate in such a way as to take over part of the demand. To the extent that such intrusions are successful, abnormal profits of the firm in question will be reduced. If the monopolist is able to prevent the entry of close

Exhibit 3

FULL EQUILIBRIUM FOR MONOPOLY

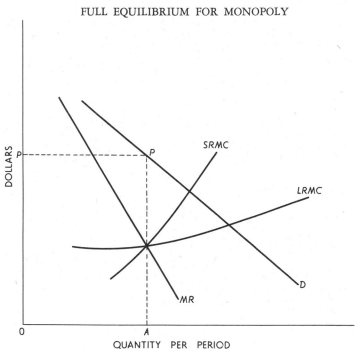

rivals, however, by political means, by patents or copyrights, by technical competence which cannot be duplicated, or by a uniquely favorable location, the abnormal level of profits may persist.

In order to secure maximum profits, the monopolistic firm, as well as the competitive one, must be of the correct size. In the case of the monopoly, however, this is unlikely to be the most efficient size in the sense of providing the lowest costs of production. Utility companies in small cities are typically too small to provide electricity, gas, water, or transportation at lowest cost through securing full "economies of scale." Or if monopoly prevails in a field which should be competitive or oligopolistic, the firm is likely to be too large for greatest efficiency.

If demand is expected to remain unchanged, determination of the best scale to which to build the firm may be shown by employing the concept "long-run marginal cost." This is the additional cost of output which is attainable by changing all inputs, including the scale of plant. In order that capacity can be optimally adjusted to the existing demand, it is necessary that long-run marginal cost be equated to marginal revenue. This means that the additional revenue from expanding output will just cover the additional cost of expanding plant capacity and associated inputs to bring about the lowest possible unit cost of producing at this rate.

Exhibit 3 shows a monopolistic firm in a position of both long-run and short-run equilibrium. Optimum output OA is determined by the intersection of both short-run and long-run marginal cost curves with the marginal revenue curve. If, instead, the long-run marginal cost curve were lower than it is, this would indicate the desirability of expanding the scale of plant. (This expansion would cause a shifting of the short-run marginal cost curve to the right until $LRMC$, $SRMC$, and MR all intersected again.)

Application to a Cartel

As it was pointed out in the preceding chapter, businessmen often attempt to increase profits by forming a cartel, especially when the power of government can be mustered to support the cartel or a cartel-like arrangement. Paradoxically, government is a foe of cartellization in some cases and a friend in others.

A leading reason for political attempts to back up cartel prices by utilizing the police power of the state is that there are many difficulties involved in securing agreement on price and other terms, sales quotas, markets, lines of authority, and other matters. If firms which desire to co-operate in a cartel are of unlike size and efficiency, have somewhat different products, or have different attitudes toward the desirability of growth, there will be strong forces at work to cause a breakdown of the cartel. The analytical tools already used in this chapter help to illustrate the nature of these forces.

Suppose that a price has been agreed upon by all members of an association, representing a compromise between the wishes of the various members. Probably the price will be lower than is desired by some

companies and higher than desired by others. Also, a price which is
initially reasonably satisfactory to all of the sellers may become quite
unsatisfactory to some after a short time because of changes in demand,
cost, or other conditions.

The situation of a single operating firm under an unsatisfactory cartel
arrangement is illustrated in Exhibit 4. The demand curve in the left-
hand figure is drawn on the assumption that all firms in the cartel
charge the same price, i.e., that the central organization is able to maintain sufficient discipline among its members. However, the established
price, P_c, is higher than that which would maximize short-run profits
for this particular firm.

Exhibit 4

THE INCENTIVE TO "CHISEL" IN A CARTEL

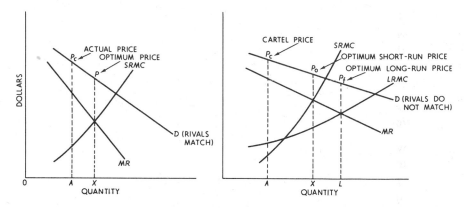

Under these conditions the firm may be hard to keep in line. If its
managers believe they can lower price without causing the other companies to follow suit, as is assumed in the demand curve in the right-
hand figure, they will be tempted to lower price to P_o, which will
sharply expand sales and maximize their profit. If an outright cut in
price is considered likely to lead to reprisals, the firm may instead use
nonprice concessions. Scores of different types of nonprice concessions
might be used, such as trading stamps, premiums, better credit terms,
better trade-ins, and others as indicated in the Appendix to the previous chapter. So many ways are available to alter the true net price
that adherence by all firms to a nominal price in dollars may not be
very significant. If all or many firms "chisel" overtly or covertly, the
cartel arrangement is likely to break down and open competition to be
restored.

There may also be an opportunity for the individual firm in a cartel to expand profit further by means of expanding capacity. This is reflected on the right-hand side of Exhibit 4 by the inclusion of the long-run marginal cost curve. If the firm in question is convinced that its rivals will adhere to the cartel price for a substantial period of time, it can, in the situation pictured increase its own profit by expanding capacity. When this expansion has been completed, optimum price for this firm will be P_f. The firm undergoes a particular risk by expanding, however, since it may be left with far too much capacity if other members of the cartel decide to cut price in order to regain some of the sales which have been lost to the "chiseler." If the latter is small compared with the industry as a whole, its actions are more likely to be successful because maintenance of the original cartel price may still appear to be preferable to opening the door to general competition among members on a price basis.

New Entrants

A cartel arrangement runs the risk not only of chiseling from within but also of the entry of new firms. Unless entry can be restricted by enlisting the power of government, by threat of reprisals, or by other means, new firms will be attracted if the cartel members appear to be securing above-normal returns. Whether such new entrants are taken into the association or remain outside, they will take sales away from the cartel members. The loss of sales will probably be greater if the newcomers remain outside because they will then be likely to charge a lower price.

If new firms can enter freely, the profits of cartel members are likely to be reduced to competitive rates. Price will exceed the competitive level, but unit costs will also be higher due to restricted sales volume. This is illustrated in Exhibit 5 for a representative firm in the cartel.

The firm which is represented would like to sell the quantity OA, where MC is equal to the established price. Its actual sales volume may be only OB after the entry of a sufficient number of new firms. This is because a larger volume than OB would bring excess profits to this firm, and these would attract new entrants, gradually reducing its available market. Despite the artificially high price (which may be maintained if new firms are taken into the cartel), both original and new entrants will secure only the competitive level of income on invested capital. This well illustrates the force which is exerted by competition in the absence of deliberate promotion of monopoly by political means.

APPENDIX TO CHAPTER 7:   GAME THEORY AND
BUSINESS DECISIONS

Suppose you are invited to be a spectator at a meeting of the board of directors of a large corporation. And suppose that soon after the meeting is called to order, each director, at the request of the chairman, begins to toss a coin into the air, and to record the resulting heads and tails on a piece of paper. You will probably conclude that

Exhibit 5

CARTEL PRICE WITHOUT PROFIT

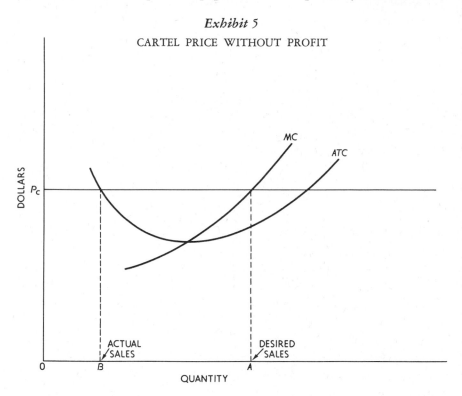

the assembled officials have suddenly felt an irresistible urge to gamble or else that the hectic pace of modern business has finally proved to be too much for the human mind. Actually, however, the directors may be engaging in a new and quite rational method of decision making according to the theory of games developed principally by a famous mathematician, the late John von Neumann.[2] As will be explained later, the purpose of the coin tossing may be to secure guidance of a

---

[2]The theory is set forth in most complete form in John von Neumann and Oskar Morgenstern, *Theory of Games and Economic Behavior* (Princeton: Princeton University Press, 1944).

pure chance (hence, unpredictable) nature as to an important business move. They may be taking the steps necessary to minimize the likelihood that their opponents will be able to guess their next move, since they themselves will not know what they are going to do until the coin-tossing ceremony is over. In the words of von Neumann and Morgenstern: "Ignorance is obviously a very good safeguard against disclosing information directly or indirectly."[3] The executive coin tossing is carried out, however, as only a part of a carefully calculated process of making a decision and differs sharply from the action of the motorist who tosses a coin to decide which fork of the road to take when he is completely lost.

Since its original promulgation the theory of games has attracted much attention in military planning circles because of its implications for certain situations encountered in war. Theoretically, it can also be useful to the gambler in guiding his play in such games as poker and in the more purely intellectual activity of chess playing. However, its actual application to such complicated games is extremely difficult and not likely to prove of practical help to the players.[4] It is especially difficult to visualize the tough, gun-toting poker player of the western movies sitting patiently while one of the players is running off on his portable electronic computer the calculations necessary to decide whether to raise, call, or drop out.

Certain simple games, however (which might conceivably be suitable for gambling), can readily be handled by means of the theory of games. The player who uses the system indicated by game theory is playing conservatively. He assumes that his opponent is skilled rather than stupid. In the words of J. D. Williams of the RAND Corporation, game theory "refers to a kind of mathematical morality, or at least frugality, which claims that the sensible object of the player is to gain as much from the game as he can, safely, in the face of a skillful opponent who is pursuing an antithetical goal."[5]

Often, the business situation in which an executive decision is required is so complex that application of the theory of games is not likely to be considered feasible. When there is a clean-cut conflict of interests between one firm and another, however, or between one firm and all

---

[3] *Ibid.,* p. 146.

[4] Von Neumann and Morgenstern devote a considerable amount of space to analysis of a simplified version of poker and conclude that "the mathematical problem of real poker is difficult but probably not beyond the reach of techniques which are available" (*ibid.,* p. 219).

[5] J. D. Williams, *The Compleat Strategyst* (New York: McGraw-Hill Book Co., Inc., 1954), p. 23. This book gives a simple and humerous exposition of the elements of the theory of games. The present Appendix is heavily indebted to this work.

other close rivals taken as a group, an optimal sort of business behavior may be calculable by the use of game theory. Even where an actual solution cannot be reached, the "way of thinking" about a problem which is suggested by game theory may be useful to the business executive. And as was suggested earlier, some knowledge of game theory should at least cause one to appreciate the possible virtue of basing an important decision on the outcome of some apparently frivolous action such as the toss of a coin or the throw of a pair of dice or a single die.

The Game of Hul Gul

This Appendix will not attempt to give any systematic or comprehensive explanation of the elements of game theory (such as is given in mathematical terms by von Neuman and Morgenstern, and more simply by J. D. Williams), but will instead apply the theory to certain simple conflict situations in such a way as to enable the reader (it is hoped) to analyze some simple business cases by this method.[6] This simple introduction may (it is also hoped) kindle some interest in further study of the theory and its possible business applications. An old game called Hul Gul, which is reputedly played by children, will first be investigated. By using the results of the analysis, one should be able to win a considerable amount of candy from even an extremely intelligent child, unless the child is too bright to stake his sweets on the outcome of the game.

The game of Hul Gul is played with beans or other small objects. In the simplest version, only two beans are used. One player holds his hands behind his back, then brings forth one fist in which he holds either one or two beans. The other player must attempt to guess the number of beans. If he does so correctly, he gets the beans or other remuneration—otherwise, he pays an amount equal to the difference between what he guessed and the actual number of beans held. It is quite obvious that the first player will wish to hold one bean more often than two beans, since when he holds only one, that is all he can lose; whereas when he holds two beans, he may lose two. He cannot hold one bean each time, however, for his strategy would quickly be figured out. To find out what proportion of the time he should hold one bean and what proportion of the time he should hold two beans in order to lose

---

[6]We shall be concerned only with "two-person zero-sum games." In such a game the interests of the players are diametrically opposed, and one player gains only at the expense of the other. The fact that collusion is unprofitable simplifies the game. On this point, see D. Blackwell and M. A. Girshick, *Theory of Games and Statistical Decisions* (New York: John Wiley & Sons, Inc., 1954), p. 10.

the smallest amount to a clever opponent is a suitable task for the theory of games. The holder of the beans is at a disadvantage compared with the guesser, since part of the time he will lose two beans on a particular play, whereas the guesser cannot lose more than one bean on a play. Consequently, a realistic objective of the holder is to minimize his loss, and a proper objective of the guesser is to maximize his gain by means of scientific play. The proportion of the time that the guesser should call "one bean" and "two beans" can also be determined by game theory.

Pay-off Matrix

The first step is to arrange gains and losses (pay-offs) in matrix form, showing who pays how much to whom under various possible circumstances. The holder of beans will be called "North," and the guesser will be called "West." Exhibit 1 shows this matrix, with positive num-

Exhibit 1

TWO-BEAN HUL GUL

NORTH HOLDS

		1	2	ROW MINIMA
WEST GUESSES	1	+1	−1	−1
	2	−1	+2	−1
COLUMN MAXIMA		+1	+2	

bers indicating payments by North to West and negative numbers denoting payments by West to North. For example, if North holds two beans and West guesses two, West receives the two beans from North. Consequently, the number +2 is in the box corresponding to "North holds 2" and "West guesses 2." The propriety of the other pay-offs can as readily be seen.

Solution of the Game

The first step in finding the solution to the game, once the pay-off matrix has been set up, is to find the minimum figure in each row and the maximum figure in each column. These are entered alongside and under the table, respectively. If the larger of the row minima were equal to the smaller of the column maxima, the game would have a "saddle point" which would immediately indicate the best strategy for each participant. (This will be explained later.) In the game of two-bean Hul Gul, however, the larger row minimum is —1, while the smaller column maximum is +1, so the game does not have a saddle point, and further calculations are necessary.

In a "two-by-two" zero-sum game, these further calculations are simple. First, subtract each figure in row 2 from the number immediately above. This gives +2 and —3. Signs are then disregarded, and these numbers are switched so that the 3 is associated with the left-hand column and the 2 is associated with the right-hand column. This solves the game for North, the bean holder. He should hold one bean three times and two beans two times out of five plays, on the average. In order to avoid falling into any sort of predictable pattern, he should ideally use a chance device of some suitable sort. For example, if North owned a miniature of the Pentagon Building in Washington, D.C., he could mark three of the sides with a 1 and two of the sides with a 2, and roll the replica on its side before each play. Each time a 1 came up, he would hold one bean; and each time a 2 came up, he would hold two beans. (It would be important, of course, to roll the building behind his back, so that his opponent would not also know the answer.)

It is also simple to find the relative use which West should make of his two alternative guesses. Subtract each figure in column 2 from the figure just to the left in column 1 to get +2 and —3. Disregard signs, and switch the numbers, so that the former is associated with the second row and the latter with the first row. This indicates that West should guess "one bean" three times out of five plays and "two beans" two times out of five plays, preferably using a suitable chance device to guide his calls also. It will be noted that this appeals quite readily to one's reason. Since North is going to hold one bean three times out of five, West should have the greatest success in guessing by using the same proportions. This helps one see how game theory is based on the assumption that each participant is intelligent. It is, of course, possible to devise a strategy superior to that suggested by this theory if one is playing with someone who "tips his hand" in any way.

Value of the Game

Even if both players follow the rules of good play as determined by game theory, the game may be biased in favor of one player or the other. The game of two-bean Hul Gul is disadvantageous to the holder and is stacked to favor the guesser, as was observed earlier. The value of the game is found by a calculation which uses the best mixture of either player against the results of either alternative action of the other player and involves an averaging process.

North's best mixture is three of "hold 1" to two of "hold 2." Used in conjunction with "West guesses 1," this gives the following calculation of average pay-off:

$$\frac{3(1) + 2(-1)}{3 + 2} = + \frac{1}{5}$$

Alternatively, the value of the game could be calculated by using North's best mixture with the "West guesses 2" alternative, as follows:

$$\frac{3(-1) + 2(+2)}{3 + 2} = + \frac{1}{5}$$

Or the value of the game can be calculated by using West's best mixture against either of North's alternatives:

$$\frac{3(+1) + 2(-1)}{3 + 2} = + \frac{1}{5}$$

$$\frac{3(-1) + 2(+2)}{3 + 2} = + \frac{1}{5}$$

The value of the game comes out $+ \frac{1}{5}$ in each of the four alternative calculations.[7] A positive value denotes that the game is unfair to North. If both players play "correctly," West will gain an average of $\frac{1}{5}$ (of whatever the unit of pay-off may be) per play. In twenty guesses, for example, West will win an average of four units, and North will lose this amount.[8]

Saddle-Point Solution

As already mentioned, the game of two-bean Hul Gul does not have a saddle point—the maximum of the row minima does not equal the minimum of the column maxima. However, the matrix shown in Exhibit 2, which is not related to any particular game, meets these requirements. Here, 3 is both the maximum of the figures to the right of

---

[7] Actually, the first and third equations are the same, and the second and fourth are the same, but each of the four equations is derived in a different way.

[8] It is, of course, possible (but extremely improbable) that all guesses will be wrong in a series of twenty guesses. In that case, West's loss would be twenty units. But the longer they play, the more likely it is that West will come out ahead.

the matrix and the minimum of those below the matrix. Pay-offs are from North to West, so North wants to keep the pay-off as low as possible, and West wants to make it as high as possible. West will always select alternative B, since both of the possible pay-offs are superior to those in row 1. North will also always select alternative B, since he assumes West to be intelligent and is therefore convinced that West would choose alternative B and gain 4 if North used alternative A. The solution of the game is, therefore, that North always uses B, and West always uses B. It would do North no good to mix his choices between A and B because, since West will stick to B, this would merely result in West's gaining more than 3 on some plays. The value of the game is 3, since that is the pay-off to West each time; 3 is called the "saddle value."

Exhibit 2

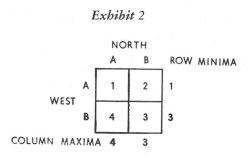

Three-Bean Hul Gul

The solution of a simple "three-by-three" zero-sum game by means of game theory can also be illustrated by reference to Hul Gul if three beans are used rather than two. The holder is permitted to have one, two, or three beans in his fist, and the guesser gets the beans (or some more interesting pay-off) if he guesses the right number. Otherwise, he pays the difference between what he guesses and the number actually held. It is at once obvious that this version is much less favorable to the guesser than is the two-bean variety, since there are two ways to miss and only one way to hit each time. Also it is by no means apparent how the game should be played against a wise opponent until one utilizes game theory. Unfortunately, the solution takes longer than that of a two-by-two game.

The pay-off matrix, with positive numbers again denoting gains by West and negative numbers gains by North, can readily be determined as shown in Exhibit 3.

Exhibit 3

NORTH HOLDS

		1	2	3	ROW MINIMA
	1	+1	−1	−2	−2
WEST GUESSES	2	−1	+2	−1	−1
	3	−2	−1	+3	−2
COLUMN MAXIMA		+1	+2	+3	

There is no saddle point, and the matrix must be solved in order to find the best "mixed strategy" for each player. The calculations are as follows:

First, subtract each row from the one above to get:

	1	2	3
(ROW 1 MINUS ROW 2)	+2	−3	−1
(ROW 2 MINUS ROW 3)	+1	+3	−4

Then, strike column 1, and the following two-by-two matrix will remain:

2	3
−3	−1
+3	−4

Take the difference in diagonal products, as follows:

$$(-3)(-4) - (+3)(-1) = +15$$

This number (15) indicates the relative frequency with which one bean should be held. To find the relative frequency with which two beans should be held by North, strike column 2 instead of column 1. This leaves:

1	2
+2	−1
+1	−4

The same sort of cross-multiplication and subtraction yields:

$$(+2)(-4) - (+1)(-1) = -7$$

(The negative sign is to be disregarded.)

Similarly, by striking column 3, one gets:

1	2
+2	−3
+1	+3

This gives:

$$(+2)(+3) - (+1)(-3) = +9$$

It has been determined that North should hold one bean 15 times out of 31 plays, two beans seven times out of 31, and three beans nine times out of 31 plays, on the average. A chance device should be used to determine each particular play but should be devised so as to secure this mixture of probabilities.

From the results of the two-bean version, one can now guess that West should also use the mixture 15:7:9 for guessing one, two, and three beans, respectively. This can be verified by a similar sort of calculation.

First, subtract each figure in each column from the figure just to the left:

1	+2	+1
2	−3	+3
3	−1	−4

Strike row 1, and there remains:

2	−3	+3
3	−1	−4

The difference in diagonal cross-products is found as follows:

$$(-3)(-4) - (-1)(+3) = +15$$

Next, strike row 2, leaving:

And get, by cross-multiplying and subtracting:

$$(+2)(-4) - (-1)(+1) = -7$$

Then, strike row 3:

And subtract one cross-product from the other:

$$(+2)(+3) - (-3)(+1) = +9$$

This verifies that West as well as North should use the mixture 15:7:9 for alternatives 1, 2, and 3, respectively.

Value of the Game

As before, the value of the game can be calculated by using the optimal mixture of either player against any of the alternative strategies of the other. For example, West's 15:7:9 mixture can be used against North's "hold 1" strategy:

$$\frac{15(+1) + 7(-1) + 9(-2)}{15 + 7 + 9} = -\frac{10}{31}$$

Or as one of the other five ways of calculating this value, try North's best mixture against West's "guess 3" strategy:

$$\frac{15(-2) + 7(-1) + 9(+3)}{15 + 7 + 9} = -\frac{10}{31}$$

The reader can easily satisfy himself that the other four calculations yield the same answer.

A negative value shows that the game is unfair to West. If both players play well, West will be more certain to lose, and to lose more, the longer they play. The game could be made fair to West by payment to him of $\frac{10}{31}$ of a pay-off unit before each guess. If the pay-off unit were 31 cents, North should pay West a dime before each play of the game.

A Loss-Leader Problem

Unfortunately, it is easier to apply game theory to games than to business. Nevertheless, there are certain types of conflict situations between firms where the theory may be helpful, provided the businessman is able to set up a reasonably accurate pay-off matrix relating to the situation. (If he has no idea of pay-offs under various courses of action open to him, he cannot make a rational decision by any other method, either.)

Suppose that two firms, which we shall rather unimaginatively call North and West, are grocery stores located in the same area but well isolated from other sellers. This makes them close rivals who watch each other's prices and selling activities warily. Every Thursday evening, each entrepreneur turns over his advertising copy to the local newspaper; included in the advertising items is a loss leader designed to attract customers to his store and away from the rival store. Experience has shown, we shall assume, that coffee and butter are the most satisfactory loss leaders; each Thursday, each manager chooses one of these to be the special bargain during the Friday-Saturday period. Suppose further that historical experience has taught each seller that the gains and losses from various possible actions are as shown in Exhibit 4, positive pay-offs being gains in total dollar sales by West and losses of sales by North, and negative pay-offs being gains in dollar sales by North at the expense of his rival, West.[9]

It is apparent that the whole practice of using loss leaders is more favorable to West than to North. However, experience has shown North that it is not wise to run no loss leader at all, in view of West's consistent policy of using leaders.[10] A glance at the row minima and

---

[9]This assumption makes it a zero-sum game. Actually, it is quite possible that total sales will be somewhat increased by the loss leaders for the two stores taken together and that the gain of one will not be entirely at the expense of the other. If the assumption is close to the truth, however, the game theory solution may be of practical utility.

[10]The strategy on North's part of using either butter or coffee as a leader may be said to be "dominant" over a strategy on his part of using no leader at all. If a third column labeled "No Leader" were added to the matrix, the pay-offs might be, for example, +80 and +200 in rows 1 and 2, respectively. This strategy is clearly so inferior from North's viewpoint that it should never be followed. Therefore, it can be eliminated from the matrix.

column maxima shows that there is no saddle point. It is clear that it would not be desirable for West to use butter each week as the loss leader, because North would do the same and no sales advantage would accrue to West. It would be undesirable for West to use coffee as the leader each week, because North would also do so and would take $50 in sales away from West. Similarly, it would be foolish for North to settle on a policy of using butter each week as the leader, because West would use coffee as the leader and gain $150 in sales at North's expense. It can similarly be seen that a constant strategy of using coffee as the leader would be unwise for North. Clearly, a mixture of strategies by each grocer is called for, with the loss-leader special for each week being kept a secret until it is too late for the rival firm to change its advertising copy in the newspaper. The optimal mixture of the two alternative actions can be calculated as in two-bean Hul Gul, since this too is a two-by-two matrix without a saddle point.

Exhibit 4

A LOSS-LEADER GAME

| | | NORTH USES AS LOSS LEADER | | |
		BUTTER	COFFEE	ROW MINIMA
WEST USES AS LOSS LEADER	BUTTER	0	+100	0
	COFFEE	+150	−50	−50
	COLUMN MAXIMA	+150	+100	

Subtracting each figure in row 2 from the figure just above it, we get −150 and +150, which means that North should use each loss leader half of the time, perhaps tossing a coin once a week and using butter as the leader when heads turns up and coffee when tails turns up.

To obtain West's optimal mixture, subtract each figure in column 2 from the figure just to the left. This gives −100 and +200. Disregarding sign and switching the numbers, it turns out that West should use butter twice for each time he uses coffee as a loss leader. His choice on any particular Thursday should be determined by using a chance device which has twice as great a probability of indicating butter as it has of indicating coffee. He might, for example, shake a cocktail shaker containing two yellow marbles and one brown marble of equal size, close his eyes and withdraw one—and then use butter as the loss leader if he comes up with a yellow marble and coffee if he picks out the brown one.

The value of the loss-leader "game" can be calculated by using the best mixture of either seller against the results of either alternative strategy of the other. The average pay-off according to the four methods of calculation is as follows:

$$1. \quad \frac{1(0) + 1(+100)}{2} = +50$$

$$2. \quad \frac{1(+150) + 1(-50)}{2} = +50$$

$$3. \quad \frac{2(0) + 1(+150)}{3} = +50$$

$$4. \quad \frac{2(+100) + 1(-50)}{3} = +50$$

Since the value of the game is positive, it is "unfair" to North and favorable to West. West should continue to use loss leaders, and this forces North to do so also. North should try to convince West that it would be better to discontinue these special bargains and even offer West some valuable consideration if he will discontinue using loss leaders (so long as this consideration is not more damaging to his net profits than the loss of $50 a week in sales).

Business Situation with a Saddle Point

The theory of games seems to hold more promise of being useful in guiding executive decisions in repetitive situations like the weekly choice of a loss leader than in one-time decisions. It may, however, logically be applied to the latter type of decisions also. Suppose that there are two large—but not entirely modern—motels so located between a mountain range on one side and a national park on the other that, while they are in vigorous competition with one another, they are well isolated from other accommodations for motorists. (This assumption makes a zero-sum game solution quite plausible, since the gains made by each will be mainly at the expense of the other.) The motels will again be named North and West.

Aware of the luxury demanded by American motorists, both motel owners begin to ponder the desirability of installing free television in all rooms and/or building a swimming pool on the premises in order to take business away from the rival firm. By chance, both hire the same management consultant, who, after considerable study, furnishes each manager with estimated pay-offs from various combinations of actions. Pay-offs are estimated increases and decreases of weekly net profits, positive figures being profit gains by West, and negative figures being profit gains by North. Each entrepreneur learns that the other has access to the same pay-off information, and each regards the other as an astute businessman. (See Exhibit 5.)

It will be noted that the installation of TV, a swimming pool, or both is somewhat more favorable to West than to North. This may be because North's location is somewhat lower and shadier than West's location, which will force North to erect higher antennas, and which

Exhibit 5

THE MOTEL GAME

		NORTH INSTALLS				
		TV	POOL	BOTH	NEITHER	ROW MINIMA
	TV	+2	−10	−20	+10	−20
	POOL	+10	+4	−10	+15	−10
WEST INSTALLS	BOTH	+15	+5	+6	+20	+5
	NEITHER	−5	−10	−15	0	−15
	COLUMN MAXIMA	+15	+5	+6	+20	

will make swimming somewhat less attractive to the guests. Nevertheless, it will not pay North to abstain entirely from these improvements. The matrix has a saddle point at "install both" for West and "install pool" for North.[11] North's weekly loss of net profits (after costs, including the new maintenance, repair, and depreciation) will be $5.00, because of the new investment by the two motels. However, if West installed both TV and a pool while his rival did nothing, he could deprive North of an estimated $20 a week in net profits.

General Observations on Game Theory and Business

A main practical difficulty in applying game theory to business decisions is that of getting reasonably accurate estimates of pay-offs under various sets of conditions. These estimates need not be perfectly accu-

---

[11] The saddle value is $5.00, because this figure is both the maximum of the row minima and the minimum of the column maxima.

rate, of course; but it is clear that if they err too greatly, they may lead to incorrect action. In this respect the estimates do not differ, however, from calculations made to guide executive decisions in nongame situations—e.g., whether or not to build an additional plant when the actions and reactions of rivals need not be considered. Any decision based on inadequate work on the part of statisticians, accountants, and engineers is apt to be nonoptimal.

Another problem is that of choosing the best pay-off criterion. In business, this is usually assumed to be net profits to the firm. Sometimes, however, the maximization of short-run profits is not consistent with maximization of long-term profits—if, for example, such earnings attract new competitors who would otherwise not enter the field, or if they bring on a union demand for a wage increase. In the case of the loss-leader problem examined earlier, the pay-offs were measured in terms of gains and losses of sales in the two stores. This tacitly assumed that profits are positively correlated with store-wide sales. Otherwise, sales do not constitute a rational pay-off criterion (unless short-run sales are considered to be positively correlated with long-run progress and profitability of the enterprise through their power to mold consumers' buying habits).

Another major problem in the application of reasonably simple game theory is the need to find situations in which the gains of one businessman are entirely, or at least almost entirely, at the expense of another. This is needed to make their competitive struggle a "zero-sum game"—one in which the gains are exactly equal to the losses. Most of the development of the theory of games refers to zero-sum games, although a chapter of von Neumann and Morgenstern's book contains a discussion of game theory for situations where this condition is not present. Most business decisions involve actions which are designed to increase the net income of the particular firm without necessarily affecting other firms in any clearly discernible manner. This is especially true in a growing economy where total dollar and physical sales are increasing in volume. Where businessmen are sharply in conflict with one another, however, simple applications of two-person zero-sum game theory may improve the quality of certain business decisions.

According to J. C. C. McKinsey,[12] the most "crying need" in game theory is development of a more satisfactory theory of nonzero-sum games and games where the number of players exceeds two. This development would be of great aid in solving certain types of economic

---

[12]*Introduction to the Theory of Games* (New York: McGraw-Hill Book Co., Inc., 1952), p. 358.

and business problems. Nevertheless, game theory in its present state has been characterized as an important "intellectual breakthrough."[13]

CASE 7–1: SOUTHWESTERN BELL TELEPHONE COMPANY VERSUS CITY OF HOUSTON

The city of Houston and Southwestern Bell Telephone Company have a long history of controversy over local-service telephone rates.[14] In December, 1917, the company filed an application for a rate increase with the City Council, and was turned down by the city in January, 1918. However, in September, 1920, the increased rates were finally put into effect after lengthy court proceedings. The final decision was by the Supreme Court of the United States on May 22, 1922.[15]

These rates remained in effect until 1941, when the city was able to obtain a reduction after informal proceedings. The new rates remained in effect until December, 1949, when the telephone company was granted an increase after several days of hearings before the City Council.

In December, 1950, the city passed ordinance No. 5759 terminating the company's franchise effective June 21, 1951, in accordance with the terms of the franchise. In October, 1951, the company filed an application for increased rates. No hearings were set by the City Council, the city taking the position that the franchise question would have to be settled before any action could be taken on the rate application. Conferences were held during the year 1952 by the city and the company; and in December, ordinance No. 8312 was passed, granting the company a new franchise effective January 23, 1953.

In March, 1953, the company filed a supplementary application for increased rates and asked that temporary rates be placed in effect under bond. In April the City Council denied rates under bond and set hearings for the proposed increases for June, 1953.

The hearings before the City Council were conducted from June 1, 1953, through August 20, 1953, and the record contains 2,414 pages of oral testimony and seventy-one exhibits. On September 9, 1953,

---

[13]A very interesting criticism of the von Neumann-Morgenstern theory of games is contained in an article by Daniel Ellsberg, "Theory of the Reluctant Duelist," *American Economic Review,* December, 1956. He points out that the conservative actions indicated by the theory are more appropriate for one who is *forced* to engage in the game than to one who enters a two-person conflict situation willingly in the hope of a big pay-off to himself. Applied to business, this suggests that the best strategy may be to try to confuse an opponent, to find out his strategy, or to tempt him into a situation where a big "killing" is possible. This is particularly the case where only one "play" is to be made, as Ellsberg points out.

[14]Texas was in 1958 one of two states without a state commission for the regulation of utilities.

[15]*City of Houston* v. *Southwestern Bell Telephone Company,* 259 U.S. 318.

the City Council enacted ordinance No. 9236 denying the company's application for an increase in revenues and giving specific findings and conclusions on the issues raised.

The company filed action on October 5, 1953, in the District Court of Harris County, 133d Judicial District of Texas, asking a temporary injunction, a permanent injunction, and the right to place higher rates in effect under bond pending the final determination of the proceedings. The District Court on November 9, 1953, found for the company, and ordered a temporary injunction restraining the city from enforcing the rate ordinance of 1949 and allowing the company to place higher rates in effect under the condition that it file a $12 million surety bond. The company put into effect an increased schedule of rates effective November 10, 1953.

The temporary injunction order was appealed by the city to the Court of Civil Appeals, but the order was affirmed on December 9, 1953, and a rehearing was denied. The Texas Supreme Court refused a writ of error on February 10, 1954.

The company requested that a master in chancery be appointed to receive evidence, hear the issues of fact and law arising in the proceedings, and report findings of fact and conclusions of law to the court. A master in chancery was appointed by the court over the objections of the city, and hearings were held.

The areas of contention were the rate base, the allowable revenues and expenses, and the allowable rate of return. The evidence and findings are presented for each of these areas.

At the outset, the parties agreed that the entire Houston District Exchange, comprising not only the city of Houston, but a number of other smaller municipalities, would serve as the basis for the data on plant, revenues, and expenses to be considered. This area is a single operations unit, that is, any local subscriber may call any other local subscriber without payment of a toll.

Rate Base

The basic area of contention between the city and the company on the rate base was in the definition of fair value. The city contended that fair value need not give predominant weight to current cost or reproduction cost. The company felt that current cost should be given predominant weight, particularly since the price level had risen greatly since much of the plant was placed into service.

Exhibit 1 shows the computation of the rate base by the company, the city, and the master in chancery. Each is discussed with more detailed discussion following on the questions of depreciation and separations.

Exhibit 1

COMPUTATION OF THE RATE BASE, HOUSTON EXCHANGE, SOUTHWESTERN BELL TELEPHONE COMPANY

(As of December 31, 1952)

COMPUTATION BY J. B. BLANTON OF THE COMPANY

Current cost of telephone plant in Houston District Exchange (before separations)	$111,475,674
Less: Deterioration and obsolescence (observed)	10,648,707
Current cost of telephone plant less accrued depreciation (before separations)	$100,826,967
Less: Portion allocable to long-distance operations as per "usage method"	17,259,386
Current cost of depreciated telephone plant allocable to local exchange service	$ 83,567,581
Plus: Cash working capital	618,005
Plus: Materials and supplies	971,061
Total Current Worth	$ 85,156,647

COMPUTATION BY JAMES HONAKER FOR THE CITY OF HOUSTON

Gross telephone plant allocable to local exchange service in Houston District Exchange (after separation of portion allocable to long-distance operations according to procedures recommended by Honaker)	$ 71,736,159
Less: A. T. & T. excess earnings through Western Electric Company included in plant	1,240,481
Adjusted gross telephone plant	$ 70,495,678
Less: Reserve for depreciation	13,405,161
Net Telephone Plant as Adjusted	$ 57,090,517

COMPUTATION BY THE MASTER IN CHANCERY

Average original cost of plant in service during 1952 (before separation)	$ 89,334,830
Less: Portion allocable to long distance in accordance with "usage method"	15,231,918
Average original cost after separations	$ 74,102,912
Less: Balance of book reserve for depreciation (based on company's special Houston study)	12,444,474
Average net plant for year 1952	$ 61,658,438
Plus: Adjustment for appreciation of land value	202,054
Fair Value as Determined by Master	$ 61,860,492

Source: *Report of Master in Chancery*, pp. 31, 125.

Two witnesses for the company testified as to the fair value of the property. Mr. Jackson Martindell, before the City Council, determined fair value by converting the additions to the plant since 1939 to 1952 dollars by use of the Consumer Price Index, in order to express the value of the plant in terms of the purchasing power of 1952 dollars. By this method, he determined the fair value of the property to be about $83 million. Mr. J. Ben Blanton of the company listed nine elements that he believed should be considered in determining the fair value of the property. These were:

. . . First would be the original cost of the property; by that I mean the number of dollars invested in and subject to all risks inherent to the operation of the business. The second item would be the number of dollars in the reserve for depreciation. . . . The next item, the net investments in the property expressed in terms of the purchasing power of the dollar as of December 31, 1952. . . . The next element that we took into consideration is the current cost of the properties used and useful in rendering telephone service, and by that I mean what it would cost to construct the properties being used in public service at the prices for wages and materials in effect December 31, 1952. . . . The next element is the present condition of the property, that is, whether there is any deterioration or obsolescence existing in the property. The next item to take into consideration is the amount of cash working capital, and the value of the quantity of materials and supplies which are required for the day to day operations of the business. . . . The next item was in the engineering of the property, that is, whether the property had been properly engineered and is adapted to meet the needs of the community. . . . The next item that we look into is to whether there is any existence of non-useful property, whether there was any waste in the building and the property. . . . The last item which we would recognize and give consideration to, is whether or not Houston is a progressive area, one in which the future of the telephone service will continue into the foreseeable future.[16]

Mr. Blanton's method of appraisal consisted of securing an inventory of all of the assets of the exchange. Equipment other than buildings and land was repriced at prices prevailing on December 31, 1952. Buildings were revalued by the use of building construction cost indices for the Houston area. The buildings were valued as if they were to be rebuilt wholesale rather than piecemeal, as they were actually constructed. Land was valued as appraised in 1949 plus the market price for land added since 1949. For right of way, vehicles, furniture, and work equipment, original cost was taken as the best evidence of the current cost of these items. Observed depreciation was deducted from this total to obtain the present value. The observed depreciation was determined by an engineering inspection of a small sample of the

---

[16]*Master's Hearing,* p. 728B–735 (transcript of hearing before the master in chancery).

property. An over-all per cent condition was then determined and applied to the current cost to obtain the depreciated current cost. The long-distance plant was separated from the local plant by means of separations studies which will be discussed later. Both Mr. Martindell and Mr. Blanton used plant as of December 31, 1952, rather than the average plant. (See Exhibit 1.)

The city, on the other hand, used average annual values for the plant instead of year-end values, and deducted the book reserve for depreciation using the state-wide ratio of reserve to depreciable telephone plant. The city used original cost according to the records of the company. The city also used a different separations procedure, which will be explained later. An adjustment was made by the city for alleged excess values of plant equipment purchased from Western Electric Company by Southwestern Bell. (The city contended that because of higher prices, Western Electric was enabled to earn a greater return than a public utility should.) (See Exhibit 1 for the rate-base computation.)

The rate base determined by the City Council after its hearings was $57,292,571. This increase over the rate base presented by the city's witness reflected the appraised value of the land acquired prior to 1949.

The master in chancery determined the rate base in a different manner than either the city or the company. He agreed with the city in the use of average values, in the exclusion of working capital from the rate base, and in interpreting the fair-value statute to permit the use of original cost for property other than land. The master sustained the company with respect to separations, Western Electric Company excess profits, and the use of a special depreciation study for the Houston District Exchange.

The master also found that if, as a matter of law, he was required to give greater weight to current cost than this, the rate base should be $68,500,000.

Since the disagreement over separation of the toll from local exchange is of fairly great magnitude, and since the question of depreciation is also very important, the evidence on these issues is presented in some detail.

Separations

The National Association of Railroad and Utility Commissioners, acting jointly with the Federal Communications Commission, in 1947 issued a *Separations Manual* designed to provide criteria for the separation of intrastate and interstate plant, revenue, and expenses. This manual was subsequently modified on March 1, 1952, resulting in more equipment being switched to interstate toll. The manual was further modified in 1956, but this last modification does not affect local jurisdiction. This *Separations Manual* was not written for the purpose of separating local exchange from toll, and states that some modification might be required for this use.

The company, using the *Separations Manual,* made studies to separate the plant on the basis of usage. The principal conflict on separations between the city and the company was the group of accounts called station equipment. These include "those telephone facilities which are ordinarily located on the customer's premises, including the apparatus itself, the cost of installation thereof, and the drop wires leading toward the distribution lines on the highways, streets, or utility easements."

The company based its separation of these accounts on a holding-time study which was conducted over a period of several months during representative hours of the day. In this study a team stationed in an exchange timed every call from every phone and determined how long the phone was in use, and noted whether the call was toll or local. An average time for toll calls and an average time for local calls were then determined. These times were then multiplied by the total of each class of calls for the year, and the ratio of toll time to local time determined the per cent of joint plant allocated to each category. In this case, this resulted in 4.25 per cent of the station equipment being classed as toll and 95.75 per cent being classed as local exchange. Much of the rest of the plant can be separated according to actual use. The over-all separation factor was 17.65 per cent toll and 82.35 per cent local exchange on original-cost, undepreciated valuation.[17]

The city, through its witness, Mr. James Honaker, objected to this method of separating the station equipment for several reasons. Most important, it was felt that because toll calls are paid for on a measured basis and because local calls are unlimited under flat-rate billing, naturally much more time will accrue to local calls. Also, Honaker felt that since this equipment was actually in use only about 2 per cent of the time, some allowance should be made for "stand-by value," that is, the value of having the phone there even if you are not presently using it. Expenses do not vary appreciably with holding time, especially where dial equipment is used.

---

[17]*Plaintiff's Exhibit No. 28, Master's Hearing.*

For these reasons the city apportioned the station equipment in the same ratio of local to toll as all other plant and equipment. This resulted in 19.7 per cent of these accounts being assigned to toll and 80.3 per cent assigned to local exchange, a substantial reduction in rate base. The company objected to this method of apportionment primarily because it had a considerable amount of toll equipment located within the Houston District Exchange that served no local purpose, being merely used for switching for toll calls for the surrounding area, resulting in an unjust apportionment of the station equipment.

The city adopted the "Honaker method" of separations in determining the rate base. The master accepted the company's method, but said that the city was not precluded from making its own apportionment, but that in this case it had failed to rationally support its findings. Mr. Honaker had made no local studies, and no adjustment was made for the toll facilities located in Houston for other areas.

Depreciation

Depreciation is important not only in determining the rate base, but also in determining expense. The expense question will be postponed until expenses in general are considered.

The company witness for the rate base, Mr. Blanton, used observed depreciation as the basis for the deduction from the valuation. He said that per cent condition or observed depreciation should be used

. . . because the amounts in the reserve for depreciation are in there anticipating the ultimate retirement of the property and they are accrued to this investment in a straight uniform method over the service life of the property. The plant itself actually does not deteriorate or become obsolete in a straight uniform line, so to reflect the true condition or the amount which should be deducted for deterioration and obsolescence it has to be done as of a specified time.[18]

The per cent condition of each category of plant was arrived at by inspecting a small sample of each and imputing the condition of the sample to the class. For example, out of 72,875 creosoted poles and 183 noncreosoted poles, Mr. Blanton personally inspected 186, and his crew (including himself) inspected a total of 296. Out of 2,505 manholes, 11 brick and 29 concrete manholes were inspected by Mr. Blanton. Some categories of plant were reduced in value for obsolescence, but in no case were they reduced below the book cost less

---

[18]*Master's Hearing,* p. 970.

accrued depreciation. The over-all per cent condition arrived at by Mr. Blanton was 90 per cent.

The city, using average original cost as adjusted for its rate base, maintained that the average balance of the reserve for depreciation determined by using the state-wide ratio of depreciation reserve to telephone plant should be used as the deduction. (The rates of depreciation are submitted to the FCC by the company engineers, and are based upon engineering studies of the service life and expected obsolescence of the various categories of plant and equipment.)

The master followed the city in the case of average depreciation, but without the adjustments which the city had made for alleged Western Electric excess profits.

Revenues and Expenses

Exhibit 2 lists the net earnings claimed by the company, the disallowances contended for by the city, and the disallowances which were approved by the master.

Items (a) and (b) were discussed previously under the rate base. They were disallowed by the master for the same reasons as before.

Items (c) and (d) both deal with depreciation. Item (d) was disallowed because the master felt that average values should be used since the earnings were based on average plant rather than year-end plant. This was consistent with the deduction of depreciation from average plant rather than year-end plant. The claim for "current cost depreciation" is based upon the theory that depreciation should recover the real physical assets rather than the dollar investment. The master felt that current cost depreciation was too "theoretical" and should not be allowed.

Item (e) was disallowed by the master, as he felt that the stockholders rather than the rate payers should be charged with contribu-

Exhibit 2

HOUSTON EXCHANGE EARNINGS AS ADJUSTED BY CITY AND BY MASTER IN CHANCERY

Net earnings as claimed by company in its original presentation before city council..$2,341,737

Less: Adjustment to give effect to August, 1953, wage increase not taken into consideration in presentation before city council ($327,824 minus 52 per cent tax credit).......   157,355

Adjusted Net Earnings Claimed by Company in Hearing before Master..$2,184,382

Exhibit 2 (Continued)

Adjustments Contended for by the City	Amount of Disallowance Contended for by City (Net after Applicable Income Tax Offset)	Amount of City's Claimed Disallowance Not Approved by Master	Amount of City's Claimed Disallowance Approved by Master (Net after Applicable Income Tax Offset)
a) To give effect to Honaker system of separations..............................	$ 318,686	$318,686	
b) To give effect to Western Electric profit disallowance........................	42,204	42,204	
c) To give effect to disallowance of so-called "current cost" depreciation.............	345,928		$ 345,928
d) To give effect to depreciation on annual average plant instead of year-end balances.	53,314		53,314
e) To give effect to disallowances of club dues, expense, and contributions to charitable organizations....................	18,874		18,874
f) To give effect to income tax reduction effected through use of 40–60 debt-equity ratio...............................	128,983	128,983	
g) To give effect to disallowance of certain pension accruals......................	11,598	11,598	
h) To give effect to disallowance of current cost adjustments included in amounts claimed as maintenance expense, including casualty and wiring loss................	71,364	71,364	
i) To give effect to disallowance of certain nonrecurring central office repairs........	5,513		5,513
j) To give effect to disallowance of certain claimed excessive strike expense.........	2,109	2,109	
k) To give effect to disallowance of certain direct and allocated advertising and business promotion expenses................	14,743	14,743	
l) To give effect to disallowance of certain allocated legal fees and expenses.........	7,599	7,599	
m) To give effect to increased rate of earnings actually enjoyed at 1953 current levels— not identified as to specific items........	159,619	159,619	
Total Disallowances Contended for by City.......................	$1,180,534		
Total Disallowances Contended for by City and Not Approved by Master......................		$756,905	
Total Disallowances Contended for by City and Approved by Master...			$ 423,629
Earnings for Test Period as Determined by Master........................			$2,608,011

Source: *Report of Master in Chancery*, pp. 146–47.

tions to charity and club dues. Decisions in Texas cases have been consistently in agreement with the master on this point.

Item (f) was not disallowed because the company actually paid substantially all of this in taxes.

The disallowance of pension accruals was not approved by the master. It is allowed by the FCC as a legitimate operating expense. The courts have uniformly reversed decisions in which this expense was disallowed.

The master felt that item (h) was reasonable. It was based on ten-year averages by both the city and the company, but the company adjusted it to current price levels. The master felt that it was reasonable, in that current prices would actually be incurred. The disallowance of item (i) was approved by the master, as it involved the repair of equipment withdrawn from service in the Houston District Exchange. Item (j) was not disallowed by the master because it was less than the increase in the wage bill would have been, had there been no strike.

Item (k) was partly due to differences in allocation methods of the company and the city, and partly due to the disallowance by the city of advertising expense incurred in bill inserts. Since the allocation method of the company was adopted by the master, the only question then is the bill inserts. This amount the master felt to be reasonable. Item (l) was the allocation of a portion of the state-wide legal expenses to the Houston District Exchange. Since the actual legal expense in Houston during 1952 was greater than this, the expense was allowed. Item (m) was not allowed, as it was not adequately developed in the record.

Thus, net earnings for 1952 were determined to be $2,608,011 by the master.

Rate of Return

The governing statute does not include any provision as to the rate of return that a utility should be allowed to earn. It is generally assumed that a "fair return" is implied by the statute. The applicable definition of fair return is:

> . . . What annual rate will constitute just compensation depends upon many circumstances and must be determined by the exercise of a fair and enlightened judgment, having regard to all relevant facts. A public utility is entitled to such rates as will permit it to earn a return on the value of the property which it employs for the convenience of the public equal to that generally being earned at

the same time and in the same general part of the country on investments in other business undertakings which are attended by corresponding risks and uncertainties; but it has no constitutional rights to profits such as are realized in highly profitable enterprises or speculative ventures. The return should be reasonably sufficient to assure confidence in the financial soundness of the utility, and should be adequate, under efficient and economical management, to maintain and support its credit and enable it to raise the money necessary for the proper discharge of its public duties. A rate of return may be reasonable at one time and become too high or too low by changes affecting opportunities for investment, the money market, and business conditions generally.[19]

There was extensive testimony as to the fair rate of return, both before the City Council and before the master. The company had two primary witnesses, Mr. Robert Moroney, a Houston investment banker, and Mr. Jackson Martindell, a financial consultant.

Mr. Moroney felt that the current cost of capital provided the best guide to determining the "fair return." To determine the current cost of capital, he made studies of the cost of debt and equity capital. The actual cost of debt capital to Southwestern Bell he determined to be approximately 3 per cent. From studies of recent debt issues of other Bell companies, he determined the current cost of new debt capital to be 3½ per cent. The prospective cost of debt capital in the next year or two he felt to be 4 per cent, because of a long-term upward trend of interest rates. He concluded that predominant weight should be given to the prospective debt cost in determining the current cost of capital.

Mr. Moroney used the earnings-price ratio of the previous twelve months as the best measure of the cost of equity capital. However, since the last direct stock issue of the American Telephone and Telegraph Company prior to this time was in 1931, he did not consider directly the earnings-price ratio of A. T. & T. The conversion of convertible debentures into common stock did not adequately represent the true cost of new equity capital to Mr. Moroney because of the "invisible" cost of going into debt incurred by A. T. & T. when it issued convertible debentures. Therefore, he considered the cost of new equity capital to the General Telephone Company, which he determined to be 10.37 per cent in 1952 and 11.33 per cent in 1953. Also, he determined the cost of new equity capital to electric utilities operating in the same area as Southwestern Bell. This was found to be 9.8 per cent, or 10.2 per cent after excluding companies which had rate increases prior to a financing, but which was not reflected in earnings.[20] The cost of new

[19]*Bluefield Water Works & Improvement Co.* v. *Public Service Commission,* 262 U.S. 679, 692 (1923).

[20]Based on 17 public offerings and 13 pre-emptive offerings during the period 1948–53.

equity capital to natural gas companies operating in the area he found to be 9.7 per cent. From these results, he estimated the cost of new equity capital to the telephone company to be 11 per cent.

In determining the over-all cost of capital, Mr. Moroney felt that a 40–60 debt-equity ratio would be the proper one to apply. (The actual A. T. & T. debt-equity ratio was very close to this.) Using this ratio and the capital costs he had developed, he determined the current cost of capital in the three ways shown below:[21]

A. At prospective debt cost of 4.0 per cent:

  Bonds...........$ 400,000 × 4.0%...........$16,000

  Stock........... 600,000 × 11.0%........... 66,000

     $1,000,000 $82,000

  $82,000 ÷ $1,000,000 = 8.2% Cost of new money

B. At spot debt cost of 3.5 per cent:

  Bonds...........$ 400,000 × 3.5%...........$14,000

  Stock........... 600,000 × 11.0%........... 66,000

     $1,000,000 $80,000

  $80,000 ÷ $1,000,000 = 8.0% Cost of new money

C. At imbedded debt cost of 3.0 per cent:

  Bonds...........$ 400,000 × 3.0%...........$12,000

  Stock........... 600,000 × 11.0%........... 66,000

     $1,000,000 $78,000

  $78,000 ÷ $1,000,000 = 7.8% Cost of new money

Mr. Moroney also presented an exhibit where he determined the cost of capital on the basis of conversion of convertible debentures, but stated emphatically that he did not believe it to be the proper method of determining capital cost. For the period 1950–52 the American Telephone and Telegraph Company obtained equity capital in the amount of $1,863,965,764 from conversion of debentures and sale of stock to employees. This was supported by earnings of $163,455,710, giving an earnings-price ratio of 8.77 per cent. Exhibit 3 shows how he determined the over-all capital cost on this basis.[22]

Mr. Martindell estimated the current cost of debt capital to be between 3½ and 4 per cent, based on the net cost to the issuer of high-grade electric utility securities during 1952–53. He determined the current cost of equity capital from seventy-three common stock issues of $5 million or more of forty electric utilities during 1952–53. Some

---

[21]*Plaintiff's Exhibit No. 45, Master's Hearing.*

[22]*Plaintiff's Exhibit No. 46, Master's Hearing.*

issues were eliminated where they were not underwritten or where the offering price was not set at the latest possible date or where a rate increase was not fully reflected in earnings. Based upon this study, he determined the cost of new equity capital to be between 9½ and 10 per cent.

Exhibit 3

1. Total money raised by issuance of A. T. & T. stock, three years, 1950–52...................$1,863,965,764
2. Dollars of earnings supporting stock money raised*.................................... 163,455,710
3. Relationship of earnings to stock money raised (item 2 ÷ item 1).......................... 8.77%

Debt........$ 400,000 × 3.00%.....$12,000
Equity.......   600,000 × 8.77%...... 52,620

$1,000,000 $64,620

$64,620 ÷ $1,000,000 = 6.46%

*Total number of shares of stock issued during each year of the three-year period divided by that year's earnings per share.

The electric utility companies used in the study had an average equity-debt ratio of 35 and 65 per cent (50 per cent debt, 15 per cent preferred stock). Mr. Martindell believed the telephone business to be more risky than the electric utility business; and therefore, in order to compensate for the difference in risk, he applied a ⅔–⅓ equity-debt ratio to the current costs he had determined. He insisted that this did not reflect his judgment as to the proper equity-debt ratio, but was done merely to equalize risks. He based his opinion as to the comparative risks upon a study purporting to show (1) that market changes between 1929 and 1940 showed telephone stocks to be twice as sensitive as electric stocks, (2) that telephone revenues are about 40 per cent more sensitive than electric revenues, and (3) less than one half of electric utility expense is relatively rigid, as compared to three fourths in the telephone industry. Exhibit 4 shows how he determined the over-all cost of new capital.[23]

Both Mr. Moroney and Mr. Martindell insisted that in order to protect historical stockholders, the current cost of capital should be applied to a current-cost rate base. If a cost rate base were used, then a relatively greater per cent return would be required.

Mr. James Honaker testified as to the fair return for the city. He submitted a study designed to determine the required rate of return to

---

[23]*Plaintiff's Exhibit No. 51, Master's Hearing*, p. 12.

provide $10.50 earnings per average share of A. T. & T. common stock.[24] (See Exhibit 5.)

Applying the earnings requirement of $501,877,000 to the net telephone plant and other investments total of $8,839,896,000, Mr. Honaker found that a return of 5.68 per cent was required to provide $10.50 per share earnings. This same amount would provide a rate of return of 5.57 upon the total capital of $9,017,871,000. A 6 per cent

Exhibit 4

Components of Total Capital	Current Cost	Capital Structure Weight	Weighted Components
Debt..............	3.50%– 4.00%	⅓	1.17%–1.33%
Equity...........	9.50%–10.00%	⅔	6.33%–6.67%
Over-all current cost of capital........			7.50%–8.00%

Exhibit 5

	Capital	Required Earnings
Funded debt:		
Amount...................................	$3,748,589,000	
Fixed charges...............................		$117,029,000
Publicly held stock of subsidiaries:		
Amount...................................	164,392,000	
Dividends and earnings applicable thereto.......		11,800,000
American component common stock:		
Amount of stock, premiums, instalments, and surplus.............................	5,104,870,000	
Dividends and earnings applicable thereto.......		373,048,000
Total...................................	$9,017,851,000	$501,877,000

return on net plant and other investments would provide earnings of $11.30 per average share, as compared with $11.45 actually earned in 1952. Mr. Honaker determined the historical pay-out between 1922 and 1952 to be 84.7 per cent; and on this basis, $10.63 earnings per average share were required for 1952. This return would be 5.73 per cent on net plant or 5.62 per cent on combined capital. If the pay-out ratio of 90.4 for 1937–52 is considered, then earnings of only $9.95

[24]Report of Master in Chancery, District Court of Harris County, Texas, 133d Judicial District, No. 426,913 (Southwestern Bell Telephone Co. v. City of Houston et al.), p. 153.

per average share would be required for 1952, giving a return of 5.45 on net plant or 5.35 on combined capital. Considering this information, Mr. Honaker felt that from 5½ to 5¾ per cent would be the fair rate of return.

Mr. Edwin Bruhl, an independent certified public accountant, also presented rate-of-return evidence for the city. Mr. Bruhl felt that the debt-equity ratio should be 40–60, even if the interest rate should be very high because of the income tax factor (e.g., for an interest rate of 3½ per cent, the net cost to the company is 1.68 cents per dollar of debt capital, whereas it is about 8⅓ cents per dollar of equity capital). Using the imbedded debt cost of 3 per cent and an equity capital cost of 7½ per cent—the average cost of obtaining equity capital from the conversion of debentures for the period 1945–52—he determined the fair rate of return to be 5.7 per cent:

$$\text{Debt} \quad \$ \ 400,000 \times 3.0\% \quad \$12,000$$
$$\text{Equity} \quad 600,000 \times 7.5\% \quad 45,000$$

$$\$1,000,000 \qquad\qquad \$57,000$$

$$\$57,000 \div \$1,000,000 = 5.7\%$$

The master in chancery did not accept any of the methods presented, but instead used his own procedure. The cost of debt capital used was the imbedded cost of the outstanding debt of Southwestern Bell. He did not give any consideration to current debt cost because the company did not plan to issue new debt in the near future, and the replacement of the present debt was still a long way off. To give effect to the 40–60 ratio of debt to equity, he considered the advances from A. T. & T. to Southwestern Bell as debt capital, and he also considered enough of Southwestern Bell's common stock to be debt to bring the total debt component up to 39.719 per cent (the actual percentage of A. T. & T.'s capital structure that was debt). This is shown in Exhibit 6. The over-all debt cost is therefore 2.936 per cent.

In determining the cost of equity capital, the master considered that the actual experience of A. T. & T. should be given greater consideration than Mr. Moroney and Mr. Martindell had given it. Since during the year 1952, total conversions of convertible debentures had been greater than total issues, the master felt that it would be appropriate to consider conversions as though they were an issue of equity capital. The proceeds of conversion for 1952 are shown in Exhibit 7. Average conversion proceeds received by company per share were $137.96.

Thus, he determined the cost of equity capital by using the ratio of 1952 earnings to net conversion proceeds of $11.45 to $138.00, which gave a cost of equity capital of 8.30 per cent. With a debt-equity ratio of 40–60, the over-all capital cost was 6.15 per cent. Any return less than this would result in confiscation. If the current cost rate base (as he determined it) were used, then the cost of capital would be 6.00 per cent.

Exhibit 6

	Debt Component in Dollars	Per Cent of Total Capital	Rate	Weighted Component
Southwestern Bell debt.....	$175,000,000	{25.410%	2.880%	$5,040,000
A. T. & T. advances........	35,370,555		3.000	1,061,117
Southwestern Bell common..	118,454,654	14.300	3.000	3,553,640
	$328,825,209	39.719%	2.936%	$9,654,757

Exhibit 7

Year of Issue	Par Value of Debenture Converted	Minimum Price at Which Converted	Minimum Proceeds of Conversion
1946............	$ 57,968,000	146	$ 84,633,000
1947............	57,230,000	140	80,122,000
1949............	9,697,000	130	12,606,000
1951............	142,360,000	138	196,457,000
1952............	260,201,000	136	353,873,000
	$527,456,000		$727,691,000

In order that a return of 6.15 per cent be earned on a rate base of $61,860,492, net earnings of $3,804,420 were required. Earnings for 1952, as determined by the master, were $2,608,011. Therefore, earnings were deficient in the sum of $1,196,409. For the company to earn this amount of net additional revenue, it must collect additional gross revenue of $2,650,046 because of taxes, etc.

The master in chancery also submitted a special report in which he recommended that the rates which had been set under bond be reduced to a scale which he proposed. The city suggested an even lower scale. The District Court felt that the proposed rates of the master were too low and that the bonded rates were too high, and said that if the injunction was to remain in effect, the rates should be set halfway between the two scales. The city gave notice of appeal and asked for several extensions. With a change in administration, the city voted to drop the appeal. The company then pledged that the basic phone rates would remain in effect for two years. Pay phone rates were later raised from 5 to 10 cents. Exhibit 8 shows the various rate schedules discussed.

Exhibit 8

HOUSTON TELEPHONE RATES

	(1) 1949 Ordinance	(2) Requested by Company, March, 1953	(3) Set under Bond	(4) Recom- mended by Master	(5) Set by Court
Business service:					
One party—flat.......	$12.00	$18.00	$17.00	$16.00	$16.50
Extension—flat.....	1.50	1.75	1.75		1.75
Semipublic..........	0.25/day	0.35/day	0.35/day		
Extension—noncoin.	1.00	1.25	1.25		
One party—measured.	6.00	8.50	8.50		
Extension—meas- ured...........	1.00	1.25	1.25		
PBX:					
Commercial:					
Trunks...........	18.00	27.00	25.50	24.00	
Stations..........	1.50	1.75	1.75		
Residence:					
Trunks...........	7.13	10.13	9.75	7.88	
Stations..........	1.00	1.25	1.25		
Hotel:					
Trunks...........	12.00	18.00	17.00	16.00	
Stations..........	0.75	1.25	1.25		
Residence service:					
One party..........	4.75	6.75	6.50	5.25	5.90
Two party..........	4.00	5.75	5.50	4.25	4.85
Four party..........	3.25	4.75	4.50	3.25	3.85
Extensions..........	1.00	1.25	1.25		1.25
Rural:					
Business............	7.50*	10.00	10.00*		
Extension.........	1.50	1.75	1.75		
Residence...........	3.25*	4.75	4.75*		
Extension.........	1.00	1.25	1.25		
Government PBX:					
Trunks..............	27.00	40.50	38.25	36.00	
Service stations:					
Residence...........	2.00	2.50	2.50		
Business............	4.00	5.00	5.00		

*Applies within four miles of the base-rate area. For each additional mile or fraction thereof, 25 cents extra. Air-line measurement used.

Sources: Columns 1, 2, and 3: *Report of Master in Chancery*, p. 165; column 4: *Special Report of Master in Chancery;* column 5: Southwestern Bell Telephone Company.

QUESTIONS

1. What should be the goal of the city of Houston in its regulation of the rates of Southwestern Bell Telephone Company?

2. Does or can regulation achieve these goals?

3. What is the relationship between the rate base, the rate of return, and the phone rates which are the end result of the regulatory process? Does the relationship change with changing definitions of the components of the formula?

4. Which of the alternative computations of rate base, rate of return, and expenses would you choose if you were on the Houston City Council or if you were a circuit court judge? Defend your choices.

CASE 7-2: INTERNATIONAL AIR FARES

Air passenger traffic has grown rapidly in the postwar period. The transatlantic route has grown particularly rapidly since the introduction of jet service. Fares have declined as more flights have been scheduled with more air lines participating in the traffic.

Most of the air lines which fly the transatlantic route are members of the International Air Transport Association (IATA), a voluntary organization of air line companies. Any air line with scheduled air service among two or more countries may join, provided it operates under the flag of a state which is eligible for membership in the International Civil Aviation Organization (ICAO), an organization primarily concerned with standardization of technical matters in international aviation.[25]

The IATA provides a means whereby air lines can attempt to solve jointly many problems which they cannot individually resolve.

It is active in the fields of traffic, finance, legal and technical matters, medicine, public information, and the like. In some cases, IATA acts as a central bank of information and technical knowledge for all member airlines; in others, IATA is preparing to publish tariffs and time-tables; it conducts such enterprises as the IATA Clearing House; it administers committees of airline experts set up to deal with continuing problems; and it represents the airlines in their dealings with other international organizations.[26]

The IATA also regularly schedules joint rate conferences of scheduled air lines to consider rates. If rate schedules are unanimously agreed upon, they become binding upon the member air lines, subject to the

---

[25] John H. Frederick, *Commercial Air Transportation* (5th ed.; Homewood, Ill.: Richard D. Irwin, Inc., 1961).

[26] *Ibid.*, pp. 309–10.

approval of their governments. However, if the agreement is not unanimous, or if all the governments involved do not agree, the result is an "open rate," and members may quote competitive rates. If agreement is reached by all parties, then the member air lines must abide by the conference rates and are subject to fines of up to $25,000 for violations of the agreement. Exhibit 1 shows a chronology of fare changes on the North Atlantic route from 1948 to 1961.

The rapid growth of traffic and the changing character of the service offered is illustrated by Exhibits 2 and 3. Exhibit 2 shows the total seats available, the number of passengers carried, and the load factor for each of the three classes of service—first class, tourist, and economy. Exhibit 3 shows total seats available, total passengers, and also information concerning the number of charter passengers.

IATA conferences in recent years have been uniformly explosive over the rate issue; in fact, open rates have almost resulted several times. An issue which has caused considerable agitation in the rate conferences is the existence of Icelandic Airlines (Loftleider), which, as a nonmember, is free to set whatever rates it chooses between Iceland and the United States, and Iceland and Luxembourg. The other countries force Icelandic to charge the same fares as their state-controlled air lines; but the United States and Luxembourg have no state-owned air lines, so that by adroit scheduling, Icelandic has been able to undercut the IATA members by about 20 per cent. Exhibit 4 shows some representative Icelandic fares. Icelandic flies no jets; and on the New York to London route, it flies from New York to Iceland at an open rate, and then from Iceland to London at the IATA rate, with the net result a very low fare. Icelandic is reported to have a load factor of about 70 per cent compared to the 50 per cent load factor of the IATA members. Sigurdur Helgason, president of Icelandic Airlines, Inc., has been quoted as saying: "Loftleider's share of the North Atlantic market has remained level at about 2%."[27]

Exhibit 5 gives some cost and revenue data for international operations by all United States air lines which should be representative of the costs of international operations on the North Atlantic run.

A third problem of IATA is the rapid growth of charter flights. This problem has resulted in a rather complicated set of rules for members on the scheduling of charter or group flights. In early 1962, special group fares were permitted only under the following conditions: (1) The group must have been in organization for at least six months prior

---

[27]*Business Week,* November 24, 1962, p. 45.

Exhibit 1

NORTH ATLANTIC CHRONOLOGY OF FARE CHANGES
(Rounded to Nearest Dollar)

		FIRST CLASS		TOURIST CLASS		ECONOMY CLASS	
DATE	ACTION	One Way	Round Trip	One Way	Round Trip	One Way	Round Trip
April, 1948..........	Transatlantic fares increased slightly less than 10 per cent.	$350	$630				
October, 1948........	Special transatlantic excursion fares introduced. Round trip within 30 days for 1⅓ way. Good only in winter, October 1, 1948, to April 1, 1949.		467				
October, 1949........	Above fare extended over another winter season, good for 60 days.		467				
January, 1950........	New excursion fare, 15-day limit. One way plus 10 per cent, January through March.		385				
March, 1950..........	Fares beyond European gateways increased.						
March, 1950..........	On-season round trip continued at 180 per cent of one way (10 per cent discount). Off-season set at 133 per cent of one way.						
	On-season....................................	350	630				
	Off-season...................................	350	467				
January, 1951........	1950 special excursion experiment repeated, January through March. One way plus 10 per cent.		413				
February, 1952.......	Tourist fares approved and tourist class established.						
	On-season (April-October).....................	395	711	$270	$486		
	Off-season...................................	395	640	270	417		
March, 1954..........	Air travel tax cut from 15 per cent to 10 per cent.						
November, 1955......	Off-season transatlantic fares increased.	n.c.*	670	n.c.	482		
November, 1955......	Off-season family plan introduced between November 1 and March 31. Head of family paid full fare, wife and						

	One way..... $150 $150					
	Round trip... 300 200					
	Children under 12 travel at 50 per cent of regular adult fare, as usual.					
April, 1956............	First-class fare increased.					
	On-season....................................	440	792			
	Off-season....................................	440	742			
	"Sleeper" surcharges increased from $50 to $55 (10 per cent).					
September, 1956.......	First-class off-season rate reduction eliminated.					
	Off-season....................................	440	792			
October, 1956.........	Year-round transatlantic excursion fare introduced on tourist class, 15-day time limit.			270	425	
April, 1957............	First-class fares reduced.	400	720			
April, 1958............	Economy fare and class introduced.					
	Less leg room, buffet snacks.					
	Tourist fares and first-class fares increased.	440	792		$252	$454
April, 1959............	Jet surcharge of $15–$20 instigated on about 6 per cent or less of previous (estimates).	460	832		267	484
June, 1961............	Flying Tiger offered European groups unprecedented bargain rates on group charters, normal cost of round trip $250–$325; Flying Tiger prorated $11,682 over 118-seat Super Constellations. If filled, this meant $99 per passenger. Offered only to balance summer season travel, terminated on August 4.					

*The letters *n.c.* indicate no change.

Exhibit 2

NORTH ATLANTIC TRAFFIC,* 1948–61, IATA MEMBER CARRIERS
Scheduled Flights (by Class)

Year	First Class			Tourist Class			Economy Class		
	Passengers	Seats	Load Factor	Passengers	Seats	Load Factor	Passengers	Seats	Load Factor
1948	240,472	n.a.†	n.a.	....	....	....	....	....	....
1949	266,535	n.a.	n.a.	....	....	....	....	....	....
1950	311,545	495,561	62.9	....	....	....	....	....	....
1951	329,656	504,185	65.4	....	....	....	....	....	....
1952	243,571	362,289	67.2	188,701	263,559	71.6	....	....	....
1953	186,072	298,452	62.3	320,529	483,285	66.3	....	....	....
1954	169,824	269,103	63.1	380,176	611,835	62.1	....	....	....
1955	189,678	290,530	65.3	462,579	715,962	64.6	....	....	....
1956	208,994	329,172	63.5	576,265	897,689	64.2	....	....	....
1957	228,648	375,274	60.9	739,498	1,075,458	68.8	....	....	....
1958	255,690	451,465	56.6	274,889	450,730	61.0	662,634	1,052,097	63.0
1959	294,160	466,271	63.1	64,362	120,224	53.5	1,008,765	1,484,546	68.0
1960	306,266	581,501	52.7	10,245	24,246	42.3	1,444,261	2,134,901	67.7
1961	244,870	653,701	37.5	....	....	....	1,674,564	3,093,742	54.1

*Between United States–Canada and Europe.
†Not available.
Source: International Air Transport Association, *World Air Transport Statistics* (Montreal, annually), issues of 1957–62.

Exhibit 3

NORTH ATLANTIC TRAFFIC, 1948–61, IATA MEMBER CARRIERS

Total Scheduled Flights and Charters

	Total Scheduled Flights				Total Scheduled and Charter Passengers Carried	Per Cent Annual Increase
Year	Passengers	Seats	Load Factor	Charter Passengers		
1948.....	240,472	n.a.†	n.a.	12,392	252,864	......
1949.....	266,535	n.a.	n.a.	6,102	272,637	+ 7.8
1950.....	311,545	495,561	62.9	5,619	317,164	+16.3
1951.....	329,656	504,185	65.4	11,867	341,523	+ 7.7
1952.....	432,272	625,848	69.1	15,684	447,956	+31.2
1953.....	506,601	781,737	64.8	16,830	523,431	+16.8
1954.....	550,000	880,938	62.4	30,858	580,858	+11.0
1955.....	652,257	1,006,492	64.8	39,543	691,800	+19.1
1956.....	785,259	1,226,861	64.0	49,531	834,790	+20.7
1957.....	968,146	1,450,732	66.7	50,638	1,018,784	+22.0
1958.....	1,193,213	1,954,292	61.1	98,953	1,292,166	+26.8
1959.....	1,367,287	2,071,041	66.0	172,647	1,539,934	+19.2
1960.....	1,760,772	2,740,648	64.2	168,207	1,928,979	+25.3
1961.....	1,919,434	3,747,452	51.2	256,478	2,175,912	+12.8

*Between United States–Canada and Europe.
†Not available.
Source: International Air Transport Association, *World Air Transport Statistics* (Montreal, annually), issues of 1957–62.

Exhibit 4

REPRESENTATIVE FARES, ICELANDIC AIRLINES (LOFTLEIDER)

(New York to London)

	Tourist Fares		
Date	All Year, One Way	Off-Season Round Trip	On-Season Round Trip
December, 1953................	$262.10	$427.20	$427.20
October, 1954.................	260.40	427.20	469.20
December, 1955................	260.40	424.40	469.20
December, 1957................	260.40	424.40	469.20
January, 1959.................	243.40	392.20	438.20
April, 1959...................	248.40	405.20	447.20
November, 1960...............	248.40	405.20	405.20
April, 1963...................	248.40	405.20	405.20

Exhibit 5

INTERNATIONAL OPERATIONS, ALL UNITED STATES AIR LINES, PASSENGER/CARGO CARRIERS

Date	Expense per Available Ton-Mile	Average Total Passenger Revenue per Passenger-Mile, Scheduled Service	Break-Even Load Factor†	Expense per Revenue Ton-Mile	Passenger Revenue per Revenue Ton-Mile				Rate of Return on International Operations
					First Class	Coach Class	Economy Class	Total Operating Revenues	
1948.........	$48.97	$8.01	61%	$86.15	$77.91	......	......	$77.91	7.32%
1949.........	46.82	7.72	61	84.29	74.93	......	......	74.93	8.58
1950.........	44.83	7.28	63	76.49	70.51	......	......	70.51	5.33
1951.........	45.69	7.10	66	70.69	n.a.§	......	......	69.18	5.98
1952.........	43.14	7.01	62	70.44	n.a.	......	......	68.06	3.59
1953.........	41.20	6.84	60	67.34	n.a.	......	......	66.86	7.01
1954.........	38.22	6.76	57	61.92	86.01	$52.41	......	66.60	9.50
1955.........	36.16	6.66	54	56.55	77.36	59.43	......	66.22	5.99
1956.........	35.59	6.68	53	55.57	79.11	60.84	......	66.62	8.28
1957.........	34.49	6.55	53	54.54	79.97	59.87	......	65.39	7.88
1958.........	33.94	6.46	53	55.16	82.14	59.82	$47.58	64.51	3.63
1959.........	34.07	6.29	54	52.11	83.39	57.51	48.96	62.92	4.51
1960.........	31.36	6.35	49	52.48	85.82	56.24	55.46	63.48	4.32
1961.........	28.29	6.08	47	51.25	79.23	......	n.a.	60.79	3.17

*Represents cost of providing transportation for one ton of cargo (passengers, freight, etc.). Thus, closer seating is one way of increasing tonnage per flight-mile and reducing cost, as well as improved economy in planes.

†Approximated by using an accepted air-line rule of thumb of 200 pounds per passenger (weight and baggage) and dividing this into one ton. Thus, one ton equals ten passengers. Average passenger revenue per passenger-mile divided into cost per available ton-mile gives the number of passengers needed for break-even, easily converted to percentage points.

‡Includes subsidies until 1954. Also includes revenue from other sources—cargo, mail, etc.—which are lower per ton-mile than is passenger revenue.

§Not available.

Source: Civil Aeronautics Board, *Handbook of Airline Statistics* (Washington, D.C.: U.S. Government Printing Office, 1962). Part II.

to the trip. (2) It must have been formed primarily for some purpose other than travel. (3) The group was required to travel together for its entire itinerary. (4) Reservations must have been made at least 30 days in advance, with 30 days' notice required for cancellations. (5) The rate did not apply between 7:00 A.M. Friday and 7:00 A.M. Monday on east bound flights during May, June, and July, and during the same week-end time periods westbound during August, September, and October. However, it was stated that groups that "assemble spontaneously" qualified, provided they were not solicited. Spontaneous groups were eliminated in a later conference.

QUESTIONS

1. What additional factors do you see that could lead to open rates in international air fares?
2. What steps can IATA take to prevent open rates?
3. What would be the effects on traffic and profits if member air lines were allowed to meet Icelandic fares?
4. From the above data, analyse the future of air fares on the North Atlantic route. Check your predictions against what has actually happened to fares since the data provided in the case.

CHAPTER 8

••••••••••••••••••••••••••

Price Discrimination

IN THE previous chapter, it was pointed out that most firms handle multiple products and that there seems to be a trend toward further diversification on the part of American industry. In part, the urge to add products reflects a desire to increase profits through "price discrimination"—the practice of selling essentially the same product at different prices in different markets. While the handling of multiple products is not always necessary to price discrimination (since *exactly* the same product can sometimes be sold at different prices), the discriminating monopolist usually finds it worth while to build certain technical differences into two or more versions of a product and to apply distinguishing names to the various versions. Sometimes the difference is only one of packaging—for example, precisely the same cornstarch may be packaged under different labels by a firm and sold at different prices.

The economic and legal distinctions between price differentials and price discriminations contrast sharply. To an economist, identical prices may be discriminatory if they are not based on identical costs. The legal viewpoint is that price differentials exist essentially for purposes of discrimination. In *Anheuser-Busch* v. *Federal Trade Commission*,[1] the Supreme Court took the position that price differences were equivalent to price discriminations but that such discriminations might well be legal if justified by costs, if there was no injury to competition, or if they were made in good faith to meet competition. Despite the poor repute of the term "discrimination," in many cases it is legal, profitable, and even socially beneficial, whether the term is being used in the legal or in the economic sense.

As already suggested, multiple-product production is not always necessary to the practice of price discrimination. A surgeon may sell the same quality of tonsillectomy or a lawyer the same legal opinion for different fees to persons who are believed to be in different income brackets. A magazine is often sold at a lower price to new subscribers and to those who are slow to renew than to the habitual and eager subscriber whose name can easily be gotten on the dotted line each year at regular rates. (Hint: Let the magazine publishers coax you.)

---

[1] 363 U.S. 536 (1960). See Case 8–5 in this text (pp. 412–16).

Price discrimination often occurs in monopolistic markets but does not exist under "perfect competition," if the latter is defined to include complete knowledge and mobility on the part of buyers in addition to the presence of a large number of sellers of a homogeneous commodity. From the point of view of economic analysis, price discrimination may be said to exist when a different mark up above marginal cost is made. for different units of the same, or much the same, commodity. This unlike markup may occur in that customers who can be served only at different marginal costs are charged the same price—as is the case whenever a commodity which is produced only in one locality is sold throughout the country at a uniform price (in spite of unlike freight or postage costs). Or it may occur through imposition of unlike prices when marginal costs of serving customers are the same. An approximate example is the charging of a higher price upstairs than in the basement of a department store when precisely the same commodity is sold on both floors.[2] Still another possibility exists. Marginal costs of serving different customers may be dissimilar, and prices may also differ, but not in such a way as to provide a uniform markup for all buyers. An example is the provision of standard and deluxe models of many commodities such as automobiles, refrigerators, and fountain pens, where sellers' margins above marginal cost are usually higher on the fancier versions.

Sometimes a commodity like aspirin, which is clearly definable chemically, is sold by different firms at very different prices. In a sense the consumers who pay the higher prices are discriminated against compared with those who buy the low-priced brands. This situation does not fall within the usual meaning of "price discrimination," however, because it is not accomplished by a single firm. On the other hand, sale of a given company's product under different brand names and through separate channels of distribution involving another firm can probably be usefully designated as price discrimination. For example, a Federal Trade Commission investigation some years ago revealed that the Goodyear Tire and Rubber Company sold tires to Sears Roebuck under the brand name "Allstate" which were of the same quality as those marketed by Goodyear under its own "All Weather" brand. The difference in wholesale prices between these two brands ranged from

---

[2]The example may be only approximate, because it may well add somewhat more to cost to sell a unit in the upstairs store. However, the main element in marginal cost—the wholesale price at which the store buys the good—would be the same whether it was sold upstairs or in the basement.

29 to 40 per cent in the period 1927–33. At retail, Allstate tires were sold at prices 20 to 25 per cent below those of All Weather tires.[3]

Separation of Markets Essential

Whether price discrimination is practiced with respect either to precisely the same commodity or to different versions of a commodity, a necessary condition is that customers be somehow segregated for different treatment. When the versions of the commodity are differentiated by means of minor technical differences, trade-marks, packaging, or other means, customers are segregated on the basis of their own preferences (their preferences being heavily influenced, however, by sellers through the forces of advertising and salesmanship). When precisely the same commodity is sold at different prices, numerous bases of separation which are under the control of the seller may be feasible. The following appear to be among the most important:

1. *Apparent Income or Wealth of the Buyer.* The man who drives a large car is often charged more for an identical repair job than the owner of a more modest vehicle. The sale of a larger house typically involves a larger commission to the real estate agent, since these fees are usually computed at a percentage of sales price, and probably the effort involved on his part does not increase so rapidly as price. Discrimination by surgeons and lawyers on the basis of income and wealth has already been mentioned.

2. *Convenience to the Buyer.* A reserved seat may sell at a higher price than an unreserved seat which is equally well located, the difference being a premium paid by the buyer in order to avoid uncertainty and possible inconvenience.[4]

3. *Quantity Purchased by Individual Buyer.* The practice of granting "quantity discounts" is a common one which takes several forms. The buyer of the large "economy size" tube of toothpaste, box of soap powder, or package of ice cream usually gets a better price in relation to cost than the buyer of a smaller amount. A large firm may get a lower price than a smaller one on a like purchase, and the large buyer of electricity usually gets a lower average price per kilowatt-hour than the small consumer.

4. *Newness of Customer's Business.* The favoritism often shown to new subscribers to magazines has already been mentioned. Similarly,

---

[3]FTC Docket No. 2116.

[4]If "convenience" is considered to be a separate commodity sold along with the seat, it may be argued that this is not a case of price discrimination.

graduate students often receive lower subscription rates on professional journals than regular buyers.[5] In other fields the established customer, however, may receive better treatment than the new buyer. Price discrimination on either basis is motivated more by long-run profit considerations than simply by a desire to maximize immediate profits.

5. *Location of Buyers.* Geographic separation of buyers often provides a convenient basis for price discrimination. When "blanket" freight rates bring about equal transportation charges over wide areas irrespective of distance, the buyers located relatively near the source of shipment are discriminated against compared with distant customers. Also, the device known as "basing-point pricing" (which will be discussed in some detail later in this chapter) discriminates against the buyer located near a source of supply which is not a basing point, since he must pay for more freight than is actually involved in the delivery.

6. *Time of Purchase.* Frequently, price is different to those who buy at various times of the day or at different seasons of the year. A motion-picture theater on 42nd Street in New York may vary its price several times during the day, charging the highest rates at night. Or a department store may charge more for the same item before Christmas or Easter than after these holidays. This basis of separation emphasizes the fact that price discrimination and multiple products may be indistinguishable from one another, since it is an arbitrary matter whether one considers an afternoon and evening showing of a given film to constitute the same or different commodities. Similarly, long-distance telephone and telegraph rates are lower at night than during the day. The monopolistic seller of such services has an incentive to lower the rates at night in order to make better use of existing capacity, just as the firm has an incentive to add new products when it has unused managerial or plant capacity.

7. *Age of Buyer.* Youthful and aged persons sometimes receive lower prices than those of intermediate ages. In part, this is a way of discriminating according to purchasing power, since incomes tend to be lower among the young and the old. The pricing of motion pictures and rides in amusement parks exemplifies discrimination in favor of children. Aged persons sometimes received such concessions as free or cheaper hunting and fishing licenses. Group life insurance plans, when they provide for payment of the same premium by persons of all ages, discriminate in favor of the older participants, for whom mortality rates are higher. When children are charged lower prices than adults (at

---

[5]This illustration is given by A. G. Papandreau and J. T. Wheeler in *Competition and Its Regulation* (New York: Prentice-Hall, Inc., 1954), p. 95.

theaters, for example), this is in part an effort to build up habits which will sustain long-run demand.

8. *Prestige of Buyer.* The influential person, such as a senior executive in a corporation, may be given an especially favorable price on property in a new real estate subdivision in order to attract ambitious junior executives to the area. Similarly, a well-known motion-picture actress may be invited to dine "on the house," whereas an unknown nonpayer would have to wash dishes. Price discrimination on this basis somewhat resembles the practice of using "loss leaders" to attract customers who will buy other items.

Resale Must Be Difficult

If buyers can somehow be segregated, services often lend themselves readily to the practice of price discrimination, because they usually cannot be resold. The tonsillectomy already referred to is an obvious example. Commodities, however, can often be resold by those who receive lower prices to those who qualify only for higher prices, thus ruining the latter market for the would-be discriminatory monopolist. That is to say, activities of an arbitrage nature may interfere with effective price discrimination. Where transportation costs constitute a substantial barrier between markets, however, resale is unprofitable so long as the price differential which is imposed does not exceed the cost of transport between the markets.[6] This is why goods can often be "dumped" abroad at prices substantially below those charged at home. Any tariff on imports then becomes an additional impediment to resale in the producing country. Similarly, a highly perishable commodity cannot readily be resold because suitable refrigerated delivery facilities are likely to be lacking; thus, it may lend itself to discriminatory pricing. Also commodities such as electricity and gas, which for technical reasons cannot readily be redistributed, are well suited for this purpose.

Even when resale is not practicable, price discrimination may not be feasible if it causes resentment on the part of those who are charged the higher prices. Such resentment may cause buyers either to demand the more favorable rates or to take their custom elsewhere. Consequently, price discrimination is apt to be more feasible when customers are geographically or temporally separated. There obviously may also be an advantage in keeping price lists secret. Similarly, technical complexity makes it difficult for the buyer to judge the propriety of price

---

[6]This point is elaborated on by C. G. F. Simkin, "Aspects of the Theory of Discrimination," *Review of Economic Studies,* Vol. XV (1), No. 37 (1947–48), p. 5.

and hence favors discrimination. This is one reason for the confusing array of policies offered by insurance companies. It also helps explain the aversion which most life insurance companies have to selling pure insurance (term insurance), which is simplest in nature and for which an appropriate selling price can most easily be judged by reference to mortality tables.

The street peddler in a Latin American country, for example, is expert in the matter of price discrimination among American tourists. He is willing to spend a considerable amount of time with each potential customer in order to test his demand function and bargaining ability. Customers are usually unable to compare prices, particularly since there are usually variations in design and quality between different items which the street peddler sells. While this type of bargaining is time-consuming, the frequency with which large markups over cost are secured justifies the practice from the seller's viewpoint.

Perfect Price Discrimination

It is instructive to consider the extreme case of "perfect" price discrimination in order to understand the motivation behind more practicable schemes of discrimination. Whereas the usual assumption employed in the economic theory of monopoly is that the *single* most profitable price under existing conditions is charged, the notion of perfect price discrimination is that every unit be sold at a *different* price and that this be the highest price at which that unit will be purchased.

The usual geometrical demonstration of perfect price discrimination is given in Exhibit 1. It should be noted that the demand curve is also the marginal revenue curve. This follows from the assumption that each unit sold is independent of the others; that is, to sell an additional unit, the monopolist does not have to take a lower price on the earlier units. Whatever price he gets for a particular unit adds exactly that amount to his revenue. The average revenue curve lies above the marginal revenue curve, since whatever quantity is considered along the horizontal axis, the earlier units in this quantity will bring a higher price than the later ones and hence will hold the average price above the price at the margin. Maximum profit is secured by selling OA units, where marginal cost equals marginal revenue. Further sales would not be profitable because more would be added to cost than to revenue. Total revenue would amount to OA times AK.

It is important to note that the "demand curve" in Exhibit 1 is not the same in nature as that which is used in either competitive or

monopoly price theory. Under the usual definition of a demand curve
the various price-quantity combinations shown are alternatives, of
which only one set can become an actuality in a given time period.
(Supply conditions determine which set this will be.) If, instead, many
different prices were charged during the same time period, the claims
on consumers' purchasing power would be entirely different than under
a single price assumption, so that quite a different sort of demand schedule would exist. In general, at a relatively low price, more could be
sold at that single price than if it were only the "marginal" price with
other units going at higher prices.

Exhibit 1
PERFECT PRICE DISCRIMINATION

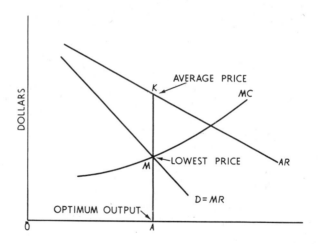

Imperfect Discrimination

In practice, a much lower degree of price discrimination is feasible.
Even an electric power company, whose product is unusually well
suited to price discrimination, uses "blocks" of substantial size when
it gives quantity discounts. When the monopolistic seller is able somehow to divide the market into two or more segments for unequal treatment, he secures maximum profit by pricing in such a way as to equalize the marginal revenue received in each submarket. Unless this
equalization is attained, he can increase profits by switching units from
submarkets where marginal revenues are lower and selling them instead where they are higher. This rule alone does not, however, tell at
what *level* marginal revenues should be equated or what total quantity
should be produced and sold. Marginal cost enters into these determina-

tions. Optimum output is the one at which marginal cost is equal to aggregate marginal revenue, and the level at which these are equated is the level to which marginal revenue must be brought in each submarket. This construction, which was originated by a well-known British economist, Joan Robinson,[7] is shown in Exhibit 2.

Demand in one submarket has been labeled D_1 and demand in the other market, D_2; corresponding marginal revenues are MR_1 and MR_2. Aggregate marginal revenue, AMR, is obtained by the horizontal summation of these marginal revenue curves. The marginal cost of production is shown by MC. Optimum output is OA, determined by the equal-

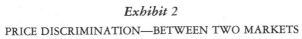

Exhibit 2

PRICE DISCRIMINATION—BETWEEN TWO MARKETS

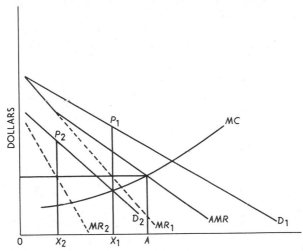

ity of MC and AMR. If the rate of production were above OA, it would be too high because units above OA would add more to the firm's cost than to its revenue, even if units were properly allocated in sale between the two submarkets (that is, allocated so as to equate marginal revenue in each).

Buyers in market 2 receive a substantially lower price (P_2) than buyers in market 1 (who pay P_1). Optimum sales in market 2 are OX_2,

[7] *The Economics of Imperfect Competition* (London: Macmillan & Co., Ltd., 1938), p. 183.

Price discrimination is more difficult to detect when marginal costs of serving different markets are not the same. Equalizing marginal revenues represents optimizing behavior only if the marginal costs are equal. In the utility cases at the end of this chapter, the marginal costs of serving different time patterns of demand differ, and part of the effort of utilities may go toward reducing discrimination through price differentials that more closely match marginal revenues with the appropriate costs.

determined by the intersection of MR_2 with a horizontal line drawn at the level at which MC equals AMR. Optimum sales in market 1 are determined by the intersection of MR_1 and the same horizontal line. (As a consequence, marginal revenues are equated in the two submarkets.) Prices in the two submarkets are those at which the optimum quantities can be sold; consequently, the prices are found on the demand curves directly above the optimum sales quantities. Although it appears in the diagram that total output will be the same under price discrimination as under a single-monopoly price, this will not be true for the reason discussed under perfect price discrimination, i.e., the relevant demand curves are not drawn using identical assumptions.

Discrimination when One Market Is Competitive

In Exhibit 2, demand at any price which is chosen for consideration is considerably more elastic in market 2 than in market 1. This is the reason for the profitability of charging less in market 2 than in the other market. Customers who make up market 2 would desert the firm more drastically (as far as percentage cutback goes) than those in the other submarket if confronted by a high price.

Sometimes a firm divides its sales of a given commodity between a monopolistic market and a highly competitive market. In this case the price is, of course, considerably higher in the former. Marginal revenue is equated in both markets, since the firm will not sell any units in the monopolistic market which will add less to revenue than they would have added if they had been sold in the purely competitive market.[8] This situation frequently occurs for commodities which are traded internationally. As already mentioned, transportation costs create a natural barrier between foreign and domestic markets, and resale by foreigners in the United States may be further impeded by tariffs and quotas imposed by this country. This creates a situation favorable to price discrimination and frequently results in the "dumping" of a product abroad at a relatively low, competitive price while at the same time price is maintained at a monopolistic level at home. Recently, an attempt has been made by cotton growers in the United States to induce the Commodity Credit Corporation to sell large quantities of stored cotton abroad at competitive prices while the domestic price is artificially maintained by the government's price-support program. The purpose of this proposed dumping would be to get rid of stored cotton which might otherwise eventually depress domestic prices. The State

---

[8]The student is advised to draw this chart for himself; this is usually the best way to make a diagram and the underlying principles "sink in."

Department has pointed out the danger of harming friendly nations who have cotton to sell by this policy.[9] In such a case, where sales are made out of stocks accumulated by a government agency over time, the price which is charged in the world market might well be considerably below its marginal cost of production in this country. Under the theory of price discrimination outlined above, which considers current production to be sold currently, no units of product are sold below marginal cost.

Discrimination when Products Are Dissimilar

The theory of price discrimination, which has been briefly described, is based on the assumption that a firm may find it possible to sell exactly the same commodity to two or more groups of buyers at different prices. More frequently, however, companies which are in a position to increase profits by means of price discrimination find it necessary or desirable to differentiate products from one another, so that similar—but not quite the same—goods are sold at two or more prices. This does much to prevent those who pay the higher price from being dissatisfied and switching their custom to other firms. When products are not quite the same, it is often very difficult for a buyer to know what a proper price differential would be. It is also impossible analytically to say whether the firm is practicing "price discrimination" or is merely a multiple-product firm.

The essence of price discrimination which is motivated by a desire to maximize short-run profit, as can be inferred from Exhibit 2, is that the excess of price over marginal cost differs in the various markets in which a good is sold. (No reference need be made to average cost.) Where products are somewhat dissimilar, separate marginal cost curves are applicable to the various products. The firm may find it possible to charge a substantially higher price in relation to marginal cost for one commodity than for the other(s); this can be considered to be price discrimination. But as already mentioned, it is not easy to say definitely where "price discrimination" ceases and the ordinary production and sale of differentiated multiple products begin.

Geographic Price Discrimination

Frequently, markets which are subjected to unlike treatment by a firm are separated on a geographic basis—that is, transportation costs

---

[9]"Government Should Export Cotton at Competitive Prices, Group Says," *Wall Street Journal,* February 7, 1956, p. 5.

impose an economic barrier between markets. The case of "dumping" a commodity abroad at a low price while the domestic price is maintained has already been mentioned. Geographic price discrimination makes its appearance in numerous other forms also. For example, "blanket" freight rates are sometimes charged by the railroads which result in the same charge for transporting a unit of commodity over a wide geographic range, irrespective of the actual length of the haul. An outstanding example is the movement of California oranges in carload lots from all points of origin in that state to any point between Denver and the North Atlantic seaboard at the same rate.[10] This means, for example, that buyers in Chicago are discriminated against compared with those in New York, in that the former are charged the same price despite the lower marginal cost of production plus transportation involved in placing California oranges in Chicago. More resources are used up in delivering a box of California oranges to New York, but price does not reflect this fact.

The same sort of price discrimination occurs whenever a commodity is "fair-traded" at the same price throughout the country (as far as the law permits), especially when the transportation cost per unit is substantial. Points close to the plant or plants in which the good is made are charged a higher markup above marginal cost, including transportation, than are more distant points. Frequently, mail-order houses do not make an explicit charge for postage to the buyer, at least on lightweight items. This, again, is a form of discrimination, though not a very serious one, against the buyers who are close to the origin of shipments. A more serious, though understandable, form of geographic price discrimination occurs through the practice of the railroads of charging lower freight rates to seaports and other places where water competition is present than to nearby cities where such competition does not prevail.

Basing-Point Pricing in Steel

A historically important, and still significant, form of geographic price discrimination is known as "basing-point pricing." The most famous example of the practice was the "Pittsburgh-plus" system of pricing used by the steel industry prior to 1924.[11] Under this system, mills all

---

[10]Kent T. Healy, *The Economics of Transportation in America* (New York: Ronald Press Co., 1940), p. 250.

[11]Steel beams were sold on this basis as early as 1880. Frank A. Fetter, *The Masquerade of Monopoly* (New York: Harcourt, Brace & Co., 1931), p. 147.

over the United States calculated prices not by reference to their own costs and shipping charges but by reference to the single set of basing-point prices at Pittsburgh, plus rail freight from Pittsburgh to the buyer's location.[12] Thus, steel delivered to Washington, D.C., for example, was priced as if it came from Pittsburgh even if, in fact, it came by boat from nearby Baltimore. The steel industry changed to a multiple basing-point system in 1924 after the United States Steel Corporation was ordered by the Federal Trade Commission to "cease and decise" from the Pittsburgh-plus system. Under the amended system the delivered price at any city was calculated by adding to the mill price the freight from the *applicable* basing point. This was done by calculating the lowest combination of mill price and rail freight for any given buyer. The "applicable basing point" would always be the one from which rail freight was lowest if mill prices were the same, but might not be if mill prices were dissimilar. Any steel mill which wished to sell in a particular locality could offer its product at the delivered price thus computed.[13] This required the absorption of part of the freight charge by more distant steel mills, however.

Under a multiple basing-point system, there is less collection of "phantom freight" than with a single basing point. Under the Pittsburgh-plus arrangement, steel buyers all over the country, except those in the area served by the Pittsburgh mills, had to pay fictitious freight charges equal to the difference between rail freight from Pittsburgh and actual freight from the source of the shipment. Even under a multiple basing-point system a buyer in the same city as a steel mill which was not designated as a basing point would have to pay phantom freight from the nearest basing point. Use of a cheaper means of transportation than rail freight also led at times to receipt of phantom freight by the seller. However, the larger the number of sources designated as basing points, the less the importance of phantom freight.

If *all* of the sources of supply of a product were designated as basing points, the system would approximate an f.o.b. mill system (in

---

[12]A few exceptions were permitted for particular locations. One of these locations was Detroit, Michigan, where the automobile industry used tremendous quantities of steel. Also, part of the Alabama output of the United States Steel Corporation was sold on a "Birmingham-plus" basis after 1908. Fritz Machlup, *The Basing-Point System* (Philadelphia: Blakiston Co., 1949), p. 65.

[13]It should be remembered that geographic distance and economic distance are often quite different. Mountains, for example, raise transportation costs, so that a short distance may actually be a considerable economic obstacle to the movement of goods. On the other hand, the possibility of water transportation renders distance less costly. The latter possibility did not, however, affect delivered prices, since *rail* freight was made a part of price.

which actual freight is paid from the actual source of supply). It would still not be precisely the same, however. For example, the basing-point system might still specify the use of *rail* freight from the nearest mill, whether or not this was the actual mode of shipment. Also, there would be a single delivered price in each city, regardless of the actual origin, instead of unlike prices for shipments from different sources. Probably the most serious objection to a multiple basing-point system with every source a basing point would derive from the interfirm collusion necessary to establish and police such a pricing system. A basing-point system of any kind, with published lists of delivered prices in each locality, serves as a strong deterrent to overt price cutting to gain additional sales.

Other Basing-Point Industries

The portland cement industry was also a well-known practitioner of the multiple basing-point system of pricing; and historically, this system was second only to that of the steel industry in importance to the American economy. Cement prices charged by different companies were thus identical at any point of delivery.[14] During the 1930's, about half of the cement mills were basing points, and about half were not. Buyers located near the nonbasing-point mills were forced to pay some "phantom freight," while those near basing points were not at this disadvantage. In 1948 the Supreme Court upheld a Federal Trade Commission order that the portland cement industry "cease and desist" from selling cement at prices calculated in accordance with a multiple basing-point system or using other means to secure identical price quotations for the product of the various companies.[15] Shortly after this decision, both the portland cement and the steel industries abandoned the basing-point method of pricing and adopted systems of f.o.b. mill pricing.

The corn-refining industry and the pulp, sugar, copper, zinc, gasoline, lead, asphalt roofing, maple and oak flooring, and other industries have also made use of basing-point systems, temporarily or perma-

---

[14]This resulted in identical bids on government contracts. For example, eleven companies bid exactly $3.286854 per barrel of cement on a contract for delivery of six thousand barrels for a federal project at Tucumcari, New Mexico (Machlup, *op. cit.,* p. 99).

[15]The wording of the order may be found in Dudley F. Pegrum, *The Regulation of Industry* (Homewood, Ill.: Richard D. Irwin, Inc., 1950), p. 337. This order was under Section 5 of the Federal Trade Commission Act directed against unfair methods of competition and clearly condemned the *collusion* necessary to maintain the multiple basing-point system rather than basing-point pricing itself.

nently.[16] While some of the most important systems from a historical viewpoint have been abandoned, the system continues to be in effect for some products.

Several years ago, the Ford Motor Company and General Motors took action to abandon a modified version of basing-point pricing.[17] Since about 1915, it had been the industry practice to charge dealers for full transportation charges, as though the car were shipped from the home plant, when it may actually have been assembled at a nearby facility. This had the effect of overpricing cars in the more distant cities compared with their prices in the Detroit area. As a result, it was often worth while for "car bootleggers" to buy new cars in or close to Detroit and to tow or haul them to the Southwest or Far West and sell them at lower prices than the authorized dealers were permitted to charge. Also, a great many individual customers living on the West Coast found it worth while to fly or take the train or bus to Detroit in order to buy and drive home a new car; this at least provided a very cheap vacation. The automobile manufacturers other than General Motors and Ford have fewer assembly plants located away from the home area and have participated less fully in the collection of phantom freight.[18]

Market Penetration

Advocates of basing-point pricing usually claim that the system is highly competitive because each seller can offer his product at the same price in any locality—that is, firms may compete freely for sales but may not compete in price. Any plant which has unused capacity, and whose owners are therefore anxious to increase sales, can offer its wares at the same price as others in any locality, although this may be possible only through "freight absorption," which means a reduction in the "mill net" price realized. Although this may help utilize the excess capacity of the mill which penetrates the usual territory of another mill, it clearly tends to cause excess capacity in the plant whose market is being penetrated. If such freight absorption were not practiced and buyers were instead given prices equivalently lower, the resulting increase in total sales would help avoid excess capacity in both plants.

---

[16]Machlup, op. cit., p. 17.

[17]"GM Says It, Too, Is Abandoning Use of Phantom Freight Charges," Wall Street Journal, February 27, 1956, p. 1.

[18]L. L. Colbert, president of the Chrysler Corporation, declared in a hearing before Chairman Monroney's Senate Commerce Subcommittee that his company in 1955 paid out more than it took in for transportation of automobiles. "President of Chrysler Is against Any Law to Bar 'Phantom Freight,'" Wall Street Journal, March 2, 1956, p. 18.

Market penetration, phantom freight, and freight absorption can perhaps be more easily understood from Exhibit 3. In this chart, A and B are mills producing the same commodity; but B is a basing point (the "applicable" one in the region considered), while *A* is not. Circles are drawn around *B* to reflect transportation costs from *B;* at each point on a circle the delivered price is the same. These delivered

Exhibit 3

MILL A COLLECTS PHANTOM FREIGHT TO LEFT OF *XY*
BUT ABSORBS FREIGHT TO RIGHT OF *XY*

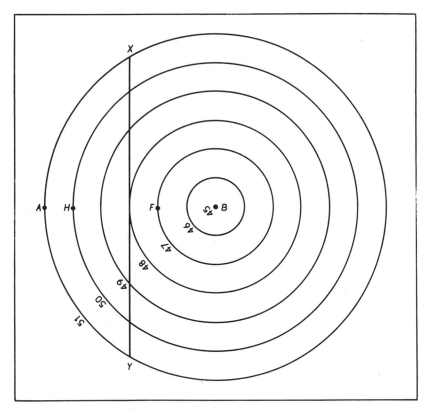

prices are shown by the numbers attached to each circle, and are calculated by assuming the mill price at *B* to be $45 and the transportation cost from one circle to the next to be $1.00 per unit.[19]

If we assume that freight costs are the same in either direction and that equal distances represent equal freight costs, it is clear that mill A

---

[19]The use of circles assumes that transportation costs are uniform in all directions. Actually, they would be affected by the availability of railroads, highways, and waterways, and by mountains, etc.; this would cause the isoprice lines to be irregular in shape.

has a very favorable mill net price in selling near home. If mill A sells at point H, for example, the price will be $50, which includes a $5.00 freight charge from the basing point. Since actual freight from A to H is $1.00, the "phantom freight" collected by mill A is $4.00. On the other hand, if mill A sells at point F, the price will be $47, which includes $2.00 of freight. Since actual freight from A to F is $4.00, mill A must absorb $2.00 in freight costs in order to make the sale. On sales anywhere between A and the vertical line XY, mill A will realize phantom freight; while to penetrate beyond line XY, it will have to absorb freight. Line XY is drawn so as to be equidistant between the two mills.

It is also apparent from the chart that the basing-point mill B can penetrate the territory of mill A without penalty. If mill B sold at point H, for example, it would secure the same mill net as on a sale at point F, because the delivered price always includes full freight cost from point B. Under the Pittsburgh-plus plan the Pittsburgh mills could sell anywhere in the country without reducing their mill net. This system was well adapted to minimizing unused capacity at Pittsburgh but tended to promote excess capacity in other districts.[20] On the other hand, mills located at the basing point do not have an opportunity to collect phantom freight, as do nonbasing-point plants.[21]

Cross-Hauling

Under any system of pricing a certain amount of "cross-hauling" is bound to occur—that is, one mill shipping the same commodity into the natural territory of another mill at the same time the other mill is delivering in the territory of the first mill. This occurs even if the term "cross-hauling" is defined strictly so as to require that a mill in city A be shipping a given commodity to a buyer in city B at the same time a mill at city B is shipping to a buyer at city A. The shipments are likely even to pass one another on freight trains headed in opposite directions. Under a basing-point pricing system, cross-hauling is especially likely to occur, because the delivered price at any destination is the same regardless of origin of shipment. If shape, size, quality, and

---

[20]In 1920 the Chicago mills, which had much unused capacity, broke away from the Pittsburgh-plus plan and established Chicago as a basing point. At about the same time the Federal Trade Commission began investigations which eventually led to abandonment of the single basing-point system in the steel industry.

[21]Except when a basing-point mill is able to use a cheaper mode of transport than the railroads.

finish of the product are precisely the same, there is an obvious waste of transportation resources when this occurs.

Some data on cross-hauling in the steel industry were collected by the Temporary National Economic Committee for 1939 (when the industry was operating under a multiple basing-point system). Detroit is a very large user of both cold-rolled and hot-rolled sheets because of its automobile plants. In February, 1939, the Detroit area received 43,671 tons of cold-rolled sheets and 46,153 tons of hot-rolled sheets. Although these quantities exceeded the amounts which can be produced in Detroit, the Detroit mills shipped out of the area 5,253 tons of cold-rolled steel sheets and 11,357 tons of hot-rolled sheets.[22] Detroit mills were shipping large tonnages to Chicago, especially, at the same time the Chicago mills were shipping to Detroit. In part, this type of persistent cross-hauling can be explained as a sort of hedge against a decline in demand. It may be useful for Detroit mills, for example, to have some regular customers who are not members of the automobile industry in the event of a severe drop in automobile production.

Basing-Point Pricing and Location of Plants

Under an f.o.b. mill system of pricing, there is an obvious cost advantage, other things equal, in being located near a mill which supplies a principal raw material. When a basing-point system is employed, however, it is necessary to be near a basing point in order to hold down the freight charge which is included in the price of the raw material. Proximity to a nonbasing-point mill does not help when freight on the raw material is calculated as if it came from another source. The Pittsburgh-plus single basing-point system thus favored the location of steel-using plants in the Pittsburgh area. A well-known economist, after an extensive study of basing-point pricing, concluded that the Pittsburgh-plus system undoubtedly handicapped the South in developing a steel fabrication business.[23] A *multiple* basing-point system also tends to impede the development of fabricating industry in the vicinity of nonbasing-point mills, although effects are less serious than under a single basing-point system.[24]

---

[22]George W. Stocking, *Basing Point Pricing and Regional Development* (Chapel Hill: University of North Carolina Press, 1954), p. 113.

[23]*Ibid.*, p. 74.

[24]As was noted earlier, the Detroit-plus system of pricing automobiles by some companies tended to curtail sales of cars in the Southwest and Far West. This effect is similar in nature to the handicapping of nonbasing-point regions, described above.

The basing-point system can also be used by a strongly led industry to discourage the construction of new capacity in the industry itself. Referring to Exhibit 3, suppose that the mill at point A is extremely prosperous and that a new firm is considering building a plant there to produce the same product. The industry may then threaten to make point A a basing point if the new plant is built there. This would immediately lower the mill net price which could be realized by sales in the area to the left of line XY, since phantom freight would be eliminated. This threat might be sufficient to keep out the new mill. Alternatively, mill B might threaten to conduct an especially aggressive selling campaign in the natural area of mill A. This it could do because it can sell as profitably in the natural market area of mill A as in its own market area. This sort of sales concentration by mill B would leave additional customers in the territory of mill B who might be served by mills at point A, but they could do so only by absorbing freight, and this prospect would not be attractive to the men considering the erection of new capacity at point A.

Price Discrimination and the Law

Section 2 of the Clayton Act (1914) prohibited discrimination in price between different purchasers of commodities "where the effect of such discrimination may be to substantially lessen competition or tend to create a monopoly in any line of commerce." This prohibition was, however, greatly weakened by the proviso "that nothing herein contained shall prevent discrimination in price between purchasers of commodities on account of differences in grade, quality or quantity of the commodity sold, or that makes only due allowance for difference in the cost of selling or transportation, or discrimination in price in the same or different communities made in good faith to meet competition. . . ."

This provision was completely rewritten in 1936, when Congress passed the Robinson-Patman Antidiscrimination Act, an amendment to the Clayton Act. This act prohibited discrimination in price between different purchasers of commodities of like grade and quality, where the effects of such discrimination might be substantially to lessen competition or create a monopoly in any line of interstate commerce. Price differentials were permitted, however, if they made only due allowance for differences in the cost of manufacture, sale, or delivery, or if they represented a "good-faith" effort to meet competition. Certain other less important provisions were also included. The Federal Trade Commission was empowered to limit quantity discounts, even where they could be shown to be consistent with differences in cost, if it concluded that differentials based on cost would give an advantage to large-scale marketing that might be injurious to competition.

The Robinson-Patman Act has often been called an "antichain store law" because of the last-mentioned provision. This was clearly an attempt to make it possible for the federal government to protect small business from competition from large, well-organized firms. As such, it is socially undesirable, unless one feels that small business has social merit which cannot be measured exclusively in terms of price to the consumer or the efficiency of resource allocation.

Basing-point pricing may be vulnerable under the Robinson-Patman Act, since different net prices are received by nonbasing-point mills on sales to buyers in different locations. Nongeographic price discrimination is, of course, also covered to the extent that it takes place in interstate commerce. (There are few effective laws against either monopoly or price discrimination in intrastate commerce.)

Average or Marginal Cost?

The Robinson-Patman Act does not specify whether "cost" means average cost or marginal cost. The theory of price discrimination as developed by Joan Robinson (not related to the legislator) indicates that an unlike markup over marginal cost constitutes the essence of price discrimination. It might theoretically be better if "cost" were clearly defined as marginal cost rather than being left indefinite, because this would plainly obviate the need to allocate the fixed costs of the firm among different groups of customers. Such allocation is likely either to be arbitrary or to be purposely made by a firm in such a way as to attempt to justify any price system which is in effect. Marginal short-run costs exclude all fixed costs, being determined by considering only expenses which are variable in the short period. Legislators tend to think only in terms of average cost; hence, when they legislate on economic matters, they are likely to cause considerable confusion in circumstances where they could actually be framing laws in terms of marginal cost. On the other hand, so many businessmen and accountants may be unaware of the meaning of "marginal cost" that they would have difficulty in complying with a properly framed law even if they wanted to do so. The two utility cases which follow are indicative of the complexities in deciding what costs should be allocated to particular segments of demand that are served.

CASE 8–1: THE COUNTRY DOCTOR[25]

Dr. Young served a rural area a substantial distance by ferry and automobile from other medical facilities. He estimated that to cover his family living expenditures and the fixed overhead connected with his small clinic, he required $15,000 gross income. On purely economic grounds, he could command more income elsewhere. Fifteen thousand dollars plus variable expenses represented a minimum gross necessary for him to continue to supply his services to the particular area, considering his sense of service and other noneconomic factors as well. In addition, he had certain variable expenses which would vary with the number of visits, and he estimated these at $1.00 a visit. (Obviously using a common unit, the visit, to describe the variety of medical services possible is a great simplification.)

Exhibit 1

HYPOTHETICAL DEMAND SCHEDULES CONFRONTING DR. YOUNG

Price	Visits, Group I	Visits, Group II	Total Visits
$18	0	0	0
15	475	25	500
12	900	100	1,000
9	1,100	400	1,500
6	1,300	700	2,000
3	1,450	1,050	2,500
0	1,500	1,500	3,000

The population of the area consisted essentially of two groups, the new inhabitants and the older inhabitants. The first group was characterized by being mostly retired, generally well off, and primarily attracted by the resort aspects of the community. The second group were permanent residents who furnished services and participated in marginal agriculture and fishing.

Assume that the effective demand for Dr. Young's services among the two groups is described by smoothly drawn demand curves through the points in Exhibit 1 and that Dr. Young can provide three thousand visits.

---

[25]With one other partial exception, all cases in this book are based on actual events. There is no Dr. Young, though there are certainly some like him. This episode is included because of the importance of the analytical points involved.

QUESTIONS

1. Evaluate the following pricing alternatives:

   a) A one-price system

   b) Perfect price discrimination

   c) A six-price system ($15, $12, $9, $6, $3, $0)

   d) One price for group I and one price for group II

2. Recognizing that none of the alternatives above are fully possible (Dr. Young would not have the perfect knowledge required for [*b*] and [*c*], and would find it professionally difficult to practice [*a*] and [*d*] without providing some free services as well), what approach would you recommend?

3. Show that under perfect price discrimination the demand curve becomes the marginal revenue curve, and construct the new average revenue curve.

4. What are the fundamental economic circumstances that make price discrimination a method for providing an economic service that could not be provided under a one-price system without subsidy? How much of a government subsidy would be required to provide the medical services under a one-price system?

5. Cite an example of a business situation with similar circumstances.

CASE 8–2: MARTIN-TURNER TOOL COMPANY

For many years the Martin-Turner Tool Company produced a wide line of small industrial tools such as saws, grinders, jigs, drills, and die cutters. In 1940 the firm introduced a number of portable power tools for distribution through retail outlets. The line of industrial tools had been sold directly to industrial users through the company's own salesmen. The distribution of portable tools at retail was established through dealers and distributors. During World War II, all production of tools for retail sale was suspended.

In the years immediately following the close of the war, there developed a rapid growth of the "do it yourself" idea. The movement provided a huge demand for power tools, and the Martin-Turner Company capitalized upon this development. By 1949 the firm had well established itself in this market as a producer of high-quality precision power tools for home use. These were sold under the brand name of "Turner Tools." The line included circular saws, jig saws, drills, lathes, band saws, grinders, sanders, polishers, and planer-joiners. The drills, grinders, and lathes were made for both metal and wood. The remainder of the line was for woodworking only. The principal retail outlets were hardware stores, lumberyards, and department stores.

As early as mid-1948 the sales manager had observed that the sales of Turner Tools were not expanding as rapidly as the sales of the entire portable tool industry. Sales were at a satisfactory level in so far as profits were concerned, but the fact that the line was not maintaining its relative share of the market was disturbing to the officers of the company.

Since the introduction of the line of Turner Tools, there began to appear, during 1946 and 1947 especially, an increasing number of competing brands of tools. There were three other brands of high-quality tools comparable to the Turner line. Like Turner Tools, they sold at a price somewhat higher than many of the other competing lines. This is indicated in Exhibit 1. It was the lower priced lines which

Exhibit 1

COMPARATIVE RETAIL PRICES OF SELECTED TURNER TOOLS AND LEADING COMPETING BRANDS

Item	Turner Tools	Brand A	Brand B	Brand C	Brand D*
Circular saws (6").......	$79.95	$79.95	$74.95	$79.95	$51.95
Drills (¼")............	59.95	56.95	49.95	54.95	32.95
Jig saws (21").........	59.95	54.95	54.95	52.50	36.95
Band saws (18")........	63.95	64.95	69.95	67.50	44.95

*Median price of the five most popular lower priced brands.

were enjoying an increasing share of the total market. These developments prompted a series of discussions among the company's executives which centered around the possibility of adjusting prices downward so as to retain at least the firm's share of the market, if not increase it.

One of the chief obstacles to a price reduction of any substance was production costs. These costs, for selected portable tools, are shown in Exhibit 2. Sales of these selected items are shown in Exhibit 3.

After several discussions the president and sales manager proposed the following plan of action, which the executive committee presented to the board of directors:

1. The Martin-Turner Tool Company should enter the lower priced tool market. Since the company had acquired a reputation for high-quality products which it was successfully selling at premium prices, the present line of Turner Tools should be retained. It was believed that any cheapening of the line by lowering its quality would result in a loss of this particular segment of the market.

At the current volume of output of these various tools, it was more economical to assemble them by benchwork rather than by an assembly line with more and simpler operations. Under the benchwork system, one employee was required to perform several operations, including some subassembly work. Some of these operations were rather complex and required some skill. This method of assembly frequently resulted in an irregular flow of products through the manufacturing process. All gears were machined. No stamped gears were used, as in the case of some of the lower priced lines. The housings of most of the line con-

Exhibit 2

COSTS, PER UNIT, OF SELECTED TURNER TOOLS

Item	Circular Saws (6″)	Drills (¼″)	Jig Saws (21″)	Band Saws (18″)
Direct labor	$12.53	$ 7.87	$ 9.01	$ 9.71
Materials	11.36	10.62	9.19	11.55
Spoilage	0.34	0.15	0.12	0.23
Indirect labor	2.19	0.46	0.44	1.00
Factory overhead	1.22	1.01	0.82	0.92
Administrative and selling expense	0.61	0.31	0.56	0.59
Total Cost	$28.25	$20.42	$20.14	$24.00
Profit	7.75	5.50	5.50	5.00
Factory Selling Price	$36.00	$25.92	$25.64	$29.00

Exhibit 3

NET SALES OF SELECTED TURNER TOOLS,
JANUARY 1 TO DECEMBER 31, 1948

Circular saws (6″) 9,371
Drills (¼″) 21,426
Jig saws (21″) 5,211
Band saws (18″) 3,608

sited of two or three steel parts which were bolted together in the assembly process. Redesign of these housings to cast them as a single piece would reduce the cost of both materials and assembly. Except for the proposed change in housing design the line would remain as presently designed.

2. The Martin-Turner Tool Company should set up a wholly owned subsidiary to market a lower priced line of tools under the brand name of "Chieftain." The use of a subsidiary with a different brand name was recommended so that the general public would not associate the lower priced tools with Turner Tools. This would protect the Turner line from suspicion of lowering quality.

This subsidiary would contract for all of its production with Martin-Turner Tool Company. It was estimated that the Chieftain Tools would, within two years, have a market at least twice the current volume of Turner Tools. If total output of the two brands reached approximately 50 per cent of this estimate, the bench method of assembly could be replaced by the line. This, it was estimated, would reduce assembly costs by at least 30 per cent, or more. In addition, the purchase of raw materials in larger quantities would result in lower unit material costs.

Exhibit 4

PROJECTED COSTS OF SELECTED TURNER TOOLS AND CHIEFTAIN
TOOLS UNDER PROPOSED ASSEMBLY LINE
METHOD OF PRODUCTION

ITEM	TURNER TOOLS		CHIEFTAIN TOOLS	
	Circular Saws (6")	Drills (1/4")	Circular Saws (6")	Drills (1/4")
Direct labor.	$ 7.51	$ 4.73	$ 7.03	$ 4.46
Materials.	9.09	8.50	8.61	7.64
Spoilage.	.19	0.08	0.19	0.08
Indirect labor*.	1.96	0.42	0.70	0.10
Factory overhead*.	1.01	0.83	0.71	0.53
Administrative and selling expense. . . .	.60	0.27	0.37	0.19
Total Cost.	$20.36	$14.83	$17.61	$13.00
Profit.	15.64	11.09	6.90	5.50
Factory Selling Price.	$36.00	$25.92	$24.51	$18.50
Suggested retail price.	$79.95	$59.95	$51.95	$36.95

*Includes amortization of the acquired plant; these amounts allocated between Turner Tools and Chieftain Tools on basis of projected volume of each.

Materials in the Chieftain line would be of the same quality as used in Turner Tools. There would be a difference in the housings of the Chieftain Tools. Not only would the designs differ somewhat, but they would be made of aluminum and plastic. All working parts of Chieftain Tools would be identical with Turner Tools. There would be no distinction between the two brands in the assembly of the chassis. Only when the chassis were mounted in the housings would there be separate assembly lines.

3. In order to obtain an immediate market for the Chieftain line, it was proposed that the subsidiary acquire ownership of a division of a firm currently producing and marketing a line of power tools. Such a purchase was available and could be obtained on a stock-exchange

basis, which would minimize the need for a large amount of cash. The manufacturing facilities of this acquired plant would be transferred to Martin-Turner Tool Company.

The company to be acquired was presently engaged in the production of several private brands of tools, as well as its own brand. These private brands were produced according to purchasers' specifications and were inferior in quality and performance to Turner Tools, yet were considered satisfactory at their prices. This acquisition would give Martin-Turner a third line of power tools which could also be produced on the proposed new assembly line, using less expensive materials.

Exhibit 4 shows the estimated costs of selected Turner Tools and Chieftain Tools when produced under the projected assembly method.

QUESTIONS

1. Which of the proposed policies would you recommend? Why?

2. One of the Martin-Turner officers objected on the ground that this was a scheme of price discrimination which was unfair to purchasers of Turner Tools. Comment.

3. Is price discrimination an effective means of contributing to profit? Explain.

CASE 8–3: COMMONWEALTH EDISON COMPANY

Proposed Cancellation of Special Off-Peak Rates in 1954

In November, 1954, Commonwealth Edison Company filed with the Illinois Commerce Commission proposed changes in its electric rates[26] which would affect certain customers located in the city of Chicago and in the Public Service Company division outside the city of Chicago. One of the main purposes of the filing was to cancel the so-called "off-peak" rates then applicable to certain customers and to establish a plan for the gradual elimination of the concessional charges granted under such rates.

The company proposed, effective with meter readings taken on and after January 1, 1955, to cancel certain rates which provided concessional charges for service received during certain hours of certain days and certain periods of the year. The off-peak rates to be canceled applied to the following categories of customers: industrial electric serv-

---

[26]The company proposed changes in "riders" as well as "rates"; although there is a distinction between the two, the purposes of the case are served as well by using the term "rates" where it would be more accurate to refer to "rates" and "riders."

ice; large light and power service; air-conditioning equipment; and ice-making, ice-cream, and cold-storage companies.

After the proposed cancellation, service would be supplied under other rates of the company not having off-peak provisions. The number of customers served under the off-peak rates involved totaled 1,239, and they were included in the commercial, industrial, and public authority customer classifications. These 1,239 customers represented only about 0.6 per cent of the 223,255 customers in these classifications served by the company as of August, 1954.

History of Off-Peak Rates

Some of the company's rate provisions for off-peak service originated during its early history. Even the latest of such provisions, relating to air conditioning, were adopted more than twenty years ago. In order to understand the desirability of these provisions at the time they were introduced in the rate schedules of the company and its predecessors, it is necessary to recognize the nature of system electrical demands at that time. For example, in the early 1930's the annual Edison system peak load occurred during the early evening hours on a business day in the winter season, usually just before Christmas. This resulted primarily from the large lighting loads in homes, offices, and stores, overlapping the then relatively large Chicago and interurban railway load which was at or near its maximum due to electric heating of cars and more frequent service provided for Christmas shoppers. Winter daytime loads, summer loads, and nighttime loads were considerably lower. In fact, substantial differentials between the evening peak loads in winter and the loads occurring in other seasons of the year were of such magnitude that the company could take capacity out of service during the nonwinter months for extended periods of maintenance and overhaul, and still have unused capacity available over and above that required for emergency outages. The annual system load factor at that time was about 50 per cent. This means that the average system load over the period of a year was only about 50 per cent of the maximum load for the year.

Because of system load characteristics as described above, the company, in the early 1930's and prior thereto, was interested in promoting seasonal business to utilize the unused capacity during the summer load "valley" in order to improve the system load factor, with a resulting increase in revenue. These types of loads included ice-making, cold-storage, air-conditioning, and stone quarry and gravel pit operations. In addition, the company was interested in promoting other types of business having loads whose heaviest demands could be scheduled during the off-peak daytime and nighttime hours when system loads were relatively low. Therefore the loads during the off-peak periods could be supplied without necessitating the addition of system capacity.

Provisions of Off-Peak Rates

The provisions of the so-called "off-peak" rates proposed for cancellation or revision were such that all of these rates provided lower billing to customers whose demands on the company's facilities were lower during the peak period than at other times. In general, one of two types of concessions was provided to customers:[27] (1) Customers who established their maximum demands outside the peak period, such peak period defined as the hours from 4:30 P.M. to 7:30 P.M. from October 15 to the following February 14, inclusive, Saturdays, Sundays, and holidays excepted, received lower billings for their electrical requirements than if their maximum demands occurred during such peak period; (2) reduced billings were provided customers who use air-conditioning equipment in nonwinter months.

Billings under the first type of concessionary off-peak rates usually provided that the demand established during the peak period would hold for twelve months unless exceeded in subsequent months of the peak period. One rate provided that any excess of daytime demand over the peak demand was billed at an intermediate level of charges, and any excess of nighttime demand over the daytime or peak demand was billed at the lowest level of charges. Daytime and nighttime demands applied for billing purposes only in the months in which they were established. For a given usage, therefore, the lowest billing was rendered to the customer whose usage was entirely within the nighttime period, no demands having been established during the peak or daytime periods. Likewise, the highest billing was rendered to the customer whose highest demand occurred during the peak period. Customers whose demands were lower during the peak period, therefore, had a lower billing than if their highest demands occurred during the peak period. Also, reduced billing resulted for the customer whose higher demands occurred during the nighttime period instead of during the daytime or peak period. Other off-peak rates had similar provisions except that there was only one off-peak period which included both daytime and nighttime hours.

[27]See Exhibit 1 for a summary of one of the company's off-peak rates.

Exhibit 1

RATE 13—INDUSTRIAL ELECTRIC SERVICE (OFF-PEAK)
(Extract—Includes Selected Paragraphs Only)

AVAILABILITY

This rate is available only to customers receiving alternating current service hereunder at their present locations on November 22, 1954, for all commercial and industrial requirements, and who have not subsequently discontinued doing so. Upon the expiration of the customer's availability period under Rider 21, or upon the discontinuance of service under this rate by the Customer for any reason, whichever first occurs, he shall not again be served hereunder. . . .

EXPLANATION OF RATE

The charge for electric service under this rate is the sum of a charge for the maximum demand created and a charge for the energy supplied. Three operating periods are specified corresponding to load conditions on the Company's system, namely, "peak," "daytime," and "nighttime," and a different demand charge is provided for demands created during each period. The peak billing demand is determined on an annual basis and the off-peak daytime and nighttime billing demands are determined on a monthly basis, as hereinafter provided.

CHARGES

Demand Charge

The number of kilowatts of peak, daytime, and nighttime billing demand shall be charged for in the order named, consecutively through the blocks of kilowatts in the following table, at the prices per kilowatt for the respective demand periods (for example—200 kilowatts of peak billing demand, 800 kilowatts of daytime billing demand, and 100 kilowatts of nighttime billing demand will be charged for at $2.15, $1.00, and $0.55, respectively):

Peak Billing Demand	*Daytime Billing Demand*	*Nighttime Billing Demand*		*Kilowatts of Billing Demand for the Month*
$2.15	$1.35	$0.75	per kilowatt for the first	200
1.50	1.00	0.60	per kilowatt for the next	800
1.40	0.90	0.55	per kilowatt for the next	2,500
1.15	0.75	0.50	per kilowatt for all over	3,500

Energy Charge	*Kilowatt Hours Supplied in the Month*
2.49¢ per kilowatt hour for the first	6,000
1.14¢ per kilowatt hour for the next	24,000
0.90¢ per kilowatt hour for the next	70,000
0.68¢ per kilowatt hour for the next	400,000
0.59¢ per kilowatt hour for all over	500,000

The energy charge for each kilowatt hour supplied in the month is subject to adjustment in accordance with the provisions of the Company's Fuel Adjustment rider.

The gross energy charge shall be ten per cent more than the sum of the net energy charge and the "Fuel Adjustment," for the first 100,000 kilowatt hours supplied in the month.

Minimum Charge

The regular minimum monthly demand charge shall be $60.00 for the first month which includes any part of the peak period and for the succeeding four months. For all other months the regular minimum monthly demand charge shall be $40.00.

DEMAND PERIODS

The peak period is the period between the hours of 4:30 P.M. and 7:30 P.M. of each day from each October 15 to the next succeeding February 14, inclusive, except Saturdays, Sundays, Thanksgiving Day, Christmas Day, and New Year's Day.

The Company reserves the right, upon giving the Customer not less than three months' advance written notice, to change the peak period to not more than eight consecutive half-hours between the hours of 8:00 A.M. and 9:00 P.M. of each day in any period of not more than 124 consecutive days, Saturdays, Sundays, and legal holidays excepted.

The daytime period is the period between 8:00 A.M. and 9:00 P.M. of each day, except that it shall not include any period which is within the peak period.

The nighttime period is the period between 9:00 P.M. of of each day and 8:00 A.M. of the following day.

Maximum Demands

The peak maximum demand in any month shall be the greater of (*a*) the average of the three highest 30-minute demands established during the peak period, if any, on different days of such month or (*b*) the number of kilowatts by which the daytime maximum demand exceeds 25,000 kilowatts.

The daytime maximum demand in any month shall be the average of the three highest 30-minute demands established during the daytime period on different days of such month.

The nighttime maximum demand in any month shall be the average of the three highest 30-minute demands established during the nighttime period on different nights of such month.

Change in Peak Loads

The off-peak provisions of the company's rates were adopted more than twenty years ago and were based on the fact that at that time, additional loads occurring during other than the early evening hours of the winter season could be supplied without necessitating the addition of system capacity.

However, from 1934 through 1954 the company's daytime loads, particularly the summer maximum loads, grew consistently at a faster rate than the winter peak loads, largely because of the great increase in daytime industrial loads. In more recent years, with the accelerated growth of air conditioning and other summer loads and with a substantial reduction in electric railway load, the differential between summer and winter maximum loads had grown progressively smaller. During the same period the annual system load factor had increased from about 50 per cent to about 60 per cent. The company noted that this improvement in load factor had been beneficial to all customers of the company because the company's investment in facilities had not increased in the same proportion as sales and revenues, and that generally the result had been a lower level of charges for customers than would have otherwise been possible.

Exhibit 2

MONTHLY SYSTEM MAXIMUM KILOWATT LOADS EXPRESSED IN
PER CENT OF PREVIOUS WINTER'S PEAK LOAD

	MONTH											
YEAR	January	February	March	April	May	June	July	August	September	October	November	December
1954.......	97.3	95.2	92.1	91.5	90.9	94.4	91.7	97.7	92.9	91.1	98.7	n.a.*
1953.......	99.7	94.6	95.4	94.4	95.7	96.0	92.0	95.4	96.4	99.5	100.7	104.5
1942.......	100.0	96.6	92.3	88.6	90.4	90.3	89.6	86.9	93.2	94.1	99.4	100.6
1932.......	99.7	91.5	85.9	77.4	77.1	69.4	67.2	67.7	77.6	90.3	91.9	94.8

*Not available.

Exhibit 2 shows for the years 1932, 1942, 1953, and 1954 through November, Commonwealth Edison Company monthly maximum system loads expressed as a percentage of the previous winter's peak load. Referring to the data for the year 1932, which typify the character of the company's system load during the period when the company's off-peak rate provisions were adopted, it is apparent that there was a large underutilization of the system during the six months April to September, inclusive. During this period the maximum monthly loads were below 80 per cent of the previous winter's peak load; and during the months of June, July, and August the maximum loads were less than 70 per cent of the previous winter's peak load. For the years 1942, 1953, and 1954, Exhibit 2 shows a progressively diminishing difference between summer monthly maximum loads and the previous winter's peak load. In 1953 the maximum load in June and September was about 96 per cent of the previous winter's peak load, and in 1954 the August maximum load was nearly 98 per cent of the previous winter's peak load. At no time during 1953 or 1954 did the monthly maximum loads fall below 90 per cent of the previous winter's peak load.

At the same time that summer system loads were growing relative to winter system loads, the system daily peak shifting from the early evening to the late morning or early afternoon for all months except January, November, and December; and in these three months the daytime maximum loads increased to about 95 per cent of the early evening maximum loads.

The company expected that summer daytime maximum loads would continue to grow faster than winter evening maximum loads and that in the relatively near future the Commonwealth Edison Company's annual system peak load would occur during the summer daytime hours. This situation had already occurred in many other utility systems. One of the main reasons for the faster growth of summer loads was the accelerated growth in air-conditioning loads. More and more commercial establishments were installing air conditioning, and the development of moderately priced, dependable room coolers had met with such general public acceptance that it appeared that the company would be faced with a mushrooming growth of air-conditioning load, not only for commercial purposes but also for residential purposes. The company expected that the result of the anticipated growth in air-conditioning load would produce an acceleration in the relative growth of summer system loads.

Summer Capability Less than Winter Capability

The company pointed out that while the character of its system load had changed over the years to the point where the maximum loads occurring during the daytime hours of hot summer months were almost as large as the maximum loads occurring during the early evening hours on a winter business day, the capability of the company's system to produce and to distribute electricity was less in the summer than in the winter, for several technical reasons. In fact, the summer maximum loads had become the critical loads which determined the amount of capacity which the company needed to have available to meet the demands of its customers, after consideration was given to the lower load-carrying capability of the system in summer.

The first of these technical limitations which prevail during the summer months is that warmer condensing water generally results in poorer vacuum and lessened efficiency, and consequently reduces the ability of the turbine to carry the system load. Another technical factor is the inherently lower load-carrying capability of electrical equipment in summer as compared to winter. The permissible load which can be carried on electrical equipment, such as transformers, regulators, circuit breakers, cables, and other conductors, is determined by the maximum allowable temperatures at which such equipment can be operated without damage. It therefore follows that in the summer when ambient temperatures are relatively high, electrical equipment has less load-carrying capability than in winter when ambient temperatures are much lower. A third item which reduces the ability of the company's system to carry load in summer is the fact that the power factor of the summer daytime loads is less because of a higher percentage of motor load and a lower percentage of lighting load.

As a result of these technical limitations, the load-carrying capability of the company's generating stations in the summer was reduced about 5 per cent, and the over-all capability of the transmission and distribution system to supply load was reduced by about 14 per cent as compared to the winter. With summer maximum loads in 1954 being approximately 5 per cent below the previous winter peak load, the company claimed that summer loads created more of a supply problem than did winter loads. Thus, the company pointed out, because the summer loads were higher in relation to the load-carrying capability of the company's system than were winter loads, it followed that the summer maximum load determined the facilities which the company needed to provide to serve its customers.

Having no significant "valley" in which to take capacity out of service for necessary overhauling and maintenance, the company found that it needed to have available generating capacity substantially greater than if pronounced summer "valleys" existed. This was in contrast to the situation prevailing at the time the off-peak provisions were initiated.

No Longer Justification for Off-Peak Rates

In consequence of the changes which had occurred in the company's system load characteristics and the fact that system load-carrying capability was less in summer, the company noted that it no longer had unused system capacity during the daytime hours of the summer months. Therefore, it felt there was no longer justification for the lower off-peak daytime charges which were based on the concept that such loads could be served without the company being required to provide additional system facilities. Also, the company felt that continuation of the off-peak rates with their concessional charges to the few customers served thereunder might be considered unjust discrimination against the 1,750,000 other customers of the company. There was still, of course, sufficient justification for concessional charges for nighttime operations; and for this reason, it proposed a new nighttime rate which would grant concessional rates to users of electricity whose nighttime demands are higher than their daytime demands.

Exhibit 3 summarizes the estimated annual savings or benefits to customers that were served under the off-peak rates[28] as compared to bill-

Exhibit 3

SUMMARY OF ESTIMATED ANNUAL SAVINGS IN BILLING TO CUSTOMERS SERVED UNDER OFF-PEAK RATES AS COMPARED TO BILLING UNDER "NEXT BEST" STANDARD RATES (EXCLUSIVE OF GOVERNMENTAL CUSTOMERS), BASED ON ACTUAL SALES FOR TWELVE-MONTH PERIOD ENDED AUGUST, 1954

	Amount	Per Cent
Present revenue, 1,216 customers..........................	$33,024,276	100.0%
Estimated amount of benefits received by customers which would be lost as a result of proposed cancellation......	2,045,524	6.2
Number of customers served under off-peak rates as of August, 1954...	1,216	
Customers served under off-peak rates but receiving no benefits..	83	
Customers served under off-peak rates and receiving benefits..	1,133	

NUMBER OF CUSTOMERS BY RANGE OF BENEFIT AS A PER CENT OF INDIVIDUAL CUSTOMER'S TOTAL BILL

Range of Benefit	Number of Customers Receiving Benefit
0.0– 5%.....................	554
5.1–10......................	215
10.1–15.....................	87
15.1–20.....................	85
20.1–30.....................	106
30.1–40.....................	49
40.1–50.....................	17
50.1–60.....................	15
60.1–70.....................	3
70.1–80.....................	1
80.1–90.....................	1
	1,133

[28]Exclusive of rate 22, which applied to governmental customers. Rate 22 and the changes proposed in this rate were somewhat different than the commercial and industrial rates and proposed changes. For purposes of simplification, governmental rates and proposed changes in governmental rates are not considered.

ing under the "next best" standard rates. The term "next best" standard rate meant the rate that had no off-peak provisions available to such customers which would have produced the lowest net billing for the test period. In the lower tabulation of Exhibit 3 is shown the number of individual customers by range of benefit.

Proposed Gradual Adjustment of Rates

Because of the relatively large increases in billing which would have immediately resulted to individual customers from the outright cancellation of the off-peak rates, the company proposed a special provision that would permit a gradual adjustment of the off-peak benefits which had been enjoyed by the customers served under the off-peak rates. The company, in making this proposal, recognized that the customers served

Exhibit 4

SUMMARY OF ANNUAL REVENUE EFFECTS OF PROPOSED CANCELLATION OF
OFF-PEAK RATES UNDER PROVISION FOR GRADUAL
ELIMINATION OF BENEFITS

(Based on Actual Sales for Twelve-Month Period Ended August, 1954)

	Amount	Per Cent
Present revenue, 1,133 customers................	$30,654,417	100.0%
First year..	88,697	0.3
Fifth year..	963,775	3.1
Tenth year.......................................	1,525,785	5.0
Fifteenth year....................................	1,831,150	6.0
Twenty-first and subsequent years..............	2,045,524	6.7

under the off-peak rates had been only partially responsible for the change in the company's load characteristics, that such customers had helped the company to utilize better its capacity which had previously been not used in the off-peak periods, and that such customers may have relied to some extent upon the benefits of the off-peak rates in the devlopment and operation of their businesses.

The special provision proposed by the company to permit a gradual decrease in the concessional benefits was such that customers who would be affected most substantially by cancellation of the off-peak rates were granted the longest period of time for the gradual elimination of benefits. The periods of time granted to off-peak customers for gradual elimination of benefits varied from a minimum of 60 months to a maximum of 240 months. During these periods of time the benefit would have been eliminated by a constantly increasing percentage, the decrease in benefit starting with the second month and continuing until the last month, after which time 100 per cent of the benefit would have been eliminated. Exhibit 4 summarizes the effect of eliminating benefits gradually.

Objections to Elimination of Off-Peak Rates

Among the customers who would have been affected by the rate change proposed by the company was a group that filed objections with the Illinois Commerce Commission.

One argument made by the objectors was that the off-peak rates were justified because the summer maximum load was less than the winter peak load. The company pointed out, however, that the objectors ignored the crucial differential between the load-carrying capability in the summer and in the winter.

The objectors also argued that the company's Exhibit 2, which was submitted to show the differential between summer maximum loads and winter peak loads by comparing the summer loads with the previous winter's peak load, should have compared the summer loads with the following winter's peak load. The objectors thought that for the years shown in the company's Exhibit 2, the method of comparison used by the company resulted in figures which overstated the disappearance of the summer "valley"; they claimed that the direction of shift in demand for electricity was such that the use of the previous winter's peak made for this overstatement.

Another argument put forth by the objectors was that elimination of off-peak rates would result in increased utilization of generating capacity during the peak periods and would therefore result in the need to install additional capacity to meet the demands of the off-peak customers during the winter's peak periods. Contrary to the objectors' contention, the company felt that this was not likely to happen since customers who were receiving substantial benefits under the off-peak rates would continue to observe the conditions of such rates in order to obtain the benefits available under the company's proposed period of gradual adjustment to the standard rates; these benefits would not be available otherwise.

Finally, the objectors argued that discrimination may not be removed by increasing discriminatory rates unless accompanied by offsetting reductions in other rates. The company pointed out that the Supreme Court of the United States had stated in several cases that discrimination in rates may be eliminated by either decreasing the rates of those customers against whom the discrimination operated or increasing the rates of those customers who have benefited from the discrimination to the level of the other customers, or by a combination of both. The company also pointed out that a very small portion of the company's service would be affected (cf. revenue in Exhibit 5) and, therefore, the adjustment of the company's entire rate schedules to offset the relatively small increase in revenues would be exceedingly difficult and not reasonable, especially since the resulting total return would still be "within the limits of reasonableness."

Exhibit 5

COMMONWEALTH EDISON COMPANY AND SUBSIDIARY COMPANIES
Statement of Consolidated Income, 1954

Electric operating revenues	$ 309,502,118
Electric operating expenses and taxes:	
Production fuel	$ 60,107,658
Other operation	73,206,489
Maintenance	20,585,436
Provision for taxes	72,073,248
Provision for depreciation	31,898,509
	$ 257,871,340
Electric net operating income	$ 51,630,778
Other income	$ 6,229,505
Gross income	$ 57,860,283
Deductions (interest, etc.)	$ 12,988,895
Net Income	$ 44,871,388
Consolidated balance sheet assets	$1,188,060,865
Kilowatt-hours of electricity sold, 1954	15,597,065,049

QUESTIONS

1. Did the special rate for air conditioning represent price discrimination—initially or in 1954?
2. What changes occurred in relevant costs as demand changed?
3. Was the company's procedure in modifying the rates an effective one, in your opinion?

CASE 8–4: THE URBAN ELECTRIC COMPANY

In 1962 the Urban Electric Company, which served both metropolitan and rural areas in the Middle West, found itself in an unfavorable operating position because of the rapid growth of summer air-conditioning load, which had resulted in increased investment in utility plant and equipment without adequate increase in income. Obviously, a compensating type of load was needed to offset the unfavorable system effects of added air-conditioning load. Therefore the president of the company authorized the establishment of a "working" committee to bring in recommendations as to what measures should be taken:

1. To review the data previously prepared in the Economic and Rate Research Department to determine whether or not the company should encourage space heating.
2. To estimate the potential rate of growth in the residential space-heating market for the purpose of determining when a balance between summer and winter peaks could again be established.
3. To propose a price policy based on the necessary costs to the company to serve a residential space-heating load.

The committee had as chairman the manager of the Rate Department and staff representatives from the Sales, Operating, Comptroller, and Economic Research departments.

During the course of the discussions, committee members developed the following attitudes:

The vice chairman, coming from the sales area, found himself on the horns of a dilemma. His evaluation of market growth, taking into consideration the intense competition to be encountered from the gas and fuel oil interests, was that it was likely to be quite slow; hence a special rate might not be justified at present. On the other hand, competition made it mandatory to be able to offer the lowest possible service rate to gain entrance into the space-heating market; hence a special rate was required.

The representative of the comptroller's office was basically opposed to offering any special rates in the first place, but if a special rate was to be offered, he insisted that investment costs be included in determining company costs of service from the outset.

The representative from the Operating Department was all in favor of any promotional effort which would at least tend to equalize the rate of growth of summer and winter loads, but was fearful that if domestic space heating once "caught on," it would have a runaway growth similar to that experienced in air conditioning in the postwar period. If this occurred, then the utility would be right back in the position it was about 1930, with winter peaks far in excess of summer peaks. While this situation would be better than a permanent summer peak, it still was an undesirable situation because, on the basis of present knowledge, there would be no compensating summer load to be developed. If this happened, an unbalanced operating condition would become a permanent characteristic of utility operation.

The research analyst from the Economic and Rate Research Department, who had been responsible for the basic technical and market research, was inclined to emphasize that the rate of growth of space-heating load seemed almost sure to be slow, while all the evidence tended to prove that the rate of growth of summer air-conditioning load for the next decade was sure to be large; hence, there would be an increasing gap between summer and winter peaks for most, if not all, of the period until 1970–75. He based his judgment that the rate of electric space-heating growth would be slow on what had actually happened, particularly in northern climatic areas, during the fifteen years elapsed since World War II. Electric space heating as the principal source of home comfort heating in the United States really had gotten its start in the Pacific Northwest, where a domestic conventional fuel shortage developed in 1942–43, and in wartime housing developments near military installations. These first systems were poorly engineered and poorly installed, so that electric space heating really had a setback in the first five years after World War II, both from the public and from the utility point of view. It was not until the very rapid rate of growth in summer air conditioning became apparent in the early 1950's that the utilities became concerned with the unbalanced seasonal load that was developing and started taking a genuine interest in electric comfort heating of homes.

The U.S. Census Bureau undertook in 1960 to conduct a housing census on a sample basis, and one item was the fuels being used in domestic comfort heating systems. A condensation of the result of the census survey is shown in Exhibit 1.

If these summer and winter growth trends were accurately forecast, space-heating load additions should not be charged with peak responsibility before at least 1970; hence a low rate covering direct incremental expenses only would be justified until the winter "valley" was again filled. In his view a new point of equilibrium, assuming no change in general load conditions, would not occur before 20 to 25 years had elapsed. The research analyst therefore favored a low incremental space-heating rate to meet gas competition, and reliance on future general load growth to balance future system peaks.

In the final analysis the chairman showed little interest in any questions but the third, and that from the viewpoint of being able to draw up a rate in line with committee recommendations as to the level that would fit into the general rate policies and structure of the company.

The committee's preliminary findings concerned the changing seasonal pattern of the demand for electricity, electrical space-heating growth possibilities, the relevant costs of serving space demand, and alternative rate structures.

Exhibit 1

PERCENTAGES OF HOUSEHOLDS USING VARIOUS SPACE-HEATING
FUELS IN 1960

By Regions of Continental United States

	PER CENT OF HOUSING UNITS HEATED BY:					
	Gas*	Petroleum†	Coal	Electric	Liquid Petroleum Gas	Other‡
1. New England states (6 states).................	12.8	77.8	6.0	0.1	1.5	1.8
2. Mid-Atlantic states (5 states and District of Columbia)...............	28.1	53.8	15.6	0.2	1.0	1.3
3. South Atlantic states (6 states).................	22.7	39.1	13.3	3.3	8.5	13.1
4. North Central states (12 states).................	45.5	30.2	17.1	0.3	4.5	2.4
5. South Central States (8 states).................	62.7	3.1	9.8	3.5	11.5	9.4
6. Rocky Mountain states (6 states)...............	73.0	7.6	7.0	1.1	7.4	3.9
7. Pacific Coast states (5 states)................	68.1	16.7	1.8	5.3	3.8	4.3
8. Total United States (including Alaska and Hawaii)....	43.5	32.6	12.3	1.8	5.1	4.7

*Includes both natural and manufactured gas.
†Includes all grades of petroleum fuels used for heating (except "bottled" liquid petroleum gas).
‡Includes all types of electric heating where electrical heating is the principal, not the auxiliary, type of heating.
Source: *1960 U.S. Census of Housing.*

The Change in the Seasonal Peak

The normal annual load pattern prior to World War II had been for an annual maximum peak to be reached in winter (usually in December), but the very rapid growth of large commercial air-conditioning loads and residential air conditioning produced summer annual peak-load conditions for many utilities, including the Urban Company. This was a disadvantage to the utilities because the efficiency of utility plant and equipment goes down as ambient temperatures rise. The transmission and distribution efficiency problem is the same for all utilities regardless of whether or not hydro or steam power is used for generation, but the generating efficiency problem is much more acute for steam-generating systems than for the hydroelectric systems. The Urban Company relied exclusively on steam generation and had testified before the state Commerce Commission that its over-all plant and equipment efficiency is 14 per cent less in hot weather than in cold weather.

Thus, in order to meet customer demands for service, 14 per cent more plant and equipment had to be provided to meet summer demands than identically sized winter demands. Therefore, as soon as the differential becomes less than 14 per cent, additional capacity would have to be provided on a summer basis rather than a winter basis. The last increment of capacity required to meet annual peak conditions also becomes unused capacity for more than half of the year; therefore, idle capacity was available in the spring, fall, and winter seasons.

Another aspect of the utility operating problem is that whereas, prior to World War II, winter peaks were sufficiently above summer peaks so that generating and transmission equipment could easily be taken out of service for periods of several weeks up to two or three months for heavy maintenance and overhaul, the postwar load developments tended to level off monthly peak demands so that no comparatively long period of the year is really available for planned heavy overhaul and maintenance. This problem is aggravated by the rapid increase in size of generating units in the large utilities from a 100,000–150,000-kilowatt capacity to 300,000– to 500,000-kilowatt capacity, with units being planned of from 800,000– to 1,000,000-kilowatt capacity. This increase in size of unit means fewer units and greater efficiency of generation, but it also means increasing total reserve requirements to meet emergency outages as well as normal maintenance and overhaul schedules. For laydowns a 12 per cent inoperable reserve would be necessary plus a 5 per cent to 10 per cent operable reserve for emergencies.

The company was just achieving a comfortable reserve position after the strains of World War II when the shift from winter to summer peaks further embarrassed the operating men because reserve capacity had been planned on a winter, not summer, basis. Exhibit 2 shows in index terms what has actually happened to the load conditions being met by the company. The Ratio of Summer Peak to Winter Peak column is the important one in this tabulation. In absolute terms, summer peaks were below winter peaks until 1957, but only in 1950 was the differential as much as 14 per cent. It was now predicted that this condition could become a permanent situation as summer temperature sensitive load had been averaging a 10.75 per cent annual rate growth as compared to an 8.5 per cent annual rate of growth for winter temperature sensitive load.

Electrical Space Heating

Electric heating had progressed to a point where quality-built equipment was commercially vendable at prices comparable to conventional heating equipment. Current equipment could be depended upon to operate satisfactorily if properly installed by an experienced installer, and if heated spaces were properly insulated. Insulation was extremely im-

Exhibit 2

GROWTH IN SEASONAL PEAK DEMANDS, 1947–60
(1947 = 100)

YEAR	RELATIVE GROWTH IN PEAK DEMAND		RATIO OF SUMMER PEAK TO WINTER PEAK
	Winter	Summer	
1947	100.0	100.0	88.8
1948	104.5	104.4	88.7
1949	110.1	108.7	87.6
1950	120.5	110.6	85.3
1951	126.0	115.8	88.1
1952	134.2	119.2	89.3
1953	138.7	146.2	93.6
1954	144.9	154.7	94.8
1955	159.2	166.9	93.1
1956	169.5	180.2	94.4
1957	172.7	196.7	101.1
1958	184.3	200.5	96.6
1959	201.4	220.2	97.1
1960	209.9	240.2	102.5

portant with electric heating, as it does not require the same volume of outside air to supply needed oxygen as was required for flame types of fuel. The cost of operating an electric heating system could vary as much as 50 per cent, depending on how well the building was insulated. Storm doors and windows would be a necessity for electrically heated homes, as well as wall, floor, and ceiling insulation.

Room or area control of resistance heating systems had been well developed, and resistance heating had been the fastest growing type of electric space heating in the past decade because it had the lowest installation costs.

Heat pumps for year-round air conditioning were little beyond the pioneering stage. One of the things holding back their development was a decision as to what source of heat, or "sink" for heat, is best. In Florida, with groundwater close to the surface, water-to-air machines were favored. In areas where the water supply is relatively deep in the ground, ground-to-air systems had been found reasonably satisfactory. The chief objection to both types was that while the component equipment parts were mostly standard items, each job had to be individually engineered and assembled. This made either ground-to-air or water-to-air installations expensive. The big equipment manufacturers came out, about 1955, with the air-to-air heat pump which, while it was the least efficient of the three types of heat pump, was the only one which could be factory-assembled into a self-contained unit. Early air-to-air heat pumps had some operating "bugs" in them but could be produced for a cost low enough to compete with the price of a conventional furnace plus central air-conditioner equipment (about $2,000 for an average-sized installation). Satisfactory "electric" furnaces for hot-air or hot-water heating systems had been available on the market only for the past two or three years and were just beginning to be used.

Off-peak hot-water (or limited heating hour) storage heating systems had been tried but were costly to install, and the large-sized storage tanks occupied considerably more space than a modern furnace. If a satisfactory chemical heat-storage material of small bulk could be found, then off-peak space-heating systems might become popular with both the public and the utilities.

Tolerable Price Differential between Electric and Gas Systems

An analysis of relative operating costs of gas and electric space heating indicated that when the price per BTU[29] consumed for electricity was not more than two to two and a half times the comparable gas price, electric heating could be sold on a nonprice competitive basis because of its greater cleanliness, safety, and flexibility. As noted previously, resistance-heating installation costs, even allowing for extra insulation, were as low as or lower than conventional hot-air or hot-water heating systems, while air-to-air heat pumps could be installed at a cost approximately equal to that of a conventional hot-air furnace plus central air conditioning.

[29]British thermal unit, the standard measure of heat.

Exhibit 3 shows the relative operating cost of heating a 1,200-square-foot home[30] with an average heat loss of 50,000 BTU's per hour at approximately current electric and utility gas rates and costs per gallon of fuel oil and liquid petroleum gas.

It also shows how this ratio between electric space heating and utility gas space heating can be lowered if the effective electric heating rate is lowered to 2 cents, 1.75 cents, 1.5 cents, or 1 cent per kilowatt hour.

Exhibit 3

COMPARISON OF FUEL COST RATIOS FOR AVERAGE RESIDENTIAL CUSTOMER
UNDER EXISTING RATES AND AT VARYING INCREMENTAL
ELECTRICITY RATES*

Fuel and Efficiency	Price and Unit	Relative Cost of Heating
Utility gas..............................	8.00 cents/therm	1.00
Fuel oil (80 per cent furnace efficiency)....	14.30 cents/gal.	1.00
Fuel oil (65 per cent furnace efficiency)....	14.30 cents/gal.	1.20
Liquid petroleum gas (80 per cent furnace efficiency).......................	14.00 cents/gal.	1.60
Liquid petroleum gas (65 per cent furnace efficiency).......................	14.00 cents/gal.	1.80
Heat pump..........................	2.45 cents/kwh	2.40
Heat pump..........................	2.00 cents/kwh	1.95
Heat pump..........................	1.75 cents/kwh	1.70
Heat pump..........................	1.50 cents/kwh	1.46
Heat pump..........................	1.00 cents/kwh	0.97
Resistance heating......................	2.45 cents/kwh	4.30
Resistance heating......................	2.00 cents/kwh	3.55
Resistance heating......................	1.75 cents/kwh	3.10
Resistance heating......................	1.50 cents/kwh	2.66
Resistance heating......................	1.00 cent/kwh	1.77

*While the relative cost of heating would hold approximately for a wide range of residences, calculations were based on a well-insulated 1,200-square-foot house. A season including 6,310 degree-days (65 degrees minus average temperature times days) would require an estimated 18,500 kilowatt-hours, and so electric resistance heating would cost approximately $450 as against a little over $100 for gas.

Prospects for Reducing Electric-Gas Differential through Rising Gas Prices

Studies of the competitive cost of fossil fuels and electricity, and the probable future price trends of fossil fuels, tended to show that there would not be an acute shortage of natural gas and/or crude oil supply in the United States at least until the 1980's and probably not until after

[30]A 1200-square-foot home is the approximate average size for a four-room, one-floor structure or a five-room apartment, and in the Midwest a 50,000-BTU heat loss per hour is considered average for well-insulated premises of this size.

the year 2000. The indigenous United States supply was already being supplemented with Canadian gas, and there was talk of building a pipe line from the Mexican gas fields to the United States. Also, new ways were being tried out to liquefy natural gas and transport it in specially built tankers from overseas sources. New ways of producing synthetic or manufactured gas from coal at the mine mouth were being experimented with and might become commercially feasible before the natural gas supply runs out. Finally, chemical fuel cells of various types and midget atomic power plants have been under experimentation.

The conclusion reached from the fuel studies was that, even assuming that natural gas rates rise more rapidly than electric rates (as they have in the past 15 years), to hope for equality of rates on a BTU basis between gas and electricity in less than 20 years was unrealistic. In fact, the more likely time for possible equalization of gas and electric rates was thought to be 40 years hence, rather than 20 years.

National Range of Space-Heating Rates

An analysis of the space-heating rates being offered by private utilities in increasing numbers across the country indicated that the range of the space-heating charges by those companies which were beginning to do considerable space-heating business was seldom higher than 1.5 cents. Rates higher than 2 cents per kilowatt-hour were producing little business. For further details, see Exhibit 4.

Cost Data

The committee considered three principal ways for determining cost to serve: (1) to charge full annual system peak responsibility to a particular type of load (as was becoming the practice for the air-conditioning load); (2) to average the chargeable responsibility for establishing the monthly maximum demands, and to charge the average monthly demand costs to the new load; and (3) to charge no peak or maximum demand responsibility to space-heating loads. The third method would produce a marginal cost-to-serve figure which includes incremental investment and maintenance charges (if any) directly chargeable to the new load and direct fuel and operating costs for the energy consumed, but does not prorate existing costs over the additional load expected.

The principal difference in these three methods was how peak or system maximum demand charges were assessed against the particular

Exhibit 4

SATURATION OF ELECTRIC SPACE HEATING IN THE UNITED STATES
As of December 31, 1961

Effective Date of Current Space-Heating Rate	Name of Electric Utility	Number of Residential Customers in Thousands	Principal State Served	Lowest Block Rate Applicable to Space and Water Heaters		Electric Space-Heating Saturation as of Dec. 31, 1961	
				Space (Cents)	Water (Cents)	Heat Pumps— Per Cent Saturation	Resistance— Per Cent Saturation
			1. New England States				
1961......	New England Electric System	756.5	Massachusetts	2.00[1]	1.30[2]	0.00	0.10
1958......	Western Massachusetts Electric Company	125.1	Massachusetts	1.30[2]	1.30[2]	0.00	0.70
			2. Middle Atlantic States				
1958......	New York State Electric and Gas Corporation	420.8	New York	1.20[2]	1.20[2]	0.00	1.00
1961......	Public Service Electric and Gas	1,253.1	New Jersey	1.50	1.03[2]	0.00	0.02
1961......	Philadelphia Electric Company[3]	926.2	Pennsylvania	2.00[4]	1.00[2]	0.00	0.01
1961......	Baltimore Electric and Gas Company[5]	492.7	Maryland	1.60[4]	1.75[1]	....[6]	0.02
			3. Southeastern States (Excluding Tennessee)				
1959[9].....	Appalachian Electric Power Company	437.7	Virginia	1.50[1]	1.10[1]	0.20	1.50
1957......	Georgia Power Company	642.1	Georgia	1.00[4]	1.00[1]	0.24	0.41
1962......	Alabama Power Company[7]	577.0	Alabama	1.00[4]	1.20[1]	0.50	0.80
1962......	Florida Power Corporation	257.9	Florida	1.60[4]	1.42[1]	3.00	5.40
			83 (a). Tennessee (TVA)				
1939......	Electric Power Board of Chattanooga	76.4	Tennessee	0.75[1]	0.40[1]	2.70	52.80
1938......	Knoxville Utility Board	71.6	Tennessee	0.75[1]	0.40[1]	0.65	43.00
1959......	Memphis Light, Gas and Water Division[8]	165.3	Tennessee	0.70[1]	0.70[1]	0.05	1.50
1939......	Nashville Electric Service	117.1	Tennessee	0.75[1]	0.40[1]	0.00	40.00
			4. Great Lakes and Upper Mississippi Valley States				
1961[9].....	Ohio Power Company	418.4	Ohio	1.40[1]	1.00[1]	0.07	1.90
1949......	Indiana and Michigan Electric Company	200.4	Indiana	1.50[1]	1.00[2]	0.10	3.50
1959......	Detroit Edison Company	1,177.0	Michigan	2.00[1]	....[10]	....[6]	0.02
1961......	Central Illinois Public Service Company	203.4	Illinois	1.90[4]	1.40[1]	0.00	0.30
1961......	Northern States Power Company[11]	654.0	Minnesota	2.00[1]	2.00[1]	0.00	0.07
1960......	Union Electric Company[12]	550.8	Missouri	1.50[4]	....[12]	....[6]	0.40

Exhibit 4 *(Continued)*

Effective Date of Current Space-Heating Rate	Name of Electric Utility	Number of Residential Customers in Thousands	Principal State Served	Lowest Block Rate Applicable to Space and Water Heaters		Electric Space-Heating Saturation as of Dec. 31, 1961	
				Space (Cents)	Water (Cents)	Heat Pumps— Per Cent Saturation	Resistance— Per Cent Saturation
		5. SOUTHWESTERN STATES					
1961......	Oklahoma Gas and Electric Company[13]	309.3	Oklahoma	1.20[4]	1.20[4]	0.23	0.12
1960......	Central Power and Light Company[14]	209.4	Texas	1.00[4]	1.90[2]	0.55	0.27
1952......	Salt River Power District[15]	92.8	Arizona	1.00[4]	1.00[4]	4.22	1.01
		6. PACIFIC COAST STATES					
1961......	Southern California Edison Company	1,470.7	California	1.40[1]	1.10[1]	0.50	1.40
1961[9].....	Portland General Electric Company	233.4	Oregon	1.10[1]	0.70[1]	0.10	16.00
1960[9].....	Tacoma City Light	57.0	Washington	1.20[1]	0.62[1]	0.00	9.60
1960[9].....	Washington Water Power	129.0	Washington	1.20[1]	0.80[1]	0.03	10.00
1960......	Idaho Power Company...	114.6	Idaho	1.75[1]	0.90[1]	....[6]	0.86
Total for United States..........		36,193.8				0.02	1.10

Notes to Exhibit 4

[1] Uncontrolled.

[2] Limited usage hours permitted.

[3] Philadelphia Electric Company seasonal space-heating rate is $2.00 per kilowatt based on 60 per cent of connected resistance heating load, plus 2 cents per kilowatt-hour for all monthly usage above 500. Applicable from October through the following May.

[4] Seasonal data, applicable in heating season only.

[5] Baltimore Electric and Gas Company seasonal space-heating rate is applicable for billing months November through May, and provides a low rate of 1.6 cents per kilowatt-hour for all over 600 kilowatt-hours being billed.

[6] Less than 0.01 of 1 per cent.

[7] Alabama Power Company's space-heating rate provides for a 0.2-cent reduction in kilowatt-hour charge for all kilowatt-hours consumed over 1,363 per month, November through April.

[8] The contract between the Memphis Light, Gas and Water Division and the TVA was renegotiated in 1959 after Congress refused to pass appropriations for TVA to build a special generating station for Memphis; hence the variation in rates.

[9] Promotional rate in effect before current rate.

[10] The Detroit Edison Company's water-heating rate is a flat monthly charge of from $4.00 to $7.00, depending on gallonage of tank. No metering is required, but a time switch is required to control heating hours to twenty per day.

[11] In Minneapolis a 1.5 per cent surcharge is applied to all bills. In St. Paul the minimum rate is 2.1 cents per kilowatt-hour. In Winona only, the company has separate water-heating rates which are 1.5 cents per kilowatt-hour for uncontrolled water heating and 1.3 cents for controlled.

[12] The Union Electric Company has established a seasonal flat rate of 2 cents per kilowatt-hour for the four summer billing periods and 1.5 cents per kilowatt-hour during the eight winter billing periods for homes having both electric water heating and electric space heating; off-peak control for either is not required.

[13] Oklahoma Gas and Electric Company allows 0.9-cent discount for all kilowatt-hours consumed over 600 per month for the period from November through April for space-heating installations of 3-kilowatt capacity or over. This, in effect, extends the year-round water-heating rate to space heating during the winter months.

[14] Central Power and Light Company has an all-purpose seasonal residential rate with a bottom charge of 1.25 cents per kilowatt-hour. It also offers an alternate combination of rates: controlled water heating (year-round), 1 cent per kilowatt-hour, and a space-heating rate of 1 cent per kilowatt-hour from approximately November 1 through April. The customer's general usage (lighting, range, appliances, etc.) is charged for on the regular residential rate.

[15] Salt River water- and space-heating rate is applicable from November through April, when water heating and space heating are separately metered. Bottom step of general residential rate applicable to general usage is 1.7 cents.

Sources: "33rd Annual Appliance Survey," *Electric Light and Power*, May and August, 1962. Rate data only: Federal Power Commission, *National Electric Rates*.

BUSINESS ECONOMICS

type of load being considered. The method of computing cost-to-serve off-peak night water-heating charges was one form of computation of incremental rates, since it was assumed that night water-heating loads did not add to system investment, but rather increased the over-all daily usage of utility facilities. In view of the finding that space-heating load was likely to have a slow rate of growth, an incremental method of computing cost to serve might be justified for the foreseeable future.

The average peak-load method of computation was a compromise between the full-peak and the no-peak charge methods. Its use was most suitable when the variation between monthly peaks was so reduced that there would be little chance for scheduling heavy overhaul in any one season of the year, thus requiring increased reserve capacity to provide overhaul periods.

If and when a substantial saturation of electric space heating could be achieved, such load would probably first become dominant during cold spells in January or February. Under already existing system conditions, as extra Christmas lighting was dropped, and early evening commercial lighting loads decreased with the increase of daylight, the time of the daily system peak of the electric system tended to shift in February from a 5:00–6:00 P.M. to a 10:00–11:00 A.M. morning peak produced by industrial load. Space-heating systems loads which would be heaviest in prolonged cold spells could conceivably be the cause for changing the hour of the monthly January or February peak from 10:00–11:00 A.M. to 7:00–8:00 A.M. before other monthly peaks were affected. On the other hand, space-heating load would contribute nothing to July-August-September monthly peak loads, and would be unlikely to change the time of May, June, and October monthly maximum demands until a very high degree of saturation was attained. Therefore, by averaging the expected contributions of space heating for each of the twelve months of the year, a basis for computing investment charges on space-heating load could be established. Such an average charge is more than the incremental cost, but smaller than full-peak responsibility charges.

Exhibit 5, based on an Urban Company space-heating cost-to-serve study, illustrates the comparatively wide spread in results obtained from computing costs on the basis of the three methods outlined. These figures do not include general administrative expenses and certain minor items which were not usually allocated by functions. In determining any rate required to meet the cost to serve, these unallocated expenses were added to the total of itemized costs on an over-all percentage basis. They amount to about one eighth of the total.

Exhibit 5

COMPARISON OF COSTS TO SERVE AN AVERAGE RESIDENTIAL ELECTRIC
SPACE-HEATING LOAD DURING A NORMAL WINTER SEASON

	CENTS PER KILOWATT-HOUR		
	Full Peak Responsibility	Average Peak Responsibility	No Peak Responsibility
1. Capacity costs:*			
Generating†............................	0.435	0.375	.....
Transmission‡............................	0.255	0.180	.....
Distribution, including customer costs§.....	0.450	0.345	0.165
Total Capacity Costs................	1.140	0.900	0.165
2. Operating and maintenance costs:#			
Generating...........................	0.075	0.060	.....
Transmission.........................	0.008	0.003	.....
Distribution, including meter reading and billing costs.....................	0.045	0.015	0.015
Total Operating and Maintenance Costs.	0.128	0.078	0.015
3. Fuel costs‖	0.450	0.450	0.450
4. Total cost to serve, excluding certain un-allocated executive and financial costs.	1.718	1.428	0.630
Percentage ratio of (1) to (2) and (3) to (2)....	120.3	100.0	0.441
Percentage ratio of (3) and (2) to (1)..........	100.0	83.0	0.334

*Capacity costs applied to plant—carrying charges of 12 per cent based on a thirty-year plant life were applied to plant costs. This percentage, computed by the level-premium method, assumes a 6.5 per cent return on equity, a 52 per cent debt ratio, a 3.85 per cent cost of debt money, and a straight-line depreciation for tax purposes. State and local tax rates vary, depending upon location of plant within the urban area or the suburban areas served by the Urban Electric Company; therefore a weighted average rate of 1.15 per cent was applied for the combined state and local rates.

†Generating capacity costs include all costs to build a generating station, including land, structures, and equipment up to and including generating station transformer yards.

‡Transmission capacity costs include all costs to build and maintain the high-voltage transmission system (66,000 volts and higher) from generating station yard terminals to and including primary distribution centers, where the current is stepped down from high to medium voltage (12,000 to 66,000 volts).

§Distribution capacity costs include (1) land, structures, and equipment from the primary distribution center terminals through the secondary substations, where voltage is again stepped down from 12,000 volts or higher to 4,000 volts or equivalent thereof; (2) from the distribution substation terminals through the alley transformers, where the current is stepped down from 4,000 volts to 110–20 to 220–40 volts (using voltages) or combinations; (3) company-owned low-voltage equipment on customer premises such as individual service drops and meter equipment.

#Operating and maintenance costs, except fuel, are all costs of labor and material used in operation and maintenance of the system, and appertain to the same segments of the electrical system as do the capacity costs. Meter reading, billing, and customer service costs are included under distribution costs.

‖Fuel charges are the cost of fuel on the kilowatt-hour basis used for generating electricity. They are normally converted to a coal-equivalent basis, although other fuels, such as natural gas and fuel oil, may be used seasonally or only during emergencies.

The Rate Structure

There are various forms in which a winter space-heating rate can be offered. First, it can be a specific single-usage or flat rate which applies only to electric space heating. Such a rate has to be made applicable in conjunction with the appropriate general service rate and also requires separate metering of heating load to administer.

Second, when the block form of rate rather than the demand form of rate is used, a new low block step can be added to an existing general service rate.[31] The problem in this type of procedure for the Rate Committee was to set the volume at which the heating step became effective great enough to insure that the bulk of all other electric services furnished the customer would be charged for at the general-service rate levels during the nonheating season. On the other hand, the effective volume of the space-heating step should be set low enough so that all space heating would fall in the space-heating step, particularly during the heavy heating season (November through March in the geographic area served by the Urban Electric Company). Inasmuch as residential summer air conditioning, per se, tends to increase customer summer usage above winter general service usage levels, the balancing point for applicability of the space-heating step was not easy to determine. The chief advantage of the all-purpose rate was that it required no special metering or billing. The rate (at least theoretically) would be available for any customer using enough kilowatt-hours for any purpose to become eligible for the low steps of the rate and, particularly in rural areas, where farms are typically on residential service, would be extended to uses other than space heating.

A third form of space-heating rates was to establish, in effect, a "larger user" rate, but restrict its applicability to customers whose principal means of space heating were all electric. It had all the advantages of the second form of rate, but could adjust the blocks more readily for general-usage and water-heating purposes, without making these adjustments available to all customers. Such a special rate could be offered only for a limited period of time and could then be dropped if found unsatisfactory for any but existing customers without further formal commission procedure.

Note on Rates

There are three usual forms of general service rates: block, demand, and flat. Governmental rates normally follow the nonresidential form

---

[31]For an explanation of rate forms, see the section entitled "Note on Rates" below.

of rates, while so-called "special" rates, when used, can be in any form, but generally are in effect special contracts applying to only one large customer whose usage needs are peculiar to himself. Such special contracts are filed with the utility commission having jurisdiction, but are normally not published as a part of the utility's rate schedule available to the public.

1. Residential rates are generally "block" rates, i.e., the total consumption of the customer as recorded by a watt-hour meter is divided into steps or "blocks," with the rate of charge per kilowatt-hour progressively declining for each block as the total consumption increases.

A hypothetical example of a block-type rate schedule is:

First	25 kwh at 5 cents per kwh
Next	75 kwh at 3 cents per kwh
All over	400 kwh at 2 cents per kwh
Minimum bill	$1.00

2. For nonresidential customers the "demand" form of rate is generally used, and it has been tried experimentally for large residential users. This form of rate differs from the block rate in that the two basic components of utility costs are separated and a separate charge is made for each component. The first component is frequently called the "readiness to serve" cost. When a customer is connected to a public utility's lines, the utility by law is required to furnish the customer with any amount of service at any hour of the day or night he desires to use it ("demand" it), up to the capacity of all of his electricity-using equipment. This means that the utility must have generating and distribution capacity available at all times to meet the customers' "demands." The utility calls these basic costs, which are incurred regardless of how much use the customers actually make of electric service, "readiness to serve" costs, or for billing purposes the "demand charge."

The second type of costs borne by a utility are the direct costs of producing and distributing electric energy. The charge made to cover these costs is called the "energy" charge.

Therefore the bill of a customer who is on a demand rate contains two charges: (a) for the "demand" he created during the billing period, usually expressed in dollars or cents per kilowatt of demand; and (b) an energy charge computed in cents or decimals thereof per kilowatt-hour of energy actually consumed.

A hypothetical example of a demand form rate for a small to medium-sized customer is shown in Exhibit 6.

Exhibit 6

1. Demand charge
   For all kilowatts of demand, $1.50 per kilowatt of demand, but not less than $7.50 per month.* (Demand is based on highest quarter-hour demand during the billing period.)

2. Energy charge
   First 100 kwh.................at 6.0 cents per kwh
   Next 400 kwh.................at 4.5 cents per kwh
   Next 2,500 kwh...............at 3.0 cents per kwh
   Next 7,000 kwh...............at 2.0 cents per kwh
   Next 20,000 kwh.............at 1.5 cents per kwh
   All over 30,000 kwh..........at 1.0 cent per kwh

3. Flat rate
   A flat rate, or an unvarying rate of charge, finds its greatest use for temporary or other usage where metering would not pay, or for some special usage auxiliary to a customer's regular usage. The form of rate may be either a flat charge per day or month where metering is not used, or a flat charge per kilowatt-hour if watt-hour meters are used to measure the services. Street lighting is frequently billed on the first basis at a flat rate per light or lighting standard (if multiple lights are used). Domestic water-heating rates, where water-heating usage is separately metered from the general service used, are an example of the second type of flat rate on a kilowatt-hour basis.

*This, in effect, is the minimum monthly charge.

QUESTIONS

1. Assuming a flat incremental rate was charged, what rate would you recommend? How could such a rate be administered? Consider the advantages and disadvantages of a flat rate against a new step in block-rate structure.

2. The committee's analysis lead it to expect a slow rate of growth in demand. What does this suggest about the relevance for costs of full peak responsibility, average peak responsibility, or no peak responsibility?

3. Would you consider it price discrimination to be charging the kilowatt-hour rate for lighting of 2.45 cents and for space heating of 1.50 cents at the same time of day? Why, or why not? What would the utility lose and gain by setting up a block-rate structure to avoid such separate rates?

CASE 8–5:   ANHEUSER-BUSCH, INC., AND FEDERAL TRADE COMMISSION[32]

At the end of 1953, Anheuser-Busch, Inc., brewers of Budweiser beer, had completed several years of close contention with Schlitz for the position of number one brewery in national market share. It held

---

[32]Most of the material in this case is drawn from *Federal Trade Commission* v. *Anheuser-Busch*, FTC Docket 6331; and *Anheuser-Busch* v. *Federal Trade Commission*, 363 U.S. 536 (1960), U.S. 7th Circuit Court of Appeals, April 5, 1959, and January 25, 1961.

about 7 per cent of the national market but was first in no major market, and in its home area around St. Louis was fourth in market share behind three regional brewers, one of which, Falstaff, was rapidly growing. (Falstaff was to become the sixth largest brewer in 1954 and fourth in 1955, even though its distribution was limited to twenty-six states.) After a wage increase in October, 1953, most national brewers increased prices generally by 15 cents a case.[33] Budweiser incurred serious sales losses in several parts of the country, partly because distributors chose to increase the spread between national and local or regional beers by as much as 50 cents a case. In the home market of St. Louis, competitors maintained their pre-October prices of $2.35 a case, and Budweiser's price was held at $2.93.

On January 4, 1954, Anheuser-Busch cut the price of Budweiser by 25 cents. On June 21, with its share up from about an eighth to a sixth of the St. Louis market, the price was cut again to $2.35, the level of competitive beer prices. After the second cut, Budweiser's share moved up to almost 40 per cent of the market, and it took first position; all competitors but Falstaff lost heavily in market share. After investigation the Federal Trade Commission issued a complaint charging Anheuser-Busch, Inc., with illegal price discrimination under Section 2 (*a*) of the Robinson-Patman Act,[34] on the grounds that it "discriminated in price between purchasers of its beer of like grade and quality by selling it to some of its customers at higher prices than to others . . . and the price cut was sufficient to direct business from its competitors . . . and there was a reasonable probability it would substantially lessen competition in the respondent's line of commerce."[35]

In March, 1955, the price of Budweiser was raised 45 cents to $2.80, and that of competitive beers by 15 cents to $2.50. Anheuser-Busch then introduced a new beer, comparable in price to its competitors, without real initial success; and its market share in St. Louis rapidly dwindled to 21 per cent by July 31, 1955, and to 17.5 per cent by January 31, 1956.[36] The changing market shares are shown in Exhibit 1. It also chose to contest the complaint but lost the trial before the Federal Trade Commission, with a cease and desist order being issued against the company in 1957.

---

[33] A case consisted of twenty-four twelve-ounce bottles.
[34] See Appendix of Chapter 16 for full text of the act.
[35] Docket 6331 cited by Circuit Court, April 4, 1959.
[36] Anheuser-Busch has continued this policy of meeting local prices not with Budweiser but with Busch Bavarian, as listeners of the ball games of the Busch-owned St. Louis Cardinals have been well aware.

The company decided to appeal the order to the circuit court; and in April, 1959, Judge Schnackenberg's decisions set aside the order on the ground that the price cuts had not been discriminatory. "Even if we assume these cuts were directed at Anheuser-Busch's local competitors, by its cuts Anheuser-Busch employed the same means of competition against all of them. Moreover, it did not discriminate among those who bought its beer in the St. Louis area. All could buy at the same prices." The decision recognized that the seldom-used criminal provisions of Section 3 of the Robinson-Patman Act specify geographical price discrimination, but the Federal Trade Commission has no jurisdiction under this section. The decision was on the narrow grounds that no

Exhibit 1

ESTIMATED MARKET SHARES FOR BEER IN ST. LOUIS MARKET, 1953–56

	For Periods Ended:				
	December 31, 1953	June 30, 1954	March 1, 1955	July 31, 1955	January 31, 1956
Anheuser-Busch..........	12.5	16.65	39.3	21.0	17.5
Griesedieck Brothers......	14.4	12.6	4.8	7.4	6.2
Falstaff.................	29.4	32.0	29.0	36.6	43.2
Griesedieck Western......	38.9	33.0	23.0	27.8	27.3
All others...............	4.8	5.8	3.9	7.2	5.8

Notes: In the period ended June 30, 1954, total sales were up by 2.7 per cent over the similar period in 1963. Assume that market shares are in physical units and that the period ended December 31, 1953, is for six months (the other periods being inclusive from previous date). Assume also that the sales in the June 30, 1954, period primarily reflect the first price reduction.

Source: Originally FTC Docket 6331; subsequently cited in all three court cases as listed in footnote 32.

price discrimination, as defined by Section 2 (*a*) of the act, had taken place, and so did not consider the company's other defenses of no injury to competition and of meeting competitors' prices in good faith.

This decision was rapidly disposed of when the FTC appealed to the Supreme Court. The Supreme Court's ruling emphasized the law's phraseology, "where the effect may be substantially to lessen competition or to create a monopoly in *any line of commerce.*" While is recognized that Congressional concern in enacting the Robinson-Patman Amendment to the Clayton Act was principally with the impact of secondary lines of competition on the bargaining power of large purchasers (notably chain stores), *any line of commerce* included primary competition as well. In this case the primary competition was among the brewers operating in St. Louis, while the secondary competition was among the distributors and retailers of beer.

The court went on to say that a price discrimination is merely a price difference; it was not necessary that different prices be charged to different purchasers in the same market. Here the price differences were between areas—while Budweiser was sold first at $2.93 and then at $2.35 in St. Louis, it was being sold at $3.44 in Chicago and $3.79 in San Francisco. Anheuser-Busch did not attempt to justify these price differences as being justified by cost differences, although with three breweries, some difference in transport costs would necessarily exist. The court then went on to state that there was no flat prohibition of price differentials, since such differentials were but one element in a Section 2 (*a*) violation. "In fact," it said, "Anheuser-Busch has vigorously contended this very case on the entirely separate grounds of insufficient injury to competition and good faith lowering of price to meet competition."[37] The case was sent back to the circuit court for findings on these grounds.

Again, in 1961, Judge Schnackenberg gave a decision on narrow grounds, ruling that there was no injury to competition and in view of this it was not necessary to determine whether the price cut was a good-faith effort to meet competition. He saw the two price reductions as a temporary "experimental method of sales promotion . . . made necessary by competitive conditions" and noted that the two competitors which lost substantial shares had problems other than Budweiser's price cut. Griesedieck Brothers had introduced a new product in 1953 which was "badly named, poorly merchandised, and bitter in taste." Griesedieck Western was purchased by Carling Brewery Company in 1954 after it had been maintaining a highly liquid position at the expense of renewal of production facilities. Thus the court found that the commission failed to prove that the "price reductions in 1954 caused any present, actual injury to competition." The commission had been concerned with potential injury as well, finding that there was "nothing in this record to show that what Anheuser-Busch did in the St. Louis market could not be done in future markets," and that as a nationwide company with assets far greater than local competitors, it could use income from the rest of its business to stabilize possible losses from a price raid. The circuit court was not persuaded by this argument. "If the projection is based upon predatoriness and buccaneering it can be reasonably forecast that an adverse effect on competition may occur, . . . [but] Anheuser Busch exercised a proper restraint in its use of competitive power, not a wilful misuse thereof." This proved to be

---

[37]Footnote 32 in this case covers the several legal quotations.

the last word on this case, though not necessarily the definitive word on the question of business actions that may injure competition.

QUESTIONS

1. Do the facts of this case indicate that there was price discrimination in the economic sense?

2. Why do you think the FTC was concerned enough about the business strategy in this case to see it through three court hearings? (Actually, the commission was probably ready for another appeal but was dissuaded by the Solicitor General.)

3. Share elasticity of demand with respect to price has been defined as the percentage change in market share (a percentage of percentage figure) over the percentage change in price. Was the demand indicated to be elastic in this sense as shown in Exhibit 1? What assumptions must be made for this conclusion?

CHAPTER 9

●◆●◆●◆●◆●◆●◆●◆●◆●◆●◆●◆●◆●

Product Line Policy

MOST OF the discussion thus far has been concerned with demand, output, and cost for a single commodity produced by a firm or industry. This is obviously an unrealistic assumption for virtually all firms engaged in the wholesaling, retailing, or transporting of goods. Manufacturing establishments more frequently specialize in only one good (e.g., bricks, Portland cement, a soft drink, airplanes, wheat, or tobacco) but, even so, usually produce the good in various sizes, models, packages, and qualities, so that it is not entirely clear whether they should be called single-product or mutiple-product firms. In recent years, there seems to have been a particular emphasis on product diversification on the part of manufacturers—single-product firms becoming multiple-product producers and those already handling multiple products adding even more lines.[1]

The assumption of one product to a firm is a simplifying abstraction which is useful in developing numerous principles applicable to multiproduct companies as well. For the most part, it is true that the entrepreneur handling many commodities should make short-run and long-run calculations in the same way as is suggested by economic theory for the single commodity firm; he should equate marginal cost and marginal revenue in short-run operational decisions with respect to every product, and should anticipate at least covering average costs (including normal returns to self-employed factors) when making new investment pertaining to any product.

The multiproduct firm is often a member of several industries when "industry" is classified according to the federal government's statistical procedure. It is equally appropriate, though usually less useful, to consider the firm to be a member of as many industries as it produces distinct commodities. Competitive conditions may differ greatly from good to good for any particular firm. Some commodities may be turned out under conditions approaching pure competition, where price is set by market forces outside the control of any individual company. Others

---

[1]This trend is interestingly described by Gilbert Burck in "The Rush to Diversify," *Fortune,* September, 1955, p. 91.

may be turned out under monopolistic conditions, where the firm can choose its price, within limits, without regard to rivals' reactions. Other goods may be supplied to oligopolistic markets, where the power to set price exists, but where rivals' reactions are of prime importance (and where the conflict of interests may sometimes by usefully viewed as a "game" between firms).

Growth through Diversification

Alert management is usually in constant search of ways to promote the growth of the firm.[2] Very often, such growth is effected by adding new products; and frequently, this is accomplished by the acquisition of entire companies. It is apparent that a systematic search for new investment opportunities will usually indicate the best opportunities to be associated with commodities other than those already being produced, rather than with current products, simply because there are so many more items in the former category. This is especially true because new goods are constantly being developed through research. The scope for useful diversification is usually somewhat limited, however, by the desirability of having the new products of a firm related in some way to the old ones. The types of relationship making for compatibility are many; and often, more than one type of relationship exists at the same time. Goods may be (1) cost-related, (2) related in demand, (3) related in advertising and distribution, or (4) related in research. (Other relations conducive to multiple products might be named, but these appear to be the most important.)

A quantitative picture of the extent of product diversification by the one thousand largest manufacturing firms is given in a voluminous compilation prepared by the Federal Trade Commission.[3] Exhibit 1 is taken from this report.

While all of the firms covered by the FTC report are large, there is a marked difference in the extent of diversification by the top 50 and the 50 which just make the list in size. It can be seen in Exhibit 1 that some of the largest 50 can scarcely be said to have a "principal industry," since such a small proportion of shipments is concentrated in one industry. Most commonly, firms in the top 50 make between 40 and 60

---

[2] Many corporations now employ a vice president who is primarily in charge of growth and development. While greater size often leads to larger and more dependable profits, part of the urge to grow is undoubtedly based on bigness as a goal in itself.

[3] *Federal Trade Commission, Report on Industrial Concentration and Product Diversification in the 1,000 Largest Manufacturing Companies* (Washington, D. C.: U.S. Government Printing Office, January, 1957), p. 15.

per cent of their shipments in their principal industry, leaving a large share for other products. Only four firms specialize almost completely in one industry.

The bottom 50 of the largest 1,000 show a substantially lower degree of diversification, although more than half are multi-industry producers. Only a few diversify to the extent of making less than half of their shipments in one industry. It should be kept in mind, however, that a great variety of products can be turned out by an industry within a given "industry" classification. This is especially true of the broad classifications such as the "chemical" industry.

Exhibit 1

MANUFACTURING COMPANIES BY PROPORTION OF TOTAL SHIPMENTS
REPRESENTED BY SHIPMENTS IN THEIR SINGLE MOST IMPORTANT
INDUSTRY, 1950

Percentage Range	Companies Ranked 1–50 in Size	Companies Ranked 951–1,000 in Size
10% or less	1	..
Over 10%, not over 20%	1	..
Over 20%, not over 30%	2	..
Over 30%, not over 40%	7	
Over 40%, not over 50%	11	4
Over 50%, not over 60%	10	7
Over 60%, not over 70%	4	4
Over 70%, not over 80%	2	4
Over 80%, not over 90%	8	8
Over 90%	4	23
	50	50

Joint Costs

The most obvious cost relationship which brings about multiple products within the firm is the situation of joint costs. These exist when two or more products are turned out in fixed proportions by the same production process. Often, proportions are variable in the long run but fixed in the short run, since it may be necessary to alter the amount of capital equipment used in order to change proportions. Fixed proportions are especially common in the chemical industry. The cracking of petroleum, for example, yields gasoline, kerosene, and other joint products. Joint products are also quite common in the processing of agricultural and fishery output. A famous example is the ginning of cotton, where cottonseed and cotton linters are produced in a weight ratio of about two to one. In processing frozen orange concentrate, the

concentrated juice, orange peel and pulp (used as cattle feed), molasses
(also used in cattle feed), essential oils (used in flavoring extracts), and
seed (used in plastics and animal feed) appear in approximately fixed
proportions. In the processing of a shark of a given variety, there are secured, in approximately fixed proportions, liver oil (rich in Vitamin
A), skins for leather, meat for dog food, bones for novelties, and fins
for shipment to the Orient for use in soup.

If joint products are sold in perfectly competitive markets, their
prices are determined by total demand and supply, and the individual
firm has only the problem of deciding upon its own rate of output.
The firm's short-run adjustment may be shown most simply if output
units are defined in such a way as to keep the quantity of each product
turned out always equal. If, for example, X and Y are joint products,
and three pounds of X are secured simultaneously with two pounds of
Y, we can usefully define three pounds of X as one unit of X and two
pounds of Y as one unit of Y. Thus defined, the output of each, measured in the new units, would always be the same. If, for example, 300
pounds of X and 200 pounds of Y were produced during a given day,
we could say that the output was 100 units of each good.

In Exhibit 2, units of output of two joint products are defined in this
special way. One marginal cost curve and one average cost curve serve
for both goods, but separate demand curves are drawn for each of the
joint products, since they are sold separately. Demand curves are horizontal lines, since the individual firm can sell all it wishes at the prevailing market prices. In addition, a line ($D_{x + y}$) which represents the
sum of the two prices has been drawn.

The optimum output of the firm is OA units of each product per
time period, since at this production rate the price OP received for the
two goods regarded as one is equal to the marginal joint cost. Any
higher rate of output would be unwise, because additional cost to the
firm would exceed additional revenue from the sale of both goods; any
smaller output would be nonoptimal, because if less than OA were
being produced, additional units could be turned out which would add
more to revenue than to cost. Since average cost (which is total cost
divided by the quantity of either good) is below OP, the operation is
yielding economic profit to the firm; that is, more than the usual returns
are accruing to those receiving income on a noncontractual basis. If
this situation is expected to persist, additional firms will enter the industry, gradually eliminating economic (but not accounting) profit.

From the point of view of an industry (rather than an individual
firm), an increase in the demand for one of two joint products increases

the price of that good but lowers the price of the other joint product, provided demand for the latter does not also rise. This is because the output of both goods will necessarily be stepped up in order to take advantage of a better demand for one good, and this will necessitate a lower price on the other in order to clear the market. Under perfect competition the price of any joint product can easily remain far below

Exhibit 2

JOINT PRODUCTS UNDER COMPETITION—FIRM
REGARDS TWO AS ONE

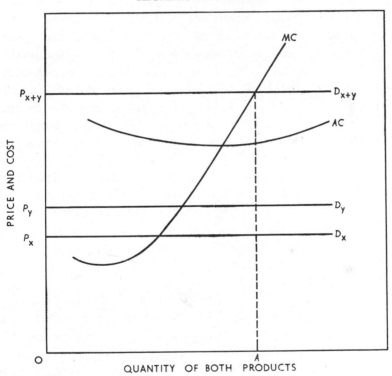

average cost of production, since as a long-run matter, average cost is covered by the *sum* of the prices of the joint products. As long as any positive price can be obtained for a good, a competitive firm has no incentive to withhold any output from the market, inasmuch as its own sales will not depress price. If the price of a joint product falls to zero, it becomes a "waste product."[4]

---

[4] A waste product may also have a negative value in the sense that additional costs must be incurred in order to get rid of it. Orange peel, pulp, and seed were formerly in this category but now constitute valuable by-products.

Joint Costs and Monopoly

When two or more joint products are produced for sale under monopolistic rather than competitive conditions, profit-maximizing behavior on the part of the firm is somewhat different. Assume again, for the
sake of simplicity, that only two joint products are turned out by a
monopolistic firm and that units are again so defined as to keep their
outputs the same. If the demand for both of these is sufficiently strong
in relation to productive capacity, the determination of optimum price

Exhibit 3
MONOPOLIZED JOINT PRODUCTS—ENTIRE OUTPUT SOLD

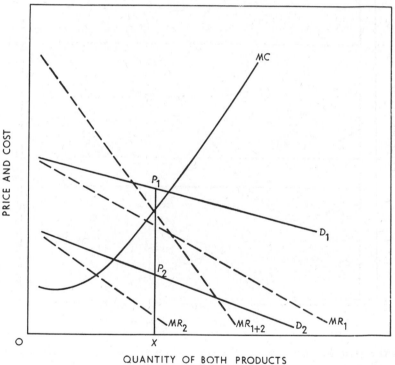

QUANTITY OF BOTH PRODUCTS

and output is much like that of the single-product monopolist. In Exhibit
3 the separate demands are represented by D_1 and D_2, marginal joint
cost is MC, and MR_1 and MR_2 are marginal revenue curves corresponding to D_1 and D_2, respectively. Combined marginal revenue, MR_{1+2},
is derived by adding MR_1 and MR_2 for each output. The best output (of
both) joint products is OX, determined by the intersection of MC and
MR_{1+2}. The separate prices P_1 and P_2 are found on demand curves

D_1 and D_2, respectively, and represent the prices at which quantity OX can be disposed of. It is worth while for the firm to sell all of both products, because marginal revenue from each is above zero at the optimum output. The "last" unit of each good makes a positive contribution to revenue, and the sum of the contributions of the last unit of good 1 and the last unit of good 2 is just equal to the addition to cost which their production entails.[5]

Exhibit 4
MONOPOLIZED JOINT PRODUCTS—PART OF OUTPUT DESTROYED

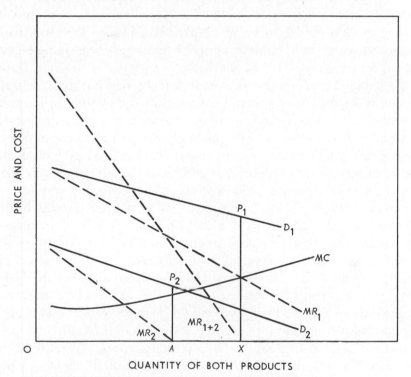

If the demand for one of two joint products is substantially lower than the demand for the other, profit-maximizing behavior on the part of the monopolistic firm is somewhat different. This behavior can be analyzed most clearly by means of Exhibit 4. The curves have the same meaning as before, the difference between Exhibits 3 and 4 being that in the latter the intersection of MC and one of the separate marginal

---

[5]Actually, any unit can be considered to be the "last" unit turned out, and this terminology has only the merit of convenience. The quantity axis measures rate of output per time period, and any particular unit can be considered marginal during that period just as well as any other one.

revenue curves (MR_1) lies to the right of the intersection of MC and MR_{1+2}. Optimum output OX in Exhibit 4 is determined by the intersection of MC and MR_1, and this is necessarily the output of both joint products, in view of the way units of quantity are defined. Marginal revenue from the sale of OX units of good 1 is positive, but marginal revenue from OX units of good 2 is negative (below the horizontal axis). It is necessary for the firm to produce OX units of good 2 in order to exploit fully the demand for good 1, but the monoplist is under no compulsion to sell all that he produces. He should sell OX of good 1 but only OA of good 2, since selling more of the latter would reduce his total revenue and reduce his profit. He will discard AX units of good 2 in each period unless he anticipates a change in cost-demand conditions which will make it worth his while to incur storage costs for this commodity.

If a monopolistic firm produces joint products which it then processes further, the graphical exposition becomes quite complex and will not be presented here.[6] It is not difficult to see, however, that the entrepreneur may find it worth while to "work up" only part of the output of one or more jointly produced raw materials, since further processing of all the output of some joint products may add more to conversion costs than sale of the associated final product would add to the firm's revenue.

Often, multiple products are turned out by a given process but in proportions which are beyond the control of the firm. In this situation the less important products may be designated as "by-products" of the manufacture of the most valuable product. Natural pearls are a by-product of the shelling of oysters, clams, and certain other mollusks; gas is a by-product in the manufacture of coke; and public recreational facilities are a by-product of power and flood-control projects. The dividing line between a joint product and a by-product is usually not sharp in practice, since absolute fixity of proportions is rare, especially in the long run. It should be apparent from the analysis of joint products that the amount of competition which exists may be a determinant of whether a commodity produced in fairly rigid proportions with another is considered by a producer to be wholly a salable joint product or in part a waste product. A monopolist will often find it advantageous to discard some units of output which would be marketed under more competitive conditions. As long as a positive price can be secured for any joint product or by-product, the competitive producer has no incentive to withhold any of it from the market, since by himself he cannot

---

[6]The interested reader is referred to M. R. Colberg, "Monopoly Prices under Joint Costs: Fixed Proportions," *Journal of Political Economy*, February, 1941, p. 109.

affect price; the monopolist, however, may find such withholding profit-able inasmuch as the quantity which he markets does clearly affect price.

Profit-maximizing behavior of a monopolist operating in a joint cost situation may bear an analytical resemblance to that of a monopolist producing under conditions where costs are separable. In the latter case, if the monopolist is able to regulate the rate of output quickly, there should be no need to produce units that will "spoil the market." However, when quantity produced depends on weather conditions, and if a considerable period of time elapses between planting and harvesting, an industry that is monopolistically controlled may find itself with too much of the product for its own good. Steps may be taken to destroy that portion which would bring in negative marginal revenue if placed on the market. Bonfires fueled by Brazilian coffee are a well-known ex-ample of a sure method of disposing of a plethora. Also, when demand for such a product as football tickets fluctuates from week to week, the monopolistic seller does not hesitate to leave seats empty for some games if this will increase revenue. In effect, a "destruction" of part of the crowd that could readily view a game is effected by means of a price policy aimed at maximizing profit. It will not be profitable to have empty seats for the most popular games, of course. The various pos-sibilities along this line were examined more fully in Chapter 7.

Multiple Products to Utilize Capacity

Frequently, goods can be turned out more cheaply together than in separate facilities, even though they do not necessarily appear as the simultaneous product of the same process. For example, unless the avail-able volume of one commodity is sufficient for a full trainload, it is ob-viously more economical to transport a number of goods at once than to have a separate train for each good. This advantage of transporting multiple products derives from the indivisibility of such resources as locomotives, engineers, and cars. If the capacity of any indivisible re-source is not being fully utilized (because the train is too short, for ex-ample, or cars are not fully loaded), additional products can be hauled at a very low marginal cost. Additional revenue in prospect need not be great to induce the railroad company to carry extra items when excess capacity is present.

Similarly, a manufacturing plant which has excess capacity may have a strong incentive to add another product or products. Excess capacity may be due to a variety of causes. A decline in the demand for the product for which the plant was originally designed is clearly a possible cause. Or a plant may have been built purposely too large for present needs in anticipation of future requirements, and this may make at least the temporary installation of another product advantageous. Excess capacity may exist for a substantial period of time even under highly competitive conditions where inefficient firms tend to be driven out of the field. But excess capacity is more likely to be chronic when collusive pricing or a cartel arrangement among sellers (e.g., motel owners) both restricts total sales and attracts additional investment because of the temporary profitability of the high prices to those already in the field.

Industry Development and Integration

It has sometimes been observed by economists that firms in relatively new industries produce multiple products simply because the demand for any one of the products is insufficient to make possible its production in a volume sufficient to secure the advantages of scale. In this situation, some of these advantages can be secured by utilizing a large plant and producing several commodities.[7] However, if the demand for the principal commodity expands sufficiently, it may become more economical to cease producing the others and to specialize in this main good. This is because the indivisible factors are seldom equally adapted to all of the goods being produced, so that it pays to specialize output further if sufficient volume can be secured in one or a few goods.

Young industries are often forced to be vertically integrated (to produce at several stages) because the economic system is not geared to produce specialized raw materials and components which they require. As an industry grows, it is often both possible and profitable to turn over the production of these special raw materials and components to other firms. Similarly, as transactions on the New York Stock Exchange have grown in volume, brokers who do not wish to engage in extensive analysis of securities have been able to omit most of this work because of the growth of specialized market advisory services.[8]

The tendency toward vertical disintegration as an industry grows depends, however, on the existence, or potential existence, of thorough-

---

[7]N. Kaldor, "Market Imperfections and Excess Capacity," *Economica,* N.S., Vol. II, No. 5 (1935), p. 47.

[8]On the other hand, the volume of "put" and "call" options on stocks has not been sufficient to support a trade journal or specialized advisory services. The individual brokers publish separate informational pamphlets regarding options trading.

going competition at all stages of production. If it is necessary for a firm to pay monopolistic prices for materials or components, it may be better to undertake their manufacture itself, even if great efficiency cannot be secured in such production. Most raw-material cartels have experienced trouble with customers who wish to integrate backward in order to avoid paying monopoly prices.[9]

During periods of war or postwar emergency, when the federal government allocates certain "scarce" materials in furtherance of its preferred programs (aircraft, atomic bombs, housing, etc.), a special advantage is inherent in integration in that the output of "captive" facilities producing in earlier stages is unlikely to be subject to allocation. Instead, such production will probably go automatically to the owning firms, just as the early items on a plant's assembly line under emergency conditions may have their impact mainly on the nonintegrated producers. Thus, vertical integration constitutes something of a hedge against emergency shortage of materials.

Integration in Food Distribution

Grocery chains in the United States are outstanding examples of integrated operations; and in this case, there does not appear to be a tendency toward disintegration as the industry grows. A & P, Kroger, and other food chains operate such facilities as warehouses, bakeries, milk-condensing plants, coffee-roasting plants, salmon and tuna-fish canneries, and plants for processing many special products such as mayonnaise, spices, jellies, and beverages.[10] Reasons which have been cited for the growth of integration in this field are several. Probably the most important pertain to the savings of costs of transfer of ownership of goods from company to company. This saving can easily be exaggerated, however, since much intracompany bookkeeping with respect to such transfers is still required in an integrated operation. Certain advertising and other selling expenses can be eliminated by means of integration, since one stage does not have to "sell" the next. Freight and cartage costs may be lower when a number of products are shipped from the company warehouse to retail outlets. Faster handling due to uni-

---

[9] George J. Stigler, "The Division of Labor Is Limited by the Extent of the Market," *Journal of Political Economy*, June, 1951, pp. 151, 191. Stigler gives historical examples of cartels which have encountered this difficulty.

[10] A. C. Hoffman, *Large Scale Organization in the Food Industries*, TNEC Monograph No. 35 (Washington, D.C.: U.S. Government Printing Office, 1941), p. 12.

formity of distribution channels under integrated operations may be especially important for fresh fruits and vegetables.

Pitfalls in Integration

It has been noted that disintegration of operations has frequently been observed, especially as industries grow in size. In part, this is to permit management to devote its time to the production and sale of the principal end product, which is apt to be very different in nature from the raw materials and transportation which are required in the production-distribution process. That is to say, the multiple products turned out at different stages by a vertically integrated firm are especially likely to be incompatible from a managerial standpoint. Capital which can be obtained by selling facilities used in the earlier stages can often be better invested in the final stage, where the chief interest of the company is likely to lie.

A leading danger in integration is that demand at the earlier levels provided by the firm's end-product operations may not be sufficient to justify production of the earlier commodities on a scale large enough to secure the full advantage of size.[11] Fixed costs are especially high in transportation and in some types of mining. Consequently, a decline in demand for these items due to a decrease in output at the final-product stage will raise unit costs sharply for the firm. Unless quite a steady rate of output of the final good can be foreseen, it is usually better for a firm to purchase inputs from other firms in order to avoid this hazard. It may, of course, be possible to sell some of the output of the earlier stages to other firms; but this is not always feasible, since selling and advertising facilities are not likely to be well developed at these levels because, typically, only an intracompany transfer is required.

There is often danger of inefficiency in the earlier stages of an integrated firm, since these stages do not have the usual competitive check of having to cover costs by their sales revenues. As a means of preventing this inefficiency, some integrated companies have made their earlier stages compete on a price basis with outside suppliers for the business of the parent firm, thus in part treating the earlier stages like separate companies. The Ford Motor Company is reported to follow this practice.[12]

---

[11]For convenience, we are referring to the "earlier" stages in an integrated operation. Actually, some of the stages may instead be "later." Transportation of bottled beer is a case in point.

[12]Burck, *op. cit.*, p. 206.

Demand-Related Goods

Often, multiple products are turned out by a firm because they are related on the demand side instead of the cost side. (Or they may be related in both respects.) The motorist who buys gasoline is obviously a likely customer for oil, grease, tires, and soft drinks. The housewife who buys groceries is an excellent prospect for meat and fish, and the man who buys fire insurance on a home is a likely buyer of burglary or liability insurance. Usually, it pays the firm—once it has established contact with a customer—to be in a position to sell him other products. The Mexican peddler, for example, is well aware of this possibility. Once he has secured a degree of attention from the tourist, he is usually prepared to present several types of jewelry or other goods rather than only one variety. Generally, he keeps his other wares hidden until he has sealed a sale on the principal item or has been definitely turned down on that item. The more difficult it is to secure contact with a customer, the greater the gain from handling a multiplicity of products is likely to be. Thus, traffic and parking congestion cause it to be difficult for the motorist to make several stops on a shopping trip. This factor leads a great many retailers to run something approaching a "general" store, where the customer can engage in satisfactory one-stop shopping. The "shopping center," however, permits stores to specialize to a greater degree by providing common parking with easy access on foot to a variety of shops.

Where parking is a municipal problem and the store is not located in a comprehensive shopping center, there is an especially strong incentive for a supermarket to carry nonfood items. This saves the customer the difficulty of going elsewhere for such items of frequent need as magazines, hair tonic, toothpaste, children's socks, and everyday glassware. It is important, however, that the nonfood items be easy to carry to the car, be difficult to steal, and have a rapid turnover, so that they do not tie up valuable space unduly. The high percentage markups on many nonfood items have been an important factor in the trend toward handling more of this merchandise in the chain grocery stores.[13]

Seasonal Demand

Frequently, multiple products are carried by the firm because they have opposite seasonal demand patterns. Coal and ice are famous

---

[13]"Shifting Shelves: Some Big Supermarkets Stop Adding Non-Food Items," *Wall Street Journal,* November 25, 1955, p. 1.

examples of this demand situation. In the past, most firms which delivered coal in the winter used the same wagons or trucks for delivering ice in the summer, and this is still done to a lesser degree. Commodities which are demand-related in this way are at the same time cost-related, since the purpose of handling multiple products is to utilize capacity which would otherwise be seasonally idle. Numerous other examples of such seasonal demand relationships can be found. An athletic stadium may be used for baseball in the spring and summer months, and for football in the fall. A clothing manufacturer changes the nature of his output from season to season in anticipation of temperature changes. The appliance dealer who stocks air conditioners in the summer may switch to heaters in the winter. In general, it is usually good business for the firm which has a seasonally fluctuating demand to install some item with an opposite seasonal demand to take up the slack. This may not be desirable, however, if the commodity is storable, since it can then be produced in the off season for sale later. The portland cement industry typically builds up inventories during the winter, to be drawn down during the spring and summer when construction is heavy. This policy is traceable to the ready storability of cement and to the desirability of limiting industry capacity, for the cement-manufacturing process uses a very high ratio of capital equipment to labor. Also, cement-producing equipment is highly specialized to that use instead of being adaptable also to other kinds of production. The industry finds the annual shutdown valuable for cleaning up the plants and making repairs.

A firm producing articles subject to sharp seasonal swings in demand sometimes finds it desirable to diversify by adding items which are stable in demand rather than opposite in seasonal demand pattern. This prevents the percentage decline in total business from being so sharp at any season. That is, a 30 per cent seasonal decline in demand for one item can be converted into approximately a 15 per cent decline for the company as a whole by adding an item of equal sales importance but with no seasonal demand pattern. An example of this sort of diversification was the addition in 1949 and 1952 of utility company equipment such as transformers and circuit breakers by McGraw Electric Company. This helped offset the seasonal fluctuations in the Toastmaster and other home appliance lines.[14] While such diversification may help only moderately in utilizing seasonally idle plant capacity, because of the specialization of machinery to certain products, it may provide fuller utilization of labor, management, sales facilities, and

---

[14]Burck, *op. cit.,* p. 92.

other more adaptable factors. This is especially true if the items of relatively stable demand are readily storable, since labor, for example, which is seasonally idle in one line can temporarily be added to the regular working force in the more stable lines. This may make it possible to carry a smaller regular labor force in the stable lines. Management as well as labor tends to gain if employment can be regularized in seasonal industries, because labor turnover is reduced; consequently, the problem of training new workers is made less difficult.

Brand-Name Carry-Over

An important force making for multiplicity of products in such fields as the manufacture of home appliances is sometimes referred to as "brand-name carry-over." That is, a customer who is satisfied with a Westinghouse, General Electric, or Philco refrigerator, for example, is quite likely to buy such items as a washing machine, range, and television receiver from the same company. Opportunity is especially great in supplying "package kitchens" of particularly compatible appliances, all turned out by the same firm. In economic terminology the demands for such items are "complementary"; an increase in the rate of sale (and home inventories) of one appliance bearing a given brand name tends to increase the demand for other appliances with the same brand name.

Numerous examples of a rapid trend toward "full-line production" can be cited. Westinghouse has introduced twenty-seven new kinds of appliances since World War II.[15] General Electric (Hotpoint appliances), Philco, General Motors' Frigidaire division, Borg-Warner's Norge division, and American Motors' Kelvinator division have all steadily expanded their lines in recent years. The full-line trend has brought on a wave of mergers of appliance makers. For example, a laundry equipment maker, a refrigerator producer, and the stove and air-conditioning division of the Radio Corporation of America have recently merged under the name Whirlpool-Seeger.

Internal Brand Competition[16]

Another force which frequently promotes multiple products within the firm is, in a sense, just the opposite of brand-name carry-over. It

---

[15]"Full-Line Fever," *Wall Street Journal*, December 6, 1955, p. 1.

[16]This section is based in part on Lowell C. Yoder, *Internal Brand Competition*, "Economic Leaflet" (Gainesville, Fla.: Bureau of Economic and Business Research, University of Florida, July, 1955).

consists in submerging the name of the company and using different brand names for two or more varieties of a product which are sold to the same group of customers. For example, two different qualities of canned corn may be turned out by a given firm under different labels. One brand may be so much poorer than the other that it is better not to emphasize that it is produced by the same company. To do so would be to run the same risk of unfavorable association as would a full-line producer of appliances who sold a decidedly inferior washing machine. When the quality of the product is not wholly under the control of the firm, as in the case of fruits and vegetables, there is likely to be especially good reason to avoid publicizing the company name. While the firm which cans tomatoes, for example, can choose to process only the best portion of its purchases, this may necessitate discarding large quantities which can instead be marketed under another brand name without greatly reducing sales of the top-quality product.

The phenomenon of internal brand competition is especially interesting when a given firm sells two or more varieties of a single product under different brand names to the same set of customers and when, further, the quality of the varieties is very much the same.[17] The following appear to be among the leading reasons for this practice on the part of some of the larger firms:

1.   Mergers or amalgamations of firms producing a given product may have occurred. Previous brand names are likely to be retained by the new company, at least in part, because of the customer following which might otherwise be lost.

2.   Often, a sizable segment of the consuming public prefers one variety of a product, even though a larger segment prefers another variety. To concentrate on the latter alone would deprive the firm of large sales which could be secured by carrying both varieties. A case in point is the production of both standard and filter cigarettes by a given cigarette company.

3.   The struggle between companies for display space in the supermarkets is a keen one. A given soap company, for example, is likely to be able to capture a larger portion of such space by producing more than one variety of soap for use in washing clothes or dishes. The various brands produced by a firm may be promoted as vigorously as if

---

[17]Yoder, *ibid.*, prefers to limit use of the term "internal brand competition" to this situation rather than including the case of the vegetable canner or other seller of two or more quite different qualities of a product. However, no sharp dividing line can be drawn between the cases, since it is only a matter of the degree of difference of the products. Similarly, it is never possible to say that two different brands of a consumer good are sold to *exactly* the same set of customers.

they were turned out by competing companies. It is generally felt that more sales are taken away from competitors than from other products of the company by such internal brand competition. Also, the various divisions of a firm are forced by both internal and external competition to be efficient in their operation. Procter and Gamble is an outstanding example of a firm which engages in vigorous internal brand competition.

4. By installing products very similar to those already being produced, a firm may be able to secure better distribution of its product than through exclusive dealerships. Regular dealers may receive only one variety of the product, while another variety is sold through discount houses or other channels. (This practice is, of course, unpopular with the "exclusive" dealers.) A manufacturer may in this way take advantage of high prices on "fair-traded" items and lower prices on much the same items in order to promote volume.

5. Under some circumstances, a firm's advertising may be more effective when it is distributed over two or more quite similar products than when it is concentrated on one brand. Two or more types of advertising appeal can be used simultaneously, and this may have greater total effect than an equal expenditure devoted to one product. Further, one product of the company can effectively be advertised on the package in which a rather similar product is sold. Armour-produced soap flakes, for example, are advertised on the can in which an Armour liquid detergent is sold.

Commodities Related in Advertising and Distribution

Frequently, firms find it advantageous to handle multiple products at least in part because they are related in advertising, even if the situation is not one of internal brand competition. The various items advertised individually by the roadside gift shop have a cumulative appeal which may cause the driver to pause in his headlong dash. A full-page advertisement may be optimal in attracting the attention of the newspaper reader; but once his attention has been gained, he is likely to be willing to read about a number of items carried by a firm rather than just one. (In fact, the housewife may be anxious to check many items at once, in order to see whether a particular store is worth visiting on a particular week end.) Also, a multiple-product firm is in a position to use coupons attached to one product to help sell another product. The coupons provide both a means of advertising and a direct financial incentive to the customer to buy the indicated commodity.

Multiple products are frequently carried by a firm largely because they are related in distribution. This factor may not be clearly separate from the relationship through advertising. For example, the salesman-driver who delivers coffee, tea, or eggs to the door can easily "advertise" (orally) all sorts of other products handled by his firm. In recent years, there has been a trend away from the specialized, motorized vendor of such commodities as coffee and toward the traveling variety store, in order to take fuller advantage of the contacts which are made with customers.

Salesmen who regularly call on drugstores, for example, can often quite easily supply these stores with other products of the same firm for which delivery facilities are suitable. The Gillette Company recently diversified its operations by entering the ball-point pen field, buying the companies which made and distributed Paper Mate pens.[18] The production and distribution facilities of Gillette were both considered by its management to be well suited to ball-point pens. Similarly, Standard Brands, Inc., is able to use a common system of distribution for a variety of products bought by bakeries and grocers, including yeast, baking powder, desserts, coffee, and tea.

Commodities Related in Research

A firm which has a strong research department is obviously apt to be frequently adding new products as these are developed. To the extent that new items can be patented, the legal system is likely to make possible substantial monopoly gains for a period of time. Even if other firms can readily add the same product or very similar items, the firm which first enters the field may reap substantial innovation profits before others are tooled up and otherwise adapted to turn out the good. Once qualified chemists, engineers, and others are hired and trained to work as a research department, a firm is likely to be making inadequate use of such a department unless it is ready to produce and distribute any promising new products which are developed. This is similar to the principle noted earlier that available unused capacity of any kind—in plant, management, or skilled labor—may lead to opportunities for product diversification on the part of the alert firm.

It has become very common in the annual reports of industries with changing product lines, such as chemicals and processed foods, to find statements that a large percentage of sales are on products introduced

---

[18]"Gillette President Says Paper Mate Companies Cost Firm $15 Million," *Wall Street Journal,* November 22, 1955, p. 1.

in the last ten years. For example: "In 1962, following a 10-year period in which 438 products were introduced by Monsanto's five chemical divisions, 293 of these products contributed 35 per cent of those divisions' total sales and 37 per cent of their gross profit. During the year, 78 new Monsanto products survived screening tests and were sold commercially."[19]

The implication, however, of these product additions is not that the product lines inevitably become larger; product abandonments are also common under the pressure of new research and technology. Du Pont, which has shown great concern over the dwindling profit margins which can accompany a mature product line, announced in late 1962 the abandonment of silicon production because of overcapacity in the business and the final termination of the rayon business which for over forty years had constituted an important company activity.

CASE 9–1:   L & M PRODUCTS CORPORATION

The L & M Products Corporation manufactured and marketed a wide line of both industrial and consumer electrical products on a nationwide basis. The main office and central plant were located in Minneapolis, Minnesota, but manufacturing of various items was carried on in plants in Newark, New Jersey; Atlanta, Georgia; and Los Angeles, California. Industrial products were sold directly to users by company salesmen. Consumer items were sold through company salesmen to jobbers and distributors, although some chain and department store accounts were handled directly.

The entire line produced by L & M was of high quality. On several items, both industrial and consumer, the company had long maintained prices above those of competing products. Quality and service had been emphasized as selling points. The company engaged in an extensive advertising program annually. Institutional-type advertisements were carried in several trade journals serving the firm's industrial customers. In the consumer field, advertisements featuring specific articles were regularly supported in several national magazines and in selected urban newspapers in co-operation with local dealers. Spot announcements on radio and television were made at various times.

In 1952, one of L & M's competitors introduced a heat-controlled electric frying pan. Shortly thereafter the largest electrical company in the nation introduced an electric frying pan of its own. Both of these items were priced identically at $29.95. Early in 1953 the originator

---

[19]Monsanto Chemical Company, *1962 Annual Report.*

of this item reduced his price to $24.95, which was almost immediately followed by the other company.

By rearranging some manufacturing operations in its Atlanta plant, L & M began the production and sale of an electric frying pan in June, 1953. It contained several features not possessed by competing frying pans. Among them was the fact that it was completely submersible in water for cleaning; it could even be placed in electric dishwashers. Another feature was free lifetime repair service when returned to the factory with a small handling charge. The pan was initially priced at $26.95. By the end of 1953, there were several brands of electric frying pans on the market, ranging in price from $13.95 to $26.95, L & M being the highest priced. The company felt that because of its reputation for service and quality, it could command a premium price, as it had done on other items in the past.

At the beginning of the Christmas shopping season in 1953 the originating company reduced its price to $21.95. One week later the largest company met this price. L & M maintained its price of $26.95. As a result of rather disappointing sales during the Christmas season, and this in spite of an intensive seasonal promotion, the company reduced its price to $23.95 on January 15, 1954. It had been learned that the two large competitors had enjoyed most satisfactory Christmas sales.

In May, 1954, the originating company reduced its price to $19.95 and introduced an identical electric frying pan, but somewhat larger in size, at $23.95. The other large competitor reduced its price to $19.95, but did not introduce a larger pan. L & M reduced its price to $21.95, and launched an advertising campaign featuring the usefulness and convenience of the pan as ideal for summer cottages as well as generating less heat in the home kitchen during the summer season.

In preparation for the 1954 Christmas season, L & M reduced its price to $19.95, the same as that of its competitors. Sales showed an increase following this price reduction. Early in 1955, it was apparent that sales needed another stimulus, since it was felt that the company was not getting its share of the market. A more drastic reduction in price, to $14.95, was ordered. Neither of the larger competitors met this price. As indicated in Exhibit 1, there was an almost immediate increase in sales until August, 1955, when a decline appeared. Following another disappointing Christmas season in 1955, the company increased its price in January, 1956, to $17.95. The two large competitors continued their price of $19.95.

The vice president in charge of production suggested that the company discontinue the line of electric frying pans. He pointed out that capacity production had been designed for 35,000 units per month, a level which had never been reached. At an output of 20,000 units per month, labor, material, and packaging amounted to $6.83 and overhead averaged $1.31 per unit. Prices to dealers and distributors averaged $9.27 per unit. This same officer noted that the small electric motor division was working two shifts and had a backlog of approximately five months. He recommended that the space currently used for frying pan production be converted to small motors. These motors were now produced at a cost of $4.01 each, including overhead, and were sold at an average price of $6.10 each. He estimated that the conversion of this space would permit the manufacture of an additional 30,000 motors per month.

Exhibit 1

L & M PRODUCTS CORPORATION

Monthly Factory Shipments, Electric Frying Pans, June, 1953, to May, 1956

Month	1953	1954	1955	1956
January....................	......	15,985*	15,330	20,005†
February...................	......	17,630	19,880‡	19,765
March.....................	......	18,315	23,525	19,755
April......................	......	17,990	24,690	19,960
May.......................	......	18,050§	25,070	19,870
June......................	7,400	19,455	24,155	......
July......................	11,150	17,360	23,650	......
August....................	11,775	16,990	21,385	......
September.................	15,160	16,340	22,100	......
October...................	17,180	17,920#	23,455	......
November	15,730	20,115	23,210	......
December.................	14,825	16,340	21,645	......

*January, 1954, price reduced to $23.95.
†January, 1956, price increased to $17.95.
‡February, 1955, price reduced to $14.95.
§May, 1954, price reduced to $21.95.
#October, 1954, price reduced to $19.95.

The president of the company, as well as the vice president in charge of sales, did not agree with this proposal. The president felt that the company should not drop a line which was showing a profit. He further believed that the company had made a mistake in lowering the price of its frying pan to that of the average popular price of competitive makes. This, he said, was contrary to the long-established price policy of the company of maintaining a higher differential price over competitive products. He suggested that the poor performance in sales was due to a departure from this policy which he stated had destroyed the preference of customers for L & M products because of their superior quality. He proposed that the price be increased to $21.95 immediately. This, he believed, would result in larger profits, although the volume might decline slightly.

The vice president in charge of sales felt that the product needed some improvement in design and construction to improve sales. He believed that the product had not yet been on the market long enough to conclude that it had reached its maximum potential of sales. Rather than discontinue the line and convert the space to small motors, he proposed that two new products, which the research department already had in the pilot-model stage, be added to the line. One was a two-quart electric saucepan, and the other was a rectangular electric grill suitable for pancakes, eggs, etc. The introduction of these products would give the company a more complete line of portable cooking equipment. It seemed to him that the conversion of existing facilities to small motors would quickly eliminate the backlog now in the department, and the company would then be faced with the same problem as now confronted it in the frying pan department. He could see no particular advantage in exchanging one problem for the other.

QUESTIONS

1. Do you think the company made a mistake by adding the electric frying pans to its line? Why?

2. Do you agree with the proposal to discontinue the line? Why?

3. What is your reaction to the proposal that the line be expanded by the addition of new products? Explain.

4. Do you subscribe to the company's policy of pricing its products slightly above the competitive price and promoting them on the basis of superior quality? Why?

5. Is product diversification always the best policy in the face of declining sales? Explain.

CASE 9–2: STANDARD PROCESSED FOODS, INC.

From its beginning as a small cannery in 1923, Standard Processed Foods, Inc., had grown to a large, integrated canned foods firm serving a national market by 1940. About 10 per cent of its output was sold in Canada, Mexico, Central America, and the West Indies. Originally, the company had canned only vegetables; but in 1928, canned fruit was added to its line. In this same year, it had shifted from selling only through brokers and wholesalers to a combination of food brokers and direct selling. In 1934 the firm entered the infant-food market with a line of strained vegetables and fruits. In 1937, canned pulverized meats were added to the infant-food line. With the growth of chain groceries in the decade of the thirties, the company soon found itself selling more than three fourths of its output through its own sales organization.

By 1940 the infant-food division accounted for more than 70 per cent of total sales. The rapid growth of this division was attributed to the wide acceptance of strained and pulverized baby foods by mothers throughout the country. To meet this demand, the company had built or purchased four plants for the processing of infant foods. Each was located in an area suitable for the growing of fruits and vegetables. Contracts for vegetables were made with farmers at the beginning of the growing season. Seed was furnished by Standard Processed Foods, Inc., and planting time was scheduled so as to control delivery of fresh vegetables to the plants during the harvest season. Fruits were purchased in season from commission houses. Both fruits and vegetables received in excess of a plant's daily operating capacity were canned in fifty-gallon barrels for later processing. This permitted operation of the plants on a more regular schedule. All foods containing meat were prepared in the Iowa plant.

During World War II the infant-food division experienced another period of rapid expansion. The sharp increase in the marriage rate during this time was accompanied by an even higher increase in the birth rate. The company experienced difficulty in meeting demand. Because of wartime restrictions, containers were more of a problem than the contents. In addition, the firm enjoyed a large increase in its sales of canned goods to military establishments. All of its products sold at retail were subject to OPA rationing controls. Upon the cessation of hostilities the company began the construction of additional facilities at three of its plants. These were completed in 1946.

Demand for infant foods continued to grow until 1948, when there was a leveling of sales. In 1949 the company reduced operations in this division because of an absolute decline in demand. In view of the apparently increasing prosperity of the nation, an investigation was initiated by the sales manager to determine the reasons for such a decline. His report contained, among other observations, the following:

1. The decline was industry-wide.

2. Infants usually begin the use of processed foods early in their first year. They consume the maximum amount of such foods during their second year. By their third year, they have begun the consumption of home-prepared foods. Usually, after their fourth year, they eat little, if any, strained food.

3. The birth rate, which reached its peak in 1943–44, declined thereafter until 1946, when it leveled at a rate substantially above the prewar rate. The leveling-off and decline in infant-food sales by 1948 could be attributed to a decrease in the number of infants under two years of age and an increase in the number over four years of age.

4. The birth rate for 1948, projected through the decade of the fifties, indicated that the number of infants under two years of age would remain level for a few years and actually decline somewhat before moving upward. This was because the new parents of this period were born during the thirties, when the birth rate was very low. This also indicated that the rate of new marriages would actually decline during the middle and late 1950's. This forebode a further decline in the sale of infant foods.

The results of the sales manager's study were presented at a meeting of the board of directors. The decline in sales had now reached approximately 15 per cent and was considered serious. Along with the report, the president of Standard Processed Foods, Inc., presented several alternative courses of action, as follows:

1. The company could attempt to secure a larger share of the market. It now supplied about 30 per cent of the infant-food market, a proportion which had remained fairly stable since 1940. An aggressive but expensive promotional campaign might enlarge its share of the market, but the president was skeptical of such an outcome. There were only three other major companies in the field, one of which also supplied approximately 30 per cent of the market.

2. The company could expand its present line. In its effort to meet the constantly increasing demand for infant foods during the thirties, the president felt that three areas of the market had been neglected: (a) processing and canning of low-calorie fruits and vegetables for dietetics, (b) promotion of the use of strained and pulverized foods by hospitals and convalescent homes, and (c) some means of retaining infants as consumers of the company's products beyond their third and fourth birthdays.

a) The first of these areas (dietetic foods) had already been entered by several small canneries with fairly satisfactory results. With the current popularity of and emphasis upon individual weight control, the president believed there were profitable possibilities in this line. Furthermore, there would be no major problems of production and distribution, since existing canning facilities and equipment, warehouses, and selling organization could be used. Capacity could easily be increased by 10 per cent without strain on resources.

b) The second area (strained and pulverized foods for institutional use) was as yet untouched. For many years, Standard Processed Foods, Inc., had packed fruits and vegetables in two- and five-gallon containers for institutional use. In the development of infant foods the company had solicited and obtained the co-operation and endorsement of pediatricians as well as several medical organizations. Preliminary research had disclosed that considerable chopping and straining of foods is done in hospital kitchens. Little or nothing is done with the pulverizing of meats. If the foods now prepared for infants were packaged in containers of convenient size, the president believed that potential sales here would more than offset the decline in sales of infant foods at retail. Also, in this case, production and distribution could be handled by existing facilities and organization.

c) The third possible area of expansion was the addition of a line of junior foods for children from three to six years of age. The firm's experimental kitchen had developed a method of chopping certain vegetables and fruits which made them "bite size" and attractive. These could be packaged in slightly larger containers than those of the infant foods. These foods had been tried with selected families, more than 90 per cent of whom had approved of them. If the junior-food line could be successfully promoted, it would add materially to the market. Infants who began on infant foods would probably continue with junior foods. If this line proved successful, it could conceivably raise total sales above their original level.

3. Another possibility for strengthening the company's position was entry into the frozen-food business. This would be an entirely new experience for the company. Although the popularity of frozen foods was increasing, there were several companies already in the field. If Standard Processed Foods, Inc., were to enter this market, additional capital in the amount of $10 million would be required. The company would have to build at least two frozen-food processing plants and arrange for adequate cold-storage space in several cities, as well as provide for frozen-food delivery to retail outlets. Because of the backlog for machinery, it would be approximately fourteen months before plants could be built and equipped. An alternative was the purchase or acquisition of an existing frozen-food business. The latter would have the advantage of an established market. Whether a plant was built or purchased, the president stated that initial expenses would rule out profits for at least two years. Beyond that period, however, he was very optimistic. The president had made some preliminary inquiries as to the possibility of purchasing a frozen-food business located in New Jersey.

This business could be acquired for $14.5 million. Standard Processed Foods, Inc., had approximately $1 million in liquid resources above its present working capital requirements. If the company expanded its present line as suggested above, working capital requirements would increase by $1 million.

QUESTIONS

1. Which course of action would you recommend? Why?
2. One of the directors recommended that the company ride out the present downward trend in sales. Do you agree? Why?
3. What do you think of the proposal of attempting to increase the company's existing share of the market?
4. Under what conditions would you recommend entering the frozen-food market? What are the disadvantages of this proposal?

CASE 9–3: DIAMOND ELECTRIC COMPANY

The Diamond Electric Company manufactured a line of radios, television sets, and industrial electrical products. The company was established in 1927 and, through merger and expansion of its markets, had grown to serve a national market. It operated seven different plants, located in California, New Jersey, Georgia, and Illinois. Of the four plants in Illinois, one was used for radio production, one for television manufacture, and two for industrial products. In addition, the firm maintained twenty-two sales and service offices in various parts of the United States.

The company organized its activities in four divisions on a product basis. These were the radio, television, light industrial, and heavy industrial divisions. The company began as a radio-manufacturing company. Light industrial products were added in 1936, heavy industrial products in 1942, and television in 1946. Research had always been carried on rather extensively, and the company was considered one of the leaders in all of its fields. It was the Diamond Electric Company which had led in the production of radios for installation in automobiles. Many of the improvements in automobile radios resulted from research in its laboratories.

From the initial introduction of automobile radios until about 1940, the Diamond Electric Company was the chief supplier of sets to the automobile industry. In the mid-thirties, several companies entered the field; some supplied automobile radios as original equipment, while others produced for sale to the public. Some companies, including Diamond Electric Company, produced for both markets. The automobile radios produced for public sale by Diamond were under its own brand name. With one exception, this was done by all companies who served both markets. In 1940 the company supplied approximately 40 per cent of automobile radios used as original equipment. One of the large automobile manufacturers, which had begun its own production of radios in 1938, supplied 10 per cent, and the remainder was supplied by several other companies.

During World War II, both automobile and radio production was suspended. In the reconversion period following the war, a major automobile manufacturer undertook the production of more than one half of its own automobile radio requirements. This reduced the proportion of the Diamond Electric Company to approximately 30 per cent of the total market. Although the proportion supplied was smaller, the total number of automobile sets produced exceeded that of 1941. This was attributed to the backlog of demand for automobiles in the first year of postwar production.

The company began the production of television sets in 1946. A great deal of research on television had been undertaken just prior to World War II, plus experiments with electronic equipment during the war. Facilities which had been expanded to meet the demands for military equipment were available for television production. Output of televisions sets by the company in 1946 was 7,292, but production was hindered by material and labor shortages. The 1947 output was 47,574, an increase of almost sevenfold. By 1948 the company was producing at the rate of approximately 120,000 sets per year. This rate was the maximum capacity of the television plant. This level of output, however, was insufficient to meet demand. Attempts to purchase or lease additional space had been unsuccessful. Consideration had been given to the construction of additional facilities, but the backlog in construction was so large that a new building could not be ready for occupancy for at least eighteen months. The problem of equipment for a new plant was equally acute. While the company could build much of its own equipment, it had a backlog of ten months in both the light and heavy equipment divisions. Efforts had also been made to subcontract television production to other companies; but they, like Diamond Electric Company, were struggling to meet their own demands and were unable to provide delivery at specified dates. It was feared that much business in the television market would be lost unless output was increased.

By July, 1948, output of automobile radios had declined. The largest customer, an automobile manufacturer, was now supplying practically all of its own requirements. With the growth of television, sales of other model radios had also declined. Exhibit 1 shows production of automobile radios and television sets by months from April, 1946, to July, 1948. Automobile radios, as original equipment, now accounted for slightly less than 15 per cent of the total market. The radio divi-

Exhibit 1

DIAMOND ELECTRIC COMPANY, MONTHLY PRODUCTION OF AUTOMOBILE RADIOS AND TELEVISION SETS, APRIL, 1946–JULY, 1948

	1946		1947		1948	
MONTH	Automobile Radios	Television	Automobile Radios	Television	Automobile Radios	Television
January........	......	.....	20,834	2,469	15,104	5,971
February.......	......	.....	20,692	2,704	15,432	6,004
March.........	......	.....	20,654	3,011	15,071	6,435
April..........	17,119	184	20,619	3,841	14,938	7,013
May..........	18,375	293	20,435	3,938	14,973	8,009
June..........	19,104	401	20,109	3,994	15,007	10,408
July..........	19,273	547	19,231	4,005	14,981	11,652
August........	20,421	628	18,414	4,119	......	......
September......	20,592	752	17,192	4,633	......	......
October........	20,672	1,097	16,452	4,821	......	......
November......	20,686	1,451	15,785	4,937	......	......
December......	20,921	1,939	15,134	5,102	......	......
Total.......	177,163	7,292	225,551	47,574	105,506	55,492

Exhibit 2

DIAMOND ELECTRIC COMPANY, COSTS AND FACTORY SELLING PRICES, TELEVISION SETS AND AUTOMOBILE RADIOS
(Per Unit)

	TELEVISION SETS			AUTOMOBILE RADIOS		
ITEM	1946	1947	1948	1946	1947	1948
Materials...........	$31.72	$32.04	$31.04	$ 9.31	$ 9.82	$10.01
Direct labor........	17.37	17.62	16.14	7.43	7.96	8.02
Depreciation........	2.14	1.89	1.23	1.12	1.17	1.21
Factory overhead....	8.90	8.41	8.05	1.62	1.65	1.72
Indirect labor........	6.51	6.43	5.72	2.19	2.23	2.28
Administration and selling expense.	3.03	2.83	2.54	0.24	0.33	0.35
Total...........	$69.67	$69.22	$64.72	$21.91	$23.16	$23.59
Factory selling prices..	$96.50	$97.25	$96.50	$27.00	$29.00	$29.50

sion occupied a plant of its own. Exhibit 2 shows the costs of production of radio and television sets.

At the August, 1948, meeting of the board of directors, the president of Diamond Electric Company proposed that the automobile radio line be dropped entirely and that the space in the radio plant be converted to the production of television sets. This would permit an increase in television output of approximately 5,000 sets per month. Radio-manufacturing equipment could be easily and quickly converted by some modifications and additions. The labor problem would be minor, since radio workers could be easily and rapidly trained to assemble television sets. Output of the light industrial division could provide all the additional parts by reducing only slightly the output of such parts for a few small television manufacturers. Two directors objected, pointing out that it was poor business to abandon a profitable line. The president stated that he believed the television market had excellent potential for growth, while the demand for automobile radios would probably shrink further as the supply of automobiles approached the level of demand. There appeared to be little possibility of additional sales to the automobile manufacturers, since most of them presently had well-established sources of supply.

QUESTIONS

1. Do you agree with the president of the company? Why?
2. In what sense is the automobile radio operation profitable?
3. What is the nature of demand for automobile radios? For television receivers?
4. Do you believe a company should always add new products rather than discontinue a current item? Why?
5. Do you believe the Diamond Electric Company should have expanded its total operations? Why?

CASE 9–4: ZENITH RADIO CORPORATION

The stockholders of the Zenith Radio Corporation received the following letter in February, 1950:

February 8, 1950

To Our Shareholders:

You have no doubt seen news items in the daily press (copy enclosed) to the effect that Zenith will shortly discontinue the manufacture of auto radios. I feel that you are entitled to a direct first hand statement as to the reasons for this decision which should have a far-reaching effect on your investment in our company.

When we originally went into the manufacture of auto radios for the automobile manufacturers, it was on the basis that such production would absorb some of our overhead and keep our people employed during the "off season," for household radio. Up until the war, when production of all radio was stopped, the anticipated results from this business were accomplished.

However, since the resumption of production at the end of the war, the auto radio business has not worked out as satisfactorily for us, due to several factors, which I will explain as follows:

The auto companies now require their peak requirements of radios at the *same* period of the year that our home radio and television are in greatest demand with the result that we have not been able to take full advantage of the overwhelming demand for these products from our distributors, dealers and the public. The terrific demand for television has greatly complicated our problem.

Immediately following the war we were limited in our pricing of auto sets by OPA restrictions, with the result that we operated at a loss on this business for the first two years. With the removal of these restrictions, and with the cooperation of the auto manufacturers, we were able to reprice our sets to them on a basis which has enabled us to recover our postwar loss.

However, the present competitive situation does not now warrant our using large valuable manufacturing space and some of our most highly skilled engineering and production personnel for this type of manufacturing at the expense of the much more lucrative television and radio production so much needed by our distributors and dealers.

We have, therefore, decided to concentrate our efforts on home radio, television and hearing aid production for which we expect Zenith will enjoy continued high public demand.

The quarter just finished January 31st, was the highest in volume of sales in our history, approximately $33 million and will, I expect, show the largest profit, when the figures are completed.

Present demand and orders on hand indicate a continuance of our present high rate of production for the next two months, with no indication as yet of any appreciable decline thereafter.

The future of our company was never brighter and we are determined to make the most of our opportunity.

E. F. McDONALD, JR.
President

The automobile radio business represented about $20 million of Zenith's $77,146,881 sales, April 1, 1948, to April 1, 1949. Zenith sales subsequently rose to $110 million in fiscal 1950 and $137 million in calendar year 1952. By 1961, when Zenith and RCA Victor were contending for the largest market share in television, sales reached $274 million and an 18.2 per cent return on net worth of $98.6 million was achieved.

Television production rose from 178,500 sets in 1947 to 945,000 in 1948 and 3,000,000 in 1949. The 1950 industry output of 7,557,000 had only been exceeded once through 1961.

QUESTIONS

1. In what way did the economically relevant costs to Zenith of producing automobile radios change from the prewar to the early postwar period (1946–48)?

2. How had the relevant costs changed from early 1948 to 1950?

3. How did both long-run and short-run considerations enter the decision?

CHAPTER 10

•••••••••••••••••••••••

Location of Plants

ALTHOUGH the problem of where to locate a new plant arises relatively infrequently for most firms, it is clearly a matter of great importance whenever it must be faced. Economic consultants are often brought in to study the problem of location and to advise management on this subject. While company officials are usually expert in the day-to-day operations of the firm, they may feel much less at home with the problem of finding an optimum location, since this involves such questions as the relative availability and cost of labor, capital, and materials at various places at which they may have had no business experience. Executives employed by large retailing "chains" are more likely than most officials to be in close touch with locational problems because of the frequency with which new outlets are established. There is seldom only one suitable location for a plant; instead, numerous locations are likely to be satisfactory, though some may be decidedly better than others. Some locations, of course, will be so poor that their selection alone would insure failure.

Location for the Long Pull

A basic assumption which underlies the economic theory of the firm is that executive decisions are motivated by a desire to maximize profits—or more accurately, to maximize the present value of the stream of net profits over the time horizon for which plans are made. However, in this connection the term "profit" must frequently be given an interpretation that is broader than monetary gain. This is especially true of a *relocation* problem, since there are few economic actions that generate such strong emotions as a decision to move a long-established major plant to a distant city. "Profit" in such a case may involve considerations of impact on workers, on company officials, and on the community. Management may find itself torn between a desire to maximize monetary profits for the benefit of stockholders and a desire to give adequate weight to other important consequences of a decision to move. These consequences can be political in nature, since numerous elected and appointed officials are certain to be extremely interested in the matter.

Even from a pecuniary viewpoint only, the optimum location for a plant is not necessarily the one which will bring the largest immediate profits. It may, for example, be better to select a suburban site for an apartment building where demand for such housing is presently somewhat inadequate, but on the way up, rather than a place in the city where immediate demand is strong but long-run prospects are poorer. The capitalized value of a similar building in the suburban location might well be larger, because the capitalization process involves anticipating income over the life of the project. Often, however, there is no conflict between securing maximum immediate and long-run returns, perhaps because forecasting the more distant future is so difficult that only near-future prospects are actually weighed.

If the long-run nature of the expectations that should govern plant location is kept in mind, it can be said that the best location is the one which will provide the most favorable relation between supply and demand for the products to be sold. In itself, this statement only says that the best location is the best location—that is, where profits will be greatest. However, analysis of some of the factors which serve to make demand stronger and costs relatively lower serves to improve one's understanding of the problem of location.

Demand

The height and shape of the demand curve that will face a seller often depends on location. If a retailer selects a spot which many potential customers pass on foot or can easily reach by car or bus, demand will be relatively favorable (unless too many close competitors are there first). At the same time, the cost of buying or renting may be so unfavorable at a high-demand location that the firm will be better off if it locates at a lower cost site and sacrifices some demand potential to gain this saving in cost.

The manufacturer of a commodity which is of a highly technical and changing nature will usually find the demand for his product to be stronger if he locates close to buyers so that technical personnel can readily consult with one another. The strong attraction of a facility such as that at Cape Canaveral, Florida, to manufacturers of missile components is an outstanding recent example.[1]

---

[1]The relative importance of various locational factors according to a comprehensive survey of new locations in Florida is set forth in M. L. Greenhut and M. R. Colberg, *Factors in the Location of Florida Industry,* Florida State University Studies, No. 36 (Tallahassee, 1962).

Frequently, a firm can secure for itself a measure of monopoly in the sale of a product within an area by locating well away from other sellers of similar products. A small producer of outdoor furniture may find it better to locate in a fairly small community where there is no competition in the line than to locate in a large city where total demand is much greater but where there are not only numerous competitors but also a greater likelihood of new entrants into the field. Cost advantages may also accrue, especially due to lower land and labor costs in areas of lower population concentration.

Importance of Personal Considerations

Personal considerations are sometimes more important factors in the location of small firms, especially, than is the quest for maximum monetary profits. A plant may be located so as to be convenient to the home of the president of the company. Or plants may locate near such cities as New York for the convenience of executives who wish to be within easy reach of urban *divertissement.* Frequently, they are located in Florida or California primarily because of favorable climatic conditions which may be sought by officials for themselves and their employees.

Favorable climatic, recreational, cultural, and educational conditions are especially important to a firm which needs to attract highly trained personnel in large numbers. When the psychic income of a location is so great to officials as to cause them to accept lower explicit or implicit salaries than they could secure at less desirable places, this personal preference can be translated into an actual cost-reducing factor.[2] Similarly, the chief official of a company may have a strong personal preference for a city where he is well known and consequently is more readily able to borrow money, secure materials, and make sales than elsewhere, on account of his personal contacts. While his personal preference for a location may be due to such sales-cost advantages, the same advantages would not accrue to another entrepreneur. These personally induced economic gains lie outside the general framework of location theory, which emphasize the demand-cost situation that would face any firm at a particular place. Nevertheless, personal considerations, and even pure chance, frequently do determine actual locational decisions.

---

[2]This is pointed out by Melvin L. Greenhut, *Plant Location in Theory and in Practise* (Chapel Hill: University of North Carolina Press, 1956).

Cost

In the theory of location, main emphasis is usually given to the cost side. The most favorable location for production is usually said to be at the place where the unit cost of gathering materials, processing them, and delivering the finished product is at a minimum. This formulation is somewhat vague, because it does not say *how many* units are produced and sold. If only a few units of finished product could be delivered cheaply from a location, this would be unlikely to make it a desirable one. A fuller explanation of plant location must consider demand as well as the cost of production. In the following discussion, demand will, however, at first be neglected.

Exhibit 1

TOTAL TRANSFER COST—USUALLY LOWEST AT ONE END

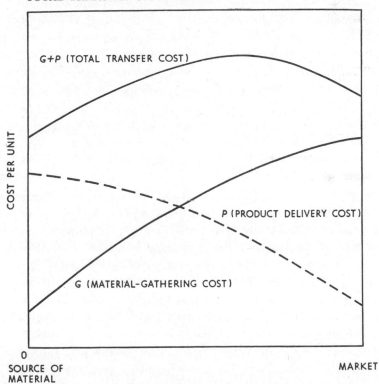

In those industries where the cost of gathering raw materials and distributing the finished product is an important part of total costs, transportation is a significant locational factor. In order to isolate the significance of the transfer factor, it is necessary to neglect processing costs, the location of competitors, and personal factors. This is the usual analytical technique of relegating to *ceteris paribus* certain variables which are of importance but which must be held constant while the effect of another variable is studied. Also, it is a useful simplification to assume that a plant uses only one raw material and turns out only one product.

The objective of the firm in locating a new plant, under the assumption described, is to minimize the combined material-gathering and product-distribution cost per unit. Usually, this will call for a location either at the source of the material or at the market for the finished good. The reason for this can be seen most easily by referring to Exhibit 1 (p. 451). Line G shows the transportation cost for the raw material at different locations between the material source and the market. This "material-gathering cost" is based on the rates applicable to the amount of the material which must be used to produce one unit of the finished product. It is lowest, of course, at the material source. It rises for locations more distant from this source, reaching a maximum at the most distant point—namely, at the market for the finished product. Line P is similar in nature, pertaining to the cost of transporting one unit of the finished product to market from various locations which might be selected for the plant. This cost would, of course, be lowest if the plant were located at the market and highest if it were at the raw-material source. Line $G + P$ is the sum of the two types of transfer costs, and thus represents the combined material and finished product transfer cost per unit of sales.[3]

As Exhibit 1 is drawn, the total transfer cost would be lowest at the source of the material; consequently, this would be the best location for a plant. Curves G and P are both drawn concave-downward, since the cost per mile of freight movement usually decreases as the length of the haul increases. The total transfer cost curve usually takes on a similar shape, with the lowest point being found either at the market or at the material source. Close inspection of Exhibit 1, and some reflection, help to disclose the factors which make for economical location at one place or the other.

The height of curve $G + P$ at the source of the material is determined in part by the cost of bringing enough of the (one) raw material to the plant to produce a unit of output, since the G curve intersects the left-hand vertical axis above the zero cost level. Even if the plant is theoretically "at" the source of the material, the assembly of material

---

[3]This chart is adapted from Edgar M. Hoover, *The Location of Economic Activity* (New York: McGraw-Hill Book Co., Inc., 1948), p. 30.

will require some transport cost. For example, a Portland cement mill located right next to a limestone quarry must incur transportation expense in loading the limestone onto a conveyor belt and bringing it into the plant on the belt. A paper mill, while it may be situated right in the forest from which it secures its supply of logs, must incur considerable transportation expense in bringing the logs by truck or railroad to the plant site. Similarly, even if the plant were located at the market, some transfer cost would normally be involved in placing the product in the wholesale or retail outlets. The principal determinant of the best location is usually the relative rise of curves G and P over the range between material source and market. That is, if curve G rises more than curve P over this range (as it does in Exhibit 1), location at the material source is usually more economical; if curve P rose relatively more over this range (and if the curves started at the same height), location at the market would be more economical.

Suppose the material source and the market are 500 miles apart. It is clear that the amount of raw material per unit of product is an important determinant of the relative rise in the two curves over the 500-mile distance. If 10 pounds of material were needed to make one pound of finished product, the material transfer cost curve would go up much more than the product transfer cost curve. That is, the cost of transporting 10 pounds of material 500 miles would probably greatly exceed the cost of moving one pound of product that distance. The smelting of most ores, the ginning of cotton, the crushing of cane sugar, the production of fruit juices, and the canning of crab meat and salmon are examples of "weight-losing" processes where it would be uneconomical to locate near the market, since this would mean incurring heavy transportation expenses on substances which are wasted or burned up in processing. A dramatic example of extreme weight loss is found in the processing of gold-containing ore, where almost all of the weight is lost. This processing takes place, of course, right at the mines.

Market Orientation

In other cases, it would cost more to move the finished product a long distance than it costs to move the material(s) the same distance. This promotes location at the market. An example is the baking industry. Flour and other components can be transported quite cheaply to the city; but bread, pies, and cakes are more costly to transport. Also, the need for freshness reinforces the desirability of urban location. The farm machinery industry tends to locate in farming areas rather than near steel mills and other sources of components, because such bulky machinery is costly to transport compared with components. The same force has led to the establishment of regional automobile assembly plants, especially by General Motors and Ford. The form, perishability, and unit value of finished products have a great influence on freight rates, and hence on location. For example, the waste space necessarily involved in transporting tin cans and bottles fosters their production near the market rather than near sources of materials.

Products which use "ubiquitous" materials—those which are available nearly everywhere—tend to locate at the market. In terms of Exhibit 1 the principal raw-material source and the market may both be considered to be at the same place (the market), so that no other location need be considered. Such products as soft drinks, beer, and ice are manufactured in cities, since it would obviously be uneconomical to transport the water incorporated in these commodities very far. At the same time, such manufacturing is usually not carried on in the very heart of cities because the competition of other uses (clothing stores, drugstores, banks, etc.) makes rental costs in central areas excessive for businesses which do not sell directly to large numbers of consumers. Sulfuric acid, an extremely important industrial material, is produced near the market. The production process adds weight, and the expense of long-distance transportation of a corrosive substance is relatively high.

Location near the market is also promoted by the production of "style goods." The demand for such products as ladies' hats and dresses is so capricious that producers must be ready to alter the nature of their output on short notice. By locating in such cities as New York and Miami, the style goods producers are able to reduce inventory losses by keeping their fingers on the pulse of demand. The locational importance of this factor has been somewhat reduced by the utilization of high-speed air transportation for style goods.

Location at Both Ends

Where the principal raw material loses very little weight, or where the higher transportation rate on the finished product quite closely compensates for the smaller weight of the finished product, it may make little difference whether processing takes place near the raw-material source or near the market. In terms of Exhibit 1 the G and P curves would rise about the same distance, so that the $G + P$ curve would be at about the same level at the market and at the material source. An example is the oil-refining industry, which has processing facilities both near the oil fields and near the large cities. The utilization of a very large part of the crude oil for a great variety of products means that the processing is not greatly weight-losing; consequently, oil may be refined at the market. At the same time, the finished products are economically transportable (by pipe line, tank car, and tanker, for example), so that processing at the source is also feasible.

The slight weight-losing property of wheat when milled into flour is quite closely compensated for by the higher transportation rate for flour. Consequently, floor milling occurs both near the wheat fields and near the markets. Changes in the relative cost of transporting wheat and flour can quickly alter the relative desirability of milling near the material source or near the market.[4]

Milling-in-Transit Privilege

The tendency which has been noted for location to be most economical either at the source of the principal material or at the market is due to the downward concavity of curves G and P in Exhibit 1—that is, to the fact that freight rates usually increase less than proportionally with distance. While a location between the material source and the market would secure some of this advantage of rate "tapering" with distance for *both* the material and the product, it would not secure so great a *total* advantage in transfer cost as location at either end. To offset this tendency, the railroads frequently grant "transit" privileges, under which a through rate is paid on both the raw material (e.g., grain) and the finished product (e.g., flour). This is usually the rate applicable to the raw material. The through rate replaces the combination of rates which would otherwise be charged; that is, it neglects the fact that a stop is made for purposes of processing.

In terms of Exhibit 1 the transit privileges would cause the total transfer cost line $(G + P)$ to be horizontal over the entire range. As a consequence, any location between the source of the material and the market would be equally feasible from a transportation point of view. It should, however, be noted that from a *social* point of view the transit privilege is not desirable, in that more resources must be de-

---

[4] D. Philip Locklin, *Economics of Transportation* (Chicago: Richard D. Irwin, Inc., 1954), p. 50, points out that the relationship between transportation rates on wheat and flour has at times determined whether flour to be consumed in Europe should be milled in the United States or abroad. Shipping rates for wheat and flour on the Great Lakes greatly affect the desirability of milling flour for the eastern markets in the Midwest or in the East.

voted to transportation to the extent that location is artificially influenced by this sort of rate. That is, if the concavity of the G and P curves is consistent with the actual cost savings due to long hauls, the transit privilege by causing the $G + P$ line to be horizontal, distorts "natural" patterns of location. It would also tend to hold down land values at the material source and at the market, and to increase land values at intermediate points.

Transit privileges apply to a large number of commodities and to quite dissimilar forms of "processing." Shippers of livestock may use the privilege to rest their stock and to test the possibilities of local sale. Soybeans and cottonseed may be converted into oil and meal under this rate system. Lumber products may be milled, iron and steel stopped for fabrication of certain kinds, and agricultural products stopped for storage under the transit privilege.

Multiple Sources of Materials

Frequently, a manufacturing process uses two or more materials in large quantities. When both are weight-losing in the process, the optimal location may be between the principal sources of these materials. If one of the materials—e.g., fuel—is more weight-losing than the other, this material will tend to exert more influence on the minimum transfer cost locaton. At the same time, the attraction of the market may also be significant.

The steel industry provides an interesting example of this situation. It is also an extremely important example because of the attraction of steel itself to a great variety of steel-using manufacturing activities.[5] Steel plants are usually located between deposits of coking coal and iron ore. Much the greater influence has been exerted by coal, in part because of the low-cost water transportation available on the Great Lakes for ore from the Lake Superior region and on the eastern seaboard for imported ore. The market exerts perhaps an even greater influence than fuel, especially since cities are the main source of the scrap used in steelmaking. That is, the best markets are also important sources of a material. Economies recently introduced in the use of coal in blast furnaces have somewhat diminished the attraction of fuel as a locational

---

[5]According to Richardson Wood, "Where to Put Your Plant," *Fortune,* July, 1956, p. 101, the existence of the steel belt stretching from Buffalo and Pittsburgh to Detroit and Chicago is the main reason why 70 per cent of the industrial labor force of the country is found in less than 10 per cent of the nation's territory.

factor for steel mills and have increased the relative locational pull of the markets.[6]

Processing Costs

In many industries, transportation is not highly significant, constituting but a small part of the total cost of putting the product into the hands of the consumer. This may lead to the establishment of a relatively small number of large plants designed to serve national or even international markets. Examples of such commodities are typewriters, alarm clocks and watches, razor blades, and bobby pins. For such goods the location which minimizes processing costs is apt to be optimal. These consist of such expenses as wages and salaries, interest on short-term funds, taxes, utility charges, and the f.o.b. cost of materials and fuel.[7]

If labor were perfectly mobile between different geographical areas, regional differences in wage and salary rates would not be an important factor in plant location.[8] Under this assumption, workers would move until no further advantage in terms of real wages could be secured. (If this is to be strictly true, real wages must be considered to include as positive or negative items such factors as climate, cultural advantages and disadvantages, traffic congestion, and recreational opportunities.) In the real world, however, labor is slow to move in adequate numbers. This is a basic reason for the "farm problem" and for the low earnings of many families in the South and Southwest, especially outside the principal cities.

The existence of regional differences in the wages of potentially equally productive workers may exert a powerful locational pull in industries where labor costs are a large part of total processing cost. Many textile and woolen mills have moved to the South and to Puerto Rico to take advantage of lower wage rates. The shoe industry has also shown a tendency to establish plants in small communities in the South, especially to utilize female labor. Frequently, firms which move to low-wage areas to take advantage of this cost saving are careful to conceal the fact, in view of the rather general feeling that there is something reprehensible in this sort of action. Actually, the only way in which low-

---

[6]Greenhut, *op. cit.*, p. 117.

[7]The f.o.b. cost of materials and fuel, rather than the delivered price, is considered a processing cost, since the transportation cost was treated as a transfer expense in the previous discussion.

[8]"Perfect mobility" does not necessitate a readiness of *every* worker to move. It implies only such readiness on the part of a sufficient number of laborers to equate wage rates for a given type of work at different places.

wage areas can improve their economic lot rapidly is through the in-movement of capital or the out-migration of labor. Each plant which is located to take advantage of cheap labor helps to raise the real income of workers in that area.

In addition to the wage rate for workers of a given ability level, prospective employers give consideration to turnover, dependability, existence or absence of unions, and local labor laws. Federal minimum-wage legislation, which receives its principal support from labor unions and from congressmen in the high-wage areas, exerts some locational influence in that it tends to reduce the attraction of surplus-labor areas to new industry. That is, the legislated minimum wage may prevent a regional or local oversupply of labor in relation to employment opportunities from exerting a normal locational attraction to new enterprise. Racial segregation tends to have a similar effect. However, it is common in the South to use white and nonwhite workers in the same plant so long as different jobs are performed. In some cases the jobs are identical, but white and colored persons work at different tables in the same room.

Land Rent

The purchase price which must be paid by a firm for the land on which it erects a plant—or alternatively, the rent which must be paid on a long-term lease for the use of land—may be an important locational factor. For convenience, we shall speak of the rent on land, since this keeps the cost on an annual or monthly basis comparable to wage and interest payments.

Land rent, like the return from any factor of production, arises from its value productivity. This productivity stems from the fertility of the soil in agricultural uses, from the minerals which it may contain, and from its location, especially with respect to markets. The last-named factor is of principal importance in location theory.

To the extent that there is active competition for land, and to the extent that landowners are well informed and rational, the rent on better sites will be higher than on poorer ones. Theoretically, the rental value of any piece of land will be determined by the best use of the land from the viewpoint of value productivity. Often, it is to the advantage of the landowner temporarily to hold his land out of use, rather than committing it to a long-term use, if prospects are good for an increase in its value.

A German economist, Johann Heinrich von Thünen,[9] was the first to describe the pattern of land use and rents which would tend to evolve from the unhampered workings of the price system. He considered a large town in the middle of a large plain, where the land was everywhere of equal fertility. The plain was assumed to be isolated from other places of economic activity by a wilderness. The town was considered to supply the farmers with manufactured items in exchange for raw materials and food.

Von Thünen concluded that the rent of land would decline with its distance from the town. Within a circle nearest the town, such commodities as green vegetables and milk would be produced. Intensive cultivation of forest lands for fuel and building materials would take place in the next circle. Such activities as grain and cattle raising would occur in the outer circles. In the most remote zone the most extensive land use—hunting—would take place. The basic principle is that different uses of the land vary in their ability to bear rental costs relative to transportation costs. Such items as milk and vegetables are perishable and are transported to market frequently. They are better able to stand high yearly rental costs than the high yearly transportation costs which would be associated with more distant hauls to market. Grains, on the other hand, are transported to market less frequently and in larger lots, so they can better bear high transfer costs than high land rents. The aim of each user of land would be to minimize the sum of land rental and transportation charges per time period.

Although based on highly abstract assumptions, the von Thünen theory discloses factors which are of importance both for agricultural and for industrial location. If fertility, land contours, and other natural features are fairly uniform, rent per unit of land tends to decline with distance from the market. Since this decline is due basically to the cost of transportation from plant or farm to the market, any change in the structure of transportation charges tends to affect land rents. It was pointed out earlier that the milling-in-transit privilege tends to increase land rents at points more remote from the market and the material source by giving the same through rate from material source to market regardless of where processing actually takes place. A general increase in freight rates tends to increase rental values near the market and to decrease the value of the more remote sites.

---

[9] *Der Isolierte Staat in Beziehung auf Landwirtschaft und Nationalökonomie* (3d ed.; Berlin: Schumacher-Zarchlin, 1875).

Once the rental value of a piece of land is established, this value can be considered to have the economic function of excluding inferior uses of the land. An ice-cream plant, while properly located in the city, is forced by the high rent on downtown property to be situated less centrally. The owner of an orange grove in an area where housing developments are spreading rapidly will find it best to sell the grove to a real estate firm and to relocate his citrus business in an area more remote from the city. A jewelry store, on the other hand, whose sales heavily depend on the number of passers-by, may find it best to pay a high rent in order to secure a downtown location.

Demand Interdependence

A good deal of modern location theory is based primarily on considerations of demand rather than cost. That is, a primary locational objective may be the carving-out of a more or less exclusive sales territory by means of securing such proximity to a group of buyers as to be able to undersell competitors. Much of this theory is similar to that of oligopoly pricing, in which the probable reactions of rivals must be considered before a price change is made. That is, in selecting a location, it may be necessary first to determine where rivals will probably locate in response to your decision. It is probable that the theory of games has useful applications to this sort of locational problem.

Because of the large number of possibilities with respect to the nature of price competition, costliness of changing location, and assumptions which a firm may make as to rivals' reactions, it is necessary to specify clearly the set of assumptions on which any theory of locational interdependence is based. It is also a convenient simplification to consider the market to lie along a straight line rather than having a circular, hexagonal, or irregular shape, as it usually would have in reality. Despite this simplification (or rather *because* of this simplification), it is possible to see some interrelationships of real-world significance.

The following assumptions make possible the study of a simple model of locational interdependence:

1. The market is linear and bounded at both ends.
2. At each point, there can be only one delivered price. The total amount purchased at that point is sold by the firm with the lower delivered price. The lower the delivered price, the greater the physical volume of sales.
3. There are two rival firms, A and B, selling the same product.
4. Marginal costs are constant, so that the desirability of increasing sales is not limited by rising production costs.

5. Freight rates per unit per mile decline uniformly as the haul increases.
6. Sales are made on an f.o.b. mill basis, so that delivered price at any point is equal to the mill price plus freight.
7. Each plant can be moved to any point, without cost.

Exhibit 2 represents the linear market by the distance CD[10] If a mill is located at point A, the f.o.b. mill price is AM; delivered prices to the left and right of A are shown by the lines MP and MR, respectively. These price lines are drawn concave-downward, to reflect the tapering

Exhibit 2

OPTIMUM LOCATIONS—TWO-PLANT MONOPOLY

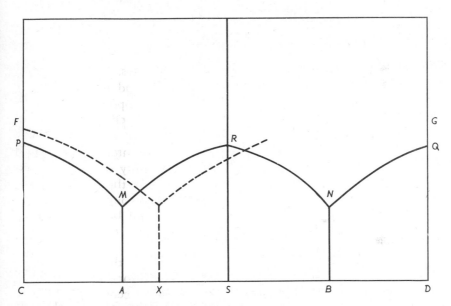

of rates with distance. If a mill is located at point B, the mill price is similarly represented by BN, and delivered prices by NR and NQ. Points F and G represent the highest price at which any sales can be made. It is clear that if demand curves are similar and downsloping at all points in the market, greater quantities will be sold near the mills than at a distance, but it will pay to make additional sales which can be secured, since the consumer is assumed to pay the freight.

If it is assumed that a single firm owns both plants—i.e., that the firm is a monopolist in the market—it is apparent that the locations A and B are optimal. These locations are at the quartiles, so that dis-

[10]Chart and analysis are adapted from Arthur Smithies, "Optimal Location in Spatial Competition," *Journal of Political Economy,* June, 1941, p. 426.

tances *CA, AS, SB,* and *BD* are all equal. Maximum sales could be secured by these locations, since lower average delivered prices can be charged than with any other locations. This can be seen by considering what the situation would be if plant A were closer to *S* than is now shown. Suppose it were located at point *X.* Plant A could then undersell plant B in the territory just to the right of *S* (as indicated by the dotted price line), but this would not help the firm, since it owns both plants. To the left of *A,* plant A would sell less than before, because delivered prices (as shown by the dotted line) would be higher. While the same amount as before could be sold between *A* and *X,* the decreased sales to the left of *A* would cause a diminution in total sales. The firm would, consequently, be better off with its plants at the quartiles.

Competition in Location

If the two plants are owned by separate companies, and if each firm believes that the other will match both its price and its location, the quartiles will again be the equilibrium location. Suppose that plant A considers a move to the center of the market in an effort to control a greater territory. Under this assumption the locator would know immediately that plant B would also move to the center. If the moves were made, both firms would then still control only half the market (as before) but would have diminished sales, since the long hauls toward *C* and *D* would reduce the quantities which buyers would purchase. The best thing for both plants to do would be to stay at the quartile locations, since they would anticipate poor results from any movement toward the center.

Under altered assumptions as to rivals' reactions the quartiles will no longer be the likely locations. If each competitor believes he can increase his sales territory by moving closer to the center, because his rival will meet price competition but will not change location, both will locate closer than the quartiles to the center. Plant A, for example, may first move from *A* to *X.* This will cause plant A to take sales away from plant B, which will move a comparable distance toward *S,* or even farther. (That is, the belief that plant B would "stay put" turns out to be erroneous.) Plant A will then locate symmetrically, or go even closer to the center. Where the move toward the center will stop depends on how quickly the competitors revise their original expectation of locational independence as they notice declining sales brought on by the rival's movements. Once they have moved toward S, locating at equal distances on either side, they will not retreat to the quartiles, since each would fear that the other would not also move away from the center. The wisest thing for the firms to do would be to come to a cartel-like agreement to move back to the quartiles. In this case a monopolistic agreement as to location (but not as to mill price) would be socially beneficial.

Location along a Highway

Those great modern institutions—the automobile and the highway— create numerous interesting locational problems. In this case the buyers transport themselves to the goods offered by the gift shop, restaurant, filling station, or other roadside facility. The most important consideration is locating and advertising in such a way as to stop a sufficient number of cars. Location at or near the intersection of highways may be advantageous not only because of the greater number of cars passing such a point but also because of the lower speeds which the intersection imposes on drivers.

Gift shops which also sell candy, soft drinks, and other items of interest to motorists often locate along a long stretch of highway well away from all other structures. This permits the purchase or lease of a substantial plot of land with ample parking space, cheaply. At the same time, a large number of passing cars carry potential customers. Where the highway is divided, or where it is a heavily traveled two-lane road, most of the cars will stop only on the right-hand side of the road. A gift shop located along a barren stretch of road will usually advertise heavily for many miles in order to build up demand—which may be the result of pressure from children who have, unfortunately, learned to read. In this situation the optimal strategy for a competitor is to locate on the same side of the road but at a point which will be reached a little sooner by the traffic stream. This permits the invader to take over part of the demand which the other firm's advertising has built up. Adoption of a quite similar name for the shop (Jones's Gift Shop versus Jane's Gift Shoppe) and the handling of similar commodities are also useful. If the first firm then adds a shop on the other side of the highway some miles away, the rival firm can again set up a shop near to it, but reached sooner by the stream of traffic. While the first firm might retaliate by erecting a third facility in front of its rival, this may not be economically feasible, since aggregate capacity could easily become too large for the market. Relocation of an existing shop is likely to be costly, so a situation of being outflanked by a rival is apt to be a serious one.[11]

Agglomeration of Sellers in Informed Markets

Where consumers are poorly informed regarding the relative quality of different goods, there is a strong tendency for sellers to hold back the information which would facilitate rational comparison.[12] Instead, advertisements are confined to generalities, meaningless statements about allegedly useful ingredients with specially coined names, and paid endorsements by famous people who may or may not actually like the product. Similarly, sellers may purposely locate their facilities at a distance from one another in order to decrease the possibility of rational comparison. For example, life insurance companies do not normally locate in the same building with the purpose of fostering easy comparison of policies by potential customers.

On the other hand, sellers who regularly deal with well-informed buyers have a tendency to locate close together, in order to facilitate a comparison of their wares. The seller who chooses to remain outside the wholesale district may find that large buyers will not bother to go out of their way to inspect his goods. The huge Merchandise Mart in Chicago dramatically illustrates the strong tendency of wholesalers to locate very close to one another, in order to facilitate the shopping of the experts.

Summary

Plant location, like most other actions by the firm, can best be understood as an attempt to maximize profits; however, nonpecuniary factors often play an important part, especially for small companies; and for companies in strong market positions, their continued existence is not contingent on profit-maximizing action. In order to maximize profits, the firm seeks to locate a new plant where the best relationship between demand and cost seems likely to exist over a sub-

---

[11]This suggests the roguish possibility of having a mobile gift shop built into a large trailer so that moving the shop would be cheap. It would also be useful if roadsigns were made as readily movable as possible. The whole project involves the further complication of making flexible arrangements with landowners on whose property the trailer and signs would rest.

[12]This is well described by Tibor Scitovsky, *Welfare and Competition* (Chicago: Richard D. Irwin, Inc., 1951), p. 402.

stantial period of time. Areas in which population is expanding rapidly are especially attractive from the demand side to businesses which are "market-oriented" because of high transportation cost on a unit of finished product or because close and frequent contact between buyers and sellers is a stimulant to demand. However, a small market where the firm has a considerable degree of monopoly power may be preferable to a large market where there are many close rivals.

Many firms sell in regional, national, and even international markets, and this may make a low-production-cost location the main consideration, although delivery costs on end items will have some weight. Where the product uses a great deal of raw material in weight and/or volume per unit of finished product, location near the source of the principal raw material is likely to be mandatory.

In some industries the market and the raw-material source may exert an approximately equal pull, so that some facilities will be found at each place. The oil-refining industry is an example, with refineries being placed both near the oil fields and near the large cities. A plant which turns out a number of different products may find it best to locate at a place which is optimal for none of its products but a good compromise for the operation as a whole.

While market or material attraction is often decisive, a great many other factors are important and may dominate particular locational choices. Labor costs and attitudes, availability and cost of borrowed capital, land costs, waste disposal facilities, availability of water for cooling and other uses, adequacy of fire and police protection, educational facilities, community attitudes, and climate may be vital.

Development commissions tend to stress cost savings and tax advantages in their efforts to attract industry. The businessman needs to be careful to see whether low taxes are accompanied by a low level of state and municipal expenditures on such items as fire and police protection and education. Also, commissions tend to neglect interdependence on the demand side of the picture. The process of plant location is often one aspect of price practice and sales policy, and thereby is part of the over-all competitive philosophy of the firm.

CASE 10–1:   REED, WAITE, AND GENTZLER

The firm of Reed, Waite, and Gentzler had for many years been engaged in the production and distribution of a line of work clothes sold under the brand name "RWG." The line consisted primarily of denim overalls and jackets, denim trousers (more popularly known as "blue jeans"), cotton twill trousers and shirts, and plain cotton trousers and shirts. A line of work hosiery was also included. These products were sold nationally, and the line was well known and popular. They were sold by department stores, chains, and specialty shops, and in smaller towns and villages were found in the "dry goods" stores.

The company operated three plants to supply its market. The shirt factory was located in a city of approximately 80,000 population in New Hampshire. The trouser factory was located in a suburb of Philadelphia, Pennsylvania. This factory produced trousers, overalls, and jackets. The hosiery mill was located in central Pennsylvania in a community of about 110,000 population. The executive and sales offices of the firm were located in New York City. Sales officers were also maintained in Chicago and Los Angeles. The location of headquarters in New York City was dictated by the long-established custom in the trade of buyers converging upon New York. There had been some modification of this practice since 1947; for this reason, sales offices had been opened in both Chicago and Los Angeles.

Like practically all industries in the postwar period, the textile industry had expanded to meet both accumulated demand and new demand resulting from population increases. It appeared, however, that the industry as a whole suffered from chronic excess capacity, which was reflected in keen price competition. A large part of the industry was affected by frequent style changes which, at the manufactured clothing level, sometimes resulted in drastic price cutting. Firms whose products were sensitive to these factors found it essential to maintain locations where such changes in demand could be most quickly perceived. The so-called "work clothes," while not subject to such frequent style changes, were nevertheless highly competitive. There were several large firms competing with Reed, Waite, and Gentzler, as well as a number of smaller firms serving regional and local markets.

In addition to the production of RWG-brand clothes, the company produced a number of private brands under contract with department stores and chains. The capacity of the company's plants was, therefore, geared to a demand consisting of RWG products plus private brands produced under contract. Placing of orders for private brands by purchasers was usually handled by competitive bidding. Securing such contracts was almost entirely a problem of competitive costs. Reed, Waite, and Gentzler experienced no more than the usual problems associated with the sales estimates of its own brands of clothing. Production of RWG clothing was planned according to sales estimates plus inventory control, and the balance of capacity was filled to the greatest possible extent by production of private brands. Certain items of work clothing

—such as blue jeans, blue cotton shirts, olive-drab twill trousers, and olive-drab cotton and twill shirts—were considered staples. These items could be produced for inventory when there was stability in the market for finished goods. Materials and labor were the two largest components of production. Instability in the finished goods market, however, seriously complicated the inventory problem.

Until 1950, Reed, Waite, and Gentzler had been fairly successful in obtaining sufficient contracts for private brands to keep the trouser factory near Philadelphia operating at or near rated capacity. Early in 1950, there was some noticeable idle capacity which had caused a reduction in the labor force. The outbreak of the Korean War in June of that year had resulted in the procurement of some military contracts which kept the plant occupied until April of 1951. Again, idle capacity began to appear. A similar situation existed among competitors of the company. This condition was reflected in keener competition for bids on private-brand production. Reed, Waite, and Gentzler were unsuccessful bidders on several contracts which they had obtained on many occasions in the past. The company reduced its bids on future contracts but still lost several to its competitors. On the latest contracts which had gone to competitors, the firm felt that it had submitted the lowest possible quotations consistent with its costs of operations. The loss of these contracts was also causing the unit costs of its own brands to rise to such an extent that competition was jeopardizing the market for RWG clothing.

An investigation of the problem was undertaken, and the following facts were revealed:

Labor Costs. It was easily and quickly determined that the labor costs of Reed, Waite, and Gentzler were higher than the costs of several of its larger competitors. Philadelphia had long been known as a "needle trades" city. During the time that a large part of the total labor force of the area had been engaged in the needle trades, the level of wages for the area as a whole had been strongly influenced by wages in the trade. While the supply of labor was adequate, there was little demand on the part of other industries to put upward pressure upon wage rates. The clothing industry had long been unionized except for a number of very small firms, so that the wage structure for the community as a whole had remained fairly stable, although it had tended upward. With the growth of "hard goods" industries in the Philadelphia area, however, the needle trades workers had become a proportionally smaller part of the labor supply, and their influence upon the wage structure had diminished accordingly. The growth of the area as an industrial center during and following World War II had diminished the influence of the trade even further. It was now quite apparent that the rise in wages of textile workers was influenced by the labor demands of other industries rather than exerting an influence upon them. To some extent the pressure of textile workers' unions was an effort to maintain their wage level consistent with that of the area. In the post-war period, growth of new industries and expansion of older ones had placed heavy demands upon the labor supply, in spite of a large population increase in the area.

The same situation existed in other textile areas of the Northeast. This was not true in all areas, however. In some isolated New England textile areas, this condition had not developed, so that some textile mills were able to enjoy a wage advantage due to the local situation. Of greater effect, however, were the differentials in wages within the clothing industry itself. During the decade of the thirties, there had begun a migration of the textile and clothing industry to the southern part of eastern United States. Some of the firms which had relocated in the Carolinas, Georgia, Tennessee, and Alabama were experiencing lower wage scales than plants of the same firms in the north. To some extent, this was because many of the workers in southern plants were not organized by labor unions, and the effects of local labor-supply situations permitted lower wages. The union had at the present time undertaken the organization of southern workers; but even where some workers were organized, there were still wage differentials as compared with the North.

Productivity. Of equal, if not greater, importance was the differential in productivity between southern and northern mills. While the differentials varied between plants and regions, it was clear that productivity was greater, on the average, in southern than in northern plants. Some of this greater productivity could be traced to more modern plants and equipment, but there were also indications that some was due to the workers themselves. In the North, productivity had actually declined with the growth of more restrictive practices negotiated by collective bargaining.

Materials. There appeared to be little differential in material costs between the two regions. In some cases of individual bargaining between clothing manufacturers and individual mills, there was some shading of prices, but the general practice of price quotations on wide regional bases tended to prevail. There was, however, one notable exception on the Pacific Coast. This area was accessible to Japanese mills, and many kinds of cotton finished goods could be obtained more cheaply

than in the eastern United States, although there was some tariff protection.

Markets. Analysis of sales of Reed, Waite, and Gentzler on a regional basis indicated that there had been a considerable shift in the
past twenty-five years. For many years the firm had marketed the
greater share of its output in the East, the Northeast, and the Midwest,
and since 1947 had moved to the Pacific Coast. The rapid growth of
chain stores in smaller cities and towns in rural areas had enabled the
company to grow into a national market. With the growth in the production of private brands the output of the firm was further diffused.
The chief markets at present were the Atlantic seaboard, the upper
Midwest and the Mississippi Valley, and the Pacific Coast. The company had always sold its merchandise f.o.b. factory. This practice should
perhaps be examined, since transportation to the Pacific Coast was an
important factor on RWG brands. On private brands, transportation
had become more important with the population shift to the Pacific
area.

Following this investigation, the company considered the relocation
of the trouser factory from Philadelphia to a point which would improve the company's competitive position. Three locations—designated
as cities A, B, and C—were suitable as possible choices. Location A
was a city of about 55,000 population in western Tennessee. This city
was provided with adequate rail and highway transportation, and was
within a radius of 200 miles of several textile mills producing the
kinds of finished cotton goods used by the trouser factory. Currently,
there was in this city a firm producing inexpensive women's dresses.
There were also several small firms assembling light electrical goods,
and a soap factory. The nearest city of comparable size was 83 miles
distant. Surrounding city A was an agricultural area of near-marginal
productivity. The city streets, water supply, and similar services were
considered adequate for the needs of the immediate future. There was
no indication that the city would experience any considerable growth
within the next 10 to 20 years. Land was available both within the
city and just outside the city limits. The trouser factory in Philadelphia
currently employed about 450 persons. It was believed that this number
of workers could be recruited from the present population of city A
without serious effect upon the existing labor supply.

Location B was in northeastern Mississippi in a city of approximately
18,000 in an area served by the Tennessee Valley Authority. At present, there was a small hosiery mill located there, as well as a meat-
packing firm, a mirror factory, a lumber mill, a small electronics plant,

and two canneries. City B was located on the main line of the Illinois Central Railroad and was served by two arterial highways. This city, in contrast to the others, had been actively engaged in a program of attracting industry, and was prepared to offer a number of concessions as to land and taxes. In three instances the city had bonded itself to erect the buildings, and it had leased the buildings to the firms currently occupying them. Upon learning of the interest of Reed, Waite, and Gentzler, similar approaches had been made. City B, however, had grown rapidly within the past 10 years. Its population had increased almost 4,000 within that period, and there were indications that growth would continue, but perhaps at a less rapid rate. About 22 miles distant was another city of 12,000 population; and Memphis, Tennessee, was 125 miles away. Jackson, the capital of Mississippi, was at a distance of 92 miles. An extensive program of street paving, sewer construction, and school building had been projected, but only the early stages had been completed. The area immediately surrounding the city was agricultural, and there appeared to be noticeable migration from this area into City B.

Exhibit 1

COMPARISON OF ACTUAL AND ESTIMATED COSTS
OF DENIM TROUSERS
(Per Dozen)

Item	Philadelphia	City A	City B	City C
Materials	$ 3.13	$ 3.14	$3.13	$ 3.11
Labor	3.21	1.53	1.49	2.04
Waste	0.59	0.61	0.60	0.60
Factory overhead*	4.08	2.97	2.27†	2.74
Indirect labor	2.01	1.62	1.65	1.81
Administration expense	0.40	0.41	0.41	0.41
Total Cost	$13.42	$10.28	$9.55	$10.71

*Includes amortization of new plant; does not include book value of Philadelphia plant.
†City B proposed certain tax and land concessions, which are taken into account.

Location C was in Georgia, about 15 miles from Atlanta. City C was also well located as to rail and highway transportation. Since the end of World War II, however, the countryside between city C and Atlanta had developed to such an extent that highway travel between the two areas was regulated by traffic lights and highway patrols. Nearer Atlanta were large housing developments. Toward city C, there were both housing and industry. The population of city C was approximately 24,000 and was still increasing. To relieve the traffic congestion, a new superhighway had been planned and approved for construction between city C and Atlanta. A number of firms had located their plants in city C in the past 10 years, and several more were currently interested. Beyond city C the area was agricultural. There was evidence of union activity in city C, and many firms in Atlanta and city C were now organized. Where comparisons could be made, there still appeared to be lower unit costs in city C than in plants in the North performing similar operations with organized labor. There was little doubt that the facilities of city C would require improvement and expansion within the next five years.

Exhibit 1 shows costs of producing blue denim trousers at the Philadelphia factory as compared with costs at the three proposed locations. Costs in the proposed locations are estimates based upon surveys of the

Exhibit 2

AVERAGE RAILROAD FREIGHT RATES TO SELECTED CITIES
FROM PHILADELPHIA AND PROPOSED LOCATIONS
(Per Dozen)

Freight Costs to:	From Philadelphia	From City A	From City B	From City C
New York	$0.39	$1.01	$1.14	$0.39
Chicago	0.86	0.99	0.99	0.86
Los Angeles	1.52	1.31	1.49	1.52

areas. Exhibit 2 shows the railroad transportation cost from the various points per dozen pairs of blue denim trousers. While these costs are not paid by Reed, Waite, and Gentzler, they are part of the delivered cost to the purchaser and thus are a competitive element of delivered price.

The market for Reed, Waite, and Gentzler is divided approximately as follows: 40 per cent is sold in the Atlantic seaboard division, 50 per cent in the Midwest and the Mississippi Valley, and 10 per cent in the Far West and Pacific Coast region.

QUESTIONS

1. Which location would you recommend? Why?
2. Would your answer be the same for both the short and the long run? Explain.
3. Is the lowest cost location always the best? Elaborate.

4. How would industry-wide bargaining affect the location of firms like Reed, Waite, and Gentzler?

5. What considerations other than those explicitly taken up in the text may influence the choice of a new location for the trouser factory?

CASE 10–2: JAYE AND COMPTON, INC.

The plant of Jaye and Compton was engaged in the printing business. For a number of years, it had confined the major part of its activities to the printing of several national magazines, mail-order catalogues, and city telephone directories. In addition, it filled large color-printing orders on a job basis. Only in certain cases did the company accept any orders for quantities under 10,000 copies.

The firm of Jaye and Compton was located in Chicago; and from the time the partnership was formed until 1937, the company had operated in leased quarters in an industrial building. In that year the partners decided that the rental on the space had reached such proportions that it would be more economical to occupy its own plant. The firm then moved to a building which had been erected in 1928 for a machine-tool company. It was four stories high and had been constructed so that all floors, including the basement, would support heavy equipment. It was equipped with two freight elevators and had its own steam power plant. The machine-tool company had failed during the depression, and the building had been unoccupied for three years prior to its purchase by Jaye and Compton. The purchase price was considerably less than its original cost, and in 1937 the building could not be duplicated at the price paid for it. Considerable renovation had been necessary, and some new equipment was acquired, but it was believed that the building would be adequate for several decades. At the same time, the company had acquired five vacant lots across the street from this building. Upon removal to these quarters the partnership was incorporated.

The present building, which occupied one city block, was fully occupied by the firm in 1953. The vacant lots, which for many years had been used as parking space for employees, were now occupied by three buildings. The company had grown to the point where it now had 4,700 employees, 3,450 of whom were working in the shops on two shifts. One of the buildings constructed on the vacant lots was used entirely for storage, which another had been constructed in 1941 as an employee cafeteria. In addition, two other buildings several blocks away had been leased for storage of paper and supplies, which were transferred by truck to the main building as needed. Four blocks from the main building the company was presently leasing, on an annual basis, a large vacant lot which had been improved for employee parking.

In the main plant itself, printing operations were carried on in the basement and on the first three floors. The top floor was used for office space. Because of lack of space on any one floor, it had not yet been possible to devise a system where any one job could be initiated and completed on the same floor. In some cases a given job would require operations on all floors. This necessitated a great deal of handling and movement from one floor to another, much of which had to be done in small lots because of the narrow space between machines. Very little power handling equipment could be used because of the crowded conditions.

Since 1947, business had been increasing, and it was anticipated that there would be further increases. Several of the national magazines which the company had printed for many years were increasing in both size of issue and quantity, which further complicated the problems of the already crowded scheduling department. The actual and prospective increases in business volume were also a strain on the apprentice-training program which the company felt it was forced to expand in order to provide adequate trained personnel. After a survey of these operational difficulties, the conclusion was reached that additional space or an entirely new plant would be necessary.

A firm of industrial engineers was retained to make recommendations for a solution. The first step was an investigation of additional space and retention of the present quarters. This line of inquiry was not very promising. There was no space available within twenty blocks of the present plant. The space which was available could be reached only by automobile and truck, and it would be necessary to travel streets which were currently overloaded with traffic. It was feared that additional space at such a distance would result in rising costs per job, a situation which was to be avoided, since it might affect bids on contract jobs. This avenue of investigation was quickly abandoned, and efforts were concentrated upon the location of an entirely new plant.

Quickly discarded was the possibility of moving out of the Chicago area entirely. This was considered, but the chief limitation was the procurement of trained personnel in a new location. A demand for approximately 3,500 printers, pressmen, typesetters, and color-press operators was one which it was felt that no one community could provide immediately. The nature of Jaye and Compton's business was not such as to permit a reduction of any size and a gradual building-up over the long run. There were some communities in which the supply of skilled workers was adequate, but they would have to be drawn away from present employment. This would probably lead to substantial increases in wages in the long run and high turnover in the short run.

A search was undertaken for a location in the Chicago area. The present plant was easily accessible by public transportation as well as private automobile. Employees of the company lived in all sections of Chicago and did not appear to be concentrated in any one particular area. A survey revealed that approximately one half of the workers used public transportation; the remainder used private cars or car pools. The company was completely unionized, except for white-collar workers, and labor problems had been negligible. The average period of service for skilled workers was fourteen years. In view of these findings, it was felt that the new location would have to be one of relatively easy access and one which would not materially increase travel time for a substantial majority of the workers.

The industrial engineering firm suggested two possible plant sites. One was located in a suburb northwest of Chicago, approximately seventeen miles from the present location, which was on the west side of Chicago about two miles west of the downtown business area. On this proposed location the company could erect a one-story plant, in which machinery could be assembled so as to minimize the amount of material handling. Conveyor belts and power handling equipment could be used. The storage section of the plant would be two or three stories and would also be suitable for power handling equipment. This section would be connected to the printing area by conveyor belts. The office portion would be four stories in height and would also house the cafeteria, lounges, and recreational space. There was adequate space for parking up to four thousand automobiles. The suburban railroad station was the equivalent of four city blocks distant. The community was primarily residential, although a number of light industries were located there. The larger share of the population of 31,000 was employed in the city of Chicago. One of the features of commuting was that Jaye and Compton employees would be riding on suburban trains at a time when the rush hour was in the opposite direction. This location would, however, entail a journey of approximately 1½ hours for employees living on the south side of Chicago. For employees living on the west side, it would increase their travel time by approximately 20 to 30 minutes. For employees living on the north side the increased travel time would average about 10 minutes.

The second location was within the city itself, on the far west side and slightly south of the main business section of Chicago, about seven miles distant. This location was much more accessible by public transportation, being served by both bus and train. The difference in travel time for employees, compared to the present location, would be negligible. The amount of land was limited, however. The printing operations would again be housed in a building of at least three stories, but the layout would be improved so as to reduce a substantial portion of the handling which occurred in the present plant. In order to provide adequate parking space, the storage facilities would be four stories in height; while the office building, with space for the cafeteria and recreational facilities, would be six stories high. This location would be more accessible for the negotiation of business, a great deal of which originated in the Chicago business area. There would also be easier access to railway transportation, since this site was adjacent to the main line of the Pennsylvania and Santa Fe railroads. The other site would be provided with a railway siding, but because it was on a railroad leading out of Chicago to the Northwest, there would be a delay of one day in delivery of freight cars to rail lines to the east and south of Chicago.

Exhibit 1

Item	Northwest Suburban Site	City of Chicago Site
Cost of new plant.............................	$20,400,000	$23,575,000
Property taxes—new plant (per year).............	961,000	1,315,000
Reduction in miscellaneous costs (per year)........	1,422,000	978,000
Estimated annual reduction in total payroll at current volume of business*.................	3,200,000	2,465,000
Estimated number of employees at current volume of business............................	4,100	4,275

*This figure includes not only the actual reduction in numbers of employees but also the increased productivity of remaining employees due primarily to new layout and use of additional equipment.

Exhibit 1 is a brief summary of the report of the industrial engineering firm. The net earnings of Jaye and Compton before federal income taxes for the year 1953 were $8,543,291.

The firm had ample resources to construct either of the proposed new plants without any external financing. It was estimated that the present plant could be sold for approximately $3.25 million.

The president of Jaye and Compton preferred the Chicago site for the new plant. He was quite concerned over employee reaction to the more distant location. Several of the directors, however, preferred the suburban location. They were of the opinion that the distance factor could be overcome to a large extent in the long run. Since it was a suburban community, the workers could be encouraged to move to the suburbs. Two directors even proposed that the company undertake the financing of the purchase of new homes for employees who had five or more years of service with the company. This would involve the commitment of about $10 million of company funds for an average period of approximately ten years. As an added inducement the interest rate could be set at about 1 per cent below the present mortgage-money market. The company at present had almost $20 million in securities, from which these funds could be taken if necessary. This commitment would not jeopardize the construction of a new plant from internal funds.

QUESTIONS

1. Which location would you recommend? Why?

2. Would you consider it profitable for the company to undertake financing of employee homes, as proposed by the two directors?

3. To what extent do transportation *costs* affect this proposed change of location?

4. Which considerations appear to be more important in this case—long run or short run?

5. Does a publishing firm usually locate near the source of its principal raw materials or near the market? Explain.

CASE 10–3:   OTIS ELEVATOR COMPANY

On Saturday, January 15, 1955, over two thousand employees of Otis' Yonkers plant and their wives, and a delegation of the principal municipal officials of the city of Yonkers, assembled in the Brandt Theater in response to an invitation sent to their homes, to hear Mr. Le Roy A. Petersen, president of the Otis Elevator Company, give the following address:

LADIES AND GENTLEMEN:

A little over a year ago, I had the privilege of talking simultaneously by long distance telephone to almost 2,000 Otis men and women who were gathered at 31 dinners in different cities throughout the United States to receive their service pins for anywhere from 25 to 55 years of service with the Otis Elevator Company.

The Yonkers Works dinner was attended by 427 employees, 239 of whom had from 25 to 30 years of service, 122 of whom had from 30 to 35 years of service and 66 of whom had service from 35 to 52 years.

To people such as these and to those who are in the process of establishing similar records, Otis is not just a place in which to work but an institution in which they have invested their lives. They have a sense of loyalty to the Company that must be matched by the Company's sense of loyalty to them.

I, therefore, feel obligated to share with you a knowledge of certain facts which have an important bearing upon your future welfare.

We have all had the privilege of working for a company which, throughout its long history, has had the enviable reputation of designing, manufacturing and installing the best elevators and escalators in all the world. This reputation is still intact, and it is the firm intention of every loyal Otis man and woman to continue to justify this reputation to the end of our working days.

Furthermore, throughout the greater part of our history we have sold not only the best elevator equipment—but the most—and, until relatively recently, have sold about as much as all of our numerous competitors combined. How numerous these competitors are is not generally recognized, and few people can name more than half a dozen elevator companies.

The fact of the matter is that, in 1946, we lost contracts for new elevators to 118 competitors and, eight years later in 1954, the number of competitors had more than doubled and had reached the startling number of 262.

The volume of elevator business available in any given year is dependent upon the number of multi-story buildings that are being built, and nothing that we or any other elevator company can do can increase the number of elevators required.

It is, therefore, apparent that, twice as many elevator contractors struggling to secure a limited volume of business, the competition for each individual contract has greatly increased.

These statements should not be interpreted as indicating that the Otis Elevator Company has ceased to be a profitable company or is on the verge of becoming an unprofitable one. One the contrary, it is anticipated that, since our income is derived from a variety of sources, including a substantial service business and extensive operations throughout the world, the annual report for 1954 will show an increase over the previous year in sales and earnings. In addition, it is believed that our backlog will assure a profitable level of operations in 1955.

However, the Yonkers Works is primarily engaged in the manufacture of equipment for new elevators for domestic use and has relatively little to do with service or foreign operations and its performance must be judged solely by the quality and cost of the products it makes.

At this point it is important that we stop and consider that what we have to sell is principally the labor of our employees and that there is nothing with which to pay the cost of labor and material except what we receive from our customers.

Our salesmen are your agents, selling your labor, and they cannot be expected to sell your labor at less than cost.

The Otis Elevator Company has prospered and has been a source of employment in Yonkers for more than a hundred years because it has continued to manufacture a high quality product at a cost sufficiently low to permit it to be sold with a fair profit at a competitive price.

Unless we can continue to do this, we will cease to be a prosperous company and will also cease to be a source of employment. It is, therefore, my duty and obligation as President of this Company to take such steps as may be necessary to maintain Otis quality and still reduce costs to the point where we can continue to secure the necessary volume at a profitable price.

[*The Cost Study.*]   Accordingly—aided in some instances by outside consulting engineers—an extensive study has been conducted as to how this necessary reduction in cost could best be accomplished. This study has covered all phases of our operations, including sales, engineering, specifying, manufacturing, and installation, and all types of cost and expense are being reduced to the maximum practical extent.

Of particular interest to you, however, is the result of the study relating to manufacture, and this study indicated that an annual saving in manufacturing costs of several million dollars could be secured by building a single plant to replace the Yonkers and Harrison plants, and that this plant should be located in the middle west near the geographical center of our elevator market.

Possible savings are attributable to a number of factors, including:

1. Reduced transportation costs
2. Elimination of duplicate managerial, accounting and stock record organizations
3. Simplified material handling
4. New and improved manufacturing methods
5. Consolidated departments
6. Fair and reasonable incentive standards

However, before deciding to embark upon such a project, involving as it would the discontinuance of the present means of livelihood of many Otis people, we concluded that careful consideration should be given to the possibility of securing a substantial part of these savings in our present plants, with the hope of preserving indefinitely an opportunity for employment for our present employees.

A further careful study has, therefore, been made which indicates that about *half* of the savings that are attributable to the new midwestern plant could be accomplished in our present plants, providing we secure the enthusiastic and understanding cooperation of our employees and the city authorities.

With the purpose of preserving as many as possible of your jobs with Otis in Yonkers and a local payroll amounting to about ten million dollars per year, we are willing and anxious to make every effort to continue the operation of the Yonkers Plant, providing we are able to accomplish, with a minimum of delay, the reduction in cost which we believe is reasonably obtainable in this location.

A definite decision to take such steps as are necessary to reduce costs substantially has already been made, and the only question remaining is which of the known methods will be chosen. If we are unable to bring about these reductions in cost in our present plants, we will have no choice but to transfer our manufacturing, as soon as possible, to a new midwestern plant—and not hesitate to do so if it becomes clearly necessary.

Whoever is in my position has an inescapable obligation to preserve our ability to manufacture and install high quality equipment which can be sold at a fair and reasonable profit. Only by so doing will we serve a useful purpose and furnish lasting employment to anyone.

[*The Cost-Reduction Program.*]   Kindly note that our plans for reduced cost are not based upon any change in our past policy of paying all who work for Otis at least as much as is paid by other reputable and comparable companies for similar jobs, both in the form of wages and salaries and in supplementary benefits. It is still our desire to keep the Yonkers Plant not only a place in which to work, but a *good* place in which to work.

Rather, our ability to secure reduced costs here and now is dependent upon our receiving your active cooperation in eliminating avoidable and unjustifiable expense and in reducing lost time and lost motion, in increasing the efficient use of existing equipment and in utilizing to the utmost the production capacity of such new equipment as we may be warranted in installing. We will welcome your suggestions.

In seeking to accomplish our objectives, we propose, of course, to work with and through the unions which you have selected as your bargaining agents and to solicit the active cooperation of their officials.

The great increase in the number of our competitors during the last 8 years has been made up almost entirely of those who buy virtually all of the component parts from other manufacturers. Many of these new competitors, therefore, have no Engineering Department, little or no fixed overhead of any kind and few, if any, supplementary benefits for their employees. Their prices are too low to support a permanent organization, and they operate on a hit and run basis— here today and gone tomorrow. Nevertheless, altogether they secure millions of dollars' worth of elevator contracts on a basis of low price, and we must keep our price within the limit of the preference we can get for Otis quality—or lose a larger and larger amount of the limited business available.

It will continue to be our policy to design all important parts of Otis equipment but, to an even greater extent than before, we must subject every component part to the question of make or buy. If, without loss of quality, we can buy a part from another reputable manufacturer for less than we can make it, we must buy rather than make, and those of you who are now engaged in making the parts which we can buy at less cost from others will have nothing left to do. The only defense against this reduction in our manufacturing volume is to keep the cost low enough so that we can afford to have you make it rather than buy it from someone else. The ultimate decision will hinge on where does it cost the least.

I trust that you will clearly understand that this is not an attempt to persuade you to do anything that you do not want to do or which you do not recognize as being clearly in your own interest.

It should be apparent that the Yonkers Works has, in effect, become a community enterprise. The Company, because of its earnest desire to retain its present organization and to continue to provide good jobs for its loyal employees, has indicated its willingness to forego some of the larger savings obtainable by other methods and to continue to operate the Yonkers Plant as long as it can afford to do so. It cannot afford to continue to operate it under present conditions—but is offering you an opportunity to help create the conditions under which we could afford to continue its operation.

We could, of course, have decided to go ahead immediately with the building of a new central plant, basing our decision solely upon the outcome of the study which clearly showed savings sufficient to justify the investment, the cost of transfer and the loss on existing plants.

We could, and some may say we should have done this without prior discussion with you. I trust that you feel, as I do, that, in fairness to you and to the City of Yonkers, this prior general discussion is desirable.

I also trust that you realize that we are trying to help you retain your jobs with Otis and that we hope that, together, we will be successful in doing so.

Next week, we will present to your union officials complete proposals outlining the conditions which we consider reasonable and essential for continued future operation in Yonkers.

We sincerely hope that these proposals will be recognized as consistent with the interests and welfare of our Yonkers employees and that agreement will be reached for their early adoption.

We are prepared to make substantial additional investment in the Yonkers Plant, if such investment appears to be clearly justified. We will do our best to further improve our methods. We will look to the city authorities for fair treatment on taxes and for a disposition to help in all other ways consistent with the welfare of the city as a whole.

The rest is up to you, and we hope that you will give the problem careful consideration.

According to press reports, there had been only scattered applause when Mr. Petersen had entered from the wings and walked to the mid-stage lectern in the big theater. Members of the audience sat through his talk quietly. There was no interruption of his speech, and no visible reaction to it. At its conclusion, his listeners filed silently from the theater.

The Company and the Industry

Origins. The Otis Elevator Company had not settled its main plant in Yonkers as a matter of deliberate choice. It was situated there because Elisha Graves Otis, a resourceful factory mechanic, lived there in 1853 when he had fashioned, from a wagon spring and a ratchet, a safety device to keep hoist platforms from falling in case their ropes snapped.

Elisha's sons, Charles and Norton, modified and improved their father's basic invention, and their elevator business grew. Hydraulic lifts replaced the steam machine, and a governor-operated safety device was developed to bring high-speed cars to a gradual stop in the event of an emergency. These developments, together with the electric motor powered elevator, changed the contour of the skyline of every metropolitan city in the land. Until now, downtown office buildings had been little more than private houses on a larger scale. Their commercial occupants, pressed for room for expansion, now found it possible to replace them with five- and six-story "elevator buildings." Hotels, whose guests found the upper floors to be the most desirable, being above the noise and dust of street traffic, pushed their buildings ever higher. These were years during which the Otis Elevator Company pioneered and developed the elevator business, and the company grew to a position of eminence in the industry.

Competition. In 1898, during the era of mergers, Otis consolidated with eight smaller concerns; and for a few years, it had a virtual monopoly on the elevator business. Its competition consisted, as Mr. Petersen had pointed out, of many small concerns, who bought their parts from others, and who were not in a position to offer technical advice, since they maintained no engineering staffs. As a result, Otis had been able to establish a reputation for quality that had been unchallenged for many years. This reputation for excellence often enabled Otis to command a higher price than its competitors—an advantage known in the trade simply as "preference." It also was a major factor in obtaining contracts for the prestige installations—the big, high-speed passenger installations such as, in their day, the Woolworth Building and the Flatiron Building. In a later era, within a period of three years, Otis installed its elevators in four successive "world's tallest" buildings which were completed in New York City: 40 Wall Street, 60 Wall Tower, the Chrysler Building, and the Empire State Building.

In 1926, Westinghouse, which had acquired the patents and engineering skills of Otis' largest competitors, entered the elevator business, and Otis met its first large-scale competition. From that time on, Otis and Westinghouse were usually the two principal contenders for any major installations. Until Westinghouse entered the field, price had been a secondary consideration in capturing the "monumental" installations. But with the total quantity of new installations becoming limited, price competition became a decisive factor, with all contenders cutting prices as far as they could.

The Market. Mr. Petersen had said in his address that there was nothing the company could do to increase the number of multistoried buildings being built in any one year. He could have gone further to say that the number had been declining, at least in this country. Otis had prospered in the era of skyscrapers and apartment hotels, but the post-World War II era had seen an exodus to the suburbs and a trend toward single-storied apartments. Its 1953 billings for new elevators and escalators were a quarter of a million dollars less than they had been in 1929, and were only about half of the unit volume. In the ensuing struggle for what business remained, Otis found its price preference to be disappearing through competitive attrition. It could no longer ignore the lower prices offered by its rivals.

Facilities and Operations

The Yonkers Works. The Yonkers Works were comprised of thirteen buildings, seven of which were major units, and some of which were six stories high. The plant covered about six square blocks of downtown Yonkers, and several city streets dissected the group. These buildings had been accumulating over the hundred years that Otis had been producing in Yonkers, with expedience dictating each expansion. While each addition had been well considered at the time it was undertaken, the total group had grown to be unwieldy, and some of the major units were quite antiquated.

Virtually all Otis installations were custom-designed, with only a few components which were standard parts, such as motors and controls. This "tailor-made" production set the job-shop nature of Otis' manufacturing operations. Scheduling and planning were extensive functions, and inventory controls were complex. A high percentage of production time was taken up by setup time, with relatively short production runs. There was a great deal of temporary storage of materials in process, and much in-plant transportation. Many components were both bulky and heavy.

Complicating the in-plant transportation problem were the multistoried buildings and the streets which separated them. The foundry was a unit in itself, for instance, and so was the machine shop. Motors were wound in one building, control panels assembled in another. All of the components had to be transported to still another building to be assembled, tested, and shipped.

Foreign Operations. While the domestic demand for elevators had been diminishing, this was not the case abroad, where construction was booming and ten-story buildings were popular. Foreign sales had boomed after World War II, thriving on the expansion of overseas industries and the rebuilding of bombed cities. The foreign share of Otis profits increased from 10 per cent in 1947 to 17 per cent in 1953 during a period when the company's gross profit margin on domestic sales was shrinking due to price competition at home.

Since the turn of the century the company had been buying established elevator concerns abroad; and by 1954, it owned a majority interest in sixteen subsidiaries with fourteen plants and 163 offices in fifty countries. These subsidiaries captured virtually all of the high-grade foreign business. Foreign operations were staffed entirely by nationals, with the home office confining itself to laying down policy and furnishing technical advice. Otis management believed that its greatest demand in the years to come would be from foreign markets. Demand was especially strong in South America and South Africa. In 1954, Otis had opened offices in Lima, Peru; in Nairobi, Kenya; and in Bombay, India.

Service Contracts. Sales of new installations were subject to the cyclical variations of the capital goods markets; and to offset these variations, Otis had been selling contracts for servicing and maintaining its installations. A "POG" (parts, oil, grease) contract usually was written at $2\frac{1}{2}$ per cent per year of the cost of the installation. A full-maintenance contract at about 5 per cent a year provided major parts replacements and around-the-clock service.

Service contracts and modernization work usually went to the producer, with Otis and Westinghouse generally servicing their own installations on the basis that they had better technical knowledge of their own elevators and could insure greater safety. It was estimated that in the course of its history, Otis had installed more than half of the 250,000 elevators in the United States, and about 70 per cent of the 3,800 escalators. Service contracts provided more than half of Otis profits and half of Otis employment during the years of the Great Depression. During 1954, Otis had service contracts covering more than a quarter of all the elevators and 30 per cent of all the escalators in the United States, and half of all its installations abroad. In the archives of its engineering department the company had a copy of the blueprints of every installation it had ever made.

The Local Situation. Yonkers, a city of 160,000, was immediately north of New York City and adjacent to it. It was a fifteen-minute ride on a public bus from the heart of Yonkers to the Bronx; it was a half-hour ride on the subway from Yonkers to Times Square; the New York Central offered commuters half-hour service from Yonkers to Manhattan. To the casual observer the city of Yonkers appeared to be an extension of New York City.

The residents of Yonkers, however, considered their city to be separate from and independent of Gotham. Some of them commuted to New York; but until recently, Yonkers had been fairly self-sufficient, supporting itself by its own industries. These had consisted of the

Alexander Smith Carpet Company, the Otis Elevator Company, and numerous smaller concerns.

The Smith Carpet Company had, however, just a few months before, closed its mill in Yonkers and moved to a new location in the South. Smith had at one time had 6,000 employees at Yonkers; but during the past few years, it had gradually reduced its Yonkers operation. At the time of its closing, it had 2,500 employees. The New York State Employment Service estimated that 1,250 of these would never be employed again because of disability or old age. The Smith plant closing had come abruptly, precipitated by the company's failure to reach an agreement with its union in the settlement of a strike.

Otis was not having any labor difficulties at the time that Mr. Petersen made his proposal. In June, 1954, the company had signed a two-year union contract which still had a year and half to run.

To the suggestion that New York City, with its innumerable opportunities for employment was within easy reach, the Yonkers residents replied that New York, with its eight million population, already had its share of unemployment. Besides, the Otis employees pointed out, while New York City might have opportunities for employment in the garment industry or the needle trades, these would be of little interest to the skilled electricians, machinists, and foundrymen of Otis. And as Mr. Petersen had emphasized, many of the Otis employees were veterans of many years of service.

Otis management made no supplementary statement or argument other than to present its proposal to the union representatives with the explanation that it was not subject to modification, and that the company was asking the employees to judge for themselves whether or not the proposal of the company to forgo some of the savings of a move to the Midwest in return for increased efficiency and reduced waste was fair, and whether or not it was what it purported to be— namely, a friendly offer to help them save their jobs.

The management of Otis, the employees of Otis, and the residents of the city of Yonkers were uniformly of the opinion that the loss of the Otis plant would result in a serious problem of unemployment for the Otis employees, and a loss of income to the city of Yonkers. The Otis payroll in Yonkers was approximately $10 million a year.

Specific Proposals

Proposals to the Union. The concrete proposals which the company made to its union officials specified that there would be no reduction in wage rates or salaries, nor any reduction of such fringe benefits as vacation, paid holidays, pensions, group insurance, hospitalization, and medical and surgical plans. The amendments which the company requested involved a revision of the wage incentive system to provide new, realistic standards and to eliminate many loose standards which the management felt had developed over the years; a concentrated effort to reduce accidents; and the right of the company to promote employees solely on the basis of ability, as determined by the judgment of management. The request for revision of the wage incentive system was considered by the Otis management to be by far the most important of the terms requested by the company.

The management also asked the support of the union in a co-operative program to reduce waste. Specific items requested included the elimination of the afternoon coffee wagon, stopping work before the recognized wash-up time, taking excessive time before the morning coffee break, lining up at the clock before the recognized quitting time, and a reduction of excessive and unwarranted absenteeism and tardiness.

Conservation of tools and equipment was also requested. The union was asked to help in the elimination of careless handling of small perishable tools and of machine tools, the use of which at high speed caused excessive wear and breakage; the elimination of improper setup and not following designated machining methods; and negligence in using company-provided measuring instruments, which included many expensive precision instruments.

Proposals to the City. The first of the two points which the Otis management wished to negotiate with the municipal officials of the city of Yonkers concerned the closing of portions of four streets which dissected the Yonkers Works. It was these streets which had multiplied the in-plant transportation problem at the Yonkers Works. Although the city had permitted Otis to bridge the streets at upper-story levels at several points, the management felt that it would improve the efficiency of its operations considerably if the city would close some of the streets entirely and sell the land to Otis, enabling it to build across these areas, and make its several plant buildings into a continuous connected unit.

The street-closing request set off some public debate. The Otis plant was centrally located in Yonkers, fronting on the north of the public square, and was within a block of the western edge of the central business district. A short block west of the plant, and separated from it by a main trunk line of the New York Central Railroad, was the Hudson

River. Of the streets in question, it was the closing of only one, Wells Avenue, which aroused opposition. Wells Avenue bisected the Yonkers Works from east to west, and carried some of the New Jersey-bound automobile traffic which went to the Yonkers Ferry, which was situated on the Hudson just west of the plant; and much of the incoming ferry traffic turned either north or south before coming to the Otis plant. These alternate routes would still be available if Wells Avenue were closed.

Debating the street closing, the Otis Employees Group stated: "Wells Avenue is not a major traffic artery. All traffic surveys indicate that it is a little-used street leading nowhere. Most of the 164,000 people living in Yonkers have never used these streets."

In an editorial on the subject, the *Yonkers Herald Statesman* disagreed:

We would prefer to have Otis remain as one of our largest industries, perhaps the largest, and to keep the Otis-Yonkers names synonymous all around the nation and the world. We do say flatly, however, that the City of Yonkers need not make its decision to close a major traffic artery under the whiplash of fear or threat.

We have come around to the conclusion that Otis will do what is best for Otis, regardless of what happens at the City Hall, and regardless of the concessions made by the organized employees. If the City of Yonkers closes all the streets that Otis wants closed, and if our busy business section accepts the major nuisance and traffic disorder that would result, there is no guarantee that Otis will remain in Yonkers for any length of time.

The second point of contention with the city of Yonkers had to do with real estate taxes. The management of Otis contended that the assessor of the city of Yonkers overvalued the Otis properties grossly, and did so as a routine practice. The management backed this statement by pointing out that every year for the past 30 years, Otis had been constrained to sue for a reappraisal of the assessed value of its properties, and it had won every court case in those 30 years. A typical settlement was a rebate of $90,000 awarded by the court in 1955 for the past five years' taxes. It cost Otis $27,000 in legal fees to win this relief. In every instance, after the court reduced the assessed value and ordered a rebate, the city promptly reappraised the properties and reset the assessed value at the higher level again.

While assessed valuations are customarily at some arbitrary figure which is less than the market value (a practice observed also in the city of Yonkers), the reverse was applied to the Otis properties. Thus a parking lot which Otis purchased for $60,000 was assessed at a value of $104,000. An addition to it, purchased for $21,000, was assessed at $46,000.

Otis requested of the city that its properties be valued fairly, at rates in keeping with the valuation placed upon other real estate in the city, so that the nuisance and expense of constant litigation might be avoided in the future.

Otis Prosperity. At the time that Mr. Petersen made his announcement, Otis was in a strong financial condition. It had assets of $86 million, a quarter of which was in cash and government securities. Abroad, it had investments of almost $10 million. In this country, it had over 10,000 employees; abroad, its subsidiaries employed another 13,000. Over the full span of its history, it had been consistently prosperous. Except in the deep depression years of 1933 and 1934 the company had earned a profit every year. It had paid dividends on its common stock for fifty-one consecutive years.

Until 1951, Otis had usually made more than half the new elevator installations in the United States; but in that year, its share dropped to 41 per cent. In 1952, it slipped again to 40 per cent. Abroad, its subsidiaries did practically all of the high-quality elevator business in the free world.

QUESTIONS

1. Petersen states: "Only half the savings of the new midwestern plant could be accomplished from our present plants." Does this necessarily indicate a decision to move would be consistent with profit-maximizing action?

2. Is the economic position of Otis such that profit maximization is necessary for it in choosing the plant location?

3. Do you think the proposals of the management adequately meet the interests of stockholding management, labor, and community?

CHAPTER 11

•◆•◆•◆•◆•◆•◆•◆•◆•◆•◆•◆•◆•◆•◆•◆•◆•

Organization and the Executive

INCREASING attention is being given by scholars to the problem of organizing activities for the accomplishment of goals. Principles in this area apply not only to the business organization but to others as well—such as a government agency, an army, an educational institution, an underworld gang, or the family. Until recently, most writers stressed the *structure* of organization, the attainment of an efficient "pyramid of control" or "organization chart." They placed emphasis on securing the proper relationship between activities to make clear who gets what type of orders from whom and to permit each unit to operate with just the right degree of independence. This traditional approach, which may usefully be designated as "administrative design theory,"[1] examines the framework within which functions and authority can be allocated correctly between units comprising an organization.

The recent work in organization theory emphasizes decision-making activities and their interdependence. Emphasis is placed on the organization as consisting of *human beings,* with their diverse backgrounds, abilities, prejudices, and motivations. Consequently, psychological and sociological theories enter into this type of analysis. "Organization theory" in its present state does not constitute a well-developed body of knowledge. It does provide interesting insights to some of the problems faced by any organization, however.

Justice cannot be done in a single chapter either to the older administrative design emphasis or to the more recent work in organization theory. Rather, some principles which appear to be useful will be set forth from both approaches. The usual admonition of the textbook writer that the student who wishes to secure a fuller knowledge of the subject should study books and articles which specialize on the subject is especially applicable here. A number of recommended references are indicated in footnotes.

---

[1]This phrasing has been borrowed from Sherman Krupp, *Pattern in Organizational Analysis* (Philadelphia: Chilton Press, 1961). In this book, Krupp develops a strong criticism of organization theory on methodological grounds.

Administrative Design

A basic principle of the older theory is that it must be made clear where responsibility for performance of any necessary function lies. In the absence of clear demarcation of responsibility, duplication, confusion, and undue rivalry will lower the efficiency of the organization. Under such conditions, much effort is likely to be devoted to ousting the competing unit from the activity—especially if the activity is an attractive one. Within the military services, tremendous energies have been expended on such questions as which types of missiles should be under the jurisdiction of the Army and which under the Air Force. Within a university, overlapping (and even contradictory) materials contained in the course offerings of various instructional units can do much to diminish the over-all quality of the education provided by the institution.

Despite the general principle that duplication should be avoided, it is sometimes desirable to introduce a measure of competition into a structure. This is especially desirable as a temporary device to enable management to determine which unit can better perform a given task. An important type of recurring report, for example, may temporarily be made the responsibility of both an operating unit and a research unit in order to determine which is better qualified ultimately to accept sole responsibility. Or a certain amount of overlapping of function may be permitted so that one unit can provide a check on the quality of certain types of important work performed by the other. In our national government, there is overlapping in the powers of the executive, legislative, and judicial branches to provide a system of "checks and balances." This was accomplished through deliberate constitutional action by the founding fathers.

Another principle of administrative design is that the organizational pyramid should not be too high if the rapid flow of information is important. That is, a shorter line of communication facilitates communication from the top down and from the bottom up. On the other hand, too low a pyramid of control may place too many persons under the direct supervision of a few men. The "span of control"[2] may become too wide to permit adequate supervision. In general, highly routinized activities (such as the billing of telephone subscribers) permit a larger span of control. The span of control may be wide when there is little

---

[2] An interesting essay on span of control is V. A. Graicunas, "Relationship in Organization," reprinted in *Papers on the Science of Administration,* edited by Luther Gulick and L. Urwick (New York: Columbia University Press, 1937), p. 181.

need for exchange of ideas between individuals. Complex activities permit only a much narrower span of supervision. For example, only a few doctoral candidates can be adequately supervised at a time by a qualified professor, while large numbers of students can be taught simultaneously at the freshman level. Here the use of closed-circuit TV can greatly increase the professor's "span" (although the "control" is more dubious).

It is usually wise to permit decisions to be made as far down and as close to the scene as possible, consistent with application of the necessary information to the problem. This may not be the case, however, when the decision to be made requires not only that adequate information be available but that high-quality managerial ability be applied to the problem. It may then be desirable to pass the information up to a higher level, at which the greater executive talent presumably resides.

A common organizational problem is whether departmentalization by "function" or by "management activity" is to be preferred. A department organized according to function may specialize in production, sales, purchases, finance, accounting, research, or personnel, for example. On the other basis a department may specialize in such activities as analysis, planning, execution, and control. When departments within the same organization are organized on both bases, conflicts arise easily. The department in charge of finance may disagree with the analysis of business prospects provided by the department of economic research, especially when the analysis of the latter is embarrassingly inconsistent with actions which have just been taken or are about to be taken by the former.

Comparative Advantage and the Organization

Some basic principles of the science of economics shed some light on the problem of organization. One of these is the concept of "comparative advantage." This principle is that it is the relative, rather than the absolute, advantage which a country, a region, a corner lot, an individual, or any other economic resource possesses which determines the best use of that resource from both a social and an individual point of view. For example, trees on a plot of land in Los Angeles County may produce the best lemons in the country for a given application of labor and water, but it may still be appropriate to convert the orchard into residential lots. The land may have acquired a comparative advantage in its residential use despite its absolute advantage in lemons. Poorer land which is not so valuable as residential property will then have a comparative advantage in lemons. Similarly, a senator may be a better typist than any whom he can hire, but it will still not be wise for him to spend his time typing letters to constituents. He has a comparative advantage as a speaker, drafter of bills, handshaker, etc.

Applied to the organizational structure, the principle of comparative advantage suggests the desirability of permitting each level of the managerial pyramid to make decisions and take action within its own province, since otherwise an undue amount of time may be spent at the higher levels in supervision and review, to the detriment of the high-level decisions. Decisions at a lower level can be "independent," however, only within the limits of the policies, plans, and rules formulated at a higher level if the operation of the firm as a whole is to be well co-ordinated. In the absence of sufficient co-ordination, various divisions of the same corporation have sometimes been found to be competing with one another in the sale of different products to the extent of reducing total profit for the company. A limited amount of such intrafirm competition is sometimes useful, however, and is actively promoted by some corporations.

The principle of comparative advantage also suggests the obvious importance of permitting an executive who is able to fill more than one spot to be placed in his most productive one. Exceptions to this rule may be found, however, especially in a "going," rather than a new, situation. It may be better to keep a man in a spot which uses the lesser of his two capabilities if the better position is filled adequately by a man who is able to function effectively only there. That is, the *total* rather than the *partial* effect of a change on organizational efficiency must be kept in mind.[3] Similarly, long-run rather than immediate efficiency may be promoted by keeping a man temporarily in less than his best spot if this is a means to giving him superior training for the more important position. "Federal decentralization," in which the various units of a firm retain a great deal of autonomy, can be a valuable device for training executives. The value of such training may have to be weighed against the possibility that more immediate efficiency might be attainable by means of a more centralized organization, with branch plants or offices, for example, making fewer important decisions.

---

[3]Similarly, there is danger in using partial equilibrium theory to make economic predictions unless the important general equilibrium consequences are kept in mind. For example, effects of the spending of a tax, as well as of its collection, must be considered in public finance.

Specialization and the Extent of the Market

Another important principle of economics which was formulated by the first great economist, Adam Smith, has relevance in this connection. This principle is that "specialization is limited by the extent of the market." Applied to the business organization, this implies that a larger firm can afford more specialized executives than can a smaller one. A large firm may have a vice president in charge of development, for example, whereas a smaller company would not be able to make full use of the talents of such an officer. Even if a policy of federal decentralization is adhered to, it follows that some executive functions will be carried out only by the headquarters organization, since separate field organizations will not be large enough to justify so much executive specialization.

In addition to being limited by the extent of the market, specialization may be limited by the problems of co-ordination which it engenders. When different individuals perform different tasks, their activities must be made consistent with one another if organization goals are to be attained. An automobile plant provides an easily visualized example.

Organization and Location

The organization of decision making within a firm bears a relationship to the factors which govern the location of plants. If a branch plant is placed in a rapidly growing population center (for reasons such as those set forth in Chapter 10, it is likely to be wise to give an official of the plant considerable autonomy in matters related to sales within that market. The ease with which an official working close to a principal market can make contact with important customers is likely to build up the total demand for the products of the firm, especially when these products are technically complex or made to order. If, on the other hand, a new plant is located primarily to be near the source of a principal raw material, it may be desirable to give plant officials less authority with respect to sales matters. In this case the primary marketing decisions will probably be better made by officials near the principal buyers. Being close to the source of raw materials, plant officials should probably be given a great deal of decision-making power in the purchasing of raw materials and in production.

When sales and production departments are geographically separated, there are likely to be conflicts between these departments. Variations in the product which make it easier to sell often make it more difficult to produce economically. Compromises on the part of both departments are then needed. These can be especially embarrassing to the sales executive who may have made promises to customers which cannot be fulfilled.

Traditional versus Organization Theory Approaches

The traditional, marginalist theory of the firm—with which this book is largely occupied—is derived from the theory of pure competition, from monopoly and oligopoly theory, and from work in the fields of "monopolistic compeition" and "imperfect competition." Except in the case of oligopoly theory, there is usually the underlying assumption of full knowledge on the part of management of pertinent demand, supply, and other functions, even though imperfect knowledge on the part of buyers is frequently mentioned. The firm, viewed in the traditional manner, is considered to be governed by a single entrepreneur who reacts rationally to the external and internal situation facing him in such a way as to maximize profits. In more careful formulations the traditional entrepreneur is assumed to maximize the present value of anticipated net profits, after taxes, over a substantial (but usually somewhat vague) period of years. This standard brand of economics of the firm is, of course, considered by the authors to be of fundamental value, since much of this book is devoted to that approach.

Recent writers on "organization theory," such as Chester Barnard and Herbert Simon, have been attempting to unearth important implications of the fact that business decisions are usually made within an organizational framework.[4] As has recently been stated by Professor Boulding: "A person acting in a role, however, is not the same as a person acting in his own behalf."[5] Organization theory studies the network of interacting roles played by persons within an organization, the communication of information into and within the organization, and the processes within the organization by which conflicts are resolved and a sufficient degree of co-operation is secured. It is by no

[4]See, for example, H. A. Simon, *Administrative Behavior* (New York: Macmillan Co., 1957), and *Public Administration* (New York: Alfred A. Knopf, Inc., 1950); C. I. Barnard, *The Functions of the Executive* (Cambridge: Harvard University Press, 1938); and R. M. Cyert and J. G. March, *The Behavioral Theory of the Firm* (Englewood Cliffs, N.J.: Prentice-Hall, Inc., 1963).

[5]Kenneth E. Boulding, "The Present Position of the Theory of the Firm," in K. E. Boulding and A. Spivey (eds.), *Linear Programming and the Theory of the Firm* (New York: Macmillan Co., 1960), p. 11.

means a well-developed body of scientific principles, nor has empirical testing been substantial.

Survival as a Goal

Most organizations of men exhibit a strong desire for survival, comparable almost to the urge of living creatures of all types to survive and to perpetuate their kind. Usually, an organization which has flourished but has passed its peak will still be capable of furnishing substantial benefits to a number of persons who will strongly support its continuance. This is one reason for the danger inherent in extensive government action in the economic sphere, i.e., that agencies once established will succeed in existing by receiving appropriations long beyond the period of real need.

Applied to the business firm, the organizational urge for survival is apt to stem from the belief of some of the executives that their present positions are more attractive than alternatives which are clearly available to them. This is particularly true of those who have been with the firm a long time and whose abilities have become highly specialized. In economic terms, their incomes consist heavily of "rent" rather than of competitively determined returns, and organization survival is vital to the continuation of such economic rents. Executives who are affiliated with flourishing enterprises are unlikely to give much thought to the problem of mere survival, of course.

A top executive who feels that he has a heavy stake in the survival of a shaky organization may adopt a "minimax" attitude toward the game of business. In the words of a recent writer, such a man "is trying to make his decisions in such a manner that if all the wrong things happen, he still would hope to salvage maximum results under the circumstances."[6] As was pointed out in the Appendix on game theory (pages 322–37), such an attitude may be considered to be that of a "reluctant duelist." This attitude is sharply in contrast with that in which primary interest centers on an all-out try for the big pay-offs.

A related idea in organization theory is that the firm will frequently attempt to "satisfice" rather than "optimize." That is, satisfactory profits are said to be a goal of a business organization. Optimizing requires processes which are much more complex than those needed to satisfice, and most human activity, whether individual or organizational,

---

[6]Sherrill Cleland, "A Short Essay on a Managerial Theory of the Firm," in Boulding 1958), p. 141.

is concerned with selection of satisfactory alternatives.[7] Optimizing activity requires that there be sufficient *search* to uncover all available alternatives and that a procedure be available for comparing these alternatives so that the best may be chosen.

If the cost of the search for more alternatives is taken into account, and if search is extended to the point where the marginal improvement in alternatives is deemed to be equal to the marginal cost of search, the behavior of the firm becomes optimizing rather than satisficing. In seeking a location for a new plant, for example, a company may rather quickly select one of the several which are already known to its executives. This would be a satisficing action. It may be more rational, however, to devote a substantial sum of money and time of executives to searching out the potentialities of a much larger number of alternative locations. Much good judgment is needed to determine when the added cost of investigation exceeds the value of uncovering new possibilities (which may be turned down, anyway). If the cost of search for alternative locations is balanced carefully against the probable gain from search, the action is of an optimizing nature. If the firm does not possess resources to devote to search, it must settle for a satisfactory, but probably nonoptimal, location.

Organizational Equilibrium

Organization theory as developed by Barnard and Simon includes the idea of "organizational equilibrium" as an important element. The organization is conceived to be a supplier of *inducements* (usually primarily pecuniary ones) and persons within the organization are conceived to be suppliers of *contributions* (usually primarily productive services). The flow of contributions by participants is the source from which the flow of inducements stems. The organization can continue to exist in a given form only if the flow of contributions can be maintained by the inducements which they generate. In addition to pecuniary inducements, business organizations can secure contributions by numerous other devices which appeal to participants. Public recognition for outstanding effort is said to be a commonly used device in the Soviet Union. Arm bands, trophies, and similar items designed to build prestige are used to secure loyalty on athletic teams, while black jackets bearing the gang name may be important in securing contributions to gang activities. Suggestion boxes may be valuable in inculcating a feel-

---

[7]J. G. March and H. A. Simon, *Organizations* (New York: John Wiley & Sons, Inc., and Spivey, *ibid.*, p. 210.

ing of "belonging" to an organization, especially if an occasional suggestion is accepted. The "beatnik" beard may make a similar contribution to its wearer and his associates. Organization pictures, picnics, and parties may have value well above their cost in gaining organizational participation, as may the effort of the "big boss" in learning and using the first names of all of his employees.

The concept of organizational equilibrium is analogous to that of market equilibrium. The demand for organizational co-operation is provided by the inducements supplied. The supply of co-operation is provided by participants in response to the pecuniary and nonpecuniary inducements. In order to maintain itself, the organization must be able at least to balance the disutility encountered in participation with the utility of the inducements provided.

Productivity of Executives

Executives within an organization have the basic function of making necessary decisions in the face of uncertainty. Despite the importance of executives both to their firms and to the economy as a whole, little theorizing or empirical study has been devoted to the subject of how executives' remuneration is determined.[8]

One difficulty inherent in measuring the marginal revenue productivity of labor to the firm is the lack of homogeneity of this factor of production. The firm may hire many different types of labor, and the measurement must be made separately for each variety. Measuring the marginal productivity of executives is obviously even more difficult. Different executives have unlike duties as a matter of policy and are apt to differ greatly in type of education and experience. Even when viewed historically, the quality of executive decisions is difficult to assess. The company may have prospered, may have declined, or may have been about an average performer; but it is usually hard to know just how this performance was related to the particular decisions which were made. If a firm possesses a good deal of monopoly power, it may prosper with only fair management, whereas management may have to be extremely capable to cause the firm to do well in the more competitive areas of the economy. The hiring of an executive obviously presents an even greater problem than assessment of his past performance, since it is necessary to anticipate in some rough way what the

---

[8] A recent exception is David R. Roberts, "A General Theory of Executive Compensation Based on Statistically Tested Propositions," *Quarterly Journal of Economics,* May, 1956, p. 270.

quality of his actions will be in the inscrutable future. Most executives are brought up through the ranks rather than being hired after they are already recognized as experienced and competent managers. This places on personnel officers the difficult job of trying to assess the executive potential of college graduates.

It is possible to define in marginal productivity terms the upper limit to the amount which a firm will theoretically pay an executive. Since his job is to produce profits for the firm by making decisions of high quality, the maximum which he will be paid can be stated in terms of profit differentials. That is, the executive's marginal revenue productivity is the excess of the firm's total profit under his direction over the total profit which would have been earned under the best alternative executive plus the amount which would have been necessary to secure the latter's services.[9] Suppose it is estimated that under Mr. X the corporation can earn $5 million a year, while under the presidency of Mr. Y it would earn $50,000 less. The maximum which the firm could afford to pay Mr. X would be $50,000 plus the salary necessary to attract Mr. Y—say, $40,000 a year. (Mr. X thus is worth a maximum of $90,000 a year, which can be called his marginal revenue productivity.) While some sort of calculation of this sort is essential to good management—lest executive compensation get completely out of line with its worth—the difficulties inherent in making the necessary estimates are quite obvious. It is difficult to know how much it would take to hire Mr. Y away from his present employer, especially since most executives are not mobile.[10] It is even more difficult to know that Mr. X's decision-making capacity is such as to bring in $50,000 more in profits than could have been garnered by Mr. Y. Since no one else is really trained to do Mr. X's job (except perhaps his assistant), the concept of the next best alternative executive is a vague one.

Actually, those who determine the compensation of an executive are often motivated by considerations other than maximizing the profits of the firm. The executive at the top may raise the pay of subordinate officers in order to make his own compensation appear to be in need of a boost. Or executives as a closely knit group may be in a position to

[9]*Ibid.*, p. 290. Roberts found size of firm to be the most important determinant of the income of the top executive officers.

[10]According to Roberts, *ibid.*, p. 291, 87 per cent of the sample of five hundred executives studied worked for only one employer after becoming corporate officers. This can create serious difficulties for executives who lose their positions through mergers. Not only do their talents become highly specialized, but they often have had no experience in looking for a job. This is described in "More Executives Start Job Hunting as Merger Pace Holds at Record," *Wall Street Journal*, August 16, 1960, p. 1.

exact a sort of monopoly tribute from stockholders by paying all executives unnecessarily large salaries. This is less likely to happen if there are important and active stockholders who are not themselves in managerial positions.

The importance of securing competent executive decisions clearly increases with the size of the firm. The officials of a large firm may, through incompetence, inflict losses on a larger group of stockholders than equally incompetent executives of a small firm. Or the former may, if capable, bring large dividends and/or capital gains to a larger body of stockholders. The number of executives per dollar of sales tends to decrease as the company increases in size.[11] Thus the financial importance of managerial decisions relating to prices, products, advertising, and so forth increases with firm size. Similarly, the importance of investment decisions increases with the size of the firm, and it is appropriate in general that executive salaries also increase with firm size.

The Remarriage of Ownership and Management

Although historically the corporation has been the device by which management has been separated from ownership, there has been a tendency to bring the two partially together again by means of compensating executives in part by granting them stock options. Such options give the right to buy a specified total of the corporation's stock at a specified price during a specified period of years. If the stock rises in market price, the holder can still purchase it at the price stated in the option. If it falls in price, he will not exercise the option. Thus the executive is given the possibility of securing a large speculative return without risk to himself (unless he chooses to hold the stock after buying it, in which case a capital loss might result from a sufficient price decline). In the event of a profit on a stock option deal, the compensation is better than straight salary from the executive's point of view because it is taxed only at the capital gains rate, meaning a maximum of 25 per cent if the gain qualifies as "long term." A much higher income tax rate applies to straight salary income received by key executives. Stock option plans are sometimes so generous to executives as to constitute something of a raid on the treasury of a corporation on the part of its

---

[11]Arch Patton, "Current Practices in Executive Compensation," *Harvard Business Review*, January, 1951, p. 62, states that in a sample of firms studied, the number of executives per $1 million of profit varied from 10.3 for firms earning less than $2 million per year to 1.5 for those earning over $7 million per year. Since profits and sales are positively correlated, the same sort of relationship could be found for executives per dollar of sales.

executives. In recent years, stockholders appear to have become more skeptical about the propriety of some stock option proposals.

The stock option device of compensating executives is supposed to improve the efficiency of such employees. Not only does an executive have the prospect to a higher salary if his work is of high quality, but he can also help himself obtain a greater capital gain by being efficient. Management and ownership tend to be rejoined to a degree. Similarly, some corporations have stock purchase plans for all employees, based on the theory that workers will be more loyal and more efficient if they participate in company ownership. Stock purchase plans for employees are popular in a rising stock market but can bring discontent in the event of a sustained downturn in security prices. In that event, employees would be paying more than the market price. If the company adjusts the purchase price to bring it below the new market price, there will be grumbles from those employees who paid the higher price. Stock option plans avoid this risk, since the options need not be exercised if they are unprofitable.

As already mentioned, the turnover of key executives is very low. Fringe benefits of various kinds are an aid in keeping down turnover at the top. For example, retirement programs are often so liberal that the executive is very reluctant to change companies after building up a substantial stake in one firm's retirement system.[12] Some contracts have provisions for the executive to remain on salary as a consultant after 65 or some other retirement age. Similarly, life insurance contracts of impressive size, some of which pledge a lifetime income to the wife, constitute an important fringe benefit and a detriment to executive mobility.

Executive compensation plans are usually based not only on reducing the temptation of a key man to leave the company, but also on reducing his personal income tax liability. As mentioned already, this is partly responsible for the popularity of stock option plans. Since the federal income tax is not really a tax on all income but only on money income, any device to give the executive benefits in nonpecuniary form, or to substitute long-term capital gains for direct payment, is likely to be seriously considered. Expense accounts which permit him to indulge in expensive entertaining and travel for the company usually bring him a great deal of untaxed satisfaction. (These have recently come under closer scrutiny by the Internal Revenue Service.) Country club mem-

---

[12]Impairment of his retirement program may be one of the most serious aspects of the involuntary separation of the executive from his position (*Wall Street Journal, op. cit.,* p. 1).

berships, free health examinations and programs, and vacations at company-owned resorts contribute to real income. Spreading out money income more evenly over the lifetime of the executive also reduces his lifetime income tax liability. This is an important reason for the popularity of deferred bonus arrangements in which a company votes an officer a bonus payable over a number of years rather than all at once. Also, the income tax favors the establishment of retirement systems, so that the executive need not save out of his salary the bulk of the funds which he will require after retirement. It should be noted, however, that income tax savings from this source can be largely or wholly lost to the executive in the long run if sufficient price inflation occurs. The real income loss due to inflation can conceivably exceed the real income gain due to the tax saving secured through the spreading-out of income over time.

CASE 11–1: TRADITIONAL DEPARTMENT STORES, INC.[13]

Traditional Department Stores, Inc., was a medium-sized chain of department stores located in the Middle West, with stores in ten cities.

Mr. Marshall Jennings, the chief men's-wear buyer for the largest store in the chain, was explaining the manner in which his buyers operated in ordering and pricing men's clothing. Mr. Jennings was a college classmate of William Griffin, who was a professor of business and economics at a nearby university. Professor Griffin was interested in determining how price and "output" decisions were made by a retail organization. Professor Griffin knew that Mr. Jennings' store competed with two other large men's clothing stores in the trading area.

Mr. Jennings was quick to point out at the beginning of the conversation that while he could only talk in detail about his department, the general practice that he and his buyers followed was a more or less standard procedure used quite widely in all departments and in most department stores.

Professor Griffin suggested that Mr. Jennings first explain how the buyer determined what quantity of goods to order (and thus what quantity the store had to sell) and then discuss normal pricing and special pricing practices.

---

[13]This case is based in large part upon the research of Dean R. M. Cyert and Professor J. G. March of the Graduate School of Industrial Administration, Carnegie Institute of Technology, as reported in *The Behavioral Theory of the Firm.* © 1963. Adapted by permission of Prentice-Hall, Inc., Englewood Cliffs, N.J.

Ordering

Mr. Jennings began by explaining that there were two kinds of orders—advance orders and reorders. The size of the advance order depended largely on the estimated sales for the season for which the goods were being ordered, but also depended on the amount of "risk" involved in advance ordering. When items were highly seasonal in nature, so that selling an overstock after the season was difficult, advance orders as a per cent of total orders were kept low, Mr. Jennings explained. Also, clothes of a very faddish or stylish nature presented a risky situation, since tastes could change easily and it was difficult to predict ahead of time what would sell well. Mr. Jennings estimated for Professor Griffin the percentage of estimated sales placed in advance orders for each of the four major buying seasons (see Exhibit 1).

Exhibit 1

Season	Per Cent	Order Dates
Easter	70%	January 15–20
Summer	50	March 10–15
Back to school	65	May 20–25
Holiday	75	September 20–25

The basic estimates of sales volume for each period were based on sales for the last period and adjusted for shifts in the timing of holidays, special sales, etc. Predictions were deliberately reduced somewhat from the last year's sales in order to decrease possible overforecasting, a mistake that was held against the buyer in judging his performance. Estimated sales forecasts did not have to be very accurate for ordering purposes, since the size of reorders could be varied to correct estimating errors.

By relying on reorders during the selling season, the buyers were able to utilize the most recent information on demand trends in terms of over-all volume and specific items. Mr. Jennings warned, however, that the buyers had to balance this advantage against the disadvantages. Manufacturers required lead times for production, with the result that "out of stocks" might occur before the reorder was delivered. Moreover, since the manufacturer based both the type and the amount of recuttings on early reorders in order to decrease his risk of obsolete inventories, the buyer who waited till too late in the season to reorder might not be able to get the required amount or the exact styles and colors he desired.

Mr. Jennings outlined the following method of determining reorder amounts. Shortly after the selling season began, the buyers checked each of their product style lines against that same line during the previous year, and then applied this ratio to the previous year's sales. For instance, if sales during the first two weeks of an item were 80 units, and sales during the same period of the previous year were 100, then the buyer calculated that sales for the remainder of the season would be 80 per cent of last year's sales during the remainder of the season.

Exhibit 2

SALES AND COMPETITION REPORT

Men's Bermuda Shorts

	Number of Pairs Sold	Traditional	Young's	Oldsfield's	Shopper's Discount
$4.95 summer line:					
1961:					
Easter..............	121	$4.95	$4.95	$4.95	.....
Summer............	459	4.95	4.95	4.75	.....
Back to school.......	315	4.25	4.25	4.50	.....
1962:					
Easter..............	110	4.95	4.95	4.95	$3.95
Summer............	200	4.95	4.95	4.95	3.95
Back to school.......	300	3.95	3.95	3.75	3.75
$7.95 summer line:					
1961:					
Easter..............	60	7.95	7.95	7.49	.....
Summer............	180	7.95	7.95	7.95	.....
Back to school.......	120	7.95	7.95	7.95	.....
1962:					
Easter..............	20	7.95	7.95	7.95	5.95
Summer............	100	7.95	7.95	7.49	5.95
Back to school.......	220	5.95	5.95	5.95	5.95

Once this new estimate of sales was determined, the inventory on hand was subtracted from this figure and any inventory desired at the end of the season added to it in order to calculate the reorder quantity. In some cases where sales had been much less than initially expected, the inventory on hand might be so large as to yield a negative reorder quantity by this calculation. In this case, past orders might be canceled or the price cut in order to move more merchandise. Once the selling season was under way and the reorder made, such a calculation was made every week to determine whether part of the reorder should be canceled, whether the price should be cut, or whether more should be ordered. This weekly check served as a control mechanism which prevented extraordinary overstocks on stock "outs" on each line.

Mr. Jennings stressed the importance of having a routinized method for handling the order problem. If each buyer had a free rein to buy as much as he wanted whenever he wanted to do so, on hundreds of items, each coming in different styles and colors, the problem of controlling purchases, sales, and inventory levels would be tremendous.

Mr. Jennings confessed that during the last year his staff had had more difficulty than usual in predicting sales volumes accurately, with the result that the department had had to cancel orders, sell goods at cut prices, and sell after the seasons were over. But occasionally, the store also found itself with too little stock. The trouble came from a new large discount store that had opened on the edge of the city, about four miles from the center of the business district. This store, according to Mr. Jennings, constantly engaged in special promotions and low markups. Mr. Jennings said he did not know how to take this store's behavior into account in forecasting sales for any one line. Prior to the opening of the discount store, he stated, he had not felt much need to take his competition into account in ordering, since the estimating method, which ignored these competitors, had in general worked satisfactorily. Professor Griffin then asked if he might see a record of an item with which Mr. Jennings had experienced trouble. Mr. Jennings had one of his assistants pull the records on men's Bermuda shorts (see Exhibit 2).

Normal Price Determination

Mr. Jennings next described for Professor Griffin the concept of retail "price lining." The store carried only a limited number of different-quality items in the same product group. This simplified choice for consumers, resulted in stable product categories for manufacturers to produce in, and ultimately increased the retail stability of prices. Since the various price lines were reasonably well standardized, as were retail markups, the manufacturer knew the maximum his costs could be in order to sell his product at a particular price in the retail market. Likewise, each retail firm knew that the cost differences were not great for merchandise in any given price line, and thus that prices in that line among different stores would not vary significantly unless intended. Thus, price lining resulted in comparability for manufacturer, retailer, and shopper, according to Mr. Jennings.

Once price lines were selected, a large part of the pricing problem was solved. Merchandise was purchased to sell within a given price line and yield a "normal" markup. Normal markup for the men's- and boy's-wear department as a whole was 40 per cent. This markup had been in existence in the industry as standard for 40 or 50 years, Mr. Jennings said. As a result of price-line standardization, the department was able to operate for the most part from a schedule of standard costs and standard prices. The schedule for the boy's section was as shown in Exhibit 3.

Exhibit 3

TRADITIONAL DEPARTMENT STORES, INC.

Boy's Wear—Normal Markup

Standard Costs	Standard Price*	Effective Markup
$ 3.00.................	$ 5.00	40.0%
3.75.................	5.95	37.0
4.75.................	7.95	40.2
5.50.................	8.95	38.5
6.75.................	10.95	38.3
7.75.................	12.95	40.1
8.75.................	14.95	41.5
10.75.................	17.95	40.0
11.75.................	19.95	41.0
13.75.................	22.95	40.0
14.75.................	25.00	41.0
18.75.................	29.95	37.4

*Calculated from the following rule: "Divide each cost by 60 per cent (one markup), and move the result to nearest 95 cents."

The selection of price lines was an infrequent policy decision. Such a decision by high-level buying and administrative personnel was based on a wide range of factors—competitive lines in other stores, the economic characteristics of the community, the store's desired image, etc. For most decisions and to most buyers the price-line structure was a "given." The problem for the buyer, then, was to find goods that could be assigned prices that would enable the department to attain or improve the markup goal.

Although the average normal markup for the department was 40 per cent, each product group had its own normal markup, which varied somewhat among product groups and which in general tended to be higher:

1. The greater the risk involved with the product.
2. The higher the costs (other than product cost).
3. The less the effect of competition.
4. The lower the price elasticity.

Risk was involved, for example, where the department dealt with foreign manufacturers. Products often varied in quality, and deliveries were not so dependable. As a result, the markup was increased 50 per cent on these items, or to 60 per cent of retail cost.

Another exceptional markup occurred when the store handled a product on an exclusive arrangement. Since the consumer was not able to make comparisons, the price and margin were set higher according to the following company rule: "When merchandise is handled on an exclusive basis, calculate the standard price from the cost, then use the next highest price on the standard schedule."

Markups were also higher on large items which used up a great deal of floor space, and on items that required considerable personal sales attention. In both cases, costs were higher.

Price decreases were automatically made to match lower prices by the store's two major competitors, although when a competitor's plans to feature an item were known in advance, the store often did not stock and never displayed the identical item. The store also met the prices of lesser competitors such as drugstores if these stores actively promoted and displayed the product. (Information about competitors was gained through newspaper advertisements, manufacturers' salesmen, customers, and professional shoppers.) Mr. Jennings stated that last year he had felt it necessary to feature a month-long "back to school" sale on many summer clothes in order to clear out large inventories built up during the spring and summer months. He blamed these overstocks on the discount house. "To tell the truth," Mr. Jennings stated, "we were all a little surprised at the results of the sale. We were actually caught short of stock after two and a half weeks, and had to rush through a special order to continue the advertised sale."

Sales Price Determination

Mr. Jennings stated that a completely different set of rules governed sales pricing in order to achieve a price appeal. Special sales were limited in number. Usually, they occurred when a buyer was able to make arrangements for lines that were exclusive in the immediate market at lower than normal cost—in other words, at a special discount.

The management had promulgated certain policy directives for the buyers to follow:

1. Whenever the normal price falls at one of the following lines, the corresponding sale price will be used:

Normal Price	Sale Price
$1.00	$0.85
1.95	1.65
2.50	2.10
2.95	2.45
3.50	2.90
3.95	3.30
4.95	3.90
5.00	3.90

2. For all other merchandise, there must be a reduction of *at least* 15 per cent on items retailing regularly for $3.00 or less and at least *16⅔* per cent on higher priced items.
3. All sales prices must end with a zero or a five.
4. No sale prices are allowed to fall on price lines normal for the product group.
5. Whenever there is a choice between an ending of 85 cents and 90 cents, the latter ending will prevail.
6. Use the standard schedule of sales pricing for prices that are slightly higher (by 5 cents) than the listed values. Thus, if the price is $3.00 retail, assume it is the same as $2.95 in computing the sales price.
7. The smaller the retail price, the smaller must be the increments between sales price endings, in order to approximate as closely as possible the desired percentage reduction. Therefore, after determining the necessary percentage reduction from normal price, carry the result down to the nearest ending specified below:
   a) Retail price greater than $5.00, reduce to the nearer of 90 cents or 45 cents.
   b) Retail price less than $5.00 but greater than $2.00, reduce to the nearest of 90 cents, 65 cents, 45 cents, or 30 cents.
   c) Retail price under $2.00, reduce to the nearer of zero or 5 cents.
   d) Reduce 5 cents more if the sale price is the same as another price line in the same product category.
8. When the special discount cost from the manufacturer is over 30 per cent less than normal, pass some of the savings on to the customer by using the following formula:

$$\frac{\text{Special discount cost}}{1 - \text{Normal markup}}$$

if the resultant sales price using the normal rule is greater. [Mr. Jennings stated that "this usually happens when our relationship with the manufacturer has been one of long standing."]

When Professor Griffin asked if competitors' reactions were considered in setting sales prices, Mr. Jennings replied that they were not. He did say, however, that his store always met the sales prices of competitors on comparable items if their prices were lower, and competitors in turn would do likewise. The store had a firm policy, however, against raising prices to match competitors' prices when they were higher than those of Traditional.

Markdowns

Mr. Jennings next went into markdown pricing procedures. He explained: "We generally consider a markdown to be a decrease in price that the buyer feels will be permanent. However, there are exceptions in practice to this definition."

Mr. Jennings said that he liked to look on markdowns as a kind of "emergency device" which the department used in its efforts to maintain sales and inventory control. Their use, he explained, could be roughly grouped into two categories—special cases and routine cases.

Special Cases

Competition. When it was determined that a recognized competitor was selling an item at a lower price, the department would mark down the item to equal the competitor's price. However, explained Mr. Jennings, if the department had reason to believe that the price was the result of a mistake, a check would be made with the competitor first before reducing the price. "Frequently," according to Mr. Jennings, "it develops that the price discrepancy is unintentional, and the competitor's price is increased."

Customer Adjustment. A returned defective item was marked down to zero and eliminated. Soiled or damaged merchandise was reduced in price. Merchandise that was returned by a customer after the line to which it belonged had been reduced in price was reduced accordingly.

Premature Depletion. If the stock for a sale was prematurely depleted, regular stock would be transferred to the sale racks and be marked down to sale price.

Promotion Item. At times during the year, as a stimulant to business, items which were in excess and also available in a large and balanced assortment were marked down by 4 per cent.

Obsolescence Differential. Some items were suitable only for one season because of a particular style, color, or material, and could not be sold in the succeeding season. To accelerate the sale of these items, they were marked down one or two dollars near the peak of the season. Said

Mr. Jennings: "We view this reduction as small enough to avoid antagonizing recent purchasers of the items but large enough to stimulate sales."

Drop in Wholesale Price during Season. When this happened, all items in stock, regardless of when they were purchased, were reduced to the appropriate level based on the new wholesale price.

Substandard Merchandise. Items which did not meet the quality standards of the original samples were either sent back to the manufacturer or, if this was not convenient, reduced in price and reimbursement sought from the manufacturer.

General Routine

This category accounted for the largest amount of dollars of markdown, according to Mr. Jennings. The items were marked down when some signal (inventory figures, reports from salesclerks, etc.) indicated that excess inventories existed. The exact nature of the price reaction depended on an analysis of the reasons for failure. Mr. Jennings outlined the pricing procedures followed for each of several common causes of excess inventories.

Normal Remnants. These were the odd sizes, less popular colors, and less favored styles remaining from the total assortment of an item which sold satisfactorily during the season. These items were considered normal, since it was impossible to order precisely the right assortment. "In fact," commented Mr. Jennings, "the complete clearance of the stock of an item by the end of the season is taken as an indication that the buyer did not buy heavily enough and that he probably suffered lost sales."

Overstocked Merchandise. These are items for which the buyer was overly optimistic—which had normal sales but still remained in a well-balanced assortment of styles and sizes at the end of the season with many acceptable items included.

Unaccepted Merchandise. This was merchandise that had "unsatisfactory" sales. During the season the sales personnel tried to determine whether the lack of acceptance was due to overpricing or poor style, color, etc. "The distinction is usually made," remarked Mr. Jennings, "by determining whether the item was ignored or whether it got attention but low sales."

The Markdown Process. Usually, Mr. Jennings said, items were not marked down right away, but were mentally "stored" in an "availability pool" until the store or department had a general clearance sale.

However, Mr. Jennings pointed out, there were times during the year when the department could not wait till the next scheduled clearance due to lack of space or lack of funds. In this case, immediate markdowns were ordered, such as the "back to school" sale of overstocked Bermuda shorts mentioned previously.

Items were marked down 33⅓ per cent in the first markdown, except in special conditions where space was extremely tight, when they were reduced 50 per cent. Mr. Jennings remarked that the 33⅓ per cent off approximated the cost of the merchandise, plus 10 cents to cover past handling costs, but that 33⅓ per cent off was an easier rule to follow. All marked-down merchandise was advertised "at least one third off." The 33⅓ per cent rule was developed into a standard "first markdown price" schedule with prices *reduced further* to the nearest 85 cents (to distinguish markdown from sale prices which ended in 90 cents). (See Exhibit 4.)

Exhibit 4

BOYS' WEAR SECTION

Regular Retail Price	First Markdown Price
$ 5.00	$3.85
5.95	3.85
(6.95)*	(4.85)
7.95	4.85
8.95	5.85
9.95	5.85
10.95	6.85
12.95	7.85

*Not considered a regular retail price.

There were two exceptions to the above rule, according to Mr. Jennings. Higher priced items were marked down by 40 per cent or more. Experience had indicated that these items (over $15) did not have high rates of obsolescence, so that when they were marked down, they were more soiled than were lower priced goods.

The second case involved manufacturers' close-outs of remnants of odd styles, sizes, colors, etc., which were purchased at low cost. In this case the department tried to sell these items for one season at the regular price, and then cut the price by one half.

Second markdowns, for merchandise still not cleared by the initial markdown, followed no rule and were left to the buyer's discretion.

At this point, Mr. Jennings felt that he could say no more about his department's operations, whereupon Professor Griffin thanked him, chatted for a few minutes longer about their college days, and took his leave.

QUESTIONS

1. How does the actual pricing practice of Mr. Jennings' department square with traditional price theory? In what ways do economic concepts apply? In what areas do they seem not to apply?

2. Could game theory be used by the department store? Explain.

3. What do you think is the reason for having such well-defined pricing practices?

4. Do you see any conflict between the "best"—i.e., optimum—economic behavior of the firm and the practical needs of the organization? Explain.

5. Do you think the buying and price decisions of this department could be made with a computer? Why, or why not?

6. What implications about the jobs of middle management (the buyers in Case 11–1) can be drawn from the above analysis?

CASE 11–2: STOCK OPTIONS

The Revenue Act of 1950 provided special tax treatment for restricted stock options, provided that certain conditions were met. Section 421 of the 1954 tax code retained this treatment. In order to qualify for special tax treatment, the following conditions must have been met:

1. The recipient must have been an employee when the option was granted, and must have exercised it while an employee or within three months after his employment was terminated. (However, the three-month requirement did not apply if the option was exercised after the death of the recipient.)

2. The option must have been nontransferable, except at death.

3. The option must not have extended for more than ten years from the time granted. However, if the optionee owned more than 10 per cent of the voting stock, the period for exercising the option was limited to five years.

4. The option price must have been at least 85 per cent of the market price at the time of grant, or 110 per cent in the case of an optionee who owned more than 10 per cent of the voting stock.

5. The price requirement could be met by a variable price formula based on the market price at time of exercise. Provision was made for resetting the option price at not less than 85 per cent of market value if the market price during the preceding twelve months averaged less than 80 per cent of the price at time of grant.

The code provided that the employee was not deemed to receive taxable income at the time of exercise. In the typical case, where the option price was at least 95 per cent of the stock's value at the date of grant, any amount over the option price realized by the employee upon sale of the stock was taxed at a capital gains rate, provided the sale took place at least two years after the option was granted and six months after it was exercised. If the stock was held until death, the gain over the option price was not taxed at all, and the employee's estate or heirs received a stepped-up basis for the stock.

The corporation received no deductible expense item at any time for issuing the option.

Exhibit 1 shows the growth in the number of companies listed on the New York Stock Exchange from 1950 to 1961 compared with stock option plans.

Exhibit 1

TOTAL NUMBER OF COMPANIES LISTED ON THE NEW YORK STOCK EXCHANGE WITH RESTRICTED STOCK OPTIONS*

Year	Cumulative Number of Plans	Cumulative Number of Companies with Plans	Number of Companies Listed on New York Stock Exchange	Percentage of New York Stock Exchange Companies with Plans
1961 (June)	1,059	714	1,128	63.3%
1960	986	693	1,121	61.8
1959	871	640	1,089	58.8
1958	759	591	1,082	54.6
1957	669	537	1,091	49.2
1956	544	463	1,071	43.2
1955	388	353	1,071	33.0
1954	287	269	1,070	25.1
1953	240	227	1,063	21.4
1952	195	183	1,061	17.2
1951	112	104	1,048	9.9
1950	27	19	1,033	1.8
Before 1950	12	8	1,009	0.8

*The data, which were compiled from public records, are limited to New York Stock Exchange companies with common stock listed as of June 30, 1961, and apply only to restricted stock option plans authorized as of that date.

Source: Reproduced from *Hearing before the Committee on Ways and Means, House of Representatives, 88th Congress, First Session, on the Tax Recommendations of the President Contained in His Message Transmitted to the Congress, January 24, 1963* (Washington, D.C.: U.S. Government Printing Office, 1963), p. 46.

These stock options aroused considerable opposition, and the resulting controversy centered around several basic issues. The purpose of the options was one of the main issues. Proponents viewed the purpose as primarily a means of enabling management to gain a proprietary interest in the corporations which they operate and secondarily as a means of attracting and retaining good management. The opponents saw stock options purely as a device to provide compensation to managers in a manner which enabled them to escape high marginal personal tax rates.

The possibility of changing the option price also aroused considerable controversy.

The following series of quotations represent some of the points of view expressed on these issues:

During the early postwar years at Ford Motor company a dozen or so skillful men—executives brought in from outside after the war—transformed a bogged-down, antiquated, money-losing company into a modern, efficient profit-making enterprise, capable of meeting the toughest kind of competition, of improving its position, and of renewing its own management resources. Largely through the efforts of these men, the company became a substantial net contributor to the managerial and technical capabilities of the economy. Furthermore, by stimulating more intensive competition in the automobile industry, the company added to the general prosperity and growth of the 1950's.

Without the guidance of these men, the stockholders' equity might be half of what it is today. The contribution of this group to the growth and profits of the company has far exceeded any financial rewards they received in return. Many of these executives were already well established, successful, and well paid. We could not have offered them enough more in salary and possible bonuses to justify the risk of leaving secure positions for the uncertainties of our situation. They joined Ford Motor Company largely upon my promise that I would do my best to give them an opportunity to acquire a stake in the company as soon as it was feasible to do so.

At the same time, we also developed a group of exceptionally able younger men who contributed materially to the company's growth and who were not being rewarded commensurately with their contribution. These young men—including a number of the leading executives of the company today—saw opportunities for realizing large capital gains outside the company. Some outstandingly capable people left us for that reason. Indeed, at one time, before we could offer stock options, we had a serious problem with sales executives leaving us to go into business for themselves as dealers.

When the Congress authorized restricted stock options by amending the Internal Revenue Code, it gave us an effective means to recognize and stimulate exceptional performance, and to protect the company's future by conserving its management "seed corn." In 1953, when our only shareholders were members of the Ford family and The Ford Foundation, the board of directors made its first grants of restricted stock options to 114 key employees, thus breaking a tradition of long standing. Stock options have since been offered from time to time to key employees.[14]

Now, the first justification of these plans was that they were supposed to make the executives partners in the business. That has gone so far by the board that Allied Chemical recently put in its proxy statement a proposal that it would no longer require the optionees to hold stock for "investment purposes." In other words, back in 1951 and 1952 and 1953 these stock option plans were sold to the stockholders—if they understood them at all, and I can't believe that

---

[14]Henry Ford II, "Stock Options Are in the Public Interest," *Harvard Business Review*, July-August, 1961.

this Congress ever understood what they were enacting when they enacted this in 1950—they were sold to the stockholders on the basis that the stock would be taken and held for investment purposes.

Now, they are frankly coming out and eliminating that from the stock option plans, eliminating it from existing stock option plans.

As people have pointed out earlier this morning, stock option plans represent a heads-I-win tails-you-lose proposition, a Monday morning quarterback, who can call the plays after the game is over.

But even this isn't enough. Assuming the corporation has done badly, management is so piggish and they have so little opinion of the intelligence of the American stockholders and the intelligence of the American public, that they then, if they find that the company had done badly and the stock has depreciated in value, they then issue a new stock option at the lower value. The rank and file of stockholders, who may have bought their stock at $40 a share when the first stock option plan came out now find that they have got a $20 loss, the stock being now worth $20 a share. But management issues new options and, if the company fares better, the stock may go back up to $40 a share. The stockholders have no profit at all, but the management now has a nice fat profit of $20 a share, with no risk, not a dime on the line.[15]

If stock options have an effective place in a company's compensation program, they are, of course, the most economical form of incentive from the standpoint of the stockholders, involving as they do, no outlay of funds. Granting a key employee the right to buy stock in the future at a price fixed in the present involves a decision to raise new equity capital if the company prospers, and therefore additional capital is needed in the business.

It is true that an option, when exercised, results in realizing a lower price for the shares than would have been obtained by waiting to sell the stock. To this extent stockholders are sharing some of the gains from the success of the enterprise with those who presumably have contributed most to achieve that success. This is both the incentive and the reward. And it is much more economical to the stockholder than a salary increase or a bonus.[16]

Seven years ago, and even now, CEIR simply could not afford to pay the salaries which a large, well-established company can pay, nor can it offer the same long-range job security. CEIR could not have obtained the highly trained professional and executive talent which is essential to a service organization such as ours, on the basis of salary alone. Nor would our company have benefited from the many hours of unpaid overtime and that extra devotion to duty which our key employees have contributed to our company because they owned a stake in its success. This was made possible only because we could offset the relatively low salaries which CEIR could afford, coupled with an uncertain future in a new company, with employee stock options, and the opportunity to become owners of increasingly valuable stock in their own company if it prospered.

---

[15]Testimony of Stanley L. Kaufman of New York, in *Hearings before the Committee on Finance, U.S. Senate, 87th Congress, First Session, July 20-21, 1961* (Washington, D.C.: U.S. Government Printing Office, 1961), pp. 72-73.
[16]Testimony of Dr. Roger Murray, Columbia University Business School, *ibid.,* pp. 108-9.

And many of our key employees had never before, and probably never would otherwise have had sufficient savings to purchase outright any substantial amount of stock in their own or any other corporation.

In a word, because it could offer restricted stock options to numerous technical and management employees, CEIR has been able to make capitalists out of each of those employees and give them a permanent stake in the future of the company they are building.[17]

In 1962, there was a dramatic drop in the stock market averages which resulted in the options granted to many executives being "under water." There was, therefore, great interest in the actions which the companies might take. It was impossible to generalize; however, the following statements were quite interesting:[18]

"A company should not reduce the option price on an existing option or cancel it and grant a new option at a lower price." Henry Ford II, Ford Motor Co.

"We don't adjust the option price. Once an option is granted, its terms should not be changed. The stockholders would have a legitimate complaint if we did." James Barr, Montgomery Ward.

"The stock market's capitalization of a company can change very suddenly, but you have got to keep the incentive feature of the plan. The carrot has always got to be in front of the officer." George Dively, Harris-Intertype.

The following statement is from the proxy statement of a corporation which did lower the option price:

. . . The Committee's action took into consideration the fact that because of a substantial decline in market price, the 1959 options had very little value as incentive to the optionees; that the decline was not due to any failure on the part of the officers or other key employees to operate the business properly or to produce earnings; and that the decline was not peculiar to this company, but rather a general, widespread revaluation of the market price of stocks. It also considered that it would be inequitable to grant options to newly eligible officers and other key employees at the current market price without modifying the 1959 options.

The 1963 tax message of the President proposed sweeping alterations in the tax laws, including the lowering of marginal tax rates, provisions for the averaging of income, and revisions to the tax treatment of restricted stock options:

I, therefore, recommend that, with respect to stock options granted after this date, the spread between the option price and the value of the stock at the date the option is exercised be taxed at ordinary income tax rates at the time the

---

[17]Statement of Dr. Herbert W. Robinson, President, CEIR, Inc., *ibid.,* p. 142.

[18]"Stock Options: Should Executives Get a Second Chance?" *Forbes* magazine, May 15, 1963, p. 13–14.

option is exercised. The averaging provision referred to above which the Secretary of the Treasury will present, will prevent a tax penalty due to bunching of income in 1 year. In addition, payment of tax attributable to exercise of the stock option would be permitted in installments over several years.

This change will remove a gross inequality in the application of the income tax, but it is not expected to yield appreciable amounts of revenue; for the gains to be taxed as compensation to the employee will, as in the case of compensation in other forms, be deductible from the income of the employer.[19]

QUESTIONS

1. Are restricted stock options compensation? Present a logical argument advancing your position.

2. Can restricted stock options enable a corporation to retain and attract management personnel? What about the economy as a whole?

3. In what ways would it be desirable to modify stock options so that stockholders would be better protected?

4. Pick one of the listed companies on the New York Stock Exchange which uses stock options, and trace the history of its stock options plans, its earnings, and the market price of its stock. (Use annual reports and the financial services.) Is there a direct relationship between these three items?

5. Compare the net cost of compensation to an executive in the 50, 70, 90 per cent tax brackets of $100 in stock options versus $100 in aftertax income.

6. If you were a congressman, how would you vote on the President's proposals? Why?

---

[19]*President's 1963 Tax Message to the Congress.*

CHAPTER 12

●◆●◆●◆●◆●◆●◆●◆●◆●◆●◆●◆●◆●

Employment of Labor

IN EARLIER chapters the relations between price and cost were described for both the short run and the long run. The description ran in terms of the output of products; for example, the optimum short-run rate of output requires that marginal cost of production be equated with the marginal revenue from the sale of this output. The firm must, of course, hire inputs in order to produce outputs. Once the appropriate rate of output has been determined, management's task can be considered to be that of minimizing the total cost of inputs required to turn out this volume of product. This requires, among other things, using the most efficient available production processes and using labor, executives, and capital in the best proportions. Actually, decisions as to what outputs to produce and what inputs to hire are not independent of one another. A decision to build a plant of a particular size implies an expectation of turning out the product within its economical output range, and a decision to step up the rate of production carries with it a decision to acquire the necessary additional units. It is useful analytically, however, to concentrate attention at any one time on either output or input. The latter will be examined in the present chapter as far as the employment of labor is concerned. Our approach will be largely theoretical rather than descriptive. Consequently, such subjects as union membership, bargaining, unemployment compensation, and "right to work" laws will not be discussed.[1]

Marginal Productivity of Labor

In the short run the capital equipment of the firm and the executive staff can be considered to be fixed, but the number of workers hired and the quantity of materials and supplies utilized are subject to variation by the firm. Additional output requires that an increased amount of these variable factors be applied to a fixed quantity of "plant."

---

[1]The reader is referred to Albert Rees, *The Economics of Trade Unions* (Chicago: University of Chicago Press, 1962), for broader, but consistently analytical, coverage of important subjects in this field.

In Exhibit 1 the total number of units of a product which would result from the employment of successive workers in a hypothetical plant is shown in column 2. Outputs and inputs should be considered to pertain to some specified time period. This is assumed to be one month. Column 3 shows the "marginal product" of labor per month— the additional physical product secured by the employment of an additional worker for that length of time. Column 3, therefore, is derived by finding the difference between successive total outputs. This process is known as "imputation." The only way to measure the importance of one man to the firm is to observe how much total output would be diminished if he were not employed—or how much total output is in-

Exhibit 1

MARGINAL PRODUCTIVITY OF LABOR IN A HYPOTHETICAL PLANT

(1) Labor Input per Month	(2) Total Output per Month	(3) Marginal Product	(4) Price per Unit	(5) Value of Marginal Product
1	25	25	$10	$250
2	53	28	10	280
3	84	31	10	310
4	118	34	10	340
5	155	37	10	370
6	191	36	10	360
7	226	35	10	350
8	259	33	10	330
9	285	26	10	260
10	305	20	10	200

creased because he is employed. Since the amount of capital utilized is held constant, the output changes can be attributed to labor alone. If seven men are utilized, for example, the marginal product is thirty-five units; this should not be thought of as the product attributable to the "last man," but rather to any one of the seven men.

The firm is assumed to be able to sell any output at a price of $10 per unit. This would occur if the company were too small to affect the price by its own output—that is, if the firm sold in a purely competitive market. Value of the marginal product is found by multiplying marginal product by $10. If the firm is considered to be in some line of manufacturing, it would need additional materials, supplies, fuel, etc., as well as additional labor, in order to increase the rate of output. The additional cost of these ancillary outputs could be deducted in each row from column 5 in order to arrive at a net value of the marginal product of labor. For the sake of simplicity, however, it is assumed that there are only two required inputs—fixed capital and labor. It is further assumed that the firm is a competitive buyer of labor—a "price taker" in the labor market, unable to affect the prevailing wage by its own actions.

Under these assumptions, how many workers should the firm hire? This depends on the monthly wage rate it must pay. Suppose the prevailing wage is $300 per month. Eight men should be hired. Output worth $330 per month would then be attributable to any one man compared with a cost of $300. It would not be desirable (from a profit viewpoint) to hire nine men because any one of these would contribute only $260 per month to revenue compared with a cost of $300. It can readily be verified by a few calculations that the revenue above the total wage cost is maximized by the employment of eight workers. This is the income available for meeting such other costs as salaries, depreciation, and interest.

The firm in Exhibit 1 seems to be doing poorly, since only $190 a month will remain to meet expenses other than wages. However, once a business is established, it is better to produce and meet some of the fixed costs rather than none if there is a good chance that the situation will improve. (Otherwise it may be better to sell out.) If the prevailing wage rate were higher, say $355 per month, it would be more economical to shut down than to operate, since the wage bill could not be covered by the revenue. In terms of output analysis, price would be below minimum average variable cost.

The general rule is that workers should be hired by a fully competitive firm until the value of the marginal product of labor is equal to the wage rate which must be paid. This equalization must take place in the region of diminishing, rather than increasing, value of the marginal product; otherwise, additional men could be hired who would add more to income than to cost. A separate calculation must be made for each type of labor hired. In Exhibit 1 (as in any table), it was necessary to proceed by finite steps, and this prevented an exact equalization of the value of the marginal product and the wage rate.[2] It may be difficult for management to compute the marginal productivity of labor, but somehow a decision must be made as to how many workers to employ, and this type of analysis indicates the correct approach. A great many other types of calculations related to decision making within the firm

---

[2]This is true unless the wage rate happens to be exactly equal to one of the values of the marginal product. In that case, it does not matter whether or not the firm hires a man who adds to revenue exactly what he costs in wages. In Exhibit 1, if the wage rate were $260 per month, it would not make any difference to profits whether eight or nine men were hired.

are difficult and subject to error, but errors are likely to be even greater if the calculations are grounded on erroneous theoretical structures or if some "rule of thumb" or intuition is followed.

If labor inputs are considered for purposes of analysis to be perfectly divisible rather than "lumpy," a smooth curve can be drawn for value of the marginal product, as in Exhibit 2. This curve tacitly assumes that the plant is "indivisible" because there is a stage of increasing marginal returns as the input of labor is increased to OA units. That is, the entire plant must be utilized for turning out the product under con-

Exhibit 2

MARGINAL PRODUCT OF LABOR—INDIVISIBLE BUT ADAPTABLE PLANT

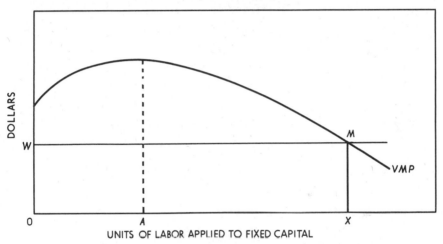

sideration, and the proportion between capital and labor becomes so much better up to input OA that increments of labor bring increasing increments of output. An example might be a cafeteria, where (conceivably) one person could serve all of the customers passing along the steam table, but where several workers can do a much more efficient job. After a certain point the additional product (measured, for example, in customers served per minute) will drop off as additional workers are put on, since each will be idle a larger part of the time.[3] The steam table is indivisible plant capacity which is adaptable to various quantities of labor.

Referring to Exhibit 2, if the prevailing wage rate is assumed to be OW, the firm will maximize profit by employing OX units of labor.

___
[3]Workers behind the steam table also have an incentive to keep up their productivity showing by attempting to sell their particular wares to passing customers.

Short of this point the number of workers would not be optimal because additional men could be hired whose added product would bring in more revenue than their pay. If more than OX are hired, the situation is nonoptimal because one or more of the workers should be considered to be adding too little to the firm's revenue.

Total revenue from the productive process is represented by the area under the VMP curve from the Y axis to input OX. Of this amount the area $OXMW$ represents total wage payments, and the remaining area represents the "quasi rent" which is available to apply toward meeting such costs as depreciation and interest.

Exhibit 3

MARGINAL PRODUCT OF LABOR—DIVISIBLE BUT
UNADAPTABLE PLANT

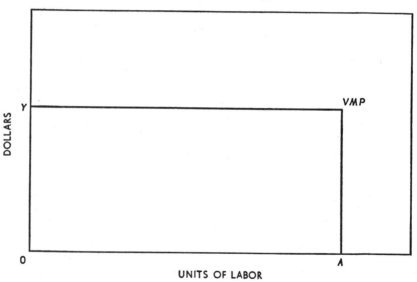

It was pointed out in Chapter 4 that marginal cost curves in manufacturing are frequently horizontal over a wide range of output. On the input side, this means that the curve in Exhibit 3 showing the value of the marginal product is horizontal over the corresponding range and then becomes vertical when maximum input is reached. This occurs when the plant is divisible but not adaptable.[4] That is, the plant may have many independent machines, each of which requires a fixed complement of labor for its operation. (A trucking firm with a large num-

---

[4] The concept of adaptability is explained in detail by George J. Stigler, *The Theory of Price* (New York; Macmillan Co., 1949), p. 122.

ber of trucks, each requiring one driver, is an example.) In this case the demand curve for labor is the vertical portion of the *VMP* curve as long as the firm desires to keep all units of the plant in operation. The number of workers hired is independent of the wage rate, unless this rate is above *OY,* in which case the firm would find it more economical to shut down because total revenue would not cover total wages. If the relation between the total wage bill and the total revenue becomes sufficiently unfavorable, there will be a tendency for capital to be withdrawn from this industry and invested elsewhere.

A plant may be both indivisible and unadaptable, and this makes the curve representing the marginal productivity of labor quite different

Exhibit 4

MARGINAL PRODUCT EQUALS TOTAL PRODUCT—
INDIVISIBLE AND UNADAPTABLE PLANT

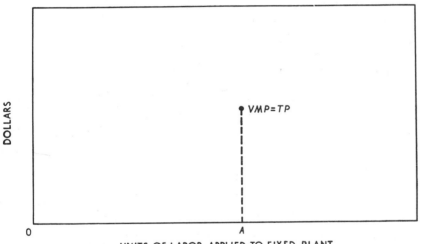

from those shown so far. This situation might exist if the plant contained a single assembly line, with each station requiring a definite complement of labor for its operation. Since every operation depends on the previous ones, there is no output at all until the employment of labor is sufficient to man all stations, but further labor input would not add to the product. The value of the marginal product of labor would then be a single point rather than a curve. This point would also represent the total product, since the addition of the last essential man brings forth the entire product, and the withdrawal of any one man would eliminate the entire product. Exhibit 4 shows this marginal productivity "curve" for labor.

In this case the firm should employ OA workers so long as the wage rate does not exceed the average product of labor. (Average product would equal the vertical value of the single point on the chart divided by its horizontal value.) If the wage rate were any higher, it would be cheaper to shut down the plant, since the wage bill would more than exhaust the total product. If the prevailing wage is less than the average product of labor, there will be some income to apply against the fixed costs. Whether or not a "profit" (in the economic sense) is earned depends on whether the return to capital exceeds or falls short of a "normal" return.

Monopolist's Demand for Labor

Only a minor modification of the marginal productivity concept is needed if the firm is a monopolistic seller of output rather than a competitive seller. As the monopolist hires more labor, his rate of output will increase, and this will lower the price at which he can sell his product. This must be taken into account in a rational decision as to how much labor to employ.

In the situation depicted in Exhibit 2, where the plant is assumed to be indivisible but adaptable, the fully competitive firm can sell any output at the market price. Consequently, diminishing VMP after input OA is due to operation of the law of diminishing returns. If the firm sold its output monopolistically, rather than competitively, the marginal contribution of labor to the revenue of the firm would be affected by the diminishing price of output in addition to diminishing physical productivity. The resulting "marginal revenue product" curve becomes the demand curve of the monopolistic firm for labor inputs. If the monopolistic seller of output is a competitive buyer of input, optimal employment from the firm's point of view requires that the marginal revenue product be equated to the wage rate which is paid.[5] It should be noted that there is no real difference in principle between the competitive and monopolistic cases. In both cases a worker should be hired if he makes an addition to the firm's gross income per period which exceeds

---

[5]This is not the optimum input if the firm is a monopsonist (the only buyer) in the labor market. Monopsony in such markets is probably uncommon in the United States and will not be examined.

Robert L. Bunting, *Employer Concentration in Local Labor Markets* (Chapel Hill: University of North Carolina Press, 1962), contains a careful empirical investigation of this matter. He found the extent of concentration of employers to be low in the unskilled labor markets. That is, few local labor markets are dominated by one or a few firms.

his wage rate per period; all workers for which this is true should be
hired.

In the event that plant capacity is divisible but not adaptable (e.g., a
trucking company), the existence of monopoly in the sale of output
causes a substantial change in the general appearance of the curve showing the marginal contribution of labor. Instead of the horizontal, then
vertical, *VMP* curve of Exhibit 3, the marginal revenue product curve
takes on the general appearance indicated in Exhibit 5. The portion of
the curve which slopes downward from left to right is traceable to the
diminishing marginal revenue obtainable from an increased rate of
output. If the prevailing wage rate is *AK* or less, the entire plant (e.g.,
all the trucks) will be utilized along with the necessary complement of

Exhibit 5

MONOPOLIST WITH DIVISIBLE AND UNADAPTABLE PLANT

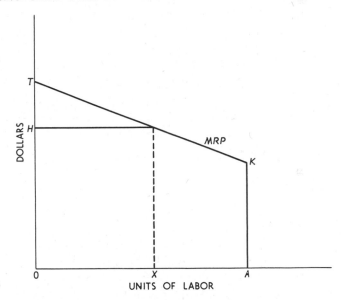

labor *OA*. At higher wage rates a smaller amount of plant and labor
will be used, the labor input at wage rate *OH*, for example, being *OX*.

The presence of monopoly in the output market does not affect the
appearance of a chart such as Exhibit 4, which pertains to a plant which
is both indivisible and unadaptable (an assembly line where a worker
is definitely needed at each station). However, the height of the single
point which represents both the value of the total output and the value
of the product of any one (indispensable) man will probably be higher
because of the firm's monopoly power in the sale of output.

Employment of Organized Labor

Once a wage rate has been established through collective bargaining with a labor union, the firm can maximize its profit, or minimize its loss, by employing workers to the point where the VMP or MRP curve reaches the wage level. The most significant consideration upon which the analysis can throw light, however, is the relationship between labor productivity curves and the relative bargaining power of unions and management.

Assuming that the union leaders are vitally interested in the employment opportunity of all members (rather than being primarily interested in those with seniority, for example), a situation in which there is a heavy investment in fixed capital and a need for a relatively fixed complement of labor to work with such capital is favorable to union bargaining power. From the union's point of view the case depicted in Exhibit 4 is ideal because no one can be laid off if the plant is to continue to operate. As long as the negotiated wage rate is less than the value of the average product per man, the firm has an economic incentive to continue to operate. In an industry which uses a great deal of capital per man (e.g., the Portland cement industry), the average product per man is attributable heavily to capital's productivity as well as to that of labor. A strong labor union in such a situation may be able to secure so high a wage rate as to appropriate for its members part or all of the normal return to owners of capital and possibly even a part of the principal.[6] Over a longer period of time, however, owners will withdraw capital from such a field.

In a tug of war between management and organized labor at the bargaining table, the financial inability of union members to stand a prolonged strike may provide a check on their capacity to exploit an otherwise strong position. Unemployment compensation, especially when the federal government stands ready to extend the period over which payments may be received, tends to strengthen union bargaining power. Employers' bargaining power is strengthened by adaptability of equipment to different complements of labor, by possibilities of moving operations overseas or to nonunionized sections of the United States, and by the threat of greater automation. Also, the rapidly growing practice of renting, rather than buying, equipment tends to strengthen the

---

[6]The power of a union that is in the position described was forcefully shown by the February, 1961, strike of flight engineers which immobilized air transportation in the United States. While this was not directly a wage dispute, the insistence of the flight engineers that they retain their own union was based on the principles discussed above.

bargaining power of employers because fixed costs associated with the equipment can more quickly be eliminated in an unfavorable situation. (A firm which owns equipment can eliminate depreciation and interest costs by selling the equipment, but a company that specializes in leasing equipment is in a better position quickly to find another user without financial sacrifices.)

In summary, the bargaining power of organized labor is increased by any forces which make the demand for labor more inelastic. These include heavy investment by firms in capital equipment, especially when it is not adaptable to different labor inputs; monopoly power of employers in output markets, with resulting abnormal profits which organized labor may be able in part to take over; restriction on entry, which reduces the number of workers whose employment is of concern to a union; and financial strength, including that which derives from a federal government that is liberal in matters of unemployment compensation. The bargaining strength of employers is increased by holding down investment in fixed capital by such means as renting equipment; keeping plant adaptable; increasing, or threatening to increase, automation; and moving, or threatening to move, operations to non-unionized areas. In recent years, labor organizations have shown increasing concern for job security in the face of rapid changes in technology. This and related issues are brought out in some detail in Case 12–2 (page 532).

Minimum Wage Adjustments

Since passage of the Fair Labor Standards Act in 1938, the federal government has set minimum wage rates in interstate manufacturing, mining, and wholesaling. Congress has recently increased the minimum to $1.25 per hour in most industries and has extended the coverage to include many retail and service workers. The effect of this type of legislation is very uneven, with many industries unaffected because their wage rates, even for the least skilled workers utilized, already exceed the prescribed minimum, while other industries must adjust their operations to a substantial increase in wage costs. Similarly, some parts of the country, especially the Southeast, are affected substantially, while other parts (e.g., the West Coast) are scarcely involved because of a higher prevailing level of wage rates. Even within an area such as the Southeast, wage rates in the rural areas tend to be lower than in urban centers. Consequently, firms in the relatively underdeveloped sections of the country, where jobs are already scarce, tend to be most affected by an increase in the federal minimum wage, and their reaction is typically to cut back employment to some extent.[7] Some states, especially outside the South, have minimum wage laws applicable to intrastate commerce.

The analysis presented earlier in this chapter can aid in prediction of the employment consequences of an increase in the minimum wage. Exhibit 6 represents a firm which is forced to pay a higher wage rate because of an increase in the legislated minimum wage. The demand for labor is provided by the VMP curve which, in this case, pertains to an indivisible but adaptable plant (e.g., a cafeteria's steam table).

Exhibit 6

EMPLOYMENT AFFECTED BY MINIMUM WAGE

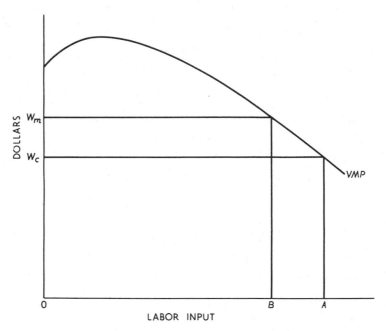

Before a change in the minimum wage law a competitive wage rate OW_c is paid, and OA workers are employed. The need to pay OW_m after the change in law will cause employment to be cut back to OB by this firm. This sort of demand curve for labor is probably quite common. On the other hand, if the demand for labor is highly inelastic, due to lack of adaptability of plant as illustrated in Exhibits 3, 4, and 5, the higher minimum wage may have no short-run effect on employment. (Over the longer run, it is likely to induce a substitution of

---

[7]M. R. Colberg, "Minimum Wage Legislation and Florida's Economic Development," *Journal of Law and Economics,* October, 1960.

capital for labor so that demand for labor does acquire some elasticity.)

Since it is theoretically possible for minimum wage boosts to have anywhere from zero to very substantial effects on employment, it is important that statistical studies be made to ascertain actual effects. The Department of Labor has been active in this field of investigation, and its work has been supplemented by the efforts of some economists outside the government service. Some of the effects which have been uncovered by the Department of Labor studies are a narrowing of differentials between occupations in affected firms; upward force on wage rates in uncovered as well as covered firms in the same industry; some reduction in employment in most of the industries studied; and a definite tendency for employment to decline more, or increase less, in the lower wage plants than in higher wage establishments. Adjustments also included greater care in the selection of employees, a rise in production standards, increased investment in machinery, and increases in prices of output.[8]

Proponents of an ever higher and broader national minimum wage almost invariably claim that the purchasing power of employees who are benefited will increase enough to shift the demand for labor upward to an extent which will prevent a reduction in employment and will even increase employment. Available statistical studies tend to disprove this "purchasing power" thesis.[9] The gains in purchasing power that are achieved by workers who receive wage increases and keep their jobs are offset by losses in wages by those who lose their jobs and by diminished returns to owners of capital. Usually, the losses of manufacturing employment are greatest in such industries as lumbering, canning and preserving, and certain textiles. There is no reason to believe that an increase in purchasing power, if it did occur, would be directed in such a way as to bolster the demand in just the right industries and areas to avoid a decrease in employment.

Viewed broadly, government interference with the price system is dangerous as a device to redistribute income, since it lowers the total output of goods and services in the economy. Some of the advantages of specialization are lost. (A minimum wage applied to commercial laundries tends to move more laundry work into the home, for example.) To the extent that a redistribution of income and wealth is desired by our selected representatives, this can be accomplished more

[8]H. M. Douty, "Some Effects of the $1.00 Minimum Wage in the United States," *Economica,* May, 1960.

[9]J. M. Peterson, *Employment Effects of Minimum Wages, 1938–1950* (Ph.D. dissertation, University of Chicago, 1956).

safely by means of fiscal devices which do not interfere with competitive prices.[10]

CASE 12–1:   MID-SOUTH PRODUCTS CORPORATION

In 1901 the Mid-South Wholesale Grocery Company was formed by
the merger of two small wholesale firms. The company acted as a
wholesale firm only until the first World War, at which time it acquired
a small fish-packing plant in New Orleans, Louisiana. Shortly after
the war a small company in Texas which milled flour and processed dry
cereals was purchased. In 1923 the firm was reorganized into the Mid-
South Products Corporation, with the main office and warehouse in
Memphis, Tennessee. A subsidiary corporation, wholly owned, was
organized to handle all food manufacturing and processing. In 1926
the company purchased a commission house dealing in fresh fruits and
produce. Another wholly owned subsidiary was organized to direct this
division. The parent company concentrated its efforts on the distribution of these various products to brokers, wholesalers, retailers, and
other manufacturing firms such as bakers, confectioners, and specialty
food processors.

Among the products handled by the company were pecans, which
were sold both in the shell and as shelled kernels. Pecans were purchased from individual growers by the commission division, and transferred for shelling and packaging to the manufacturing division, which
turned them over to the parent company for distribution. About
90 per cent of all nuts handled were shelled. Shipments were made
from the home office and also direct from the processing plants, as
described below. Purchasers of pecans were located in various parts of
the United States. The company had no retail outlets of its own. Pecans were processed and packaged for several grocery chains under
their respective labels, as well as under the brand name of Mid-South
Products Corporation.

Prior to 1932 the company had purchased pecans in the shell
through its commission division and resold about 60 per cent of them
without further processing. Those that were processed were shipped by
truck or train from the chief growing areas in southern Mississippi,
northern and central Florida, Georgia, and eastern and southern Texas.
Processing was done by hand, except that shells were cracked by hand-
operated machines. Since highest prices were obtained for whole kernels, efforts were made to crack the shells without damaging the kernel.

---

[10]This position is set forth with particular clarity by Henry Simons, "Some Reflections
on Syndicalism," *Journal of Political Economy,* March, 1944.

Kernels which were broken were sold ungraded, primarily to bakers and confectioners. Hand processing was a high-cost operation, but up to 1932 the price had been high enough to cover this high labor cost and show a profit.

In 1932, however, the price of shelled pecans dropped sharply in relation to costs of processing. Although labor was relatively cheap in Memphis at the time, the prevailing wage was still such that the company could barely cover variable costs in the processing of pecans. On a total-cost basis the operations were carried on at a loss for the years 1931 and 1932. In an effort to cut costs, the company decided to decentralize the processing operations. It was observed that the wage level in smaller towns and villages in the South was lower than in Memphis. As a result of several investigations, the company moved its pecan processing to three different locations—one in Quitman, Georgia; another in Crockett, Texas; and the third in Picayune, Mississippi. All locations were in pecan-growing areas, and all were towns of a few thousand population. In these small towns, it was possible to secure a considerable amount of part-time labor at very low wages. In Picayune, Mississippi, for example, all the employees were women who worked as domestics part of each day and could be secured for 20 cents per hour for three to four hours each afternoon to shell and clean pecans. The rate of turnover was high, but the nature of the labor was unskilled, so that this factor was not serious. About three hundred part-time workers were used in this plant for six or seven months each year.

Since pecans are harvested in the autumn season within a period of about two months, they must be stored in warehouses and withdrawn as needed. Prior to decentralization of operations, this necessitated the use of expensive warehouse space in Memphis, until the nuts were processed and again stored. Since substantially less space is required to store the shelled kernels, there was considerable pressure upon the manufacturing division to process the pecan stocks as rapidly as possible. Frequently, it was necessary to employ overtime to hasten the processing. In the new locations the company was able to acquire satisfactory existing structures for storing the newly harvested pecans which were less expensive than the urban location in Memphis. In addition, the net freight charges were less on shelled pecans, plus the fact that the shells were more easily disposed of in the rural locations. In the latter places the processing could be spread over a much longer period of time. Pecans were shelled and shipped in 50-pound containers to the main plant in Memphis, where they were graded and repacked for distribution.

This decentralization permitted the company to show a profit on a total-cost basis. In 1933 the company processed approximately 16,000 pounds of shelled pecans at a net profit of 21 cents per pound. By 1937 the company was processing about 24,000 pounds of shelled pecans annually at a profit of 20 cents per pound. The largest item of cost in the processing was labor. A good worker could shell about one and a half pounds of whole kernels per hour and about three quarters of a pound of broken kernels. In view of hand operations the rate of broken kernels was not considered too high.

In 1938 the President of the United States signed the Fair Labor Standards Act, which required, among other things, a minimum wage of 40 cents per hour for labor engaged in or affecting interstate commerce. In addition, the act contained provisions for payment of overtime in excess of forty hours per week. Upon recommendation of legal counsel the company decided to comply with the provisions of the act. In the pecan-processing operations, this would require a wage increase in excess of 100 per cent.

Coincident with the passage of this act, there was a sharp decline in economic activity and prices. Coupled with an unusually large walnut and almond crop in California, the price of pecans declined so that the profit per pound decreased to 4 cents. The price of pecans tends to conform in movement to the prices of nuts which are fairly good substitutes, such as walnuts, almonds, cashews, Brazil nuts, etc. The Mid-South Products Corporation distributed all kinds of nuts, but processed and packaged none other than pecans.

The executive committee called a meeting of the board of directors to consider the status of the pecan-processing operations. To pay the required minimum wages and overtime would involve the company in a substantial loss at the existing market prices of shelled pecans. There was divided sentiment among the directors as to what should be done. One suggestion was to abandon the pecan business entirely, since it constituted such a small part of the business, although it was growing in size. Another was to deal only in pecans in the shell. One director suggested raising the price to cover the new labor costs.

Early in 1937 the vice president of the company had investigated the possibilities of mechanical processing of pecans. There was little standard equipment available which the company did not already possess. However, a large eastern electrical manufacturing company had, at the request of the vice president, drawn up plans for a machine which would crack, shell, grade, and package pecans in containers of various sizes. It was designed to operate by means of a battery of electric "eyes." Since the machine was a specially designed affair and many parts would have to be made by hand, it was estimated to cost approximately $35,-000. It would, however, have a capacity of 10,000 pounds of shelled pecans per week and would require two highly skilled operators in addition to several laborers to close the containers as they were filled. The cost of constructing a machine of half that capacity was estimated to be only $2,000 less. The idea was rejected at the time because of the high cost. The cost accounting department had calculated that, with the current volume of operations, the installation of such a machine in any one of the three locations would result in a cost per pound higher than that incurred by hand operations.

The Mid-South Products Corporation competed with five other similar food-processing and -distributing companies in the sale of shelled pecans. Two of these companies were much larger than the Mid-South Corporation. In addition, there were numerous smaller companies which also sold small quantities of shelled pecans. These companies "farmed out" their shelling operations to individuals who performed the work in their homes. The Mid-South Corporation had experimented with this method at one time but had found it unsatisfactory for large-scale operations. The vice president of the company had discussed the labor problems occasioned by the new law with three of his larger competitors and found that they faced the same problems. The two larger competitors each sold about 40,000 pounds of shelled pecans annually, while the third sold about the same volume as the Mid-South Corporation.

The cost accounting division of the Mid-South Corporation reported in 1938 that if a volume of 75,000 pounds of shelled pecans could be sold annually, the company could reduce labor costs to approximately 8 cents per pound for the entire pecan operations if the machine were purchased. This included amortization of the purchase price, a special building to house the equipment, and wages of the skilled operators. At the price of pecans in 1938, this would produce a profit of about 16 cents per pound on a total-cost basis.

QUESTIONS

1. What action would you recommend for the company? State your reasons.
2. If the machine were purchased, what considerations would affect your choice of its location?
3. If the machine were purchased, should the book value of the three existing processing plants be added to the cost of the machine?
4. Does this case introduce any relationship between size of market and unit cost? Explain.

5. Adam Smith said: "Specialization is limited by the extent of the market." Can you apply this principle to the present case?

6. What is the present minimum wage? On what sections of the country do you believe the latest increase had its greatest effects? Give arguments both for and against the minimum wage.

CASE 12-2: KAISER STEEL CORPORATION–UNITED STEELWORKERS OF AMERICA LONG–RANGE SHARING PLAN

During World War II, Kaiser Steel Corporation built near Fontana, California, the only fully integrated steel mill on the West Coast. In 1963, it remained the only fully integrated producer on the West Coast. Its 1962 capacity was three million ingot tons, which put it in the smaller group of large steel companies. Exhibit I shows steel production by Kaiser in tons since 1955, net sales, and net income.

Exhibit 1

KAISER STEEL CORPORATION

Year	Steel Ingots Produced (Tons)	Net Sales	Net Income*
1957	1,590,322	$208,307,615	$21,438,507
1958	1,966,278	181,179,192	3,422,271
1959	1,537,802	201,939,440	(7,401,076)
1960	1,706,826	207,116,051	(8,215,842)
1961	1,403,000	265,973,000	17,103,000
1962	1,290,000	232,316,000	(5,207,000)

*Parentheses indicate deficit.
Source: Annual reports of Kaiser Steel Corporation.

Kaiser broke away from the industry bargaining group during the 1959 strike of the United Steelworkers and signed a separate agreement with the union. Among the provisions, this contract provided for the establishment of a committee to study the sharing of gains from productivity.

In 1962, Kaiser also virtually eliminated the historical differential in steel prices between the West Coast and the remainder of the country. The average price reduction was $12 a ton. Kaiser believed that this would not only make Kaiser more competitive domestically but would assist in meeting the competition from imports.

The following is an announcement and summary of the proposed long-range sharing plan developed by the Long-Range Committee of Kaiser Steel and the United Steelworkers.

Long-Range Sharing Plan

(Announcement by members of the long-range committee, Kaiser Steel Corp. and the United Steelworkers of America, AFL-CIO, December 17, 1962)

The long-range committee of Kaiser Steel Corp. and the United Steelworkers of America, AFL-CIO, today announced their recommendation of a plan for equitable sharing of economic progress by employees, the company, and the public.

The plan has been accepted by officials of Kaiser Steel and the international union. It will become effective only with approval of employees represented by the union at the Kaiser Steel plant in Fontana.

Announcement was made at a public meeting by Dr. George W. Taylor, Chairman of the Committee, by David J. McDonald, president of the United Steelworkers of America, AFL-CIO, and Edgar F. Kaiser, chairman of the board of Kaiser Steel Corp. The meeting was held at Swing Auditorium on the Orange Show Grounds, San Bernardino, California and was attended by several thousand employees and their wives and husbands.

Coverage of USWA Employees

The plan will cover all Steelworkers Union employees at the plant, including some 6,500 members of the Production and Maintenance Local No. 2869 and 500 members of Clerical and Technical Local No. 3677, employed at the Fontana steel plant.

Protection against Automation

The plan provides protection against the loss of employment because of any technological advance (automation) or new or improved work methods, and also against the loss of income that an employee might otherwise suffer because of such changes. Appropriate protection is provided against loss of opportunity for employment for all reasons except a decrease in the production or demand for finished steel products, a change in products, and the like. Protection against unemployment for such reasons is already provided by the supplemental unemployment benefits plan and other provisions in the existing collective bargaining agreement.

Monthly Sharing of Savings

The plan provides for a monthly sharing with employees of all savings in the use of materials and supplies, and from increased productivity of labor. The sharing takes place whether the increased productivity comes about by direct effort of employees, by the use of better equipment, newer processes, better materials, or through improved yields. Formula for sharing provides that about one-third of any dollar gains made under the plan will be shared by employees. The balance is shared by the company and by the public through taxes. The plan is not a profit-sharing plan—the amount of sharing is not dependent in any way on the level of company profits.

Minimum Guarantee

The plan guarantees that the employees will receive, as a minimum, any economic improvements which may be negotiated in the future in the basic steel industry. This provision is essential in order to encourage full employee participation and to obtain the maximum benefits from the use of technological improvements, including automation. The parties are confident, however, that this minimum guarantee always will be exceeded because the employees' share of economic gains generated by the plan will be greater than the gains that might result from periodic negotiations between the union and the industry generally.

Industrial Peace

The plan will do away with contract deadlines with respect to economic issues and will contribute greatly to the objective of industrial peace. Normal collective bargaining procedures are retained with respect to all other matters.

Results of 3 Years of Study and Research

The plan was developed during nearly 3 years of joint study by long-range committee members and staffs of the United Steelworkers and Kaiser Steel. In addition to committee members named above, also participating in the development of the program were David L. Cole, arbitrator and former Director of the Federal Mediation and Conciliation Service, and Dr. John T. Dunlop, professor, Harvard University, as public members; Marvin J. Miller, assistant to the president, and Charles J. Smith, director of district 38 (west coast area), for the United Steelworkers of America; and E. E. Trefethen, Jr., vice chairman of the board, and C. F. Borden, executive vice president, for Kaiser Steel.

Based on Contract Objective

The committee dates back to October 26, 1959, when Kaiser Steel and the Steelworkers ended a 3½-month strike. At that time the company and union entered an agreement to establish a joint nine-man committee representing the public, the company, and the union, to develop a long-range plan for the equitable sharing of economic progress. It was agreed in the contract, "The formula shall give appropriate consideration to safeguarding the employees against increases in cost of living, to promoting stability of employment, to reasonable sharing of increased productivity, labor-cost savings, to providing for necessary expansion and for assuring the company's and employees' progress."

Technological Progress and Protection of Work Practices

The plan recognizes that, in a free enterprise system, economic progress can only be achieved by practical utilization of equipment and materials in order to provide good service and a consistently high quality product. It also recognizes that human values must be conserved in the production process and that the best method of achieving efficiency is by joint effort—not by unilateral change. The plan, therefore, makes no change in existing contractual protections of work practices. It provides, instead, a framework which is designed to lead to increased productivity. This framework consists of the provision for the sharing of gains of increased productivity and the guarantee, which the plan provides, against unemployment due to technological change or such changes in work practices as may mutually be agreed.

Plan Based on Existing Costs

Four steps were taken by the committee in order to meet the requirements for the plan. First step was to establish the present level of costs (not prices) of products that are sold at the steel plant in Fontana in terms of labor costs and material and supply costs for each ton of finished steel produced. This was done in such a manner as to recognize the differences in operating levels as well as in the amount of processing required in producing the various products made by Kaiser Steel. These factors provide the base point or standard against which future improvements in productivity will be measured.

Recognizes Industry and National Economic Factors

The second step was to provide for changes in the price level of purchased materials, for safeguarding employees against cost-of-living increases and comprehending the company's practical ability to pay. The committee chose as the most desirable method of measuring these basic factors two broad economic indexes, which include these considerations. It was agreed that the wholesale price index of industry steel prices and the Consumer Price Index issued by the Bureau of Labor Statistics would fulfill this requirement. Movements of these indexes will be reflected in the standards.

32.5 Per Cent of Gains Shared by Employees

The third step taken by the committee was the development of a formula for sharing the improvements. The formula is simple and equitable. The employees' share of the total net dollar gains generated under this plan is 32.5 per cent. This sharing relationship is consistent with the past ratio of labor costs to total manufacturing costs at Kaiser Steel.

Monthly Sharing by Employees

Finally, the plan provides distribution of the employees' net share in the gains on a monthly basis. The plan thus offers employees potential new sources of income by sharing savings as they occur during the actual course of production. It also permits the parties to agree on the use of a portion of the gains produced by the plan for making improvements or adding to insurance, retirement, vacation, holiday and other benefits not provided generally in the industry. The remaining net gains will be distributed in paychecks directly to the employees each month as an addition to their regular pay, through the receipt of payments under the long-range sharing plan.

Sharing by Incentive Employees

Employees now on incentives may transfer to the long-range sharing plan in a variety of ways.

1. The employees on any incentive plan may decide, by majority vote, to cancel the existing incentive and transfer to the long-range sharing plan.

2. When the company so offers, the employees on an incentive plan may decide, by majority vote, to accept a lump sum payment roughly equivalent to 2½ years' incentive earnings and to participate in the long-range sharing plan. If the employees reject the lump sum payment, present incumbents will continue to receive the same incentive earnings as in the past, through conversion of such incentives to plans paying no more than 35 per cent and differential payments to equal prior earnings. Any savings made by the company as a result of the acceptance of lump sum payments, or as a result of the elimination of incentive earnings for new employees, will be added to the overall employees' share under the plan.

3. Incentive employees who are not offered a lump sum payment, and who do not elect to transfer to the long-range sharing plan because their incentive earnings exceed the shares payable under the plan, will continue on incentive and, after 2 years, will also participate, on an adjusted basis, in the long-range sharing plan.

In Keeping with Basic Agreement

The committee said this long-range sharing plan is in harmony with the spirit and intent of the basic labor agreement. It provides a motivation for insuring the future economic progress of the company and its employees, and at the same time, preserves the normal union and company roles.

Members to Vote on Plan

The plan is in the process of being printed and will be distributed to the membership as soon as practicable. In the meantime, the company and the union have arranged to conduct briefing sessions for both union members and management personnel on details of application of the plan. Voting on the plan by union members will take place after these sessions.

The plan would be effective for a 4-year period, subject to review and revision by the company and the union annually. The plan can be terminated by either party on 4 months' notice, following the fourth anniversary date of the plan.

The proposal was submitted to the locals and ratified by secret ballot on January 11, 1963, by a vote of 3,966 to 1,383. The plan went into effect on March 1, 1963.

In late April, 1963, the first payments under the plan were announced. Total savings over the 1961 rate for the month of March were $962,000, of which $312,000 went to the 3,930 participating workers, with the bonus averaging $79 a man. Not all workers participated, since some chose to remain under existing incentive programs. It was estimated by a United Steelworkers official that payments varied from 15.1 per cent to 45.1 per cent of wage rates. The lowest payment was 31.5 cents an hour for an employee in the lowest category earning $2.10 an hour. An employee in the highest category, earning $3.00 an hour, received an extra $1.35 an hour.

QUESTIONS

1. In what ways could the theory of employment, as developed in this chapter, have been of use to the committee as it developed this plan?

2. What aspects of the plan suggest that the theory is perhaps too narrow for such a dynamic response to changing production techniques?

3. From your own knowledge or from studying the steel industry, are there any factors which might make this plan successful at Kaiser and perhaps not successful at other steel companies?

4. What alternative solutions are possible to the problems of technological change and automation?

CASE 12–3:   LABOR IN THE BITUMINOUS COAL INDUSTRY*

Since the early thirties, the major coal producing companies have had contracts with the United Mine Workers Union. The union has

Exhibit 1

EMPLOYMENT AND PRODUCTIVITY DATA FOR THE
BITUMINOUS COAL INDUSTRY

		Output per Man per Day			
Year	Total Employment (000)	Underground	Strip	Auger	Average All Mines
1924.............	n.a.	4.50	9.91		4.56
1936.............	457	4.42	13.91		4.62
1937.............	470	n.a.	n.a.		4.69
1938.............	416	4.60	15.00		4.89
1939.............	381	4.92	14.68		5.25
1940.............	439	4.86	15.63		5.19
1941.............	452	4.83	15.59		5.20
1942.............	480	4.74	15.52		5.12
1943.............	434	4.89	15.15		5.38
1944.............	415	5.04	15.89		5.68
1945.............	388	5.04	15.46		5.78
1946.............	391	5.43	15.73		6.30
1947.............	429	5.49	15.93		6.42
1948.............	442	5.31	15.28		6.26
1949.............	434	5.42	15.33		6.43
1950.............	416	5.75	15.66		6.77
1951.............	n.a.	6.08	16.02		7.04
1952.............	335	6.37	16.77	20.07	7.47
1953.............	n.a.	7.01	17.62	25.30	8.17
1954.............	227	7.99	19.64	24.12	9.47
1955.............	225	8.28	21.12	22.22	9.84
1956.............	228	8.62	21.18	24.85	10.28
1957.............	229	8.91	21.64	26.19	10.59
1958.............	197	9.38	21.54	28.15	11.33
1959.............	180	10.08	22.65	28.77	12.22
1960.............	169	10.64	22.93	31.36	12.83

Source: U.S. Bureau of Mines cited in *Bituminous Coal Facts*, 1962.

*See Case 5–3 for additional information about the bituminous coal industry.

achieved significant gains in wages and fringe benefits since that time, but total employment has diminished in the mines as new processes of mining have been installed which involve considerable substitution of machinery for labor.

The resulting productivity increases, plus continued and increasing competition from competitive fuels has resulted in a decrease in the price of coal at the mine of 34 cents per ton since 1948, despite an increase in the daily wages of the miners of $10.20.

Exhibit 2

AVERAGE HOURLY EARNINGS IN COAL,
OTHER INDUSTRIES, 1939–61

Year	Bituminous Coal	Chemicals	All Manufacturing	Automobiles	Textile Mills
1939............	$0.86	n.a.	$0.63	$0.92	n.a.
1942............	1.03	n.a.	.85	1.17	n.a.
1943............	1.10	n.a.	.96	1.24	n.a.
1944............	1.15	n.a.	1.01	1.27	n.a.
1945............	1.20	n.a.	1.02	1.27	n.a.
1946............	1.36	n.a.	1.08	1.35	n.a.
1947............	1.58	$1.22	1.22	1.47	$1.04
1948............	1.84	1.34	1.33	1.61	1.16
1949............	1.88	1.42	1.38	1.70	1.18
1950............	1.94	1.50	1.44	1.78	1.23
1951............	2.14	1.62	1.56	1.91	1.32
1952............	2.22	1.69	1.65	2.05	1.34
1953............	2.40	1.81	1.74	2.14	1.36
1954............	2.40	1.89	1.78	2.20	1.36
1955............	2.47	1.97	1.86	2.29	1.38
1956............	2.72	2.09	1.95	2.35	1.44
1957............	2.92	2.20	2.05	2.46	1.49
1958............	2.93	2.29	2.11	2.55	1.49
1959............	3.12	2.40	2.19	2.71	1.56
1960............	3.15	2.50	2.26	2.81	1.61
1961............	3.13	2.58	2.32	2.86	1.63

Source: U.S. Bureau of Labor Statistics, cited in *Bituminous Coal Facts*, 1962.

Although 68 per cent of coal in the United States is still mined underground, 95 per cent of this coal is cut, drilled, blasted, and loaded by machines. Three fourths of the underground mining is accomplished by using cutting machines, which undercut the coal face to facilitate blasting. The explosive is placed in holes bored by mechanical drills and the coal is "blown down." Mechanical loaders and conveyor belts are used to bring the coal to the surface. In other underground mines, continuous mining machines chew the coal from the earth at a rate of up to eight tons per minute, at the same time carrying the coal out to the surface.

Very large machines have been constructed for use in surface or strip mining—some electrically driven shovels close to 14 stories high with tremendous capacities. Surface mining, which accounts for almost 30 per cent of coal production in the United States, had a 1960 average output per man-day of 22.9 tons, compared to 10.6 for underground mines. In hilly coal areas, huge augers are being used to bore coal out of the sides of hills at output rates of over 31 tons of coal per man per day.

A unique feature of the union agreements in the coal industry is the welfare fund contribution which the mine operators have agreed to make. This presently amounts to 40 cents per ton. The fund supports a large number of benefits for mine workers, including medical care and pensions.

Although most of the large coal producers are organized, a proportion of the mines still employ nonunion miners at wages below the union scale and do not make the 40-cent per ton contribution to the welfare fund. Data are not available on the extent to which these nonunion mines operate.

Exhibits 1 and 2 show some basic data concerning employment, output, and wages in the coal mining industry.

Questions

1. What is the significance of the welfare fund contribution to the mine owners attempts to reduce labor costs through mechanization?

2. Although average output per man per day has increased dramatically in strip and auger mines, the over-all average has increased only slightly in recent years. Why?

3. Compare the necessary marginal revenue product to hire an additional miner in an average productivity nonunion mine with that of an average productivity union mine.

4. How do you account for the differences in the relative wage increases in the industries given in Exhibit 2?

CHAPTER 13

•••••••••••••••••••••••••

Taxation and the Firm

IN AN economy where federal tax collections amount to about one fifth of the gross national product and where state and local taxes are increasing steadily, a great many business decisions are affected strongly by tax considerations. Personal decisions are also based on tax liability to a much greater extent than was the case before World War II. Some well-known motion-picture actors have limited themselves to two new films per year due to the high tax rates on additional income. Recently, the 50-year-old president of a corporation gave up his $50,000-a-year salary because the position netted him only $4,500 after taxes.[1] This was due to his large income from investments which put his entire salary into the top income tax bracket. The federal income tax can in such a case be aptly described as a "subsidy to leisure." It is also a subsidy to home ownership, in that property taxes are deductible from gross income, and because no tax is assessed against income received in the form of housing services from an owner-occupied dwelling.[2] On the other hand, a renter who keeps an equivalent amount invested in securities or other income-earning assets usually pays an income tax on such income and is unable to deduct property taxes which enter into his rental costs.

Corporation Income Tax

The magnitude of the tax on corporate net income (30 per cent on the first $25,000 and 52 per cent on the remainder) makes it a major factor in many business decisions. It was pointed out in Chapter 1 that, in theory, this tax should be assessed against economic profit rather than against accounting profit. This reform is probably not administratively practicable; but if it could be put into effect, it would discontinue the unfortunate stimulus now given to debt financing instead of equity financing, due to the deductibility of explicit interest payments

---

[1] "Tax Angles: Federal Levies Push More Americans into Unusual Decisions," *Wall Street Journal,* January 3, 1956, p. 1.

[2] The Department of Commerce, however, imputes a value to such housing services in arriving at national income estimates.

only, in arriving at net income. (It has also been pointed out that the chronic inflation since the outbreak of World War II has tended to make bond issues preferable to stock issues from the point of view of firms in need of capital; that is, a debtor status is desirable if inflation is in the offing.) A more nearly practicable reform in the corporate income tax law would consist of eliminating the deductibility of interest in arriving at net income for tax purposes. This change would, of course, permit a substantial lowering of the tax rate.

The existence of a high tax on corporate income gives some stimulus to use of the partnership form and to the individual proprietorship as a means of avoiding this impost. Income received under these forms of business organization is taxed only as personal income, while the net profit received by a corporation is first taxed as corporate income and then as personal income, to the extent that it is paid out as dividends. This is frequently criticized as "double taxation," and the criticism has led to recent amendment of the federal tax regulations to permit a limited deduction of dividend income in arriving at taxable personal income. To the extent that income is retained by the corporation through the reinvestment of profits, there is some avoidance of this double taxation; but since plowing back profits tends to increase the market value of stock, a capital gains tax of 25 per cent will eventually have to be paid by the owner when he sells his shares.[3] The advantage of the corporate form in raising capital, its limited liability, and the relative independence of its existence from the life of any individual are of such importance that the corporate form of organization retains its popularity in spite of the high corporate income tax.

The small corporation, however, may be quite seriously hampered by this tax compared with the large corporation. To the extent that the corporate income tax is absorbed by the firm rather than passed forward to the consumer or backward to suppliers of inputs, it directly reduces the profits which can be retained by the corporation. This probably hinders the growth of smaller corporations more than that of larger ones, due to the greater ability of the latter to secure additional funds through the sale of new securities. Also, the growth of corporations in the more risky lines of business is probably hampered more than that of other corporations, because the former tend to sell common stock rather than bonds to a greater degree.

This problem has been examined by John Lintner and J. Keith

---

[3]If the stock is retained until the death of the owner, no tax on the capital gain need be paid by the estate. This value will, however, enter into the estate and inheritance tax liability, and the need to pay these taxes may require liquidation of some securities.

Butters.[4] They found through empirical study that the average retained earnings of profitable smaller manufacturing companies regularly constituted a much larger percentage of their net worth than did the retained earnings of larger manufacturers. They point out further that even when outside capital is *available* to small firms, it is often less acceptable to them than to large corporations, because terms may be less favorable, and because there is more fear of weakening the control position by selling additional securities with voting privileges.[5]

Is the Corporate Income Tax Shifted?

Conclusions as to the effect of the corporate income tax usually rest on the assumption that the burden of the tax falls on the corporation rather than upon customers, workers, and others. If, instead, it were possible to shift the tax completely, dividends and retained profits would not be decreased by the existence of the tax. In that event, there would not actually be any impact on the relative rate of growth of small corporations compared with large ones, or on risky activities compared with others. The question of the incidence of the corporation income tax is therefore important, and it is one which has received a good deal of attention from economists. There is little consensus among the experts, however.

The traditional view has been that the corporate income tax is not an element in costs, since it is assessed only on net profit; that it consequently will not affect the inputs or outputs of firms; and that it cannot, therefore, be shifted. That is, if corporations turn out the same volume of goods with the tax in existence as they would in the absence of the tax, selling prices will be the same, so the tax will not be borne by consumers. And if corporations faced with this tax will utilize the same volume of resources as otherwise, they will have to pay the same amount for these inputs and consequently cannot shift the tax "backward." Marginal cost curves of firms are, in this traditional view, unaffected by the income tax. As a consequence, a perfectly competitive industry will have no reason to change output in the short run. Similarly, a monopolistic firm, assuming that it is already charging the most profitable price, will have no incentive to change that price, even though it is forced to share its profits with society.

Most businessmen share the opinion that the corporate income tax

---

[4] "Effects of Taxes on Concentration," *Business Concentration and Price Policy* (Princeton: Princeton University Press, 1955), pp. 239–80.

[5] *Ibid.*, p. 258.

is not shifted, according to two surveys by the National Industrial Conference Board.[6] It should be recognized, however, that answers to such a question may be more nearly propaganda than honest conviction. Most people like to claim that their own tax burden is heavier than it should be and to imply that it should therefore be lowered. On the other hand, some businessmen feel that the best attack on the corporation income tax is to claim that it really hits consumers and workers.

To the extent that the corporate income tax reduces the supply of capital to enterprises, it can be said to be shifted forward to consumers through higher prices. That is, output will be lower and prices higher than in the absence of the tax. Individuals will tend to invest less in corporate equities and more in other types of assets, thus distorting somewhat the allocation of resources in the economy. In addition, some reduction in the rate of real capital formation probably results from the corporate income tax, and this tends to keep prices of goods higher than they would otherwise be. In the main, however, incidence of this tax appears to rest on stockholders.

This conclusion is not necessarily applicable in the case of oligopolistic industries. If it is the accepted pricing practice in an industry to add to prime cost a certain percentage markup for overhead and another markup for profit, it is probable that the corporate income tax causes the last-named percentage to be larger and thereby causes a shifting of the tax to consumers. Such industries are said by some analysts frequently to "satisfice" rather than "optimize," that is, to take a long-run view of earning satisfactory profits rather than striving to maximize profits.[7] If this has been the case, the industry will have less difficulty in shifting a major part of a corporate income tax to consumers.

The possible patterns of oligopolistic behavior are so numerous that it is difficult to reach useful generalizations regarding the probable effects of the corporate income tax as far as oligopoly characterizes industries in which corporations dominate. The difficulty of assessing its incidence, along with its great importance to the federal government as a revenue raiser, suggests that this tax will be a part of the American business scene for a long time. The major questions for the immediate future seem to be whether to make the tax a progressive one

---

[6] National Industrial Conference Board, *The Shifting and Effects of the Federal Corporation Income Tax*, Vol. 1 (New York, 1928); and *idem, Effects of Taxes upon Corporate Profits* (New York, 1943). Over 75 per cent of the top men in 10,000 corporations surveyed in the earlier questionnaire felt that the tax was not shifted.

[7] See J. G. March and H. A. Simon, *Organizations* (New York: John Wiley & Sons, Inc., 1958), p. 141.

rather than charging a flat 52 per cent on most income, and whether to change the percentage if a single rate is kept in effect.[8]

Taxation and Mergers

Business mergers are motivated by numerous considerations in addition to the tax advantages which may be gained.[9] Tax motives constitute an important and often dramatic reason for mergers, however. This arises mainly from the provisions of the federal tax law which permit the "carry-back" and "carry-forward" of losses incurred in a particular year. A loss incurred in 1960 can be used to secure a refund on 1957, 1958, and 1959 corporate income taxes—if those were profitable years—or to reduce the tax during the years 1961 through 1965 if those years are profitable. That is, losses can be carried back three years and forward five years as an offset against profits. A loss in 1960 can be carried back to 1957, and the taxpayer then secures a refund equal to the difference between the tax which was paid in 1957 and the amount which would have been paid that year if the 1960 loss had been incurred in 1957.[10] If this does not exhaust the 1960 loss, the unused portion is applied against 1958 income, and then 1959 income. If the three-year carry-back does not absorb the entire loss, it may be carried forward to 1961 and then for four more years.

This provision has given a peculiar value to unprofitable operations, increasing the selling value of a firm which has unused tax losses on its books above what it would otherwise be. Frequently, firms with tax losses are advertised for sale—and the existence of the losses is stressed in the advertisements. Profitable firms often run advertisements showing that they want to buy unprofitable companies. Also, firms with tax losses frequently look for profitable companies to buy, so that the loss can be offset against the profits of the merged firms.

It should not be inferred that it is just as good for a corporation to have a loss as a profit, of course. A loss means an impairment in the

[8]For a discussion of the corporate income tax from a broader point of view, see J. M. Buchanan, *The Public Finances* (Homewood, Ill.: Richard D. Irwin, Inc., 1960), chap. xxiv.

[9]These are summarized by J. Keith Butters, John Lintner, and William L. Cary, *Effects of Taxation: Corporate Mergers* (Boston: Harvard University, 1951), p. 232, as the "desire for a new product, plant, or production organization, for greater vertical integration, including both new marketing outlets and sources of supply, and for financial advantages of various sorts." They found that taxes constituted an important reason for about one fourth of the mergers involving selling companies with assets over $1 million.

[10]Information in this paragraph was obtained from "Notes and Comments, *Yale Law Journal,* June, 1960, pp. 1202–4.

net asset position of a firm. (The excess of total assets over total liabilities is decreased.) But if there are profits against which the loss can be fully offset, the ill effects of the bad year on the net assets of the firm can be cut approximately in half. This is why the carry-back and carry-forward tax provisions are considered by many to be an appropriate way to foster risk taking on the part of corporations and to promote innovations which may at first produce losses.

Assuming, for convenience, a 50 per cent corporate income tax and a three-year carry-back privilege, suppose that profits and taxes were as shown in Exhibit 1. There would then have occurred no change in the net asset position for the four-year period as a whole. Without the carry-back provision, there would have been a $3-million impairment of assets. The damage caused by the 1960 experience has been cut in half by the carry-back possibility.

Exhibit 1

Year	Net Income (in Millions)	Tax (in Millions)
1957	$2	$1
1958	2	1
1959	2	1
1960	−6	3 (refund)

If a firm has a large tax loss that cannot usefully be carried back, it is especially important that it resume profitable operations quickly and substantially enough to be able to make full use of the loss carry-forward privilege. If it seems unlikely that this can be done, a solution may lie in merger with a company which promises to earn steady profits in the near future. If the latter firm buys the tax-loss firm, the net price which it must pay for the acquisition is, in effect, substantially reduced by the tax saving which will accrue. It is important, of course, that the unprofitable company be made profitable again, or the temporary tax gain to the buying firm can turn into a long-run loss.

In 1954, Congress clarified the rules on tax-loss mergers, making it illegal to merge companies where the action is aimed overtly at tax reduction. Also, the United States Treasury has been working on new regulations, in order to clarify what can and cannot be done for tax-reduction purposes. The whole matter is difficult to handle administratively because tax saving is likely to be only one of several important considerations in a merger, and it is usually hard to show that it is really the basic motive.

Accelerated Depreciation

Since 1913 the income tax laws have permitted a reasonable deduction for depreciation of durable assets. There has been fairly general use of the straight-line formula, where original cost less salvage value is written off at a uniform absolute rate over the life of the asset.[11] The straight-line method is becoming less popular, however, because of a very important change in the law in 1954, which now allows accelerated depreciation according to specified formulas. The principal interesting fact about the new law is that it allows firms to compute depreciation according to either the "declining balance" or the "sum of the years' digits" method, as well as by the straight-line method. Both provide larger depreciation deductions in the early years of life of a durable asset, and both usually provide tax savings compared with the straight-line method.[12]

Depreciation Allowances for Defense Facilities

A special sort of accelerated depreciation is allowed for facilities which receive the necessary certification as important to the national defense. Under the rapid write-off program a portion of the cost of a new project may be charged off in five years. As of July 8, 1956, a total of 21,326 projects had been certified for rapid amortization.[13] This program is based on World War II experience with accelerated depreciation of emergency facilities.[14] A large number of certificates have been issued to utility companies and railroads. Oil companies, metals producers, shipbuilders, air lines, freight-car builders, and other industries have also received large numbers of certificates. The effects on

---

[11] William J. Edmonds, "The Effect on Business Decisions of Changes in Tax Depreciation Policy," *National Tax Journal,* March 1955, p. 99.

[12] The law allows use of the declining balance method at a rate up to twice the straight-line rate. For example, an asset with an estimated life of 10 years could be depreciated at a yearly rate of 20 per cent—this rate being applied each year to the undepreciated balance. If the asset cost $1,000, the first year's depreciation charge would be $200; the second year's, $160; etc. The act permits the firm to shift at any time to a straight-line basis on the balance of unrecovered costs less salvage. Otherwise, the asset would never be fully written off.

Under the "sum of the years' digits" method a complete write-off does occur. If the asset will last 10 years, the allowable depreciation charge in the first year is 10 divided by the sum of digits from 1 to 10—that is, 10/55; the second year, it is 9/55; and the tenth year, it is 1/55. The cost minus the salvage value of the asset is multiplied by these fractions.

[13] *New York Times,* July 8, 1956.

[14] The wartime program is described and analyzed by E. Cary Brown and Gardner Patterson, "Accelerated Depreciation: A Neglected Chapter in War Taxation," *Quarterly Journal of Economics,* August, 1943, p. 630.

tax liability of this sort of emergency amortization are quite similar to the tax results of regular accelerated depreciation as provided in the 1954 Revenue Act. Consequently, the effects will not be separately examined.

Interest Saving

The financial newspapers and popular discussions usually emphasize that accelerated depreciation results only in a deferral of tax liability, because the heavy depreciation charges in the early years of an asset's life will be counterbalanced by correspondingly smaller write-offs in later years, thus increasing the tax liability in later years. One error in this observation is that it neglects the permanent saving in interest which results from accelerated depreciation. Assets which can be tem-

Exhibit 2

DEPRECIATION OF A SINGLE PROJECT BY TWO METHODS

Depreciation by:	Year 1	Year 2	Year 3	Year 4	Year 5
Straight-line method...........	$300	$300	$300	$300	$300
"Sum of years' digits" method...	500	400	300	200	100
Difference................	+$200	+$100	$ 0	−$100	−$200

porarily retained in a company by reducing early tax liability will normally earn an interest income for the firm—an income due entirely to the deferral of taxes. A dollar on hand today is worth more than a dollar which will not be received for a number of years, since if it is on hand today, it can begin immediately to earn interest. Consequently, a tax saving today is better than a tax saving in the future.

The tax benefits from accelerated depreciation are, in practice, usually not limited to the extra interest income which it generates. If only a single investment project is considered, the interest saving is actually the only saving. This is illustrated in Exhibit 2, which shows annual depreciation charges under the straight-line and "sum of the years' digits" methods against a $1,500 project. To keep this calculation simple, a five-year life span is assumed; salvage value is assumed to be zero; and the projects are completed at the beginning of year 1, so that full depreciation can be charged for that year. While annual depreciation is greater in the first two years when the "sum of the years' digits" formula is used, this is exactly counterbalanced in the last two years. The only permanent advantage comes from interest on the early tax saving.[15]

Continuous Investment

If a firm is a progressive one, its yearly gross investment (including the reinvestment of funds made available through depreciation charges)

Exhibit 3

ANNUAL STRAIGHT-LINE DEPRECIATION WITH CONSTANT RATE OF INVESTMENT

Project No.	Year 1	Year 2	Year 3	Year 4	Year 5	Year 6
1................	$300	$300	$300	$ 300	$ 300	
2................		300	300	300	300	$ 300
3................			300	300	300	300
4................				300	300	300
5................					300	300
6................						300
Annual Total..	$300	$600	$900	$1,200	$1,500	$1,500

Exhibit 4

ANNUAL "SUM OF THE YEARS' DIGITS" DEPRECIATION WITH CONSTANT RATE OF INVESTMENT

Project No.	Year 1	Year 2	Year 3	Year 4	Year 5	Year 6
1................	$500	$400	$ 300	$ 200	$ 100	
2................		500	400	300	200	$ 100
3................			500	400	300	200
4................				500	400	300
5................					500	400
6................						500
Annual Total..	$500	$900	$1,200	$1,400	$1,500	$1,500

is likely to have an upward trend. Even if the annual gross investment is constant rather than increasing, the results of accelerated depreciation are considerably more favorable than when only an individual investment project is considered.

---

[15]The capitalized value of the anticipated tax saving at the beginning of year 1 would be positive, since the negative savings in years 4 and 5 would be discounted more heavily than the positive savings of the first two years.

Exhibits 3 and 4 show yearly depreciation charges under the straight-line and "sum of the years' digits" methods, respectively, when there is a gross investment of $1,500 a year, other assumptions being the same as were used in connection with Exhibit 2. It can be seen that in the fifth year and thereafter, the annual depreciation charge will level out at $1,500 under both methods of depreciation. However, the larger total depreciation charges in the first four years under the "sum of the years' digits" method mean not only a saving of interest but a permanent retention of more profits than could have been retained under straight-line depreciation. A similar permanent saving of assets can be shown to take place with utilization of the declining balance formula.

If yearly gross investment tends to increase from year to year, the new accelerated depreciation methods will result in *permanently* higher yearly depreciation charges, and hence tax savings.[16] Firms which are able to grow rapidly and steadily stand to profit most by changing over to accelerated depreciation for tax purposes. Also, firms which are heavy users of fixed capital in relation to sales will gain more by the switch than those which have relatively little fixed capital. In general, such industries as manufacturing, railroads, and utilities seem to have more to gain from the 1954 Revenue Act than retailing, wholesaling, financial, or personal service activities.

Expectations regarding future tax rates also play a part in the making of rational decisions as to whether to switch from straight-line to accelerated depreciation. If it is anticipated by corporate officials that the present 52 per cent rate will probably be lowered in the future, the advantages of accelerated depreciation are even greater. At the time of this writing (Spring, 1963), such a cut appears likely. It is then especially desirable to take the largest possible depreciation deductions when tax rates are high. This would be true even if there were only a single investment project, such as was assumed in Exhibit 2.

Accelerated depreciation of the emergency type, which requires special certification, has apparently had a great effect on investment in the postwar period. According to the *U.S. News and World Report*,[17] the after-tax profit of all corporations except banks and insurance companies declined from $17.5 billion to $16.7 billion between 1947 and 1954. Yet corporations were able to increase dividend payments by

---

[16]This is pointed out in an excellent article by Robert Eisner, "Depreciation under the New Tax Law," *Harvard Business Review*, January-February, 1955, p. 70. Eisner says that continued inflation may in itself bring about a growing annual rate of investment by most firms.

[17]"Why Business Spending Is Going to Stay High," May 27, 1955, p. 89.

$3.2 billion and to step up the rate of investment of internally gen-
erated funds because bigger depreciation allowances contributed an
extra $7.4 billion to such investment.

Investment Tax Credit

An important recent innovation in federal income tax law is of decided importance to business decisions. This is the "investment tax
credit," equal to 7 per cent of the amount invested by the firm in certain qualified depreciable property. The basic purpose of the credit is
to stimulate economic growth by providing more internally generated
funds for investment. A great deal of discussion in accounting and
other related fields has been generated by the complex provisions and
interpretations of the investment tax credit.[18]

Regulations provide that the entire amount of an income tax of
$25,000 or less can be canceled if the investment tax credit amounts
to $25,000 or more. (This requires investment of about $357,143—
which is a large sum for a firm with so small a tax liability.) If the tax
liability exceeds $25,000, the first $25,000 can be canceled by a tax
credit of this size; and in addition, 25 per cent of the tax liability in
excess of $25,000 can be canceled. Unused investment tax credits may
be carried forward and backward.

Suppose a firm has invested $1 million during the year in qualified
types of property. The tax credit is $70,000. Suppose the computed
income tax liability is $140,000. Then the actual tax payment to be
made will be $140,000 minus $25,000 minus one quarter of $115,000,
or $86,250. Since the amount of investment tax credit used up is
$53,750, a carry-forward or carry-back credit of $16,250 still remains.

Excise Taxes

It has been indicated that the corporation income tax poses extremely
important problems for management. Another important levy in this
respect is the manufacturers' excise tax, which ranks second among
business taxes only to the corporate income tax as a revenue raiser for
the federal government. Some use is also made of this tax by state
and local governments, but these fiscal bodies make greater use of gen-

---

[18]Information on this subject has been obtained from Prentice-Hall, Inc., *Federal Taxes,*
Report Bulletin 13 (Englewood Cliffs, N.J., March 28, 1963). The reader is referred to
this loose-leaf publication for up-to-date information.

eral sales taxes than of imposts directed at particular types of manufacturing. The reason is clear. A state using such a tax is likely to repel
new firms and may even lose established ones if it levies such an impost
on goods manufactured within its borders, especially when they are
sold in interstate commerce. Federal excise taxes on liquor, gasoline,
cigarettes, and other tobacco products are well known and very important in this category.

When a new excise tax is levied, or when the rate of an existing one
is increased, the firm has to decide whether to attempt to pass the levy
on to consumers in whole, in part, or not at all. If the firm is operating
in a purely competitive situation, it does not have the option of deciding how much to change its price. Instead, this will be decided for the
individual seller by the combined actions of a great many competing
enterprises.

Shifting of an Excise Tax by a Competitive Industry

The basic means by which an excise tax can be passed forward to
consumers is through a reduction in supply. Assuming that the demand
curve for a product will be unaffected by the tax, the only way in which
price can be raised is through a decrease in supply. Usually, this reduction will be greater in the long run than immediately, because it takes
some time to shift resources to an untaxed use.

Suppose an excise tax of 5 cents a dozen were levied on farmers
who produce and sell eggs. This is a highly competitive industry, and
the effects of the tax can best be divined through use of the economists'
pricing model for perfect competition. Since the farmers would have to
pay the government 5 cents for each dozen of eggs produced, the marginal costs of each firm would be that much higher than before. The
short-run supply curve for the entire egg industry would shift upward
by a like amount. Price to the consumer would go up, but not by a
full 5 cents per dozen.

The short-run effect of an (unanticipated) excise tax can most
easily be seen with the aid of a diagram such as Exhibit 5. Straight-line
demand and supply "curves" are used for convenience. The posttax supply curve S' lies above the pretax supply curve by 5 cents at each possible output. This shift in supply raises the price of eggs from P_1 to P_2
—an amount less than the tax, but only a little less, in view of the
way the chart is drawn. Determinants of the short-run price increase
are the size of the tax, the slope of the demand curve, and the slope of

the supply curve. The change in price can most conveniently be calculated from the formula

$$\triangle P = \frac{t}{1 + \left(\frac{c}{b}\right)}$$

where $\triangle P$ is the price increase, t is the amount of the tax, c is the slope of the supply curve and b is the slope (disregarding sign) of the demand curve.[19] If the supply curve were horizontal (had a zero slope), the formula readily shows that price would rise by the full amount of

Exhibit 5

TAX SHIFTING UNDER COMPETITION—PART OF TAX SHIFTED
IN SHORT RUN

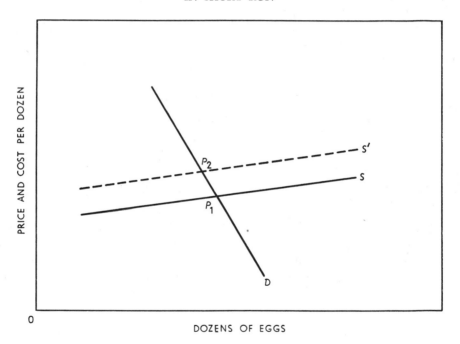

the tax. If the demand and supply curves had equal numerical slopes, the price would rise by one half the amount of the tax. Any other combination of slopes can be as readily handled by means of the formula.

Economic factors which underlie the slopes of the demand and supply curves actually determine the incidence of an excise tax. The more readily consumers will be willing and able to substitute other goods

[19]For the derivation of the formula, see M. R. Colberg, "Shifting of a Specific Excise Tax," *Public Finance: Finances publiques,* Vol. IX, No. 2, p. 168.

for the taxed one, the smaller will be the slope of the demand curve for the taxed good, and the smaller the proportion of the tax which will be immediately shifted to buyers. That is, the taxed industry will not find it economical to raise price very much if close substitutes are available toward which buyers can divert their custom.

On the supply side, factors which make plant relatively "flexible" are conducive to the ready reduction in amount supplied, and hence to a passing-forward of most of the tax. As was pointed out earlier in this volume, the use of relatively little fixed capital compared with variable inputs makes for flexibility. Also, divisibility of the plant increases flexibility (i.e., makes for relatively horizontal short-run supply curves). In the case of the tax on egg production the plant can be thought of as consisting mainly of a large number of separate egg-producing machines (i.e., chickens). These can quite economically be withdrawn from productive use, reducing the supply of eggs and raising market price. The chickens which are withdrawn from egg production can readily be put to another use—they can be sold as food. Also, the farmer and his family are likely to eat into their capital.

Shifting in the Long Run

In the long run, it is likely that an excise tax levied on a competitively produced commodity will be wholly, or almost wholly, included in the price which consumers must pay. Long-run supply curves are usually horizontal or upsloping only slightly—the latter occurring if some resources are bid up in price by firms within the industry as the industry expands in size.

It can readily be seen by reference to the formula that if the long-run supply curve is horizontal (has a zero slope), the price increase due to the tax will be equal to the full amount of the tax, regardless of the slope of the demand curve.[20] The complete shifting of the tax will have been accomplished by means of firms leaving the industry to enter untaxed activities. In addition to being reflected fully in price, the excise tax will be harmful to the owners of resources which are forced into other fields, to the extent that earnings are less favorable in the new occupations. If the long-run supply curve is slightly upsloping, the price to consumers will be raised by not quite the full amount of the tax.

---

[20]Substituting zero for c in the formula, we have $\triangle P = \dfrac{t}{1 + \left(\dfrac{0}{b}\right)}$ which equals t regardless of the amount of slope in the demand curve.

A firm selling in a highly competitive market can do little to alleviate the adverse effects of an excise tax. (Members of the industry may, of course, lobby for reduction or repeal of the tax.) Nevertheless, an understanding of economics of the long run may be helpful in showing an entrepreneur that surviving firms will be in about the same position as they were prior to the tax. This understanding may lead him to take steps to be among the survivors.

Shifting under Monopoly

Paradoxically, a monopolistic firm is apt to absorb a greater part of an excise tax than will a competitive firm. This conclusion, however,

Exhibit 6
EXCISE TAX ON MONOPOLY—MAY BE LARGELY ABSORBED

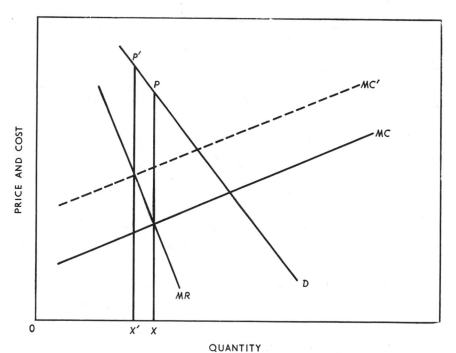

rests on the assumption that the monopolistic firm was charging a profit-maximizing price before the tax was levied. If his price was below this level—due, for example, to fear of antitrust action by the federal government—the tax is likely to be fully passed on to the buyer, since this action would not seem unreasonable.

If it is assumed that an optimum price was in force before the tax, the motive to increase price can be shown in Exhibit 6. Marginal costs will be higher by exactly the amount of the excise tax, since the firm must pay this amount to the government on each unit produced. The upward shift in marginal costs will cause the optimum price to rise from XP to $X'P'$ and the rate of production to fall from OX to OX'. It will be noted that the price increase is considerably less than the tax.

As in the competitive case the change in price due to the tax can most conveniently be stated by means of a formula. Again, it is the relative slopes of the (linear) demand and marginal cost curves which determine the price increase, the formula being

$$\triangle P = \frac{t}{2 + \left(\frac{c}{b}\right)}$$

where the symbols have the same meaning as before, except that c denotes the slope of the marginal cost curve rather than the supply curve.[21] The figure 2 in the denominator causes the price increase under monopoly to be less than it would have been under competition with the same demand and cost curves in existence. If, for example, the marginal cost curve is horizontal (slope of zero), the price increase under monopoly equals half of the tax. Under competition, it is equal to the entire tax.

Miscellaneous Tax Effects

Emphasis has been placed in this chapter on the corporate income tax and on excise taxes. Many other types are, of course, of importance to businessmen. These include general sales taxes, property taxes, licenses, utility taxes, and others. It was pointed out in Chapter 10 that state and local taxes may be an important consideration in locational decisions. This is especially true of levies such as the property tax which are difficult to shift. A property tax does not affect short-run marginal costs of the firm and hence does not cause a reduction in output whereby price can be immediately raised. Over the longer run, however, property taxes on business tend to raise prices to consumers by restricting somewhat the quantity of resources going into business employment and in this way reducing supplies of goods. Fuller analysis, however, requires a consideration of the ways in which government expenditures aid business, alternative ways in which government reve-

---

[21]Under monopoly, there is no supply curve, but the marginal cost curve is influential in determining output. The formula and its derivation can be found in Colberg, *op. cit.*, p. 171.

nue can be raised, and other matters beyond the scope of this brief treatment.

Note: Depreciation issues discussed in this chapter are covered in the capital-budgeting cases that follow Chapter 15.

CASE 13–1:   HENRY W. SILASH

Shortly after Henry W. Silash moved to Chicago from Buffalo, New York, in 1922, he purchased a 332-acre farm northwest of Chicago, about 23 miles from the center of the city. This farm was situated at the northern edge of the "black belt," a highly fertile area of black soil extending from Ohio into Iowa. While not the best farmland in the area, the soil yielded a living for Mr. Silash and his family as long as it was tilled. Mr. Silash paid $14,000 for this farm. It included a nine-room house, two barns, and a few smaller sheds.

As shown in Exhibit 1, Mr. Silash's farm was bounded on the north by Appleton Road, on the east by Town Line Road, and on the west by Carson Street. Appleton Road was the extension of Appleton Street, which originated in a suburb of Chicago, about five miles to the east. Carson Street was an extension of a street by the same name in the city of Chicago. Town Line Road began at the northern city limits of Chicago and ran directly north, terminating at an east-west highway about 15 miles to the north. The southern boundary of the Silash farm adjoined the farm of Dorson Cronkhite.

During the decade of the twenties, there occurred a housing boom in this particular area. As a result, a number of homes were built west of the suburbs north of Chicago, and to the north of Chicago itself, in the general direction of the Silash farm. Appleton Road became one of the main traffic routes east and west. Both Town Line Road and Carson Street carried increasing traffic loads. No homes were built within a mile or two of the Silash farm, but Mr. Silash did lease a small parcel of his property at the corner of Appleton Road and Town Line Road to an oil company, which erected a gasoline service station on the corner in 1928.

As a result of the WPA road-building program in the years of the Great Depression, Carson Street was reconstructed and became the main highway northwest from Chicago. In 1937, Appleton Street was also improved. In 1939, Town Line Road was widened and became a main route for traffic between Chicago and points in eastern Wisconsin. In 1938, Mr. Silash leased two more parcels of land for commercial purposes and renewed the 1928 lease with the oil company. He leased the parcel at the corner of Carson Street and Appleton Road to an individual who constructed a golf driving range and putting green. On Carson Street, where the Silash and Cronkhite farms adjoined, he rented a small parcel to a firm which erected a small restaurant and ice-cream stand to serve "drive-in" customers.

While these developments were going on with Mr. Silash, several commercial establishments of relatively small size sprang up on Appleton Road and Town Line Road. These are identified in Exhibit 1.

Following World War II, a housing boom of substantial proportions developed in the general area of the Silash farm. By 1952 the vicinity of the Silash farm was surrounded with new homes, both finished and under construction. Little development of home building had occurred along Carson Street and Town Line Road north of Appleton Road. Apparently, the presence of commercial establishments of many kinds had discouraged the use of this land for home building. Late in 1951, however, a large parcel of land—extending from Town Line Road along Appleton Road to Carson Street, then north to Avery Road, thence east to Town Line Road—was leased by a development company for the purpose of constructing a shopping center to serve the newly developed area. This area contained 97 acres, and the purchase price was $1,271,350. Shortly after the initial construction was begun on this center in 1954, Mr. Silash was approached by a real estate company which wished to lease the entire frontage of his farm on Appleton Road, from Town Line Road to Carson Street, to a depth of 375 feet. This would include the land now leased by the oil company and the golf driving range. The real estate company proposed a 24-year lease at the annual rate of $42,500 per year, with an option to renew for an additional 20 years at a rate to be determined at renewal.

All present leases on the Silash farm had been renewed and ran until 1958. The lease to the oil company was yielding $175 per month for a plot 125 by 110 feet. The golf driving range was yielding $215 per month for an area of approximately nine acres, while the restaurant and drive-in yielded $100 per month. This latter area was not affected by the proposed lease.

Mr. Silash consulted an appraiser to determine the value of the land for which the lease had been proposed. The report of the appraiser stated that the total amount of land involved was 219.4 acres and placed upon it a valuation of $810,000.

Exhibit 1

VICINITY OF HENRY W. SILASH FARM

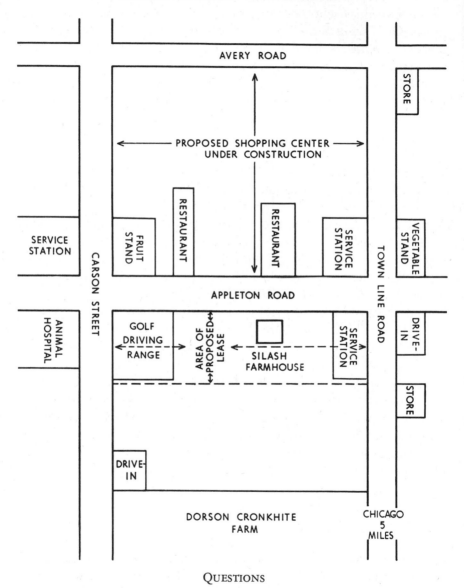

QUESTIONS

1. Should Mr. Silash accept the lease as proposed by the real estate company? If not, what amount would you suggest?

2. On the basis of the valuation, would you say that the lessees of the parcels of the Silash farm were getting a bargain? Explain.

3. In order that Mr. Silash can accept the new lease offer, it will be neces-

sary to make a settlement with the driving range lessee and the oil company. What amounts would you suggest for settlement?

4. If Mr. Silash had an offer to sell or lease, which would you recommend? Why?

CASE 13–2: STUDEBAKER CORPORATION

On Friday, November 16, 1962, the stockholders of the Studebaker Corporation met in Minneapolis, Minnesota, and voted to purchase the business and assets of the Franklin Manufacturing Company for cash in the amount of $29 million plus the unpaid 1962 income tax of Franklin, 1,333,333 shares of Studebaker common stock, and the assumption by Studebaker of certain liabilities of Franklin. The vote was 7,297,541 shares in favor and 218,452 against, out of 12,357,830 shares outstanding.

This brought the number of companies acquired by Studebaker to ten since it announced a diversification program in 1958. One company was later sold. These acquisitions are described briefly in Exhibit 1.

When Studebaker announced its diversification program in 1958, it had available $134 million in tax credits. By the end of 1961 the five-year time limit had run out on $46.3 million. Earnings of $31.7 million during the years 1959, 1960, and 1961 had further reduced the credits to $56 million. At the end of 1962, $27 million of additional tax credits were due to expire, and the other $29 million would expire at the end of 1963. Mr. Sherwood H. Egbert, President of Studebaker Corporation, has been quoted as saying: "We're not going after acquisitions with the single-minded objective of using up those tax credits. We don't want something that will blow up on us later."[22]

The following information concerning the Franklin merger has been extracted from the Studebaker Corporation's proxy statement to its shareholders dated October 16, 1962.

REASONS FOR THE FRANKLIN ACQUISITION PROPOSAL[23]

In 1958, Studebaker adopted a Diversification Program designed to diversify beyond its traditional automotive activities into the manufacture and sale of other types of products. Of the several businesses acquired by Studebaker, Franklin would be the largest and most important. Franklin designs, manufactures and sells primarily household freezers and refrigerators and also automatic washers and dryers. All such products are sold for resale under private brand names of major mail-order and retail companies. For its fiscal year ended March

---

[22]*Wall Street Journal,* October 16, 1962.

[23]All information relating to Franklin in this proxy statement has been furnished by the management of Franklin to Studebaker for such use.

Exhibit 1
STUDEBAKER DIVERSIFICATION PROGRAM

Date	Name of Business	Type of Business	1961 Sales
May, 1959	Gering Products, Inc.*	Manufacturer of plastic molding powder and compounds, films, wrappings, and plastic garden hose.	. . . .
August, 1959	C. T. L., Inc.	Research projects related to reinforced plastics designed to withstand high temperatures. For missile nosecovers, etc.	n.a.†
May, 1960	Gravely Tractors, Inc.	Manufacture and sale of 6.6-h.p. hard tractors with power take-off in the front end.	$11,500,000
September, 1960	Clarke Floor Machine Co.	Commercial floor-maintenance equipment—power and hand sanders and edgers, etc.	9,500,000
October, 1960	D. W. Onam & Sons, Inc.	Manufacturers of specialized electric generating equipment and related products.	15,500,000
March, 1961	Chemical Compounds, Inc.	An oil additive, "STP," marketed through service stations and garages.	6,000,000
March, 1962	Schaefer, Inc.	Manufactures low-temperature refrigeration equipment for commercial uses.	10,000,000
March, 1962	Paxton Products	Assembles superchargers for automotive and industrial applications. Performs automobile engine customizing work.	n.a.
October, 1962	Trans International Airlines, Inc.	A contract air line which contracts with the Military Air Transport Service, primarily on transpacific routes.	6,000,000

*Sold by Studebaker in December, 1961, for cash at a profit of $5,668,867, after paying the unpaid balance of the note.
†Not available.
Sources: Studebaker Corporation proxy statement dated October 16, 1962; *Wall Street Journal*, October 16, 1962.

31, 1962, Franklin reported net sales of approximately $69,000,000 and Income Before Income Taxes of approximately $7,240,000. See the information set forth herein under the heading "Franklin Consolidated Statements of Income."

The terms of the proposed transaction were determined by arm's-length bargaining between representatives of Studebaker and Franklin, have been the subject of careful consideration by the officers and directors of Studebaker and are, in the opinion of the Studebaker Board of Directors, fair and equitable to the shareholders of Studebaker. In negotiation of the Purchase Agreement, among the factors considered by the Studebaker management were the financial condition, past and current earnings, potential earning power and growth possibilities of Franklin.

The Studebaker Board of Directors and Management recommend a vote "FOR" the Franklin Acquisition Proposal.

SUMMARY OF THE PURCHASE AGREEMENT

The Purchase Agreement provides that Franklin will transfer to Studebaker the assets, properties and business of Franklin and that in payment therefor Studebaker will pay cash in the amount of $29,000,000 plus the unpaid 1962 Income Tax of Franklin (as defined) and will deliver 1,333,333 shares of Studebaker Common Stock to Franklin and will assume certain obligations and liabilities of Franklin. The Purchase Agreement provides that on the Closing Date Studebaker will pay $25,000,000 cash to Franklin and assume certain liabilities of Franklin. The balance of the cash purchase price, $4,000,000 plus the Unpaid 1962 Income Tax of Franklin (as defined), will be paid to Franklin after completion of a joint audit of Franklin as of the last business day prior to the Closing Date; such audit will be conducted by the accountants for each of Studebaker and Franklin with any differences between them to be resolved by a third national accounting firm. The Purchase Agreement provides that such cash purchase price is to be reduced dollar for dollar by the amount by which the Closing Net Worth of Franklin (as defined) is determined by such audit to be less than $38,000,000. The 1,333,333 shares of Studebaker Common Stock will be delivered to Franklin following the listing of such shares on the New York Stock Exchange.

The Purchase Agreement provides for the assumption by Studebaker of certain disclosed liabilities and obligations of Franklin. Among the liabilities and obligations of Franklin which Studebaker will not assume are those (*a*) incident to the Purchase Agreement or in connection with the liquidation and dissolution of Franklin; (*b*) to the stockholders of Franklin; (*c*) for any income taxes of Franklin for any period prior to the Closing Date or for any income taxes of its subsidiaries with respect to periods prior to the 1962 fiscal years of such subsidiaries; (*d*) attributable to action of Franklin after the Closing Date; and (*e*) not disclosed in the Purchase Agreement and which are inconsistent with any representation or warranty or which violate any condition contained therein (other than obligations under contracts entered into in the ordinary course of business).

The obligations of Studebaker under the Purchase Agreement are subject, at the option of Studebaker, to certain conditions, among which are the following: (i) approval by Studebaker shareholders of the Franklin Acquisition and Employee Stock Proposals; (ii) the absence of adverse material changes in the business, properties, operations or financial condition of Franklin since March 31, 1962; (iii) approval by counsel for Studebaker of certain legal matters relating to the transaction; (iv) delivery of opinions of counsel for Franklin as to the validity of certain corporate actions of Franklin and as to the title to certain real properties to be transferred to Studebaker; (v) the truthfulness and correctness of the representations and warranties made by Franklin in the Purchase Agreement; and (vi) the availability to Studebaker of credit pursuant to the Revolving Credit Agreement hereinafter described.

The obligations of Franklin under the Purchase Agreement are likewise subject to certain conditions, among which are the following: (i) approval of the transaction by the stockholders of Franklin; (ii) approval by counsel for Franklin of certain legal matters relating to the transaction; (iii) delivery of an opinion of counsel for Studebaker as to the validity of certain corporate actions of Studebaker; and (iv) the truthfulness and correctness of the representations and warranties made by Studebaker in the Purchase Agreement.

The Purchase Agreement provides that the covenants, representations and warranties made by Studebaker and Franklin shall survive the closing of the purchase and sale therein provided. In addition, the holders of more than 75% of the Common Stock of Franklin have entered into a separate Indemnity Agreement with Studebaker in effect guaranteeing such obligations and also providing, among other matters, for cross indemnities in respect of the Registration Statement to be prepared and filed by Studebaker (at its own expense) under the Securities Act of 1933 in connection with disposition by stockholders of Franklin of the shares of Studebaker Common Stock to be received by them upon the liquidation of Franklin.

Studebaker and Franklin may, by mutual consent of their respective Boards of Directors, amend, abandon or terminate the Purchase Agreement at any time. For a complete description of the terms and provisions of the transaction and of the conditions to the obligations of Studebaker and Franklin, reference is made to the Purchase Agreement.

FINANCING ARRANGEMENTS

To provide necessary financing for a portion of the cash purchase price to be paid by Studebaker to Franklin, Studebaker has entered into a revolving credit agreement (hereinafter called the Revolving Credit Agreement) with the Chase Manhattan Bank, First National City Bank, Bank of America National Trust and Savings Association, Continental Illinois National Bank and Trust Company of Chicago, The First National Bank of Chicago and First National Bank of Minneapolis (hereinafter called the Banks). The maximum amount available under the Revolving Credit Agreement is $25,000,000 through January 31, 1964, and thereafter $17,500,000 to January 29, 1965; availability of credit is conditioned upon continued accuracy of certain representations as to financial condition and other matters. Borrowings will be evidenced by 90-day notes (hereinafter called the Revolving Credit Notes) bearing interest at 1/2% over the prime commercial rate of The Chase Manhattan Bank at the date of borrowing, but not more than 5 1/2% nor less than 4 1/2% per annum; the commitment fee is 1/4% per annum of the average unborrowed amount.

Studebaker may without penalty prepay the Revolving Credit Notes on 4 days' notice and terminate or reduce the Banks' commitments on 30 days' notice. In the Revolving Credit Agreement, Studebaker covenants that it will, unless otherwise consented to by the Banks holding at least 80% of the Revolving Credit Notes (or the aggregate commitment under the Revolving Credit Agreement), maintain consolidated working capital in excess of $48,000,000 and consolidated current assets not less than 150% of consolidated current liabilities, with current liabilities to include all borrowings pursuant to the Revolving Credit Agreement. Studebaker also covenants, among other matters, that, unless similarly consented to by the Banks, it will not, nor will it permit certain subsidiaries to, except within specified limits and exceptions, (a) create or suffer to exist any security interests covering any property of Studebaker or its consolidated subsidiaries; (b) create, assume or incur any indebtedness; (c) become or be liable by guaranty or otherwise in respect of any indebtedness; (d) engage in any mergers, acquisitions or dispositions; or (e) incur rental obligations, enter into any sale and leaseback transaction, dispose of fixed assets, or make any outside investments. . . . The events of default permitting acceleration of the Revolving Credit Notes and termination of the commitments of the Banks under the Revolving Credit Agreement include breach of the foregoing covenants. During an event of default, Studebaker is required, at the request of the Banks, to mortgage and pledge its free assets as security for the Revolving Credit Notes. Giving effect to the payment by Studebaker to Franklin of the purchase price provided in the Purchase Agreement and the borrowing by Studebaker of $25,000,000 pursuant to the Revolving Credit Agreement, on the basis of the pro forma condensed balance sheet of Studebaker (as of June, 30, 1962) and Franklin (as of March 31, 1962) as hereinafter set forth [Exhibit 9], baker's working capital would have been approximately $67,000,000 and its current ratio approximately 1.89 to 1, as defined in the Revolving Credit Agreement.

PRICE RANGE OF STUDEBAKER COMMON STOCK

The range of market prices of Studebaker Common Stock on the New York Stock Exchange for the periods indicated was as [shown in Exhibit 2].

[*Exhibit* 2]

Year	High	Low
1962 (to October 15)...........	10¾	6
1961........................	13¼	7
1960........................	24½	6½
1959........................	29¼	9¾
1958........................	16	2⅞
1957........................	8¼	2⅝
1956........................	10⅝	5¼

On October 15, 1962, the closing price was 7⅞.

Studebaker has not paid any dividends on its Common Stock since the combination of the Studebaker and Packard businesses in 1954 and the payment of

[Exhibit 3]

	Outstanding as of August 31, 1962	As Adjusted
Long-Term Debt:		
Notes payable...............................	$ 48,560	$ 48,560
5% Secured Notes, dated October 16, 1958, due September 1, 1973 (1)......................	16,500,000	16,500,000
Other, less current maturities (2)................	3,836,187	3,836,187
Revolving Credit Notes (3)......................	0	25,000,000
Total Long-Term Debt......................	$ 20,384,747	$ 45,384,747
Shareholders' Equity:		
$5 Convertible Preferred Stock, $100 par value, 8,628 shares authorized and outstanding (4)....	$ 862,800	$ 862,800
Second Preferred Stock, $100 par value, issuable in series, authorized 500,000 shares, outstanding 30,000 shares (5)..........................	3,000,000	3,000,000
Common Stock, $1 par value, authorized 23,000,000 shares, outstanding at August 31, 1962, 12,349,514 shares, as adjusted 13,682,847 shares (6).................................	12,349,514	13,682,847
Capital Surplus (7).............................	46,733,928	57,400,595
Retained Earnings.............................	37,329,076	37,329,076
Total Shareholders' Equity....................	$100,275,318	$112,275,318
Total Capitalization.......................	$120,660,065	$157,660,065

(1) The 5% Secured Notes are payable in annual installments of $1,650,000 beginning on September 1 1964. Substantially all of the properties of Studebaker at South Bend, Indiana, with a net carrying amount of approximately $18,000,000 at August 31, 1962, have been mortgaged as security. Additional security consists of the capital stock of two wholly-owned consolidated subsidiaries, Studebaker of Canada, Limited and Mercedes-Benz Sales, Inc., which had combined net assets of $15,430,781 at August 31, 1962. With respect to the 5% Secured Notes, Studebaker has agreed, among other covenants, to maintain consolidated net current assets of at least $25,000,000.

(2) Such liability consists primarily of non-interest-bearing indebtedness incurred in connection with business acqusition contracts payable in annual installments dependent upon earnings of the acquired divisions, and subject to possible adjustments dependent upon such earnings.

(3) It should be noted that for purposes of the working capital and current ratio covenants of the Revolving Credit Agreement, the Revolving Credit Notes constitute current liabilities.

(4) Convertible into 287,600 shares of Common Stock; dividends are cumulative and have been paid through the most recent dividend payment date.

(5) The only shares of Second Preferred Stock outstanding are Series A which may be converted into 123,558 shares of Common Stock prior to May 1, 1965; dividends are cumulative and have been paid through the most recent dividend payment date. Issuance of more than 150,000 shares of Second Preferred Stock requires the consent of the holders of ⅔rds of the ($5 Convertible Preferred Stock.

(6) 355,170 shares of Common Stock have been reserved for issue upon exercise of employee stock options under the Studebaker Stock Ownership Plan and 88,399 are held in treasury. Pursuant to the acquisition of Trans International Airlines, Inc., additional shares of Common Stock up to a maximum of 606,060 may be issued. In accordance with the Employee Stock Proposal, an additional 500,000 shares of Common Stock will be reserved for the Studebaker Stock Ownership Plan.

(7) To reflect the issue of 1,333,333 shares of Studebaker Common Stock to Franklin, a value of $9 per share has been assumed and $10,666,667, the excess of such total assumed stock value of $12,000,000 over the aggregate par value of such shares, is credited to Capital Surplus. Final determination of the consideration received by Studebaker will be made by its Board of Directors following the date of acquisition of Franklin.

dividends is subject to the restrictions described [elsewhere]. The Board of Directors does not presently contemplate the payment of any dividends on the Common Stock in the near future.

The Common Stock of Franklin is closely held and not publicly traded.

STUDEBAKER CAPITALIZATION

The capitalization of Studebaker as of August 31, 1962, and as adjusted to give effect to the consummation of the Franklin acquisition and the borrowing of $25,000,000 pursuant to the Revolving Credit Agreement [is] summarized [in Exhibit 3].

STUDEBAKER CONSOLIDATED STATEMENTS OF INCOME (LOSS)

The . . . consolidated statements of income (loss) [Exhibit 4] of Studebaker and consolidated subsidiaries for the five years ended December 31, 1961, have been examined by Ernst & Ernst, independent certified public accountants. . . . The statements for the periods of six months ended June 30, 1961, and June 30, 1962, respectively, which are unaudited, include all adjustments (consisting only of normal recurring accruals) which, in the opinion of Studebaker, are necessary to a fair statement of the results for such interim periods. . . .

During the months of July and August, 1962, Studebaker's net sales were approximately $40,800,000 as compared to approximately $23,900,000 for the same two months of 1961, and its net loss was approximately $4,200,000 as compared to approximately $3,200,000 in the same two months of 1961. During a substantial part of such months in 1961 and 1962, automobile production was suspended primarily in connection with annual model changeovers. The foregoing figures are unaudited but include all known adjustments (consisting only of normal recurring accruals) which, in the opinion of Studebaker, are necessary for a fair statement thereof.

FRANKLIN CONSOLIDATED STATEMENTS OF INCOME

The . . . consolidated statements [Exhibit 5] of income of Franklin and subsidiaries so far as they relate to the three years ended March 31, 1962, have been examined by Peat, Marwick, Mitchell & Co., independent certified public accountants . . . . The statements for the two years ended March 31, 1959, include adjustments which, in the opinion of Franklin, are necessary to a fair statement of the results for such years. . . .

The decline in Franklin's sales and earnings in 1961 and 1962 is attributable to several factors, including reduced consumer demand and a corresponding impact upon prices as well as production shifts and start-up expenses relating to the new Bloomington, Indiana, plant.

FINANCIAL EFFECT OF THE ACQUISITION

Based upon the Pro Forma Condensed Balance Sheet (unaudited) appearing [as Exhibit 9] in this Proxy Statement, the total purchase price, including the 1,333,333 shares of Studebaker Common Stock at an aggregate fair market value of $11,999,997 (based upon $9 a share subject to final determination following date of acquisition) exceeds the book value of the net assets to be acquired by Studebaker from Franklin by $2,999,997. It is expected that this

[*Exhibit 4*]

	Year Ended December 31					Six Months Ended June 30 (Unaudited)	
	1957	1958	1959	1960	1961	1961	1962
Net sales....................	$213,203,741	$180,657,592	$387,372,375	$323,226,663	$298,475,738	$134,436,137	$180,433,979
Rental income, interest, and miscellaneous income........................	2,723,378	3,022,033	3,484,270	4,343,843	3,882,132	1,753,838	1,800,591
	$215,927,119	$183,679,625	$390,856,645	$327,570,506	$302,357,870	$136,189,975	$182,234,570
Cost and expenses . . .:							
Cost of products sold.................	$198,139,488	$169,335,476	$323,347,709	$281,706,188	$256,030,456	$120,996,377	$155,585,766
Selling, administrative and general expenses......................	26,758,978	25,642,224	35,383,242	43,082,915	45,124,010	22,418,879	23,129,709
Incentive compensation awards.........			1,248,000				
Interest expense (principally on long-term debt)........................	2,076,593	1,844,628	922,316	907,273	889,792	452,214	417,656
Amortization of intangibles............			283,151	637,553	1,845,299	749,336	1,105,594
Other deductions.....................	87,168	175,938	329,540	320,694	1,335,873	231,351	803,375
	$227,062,227	$196,998,266	$361,513,958	$326,654,623	$305,225,430	$144,848,157	$181,042,100
Income (Loss*) Before Income Taxes and Special Credit................	$ 11,135,108*	$ 13,318,641*	$ 29,342,687	$ 915,883	$ 2,867,560*	$ 8,658,182*	$ 1,192,470
Taxes on income, principally foreign.......		72,296	798,349	207,033	265,583	181,990	416,040
Net Income (Loss*) Before Special Credit...........................	$ 11,135,108*	$ 13,390,937*	$ 28,544,338	$ 708,850	$ 3,133,143*	$ 8,840,172*	$ 776,430
Special credit—gain on sale of Gering Plastics Division..................					5,668,867		
Net Income (Loss*) and Special Credit.	$ 11,135,108*	$ 13,390,937*	$ 28,544,338	$ 708,850	$ 2,535,724	$ 8,840,172*	$ 776,430
Net income (Loss*) per common share, before special credit of $0.45 per share in 1961	$ 1.73*	$ 2.08*	$ 2.37 (1)	$ .05 (1)	$ .26* (1)	$ .70* (1)	$ .06 (1)
Dividends declared and paid:							
Common...........................	—0—	—0—	—0—	—0—	—0—	—0—	—0—
$5 Convertible Preferred...............	—0—	—0—	—0—	—0—	70,014	40,900	23,564
5% Convertible Second Preferred Series A.	—0—	—0—	—0—	—0—	150,000	75,000	75,000

after giving effect to the full conversion of the 165,000 shares of $5 Convertible Preferred Stock, which became convertible on January 1, 1961, into 3,300,000 shares of Common Stock. Net income used in the calculation of net income per common share has been calculated after deducting dividends on the 5% Convertible Second Preferred Series A Stock.

(2) No provision for federal income taxes was necessary in 1959, 1960, 1961, and 1962 because of accumulated tax loss carry-forward credits as explained elsewhere herein under the heading "Tax Loss Carry-Forward Credit." The aggregate and per share amount of tax loss carry-forward benefits in 1959, 1960, 1961 and 1962 [was] as follows:

Year	Aggregate Amount	Amount Per Common Share
1959	$14,483,000	$1.20
1960	336,000	.03
1961 (applicable to special credit)	1,180,000	.09
1962 (six months)	230,000	.02

[Exhibit 5]

	YEAR ENDED MARCH 31				
	(Unaudited) 1958	(Unaudited) 1959	1960	1961	1962
Net Sales	$54,637,030	$63,653,434	$82,345,931	$71,659,805	$69,320,731
Royalties and miscellaneous income	9,007	184,414 (a)	104,550 (a)	20,484 (a)	358,515 (a, c)
	$54,646,037	$63,837,848	$82,450,481	$71,680,289	$69,679,246
Costs and expenses					
Cost of products sold	$43,539,485	$47,339,649	$66,060,492	$56,219,857	$57,028,491
Selling, administrative, and general expenses	2,639,551	3,687,325	4,765,980	5,256,577	5,196,857
Other Deductions	33,187	23,988	19,443	90,594 (b)	210,011 (b)
	$46,212,223	$51,050,962	$70,845,915	$61,567,028	$62,435,359
Income Before Income Taxes	$ 8,433,814	$12,786,886	$11,604,566	$10,113,261	$ 7,243,887
Taxes on Income	4,575,000	6,910,000	6,320,827	5,559,129	3,833,569
Net Income	$ 3,858,814	$ 5,876,886	$ 5,283,739	$ 4,554,132	$ 3,410,318

(a) Includes royalty income of $176,983 in 1959, $98,996 in 1960, $12,946 in 1961 and $87,032 in 1962.
(b) Includes realized and unrealized losses (net) on foreign exchange of $66,063 in 1961 and $210,011 in 1962.
(c) Includes $246,205 excess of life insurance proceeds over cash surrender value of life insurance.

excess will be ascribed to properties on the basis of appraisals as of the acquisition date.

The annual depreciation on the additional amount ascribed to properties is estimated at approximately $250,000. The annual interest on the Revolving Credit Notes at the maximum rate of 5½% would be $1,375,000. If Franklin's income for the year ended March 31, 1962, were adjusted to reflect these additional charges, Income Before Income Taxes would be approximately $5,618,000 and Net Income would be approximately $2,630,000 (which amounts may be attributed to the 1,333,333 shares being issued which constitute approximately only 9% of the shares of Studebaker Common Stock to be outstanding). Until December 31, 1963, Studebaker tax loss carry-forward credits are available to offset Federal income taxes that would otherwise be payable.

DESCRIPTION OF FRANKLIN

General

The business of Franklin was founded in 1929 and consisted of the manufacture of small electrical transformers; battery chargers and battery testing equipment were subsequently added to the product line. In 1941 a new fast charger for automotive batteries was introduced and annual sales increased to approximately $1,000,000. During World War II the Company's production facilities were devoted entirely to defense work in the manufacture of quartz crystals and special battery charging equipment.

Upon the termination of war restrictions in 1946, Franklin entered the consumer durable goods field with the production of home appliances. The electrical division continues to make battery chargers, transformers and testing equipment, but these products currently account for less than 2% of total sales.

Principal Products

The appliance division started with the production of home freezers in the fall of 1946. In 1948, household refrigerators were added as a major appliance line. In 1955, Franklin added automatic home washers and gas and electric clothes dryers to its line through the acquisition of the assets of Beam Manufacturing Company (then a division of another corporation). Franklin now produces a complete line of household chest freezers, vertical freezers, refrigerators, combination refrigerator-freezers, automatic washers and automatic gas and electric clothes dryers to expand its product line a portable dishwasher is scheduled to be introduced in early 1963.

Products in the refrigeration field (freezers and refrigerators) accounted for approximately 85% of Franklin's sales during the last fiscal year. Freezers, the first appliances made by Franklin, continue to generate the largest sales volume.

In the fiscal year ending March 31, 1947, the first year in which appliances were produced, Franklin's sales were approximately $8,000,000. Fifteen years later, in the fiscal year ending March 31, 1962, sales had increased almost nine times to approximately $69,300,000, with the highest volume being in the 1960 fiscal year when sales were approximately $82,300,000. See the information set forth herein under the heading "Franklin Consolidated Statements of Income."

Franklin customarily makes major changes in its appliance products every three to five years with minor model changes being made yearly.

Distribution of Products

Since its formation, Franklin has designed and manufactured its products entirely for major marketing organizations. Franklin has not and does not manufacture anything for sale under its own name or under any trade name owned by it. In the fiscal year ended March 31, 1962, Franklin's largest customer accounted for approximately 29% of total appliance sales and the next four largest customers accounted for approximately another 60% of total appliance sales.

A number of these companies have been customers of Franklin since it entered the appliance field. Certain of them buy their entire requirements of one or more appliances from Franklin. Customers ordinarily place firm orders at the first of the month for delivery during the second month following. Franklin ordinarily does not purchase or commit itself to purchase raw materials except to meet the requirements of firm customer purchase orders. At August 31, 1962, Franklin had firm orders totalling approximately $12,300,000 as compared with $15,200,000 a year earlier.

Competition

The household appliance field is highly competitive both at the production and retail levels. At the production level, Franklin competes for the business of its customers with other manufacturers of private brand appliances. At the retail level Franklin's customers compete with other retailers of private brand appliances and nationally advertised appliances. A number of other appliance manufacturers have substantially greater resources than Franklin. Set forth [in Exhibit 6] is a table of certain industry statistics.

[Exhibit 6]

INDUSTRY STATISTICS FOR RETAIL VALUE OF HOME APPLIANCE SALES
(000,000 Omitted)

	YEAR				
PRODUCT	1957 (a)	1958 (b)	1959 (b)	1960 (c)	1961 (c)
Home Freezers.	$ 347	$ 385	$ 397	$ 308	$ 278
Electric Refrigerators.	1,072	977	1,272	1,129	1,027
Washing Machines (automatic and semi-automatic).	802	793	832	697	697
Total.	$2,221	$2,155	$2,501	$2,134	$2,002

(a) Source: U.S. Bureau of the Census, *Statistical Abstract of the United States* (hereinafter cited as *Statistical Abstract*): 1958 (79th ed.), p. 822.
 (b) *Statistical Abstract:* 1961, p. 821.
 (c) *Statistical Abstract:* 1962, p. 815.

Property

The administrative, sales and engineering offices of Franklin are situated at 65—22nd Avenue Northeast, Minneapolis, Minnesota. Data regarding the location, products and size of the various manufacturing plants are [shown in Exhibit 7].

The plant buildings and their sites are owned by Franklin, except for a portion of the Webster City plant, which is leased. The buildings are of various forms of construction and ages. The new Bloomington plant was designed to achieve important operating economies as well as to provide increased refrigeration capacity. Production was commenced in June, 1961. The new Jefferson plant began operations in October, 1960. Other plants have been added to or

[Exhibit 7]

Location	Products	Approximate Area Used by Franklin
St. Cloud, Minnesota...	Refrigerators and Freezers	613,000 sq. ft.
Bloomington, Indiana...	Freezers	340,000 sq. ft.
Galt, Ontario, Canada...	Refrigerators and Freezers	228,000 sq. ft.
Webster City, Iowa.....	Washers and Dryers	140,000 sq. ft.
Minneapolis, Minn......	Electrical Products	74,000 sq. ft.
Jefferson, Iowa.........	Automatic washer transmission assemblies	58,000 sq. ft.
Minneapolis, Minn......	Plastic components for appliance division	36,000 sq. ft.

modernized in recent years. Manufacturing equipment is well maintained and highly automated. Franklin does substantially all of its own fabrication except for compressors and certain controls for refrigeration units and motors and some controls for laundry appliances. Franklin believes that its plant and equipment are in good condition and suitable and adequate for their intended uses. The productive capacity is generally fully utilized on a one shift basis. . . .

DESCRIPTION OF STUDEBAKER BUSINESS

Automotive Division—Current Operations

With the introduction of the Lark in November 1958, Studebaker switched substantially to production of compact cars. The Lark is now produced in a variety of models including a luxury convertible, sliding sunroof hardtop and station wagon as well as an economy type vehicle designed for fleet sales. The Avanti by Studebaker is a new four passenger sport touring car first introduced for the 1963 model year in limited quantity. Other Studebaker motor vehicles include the Hawk four passenger family sport touring car as well as trucks for military and commercial use.

Consolidated net sales of Studebaker for the eight months ended August 31, 1962, amounted to $221,248,698; in the comparable period in 1961, consolidated net sales were $158,400,573. See the information set forth herein under the heading "Studebaker Consolidated Statements of Income (Loss)." Sales of domestically manufactured passenger cars and trucks, and related parts and accessories, accounted for approximately 48% of the Studebaker consolidated net sales for the first eight months of 1961, 59% for the year 1961 and about 63% for the first eight months of 1962.

During the 1962 model year (which began September 1, 1961) total factory sales from Studebaker's United States plant of the Lark and other passenger car models were about 93,000 units compared with sales of about 68,000 units during the 1961 model year. Production of passenger cars for the third quarter of calendar 1962 (during part of which the plant was shut down for annual model change) was approximately 8,000 units compared with 16,136 units for the comparable period of 1961. Production of passenger cars for the fourth quarter of calendar 1962 (the first full quarter of the 1963 model year) has been scheduled at approximately 41,500 units compared with 32,905 units produced during the comparable period of 1961.

An automotive reporting service estimated that dealers' stocks of new cars (excluding imported cars) for the industry as a whole were 654,846 units at August 31, 1962. In terms of days' supply, which at the end of any month is expressed in relation to retail sales during that month, such dealers' stocks represented about a 36-days' supply. Dealers' stocks of new passenger cars manufactured by Studebaker approximated 10,400 units on August 31, 1962, which represented about a 56-days' supply.

Unit factory sales of passenger cars and trucks from United States plants by Studebaker and by the automotive industry, aggregate motor vehicle registrations, and the Studebaker percentage of industry sales for 1957 and subsequently are set forth in [Exhibit 8]. Attention is directed to the fact that Studebaker's position in the automative industry improved considerably as a result of the introduction of the smaller car late in 1958 and the substantial discontinuance of standard-size passenger cars. Thereafter, increased competition generated by the introduction of smaller cars by the three major domestic manufacturers resulted in an adverse change in Studebaker's position. During the 1962 model year, the automobile industry sold the largest number of cars since 1955. Although Studebaker's market penetration did not materially change, total sales were higher in accordance with the higher volume of industry sales. Trade sources anticipate lower industry sales for the 1963 model year. Accordingly, as indicated below under "Competition in the Automotive Industry," it is expected that competition will continue to be intense. Therefore, these comparative data must be viewed solely as a summary record of results in the past and not as a prediction of future results.

Foreign Cars—Exclusive Distribution Rights

Since 1957 Studebaker has been the exclusive distributor in the United States and its territories of passenger cars and trucks, and related parts and accessories, manufactured by Daimler-Benz, A.G. of Stuttgart, Germany. In 1958, this exclusive distributorship was transferred to a wholly owned subsidiary of the Corporation, Mercedes-Benz Sales, Inc. Total unit sales of Mercedes-Benz and DKW vehicles (including 4,635 tourist deliveries) aggregated approximately 15,213 units in 1961. Foreign car operations accounted for approximately 14% of consolidated net sales in 1961, and 13% for the first six months of 1962.

The Mercedes-Benz exclusive distribution rights terminate on December 31, 1971, subject to earlier termination should certain events occur. They may be

[Exhibit 8]
FACTORY SALES BY AUTOMOTIVE INDUSTRY AND REGISTRATIONS IN THE UNITED STATES; FACTORY SALES OF STUDEBAKER COMPARED WITH AUTOMOTIVE INDUSTRY

Year	Studebaker (in Thousands of Units)	Industry (a) (in Thousands of Units)	Studebaker as Percentage of Industry	Studebaker (in Thousands of Units)	Industry (a) (in Thousands of Units)	Studebaker as Percentage of Industry	Aggregate Motor Vehicle Registrations at Year End (b) (in Thousands of Units)
1957..................	74	6,113	1.2	14	1,107	1.2	67,131
1958 (c)...............	56	4,258	1.3	10	877	1.2	68,299
1959 (c)...............	152	5,591	2.7	10	1,137	.9	71,497
1960 (d)...............	103	6,675	1.5	12	1,194	1.0	73,941
1961:							
1st Quarter...........	15	1,196	1.3	2	265	0.8	
2nd Quarter...........	17	1,561	1.1	2	310	.6	
3rd Quarter...........	15	947	1.6	1	245	.4	
4th Quarter...........	30	1,839	1.6	2	314	.6	
Total 1961..........	77	5,543	1.4	7	1,134	.6	75,847
1962:							
1st Quarter...........	18	1,750	1.0	2	303	.7	
2nd Quarter...........	25	1,857	1.3	6	327	1.8	

(a) Source: Automobile Manufacturers Association, Inc.

(b) Includes publicly owned vehicles but excludes Alaska and Hawaii for years prior to 1959. Source: U.S. Bureau of the Census, *Statistical Abstract of the United States: 1962 (83rd ed.)*, p. 562.

(c) Studebaker's percentage of industry sales of passenger cars and trucks may have been affected by the fact that one of the three largest companies in the industry experienced work stoppages due to labor disputes during the fourth quarter of 1958 and due to shortages of materials during the first quarter of 1959.

(d) Studebaker's percentage of industry sales of passenger cars may have been affected by the impact of the steel strike on the production of the three largest companies during the last quarter of 1959 and part of the first quarter of 1960. During the steel strike, Studebaker suspended truck production and utilized all its steel supplies in the production of passenger cars.

terminated if annual sales of Mercedes-Benz products are less than $35,000,000. Total Mercedes-Benz sales were well in excess of such minimum for the year 1961 as well as, on a proportionate basis, for the six months ended June 30, 1962.

Automotive Sales Organization

Studebaker's automotive products are marketed in the United States primarily through retail dealers under franchise agreements with Studebaker. These dealers are independent merchants who purchase from Studebaker and sell to retail customers. As of August 31, 1962, Studebaker had 2,112 dealer franchises outstanding as compared with 2,102 at December 31, 1961. As of August 31, 1962, approximately 490 dealers franchised by Studebaker also held franchises with other domestic automobile manufacturers. The process of obtaining and holding dealers in the automobile industry is highly competitive; accordingly, the number of dealer franchises outstanding at a particular date is given for statistical purposes only and should not be considered necessarily indicative of the number of dealer franchises which will be in effect in the future. Moreover, there is wide variation in the activity, ability, financial resources and performance of those holding outstanding dealer franchises.

Mercedes-Benz vehicles are sold in the United States directly to authorized dealers who number approximately 357, of whom about 204 also hold franchises from Studebaker for the Lark.

Competition in the Automotive Industry

The automotive industry in the United States is highly competitive and Studebaker's position therein has been relatively small. Unit factory sales of cars and trucks by the three largest companies in the industry were about 90% of the industry's total sales for the 1962 model year (excluding August, 1962) and Studebaker's percentage was 1.33% for the same period. During the months of June and July, 1962, Studebaker's percentage of the domestic industry's total sales was 1.0%. Operations relating to domestically produced automotive products manufactured by Studebaker were not profitable for the eight months ended August 31, 1962.

Tax Loss Carry-Forward Credit

As of December 31, 1961, Studebaker had a tax loss carry-forward resulting from operating losses incurred in 1958 and prior years of approximately $56,-000,000, based upon tax returns filed which are subject to audit by the Internal Revenue Service. Of this amount, approximately $27,000,000 will expire in the year ending December 31, 1962 and approximately $29,000,000 will expire in the year ending December 31, 1963. In the opinion of Studebaker's counsel, Messrs. Cravath, Swaine & Moore, Studebaker under the provisions of the Internal Revenue Code of 1954 now in effect (and assuming the non-applicability of Sections 269 and 382 thereof), will be able to apply its tax loss carry-forward as a net operating loss deduction against its own taxable income for 1962 and 1963, including the income of the Franklin Division of Studebaker after the Closing Date under the Purchase Agreement. From time to time various recommendations have been made and bills have been introduced in Congress to limit or restrict the availability of net operating loss carry-forwards.

The pro forma condensed balance sheet [Exhibit 9] gives effect to the proposed acquisition by Studebaker Corporation of the assets and business and the assumption of certain liabilities of Franklin Manufacturing Company.

[*Exhibit 9*]

PRO FORMA CONDENSED BALANCE SHEET (UNAUDITED)
COMBINING THE ACCOUNTS OF STUDEBAKER CORPORATION
AND ITS SUBSIDIARIES AS OF JUNE 30, 1962
WITH THOSE OF FRANKLIN MANUFACTURING COMPANY
AND ITS SUBSIDIARIES AS OF MARCH 31, 1962

	Studebaker	Franklin	Pro Forma Adjustments— Addition (Deduction)	Combined Pro Forma
ASSETS				
Current Assets:				
Cash..........................	$ 12,514,930	$10,689,765	($ 3,914,583)	$ 19,290,112
Marketable securities............	18,194,648	8,430		18,203,078
Accounts receivable—net.........	25,905,920	6,651,134		32,557,054
Inventories......................	60,180,855	10,984,531		71,165,386
Prepaid expenses................	1,309,147	92,845		1,401,992
Total Current Assets...........	$118,105,500	$28,426,705	($ 3,914,583)	$142,617,622
Other Assets.....................	8,372,428	663,620		9,036,048
Properties—at cost, less allowances for depreciation.................	43,726,582	13,994,784	2,999,997	60,721,363
	$170,204,510	$43,085,109	($ 914,586)	$212,375,033
LIABILITIES				
Current Liabilities:				
Accounts payable and accrued expenses......................	$ 42,119,318	$ 4,768,033		$ 46,887,351
Notes payable...................	47,919			47,919
Current payments on acquisition contracts......................	875,513			875,513
Reserve for product warranty......	2,350,466			2,350,466
Estimated taxes on income........	—0—	1,651,184	($ 1,248,691)	402,493
Total Current Liabilities.........	$ 45,393,216	$ 6,419,217	($ 1,248,691)	$ 50,563,742
Other Liabilities:				
Deferred installments of incentive compensation awards..........	$ 235,000			$ 235,000
Long-term debt:				
5% secured notes payable........	16,500,000			16,500,000
Revolving credit notes...........	—0—		$25,000,000	25,000,000
Other, less current maturities.....	3,601,187			3,601,187
	$ 20,336,187		$25,000,000	$ 45,336,187
Shareholders' Equity:				
$5 Convertible Preferred Stock.....	$ 905,300			$ 905,300
5% Convertible Second Preferred Stock......................	3,000,000			3,000,000
Common Stock..................	12,335,351		$ 1,333,333	13,668,684
Capital surplus..................	46,705,602		10,666,664	57,372,266
Retained earnings................	41,528,854			41,528,854
Franklin book value of net assets...		$36,665,892	($36,665,892)	
	$104,475,107	$36,665,892	($24,665,895)	$116,475,104
	$170,204,510	$43,085,109	($ 914,586)	$212,375,033

The proposed acquisition would be reflected by the following transactions as indicated in the Pro Forma Adjustments:

(1) The borrowing by Studebaker of $25,000,000 under a revolving credit agreement (see description under the heading "Financing Arrangements" in this proxy statement for restrictions imposed by such agreement).

(2) The issuance of 1,333,333 shares of Studebaker Common Stock at a fair market value of $9 a share (final determination of fair market value to be made following the date of acquisition) and payment by Studebaker of $28,-914,583 representing the balance of the purchase price (based upon book value of Franklin's net assets at March 31, 1962) plus $1,248,691 which at March 31, 1962, was the unpaid Federal income tax of Franklin and is assumed for this purpose to be equal to the amount (final determination of which will be made following the date of acquisition) of the Unpaid 1962 Income Tax of Franklin as defined in the Purchase Agreement. The unpaid Canadian taxes ($402,493) are being assumed by Studebaker.

The difference of $2,999,997 between the purchase price and the net assets of Franklin has been ascribed to the properties acquired from Franklin. This amount is subject to adjustment due to change in net book value of Franklin between March 31, 1962 and date of closing, and the final determination of the fair market value of the Studebaker Common Stock.

QUESTIONS

1. What are the advantages to Studebaker of this merger? Make quantitative estimates.

2. Would you recommend this merger if there were no tax credits available? On what terms?

CHAPTER 14

◆◆◆◆◆◆◆◆◆◆◆◆◆◆◆◆◆◆◆◆◆◆◆◆◆◆

Investment Decisions of the Firm

WHEN AN executive or a research worker is hired, his worth—in the sense of his potential marginal revenue productivity to the firm—is difficult to anticipate. This is less true of a piece of capital equipment, since technical performance specifications are apt to be quite dependable. However, decisions regarding the purchases of equipment are among the more difficult ones which management must make. This is because a machine represents a stock of productive services which will be utilized over a considerable period of time, usually many years, but which must be contracted for at a specific price at the time of purchase. This long-time commitment can sometimes be avoided by renting the equipment on a short-term lease, but careful calculation is required in order to make a wise decision as to whether it is more economical to buy or to rent.

While the volume of services which a given piece of equipment is physically capable of turning out is usually quite predictable, the economic circumstances in which it will operate are more uncertain. These will determine the rate at which the equipment is used and the value of its services based on the net value of its output. Output prices may change a great deal over the life of the equipment, and such changes may, of course, be unfavorable in direction. The invention of an improved machine to do the same sort of job is a particular hazard, since this can quickly lower the value of output by cutting competitors' costs of producing the same product and permitting them to lower their selling prices. Decisions in this field are hard to make, at best; but they are more likely to be correct if use is made of the relevant theory, since this pinpoints some of the basic considerations which should not be neglected. The alternative is to use some rule of thumb which may omit variables of special importance to the case in question.

Capitalization

The concept of capitalization is extremely important to the calculations which enter into a rational decision with respect to the purchase of any capital good. Capitalization is the mathematical process of finding the present value of a future stream of income. The calculation is simplest if this income stream is one without end—an income in perpetuity. Suppose a public utility company has paid a dividend of $5.00 per year per share on its common stock for many years, and will—as far as can be seen—continue to do so indefinitely. The market price of the stock should then depend almost entirely on the interest rate which is considered appropriate for this sort of investment.[1] (This percentage yield will be lower than on most stocks, because of the relatively low risk of loss of interest or principal due to the stable nature of the company.) Suppose that the appropriate interest rate is 5 per cent per year. The stock would then sell at about $100 per share. This is determined by the capitalization formula for a perpetual income, where V is the present value of a share, I is the anticipated income, and r is the market interest rate on investments of this quality.

$$V = \frac{I}{r}$$

The formula is appropriate only if no change is anticipated in either I or r. Suppose that I is expected to remain at $5.00 per year, but that most buyers anticipate that interest rates in general will rise slightly in the near future. They would then be unwilling to pay quite as much as $100 per share, since they believe that by waiting a while, they can secure a little more than $5.00 a year on $100 invested in a security of this grade (or even in this same security). On the other hand, if there is a general expectation of a decline in interest rates, the stock should now sell at a little more than $100 a share. This simple capitalization formula is also applicable to evaluation of a piece of land which is expected to yield a steady and perpetual income above taxes and all other costs. For example, the value of a piece of city land recently rented on a ninety-nine-year lease to a dependable firm which pays the owner a yearly rental of $10,000 would be $200,000 if, again, 5 per cent were considered the appropriate rate of interest on such an investment. If the land changed hands at this price, the new buyer would, of course, receive a 5 per cent return on his investment of $200,000, since this is just another view of the same problem.

The capitalization calculation is somewhat more complicated when the income will be received only for a finite number of years instead of in perpetuity. Income received today is more valuable than the same amount of income received a year from now because if it is received today, it can begin immediately to earn interest for the owner. There-

---

[1] The market price is also affected by the number of dividends paid per year and by brokerage fees and transfer taxes, but these will have a relatively minor effect on market price and are disregarded for purposes of simplification.

fore, its additional worth is just the amount of interest which it will earn in a year. By the same token, income which is still a year away must be discounted—a year's interest must be taken away—in order to find its present value. If the income is more than a year away, it must be discounted more heavily.

Suppose that a merchant has a claim to three $1,000 payments which are due to him one year, two years, and three years from today, respectively. He may wish to sell this claim in order to secure all of the cash immediately (from someone else who will look upon the claim as a suitable investment). The amount for which he can sell the claim depends on the risk which is deemed by potential buyers to be associated with the claim—that is, by the apparent degree of danger of non-payment or slow payment of an installment when due.

The present value of this claim can be found from the formula:

$$V = \frac{\$1,000}{1 + r} + \frac{\$1,000}{(1 + r)^2} + \frac{\$1,000}{(1 + r)^3}$$

This formula discounts each successive payment more heavily. The first payment is now worth the sum which will build up to $1,000 in one year, without compounding the interest. The second payment is now worth the sum which will build up to $1,000 in two years, with interest compounded at the end of the first year; while the third payment is now worth the amount which would build up to $1,000 in three years if compounded at the end of the first and second years. Suppose r is 6 per cent. The first $1,000 installment is now worth $943.40, the second installment is worth $890.00, and the third is worth $839.62. The entire claim is worth the sum of these amounts, or $2,673.02. This worth would, of course, be greater if the relevant interest rate were deemed to be less than 6 per cent, and it would be lower if a higher discount rate were used. Also, the claim would be worth less today if a period shorter than a year were used for compounding interest. (See Exhibits 1 and 2 in the Appendix to this chapter for present value of a single payment of $1.00 in future years and of an annual payment of $1.00 at various interest rates. The calculations in the present paragraph may be checked in Exhibit 1.)

Value of a Machine

The same sort of calculation is involved in finding the present value of a machine. In this case the annual income is the "quasi rent"[2] derived

---

[2]This name was given by Alfred Marshall to the "income derived from machines or other appliances for production made by man" (*Principles of Economics* [8th ed.; London: Macmillan & Co., Ltd., 1930], p. 74).

from its productive contribution. Annual quasi rent is found by deducting from the value of the annual product of the machine all variable costs (labor, materials, fuel, etc.) incurred in the same process. No deduction is made, however, for depreciation on the machine or for interest on its cost. The term "cash flow" is often used in this connection in place of "quasi rent." While it brings to mind approximately the correct picture, this term is not an entirely accurate one because in a given year the inflow of funds may take the form of increases in accounts receivable, reductions in liabilities of the firm, or some other change in noncash accounts.

Suppose a machine has three years of productive life remaining and that at the end of that time, it will have no scrap value. Assume also that (like an electric light bulb or, perhaps, a TV picture tube) it gives satisfactory service until it expires, rather than gradually running down or requiring ever-increasing maintenance expenditures. If the product turned out by the machine is worth $4,000 a year and variable expenses of $3,000 a year are incurred in its operation, the machine has a present value of $2,673.02, if a 6 per cent rate is used in discounting. (This is the same calculation as made previously—a trick which saves the writers a bit of time.)

Usually, a machine will have scrap value or trade-in value at the end of its productive life. This requires only the modification of adding in the discounted value of this last-ditch contribution of the machine. The scrap value is assumed to be realized as soon as the last output is sold (at the end of the nth year). Letting Q stand for quasi rent received at the end of each year and S for scrap value, the formula for the present value of a machine is:

$$V = \frac{Q_1}{1+r} + \frac{Q_2}{(1+r)^2} + \frac{Q_3}{(1+r)^3} + \cdots + \frac{Q_n}{(1+r)^n} + \frac{S}{(1+r)^n}$$

It is not necessary that the quasi rent be the same each year. Normally, it will decrease with time as maintenance and repair expenses connected with the aging machine increase. It is implicity assumed, however, that quasi rent is maximized each year by the operation of the machine at the output rate where marginal cost equals marginal revenue. It has been pointed out that a plant is operated optimally only when marginal revenue and marginal cost are equated, and the same is true of an individual machine. The correct present value of the machine can only be derived on the assumption that its earnings will be maximized through correct management.

It should be realized that regardless of the arithmetical care with which the present value of a machine is calculated, much uncertainty is present in the calculation. The stream of quasi rents will be affected by the price of the output; by prices which will be paid for materials, labor, etc., in the future; and by possible breakdowns of the machine itself. Its scrap or trade-in value is probably not definitely ascertainable if the machine has a number of years of life remaining. Also, the selection of the interest rate to be used in discounting requires much information and judgment. Usually, it is correct to utilize an interest rate which reflects the market-determined rate at which the firm could lend its money, the degree of risk being the same.[3]

A further complication involved in estimating V is that the present value of income taxes attributable to the earnings of the machine must be deducted. Perhaps the simplest way to make the necessary calculation is to deduct the anticipated income tax from each quasi rent before discounting the "cash flow" stream in order to find its present value. If $\overline{Q}_1$ is such a net quasi rent in period 1 and d_1 is the depreciation charge for that period, we can write:

$$\overline{Q}_1 = Q_1 - [(\text{Tax rate})\,(Q_1 - d_1)]$$

This formula is based on the deductibility of depreciation for tax purposes. Similar equations would apply to each of the periods of expected life of the asset. The present value becomes:

$$V = \frac{\overline{Q}_1}{1+r} + \frac{\overline{Q}_2}{(1+r)^2} + \frac{\overline{Q}_3}{(1+r)^3} + \cdots + \frac{\overline{Q}_n}{(1+r)^n} + \frac{S}{(1+r)^n}$$

An alternative and equivalent expression[4] for "quasi rent after taxes" in period 1 is:

$$\overline{Q}_1 = (1 - \text{Tax rate}) \times (\text{Revenue} - \text{Expenses other than depreciation} - \text{Depreciation}) + \text{Depreciation}$$

While the same tax rate will ordinarily be used in estimating each year's "after-tax cash flow," the analyst may substitute other rates if he strongly anticipates a change in the tax law (as is likely at the present time—early 1963). It is also clear that the method of computing depreciation allowances enters into the problem. Accelerated depreciation tends to increase the present value of assets by lowering income taxes in the early years when net quasi rents are subjected to smaller dis-

[3]For more accurate criteria under various conditions, see Harry V. Roberts, "Current Problems in the Economics of Capital Budgeting," *Journal of Business*, January, 1957.

[4]This formula is shown in H. Bierman, Jr., and S. Smidt, *The Capital Budgeting Decision* (New York: Macmillan Co., 1960), p. 105.

counts. Both the use of accelerated depreciation and the anticipation of lower income tax rates can be seen as favorable to a greater present rate of investment.

Decision to Purchase a Machine

Estimating the worth of a machine involves difficulties but must somehow be accomplished, at least roughly, if a rational decision to purchase or not to purchase a machine is to be made. Once the present value (V) has been determined, it is only necessary to compare this with the cost of the machine. If its value is greater than its cost, it should be purchased; if its value is less than its cost, it should not be purchased; if its value is just equal to its cost, it is a matter of indifference whether it is purchased, since funds invested in the machine will bring the same return as they could earn in an alternative investment.[5]

If V exceeds the cost of the machine, it means that according to the best calculation which can be made, the returns from the machine will more than cover all variable costs, depreciation on the machine, and a normal interest return on the capital tied up in the machine. The investment opportunity then appears to be a good one, and management is likely to buy the machine (unless a still better one is available for the job). Sales opportunities may be such that additional machines would also be expected to have a present worth greater than their cost. In this event, management should purchase additional machines as long as the value added by another machine to the present value of the whole stock of machines exceeds the cost of the machine. In this calculation, account must be taken of the fact that each machine which is added may lower the present value of the earlier machines by lowering the market price at which the output can be disposed of. It is also possible that "quantity discounts" can be secured on larger orders for machines, and this further complicates the calculation. These complications are greater than we wish to enter into in this elementary and partial treatment[6] of a difficult subject.

---

[5]This is not strictly true when the possession of the machine permits some other factor of production in which the owner has an interest to earn an income. For example, a man may be able to put his wife to work by buying her a washing machine, whereas she would otherwise send out the laundry and spend the time playing bridge. The present value of the machine to the husband would exceed its discounted stream of quasi rents plus its discounted trade-in value when quasi rents are computed by deducting normal wage costs. This is because the wife's labor can be considered to be free.

[6]An excellent book which should be studied by the reader desiring a thorough training in this subject is Friedrich A. and Vera C. Lutz, *The Theory of Investment of the Firm* (Princeton: Princeton University Press, 1951). Such problems as optimum productive techniques, optimum size of firm, optimum length of life of equipment, and optimum method of finance are treated mathematically.

Should a New Model Be Purchased?

Management faces a slightly different sort of investment decision when confronted with a problem of whether to replace machinery which is still usable with a new, improved model. The problem is similar to that of the fairly opulent family which has to decide each year whether to buy a new-model automobile or to continue to drive the old car. (The firm is more likely than the household to make a rational decision, however.) The development of a dramatically altered model, such as a jet-propelled air liner or an atom-powered ocean liner can bring this question forcibly before a great many firms at the same time.

It would seem at first glance that a new type of machine which becomes available should be purchased if it will lower the unit cost of production. Comparison of the average cost of production using different machines is valid, however, only if neither is already owned by the firm. In that case, all costs (including depreciation) should be counted. If investment has already been made in one machine, however, it is often correct to compare the *variable operating costs* per unit using the old machine to the *total cost* per unit using the new machine. This is the principle which was emphasized in Chapter 4—namely, that costs which are already sunk should not enter into decisions regarding new steps to be taken or avoided. They are bygones which should remain bygones.

This comparison is not entirely correct, however, because the sunk costs are really not lost, to the extent that they can be partially recovered through the sale or trade-in of the old machine. As long as variable operating costs using the old machine are below the selling price of the product, it can continue to yield an annual quasi rent. If this quasi rent is sufficient to cover interest on its own scrap value plus interest on the difference between the value and cost of a new machine, use of the old machine should be continued.[7]

Like most calculations involving interest, the appropriateness of this formulation is not easy to see. The following may help. If the old machine is continued in use, the firm sacrifices during each time period the interest which could otherwise be earned on its market value. This is one cost of keeping the old machine. Also, by retaining the old machine, the firm sacrifices interest income on the difference between the present value and the cost of the new machine. This interest would actually be secured from the quasi rents which would be returned by the new machine over time. If the new machine is markedly superior to the old

---

[7]This formulation is given by Lutz, *ibid.*, pp. 113–14.

one, this will be a large item and will make it desirable to replace the old machine with the new one immediately. If, however, the new machine is only a slight improvement over the old one, this will not be a large amount. In that event, it is quite possible that for some years to come, the annual quasi rent returned by the old machine will exceed the sum of the annual interest on its disposal value and the annual interest on the difference between value and cost of a new machine. Eventually, of course, the old machine should be replaced, but premature replacement by a model which is only slightly better is both common and uneconomical.

Alternative Formulation of Replacement Criterion

The complex-sounding considerations which have been set forth for deciding rationally between retaining and replacing old machinery can be restated in a somewhat simpler way if "average cost" is redefined for purposes of this sort of decision. Ordinarily, average cost is made up of variable cost per unit and fixed cost per unit, including in the latter depreciation based on the original cost of the asset. However, it will seldom happen that the market value of an old machine will exactly equal its original cost less depreciation as charged off on the books from the time of acquisition to the time at which a decision to keep or replace is to be made.

A direct comparison of the average cost of production using the new machine and using the old machine may be appropriate if three things are done: (1) Average cost of producing with the old equipment must include depreciation based not on original cost but on present market value less estimated scrap value; (2) interest must be added in as a cost, with its amount being computed on the cost and market value, respectively, of the new and the old equipment; and (3) the average cost calculation using both old and new equipment must be made in each case for the expected optimum output—i.e., where marginal cost equals marginal revenue. This may not be the same output in both cases. If it is expected that demand will fall off, replacement of the old machinery becomes less desirable, since a reduction in output will raise average cost of output more sharply for the new machinery than for the old. This is due to the higher fixed costs which will be associated with the new equipment.

In summary, the decision whether to replace existing machinery with new machinery usually cannot be made simply by comparing expected average cost of production by the two methods. Capital will have been sunk in the old equipment, but this historical event is irrelevant to a present decision except to the extent that capital could now be recovered by selling or trading in the old machinery. This requires an amended calculation of average cost of production using the old machinery. In addition, interest must be included as a cost of production. This is normal procedure for the economist but not for the accountant, except where the interest payment is explicit. Also, the average cost of production using either old or new equipment will depend on the rate of production; consequently, not a single average cost but instead an average cost *curve* should be computed for output from both old and new machinery. The optimum rate of output which is anticipated for each of the two productive processes then determines an average cost for each, and these averages can be directly compared to judge whether replacement is desirable. If *none* of the capital sunk in the old machinery can be recovered by its sale or trade-in, the relevant comparison is simply average cost at the expected output with the new machine versus average variable cost at the expected rate of output using the old machine. Interest is an element in the former but not in the latter.

Revenue Considerations

In the preceding discussion, it was implicitly assumed that the revenue received by the firm will be the same whether or not old equipment is replaced. Frequently, however, a better product is turned out by the new equipment, and income is thereby increased. This is especially easy to see in the case of new transportation equipment which will attract customers through greater speed, convenience, etc. When revenue is affected, the replacement calculation is more difficult than was indicated by the suggested comparison of average cost of production with new and old equipment (adjusted for the old equipment to include depreciation and interest based on present market value). Instead, for the rate of operation expected in each case, net earnings after income taxes must be compared, total income being computed by multiplying output by price per unit and total cost being computed by multiplying output by adjusted cost per unit. (The income tax is computed with the use of accounting costs as permitted for tax purposes, and these will differ from the costs just mentioned.)

The foregoing reduces to the rather obvious statement that old equipment should be replaced by new equipment if annual net income after taxes can thereby be increased. It should be noted, however, that the relevant net income as computed for the alternative of retention of old equipment involves the basic economic concept of disregarding sunk costs based on *previous* decisions. Instead, only *present* alternatives are involved, since average cost is derived in part from the present disposal value of old equipment.[8] In some cases, another firm can make especially good use of secondhand equipment (due perhaps to a very limited capital budget), and in such a case the firm which owns such equipment may have an especially good opportunity to modernize its own plant.

Broader Investment Decisions

So far, the discussion in this chapter has considered mainly the questions (1) when the purchase of a machine is economical and (2) whether replacement of a machine is desirable. The same principles are applicable to investment decisions considered more broadly, such as questions of the addition to a plant or construction of a whole new plant. For broader decisions, there are usually additional factors which must be taken into account, however. If a new plant turning out the same commodity is erected, sales of the product in its "natural" market area may reduce the demand for the product of the older plant. Revenue-cost considerations applied to the new plant alone are not sufficient for the making of a rational decision. Also, outlays for a major investment project are likely to be made over a period of time. This requires a discounting of the outlays to determine their present value. This present value may then be compared with the discounted value of the stream of quasi rent expected to be received after the new project is put into operation.

Abandonment of a Project

Efficient management, especially of a multiple-product firm, requires alertness to the possibility of increasing net earnings by abandoning entire activities from time to time. The information needed for a rational decision in this area is comparable in complexity and quite similar in nature to information needed for a replacement decision. That this should be the case is not surprising, since replacement of an old ma-

---

[8]The reader should realize that like any other brief statement of a principle in this complex field, the above is an oversimplification which can be applied only if circumstances warrant. It is implicitly assumed, for example, that availability of a still better machine in the near future cannot be foreseen, that prices of co-operating factors are not expected to change so as to favor one machine over the other, etc.

chine by a new one requires that the old machine be "abandoned" as far as the firm in question is concerned.

If an activity—production of a particular commodity, for example— is abandoned, the firm will lose a future stream of quasi rents (or cash flow) which could be gained from sale of the commodity. Discounting this stream of gross earnings (after taxes but before depreciation or interest charges on associated capital assets) by the minimum rate of return acceptable to the firm in view of alternative investment opportunities, one secures a figure for the present value of the income which would be lost by abandoment. This should be compared with the present disposal value of the equipment, inventories, and any other assets which would be released from use. If the disposal value exceeds the retention value, the activity promises to yield less than an acceptable rate of return and should be abandoned.

The decision is relatively easy to make, of course, if the present value of the anticipated quasi rents from retention is negative. This means that expected variable costs will exceed total income so that the return on the fixed investment is negative. The activity should then clearly be abandoned unless the present value recoverable from the fixed capital is negative due to extremely high abandonment costs (such as the need to dig up and haul away an entire pipe line).

In making estimates related to the question of abandonment, it is important for management to keep a firmwide view. That is, the shutting-down of one plant may not result in the loss of all sales formerly contributed by that facility, since other plants belonging to the same firm may be able to take over some of its customers. (This is especially easy to observe in the case of ownership by the same firm of more than one theater in the same small city.) On the other hand, the closing-down of one operation may adversely affect others of a complementary nature. Discontinuation of production of a bicycle headlight may hurt the sale of replacement batteries and lamps by the same firm, for example.[9]

It was pointed out in an earlier chapter that the competitive firm should continue to produce if price is high enough to cover average variable cost. In this way, it will meet all variable expenses and (usually) earn something toward meeting fixed costs, which will go on in any case. It can now be seen that the earlier formulation is strictly true only when none of the investment responsible for the fixed costs can presently be recouped. If some recovery of capital is possible through

---

[9]For a fuller discussion of relevant considerations, see Gordon Shillinglaw, "Profit Analysis for Abandonment Decisions," *Journal of Business,* January, 1957.

abandonment of the activity, it may be desirable to shut down permanently, even though all variable costs are being covered and some quasi rents could be secured through continued operation. This suggests the desirability of using equipment which is not too highly specialized to one commodity when the venture is a particularly risky one. In short, purchase of multipurpose equipment may help the firm hedge against uncertainty.

APPENDIX TO CHAPTER 14

(See Exhibits 1 and 2 on pages 588 and 589.)

CASES

Cases for Chapters 14 and 15 are placed at the end of Chapter 15 because the subject matter of these chapters is sufficiently similar that both should be studied before cases are analyzed.

Exhibit 1

PRESENT VALUE OF $1.00

Years Hence	1%	2%	4%	6%	8%	10%	12%	14%	15%	16%	18%	20%	22%	24%	25%	26%	28%	30%	35%	40%	45%	50%
1	0.990	0.980	0.962	0.943	0.926	0.909	0.893	0.877	0.870	0.862	0.847	0.833	0.820	0.806	0.800	0.794	0.781	0.769	0.741	0.714	0.690	0.667
2	0.980	0.961	0.925	0.890	0.857	0.826	0.797	0.769	0.756	0.743	0.718	0.694	0.672	0.650	0.640	0.630	0.610	0.592	0.549	0.510	0.476	0.444
3	0.971	0.942	0.889	0.840	0.794	0.751	0.712	0.675	0.658	0.641	0.609	0.579	0.551	0.524	0.512	0.500	0.477	0.455	0.406	0.364	0.328	0.296
4	0.961	0.924	0.855	0.792	0.735	0.683	0.636	0.592	0.572	0.552	0.516	0.482	0.451	0.423	0.410	0.397	0.373	0.350	0.301	0.260	0.226	0.198
5	0.951	0.906	0.822	0.747	0.681	0.621	0.567	0.519	0.497	0.476	0.437	0.402	0.370	0.341	0.328	0.315	0.291	0.269	0.223	0.186	0.156	0.132
6	0.942	0.888	0.790	0.705	0.630	0.564	0.507	0.456	0.432	0.410	0.370	0.335	0.303	0.275	0.262	0.250	0.227	0.207	0.165	0.133	0.108	0.088
7	0.933	0.871	0.760	0.665	0.583	0.513	0.452	0.400	0.376	0.354	0.314	0.279	0.249	0.222	0.210	0.198	0.178	0.159	0.122	0.095	0.074	0.059
8	0.923	0.853	0.731	0.627	0.540	0.467	0.404	0.351	0.327	0.305	0.266	0.233	0.204	0.179	0.168	0.157	0.139	0.123	0.091	0.068	0.051	0.039
9	0.914	0.837	0.703	0.592	0.500	0.424	0.361	0.308	0.284	0.263	0.225	0.194	0.167	0.144	0.134	0.125	0.108	0.094	0.067	0.048	0.035	0.026
10	0.905	0.820	0.676	0.558	0.463	0.386	0.322	0.270	0.247	0.227	0.191	0.162	0.137	0.116	0.107	0.099	0.085	0.073	0.050	0.035	0.024	0.017
11	0.896	0.804	0.650	0.527	0.429	0.350	0.287	0.237	0.215	0.195	0.162	0.135	0.112	0.094	0.086	0.079	0.066	0.056	0.037	0.025	0.017	0.012
12	0.887	0.788	0.625	0.497	0.397	0.319	0.257	0.208	0.187	0.168	0.137	0.112	0.092	0.076	0.069	0.062	0.052	0.043	0.027	0.018	0.012	0.008
13	0.879	0.773	0.601	0.469	0.368	0.290	0.229	0.182	0.163	0.145	0.116	0.093	0.075	0.061	0.055	0.050	0.040	0.033	0.020	0.013	0.008	0.005
14	0.870	0.758	0.577	0.442	0.340	0.263	0.205	0.160	0.141	0.125	0.099	0.078	0.062	0.049	0.044	0.039	0.032	0.025	0.015	0.009	0.006	0.003
15	0.861	0.743	0.555	0.417	0.315	0.239	0.183	0.140	0.123	0.108	0.084	0.065	0.051	0.040	0.035	0.031	0.025	0.020	0.011	0.006	0.004	0.002
16	0.853	0.728	0.534	0.394	0.292	0.218	0.163	0.123	0.107	0.093	0.071	0.054	0.042	0.032	0.028	0.025	0.019	0.015	0.008	0.005	0.003	0.002
17	0.844	0.714	0.513	0.371	0.270	0.198	0.146	0.108	0.093	0.080	0.060	0.045	0.034	0.026	0.023	0.020	0.015	0.012	0.006	0.003	0.002	0.001
18	0.836	0.700	0.494	0.350	0.250	0.180	0.130	0.095	0.081	0.069	0.051	0.038	0.028	0.021	0.018	0.016	0.012	0.009	0.005	0.002	0.001	0.001
19	0.828	0.686	0.475	0.331	0.232	0.164	0.116	0.083	0.070	0.060	0.043	0.031	0.023	0.017	0.014	0.012	0.009	0.007	0.003	0.002	0.001	
20	0.820	0.673	0.456	0.312	0.215	0.149	0.104	0.073	0.061	0.051	0.037	0.026	0.019	0.014	0.012	0.010	0.007	0.005	0.002	0.001	0.001	
21	0.811	0.660	0.439	0.294	0.199	0.135	0.093	0.064	0.053	0.044	0.031	0.022	0.015	0.011	0.009	0.008	0.006	0.004	0.002	0.001		
22	0.803	0.647	0.422	0.278	0.184	0.123	0.083	0.056	0.046	0.038	0.026	0.018	0.013	0.009	0.007	0.006	0.004	0.003	0.001	0.001		
23	0.795	0.634	0.406	0.262	0.170	0.112	0.074	0.049	0.040	0.033	0.022	0.015	0.010	0.007	0.006	0.005	0.003	0.002	0.001			
24	0.788	0.622	0.390	0.247	0.158	0.102	0.066	0.043	0.035	0.028	0.019	0.013	0.008	0.006	0.005	0.004	0.003	0.002	0.001			
25	0.780	0.610	0.375	0.233	0.146	0.092	0.059	0.038	0.030	0.024	0.016	0.010	0.007	0.005	0.004	0.003	0.002	0.001	0.001			
26	0.772	0.598	0.361	0.220	0.135	0.084	0.053	0.033	0.026	0.021	0.014	0.009	0.006	0.004	0.003	0.002	0.002	0.001				
27	0.764	0.586	0.347	0.207	0.125	0.076	0.047	0.029	0.023	0.018	0.011	0.007	0.005	0.003	0.002	0.002	0.001	0.001				
28	0.757	0.574	0.333	0.196	0.116	0.069	0.042	0.026	0.020	0.016	0.010	0.006	0.004	0.002	0.002	0.002	0.001	0.001				
29	0.749	0.563	0.321	0.185	0.107	0.063	0.037	0.022	0.017	0.014	0.008	0.005	0.003	0.002	0.002	0.001	0.001	0.001				
30	0.742	0.552	0.308	0.174	0.099	0.057	0.033	0.020	0.015	0.012	0.007	0.004	0.003	0.002	0.001	0.001	0.001					
40	0.672	0.453	0.208	0.097	0.046	0.022	0.011	0.005	0.004	0.003	0.001	0.001										
50	0.608	0.372	0.141	0.054	0.021	0.009	0.003	0.001	0.001	0.001												

Exhibit 2

PRESENT VALUE OF $1.00 RECEIVED ANNUALLY FOR *n* YEARS

Years (n)	1%	2%	4%	6%	8%	10%	12%	14%	15%	16%	18%	20%	22%	24%	25%	26%	28%	30%	35%	40%	45%	50%
1	0.990	0.980	0.962	0.943	0.926	0.909	0.893	0.877	0.870	0.862	0.847	0.833	0.820	0.806	0.800	0.794	0.781	9.769	0.741	0.714	0.690	0.667
2	1.970	1.942	1.886	1.833	1.783	1.736	1.690	1.647	1.626	1.605	1.566	1.528	1.492	1.457	1.440	1.424	1.392	1.361	1.289	1.224	1.165	1.111
3	2.941	2.884	2.775	2.673	2.577	2.487	2.402	2.322	2.283	2.246	2.174	2.106	2.042	1.981	1.952	1.923	1.868	1.816	1.696	1.589	1.493	1.407
4	3.902	3.808	3.630	3.465	3.312	3.170	3.037	2.914	2.855	2.798	2.690	2.589	2.494	2.404	2.362	2.320	2.241	2.166	1.997	1.849	1.720	1.605
5	4.853	4.713	4.452	4.212	3.993	3.791	3.605	3.433	3.352	3.274	3.127	2.991	2.864	2.745	2.689	2.635	2.532	2.436	2.220	2.035	1.876	1.737
6	5.795	5.601	5.242	4.917	4.623	4.355	4.111	3.889	3.784	3.685	3.498	3.326	3.167	3.020	2.951	2.885	2.759	2.643	2.385	2.168	1.983	1.824
7	6.728	6.472	6.002	5.582	5.206	4.868	4.564	4.288	4.160	4.039	3.812	3.605	3.416	3.242	3.161	3.083	2.937	2.802	2.508	2.263	2.057	1.883
8	7.652	7.325	6.733	6.210	5.747	5.335	4.968	4.639	4.487	4.344	4.078	3.837	3.619	3.421	3.329	3.241	3.076	2.925	2.598	2.331	2.108	1.922
9	8.566	8.162	7.435	6.802	6.247	5.759	5.328	4.946	4.772	4.607	4.303	4.031	3.786	3.566	3.463	3.366	3.184	3.019	2.665	2.379	2.144	1.948
10	9.471	8.983	8.111	7.360	6.710	6.145	5.650	5.216	5.019	4.833	4.494	4.192	3.923	3.682	3.571	3.465	3.269	3.092	2.715	2.414	2.168	1.965
11	10.368	9.787	8.760	7.887	7.139	6.495	5.988	5.453	5.234	5.029	4.656	4.327	4.035	3.776	3.656	3.544	3.335	3.147	2.757	2.438	2.185	1.977
12	11.255	10.575	9.385	8.384	7.536	6.814	6.194	5.660	5.421	5.197	4.793	4.439	4.127	3.851	3.725	3.606	3.387	3.190	2.779	2.456	2.196	1.985
13	12.134	11.343	9.986	8.853	7.904	7.103	6.424	5.842	5.583	5.342	4.910	4.533	4.203	3.912	3.780	3.656	3.427	3.223	2.799	2.468	2.204	1.990
14	13.004	12.106	10.563	9.295	8.244	7.367	6.628	6.002	5.724	5.468	5.008	4.611	4.265	3.962	3.824	3.695	3.459	3.249	2.814	2.477	2.210	1.993
15	13.865	12.849	11.118	9.712	8.559	7.606	6.811	6.142	5.847	5.575	5.092	4.675	4.315	4.001	3.859	3.726	3.483	3.268	2.825	2.484	2.214	1.995
16	14.718	13.578	11.652	10.106	8.851	7.824	6.974	6.265	5.954	5.669	5.162	4.730	4.357	4.033	3.887	3.751	3.503	3.283	2.834	2.489	2.216	1.997
17	15.562	14.292	12.166	10.477	9.122	8.022	7.120	6.373	6.047	5.749	5.222	4.775	4.391	4.059	3.910	3.771	3.518	3.295	2.840	2.492	2.218	1.998
18	16.398	14.992	12.659	10.828	9.372	8.201	7.250	6.467	6.128	5.818	5.273	4.812	4.419	4.080	3.928	3.786	3.529	3.304	2.844	2.494	2.219	1.999
19	17.226	15.678	13.134	11.158	9.604	8.365	7.366	6.550	6.198	5.877	5.316	4.844	4.442	4.097	3.942	3.799	3.539	3.311	2.848	2.496	2.220	1.999
20	18.046	16.351	13.590	11.470	9.818	8.514	7.469	6.623	6.259	5.929	5.353	4.870	4.460	4.110	3.954	3.808	3.546	3.316	2.850	2.497	2.221	1.999
21	18.857	17.011	14.029	11.764	10.017	8.649	7.562	6.687	6.312	5.973	5.384	4.891	4.476	4.121	3.963	3.816	3.551	3.320	2.852	2.498	2.221	2.000
22	19.660	17.658	14.451	12.042	10.201	8.772	7.645	6.743	6.359	6.011	5.410	4.909	4.488	4.130	3.970	3.822	3.556	3.323	2.853	2.498	2.222	2.000
23	20.456	18.292	14.857	12.303	10.371	8.883	7.718	6.792	6.399	6.044	5.432	4.925	4.499	4.137	3.976	3.827	3.559	3.325	2.854	2.499	2.222	2.000
24	21.243	18.914	15.247	12.550	10.529	8.985	7.784	6.835	6.434	6.073	5.451	4.937	4.507	4.143	3.981	3.831	3.562	3.327	2.855	2.499	2.222	2.000
25	22.023	19.523	15.622	12.783	10.675	9.077	7.843	6.873	6.464	6.097	5.467	4.948	4.514	4.147	3.985	3.834	3.564	3.329	2.856	2.499	2.222	2.000
26	22.795	20.121	15.983	13.003	10.810	9.161	7.896	6.906	6.491	6.118	5.480	4.956	4.520	4.151	3.988	3.837	3.566	3.330	2.856	2.500	2.222	2.000
27	23.560	20.707	16.330	13.211	10.935	9.237	7.943	6.935	6.514	6.136	5.492	4.964	4.524	4.154	3.990	3.839	3.567	3.331	2.856	2.500	2.222	2.000
28	24.316	21.281	16.663	13.406	11.051	9.307	7.984	6.961	6.534	6.152	5.502	4.970	4.528	4.157	3.992	3.840	3.563	3.331	2.857	2.500	2.222	2.000
29	25.066	21.844	16.984	13.591	11.158	9.370	8.022	6.983	6.551	6.166	5.510	4.975	4.531	4.159	3.994	3.841	3.569	3.332	2.857	2.500	2.222	2.000
30	25,808	27.396	17.292	13.765	11.258	9.427	8.055	7.003	6.566	6.177	5.517	4.979	4.534	4.160	3.995	3.842	3.569	3.332	2.857	2.500	2.222	2.000
40	32.835	27.355	19.793	15.046	11.925	9.779	8.244	7.105	6.642	6.234	5.548	4.997	4.544	4.166	3.999	3.846	3.571	3.333	2.857	2.500	2.222	2.000
50	39.196	31.424	21.482	15.762	12.234	9.915	8.304	7.133	6.661	6.246	5.554	4.999	4.545	4.167	4.000	3.846	3.571	3.333	2.857	2.500	2.222	2.000

CHAPTER 15

Corporate Capital Budgeting

IN THE previous chapter, it was pointed out that investment in capital equipment can rationally be made if its calculated present value exceeds its present cost. It is obvious that fairly long-term forecasting is required in order to compute the present value, since, it will be remembered, this is the discounted value of quasi rents expected to accrue over the entire useful life of the machine (or other form of capital good). If the investment in question is an apartment building with an expected useful life of fifty years, for example, the forecast of rental returns must be made for a period of half a century. Fortunately, the more distant expected quasi rents are discounted so heavily that they are not very significant in the calculation of present value, while the near-future returns, which are easier to estimate, have more weight in the calculation.

The present chapter will examine the same problem in a broader context, including the question of the sources and cost of capital to the corporation. Emphasis in this chapter will be placed on comparisons of the annual rate of return on investments with the annual rate of interest at which funds will be supplied. This is the usual approach to the problem of "capital budgeting" by the firm. It is important to realize, however, that the approaches used in the two chapters are identical, if sufficient care is used in the definition of relevant terms.

Rate of Return on a Project

It will be remembered that the present value of a project can be found from the formula:

$$V = \frac{Q_1}{1+r} + \frac{Q_2}{(1+r)^2} + \frac{Q_3}{(1+r)^3} + \cdots + \frac{Q_n}{(1+r)^n} + \frac{S}{(1+r)^n}$$

Comparison of V with the present cost (C) of a machine or other capital good, when the r which is used is a minimum acceptable rate of return to the firm, determines whether the investment is worth while. Instead of inserting an "acceptable" r in the equation, it is possible to solve for the actual r in the equation:

$$C = \frac{Q_1}{1+r} + \frac{Q_2}{(1+r)^2} + \frac{Q_3}{(1+r)^3} + \cdots + \frac{Q_n}{(1+r)^n} + \frac{S}{(1+r)^n}$$

The lower the cost of the project, the higher r becomes for any given flow of quasi rents and anticipated scrap value. This rate is sometimes called the "internal rate of return" or the "marginal efficiency of capital." If the annual rate of return calculated in this way exceeds the annual rate of cost of capital to the firm, the investment promises to be an acceptable one. The two approaches—comparison of V and C, and comparison of the annual rate of return with the annual cost of capital to the firm—are identical because present value will exceed present cost for any project which promises an internal rate of return in excess of the rate of cost of capital. This can be seen most easily by considering that if V and C were exactly equal, r would have to be the same in each of the equations just presented.

Demand for Capital Funds

A useful way to view the capital-budgeting process is to construct schedules of the demand for and supply of capital funds from the firm's point of view. These schedules may be used to construct a chart which is somewhat similar to an ordinary supply-demand exhibit in economics.

The demand for capital funds derives from the anticipated annual rate of return on various investments open to the firm. This "internal rate" is calculated by solving for r in the second of the two formulas just shown. It is quite obvious that, other things equal, the rate of return will be higher the greater the expected annual quasi rents, the shorter the pay-off period, the lower the cost of purchasing or constructing the asset, and the greater the probable scrap or trade-in value.

A demand for capital funds can be formed by ranking projects for which such funds are needed, starting with the project which promises the highest return. In a "going" company the very highest rate of return may often come from replacement of a machine or other capital asset which is crucial to the continued use of other equipment that is on hand. Other promising projects may involve expansion of capacity for a product already being produced (e.g., doubling the size of a motel), acquisition of capacity for turning out wholly new products (perhaps by purchasing other companies), acquisition of earlier or later stages in the production-distribution process, or some other activity.

A hypothetical demand schedule for capital funds is shown in Exhibit 1. The arbitrary cutoff point in this schedule is 6 per cent; usually a large number of additional projects could be listed at low rates, but these have little prospect of becoming actualities. An implicit assumption made in compiling this sort of schedule is that each project is independent of those which rank lower. Otherwise, it would not be possible to adopt only projects above any desired point without an effect on the expected rate of return. Projects need not be independent of those which rank higher, since it is assumed that all projects down to the actual cutoff point will be carried out. An investment project which depends on one lower in the scale is not really a separate project and should be combined with the lower one and the combination entered at the appropriate place.

Exhibit 1

DEMAND FOR CAPITAL FUNDS

Expected Rate of Return	Cost of Project (in Millions)	Cumulative Demand for Funds (in Millions)
50%.	$5	$5
46.	4	9
35.	10	19
24.	6	25
15.	2	27
10.	10	37
8.	3	40
6.	12	52

Supply of Capital Funds

Concepts involved in an accurate statement of the nature of the supply of capital funds to the firm are more difficult than the concepts on the demand side. The supply curve of funds must be considered to be a curve of the "cost of capital" expressed as an annual interest rate. As long as investment projects promise to yield higher internal rates of interest than the rate of cost of the associated capital funds, they should be carried out. While the interest rate paid on borrowed funds is a simple idea, the same is not true of the cost of using funds owned by the firm.

Sources of Funds

The usual sources of funds to the corporation are depreciation allowances, retained profits, equity financing, and debt financing. Yearly depreciation charges made by a firm have the effect of reserving within the firm assets which are (very roughly) equal to the value of the productive capacity of capital goods that is used up during the year. The depreciation charges in themselves are not a source of funds. Rather, it is revenue that has been brought in which builds up company assets; the depreciation charges merely prevent these assets from being paid out as dividends or income taxes. To the extent that these assets are liquid (rather than being in the form of slow-moving accounts receivable, for example), they can be converted into capital goods in a given year in furtherance of the firm's investment program. Similarly, profits earned and retained by the firm during a given year are usually available for investment. This is not always the case, however. If the year's profits show up on the balance sheet in a diminution of liabilities rather than in an increase in assets, no actual funds will have been made available for investment, although it may then be easier to borrow again in order to secure capital assets. If additional equity capital has been raised by selling shares of stock during the year, funds will obviously have been made available for investment by the firm. This will also be the case if bonded indebtedness has been increased, or if there has been short-term borrowing from the banks.[1]

Depreciation Reserves

If depreciation charges made during a given year happen to be equal to the actual loss of value of capital equipment in use during the same period, the reinvestment of this amount is needed merely to keep productive capacity at a level. Most corporate officials are reluctant to permit the firm to diminish in size if prospects are at all good, partly because their own salaries are positively correlated with the size of the firm which they manage. If maintenance of existing size is a strong motivation, it is likely that assets retained in the company by means of depreciation charges will be reinvested quite automatically in the firm.

Retained Earnings

Most corporations regularly retain a part of their earnings, both as a means of acquiring new capital equipment and as a reserve to permit

---

[1]Sometimes a firm is in the position of having accumulated an unusually high cash balance that is available for investment. This was true of Montgomery Ward which, under the leadership of Sewell Avery, accumulated $327 million in cash and government bonds. However, this would not be a *source* of liquid funds during the year. Nevertheless, officials might be affected strongly in their investment decisions by an unusually high cash balance. This serves to emphasize that the capital-budgeting approach used in the text is based on the assumption that only funds made available during a particular period (usually a year) are being considered in relation to projects then available.

the same dividend rate to be maintained in the face of a temporary dip in earnings. The average proportion "plowed back" differs markedly from firm to firm, however, depending upon the rate at which officials want the company to grow. Where most of the stock is held by a limited number of wealthy individuals, the regular retention of most, or even all, earnings is likely as a means of reducing personal income taxes. This is because only a 25 per cent tax is paid by high-income families on long-term capital gains. Where the practice can be shown to be based primarily on this tax motive, however, profits become subject to an accumulated earnings tax as well as to other corporation taxes.

The welfare of stockholders is enhanced by any corporate investment which increases the prospective earnings per share. Such an increase will permit larger dividends or a more rapid rate of company growth, or both. In order to express earnings per share as an annual rate of return for purposes of capital budgeting, it is necessary to divide by the market value per share. This gives the earnings-price ratio, which is a popular measure in security analysis. "Growth stocks" tend to sell at prices which bring about low earnings-price ratios because such great improvement in earnings per share are expected. (When such expectations are suddenly dashed, the price decline is likely to be drastic.) This points to the importance in capital budgeting of using expected *future* earnings per share in relation to present price.[2] While these earnings may not differ from present earnings for most companies, the measure is more correct, since it is applicable also to growth situations.

Correct capital-budgeting decisions require a comparison of the probable rate of return on a project and the probable earnings per share in relation to present market price if the project is not adopted. For example, if expected earnings per share without a new project are $4.00, and present market value of the stock is $40.00, the "cost of capital" may be considered to be 10 per cent. This determines the minimum rate at which the corporation should supply new capital funds to itself by retaining earnings for expansion purposes. If retained earnings can be placed into a project which will apparently earn 15 per cent, the earnings per share should rise by its adoption, and the stockholders should gain. An 8 per cent project should be rejected because it would lower earnings per share and tend to depress the price of the stock. Stockholders should be able to invest cash dividends to greater advantage in other

---

[2]This is emphasized in an excellent article by Ezra Solomon, "Measuring a Company's Cost of Capital," in a volume entitled *The Management of Corporate Capital*, edited by Ezra Solomon, Graduate School of Business, University of Chicago (Glencoe, Ill.: Free Press, Inc., 1959).

companies (where presumably they would be able to obtain a 10 per cent earnings-price ratio with about an equal risk level and growth prospects).

New Equity Financing

Approximately the same principles are applicable in determining the cost of capital derived from a new issue of common stock. An added element, however, is the cost of underwriting and flotation and the greater annual cost of bookkeeping in connection with the greater number of shares and shareholders. Stockholders are often apprehensive of a new issue of stock, fearing that the newly acquired funds cannot be invested by the company as favorably as those already on hand. (The issuance of "rights" to present stockholders, which can either be sold or be used to buy new shares below the market value, tends to assuage their feelings.)

The cost of new equity capital is, consequently, the expected earnings-price ratio per share which would exist if new stock were not sold but if all desirable investments were financed out of funds derived from depreciation reserves and retained earnings. If new stock *is* sold, the net proceeds to the firm will be reduced by underwriting and flotation costs, and the annual costs of servicing the larger number of outstanding shares will be increased. The latter cost can most easily be considered to be a factor which reduces (very slightly) the annual rate of return from any project which requires new equity financing. That is, it reduces slightly the annual quasi rent which such a project will earn. Flotation and underwriting costs seem best treated as factors which reduce the net amount of funds secured from new equity financing. Treated in this way, they do not affect the "cost of capital," but rather the amount secured from a new stock issue.

In accordance with the above, an investment project which requires exactly the net amount of funds obtained from a new issue of common stock will be worth undertaking if it promises to increase the earnings-price ratio per share. This will occur if it yields a higher rate of return (after all costs including depreciation and the increase in service costs for the new shares are deducted) than the earnings-price ratio anticipated without the new financing.

Debt Financing

So far, only funds which are "owned" by the corporation have been considered to be available for investment. Borrowed funds may also be so used, as every homeowner with a mortgage knows. It is difficult, however, to combine borrowed funds and equity funds into a single schedule. If the entire amount of capital funds needed by a firm were secured by borrowing, the annual interest rate paid on the loan would clearly be the "cost of capital." When a combination of equity and borrowed funds is used—as is the usual case—the proper concept is less clear. A brief consideration of some principles of accounting is helpful in this connection.

A "net profit" from the point of view of the accountant's profit and loss statement occurs when there is a positive difference between all income and all costs (with interest considered to be a cost only when it is an explicit payment). A net profit is also reflected in a change in the firm's balance sheet from the beginning to the end of the same time period. If the *difference* between total assets and total liabilities increases, the firm has made a net profit, and the amount of the profit will be equal to this increase. (This assumes no new investment by the owners.) This balance sheet view shows that a profit may show up entirely as an increase in assets, entirely as a decrease in liabilities, or in any combination of change in the two. It is even possible that assets will decline in the face of a net profit. This can occur if a reduction of liabilities of greater magnitude than the net profit is effected.

The above view shows that one important task of management is to manage the business in such a way as to maintain the most profitable arrangement of assets and liabilities within the firm. If funds are borrowed from banks or through the sale of bonds during a given period, this can be considered to be part of the job of management of assets and liabilities, just as a decision to use net profits to reduce liabilities may be considered to be a decision of this type. Viewed in this way, borrowing by a corporation is a way of freeing equity funds from other uses so that they may be invested in new projects. Equity funds may, for example, be considered to be released from use as cash balances, from carrying accounts receivable, from investment in government bonds, and similar uses.

Capital-Budgeting Chart

If investment projects are ranked according to their prospective rate of return, and equity funds are arranged according to their sources, with the lowest cost source first, a capital-budgeting chart of the sort shown in Exhibit 2 may be drawn. In this chart the demand for funds is taken from Exhibit 1, which pertained to a hypothetical set of investment opportunities and their expected rates of return.

The supply schedule is shown as horizontal at a rather low level up to about $12 million. This follows the idea, already explained, that depreciation allowances are likely to be reinvested rather automatically in the corporation, since officials are unlikely, as a matter of self-interest, to want a company to shrink in size. To the right of $12 million, equity funds secured from retained earnings and the sale of new common stock, or released by borrowing, are involved in the supply curve. This supply curve is not entirely independent of the demand curve because

Exhibit 2

DEMAND AND SUPPLY OF CAPITAL FUNDS

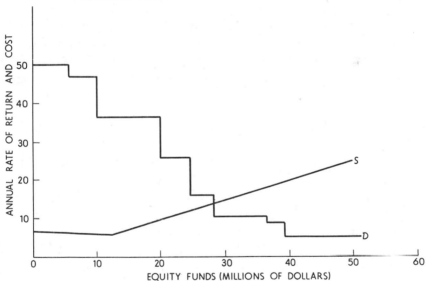

the cost of capital funds for any quantity read on the X axis depends on the projects accepted up to that point. For example, the height of the supply curve at a quantity of $20 million is in part dependent on the expected return from new projects in the demand curve up to that amount. This is because the cost of capital is based on the expected earnings-price ratio per share, and this will be increased by the adoption of worth-while projects during the present budgeting year. The upward slope of the supply curve will not be sharp, however, because earnings-price ratios per share will depend mainly on previous capital investments rather than on those of the current period. As stated earlier, underwriting and flotation costs are considered to be taken from the amount of funds raised by a given issue of common stock. Annual service charges for an augmented number of shares of stock (or bonds) are assumed to have been deducted in arriving at the expected annual rate of return from projects which cannot be financed from depreciation reserves or retention of profits.

According to the curves of Exhibit 2, all projects which promise to yield 15 per cent or more will be adopted, and poorer ones rejected. A total of $27 million will be invested in this period. The extent, if any, to which new common stock or borrowing will be required depends on how much is available from internal sources (depreciation and retained profits). The chart does not attempt to show this breakdown. Rather, equity funds are treated as a common pool regardless of their origin, since rather arbitrary considerations are involved in distinguishing these origins.

Corporations which are considered to be outstanding growth prospects will have a low cost of capital because their common stock will sell at a high price in relation to earnings per share. Thus the general reputation of a firm as a prime growth prospect will help it actually to grow.[3]

Some Complications

The foregoing treatment of corporate capital budgeting contains some shortcomings that are inevitable in a brief treatment but which would be difficult to overcome even in an extensive one. The analysis assumes that funds which become available in a given year are reinvested in the same year; this is not necessarily so. It also assumes that equity funds will be available for all desirable projects, especially if they are released for this purpose by borrowing. Finally, it neglects the possibility that particular types of loans will be secured by using specific assets as collateral, as is the case with a mortgage on a building.

On the demand side, a problem may arise because an investment is not of such a nature as to yield a measurable rate of return. A research facility is an outstanding example. The entire success of a firm may depend on the development of new products by research, but it is difficult to calculate the probable return. Similarly, the rate of return from a new recreational facility for the employees of a plant must be gauged in subjective terms which do not fit readily into a specific capital-budgeting plan.

---

[3]Among the best articles dealing with the complex problem of cost of capital to the firm are F. Modigliani and M. H. Miller, "The Cost of Capital, Corporation Finance, and the Theory of Investment," *American Economic Review*, June, 1958; and H. Benishay, "Variability in Earnings-Price Ratios," *American Economic Review*, March, 1961.

Bonds versus Stocks for External Financing

Economists have usually considered the sale of common stock to be the normal way to raise capital for expansion purposes. Investment by the firm should be based mainly on *anticipated* profits rather than on realized profits. It is theoretically better to have the public voluntarily purchase new shares when the company's outlook is bright than to have management in a position to expand because of its *past* success in earning profits. Actually, however, common stock issues resulted in gross proceeds of only about $2 billion in 1959, as shown in Exhibit 3. The sale of additional common stock may jeopardize the control of a corporation, and this may cause corporate officials to seek funds elsewhere.

Exhibit 3

GROSS PROCEEDS FROM SECURITY SALES, ALL CORPORATIONS—1959

(In Thousands)

Bonds:	
Publicly offered	$3,555,954
Privately offered	3,696,590
	$7,252,544
Common stock	$2,015,353
Preferred stock	535,141
	$2,550,494

Source: Securities and Exchange Commission, *Statistical Bulletin*, March, 1960, p. 8.

(The device of selling additional stock to the present stockholders through "rights" reduces this risk.) Also, it is difficult to select the proper time to sell new stock because of the rapid price fluctuations which occur. A new issue must be planned well in advance, and market prices may not be as favorable as were anticipated. Existing stockholders are often fearful of a dilution in their equity per share if new shares are issued, since the new investments made by the corporation may be less profitable than existing investments. (The rate of return may not exceed the cost of capital.) A further reason for reluctance to use equity financing is found in the high flotation costs of new stock.

In recent years the sale of bonds has been more popular with corporations than the sale of stock. Preferred stock has even less popularity than common stock. Utility companies, however, have made quite substantial use of preferred stock, accounting for about half of the use of this form of security. Public offerings of bonds in 1959 were about equal to private offerings (to insurance companies, industrial corporations, etc.), and each exceeded in value all sales of new stock. (See Exhibit 3.)

An important factor in the preference for selling bonds rather than stock is the high corporate income tax (52 per cent on net income above $25,000). Interest payments on bonded indebtedness are deductible as expenses, thus reducing taxable income, while dividends are considered a distribution of profits. A corporate income tax should, in theory, be levied against economic profit rather than on accounting profit, in order to avoid this discrimination against equity financing. It should be remembered from the first chapter that a "normal" return on capital stock is deductible in calculating economic profit. Unfortunately, this more defensible procedure would be difficult administratively.

The principal danger inherent in debt financing is that interest must be paid even in years of depressed business, whereas dividends on stock can be skipped. (Dividends missed on cumulative preferred stock have to be paid at a later date before common dividends can be paid.) The high level of economic activity in the United States since 1940 has probably diminished the fear of debt on the part of most businessmen— although some firms still shun debt. Another general economic force has made bonded indebtedness relatively desirable. Our federal fiscal and monetary policy, influenced by the strains of World War II and the Korean War, has for the most part been such as to bring about persistent inflation. Like other debtors, business firms which are net debtors tend to profit from inflation. Since bonded indebtedness is fixed in monetary terms, its *real* burden diminishes with inflation. It has been shown empirically that the market value of stocks of corporations which are net debtors has gone up more in years of inflation than that of the companies which are net creditors.[4]

If year-to-year earnings tend to be relatively steady, there is a particular incentive to raise additional capital by selling bonds rather than stock. Utility companies make much use of bonded indebtedness for this reason. As already noted, utilities also make more use of preferred stock than do other corporations. This is because the fixed dividend

---

[4]Reuben A. Kessel, "Inflation-Caused Wealth Redistribution: A Test of a Hypothesis," *American Economic Review,* March, 1956, p. 128. Kessel found that in a sample of 30 industrial corporations, shares of 15 creditor corporations declined in real value by 13 per cent, while shares of 15 debtor corporations increased in real value by 81 per cent from 1942 to 1948—a period of inflation.

requirement is not so apt to be bothersome. Most other types of firms have come to consider preferred stock virtually as high-cost debt financing rather than equity financing. While dividends may theoretically be skipped or deferred, they are in practice usually paid and, unlike bond interest, do not reduce a corporation's income tax liability.

Bonds have a special advantage over stock for financing an investment project which promises to be a temporary one, to be followed by a contraction in total investment by the firm. In this situation, equity financing would leave a permanently expanded number of shareholders. If, instead, bonds of relatively early maturity were issued so as to cover the period of temporary need for more capital, the capitalization of the corporation would not have to be permanently increased. This is similar to the well-established practice of borrowing from the banks to meet seasonal or other temporary needs for working capital.

Convertible bonds sometimes offer a worth-while compromise between equity and debt financing. Such bonds may be converted into stock at a specified price. If the corporation's stock rises in market price, many owners of convertible bonds will find it advantageous to exercise the privilege of conversion. Prior to conversion the interest on the bonds will be tax-deductible, and this advantage need not be given up unless a favorable price (as specified on the bond) can be secured. Also, the possibility of substantial capital gain on stock enjoyed by the holder of the convertible bond makes it possible to sell the bonds at favorable interest rates. A special use of the convertible bond is to provide funds during a long period of construction of a plant. If the bonds are made convertible only after two years, for example, a corporation may utilize low-cost capital to construct the facility, but be in a position to earn dividends on stock by the time conversions are made, since the plant will then be in operation. In an era of chronic inflation (such as we seem to be in), there is much to be said for using convertible bonds as a method of taking at least temporary advantage of the tax deductibility of bond interest and also taking advantage of the popularity of the stock market.

Timing of Borrowing

It is important that the corporate officials in charge of finance be extremely well acquainted with the capital markets in both a theoretical and a practical way. Once it has been decided that the firm should secure additional capital by borrowing, it is necessary to decide whether a public or a private offering is more satisfactory, what specific form or forms of bond to sell, and just when and how to float the loan. The executive who is able accurately to feel the pulse of the capital market (or who is lucky) may save his company very important sums of money by securing lower interest rates on borrowed capital. United States Steel wisely borrowed $300 million in 1954 when interest rates were low, despite its usual policy of internal financing. Whirlpool-Seeger could have saved $60,000 per year in interest charges by selling $30 million in debentures just two weeks earlier in 1955. On the other hand, a two-week delay saved Niagara Mohawk Power $67,500 a year in interest cost on a $30 million issue.[5] These latter situations arose because of a particularly turbulent capital market during the spring of 1955.

The general state of demand for external financing can, perhaps, be predicted from the surveys of anticipated capital expenditures made by McGraw-Hill, and jointly by the Securities and Exchange Commission and the Department of Commerce. A prediction of increased capital expenditures suggests an increased demand for loanable funds and higher interest rates. An upturn in orders for durable producers' goods would carry the same suggestion. Federal Reserve actions must be watched carefully and anticipated whenever possible by an acute vice president in charge of finance. For example, the rediscount rate was reduced from 4 per cent to 3½ per cent at all Federal Reserve banks in June, 1960. This action was a reflection of the general decline in interest rates which was brought about by changes in the demand-supply situation for loanable funds—especially a decline in demand. This development would tend to cause the deferral of a new bond sale by a firm if it induced an expectation of a further decline in interest rates, despite the fact that lower interest rates in themselves are conducive to the issuance of new bonds.

A modern trend in economics is to emphasize the importance of economic growth rather than just the present capability of an economic system to satisfy wants. Similarly, many corporation officials feel that the only way to insure the success of their firms is to keep them growing rather than simply maximizing immediate profits. This penchant for growth has brought the financial expert into a more prominent position in the American corporation. A special vice president in charge of finance is increasingly common. As a consequence, the intensive study of capital budgeting, securities, and interest rates may ultimately yield

---

[5]These examples are from Charles E. Silberman, "The Fine Art of Raising Capital," *Fortune,* July, 1956, p. 97.

rich dividends on "human capital" built up in the mind of the student who has ambitions to become an executive.[6]

CASE 15-1: NORTH-SOUTH NATIONAL BANK

Late in 1962, the North-South National Bank was considering the conversion of its trust, savings, and instalment loan records to a machine accounting system. The following is a chronological listing of the predicted costs and potential savings from such an installation.

1. January 1–June 30, 1963

During this period, procedures, forms, cards, and codes would be planned in detail. The training of personnel would begin, and space would be provided for the machines. Work would be begun primarily in the Trust Department.

Cost estimate:

Preparation of space	$1,000
Furniture	400
Development of forms	500
Wiring	925
Salaries:	
Manager	3,750
Machine operator	435
Total	$7,010
Savings estimate	$ 0

2. July 1–September 30, 1963

This period will be devoted to development and training. A key punch and an interpreter are to be used.

Cost estimate:

Freight charges for machines	$ 500
Machine rent	472
Cards	100
Electroplates	225
Salary (add key punch operator)	4,080
Total	$5,377
Savings estimate	$ 0

---

[6]Some recommended readings are Solomon (ed.), *op. cit.;* Friedrich A. and Vera C. Lutz, *The Theory of Investment of the Firm* (Princeton: Princeton University Press, 1951); and Joel Dean, *Capital Budgeting* (New York: Columbia University Press, 1951).

For additional explanation of capital-budgeting computations from the accounting point of view, see Homer A. Black and John E. Champion, *Accounting in Business Decisions* (New York: Prentice-Hall, Inc., 1961), chap. xxii.

3. *October 1, 1963–March 31, 1964*

During this period the system would be refined, and some personnel would no longer be required in the Trust Department.

Cost estimate:

Machine rent (add sorter, collator, accounting machine, and document-originating machine)	$ 8,586
Salaries (add control clerk)	9,960
Cards	100
Total	$18,646

Savings estimate:

Salary (positions replaced)	$ 7,925

4. *April 1, 1964–June 30, 1964*

The emphasis during this period would be in the Savings Department. Adjustment and training of personnel would be completed in this department.

Cost estimate:

Machine rent (add calculator)	$ 5,019
Salary	4,980
Cards	100
Wiring	500
Electroplates	225
Development of forms	100
Total	$10,924

Savings estimate:

Salary	$ 4,755
Savings interest computation	200
	$ 4,955

5. *July 1, 1964–September 30, 1964*

The Instalment Loan Department would be converted during this period.

Cost estimate:

Machine rent	$ 5,019
Salary	4,980
Cards	100
Wiring	500
Development of forms	100
Total	$10,699

Savings estimate:

Salary	$ 4,755
Savings interest computation	300
Instalment Loan Department	570
	$ 5,625

6. *October 1, 1964–Indefinitely*

	Monthly	Annually
Cost estimate:		
Machine rent	$1,673	$20,076
Salary	1,660	19,920
Cards	20	240
Total	$3,353	$40,236
Savings:		
Salary	$1,585	$19,020
Savings Department	100	1,200
Instalment Loan Department	190	2,280
	$1,875	$22,500

7. *October 1, 1964–Indefinitely*

The machine accounting system will prepare all the bookkeeping records and reports in addition to the trust, savings, and instalment loan department records.

	Monthly	Annually
Cost estimate:		
Machine rent	$3,765	$45,180
Salary	840	10,080
Cards	5	60
	$4,610	$55,320
Savings:		
Salary	$7,625	$91,500

These estimates are presented in summary form below:

First year:

	Cost	Savings
Step 1, 6 months	$ 7,010	$ 0
Step 2, 3 months	5,377	0
Step 3, 3 months	9,323	3,170
	$21,710	$ 3,170
Net savings (loss)		($18,540)

Second year:

	Cost	Savings
Step 3, 3 months........................	$ 9,323	$ 4,755
Step 4, 3 months........................	10,924	4,955
Step 5, 3 months........................	10,699	5,625
Step 6, 3 months........................	10,059	5,625
Step 7, 3 months........................	13,830	22,975
	$54,835	$43,975
Net savings (loss).....................		($10,900)

Third and subsequent years:

	Cost	Savings
Step 6, 12 months.....................	$40,236	$ 22,500
Step 7, 12 months.....................	55,320	91,500
	$95,556	$114,000
Net savings (loss).....................		$ 18,444

These estimates assume that the machinery would be rented. The machinery could also be purchased for $110,380. The bank would use a seven-year life for depreciation purposes and uses the "sum of the years' digits" method of depreciation. (The depreciation charge the first year would be 7/28 of the purchase price, the second year 6/28, the third year 5/28, etc.)

QUESTION

1. Should the machine accounting system be installed? If so, should it be purchased outright?

CASE 15-2: THE COMPONENT MANUFACTURING COMPANY

The Component Manufacturing Company, located in Oakland, California, was a medium-sized producer of parts for the aircraft industry. Prior to 1958, operations were conducted at four plants scattered throughout the city of Oakland.

The dispersion of these plants had been a matter of vital concern to the board of directors for some time. Costs had been rising rapidly and had begun to endanger the competitive pricing position of the company. The board felt that the consolidation of operations under one or possibly two roofs could do much to alleviate the situation.

So, in the spring of 1958 the company entered into a contract with the Acme Construction Company to build a plant on a site in the city of Stockton, sixty miles from the Oakland plants. The financing was arranged through the company's bankers acting as intermediaries with a financial holding company. Under the terms of the deal, the Component Manufacturing Company entered into a seventeen-year lease agreement with a $250,000 "buy back" provision. It was contemplated that the transfer of manufacturing facilities and operations would be conducted in phases, with the final move occurring by 1964.

The first section of the new plant was completed and operations commenced in August of 1960. It had now become apparent that it was not feasible to transfer all operations to this plant. Certain administration and sales functions were better co-ordinated in Oakland. In addition, it was discovered that the disposal of waste from plating operations could not be handled without a major capital expenditure. So the long-range policy now became firmly established as envisioning a two-plant operation.

To implement this objective, a new plant, contiguous to a super-highway leading to Stockton, was leased for a ten-year period in December of 1960.

Between 1960 and 1962 the company suffered severe losses due to quality problems in the field, training costs at the new plant, and a heavy litigation claim. As a result, the company had a $400,000 carry-forward loss for tax purposes.

By now, operations were conducted in three plants:

Plant No. 1—Owned by the company, encumbered with a $200,000 mortgage. Fully depreciated as war facility. Located in Oakland in generally undesirable area.

Plant No. 2—Leased in December, 1960, Approximately eight years of lease remaining. Located in Oakland.

Plant No. 3—Lease commenced in August of 1960 to continue for seventeen years. Located in Stockton.

In September of 1962 the company received an offer of $200,000 for plant No. 1. The offer was considered quite substantial, considering the general deterioration of real estate values in the neighborhood. Further, acceptance would enable the company to consolidate operations into two plants.

However, before the consolidation could be accomplished, an extension had to be built on plant No. 2. The Treasurer, R. C. Baker, was

Exhibit 1

SALE OF BUILDING AND MOVE PROPOSAL:
ANALYSIS OF COST SAVINGS

	Present Cost	Proposed Cost
Rent...	....	$48,000
Taxes and insurance........................	$15,200	7,000
Heat..	6,800	4,500
Power, light, and water.....................	9,400	8,000
Guards..	12,000	4,000
Porters..	12,000	9,000
Building repair..............................	4,000	1,000
Parking.......................................	900	3,900
Interest.......................................	12,000	....
Maintenance.................................	16,200	2,500
Total Operating Cost....................	$88,500	$87,900
Gross cost saving............................		$ 600
Additional savings:		
Labor rate revision........................		9,000
Trucking costs.............................		6,000
Plating maintenance reduction..............		4,000
Company-wide improved efficiency.........		10,400
Net Savings from Move...............		$30,000

Exhibit 2

COMPONENT MANUFACTURING COMPANY
Schedule of Capital Expenditures

Item	Amount
Depreciable items:	
Plating Department.........................	$43,000
Switchboard................................	5,000
Laboratory equipment......................	1,000
Electric wiring.............................	5,000
Total Depreciable Items................	$54,000
Moving costs:	
IBM...	$ 4,000
Level plating floor..........................	2,000
Clean up plant No. 1.......................	2,000
Office.......................................	3,000
Model room.................................	2,000
Miscellaneous and extras...................	3,000
Total Moving..........................	$16,000
Total Expenditures.....................	$70,000

Exhibit 3

COMPONENT MANUFACTURING COMPANY
Cash Flow

	Amount Paid Out	Savings before Tax	Less 50% Income Tax	Less Carry-Forward Tax (000)	Savings after Tax	Add Back Depreciation	Net Cash Savings	Adjustment for Loss Carry-Forward	Adjusted Cash Savings
Capital expenditures*.....	$70,000						($ 70,000)		($ 70,000)
First-year savings.........		$ 30,000	$ 7,000*	0	$23,000	$ 5,400	28,400		28,400
Second-year savings.......		30,000	15,000	(100)	(85,000)	5,400	(79,600)	$100,000	20,400
Third-year savings........		30,000	15,000	50	65,000	5,400	70,400	(50,000)	20,400
Fourth-year savings.......		30,000	15,000	0	15,000	5,400	20,400		20,400
Fifth-year savings........		30,000	15,000	0	15,000	5,400	20,400		20,400
Sixth-year savings........		30,000	15,000	0	15,000	5,400	20,400		20,400
Seventh-year savings......		30,000	15,000	0	15,000	5,400	20,400		20,400
Eighth-year savings.......		30,000	15,000	0	15,000	5,400	20,400		20,400
Ninth-year savings........		30,000	15,000	0	15,000	5,400	20,400		20,400
Tenth-year savings.......		30,000	15,000	0	15,000	5,400	20,400		20,400
	$70,000	$300,000	$142,000	(50)	$108,000	$54,000	$92,000	$ 50,000	$142,000

*Sixteen thousand dollars of capital expenditure will be written off against current operations. Therefore, 50 per cent, or $8,000, is recovered as income tax reduction.

directed to negotiate this possibility with the owners of the plant. He was further directed to make a thorough study of the cost and cash flow implications of the sale.

Mr. Baker realized that the tax carry-forward position of $400,000 would be very important in the cash flow analysis. Selling the building now would result in a $200,000 capital gain, since the plant was fully amortized. Capital gains would be applied to an ordinary loss, and the company would lose 25 cents on the dollar (assuming a tax rate of 50 per cent for ease of calculation). This loss would amount to $50,-000. If the building were not sold, it would take two years to use up the loss carry-forward.

The owners of plant No. 2 will make the necessary extensions at an annual rental of $48,000, provided Component Manufacturing Company agrees to an extension of the lease to ten years.

On the basis of these preliminary considerations, Mr. Baker decided to analyze two alternatives: (1) sale of the plant immediately and (2) sale of the plant in two years.

Exhibits 1, 2 and 3 were prepared by Mr. Baker's staff with the assistance of the Industrial Engineering Department to facilitate the analysis of the two alternatives.

Exhibit 4

	ALTERNATIVE I		ALTERNATIVE II	
YEAR	Profits	Cash Flow (50% after $400,000)	Profits	Cash Flow (50% after $400,000)
1	$400,000*	$400,000	$200,000	$200,000
2	200,000	100,000	200,000	200,000
3	200,000	100,000	400,000*	250,000†
Total	$800,000	$600,000	$800,000	$650,000

*Includes $200,000 normal profits plus capital gains.
†Capital gains tax at 25 per cent on $200,000.

Exhibit 1 shows the estimated cost savings from consolidation on a pro forma basis. Exhibit 2 is the schedule of capital requirements. Depreciable items are separated from moving costs to facilitate cash flow computations.

Exhibit 3 shows the cash flow under the two alternatives. Net Cash Savings refers to the first alternative, while the sale in two years is headed Adjusted Cash Savings. The cash flow adjustments for capital loss carry-forward were calculated as shown in Exhibit 4.

QUESTION

1. Consider the conversion decision and the sell now or later decision as separate decisions and analyze each. What actions should the firm take? What qualifications are necessary?

CASE 15-3: IMPERIAL COMPANY

The Imperial Company, a small Detroit fruit juice company, was considering two investment alternatives in January of 1962. Since both alternatives concerned products with the same seasonal pattern, it was decided to undertake only one of the projects in order to fit personnel requirements. The time limit on the decision was very short, as both projects required deliveries no later than April 15.

The first alternative considered by the company was the production, packaging, and sale of "chilled orange juice." This juice would be sold directly to retail stores and to dairies for home delivery.

Other brands of chilled orange juice had already secured some brand identification and some measure of success with the trade by quality control of the product and considerable advertising expense. The company felt that it would have to sell its juice under the private labels of dairies and retailers or as an "off" brand. In either case, the company felt, the price it obtained would be somewhat less than that of better known brands.

The company estimated sales volume as shown in Exhibit 1 if it entered production.

Exhibit 1

1962:

April	6,000 units
May	12,000
June	18,000
July	24,000
August	30,000
September	30,000
October	24,000
November	18,000
December	12,000

1963:

January	12,000
February	12,000
March	12,000

210,000 units in first year
300,000 units in second year

Selling price and direct product costs were estimated by the company to be 24 cents per unit and 21 cents per unit, respectively. Direct product costs were as shown in Exhibit 2.

Exhibit 2

Raw materials	$0.125
Package	0.025
Labor	0.010
Overhead (additional only)	0.010
Outside container	0.010
Delivery	0.010
Advertising allowance	0.010
Brokerage	0.010
	$0.210

The company believed it was impossible to predict profit margins beyond the second year, since the prices of the raw materials fluctuated widely on a yearly basis, depending on crop yields. Imperial felt it could forestall price fluctuations for a period of up to one year by buying ahead, but it pointed out that the risk was considerable in doing this, since prices might be lower in the next year.

The capital investment required to produce and sell the chilled orange juice was easily determined by the company (see Exhibit 3).

Exhibit 3

Plate design charges		$ 350
Packaging machine	$4,550	
Electrical installation	125	
Transportation	135	
Spare parts	240	5,050
Carton inventory		2,500
Used refrigerated truck		2,500

The company felt that it would wish to retain an inventory of 60,000 finished cartons of juice. It estimated that this inventory would cost $1,500 to maintain for a year. It also pointed out that it expected a base amount of $6,000 of accounts receivable to be outstanding at all times.

The packaging machine required for the chilled juice was a special type designed to handle one type of plastic-coated carton made by one manufacturer. The company pointed out that historically, there had been an ever-increasing technological advancement in this type of container packaging. In view of this rapid change the company felt that depreciation charges should be rapid and that useful economic life should be no more than five years.

The company felt that a refrigerated truck was necessary to ship the chilled juice. It was able to purchase a used one and considered its useful life to be four years. Tax rules permitted a 150 per cent declining balance to be used to depreciate the truck.

The second alternative under consideration by the Imperial Company was the production and sale of an orange drink packed in half-gallon, nonreturnable decanter bottles. The product was considered of low quality and in the imitation class, the juice content being only 5 per cent.

In this field, one or two brands had established only a token following among the trade. Imperial executives attributed this to poor quality control and problems concerning labeling requirements. Each of the two products on the market had been seized more than once within the last year for mislabeling. In addition, Imperial had determined that advertising allowances and expenditures for this product had been very small and not directed to the consumer. Therefore the company concluded that there had been little chance to build a following among retail consumers.

The company had conducted trade research which led it to believe that it could sell orange drink at the same price as that of the market leaders, provided it sold on a guaranteed sales basis. The company executives felt that with adequate quality control, they should be able to establish a brand name in the orange drink line. Under these circumstances, they would be willing to accept a lower than normal profit margin.

Selling price and direct product cost for the orange drink were estimated as shown in Exhibit 4.

Exhibit 4

Selling price	$0.31 per unit
Production cost:	
Raw material	0.090
Package	0.100
Cap	0.010
Label	0.010
Overhead (additional only)	0.020
Delivery	0.020
Brokerage	0.010
Advertising	0.010
	$0.270 per unit

The raw-material costs for the orange drink, as opposed to the costs for orange juice, were much more stable and presented no problem, the company decided.

The company decided it could expect to obtain the sales shown in Exhibit 5 if it adopted the orange drink.

Exhibit 5

April, 1962	4,000 units
May	8,000
June	12,000
July	16,000
August	16,000
September	8,000
October	2,000

66,000 units in first year
130,000 units in second year

Capital costs were considerably less than for the investment in chilled juice, with most of the difference attributed to the difference in cost of the two packaging machines and the fact that no truck would be purchased (see Exhibit 6).

Exhibit 6

Art charges and plate for label		$ 200
Packaging machine	$2,400	
Transportation	125	
Electric installation	125	2,650
Bottles and caps		1,320
Labels		500

Management figured that an inventory of eight thousand bottles of orange drink would have to be maintained at a cost of $800 per year. The average level of accounts receivable was expected to be about $3,600.

As opposed to the rather specialized packaging machine required for orange juice, the packaging machine for orange drink was designed to handle a large number of sizes and shapes of bottles and was considered a standard machine, having been in production for more than ten years without major modifications. The company management estimated its useful life at ten years.

Delivery of the orange drink could be made in regular company trucks, so that no new truck would be needed.

Imperial's management believed that there would be much less of a spoilage problem with the orange drink than there would be with the chilled juice. Temperature was not critical, and the drink could be stored for extended periods of time. The chilled juice was somewhat perishable and could not be stored for long periods of time. It required refrigeration both in storage and in delivery. The company had some excess refrigerator space, however, and management decided that by economizing space, an inventory of chilled juice could be squeezed in without the addition of more lockers.

QUESTIONS

1. Which alternative should the Imperial Company management choose?
2. What assumptions have you made about the future?

CASE 15-4: ROBERT C. DAVIS COMPANY

In 1926, Robert C. Davis purchased three variety stores located in small cities in central Ohio. These stores carried the usual line of merchandise handled in the traditional five- and ten-cent store, and no merchandise was sold at a retail price of more than $1.00. In 1930, Mr. Davis was operating a chain of 11 stores in Ohio and Indiana. These additional stores had been financed out of the earnings of the company.

During the decade of the thirties the Robert C. Davis Company was incorporated and began a period of expansion. Throughout the East and the Middle West, there were a number of small local chains of ten-cent stores, some of which were in financial difficulty as a result of the financial collapse in 1929 and the years of depression immediately following. Mr. Davis had survived this period without severe losses and had observed that, relatively, the ten-cent store was enjoying business better than some firms carrying higher priced lines of merchandise. Between 1930 and 1938, Mr. Davis acquired nine small chains, which gave his company a total of 73 stores. These acquisitions had been accomplished largely by the issue of cumulative preferred stock in the Robert C. Davis Company. This stock had a par value of $100 and carried an interest rate of 4¾ per cent. It was redeemable by the company at $105 per share. Although the rate was considered rather high at the time, Mr. Davis had found that it enabled him to acquire most of these chains at attractive prices and involved little cash in most instances.

As a result of reduced capitalization and overhead on the acquired chains, Mr. Davis was able to realize adequate profits, until, 1938, to pay dividends on the preferred stock. In 1938, however, shortly after he had purchased a chain of nine stores, there was a severe setback in business activity, which forced him to pass preferred dividends in 1939. At the time, all of the common stock was held by Mr. Davis personally. In 1940, another chain of 17 stores in Illinois and Kentucky was purchased by a combination of preferred stock, common stock, and cash. About one half of the cash was obtained through a mortgage loan on store properties.

No further dividends were paid on the preferred stock until 1947. During the wartime period of 1941–45 the company introduced higher priced articles of merchandise, with some items selling as high as $24.95. In spite of restrictions on many types of goods during the war, the company emerged from that period with a substantial surplus. Much of this had been the result of deferred maintenance as well as earnings on sales. As a result of the decline in the market value of the preferred stock, 10,000 shares had been redeemed through purchase in the market. Dividends were resumed in 1947; by 1950, all accumulated dividends had been paid in full. The company had also, by 1950, built and acquired more stores, so that it then had 161 outlets between the Mississipppi River and the Atlantic Coast. In order to finance this expansion, the company had issued one million shares of common stock, part of which had been issued to the vendors of stores purchased and part sold in the over-the-counter market. The common stock had a par value of $1.00. Between 1950 and 1954, another one million shares of common stock had been issued to finance additional stores and to provide working capital. In 1954 the stock was selling at approximately $39 per share. In the same year the dividend was increased to $2.00 per share.

With the development of a boom in the construction of private dwellings in the postwar period, large suburban areas began to appear around the larger cities where the Robert C. Davis Company had many of its stores. Traditionally, the company had located its stores in the heart of the shopping districts in the downtown sections of cities. In the larger cities, stores had also been located in some of the larger outlying shopping areas within the city limits. In 1952 and 1953, there began to appear shopping centers in the suburban areas. Such a center was usually promoted by a development company which constructed a complete shopping area consisting of stores of many kinds, one of which was almost invariably a ten-cent store. As large new housing developments were planned, these centers became an integral part of such plans. In some instances the property was built and constructed jointly by stores which became part owners of the project; in other cases the construction was planned and financed by the promoters, and space was leased to stores on a long-term basis.

The Robert C. Davis Company presently had stores in 11 such centers, and, with the exception of one, all were profitable. In nine of

Exhibit 1

ROBERT C. DAVIS COMPANY

Statement of Assets and Liabilities, December 31, 1954, and December 31, 1955

Item	1955	1954
ASSETS		
Cash	$19,470,223	$23,439,017
U.S. government securities, at cost and accrued interest	10,005,845	7,832,606
Merchandise inventories, at the lower of cost or market:		
Stores and warehouses	23,939,851	21,138,020
In transit	3,011,905	3,539,826
Total Current Assets	$56,427,824	$55,949,469
Property and equipment, at cost:		
Buildings	$ 7,531,293	$ 7,725,392
Improvements to leased properties	25,377,587	24,542,840
Fixtures and equipment	23,070,003	21,804,529
	$55,978,883	$54,072,761
Less: Allowances for depreciation and amortization	27,614,301	25,509,763
	$28,364,582	$28,562,998
Land	1,734,719	1,532,069
Total Property and Equipment	$30,099,301	$30,095,067
Prepaid expenses	$ 1,013,101	$ 1,159,864
Miscellaneous accounts receivable and sundry investments	591,649	543,507
Total Assets	$88,131,875	$87,747,907
LIABILITIES		
Accounts payable, including merchandise in transit	$ 3,639,541	$ 4,133,699
Taxes withheld or collected	626,856	787,899
Dividend on preferred stock	106,879	106,879
Accrued compensation and other expenses	3,476,833	3,572,519
Accrued state, social security, and other taxes	824,056	1,149,063
Provision for federal taxes on income	7,788,116	9,015,967
Mortgage installments payable within one year	30,252	41,450
Total Current Liabilities	$16,492,533	$18,807,476
Mortgage installments payable after one year	32,208	67,159
Total Liabilities	$16,524,741	$18,874,635
CAPITAL		
Preferred stock, par value $100 per share:		
Authorized, 100,000 shares, issuable in series; issued, $4\frac{3}{4}$ per cent cumulative series, 90,000 shares (redeemable at $105 per share)	$ 9,000,000	$ 9,000,000
Common stock, par value $1.00 per share:		
Authorized, 3,000,000 shares; issued, 2,129,500 shares	2,129,500	2,129,500
Paid-in surplus	11,917,891	11,917,891
Earnings retained in the business	48,557,743	45,825,881
Total Capital	$71,605,134	$68,873,272
Total Liabilities and Capital	$88,129,875	$87,747,907

these centers, there were no ten-cent stores other than the Davis store. During 1955, many new centers were planned and being built. Mr. Davis believed that stores in the downtown shopping areas would eventually show some declines in operations, especially in those areas where large suburban shopping centers were being developed. He therefore negotiated for the construction of five Davis stories in such centers and for the lease of space on a twenty-five-year basis in 23 other centers. All of these shopping centers were expected to be completed and ready for occupancy by June 1, 1956. It was estimated that the cost of construction of the stores and two warehouses, cost of additional inventory, and provision of additional working capital would amount to $35 million.

The problem of financing this expansion was presented to the board of directors. Exhibit 1 shows the company's balance sheet as of December 31, 1955. Exhibit 2 is the profit and loss statement for the period

Exhibit 2

ROBERT C. DAVIS COMPANY

Statement of Earnings for January 1–December 31, 1954 and 1955

Item	1955		1954	
Sales.............................		$182,172,687		$187,163,824
Cost of goods sold and operating expenses......................	$160,995,574		$164,072,441	
Provision for depreciation and amortization.......................	3,280,294		3,155,520	
Taxes, other than federal taxes on income......................	1,992,116		2,201,798	
Employees' retirement plan costs.......	1,054,181	167,322,165	1,100,672	170,530,431
		$ 14,850,522		$ 16,633,393
Other income, less other deductions....		290,885		263,021
Earnings before Federal Taxes on Income......................		$ 15,141,407		$ 16,896,414
Provision for federal taxes on income:				
Normal and surtax.................	$ 7,723,000		$ 8,765,000	
Excess profits tax.................		7,723,000	160,000	8,925,000
Net Earnings for the Year.........		$ 7,418,407		$ 7,971,414
Earnings retained in the business, beginning of year.................		45,825,881		42,541,012
Deduct: Dividends paid or declared:				
4¾ per cent preferred stock, $4.75 per share.....................	$ 427,514		$ 427,514	
Common stock, $2.00 per share....	4,259,031	4,686,545	4,259,031	4,686,545
Earnings Retained in the Business, End of Year..............		$ 48,557,743		$ 45,825,881

from January 1, 1955, to December 31, 1955. Several plans were presented for raising the necessary funds to meet the anticipated expenditures. As noted in Exhibit 1, the company had $10,005,845 invested in government securities. These bonds were at present yielding an average net of 2.78 per cent. It was recommended that $7.5 million of this amount be used for addition to working capital. The present Cash account was considered the minimum at the present level of operations.

Among the proposals mentioned was an increase in the common stock outstanding. The stock was currently selling around $51 per share. An additional issue of 600,000 share would yield approximately $25 million, after underwriting expenses. Mr. Davis was opposed to this proposal on personal grounds. He presently held 425,375 shares of stock, and to increase the amount outstanding by the proposed amount would dilute his ownership and possibly his control of the company if the larger share were purchased by a small group of individuals or an institutional investor. Another objection raised to the proposal was that the earnings on the additional investment would be subject to income taxes before the payment of dividends.

Still another proposal was the issue of additional shares of preferred stock. This would require an amendment to the charter, but this could be obtained easily. None of this stock had been offered for sale in more than two years. The last transfer had been priced at $114 per share. This met Mr. Davis' argument of dilution of ownership, but the dividend rate was an objection. There was also the tax problem in this instance, as in case of the common stock. Several directors objected to this proposal because of the inflexibility it might impose upon the declarations of dividends on the common stock. One director proposed that this might be the proper time to obtain enough funds to retire the outstanding preferred stock and thus relieve the company of the annual charges to meet the dividends. He pointed out that this stock could be redeemed at $105 per share, as stated in the provisions of its issue.

A third proposal was that the funds be sought from an institutional investor by means of a term loan. The current rate on such loans was about 3¾ per cent. If such a loan could be obtained on a 15- or 20-year basis, it would meet the company's needs. Furthermore, the interest on such a loan could be deducted from income before taxes as a business expense. A disadvantage was the fixed charge which the company would have to meet during the lifetime of the loan.

Closely related to the preceding proposal was another that the company issue mortgage bonds or debentures to raise the necessary funds.

At present, none of the company properties were indentured except four warehouses which had been built since 1950. Either mortgage bonds or debentures, or a combination of such bonds, would involve the problem of fixed charges, but each had the advantage that the interest was deductible for tax purposes. It was also doubtful if the company possessed enough real property to issue mortgage bonds for the full amount.

A fourth proposal was that the company sell convertible debentures in the amount of $28 million which would be convertible into common stock within two or three years. This arrangement would give the company the advantage of tax deduction for the interest during the life of the debentures; and when conversion took place, the company would be relieved of the liability of the fixed charges. It was anticipated that such debentures could be sold at par if they were offered at a rate of 3½ to 4 per cent. It was proposed that the conversion rate be set at $45 per share of common stock in order to insure conversion.

QUESTIONS

1. Which of the above methods of financing would you recommend? Why?

2. Would you recommend that the new financing include sufficient funds to retire the outstanding preferred stock? Explain.

3. Would you recommend any other method of financing than those proposed? Why?

CASE 15–5: DUFF AUTO STORES, INC.

Duff Auto Stores, Inc., operated a nationwide chain of automobile supply stores at retail. The company owned 534 stores of its own and had franchise arrangements with 1,131 independently owned stores. The company-owned stores were located in the larger cities, while the franchise stores were in the smaller cities and towns. All stores carried a fairly complete line of automobile replacement parts and accessories. In addition, a majority of them sold many kinds of hardware and tools. In the postwar period, lines of household appliances had been added.

During the early period of growth and expansion, Duff stores had sold automobile accessories only. The company began during the depression of the early thirties, when the sales of new cars declined sharply and there was a demand for replacement parts to keep them running over longer periods of time. Until 1937 the company had purchased its entire stock from manufacturers and merchandised many nationally advertised brands of parts and accessories. In 1937, when the firm was operating about 100 stores, it arranged to have tires manufactured under its own brand name. This enabled the company to purchase on more advantageous terms and also permitted it to offer tires at prices under those of the nationally advertised brands. By 1940, it had made arrangements with a number of manufacturers for the production of many replacement parts under the brand name of Duff. Late in 1940 the company began production of its own batteries and several accessories such as points, distributors, spark plugs, floor mats, and seat covers. In 1939 a national advertising campaign was undertaken. All merchandise was sold for cash.

During World War II the firm enjoyed an unprecedented growth of business. The manufacture of new automobiles was halted, so that the demand for automobile replacement parts increased sharply. Under authority of the War Production Board, certain replacement parts were given priority of materials, although production of many accessories was either forbidden or sharply curtailed. In 1945 at the end of the war, Duff Auto Stores had more than one thousand stores and affiliated dealers. It emerged from this period with a substantial cash surplus.

The period following the war was one of even greater growth and expansion. It was not until 1949 that the production of new cars began to catch up with the pent-up demand. With restrictions removed, the company opened more stores; and to take advantage of the household market, it added a line of appliances and hardware. All appliances and tools were under the Duff brand name. All items, with a few exceptions, were manufactured for Duff by contract with various manufacturers. This rapid growth had, however, raised some problems of finance. In order to obtain supplies of various items, the company had in some cases been forced to finance—both wholly and partially— a number of its suppliers. Many of these suppliers had to build additional facilities in order to produce the desired quantity for Duff.

It had also become necessary to finance partially almost all of the affiliated dealers. A store in a community of ten thousand people required an inventory of approximately $20,000, in addition to costs of leases and property. In some cases, it had been necessary to finance the construction of these stores. In order to obtain as many outlets as possible, the company curtailed the opening of its own stores and encouraged the growth of affiliated stores. Under a franchise arrangement the store was independently owned. The owner or proprietor had to provide at least 35 per cent of the total capital required. Duff Auto Stores, Inc., would finance the balance at current rates of interest, plus 1 per cent of net sales until the balance was repaid. In addition, the owner of the store would agree to purchase all merchandise from Duff. Such a store was known as the local Duff Auto Stores Affiliate.

Shortly after the close of the war, it became apparent that if Duff Auto Stores expected to share in the market for appliances and major automobile accessories and parts, it would be necessary to modify its policy of cash sales only. The growth of instalment sales was both rapid and large. In 1947 a program was worked out so that merchandise could be sold for as little as 10 per cent down, with the balance on an instalment basis. This meant that some arrangement had to be made to finance the instalment sales of all stores. Some affiliated stores made their own arrangements with local banks to carry such paper. At company-owned stores, this paper was accepted in payment of new merchandise. As the amount increased, it was discounted at banks by Duff Auto Stores, Inc., in order to obtain funds.

The postwar expansion of the company had been financed by retained earnings, three sales of common stocks, and two term loans from insurance companies. In 1955, however, it was observed that the amount of instalment paper being discounted amounted to more than $200 million. As the sales of the stores had grown, many local banks were unable to accommodate the owners with further advances; and the company had extended, on a selective basis, the privilege of submitting instalment paper in payment for new mechandise. It was the inclusion of this group which had caused the rapid growth of the discounting of this paper by Duff Auto Stories, Inc.

The terms of instalment sales were the same in all stores. After the required down payment, which varied for different sales, the balance was payable on a monthly basis, not to exceed 24 months. Carrying charges were computed on a block basis—that is, on amounts from $20 to $40 the charge was $3.50 for 24 months. In effect, the charge was about 10 per cent of the total sale for a 24-month period. There were no refunds for prepayment of the account before the end of the payment period. This paper, when forwarded to Duff Auto Stores, Inc., was discounted in various banks throughout the country where the company had established lines of credit. The average rate of discount was 4½ per cent. Although this paper passed in title to banks, payments by customers were still made to Duff Auto Stores, Inc., which redeemed the individual notes from the banks upon payment in full by customers. As payments were received on accounts from customers, they were passed on to the banks. In brief, Duff Auto Stores acted as a collection agency, since all discounted paper was endorsed by Duff, with full recourse.

Exhibit 1

DUFF AUTO STORES, INC.

Statement of Assets and Liabilities, December 31, 1955

ASSETS

Cash..		$ 47,469,523.52
Short-term securities..........................		24,623,487.00
Merchandise inventory (at lower of cost or market):		
Stores and warehouses.......................	$111,382,779.23	
In transit..................................	15,751,162.55	
On consignment of affiliates.................	56,356,115.67	
In process.................................	8,231,666.51	191,721,723.96
Accounts receivable...........................		5,279,542.75
Total Current Assets....................		$269,094,276.23
Property and equipment:		
Stores....................................	$ 5,321,154.35	
Factories.................................	17,442,557.91	
Fixtures and equipment.....................	43,477,327.50	
	$ 66,241,039.76	
Less: Depreciation.........................	15,386,127.33	50,854,912.43
Prepaid expenses..............................		3,652,914.75
Total Assets............................		$323,601,103.41

LIABILITIES

Accounts payable.............................	$ 7,649,325.51
Notes payable:	
Ten-year term loan at 3½ per cent............	14,591,781.45
Short-term bank loans.......................	4,122,525.00
Accrued interest..............................	421,652.62
Accrued taxes................................	2,121,579.86
Accrued compensation........................	8,465,233.72
Provision for federal income taxes..............	23,295,742.55
Other accrued expenses........................	4,661,922.07
Total Liabilities..........................	$ 57,680,437.28

Capital account:		
Preferred stock, par value $100:		
Series A, 4½ per cent cumulative, 100,000 shares...............................	$ 10,000,000.00	
Series B, 4½ per cent cumulative, 50,000 shares	5,000,000.00	
Common stock, no par value, 22,152,475 shares outstanding.......................	154,635,452.75	
Paid-in surplus............................	11,549,369.45	
Earnings retained in business...............	84,735,843.93	
Total Capital Account..................		265,920,666.13
Total Liabilities and Capital...........		$323,601,103.41

The vice president and treasurer of the corporation, after a study of the instalment sales program of the company, concluded that the present arrangement was one which did not fully take advantage of potential profit possibilities. He pointed out that while the instalment terms were 5 per cent per year on the balances, the company was paying banks 4½ per cent per year, and at the same time assuming all the expenses of collection as well as assuming full liability for payment of the notes to banks. He therefore proposed that the firm set up a wholly owned subsidiary, to be known as Duff Discount Corporation, for the purpose of financing the time sales of Duff Auto Stores, Inc. In order to finance this subsidiary, he recommended that Duff Auto Stores, Inc.,

Exhibit 2

DUFF AUTO STORES, INC.

Statement of Earnings, January 1, 1955—December 31, 1955

Net sales.....................................		$598,611,352.57
Cost of goods sold............................	$320,377,135.61	
Operating expenses............................	71,325,455.92	
Taxes (other than income).....................	2,732,613.73	394,435,205.26
Earnings before federal income taxes.............		$104,176,147.31
Less: Federal income taxes.....................		54,158,596.60
Net earnings..................................		$ 50,017,550.71
Earnings Retained in Business, Beginning of Year.		68,622,005.72
		$118,639,556.43
Less: Dividends paid or declared:		
Series A, 4½ per cent preferred...............	$ 450,000.00	
Series B, 4½ per cent preferred...............	225,000.00	
Common stock, $1.50 per share...............	33,228,712.50	33,903,712.50
Earnings Retained in Business, End of Year......		$ 84,735,843.93

acquire the entire authorized issue of common stock of Duff Discount Corporation. In exchange for this stock, Duff Auto Stores, Inc., would guarantee the principal and interest of a 3¾ per cent debenture offering by Duff Discount Corporation in the amount of $10 million. In addition, lines of credit would be arranged with several banks in the total amount of $150 million, to be used as needed. Under a line of credit the company would be charged interest at the rate of 3½ per cent per year on the amount of credit actually used.

If this recommendation were carried out, Duff Discount Corporation would purchase all of the instalment paper of Duff Auto Stores, Inc., for the principal amount of each sales. The carrying charges would remain the same as currently charged, but would be revenues of Duff Discount Corporation. Duff Discount Corporation would not redeem any of the paper currently held by banks but, upon beginning its operations, would finance all new sales, so that within twenty-four months, all instalment paper of Duff Auto Sales, Inc., would be held by it.

Duff Discount Corporation was organized as proposed and began business on March 1, 1956. On that date the total amount of instalment sales held by banks for Duff Auto Stores, Inc., amounted to $201,174,-239.64. Exhibits 1 and 2 show the balance sheet and earnings statement for the year ended December 31, 1955.

QUESTIONS

1. Do you think the move was a profitable one? Explain.

2. Do you think Duff Auto Stores, Inc., was "spreading itself too thin" by this proposed arrangement?

3. Should Duff Auto Stores, Inc., have invested more heavily in Duff Discount Corporation than it did? Why?

CASE 15–6: DIVERSIFIED MANUFACTURING COMPANY

In 1947, after twenty years' experience in the field of job-shop manufacturing, Mr. Frederick Burke, Sr., organized the Diversified Manufacturing Company (DMC) in Los Angeles, California. Mr. Burke's sons —Frederick, Jr., and Peter—joined the management of the firm in 1955 and 1962, respectively.

Mr. Burke began by purchasing a 4,000-square-foot building, an adjacent 4,000-square-foot vacant lot, and general-purpose production machinery. The building was expanded in 1954 to 7,500 square feet of production area and 500 square feet of office area.

DMC has been basically a metal-fabricating job shop, but has developed a line of metal smoke stands which are sold nationwide through jobbers. It also produces a large share of ice-cream-cone dispensers and -cup dispensers for the ice-cream-cone and -cup industry. DMC has recently become a major supplier of equipment for a leading mobile ice-cream and food-vending company. In 1962, these products accounted for approximately 75 per cent of the company's sales. Exhibits 1, 2, and 3 show the 1962 balance sheet, income statement, and additional data concerning 1962 operations.

In 1962 the officers of DMC were considering a number of problems concerning the future of the company. Additional manufacturing area was necessary to achieve the forecasted future sales (see Exhibit 4).

Exhibit 1

DIVERSIFIED MANUFACTURING COMPANY
Balance Sheet, December 31, 1962

Cash	$ 11,470	Accounts payable	$ 4,736
Securities	5,000	Accruals	2,471
Accounts receivable	18,723	Notes payable	950
Inventory	17,471		
	$ 52,664		$ 8,157
Plant and equipment	64,308	Shareholders' undistributed income*	27,100
		Earned surplus	1,715
		Common stock	80,000
	$116,972		$116,972

*DMC is a corporation with a proprietorship tax structure. See exhibit 2.

Exhibit 2

DIVERSIFIED MANUFACTURING COMPANY
Statement of Earnings, December 31, 1962

(In Thousands)

Sales	$208
Cost of goods	109
Gross Profit	$ 99
Factory burden, sales, and administrative expense	72
Net Profit	$ 27

Exhibit 3

DIVERSIFIED MANUFACTURING COMPANY
Additional 1962 Data

Average hours per week per man	42.7 hours
Total direct labor	22,300 hours
Average number of production men—22,300/(42.7 × 50)	10.5 men
Estimated monthly production (at 100 per cent capacity) with present plant and equipment	$20,000
Estimated average minimum work area per production worker	500 square feet
Maximum production workers based on space limitations—8,000/500	16 men
Sales dollars per square foot—$208,000/8,000	$28.60 per square foot
Sales dollars per man-hour	$9.35 per hour

The financing of the expansion was also a question to be resolved. Several new products were being considered to help even out the rather large monthly fluctuations in production (see Exhibit 5).

Exhibit 4

DIVERSIFIED MANUFACTURING COMPANY
Actual and Forecast Annual Sales (1953–65)

Year	Sales	Year	Sales
1953..............	$ 91,000	1960..............	$121,000
1954..............	80,000	1961..............	142,000
1955..............	89,000	1962..............	208,000
1956..............	93,000	1963..............	275,000*
1957..............	101,000	1964..............	300,000*
1958..............	95,000	1965..............	350,000*
1959..............	107,000		

*Forecast. Rapid growth is expected because of an expanded sales promotion plus normal growth.

DMC determined that a plant with 15,000 square feet of manufacturing area would be sufficient for the next five years. This was derived from the data given in Exhibit 3 as follows:

Maximum monthly sales with 8,000 square feet...........$ 20,000
Maximum annual sales with 8,000 square feet............ 240,000
At 80 per cent of capacity, annual sales.................. 192,000
Forecast of 1965 sales................................. 350,000

$$\frac{350,000}{192,000} = \frac{x}{8,000}$$

$x = 14,600$ square feet (80 per cent of capacity)

DMC also determined that additional equipment equal to approximately 80 per cent of current equpment would be needed by 1965, but that it could be added gradually over the next three years. The replacement value of the current equipment was $40,000. The new

Exhibit 5

DIVERSIFIED MANUFACTURING COMPANY
Monthly Sales, 1961–62
(In Thousands)

Month	1961	1962	Month	1961	1962
January............	$ 7.3	$12.7	July..............	$ 8.4	$20.3
February...........	15.4	20.7	August............	9.1	7.7
March.............	11.1	19.0	September.........	8.6	8.5
April..............	18.5	18.9	October...........	13.2	18.2
May...............	12.4	17.1	November.........	18.1	27.2
June..............	13.0	16.9	December.........	8.6	20.8

building was expected to cost $80,000, the additional equipment $32,000 (80 per cent of $40,000); it was expected that the old building could be sold for $40,000. The required financing would then be $72,000. Exhibit 6 shows the balance sheet of DMC revised to reflect a $72,000 term loan which the management believed would be repaid from earnings over the next three years if only nominal dividends were declared.

Exhibit 6

DIVERSIFIED MANUFACTURING COMPANY
Revised Balance Sheet
(Figures Rounded to Nearest Thousand)

Cash........................	$ 11,000	Accounts payable............	$ 5,000
Securities...................	5,000	Accruals....................	2,000
Accounts receivable..........	19,000	Notes payable..............	1,000
Inventory...................	17,000	Shareholders' income........	27,000
	$ 52,000		$ 35,000
Plant and equipment........	136,000	Term loan..................	72,000
		Common stock and retained earnings.................	82,000
	$188,000		$189,000

In order to level monthly production, three products were considered, each of which required some additional development. As patents had not yet been obtained, these were described only as A, B, and C. Any one or a combination of these products could be produced, as they were independent.

Exhibit 7

Product	Cost of Additional Development	Cost of Initial Marketing
A........................	$2,000	$ 3,000
B........................	4,000	10,000
C........................	7,000	15,000

Exhibit 7 gives expected additional development and initial marketing costs for each of these products. Exhibit 8 shows expected sales and profit contributions for these products.

Mr. Burke and his sons decided to study these proposals and determine what action to take.

Exhibit 8

DIVERSIFIED MANUFACTURING COMPANY

Proposed Products—A, B, and C

PRODUCT	FORECAST SALES			EXPECTED GROSS PROFIT		
	1963	1964	1965 and After	1963	1964	1965 and After
A........	$10,000	$15,000	$20,000	$1,500	$2,250	$3,000
B........	20,000	40,000	40,000	3,000	6,000	6,000
C........	....	30,000	50,000	......	4,500	7,500

QUESTION

1. What action should DMC take?

CHAPTER 16

•••••••••••••••••••••••••

Government and Business

DURING the last three decades especially, business in the United States has found it necessary to take special cognizance of the role of government—particularly the national government—in economic affairs. Not only is it necessary for the firm to adjust to particular supply-demand conditions and to the over-all state of economic activity, but it must gear its actions to current and prospective laws and rulings which will impinge on its operations for better or for worse. In addition, of course, business firms, along with other powerful groups, try to influence legislation and executive actions such as the awarding of government contracts. Substantial notice of the economic role of government has already been taken in this book in discussions of taxation, price discrimination, minimum wages, and regulation of utilities. The remaining field of government and business is far too large to handle adequately in a single chapter, but at the same time is much too important to neglect in a book of this sort. As a compromise, the discussion will be limited to antitrust and related legislation because of its importance in establishing the climate for business and because significant economic issues of market structure and behavior are involved.

Antitrust Laws

The Sherman Act of 1890 made the federal government the umpire in the great game of business, giving it the responsibility of preventing monopoly in interstate commerce. Congress used broad language in describing the nature of illegal monopoly, leaving it up to the administrative agencies and the courts to determine more explicitly what will not be permitted. The main provision of the Sherman Act states that "every contract, combination in the form of trust or otherwise, or conspiracy in restraint of trade or commerce among the several states, or with foreign nations is hereby declared to be illegal . . . ."

The Sherman Act was reinforced in 1914 by the Clayton Act, which —in addition to covering such practices as price discrimination, interlocking directorates, tying contracts, and exclusive-dealer arrangements—gave the federal government more explicit power over monopoly by merger. The principal provision of this sort (Section 7, as amended in 1950) states that "no corporation engaged in commerce shall acquire, directly or indirectly, the whole or any part of the stock or share capital. . . (or) the whole or any part of the assets of another corporation also engaged in commerce, where in any line of commerce in any section of the country, the effect of such acquisitions may be substantially to lessen competition, or to tend to create a monopoly."

For the most part, enforcement of these basic antimonopoly laws has been sporadic and limited, but the constant threat imposed by their existence has probably forestalled many combinations, overt price agreements, and other restraints on competition which would otherwise have been put into effect. The antimonopoly laws have caused some firms to attempt to hold down their share of an industry's business. Others have held prices below those which would maximize short-run profits. The long waiting periods which buyers of new cars had to endure just after World War II were a manifestation of such a policy on the part of automobile companies and their dealers. Many firms are persuaded to take a long-run view, prospering more moderately and avoiding antitrust prosecution, rather than a short-run view of pushing a business advantage to its utmost.

Dissolution and Divestiture

The most spectacular action which can occur under the Sherman Act is dissolution of a huge corporation. This is, however, an extremely rare event. In 1911 the Supreme Court, in two extraordinarily important decisions, ordered the dissolution of the Standard Oil Company of New Jersey and the American Tobacco Company. The latter controlled about 95 per cent of the cigarette business as well as high proportions of smoking tobacco, plug tobacco, and snuff production.[1] Standard Oil was broken up into a number of regional companies, while American Tobacco's assets were assigned to three full-line companies and eleven smaller ones. In both cases the previous large stockholders retained control, reducing the power of the dissolution actually to increase competition greatly.

A more recent (1952) dissolution of large magnitude involved the "Big Five" motion-picture producers. Major producers were forced to sell all their affiliated exhibition outlets. The court decrees ordered

---

[1]Vernon A. Mund, *Government and Business* (3d ed.; New York: Harper & Bros., 1960), p. 208.

that about 1,300 theaters be operated by newly formed theater companies, and that more than 1,200 theaters be sold to independent exhibitors.[2] (In view of the difficulties caused by the rapid growth of television around 1952, the sale of many theaters by the producers may actually have been good business, anyway.) The magnitude of the divestiture in the motion-picture industry was unusually great. A well-known antitrust economist has characterized this as "probably the government's greatest economic victory in the 60-year history of antitrust enforcement."[3] Usually, the judgments rendered by the courts require only partial divestiture by large corporations of interests held in other firms. Even partial divestiture judgments are not common, however.

In the United States Steel case of 1920 the Supreme Court decided that "mere size is no offense." No attempt to monopolize was found in this case because of lack of evidence of coercive, predatory, or exclusive tactics.[4] This dictum prevailed for about a quarter century but was finally reversed in the Alcoa case, which was won by the government after thirteen years of litigation. Here, size *was* considered to be the essence of an individual firm's monopoly power. (This decision is probably largely responsible for the popularity in recent years of measures of "concentration" by the Federal Trade Commission, since these relate directly to the problem of bigness of the individual company in relation to the national market.) Nevertheless, the Aluminum Company of America was not broken up into smaller units. Instead, it was decided that the War Assets Administration should sell the surplus government-owned aluminum capacity to the Reynolds Metal Company and the Kaiser Aluminum and Chemical Company in order to provide some competition for Alcoa. The latter's market position in primary aluminum was reduced from one of virtually complete monopoly to approximately 50 per cent of the industry's total.[5]

The New View of Monopoly

In recent years, there has been a tendency for the administrative agencies and the courts to examine market structures and the behavior

---

[2]*Ibid.*, p. 201.

[3]Walter Adams, "The Aluminum Case: Legal Victory—Economic Defeat," *American Economic Review*, December, 1951, pp. 915–16.

[4]J. B. Dirlam and A. E. Kahn, *Fair Competition: The Law and Economics of Antitrust Policy* (Ithaca: Cornell University Press, 1954), p. 45.

[5]John V. Krutilla, "Aluminum—A Dilemma for Antitrust Aims?" *Southern Economic Journal*, October, 1955, p. 165.

of prices in order to find circumstantial evidence of market domination. Specific *intent* to monopolize and the use of predatory practices to achieve market domination may no longer be necessary factors in determining when the existence of monopoly power falls under the Sherman Act's prohibition of restraint of trade.

This tendency was manifest in the Alcoa case, already mentioned, and in the American Tobacco decision of 1946. The court upheld a finding of conspiracy among three separate tobacco companies to fix prices, even though there was no direct evidence of collusion among the companies. The main evidence was circumstantial, in that prices charged by the separate firms tended to move together. The entire practice of price leadership in interstate commerce now appears to run the risk of being determined to be "conscious parallelism of action," even when such parallelism is not established by an explicit "agreement to agree" on prices.

The new antitrust attitude seems to have been reflected also in a 1953 case, *United Shoe Machinery Corporation* v. *United States.* This company, which produces 75 to 95 per cent of the shoe machinery turned out in the country, had followed the policy of leasing rather than selling the machinery. The court found United Shoe Machinery's practices to be "not predatory but instead to be those of a normally aggressive firm." The corporation was ordered to offer its machinery for sale on terms that would not substantially favor leasing, and prohibited any lease in excess of five years.

In this case the former refusal to sell outright had prevented the creation of a secondhand market. (As is very evident in the automobile industry, the sellers of used cars may offer substantial competition to the sellers of new ones.) Also, United Shoe Machinery, by tying in repairs with its rental contracts, was found to have prevented the growth of independent repair services.[6]

Economies of Size

In considering the wisdom of dissolution of large corporations holding substantial monopoly power, judging when "big" is "too big" is most difficult. Economies of scale with respect to plant arise from the increased specialization of productive processes and the use of large machines. A machine capable of turning out twice as much output as a smaller one usually does not cost twice as much. In order to use

---

[6]"The Supreme Court, 1953 Term," *Harvard Law Review,* Vol. LXVIII (1954-55), p. 142.

highly specialized processes of production and the largest available machinery, a plant frequently must be very large. The economies of scale differ greatly, however, from industry to industry.

While economies of scale are most spectacular with respect to plants, they exist also with respect to firms. A large multiplant firm is able to diversify its production so as to secure a stability of profits greater than would be likely with a single line (unless that line had an extremely dependable demand, such as exists for electricity). Also, a large firm usually enjoys substantial economies in purchasing, in marketing its products, and in advertising, financing, and research. (Research cost per unit is lower when a newly discovered product can be sold in large volume.) Integration to insure dependable supplies of materials and components at cost often provides a further economy related to scale of firm.

In any antitrust case, it is possible for the large firm to show the existence of competition, since *some* substitution is always possible. This may come from identical products turned out by other domestic firms, similar products which are substitutes in at least some uses, imports, or the secondhand market. It can also demonstrate economies of scale which could not be secured by a smaller company. Such *diseconomies* as may exist due to the difficulty of co-ordinating a far-flung industrial empire are not likely to be obvious. Also, the greater compulsion toward efficiency which would be brought about by more thoroughgoing competition is not likely to be clearly demonstrable, since even a firm with great monopoly power has the profit motive to spur its efficiency.

Natural Monopolies Treated Differently

When firms are deemed to be "natural monopolies" because of the clear advantages of large-scale company operations in relation to total demand, it is the prevailing public policy not to enforce the antitrust laws but instead to encourage monopoly by means of exclusive franchises, and to regulate maximum rates through administrative commissions. Or direct government ownership may be resorted to, with rates set directly by public authorities, with or without the check of a regulatory commission. In the case of the railroads and truckers especially, public regulation has also taken the form of shielding firms from the full effects of competition by fixing minimum rates as well as maximum rates. The category of "natural monopolies" which are properly subject to regulation is not clear-cut. Some industries (e.g., trucking and taxicabs) have been considered by government to be properly subject to rate regulation, even though price competition might be effective.

Workable Competition

In recent years the concept of "workable competition" has been improvised to denote a situation in which there are a number of non-colluding firms in each market area, where no one firm occupies a large part of the market, and where new firms can enter on approximately even terms. This situation can provide the consumer with many of the advantages which could be derived from pure competition—as long as rivalry remains genuine in important respects. Unfortunately, the concept of workable competition is a vague one. What will be deemed by one investigator to provide sufficient protection to the consumer may be considered by another to be an intolerably monopolistic situation. An example of conflicting views in what amounted to workable or effective competition is contained in the so-called "Cellophane case" at the end of this chapter.

Usually, different firms do not turn out exactly the same product or set of products, making it difficult to say what constitutes the "industry" or "group" within which there is supposed to be a sufficient number of firms to provide workable competition. Also, it is unclear just how many firms are needed within an industry—once a definition has been arrived at—to provide substantial competition. A duopolistic (two-firm) industry may be more competitive than one consisting of a dozen firms if the two are genuine rivals in important matters (especially in price) while the twelve co-operate in some important respects. However, the likelihood of securing substantial competition increases as the number of firms increases, since it is harder to keep all members of a larger group "in line" through trade association activity or other means. As the group becomes larger, the potential gain in sales by a price "chiseler" becomes greater, and the danger to him of retaliatory price cuts by all the other firms becomes smaller. Consequently, antitrust policy which succeeds in establishing or keeping a larger number of firms in any given field may not guarantee that the field will be made or kept workably competitive; but at least, it tends to decrease the likelihood of full collusion on basic matters.

Mergers

The strong merger movement among American corporations in recent years has greatly increased antitrust interest in the effects of this activity on the competitiveness of industry. It can be readily seen in Exhibit 1 that the number of mergers and acquisitions in manufacturing and mining increased between 1949 and 1954. Between 1955 and 1958, more than 2,600 locally operated food stores were acquired by merger.[7]

Exhibit 1

NUMBER OF MERGERS AND ACQUISITIONS IN MANUFACTURING AND MINING

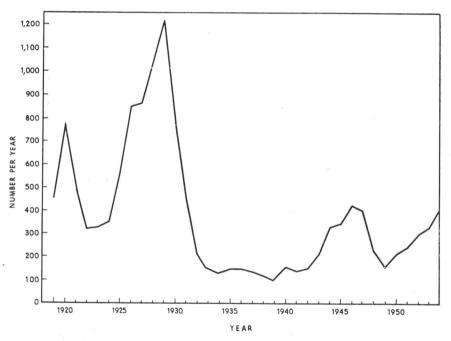

Source: Federal Trade Commission, *Report on Corporate Mergers and Acquisitions* (Washington, D.C.: U.S. Government Printing Office, May, 1955).

The upward trend in mergers and acquisitions has continued. The annual report of the Federal Trade Commission for 1962 stated that 1,032 mergers and acquisitions were recorded in 1961 and 1,633 in 1962. The Federal Trade Commission, which shares antitrust jurisdiction under the Clayton Act with the Antitrust Division of the Department of Justice, has been particularly concerned with the multiple acquisitions that have occurred in such industries as dairy products and food distribution. In its 1962 report, it cited its complaints against the Borden Company, which has acquired 80 dairy concerns, and National

[7]Mund, *op. cit.*, p. 78.

Dairy Products, which has 40 acquisitions, as two of its important continuing cases. Two more in the same classification concern Kroger and Grand Union for multiple acquisitions of smaller grocery chains.

Nature of Gains to Firms

The Federal Trade Commission's analysts found six advantages to the acquiring firm which were frequently apparent as important motives in mergers and acquisitions:[8]

1. A larger capacity may be more quickly secured by merger than by new construction.
2. A larger line of products in the same general business is often secured by retaining items already being turned out by the acquired firm.
3. Diversification of products can often be most easily and safely effected by taking over lines which are already successful.
4. Vertical integration is sometimes achieved by merger as a way of assuring dependable supplies of materials and components at cost.
5. Vertical merger, looking instead toward sale of final products, is sometimes advantageous, especially when the existing facilities for distribution can readily handle additional products.
6. Geographic coverage can quickly be expanded by taking over facilities located in regions not already covered.

It is desirable to look at the motivation for mergers from the point of view of the *selling* firm as well as the acquiring firm. Tax motives were discussed in an earlier chapter. Among the nontax motives the following have been listed by the author of a study of corporate mergers:[9] the desire to retire; loss of key management personnel by death; desire to reduce the load on key executives; inability of top management to keep up with its competition; desire to become connected with larger companies; dissension among owner-managers; anticipation by owners of a decline in the value of owner contributions where this value was highly dependent on active owner participation in management; and desire for greater diversification to improve the quality and marketability of investment holdings.

---

[8]Federal Trade Commission, *Annual Report, 1955* (Washington, D.C.: U.S. Government Printing Office, 1956), p. 59.

[9]J. Fred Weston, *The Role of Mergers in the Growth of Large Firms* (Los Angeles: University of California Press, 1953), pp. 72–73. Weston concluded that internal expansion has been of more importance since the turn of the century than mergers in explaining the present size of the large firms studied.

Mergers and the Public Interest

No valid generalization can be made regarding the effects of mergers on the public interest. Each particular acquisition must be separately considered in the light of the market situation which it affects. In the automobile industry, where most smaller companies seem to be at a serious disadvantage relative to the "Big Three," the merger of small firms has been encouraged by the government as a means of improving their competitive positions. This attitude was manifest in the Nash-Hudson, Kaiser-Willys, and Studebaker-Packard mergers. Conflicting business, economic, and legal arguments on the probable effect of an important merger are presented in the Bethlehem-Youngstown case at the end of the chapter.

Where only small companies are involved, the Federal Trade Commission usually considers that the merger or acquisition does not tend to create a monopoly. Also, the antimerger provisions of the Clayton Act are not applicable to acquisitions by or from noncorporations, or to acquisitions which are made solely for investment. However, when a large corporation shows a disposition to acquire numerous smaller corporations in the same—or nearly the same—line of business, thus removing them as competitors, the Federal Trade Commission is apt to place its activities under close scrutiny for possible antitrust violation.

Even when a large corporation is active in acquiring other corporations, the consequences may range anywhere from no effect on competition to a severe loss of competition, depending on the exact nature of the acquisitions. If a "vertical" acquisition of a parts supplier who has produced exclusively for the acquiring firm occurs, there is no effect on the immediate extent of competition at either level. A certain amount of potential competition may be eliminated, since the "captive" parts supplier will now probably be unavailable as a source of components to any new entry into the field of the acquiring corporation. More immediate and possibly serious repercussions on competition can occur if a vertical acquisition involves a raw-material or parts supplier who also supplies other firms, particularly when the latter are competitors of the acquiring firm. Much depends on the availability of alternative sources of the material or components. If these are available only at higher cost from another source—due, for example, to their having to be shipped a greater distance—the damage to competition may be substantial. The great complexity and variety of market situations which are involved make the commission's job of policing mergers which may be contrary to the public interest an extremely difficult one.

Intercompany Stock Acquisitions as a Form of Merger

Section 7 of the Clayton Act, which has recently been characterized as possibly a "sleeping giant" of the antitrust field,[10] contains a prohibition of intercorporate stock acquisitions which have the effect of substantially lessening competition or tending to create monopoly in any line of commerce. After a series of court cases which began in 1949, the U.S. Supreme Court, in the du Pont decision of 1957, held that the purchase by that company in 1917–19 of a 23 per cent stock interest in General Motors violated Section 7. In reaching the four-to-two decision the majority of the court extended the scope of the Clayton Act in three ways:[11] (1) The act was held to apply to vertical acquisitions, whereas previously it has usually been applied only to acquisitions in the same line of industry; (2) the threat to competition need not be present at the time of stock acquisition but can be found to exist at any later time; and (3) the "market" in which competition is found to have been reduced was defined narrowly to include only automobile finishes and fabrics rather than the entire market for all sorts of finishes and fabrics.

Among the interesting aspects of this important case is the connection between the legal and economic views of what constitutes a "market" or a "commodity." Economists who are impressed with the importance of brand names and fewness of sellers and buyers as a source of monopoly power would tend to agree with the majority finding in the du Pont case. Economists who are more impressed with the omnipresence of substitute commodities and the ability of new firms to enter a general field of activity will tend to be more skeptical of the decision. A much broader concept of the relevant market is contained in the Cellophane case at the end of this chapter. Economic theory and statistical investigations of economic matters can have an important effect on legal opinion as well as on legislation.

Interlocking Directorates

Another of the prohibitions of the Clayton Act is directed at interlocking directorates among corporations. Section 8 provides, in sub-

---

[10]Robert W. Harbeson, "The Clayton Act: Sleeping Giant of Antitrust?" *American Economic Review,* March, 1958.

[11]*Ibid.,* pp. 93–94.

stance, that no person may be a director in two or more competing corporations, any one of which has capital, surplus, and undivided profits aggregating more than $1 million, the prohibition not being applicable, however, to banks and common carriers.[12] Antitrust enforcement on this front has not been vigorous, but the existence of the prohibition has probably reduced somewhat the direct use of this device, which may, quite obviously, lead to collusive rather than competitive activities. Section 8 does not prohibit interlocks between suppliers and corporate customers, and this is a very common situation.

In 1946, the year to which the Federal Trade Commission study applies, the food industry was one of the outstanding exhibitors of interlocking directorates. For example, three of the ten largest dairies were directly or indirectly interlocked with one another. (Indirect interlocking occurs, for example, when two corporations each have a director who is also on the board of a third corporation.) The three largest dairies were also indirectly interlocked with General Foods Corporation, Standard Brands, and Best Foods. The largest of the dairy companies was indirectly interlocked with two large baking companies, which were potential customers, and with a large manufacturer of metal and paper containers.

Heavy interlocking was found to exist among sugar companies. Sixteen of the 23 largest sugar companies had direct or indirect ties. American Sugar Refining alone had direct and indirect interlocks with 16 potential customers.

The nonferrous metals industry was indirectly interlocked through financial institutions and also through some leading industrial corporations. American Metal Company was interlocked with 10 companies within the industry; Kennecott Copper Corporation and Phelps Dodge Corporation, with eight; and Anaconda Copper Mining Company, St. Joseph Lead Company, and American Smelting and Refining Company, with seven.

In the electrical machinery industry, the "Big Four" manufacturers —General Electric, Westinghouse, Western Electric, and Radio Corporation of America—were indirectly interlocked through six large commercial banks, two of the largest life insurance companies, a public utility, a railroad, and an industrial company. They also had backward interlocks to suppliers and forward ones to customers.

---

[12]Federal Trade Commission, *Annual Report, 1950* (Washington, D.C.: U.S. Government Printing Office, 1951), p. 27. All of the information on interlocking directorates presented here is from that report.

The leading petroleum companies—Standard of New Jersey, Socony-Vacuum Oil Company, Texas Company, Standard of California, Standard of Indiana, Gulf Oil Corporation, and others—were found by the Federal Trade Commission to be closely tied together by means of interlocking directorates or by joint ownership of affiliates. The most significant interlocking directorates were through a leading New York bank.

None of the rubber companies had directors in common in 1946. The most significant of the interlocking relations were apparently those between U.S. Rubber and General Motors, resting on heavy du Pont investments in both companies and the presence of the du Pont directors on both boards.

Significance of Interlocking Directorates

The significance of interlocking directorates cannot be simply assessed. Much depends on the power exerted by the directors through whom the relations are established. This may range from great power all the way down to mere observation. Much depends also on the nature of the companies which are thus linked. If the firms are rivals in an industry which has a small number of firms, collusive actions are likely to result. If the firms have related but not identical lines of products, the interlocking is apt to forestall the encroachment of each upon the other through the addition of new products.

Interlocking directorates between a company and its suppliers or customers may bring about preferential treatment in prices, in allocation of materials in short supply because of a strike or other emergency, or in special access to market outlets. When manufacturing companies are linked with financial institutions, they may be given preferred access to credit compared with a newcomer to the field, thus putting a potential competitor at a disadvantage. As was pointed out in the chapter on plant location, the local availability of credit is quite often an important factor in causing a firm to choose one city rather than another as the site for a new facility.

Conspiracy in Electrical Equipment

Price conspiracy in violation of the Sherman Act was in February, 1961, proved by the federal government in "the largest of all criminal antitrust cases." This case involved twenty-nine manufacturers of heavy electrical equipment and forty-five executives of these companies. All pleaded guilty or offered no defense to charges of conspiring to fix prices and to rig bids on sales to the government.

Seven executives were sent to prison to serve thirty-day sentences, and fines totaling $1,924,500 were imposed by the federal court that handled the case.[13] The largest fines were assessed against General Electric and Westinghouse Electric Corporation. Of the seven officials who were sentenced to jail terms, three worked for General Electric, two for Westinghouse, one for Cutler-Hammer, and one for Clark Controller Company. General Electric, however, issued a statement that the actions of its executives were not in conformance with company policy and were carried out without the knowledge of any member of the board of directors.

It appears likely that this strong antitrust action will do much to prevent price conspiracies in the future. In addition to the direct penalties levied by the courts, companies are exposed to civil damage suits from customers. Normally, federal agencies can sue for damages, while other customers can sue for triple damages.

The Fair-Trade Philosophy

At the same time that the federal government seeks to keep business competitive by means of antitrust activity, the "fair-trade" laws tend to have the opposite effect—namely, that of preventing thorough-going competition. These laws permit manufacturers to establish resale prices on certain items. They represent one of the many exemptions from the antitrust laws, since any price fixing, whether horizontal or vertical, is banned under the Sherman Act as a restraint of trade. Like some other laws affecting price, their effects are not entirely in one direction. There is some validity to the claim that the fair-trade laws actually promote the preservation of competition by preventing large retailers from using well-advertised products as loss leaders to attract business away from smaller firms. The latter cannot use loss leaders so effectively, since they have fewer other products to which to "lead" customers. Also, there is some validity to the argument that use of a nationally advertised brand as a loss leader may "cheapen" the product unduly in the public mind.

Resale price maintenance has been applied most extensively to commodities possessing distinctive characteristics in the minds of consumers. Proprietary items produced under secret formulas and trade-marked

[13]*New York Times,* February 8, 1961, p. 1. All of the information presented on this subject is from this source.

items sold directly to consumers are most suitable for this purpose. Durable items like farm machinery, household electrical appliances, radios, and television sets are not very suitable, because effective retail prices can so readily be altered by means of the trade-in allowance given to the buyer. Drugs, toilet goods, cosmetics, liquor, and sporting goods have been subjected extensively to fair-trade pricing.

The driving force behind enactment of the fair-trade laws was the National Association of Retail Druggists. Beginning in 1935, this association made enactment of state resale price-maintenance laws and the passage of a national fair-trade law its main objective; a secondary objective was obtaining at least a 50 per cent markup on drugstore items.[14] Led by California, which passed a fair-trade law in 1931, forty-four other states enacted similar legislation by 1941. In 1937, Congress amended the Sherman Act by passing the Miller-Tydings Resale Price Maintenance Act. This legalized retail price fixing in interstate commerce where a state fair-trade law existed. The Supreme Court found the Miller-Tydings Act to be unconstitutional in 1951, but passage of the McGuire Act in 1952 again put on the books a federal fair-trade law—with revised wording to meet the objections of the court. Without a federal law exempting firms which use fair-trade contracts from prosecution under the antitrust laws, the state laws would be of very limited significance.

Operation of the fair-trade laws has been hampered very substantially during the past decade by both legal and economic forces. As of late 1959, courts in seventeen states had effectively eliminated fair trade. In addition, the federal courts had held application of state fair-trade laws to interstate mail-order sales in nonfair-trade areas to be beyond the scope of the McGuire Act.[15] The principal legal attack in state courts has been directed at the "nonsigner" clause in state laws. This clause makes binding on nonsigners a minimum resale price specified on a particular item if a contract is signed with just one retailer in the state. This clause has often been found to be in violation of state constitutions.

Economic Forces Hampering Fair Trade

The basic economic force of substitution has been the main detriment to the fair traders. The manufacturer who sets a retail price at a high

---

[14] Federal Trade Commission, *Report on Resale Price Maintenance* (Washington, D.C.: U.S. Government Printing Office, 1945), p. xxxi.

[15] *Yale Law Journal*, November, 1959, p. 168.

level on his product invites into the market entry of technically similar commodities by other manufacturers. These may be fair-traded at a lower level, or not fair-traded at all. Many manufacturers have attempted to "have their cake and eat it, too," by selling the same commodity under different brand names, fair-trading one and selling the other through different outlets without fair-trade contracts. This is a variety of price discrimination which may be effective to the extent that consumers do not realize the similarity of the products, or to the extent that they are not careful in spending their money.

Frequently, the lower priced version of the same good is sold through "discount houses," which have had a phenomenal rise in recent years. These stores make a feature of selling branded lines at a large reduction in price. The United States Chamber of Commerce in 1954 estimated that fully 18 per cent of all retail sales were made by discount outlets of some type.[16] In such cities as New York and Los Angeles the discount houses sell well over half of the major appliances. In the latter city, some gasoline service stations compete with the discount houses. The motorist can now buy at cut rates such items as television sets, vacuum cleaners, and nylon stockings while having his car serviced. The attraction of the discounted merchandise seems also to have increased the volume of gasoline and oil sales.

Retail jewelers have been among the groups to complain that some manufacturers have used them as a "show case stimulus of the business of discount houses." The complaint, which was filed with the Federal Trade Commission, has been that jewelry manufacturers have deliberately sold watches, silverware, and related goods to discount houses without requiring adherence to fair-trade prices while at the same time enforcing fair-trade laws. The commission's advice to the retail jewelers was to sue for enforcement of the fair-trade prices against the discount houses or, alternatively, to disregard fair-trade prices themselves. A manufacturer who discriminates in the enforcement of his fair-trade prices among different types of sellers is unlikely to win a suit against a seller who disregards fair-trade prices.

Manufacturers' Actions Regarding Fair Trade

To date, some manufacturers have adhered as strictly as possible to the fair-trade philosophy; others have fair-traded and not fair-traded at the same time; and still others have completely abandoned the setting

---

[16] *Wall Street Journal,* November 14, 1954.

of resale prices. Westinghouse, which started fixing retail prices on its appliances in 1949, abandoned fair-trade prices on its line of electric housewares and bed coverings in 1955, being the first major appliance dealer to do so.[17] Among the important manufacturers who have abandoned the practice of fair-trading are General Electric, the Sunbeam Corporation, Ronson Corporation, Royal McBee Corporation, and the Toastmaster Division of McGraw-Edison.[18]

A basic lesson to be learned from the recent history of the fair-trade movement is that competition is so vigorous a force in the American economy that legislative attempts to thwart its operation often meet with insuperable obstacles. Also, experience confirms the observation that the courts, in seeking to preserve our constitutional rights, often manifest more economic wisdom than our legislatures. As long as private economic initiative and constitutional government are allowed to flourish, the nation will continue its rapid economic growth.

APPENDIX TO CHAPTER 16:   A SHORT SURVEY OF ANTITRUST[19]

As a background for recent cases in which the government has attacked what its antitrust agencies considered excessive corporate power, it is important to examine the laws, their administration and their development through judicial interpretation. The major provisions of the laws and the antitrust chronology will gain greater meaning as future reference is made to them.

THE FORMULATION OF ANTITRUST POLICY

The formulation of policy for the federal regulation of competition and monopoly reflects the separation of power in our structure of government; the legislative, administrative, and judicial branches have all appreciably influenced antitrust policy. In many areas of regulation the three co-ordinate branches of government share the policy-making function, but in antitrust the judiciary has played a particularly powerful role. At least three reasons can be cited for the importance of federal judges as policy makers. First, the basic legislation was broad and made little attempt to set up standards as to what constituted illegal activities. The Sherman Act condemned "restraints of trade" and "mon-

---

[17] *Wall Street Journal,* September 1, 1955, p. 18.
[18] *Yale Law Journal,* November, 1959, p. 170.
[19] Highly recommended supplementary reading may be found in *Public Policies toward Business,* by Clair Wilcox (Homewood, Ill., Richard D. Irwin, Inc., 1955; rev. 1958).

opolizing," and the Federal Trade Commission prescribed "unfair competition" with little further definition. Second, the Sherman Act depended entirely upon litigation for enforcing its provisions. Third, the Supreme Court read a "rule of reason" into the Sherman Act, which meant that the ultimate legality of possibly monopolistic activities would hinge on judges' views as to the reasonableness of the business behavior involved.

Legislation

Of sixty-odd antitrust laws, three, plus three amendments, are of greatest importance:

1. The Sherman Antitrust Act, July 2, 1890, forbade "every contract, combination or conspiracy in restraint of trade" (Section 1) and specified punishment for every person who shall monopolize or attempt to monopolize (Section 2).
2. The Federal Trade Commission Act (1914), as amended by the Wheeler-Lea Act (1938), prohibited "unfair methods of competition" and "unfair or deceptive acts or practices," and set up the Federal Trade Commission with broad investigatory powers.
3. The Clayton Act (1915) made several practices unlawful: price discrimination (Section 2), exclusive dealing or tying contracts (Section 3), acquisitions of stock of other corporations (Section 7), and interlocking directorates (Section 8), subject to the qualifications (or a similar one) that the acts "may substantially lessen competition or tend to create a monopoly in any line of commerce." The Robinson-Patman Amendment of 1936 and the Celler Antimerger Amendment of 1950 tightened the provisions against price discrimination and corporate acquisitions.

The Federal Trade Commission and Clayton acts, with their amendments, represent some strengthening of the Sherman Act to take care of incipient monopoly situations. A second and somewhat contradictory legislative development has been the granting of exemptions for particular industrial groups, usually in response to the pressures of the groups who were able to develop plausible and sometimes compelling reasons for the unsuitability of antitrust regulation in their areas. Section 6 of the Clayton Act itself exempted labor, agricultural, and horticultural organizations; the Webb-Pomerene Law (1918) exempted export trade associations; the NRA represented a temporary suspension of antitrust for the many industries which drew up codes. Fair-trade legislation by the federal government constitutes such an exemption by allowing price-maintenance agreements, which otherwise would be antitrust violations, to be permitted by state legislation.

Administrative Enforcement

Dual Enforcement Responsibilities. Administration of the antitrust laws is primarily vested in two agencies, the Antitrust Division of the Department of Justice and the Federal Trade Commission. The former was set up as a special division in 1903; the latter was established by the Federal Trade Commission Act in 1914. Both are responsible for enforcement of the Clayton Act. Moreover, although the Sherman Act specifies enforcement responsibility only for the Attorney General, the Supreme Court has held that "the Commission has jurisdiction to declare that conduct tending to restrain trade is an unfair method of competition (under Section 5 of the Federal Trade Commission Act, the bailiwick of the Commission) even though the self-same conduct may also violate the Sherman Act."[20]

The Attorney General, through the Antitrust Division, seeks enforcement through litigation, either civil or criminal suits. In addition, private corporations or individuals may sue for triple damages. Criminal actions can lead to fines, adverse publicity for defendants, and occasionally to imprisonment. The maximum fine assessable against both corporations and executives has been raised to $50,000 from $5,000; the maximum jail sentence is one year. The criminal suit also allows the government to subpoena witnesses and documents which may provide the evidence for subsequent civil proceedings. Thus, after the government won a criminal case against A & P, it filed a civil suit which ended in a *consent decree.* The consent decree represents a bargain between attorneys for the Antitrust Division and the defendant, which is subject to approval by a district court (usually without changes). Whether to settle in this way poses an important problem for the firm. It may save trial costs, executive time, unfavorable publicity, and a written court record that may subsequently serve as a basis for a treble-damage suit. On the other hand, it may grant concessions which the government would not have obtained. An increasing majority of civil antitrust suits have been settled recently by consent decrees. Similar considerations may lead a corporation to plead *nolo contendere* ("I do not wish to contest") in a criminal suit.

Economic remedies can be provided only through civil proceedings and may range from a court injunction against the continuation of illegal practices to a court decree calling for dissolution of the defendant, as was used against the tobacco and oil trusts in 1911.

---

[20] *Federal Trade Commission* v. *Cement Institute,* 333 U.S. 683, 693 (1948).

The Federal Trade Commission was designed to approach antitrust enforcement in a different way, through administrative processes. Its only formal action is an order to "cease and desist" against a particular offender for a specified offense. Usually, after an investigation of charges brought by an injured firm, the commission may issue a complaint which is followed by hearings in which it acts both as prosecutor and as judge. These may result in dropping the *complaint,* in issuing a *cease and desist order,* or in settlement by the *stipulation* in which the respondent promises to abstain from illegal practices without admitting guilt. The commission must go to the courts to enjoin violations of its orders, which in turn may be challenged by companies in the courts. Of more potential importance in complementing the Antitrust Division's efforts are the commission's broad powers of investigation given in Section 6 of the Federal Trade Commission Act, and the role, intended by the sponsors of the act, as an expert assistant in preparing antitrust decrees. (The Antitrust Division depends upon the FBI for case investigation.)

Adequacy of Enforcement Efforts.   Only in recent years, since Thurman Arnold headed the Antitrust Division in the late thirties, has the manpower commitment to enforcement been substantial. The 1952 budget of $3,420,000, with 209 attorneys on the staff, can be compared with the $100,000 annual budget and five employees representing the average from 1903–8 just subsequent to the great era of trust formation. Serious questions as to the present quantitative adequacy of our recent efforts have been raised by many students in the field, such as Corwin Edwards, who in 1950 called for a quadrupling of the manpower of both agencies.

The problem of nonenforcement has been particularly acute during certain administrations, sometimes because of active hostility of enforcement officers to the antitrust laws, more often because of the acceptance of the Sherman Act as a great moral gesture which needed little application. Thus, in the inaugural nine years from Harrison's administration through McKinley's, only 18 cases were brought, and under the Hoover administration, only 38.

Judicial Interpretations

Common-Law Background.   Interpretations of the Sherman Act, such as the "rule of reason," have been based upon strictures against restraints of trade in the common law. Senator Hoar, one of the act's sponsors, saw the purpose of the act as "to establish the common law principles which protected fair competition in trade in old times in England." Going to the common law did not give an unambiguous interpretation because of the divergence of common-law rules in various jurisdictions and at different times.

Illegality of Collusive Activities. Since 1898 the illegality of price-fixing and market-sharing arrangements per se has been generally held. Its definitive statement is that of Mr. Justice Stone in the Trenton Potteries case (1927), which held that price-fixing agreements in themselves are unreasonable restraints regardless of the reasonableness of the price. The very real problem remains as to how far a trade association or other group may legally go in jointly influencing price through such activities as price reporting and common methods of computing cost.

"Close-Knit" Combinations and Monopolizing. The judicial interpretations as to the applicability of the Sherman Act to "close-knit" rather than "loose-knit" combinations have followed quite a different course. The government had a few belated successes in getting "trusts" dissolved: the "Powder Trust case," in which Hercules Powder Company and the Atlas Powder Company were split off from du Pont; the Standard Oil case; and the American Tobacco case.[21] But the "rule of reason" laid down in the last two cases (that restraints of trade were illegal only if they were unreasonable) developed into an abuse theory of mergers in *United States* v. *United States Steel Corp.* (1920).[22] Such a theory held that in the absence of predatory acts or possibly "unworthy motives" the court was unwilling to dissolve the giant corporation formed by merger. From the standpoint of the economic power to fix prices, the difference in interpretations for loose and tight combinations is somewhat anomalous. A single firm arising out of the merger of several independents should generally be expected to have greater control over prices than the same independents acting collusively, since frictions, compromises, and departures from agreements will be avoided. Yet it is the independents acting in collusion who have more certainly fallen afoul of the antitrust laws.

Since 1938 the Antitrust Division has given greater attention to prosecutions against monopolizing under Section 2 of the Sherman Act. The Alcoa case,[23] decided in 1945, represented a close approach to a decision based on market control alone (over 90 per cent of primary alum-

---

[21]*United States* v. *E. I. Du Pont de Nemours & Co.*, 188 F. 127 (Circuit Court for Delaware, 1911); *Standard Oil Co., of New Jersey* v. *United States*, 221 U.S. 1 (1911); *United States* v. *American Tobacco Co., et al.*, 221 U.S. 106 (1911).

[22]251 U.S. 452.

[23]*United States* v. *Aluminum Co. of America*, 148 F. (2d) 416 (1945).

inum ingots). Such clear-cut control, however, is a rare species for American industry where "Big Threes," "Big Fours," and "Big Fives" are common.

This case is illustrative of the important part judicial discretion can have in shaping antitrust policy outside of the mere finding of violation or no violation. What remedies the courts are willing to allow greatly influence the significance of a decision. Donald Dewey has pointed out that under the "new Sherman Act" the government has won opinions but lost the decrees, particularly when dissolution of or divestiture by the defendant is requested. The government proposed 44 rearrangements of corporate structures from 1945 to 1954 and gained but two decisions for such alteration. Dewey explains this discrepancy partly on the ground that the company, led by corporate management, is found guilty of the violations but the impact of dissolution is likely to fall on stockholder and worker interests.[24]

The reluctance of the court to apply the "three D's" of divestiture, dissolution, and divorcement is one influence toward the extensive anti-merger activity of the antitrust agencies in the last few years. The first major court decision, however, under the 1950 antimerger amendment, was that in late 1958, denying the Bethlehem-Youngstown merger.

THE ANTITRUST LAWS

The Sherman Antitrust Act (1890)

An Act to protect trade and commerce against unlawful restraints and monopolies.

Be it enacted by the Senate and House of Representatives of the United States of America in Congress assembled.

Sec. 1. Every contract, combination in the form of trust or otherwise, or conspiracy, in restraint of trade or commerce among the several States, or with foreign nations, is hereby declared to be illegal. Every person who shall make any such contract or engage in any such combination or conspiracy, shall be deemed guilty of a misdemeanor, and, on conviction thereof, shall be punished by fine not exceeding five thousand dollars, or by imprisonment not exceeding one year, or by both said punishments, in the discretion of the court.

Sec. 2. Every person who shall monopolize, or attempt to monopolize, or combine or conspire with any other person or persons, to monopolize any part of the trade or commerce among the several States, or with foreign nations, shall be deemed guilty of a misdemeanor, and, on conviction thereof, shall be punished by fine not exceeding five thousand dollars, or by imprisonment not exceeding one year, or by both said punishments, in the discretion of the court. . . .

---

[24]"Romance and Realism in Antitrust Policy," *Journal of Political Economy,* April, 1955, pp. 93–102.

Sec. 4. The several circuit courts of the United States are hereby invested with jurisdiction to prevent and restrain violations of this act; and it shall be the duty of the several district attorneys of the United States, in their respective districts, under the direction of the Attorney General, to institute proceedings in equity to prevent and restrain such violations. Such proceedings may be by way of petition setting forth the case and praying that such violation shall be enjoined or otherwise prohibited. When the parties complained of shall have been duly notified of such petition the court shall proceed, as soon as may be, to the hearing and determination of the case; and pending such petition and before final decree, the court may at any time make such temporary restraining order or prohibition as shall be deemed just in the premises. . . .

Sec. 7. Any person who shall be injured in his business or property by any other person or corporation by reason of anything forbidden or declared to be unlawful by this act, may sue therefore in any circuit court of the United States in the district in which the defendant resides or is found, without respect to the amount in controversy, and shall recover threefold the damages by him sustained, and the costs of suit, including a reasonable attorney's fee.

Note: Section 3 makes the act applicable to territories and the District of Columbia, Section 5 deals with subpoena power of court; Section 6 gives right to seize property of violators in transit; and Section 8 defines "persons" to include associations and corporations.

The Federal Trade Commission Act (1914)

An Act to create a Federal Trade Commission, to define its powers and duties, and for other purposes.

Be it enacted by the Senate and House of Representatives of the United States of America in Congress assembled, That a commission is hereby created and established, to be known as the Federal Trade Commission (hereinafter referred to as the commission), which shall be composed of five commissioners, who shall be appointed by the President, by and with the advice and consent of the Senate. Not more than three of the commissioners shall be members of the same political party. The first commissioners appointed shall continue in office for terms of three, four, five, six, and seven years, respectively, from the date of the taking effect of this Act, the term of each to be designated by the President, but their successors shall be appointed for terms of seven years, except that any person chosen to fill a vacancy shall be appointed only for the unexpired term of the commissioner whom he shall succeed. The commission shall choose a chairman from its membership. . . .

Sec. 5. That unfair methods of competition in commerce are hereby declared unlawful.

The commission is hereby empowered and directed to prevent persons, partnerships, or corporations except banks, and common carriers subject to the Act to regulate commerce, from using unfair methods of competition in commerce.

Whenever the commission shall have reason to believe that any such person partnership, or corporation has been or is using any unfair methods of competition in commerce, and if it shall appear to the commission that a proceeding by it in respect thereof would be to the interest of the public, it shall issue and serve upon such person, partnership, or corporation a complaint stating its charges in that respect, and containing a notice of a hearing upon a day and at a place therein fixed at least thirty days after the service of said complaint. The person, partnership, or corporation so complained of shall have the right to appear at the place and time so fixed and show cause why an order should not be entered by the commission requiring such person, partnership, or corporation to cease and desist from the violation of the law so charged in said complaint. . . . If upon such hearing the commission shall be of the opinion that the method of competition in question is prohibited by this Act, it shall make a report in writing in which it shall state its findings as to the facts, and shall issue and cause to be served on such person, partnership, or corporation an order requiring such person, partnership or corporation to cease and desist from using such method of competition. . . .

If such person, partnership, or corporation fails or neglects to obey such order of the commission while the same is in effect, the commission may apply to the circuit court of appeals of the United States, within any circuit where the method of competition in question was used or where such person, partnership, or corporation resides or carries on business, for the enforcement of its order. . . .

The findings of the commission as to the facts, if supported by testimony, shall be conclusive. . . .

Sec. 6.   That the commission shall also have the power—

(*a*) To gather and compile information concerning, and to investigate from time to time the organization, business, conduct, practices, and management of any corporation engaged in commerce, excepting banks and common carriers subject to the Act to regulate commerce. . . .

(*b*) To require, by general or special orders, corporations engaged in commerce to file with the commission in such form as the commission may prescribe annual or special reports or answers in writing to specific questions, furnishing to the commission such information as it may require. . . .

(*c*) Whenever a final decree has been entered against any defendant corporation in any suit brought by the United States to prevent and restrain any violation of the antitrust Acts, to make investigations, upon its own initiative, of the manner in which the decree has been or is being carried out, and upon the application of the Attorney General it shall be its duty to make such investigation.

(*d*) Upon the direction of the President or either House of Congress to investigate and report the facts relating to any alleged violations of the antitrust Acts by any corporation.

(*e*) Upon the application of the Attorney General, to investigate and make recommendations for the readjustment of the business of any corporation alleged to be violating the antitrust Acts, in order that the corporation may thereafter maintain its organization, management, and conduct of business in accordance with law.

(*f*) To make public from time to time such portions of the information obtained by it hereunder, except trade secrets and names of customers, as it shall deem expedient in the public interest; and to make annual and special reports to the Congress and to submit therewith recommendations for additional legislation; and to provide for the publication of its reports and decisions in such form and manner as may be best adapted for public information and use.

(*g*) From time to time to classify corporations and to make rules and regulations for the purpose of carrying out the provisions of this Act.

(*h*) To investigate, from time to time, trade conditions in and with foreign countries where associations, combinations, or practices of manufacturers, merchants, or traders, or other conditions, may affect the foreign trade of the United States, and to report to Congress thereon, with such recommendations as it deems advisable. . . .

Sec. 10. That any person who shall neglect or refuse to attend and testify, or to answer any lawful inquiry, or to produce documentary evidence, if in his power to do so, in obedience to the subpoena or lawful requirement of the commission, shall be guilty of an offense and upon conviction thereof by a court of competent jurisdiction shall be punished by a fine of not less than $1,000 nor more than $5,000, or by imprisonment for not more than one year, or by both such fine and imprisonment.

The Clayton Act (1915)

An Act to supplement existing laws against unlawful restraints and monopolies, and for other purposes.

Sec. 2. That it shall be unlawful for any person engaged in commerce, in the course of such commerce, either directly or indirectly, to discriminate in price between different purchasers of commodities, which commodities are sold for use, consumption, or resale within the United States or any Territory thereof or the District of Columbia or any insular possession or other place under the jurisdiction of the United States, where the effect of such discrimination *may be to substantially lessen competition or tend to create a monopoly in any line of commerce:* Provided, That nothing herein contained shall prevent discrimination in price between purchasers of commodities on account of differences in the grade, quality, or quantity of the commodity sold, or that makes only due allowance for differences in the cost of selling or transportation, or discrimination in price in the same or different communities made in good faith to meet competition: And provided further, That nothing herein contained shall prevent persons engaged in selling goods, wares, or merchandise in commerce from selecting their own customers in bona fide transactions and not in restraint of trade.

Sec. 3. That it shall be unlawful for any person engaged in commerce, in the course of such commerce, to lease or make a sale or contract for sale of goods, wares, merchandise, machinery, supplies, or other commodities, whether patented or unpatented, for use, consumption, or resale within the United States or any Territory thereof or the District of Columbia or any insular possession or other place under the jurisdiction of the United States, or fix a price charged therefor, or discount from, or rebate upon, such price, on the condition, agreement, or understanding that the lessee or purchaser thereof shall not use or deal in the goods, wares, merchandise, machinery, supplies, or other commodity of a competitor or competitors of the lessor or seller, where the effect of such lease, sale, or contract for sale or such condition, agreement, or understanding may be to substantially lessen competition or tend to create a monopoly in any line of commerce.

Note: Sections 4 and 5 provide, respectively, for triple damage suits by private injured parties and for final judgments in a suit brought by the government as being prima-facie evidence in private suits in the matters involved.

Sec. 6. That the labor of a human being is not a commodity or an article of commerce. Nothing contained in the antitrust laws shall be construed to forbid the existence and operation of labor, agricultural, or horticultural organizations, instituted for the purposes of mutual help, and not having capital stock or conducted for profits, or to forbid or restrain individual members of such organizations from lawfully carrying out the legitimate objects thereof; nor shall such organizations, or the members thereof, be held or construed to be illegal combinations or conspiracies in restraint of trade under the antitrust laws.

Sec. 7. That no corporation engaged in commerce shall acquire, directly or indirectly, the whole or any part of the stock or other share capital of another corporation engaged also in commerce where the effect of such acquisition may be to substantially lessen competition between the corporation whose stock is so acquired and the corporation making the acquisition or to restrain such commerce in any section or community or tend to create a monopoly of any line of commerce. . . .

Sec. 8. . . . That from and after two years from the date of the approval of this Act no person at the same time shall be a director in any two or more corporations, any one of which has capital, surplus, and undivided profits aggregating more than $1,000,000, engaged in whole or in part in commerce, other than banks, banking associations, trust companies, and common carriers subject to the Act to regulate commerce, approved February fourth, eighteen hundred and eighty-seven, if such corporations are or shall have been theretofore, by virtue of their business and location of operation, competitors, so that the elimination of competition by agreement between them would constitute a violation of any of the provisions of any of the antitrust laws. . . .

Sec. 11. That authority to enforce compliance with sections two, three, seven, and eight of this Act by the persons respectively subject thereto is hereby vested: in the Interstate Commerce Commission where applicable to common carriers, in the Federal Reserve Board where applicable to banks, banking associations, and trust companies, and in the Federal Trade Commission where applicable to all other character of commerce. . . .

Sec. 14. That whenever a corporation shall violate any of the penal provisions of the antitrust laws, such violation shall be deemed to be also that of the individual directors, officers, or agents of such corporation who shall have authorized, ordered, or done any of the acts constituting in whole or in part such violation, and such violation shall be deemed a misdemeanor, and upon conviction therefor of any such director, officer, or agent he shall be punished by a fine of not exceeding $5,000 or by imprisonment for not exceeding one year, or by both, in the discretion of the court.

Sec. 15. That the several district courts of the United States are hereby invested with jurisdiction to prevent and restrain violations of this Act, and it shall be the duty of the several district attorneys of the United States, in their respective districts, under the direction of the Attorney General, to institute proceedings in equity to prevent and restrain such violations. . . .

Robinson-Patman Amendment to the Clayton Act (1936)

An Act to amend section 2 of the Act entitled "An Act to supplement existing laws against unlawful restraints and monopolies, and for other purposes," approved October 15, 1914, as amended (U.S.C., title 15, sec. 13), and for other purposes.

Be it enacted by the Senate and House of Representatives of the United States of America in Congress assembled, That section 2 of the Act entitled "An Act to supplement existing laws against unlawful restraints and monopolies, and for other purposes" approved October 15, 1914, as amended (U.S.C., title 15, sec. 13), is amended to read as follows:

"Sec. 2. (a) That it shall be unlawful for any person engaged in commerce, in the course of such commerce, either directly or indirectly, to discriminate in price between different purchasers of commodities of like grade and quality, where either of any of the purchases involved in such discrimination are in commerce, where such commodities are sold for use, consumption, or resale within the United States, or any Territory thereof or the District of Columbia or any insular possession or other place under the jurisdiction of the United States, and where the effect of such discrimination may be substantially to lessen competition or tend to create a monopoly in any line of commerce, or to injure, destroy, or prevent competition with any person who either grants or knowingly receives the benefit of such discrimination, or with customers of either of them: Provided, That nothing herein contained shall prevent differentials which make only due allowance for differences in the cost of manufacture, sale, or delivery resulting from the differing methods or quantities in which such commodities are to such purchasers sold or delivered: Provided, however, That the Federal Trade Commission may, after due investigation and hearing to all interested parites, fix and establish quantity limits, and revise the same as it finds necessary, as to particular commodities or classes of commodities, where it finds that available purchasers in greater quantities are so few to render differentials on account thereof unjustly discriminatory or promotive of monopoly in any line of commerce; and the foregoing shall then not be construed to permit differentials based on differences in quantities greater than those so fixed and established: And provided further, That nothing herein contained shall prevent persons engaged in selling goods, wares, or merchandise in commerce from selecting their own customers in bona fide transactions and not in restraint of trade: And provided further, That nothing herein contained shall prevent price changes from time to time where in response to changing conditions affecting the market for or the marketability of the goods concerned, such as but not limited to actual or imminent deterioration of perishable goods, obsolescence of seasonal goods, distress sales under the court process, or sales in good faith in discontinuance of business in the goods concerned.

"(b) Upon proof being made, at any hearing on a complaint under this section, that there has been discrimination in price or services or facilities furnished, the burden of rebutting the prima-facie case thus made by showing justification shall be upon the person charged with a violation of this section, and unless justification shall be affirmatively shown, the Commission is authorized to issue an order terminating the discrimination: Provided, however, That nothing herein contained shall prevent a seller rebutting the prima-facie case thus made by showing that his lower price or the furnishing of services or facilities to any purchaser or purchasers was made in good faith to meet an equally low price of a competitor, or the services or facilities furnished by a competitor.

"(c) That it shall be unlawful for any person engaged in commerce, in the course of such commerce, to pay or grant, or to receive or accept, anything of value as a commission, brokerage, or other compensation, or any allowance or discount in lieu thereof, except for services rendered in connection with the sale or purchase of goods, wares, or merchandise, either to the other party to such transaction or to an agent, representative, or other intermediary therein where such intermediary is acting in fact for or in behalf, or is subject to the direct or indirect control, of any party to such transaction other than the person by whom such compensation is so granted or paid.

"(d) That it shall be unlawful for any person engaged in commerce to pay or contract for the payment of anything of value to or for the benefit of a customer of such person in the course of such commerce as compensation or in consideration for any services or the processing, handling, sale, or offering for sale of any products or commodities manufactured, sold, or offered for sale by such person, unless such payment or consideration is available on proportionally equal terms to all other customers competing in the distribution of such products or commodities.

"(e) That it shall be unlawful for any person to discriminate in favor of one purchaser against another purchaser or purchasers of a commodity bought for resale, with or without processing, by contracting to furnish or furnishing, or by contributing to the furnishing of, any services or facilities connected with the processing, handling, sale, or offering for sale of such commodity so purchased upon terms not accorded to all purchasers on proportionally equal terms.

"(f) That it shall be unlawful for any person engaged in commerce, in the course of such commerce, knowingly to induce or receive a discrimination in price which is prohibited by this section."

Note: Section 3 of the act, which has not been used, prohibits regional price discrimination for the purpose of "destroying competition or eliminating a competitor."

Wheeler-Lea Amendment to the Federal Trade Commission Act (1938)

To amend the Act creating the Federal Trade Commission, to define its powers and duties, and for other purposes.

Sec. 3. Section 5 of such Act, as amended (U.S.C., 1934 ed., title 15, sec. 45), is hereby amended to read as follows:

"*Sec. 5.* (*a*) Unfair methods of competition in commerce, and unfair or deceptive acts or practices in commerce, are hereby declared unlawful."

Sec. 4. Such Act is further amended by adding at the end thereof new sections to read as follows:

"*Sec. 12.* (*a*) It shall be unlawful for any person, partnership, or corporation to disseminate, or cause to be disseminated, any false advertisement—

"(1) By United States mails, or in commerce by any other means, for the purpose of inducing, or which is likely to induce, directly or indirectly, the purchase in commerce of food, drugs, devices, or cosmetics, or (2) By any means, for the purpose of inducing, or which is likely to induce, directly or indirectly, the purchase in commerce of food, drugs, devices, or cosmetics.

"(*b*) The dissemination or the causing to be disseminated of any false advertisement within the provisions of subsection (*a*) of this section shall be an unfair or deceptive act or practice in commerce within the meaning of section 5."

Antimerger Amendment of 1950

To amend an Act entitled "An Act to supplement existing laws against unlawful restraints and monopolies, and for other purposes," approved October 15, 1914 (38 Stat. 730), as amended.

Be it enacted by the Senate and House of Representatives of the United States of America in Congress assembled. That sections 7 and 11 of an Act entitled "An Act to supplement existing laws against unlawful restraints and monopolies, and for other purposes," approved October 15, 1914, as amended (U.S.C., title 15, secs. 18 and 21), are hereby amended to read as follows:

"No corporation shall acquire, directly or indirectly, the whole or any part of the stock or other share capital and no corporation subject to the jurisdiction of the Federal Trade Commission shall acquire the whole or any part of the assets of one or more corporations engaged in commerce, where in any line of commerce in any section of the country, the effect of such acquisition, of such stocks or assets, or of the use of such stock by the voting or granting of proxies or otherwise, may be substantially to lessen competition, or to tend to create a monopoly. . . ."

AN ANTITRUST CHRONOLOGY

The pitfalls in any brief chronology are many: Any selection of particular events as noteworthy leaves out others with almost equal claim; important developments span many years with no definite cutoff points; the division of time into one set of "periods" is unlikely to be unique partly because the various currents influencing the history do not ebb and flow together. A chronological framework known to be somewhat inadequate, nevertheless, is better than none. The value of some knowledge of sequence for an orderly consideration of the antitrust problem is great.

Our outline distinguishes four major periods since the enactment of the Sherman Antitrust Law in 1890. The period 1890–1902 was one in which minimum efforts to enforce the Sherman Act proved almost totally inadequate to cope with the peak of the combination movement; 1903–20 was a period of supplementary legislation and "trust-busting" efforts which were largely terminated with the adverse decision in the Steel case in 1920; 1920–37 was a period of boom and bust with little government interference with a second wave of mergers in the prosperous twenties and an almost total cessation of antitrust action under the price-fixing activities of the NRA; 1938 to date has been a period of resurgence in antitrust activity (outside of the war years), with provocative attempts by judges, administrators, and economists to forge satisfactory economic and legal standards. The four periods represent two swings in antitrust activity from little to more.

Before the Sherman Act

1776 Adam Smith's *Wealth of Nations* published, with its strong attack on monopolies, particularly those buttressed by government action.

1837 Start of wave of general incorporation acts by states, paving way for large-scale business organizations.

1859 First integrated steel mill, one step in technological revolution proceeding throughout nineteenth century.

1873 First year of depression of the 1870's with its encouragement of the Granger and Populist movements which were active in drive against "monopoly."

1879 "Trust" form devised by Standard Oil, widely used in 1880's; frequently used commencement date for "early merger" movement, 1879-96.

1884 Antitrust plank in Democratic platform.

1887 Interstate Commerce Act to regulate railroad "monopolies."

1887 Wave of antitrust laws in agrarian states (1887-90).

1888 New Jersey act permitting unrestricted intercorporate stockholding and thus the "holding company"—a big step in the competitive liberalization of corporate charters by the states.

1890–1902: Peak of Corporate Combination Movement despite Sherman Act

1890   Sherman Act passed with but one dissenting vote. Only eighteen prosecutions under it through 1901.

1895   *United States* v. *E. C. Knight Co.,* 156 U.S. 1. Sherman Act held not applicable to firm controlling 98 per cent of sugar refining on ground that manufacture was not interstate commerce.

1895   *In re Debs,* 158 U.S. 564. Labor unions included under Sherman Act.

1899   *United States* v. *Trans-Missouri Freight Association,* 166 U.S. 290. Railroad price-fixing agreement held illegal on ground that Sherman Act applied to every restraint.

1899   *United States* v. *Addystone Pipe & Steel Co.,* 75 U.S. 211. Pooling agreement by pipe manufacturers invalid. First really successful application of act to a manufacturer. Probably encouraged mergers by indicating that pools were illegal.

1901   Formation of United States Steel. "A combination of combinations" with capitalization of $1.4 billion (about half was "water"). Climax of 1890–1904 merger movement leading to more than three hundred combinations with combined capitalizations of $7 billion.

1903–20: Some "Trust Busting," but Basic Corporate Structure Unchanged

1903   Bureau of Corporations set up under Roosevelt for "diligent investigation . . . into business of any corporation or corporate combination." Antitrust Division established in Department of Justice.

1904   *Northern Securities Co.* v. *United States,* 193 U.S. 197. First "trust" (holding company for Northern Pacific and Great Northern railroads) broken up.

1904   Ida M. Tarbell's *History of the Standard Oil Company* published in *McClure's Magazine.* First decade of the twentieth century has been called "the era of the muckrakers" with its many popular exposés of monopolistic abuses, political corruption, etc.

1904   Introduction of suits against the American Tobacco and Standard Oil combinations.

1908   *Loewe* v. *Lawlor,* 208 U.S. 274 (Danbury Hatters case). The hat manufacturers recovered treble damages ($220,000) from a boycotting union.

1905   *United States* v. *Swift & Co.,* 196 U.S. 375. Injunction against market sharing, and quota and price-fixing agreements, against large meat packers.

1911   *United States* v. *Standard Oil Co. of New Jersey,* 221 U.S. 1; *United States* v. *American Tobacco Co.,* 211 U.S. 106. Two combinations with long records of predatory practices dissolved in "rule of reason" cases. The du Pont explosives combination was dissolved a few months later by a circuit court. Prosecution of United States Steel and United Shoe Machinery combinations started.

1912   Wilson elected; stressed antitrust action as part of the "New Freedom." The defeated Roosevelt on Progressive ticket favored continuous government regulation of "big business" rather than antitrust suits looking toward dissolution.

1913   Opening of Ford Motor Company Highland Park plant. Its assembly line methods represent a climax in the move toward mass production in the twentieth century.

1914   Passage of the Federal Trade Commission and Clayton acts aimed at "unfair competition" and incipient monopoly. Former act established the Federal Trade Commission.

1918   Webb-Pomerene Act passed. It constituted a major exemption from antitrust laws by exempting export associations.

1918   *United States* v. *United Shoe Machinery Co.,* 227 U.S. 202. Major setback for government in suit against firm with about 95 per cent of market. Ruling stated power was not "oppressively used."

1919   *United States* v. *Swift & Co. et al.,* consent decree in the Supreme Court of the District of Columbia, February 27, 1920. Meat packers disposed of interest in public stockyards and grocery products. In 1959, companies were seeking relief from provisions keeping them out of other grocery lines.

1920   *United States* v. *United States Steel Corp.,* 251 U.S. 417. Government dissolution suit failed by four-to-three Supreme Court vote. Seemed to legalize any merger short of complete monopoly as long as firm is innocent of predatory practices at time of prosecution (the "abuse theory").

1920   Harding elected with promise of "return to normalcy."

1920   *Federal Trade Commission* v. *Gratz,* 253 U.S. 421. Courts, not commission, must ultimately determine what are "unfair methods of competition" prescribed by Federal Trade Commission Act.

1921–37: Antitrust to the Background—Business First Too Good and Then Too Bad

1921   Three unsuccessful cases under Section 7 of the Clayton Act, 272 U.S. 554, which proved useless against the secondary wave of mergers in the prosperous 1920's.

1922   *United Shoe Machinery Corp.* v. *United States,* 258 U.S. 451. Clayton Act invoked successfully against tying agreements.

1925   *Maple Flooring Manufacturers' Association* v. *United States,* 268 U.S. 563; *Cement Manufacturers' Protective Association* v. *United States,* 268 U.S. 606. Two decisions indicating that the rapidly increasing group of trade associations had considerable latitude in the exchange of price information which fell short of price fixing.

1927   *United States* v. *International Harvester Co.,* 274 U.S. 693. Restatement of Steel case thesis that "mere size" or "unexerted power" (65 per cent of market) is not an offense.

1927   *United States* v. *Trenton Potteries Co. et al.*, 273 U.S. 392. Classic state-
       ment that a combination to fix prices is illegal per se, regardless of
       reasonableness of prices. Together with Harvester case above, the de-
       cision indicates well the contrast between the application of the Sher-
       man Act to "loose-knit" rather than "close-knit" combinations.
1929   Stock market crash. Start of the Great Depression which later had the
       effect of cutting down restrictions on business co-operation.
1932   A. A. Berle and Gardiner C. Means, *The Modern Corporation and
       Private Property,* created a new awareness of economic concentration
       as a problem area with finding that two hundred largest corporations
       controlled half of corporate wealth.
1933   Passage of the National Industrial Recovery Act. Section 5 provided
       exemption from antitrust laws for codes and agreements under the act.
       Practical effect was a virtual suspension for all business of antitrust
       laws from 1933 to 1935.
1933   E. H. Chamberlin's *Theory of Monopolistic Competition* published.
       Wide acceptance among economists because of its recognition that most
       markets contained both monopolistic and competitive elements.
1935   *Schechter Brothers* v. *United States,* 295 U.S. 495. The NIRA was de-
       clared illegal in the "chicken" case involving a local business violating
       the poultry code.
1936   Robinson-Patman Act passed—an amendment strengthening Section 2
       of the Clayton Act (price discrimination).
1937   Miller-Tydings Act passed, exempting retail price-fixing agreements
       under the states' "fair-trade" laws from the antitrust laws.

1938 to Date: Antitrust Enforcement Activities at a Peak Aided by Some Broader Interpretations of the Laws

1938   Thurman Arnold appointed Assistant Attorney General to head the
       Antitrust Division. Division embarks on stepped-up program including
       industry-wide attacks. Start of case against Alcoa.
1938   Temporary National Economic Committee, with Congressional and
       executive members, set up to make "full . . . study [of] . . . concentra-
       tion of economic power in . . . production and distribution."
1938   Wheeler-Lea Act, amending the Federal Trade Commission Act, to
       prohibit "unfair or deceptive acts or practices."
1940   *United States* v. *Socony-Vacuum Oil Co.,* 310 U.S. 150. The illegality of
       collusive price fixing is extended to a scheme by major oil refiners to
       purchase "distress" gasoline.
1942   Statute allowing certificates of immunity to firms in war production.
       Chairman of War Production Board granted such certificates, giving
       broad exemption from antitrust action.
1945   Alcoa case (*United States* v. *Aluminum Co. of America,* 148 F. [2d]
       416). Alcoa found guilty of Section 2 (monopolizing) violation on
       basis of market control and acts to exclude competitors.
1945   *Hartford-Empire Co.* v. *United States,* 323 U.S. 386. Supreme Court
       ruled that patent-pooling arrangement used to monopolize the glass

container industry was illegal and required compulsory licensing of patents.

1946   *American Tobacco Co.* v. *United States,* 328 U.S. 781. Emphasized the power to exclude competitors and "community of interest" of "Big Three" cigarette companies in finding of a Section 2 violation.

1948   Federal Trade Commission report, *The Merger Movement,* published. Noted with concern new merger movement from 1940 to 1947.

1948   *Federal Trade Commission* v. *Cement Institute,* 333 U.S. 683. Collusive use of basing-point pricing held illegal under the Federal Trade Commission Act.

1948   *United States* v. *Paramount Pictures,* 334 U.S. 131. Divestiture of theater holdings ordered for major motion-picture distributors.

1948   *United States* v. *Columbia Steel Co.,* 334 U.S. 495. United States Steel's acquisition of the assets of Consolidated Steel Co., a West Coast fabricator, was upheld in a four-to-three decision against Sherman Act charges. Decision seemed to have influence in getting Congress to amend Clayton Act to meet asset acquisitions.

1948   *Federal Trade Commission* v. *Morton Salt Co.,* 334 U.S. 37. A "per se" decision against price discrimination which raised controversy over its ruling that the government had only to show a "possibility" of injuring competition.

1949   *Standard Oil of California* v. *United States,* 337 U.S. 293. This Standard Stations case seemed to indicate that all exclusive-dealing agreements involving a "substantial" amount of commerce were illegal.

1950   Antimerger amendment of 1950 which amended the Clayton Act's Section 7 to include mergers by acquiring assets as well as stock to close a notable loophole in the antitrust laws.

1952   First case under the new antimerger amendment brought against Pillsbury Mills for acquiring Ballard & Ballard Co. and Duff's Baking Division of American Home Products (FTC Docket 6000).

1952   Passage of the McGuire Act, which again permitted antitrust action for price-maintenance agreements in "fair-trade" states.

1953   Consent decree accepted by Great Atlantic & Pacific Tea Company, one of some 150 such decrees since 1938. Government had won criminal case, a widely criticized victory since many of the practices complained of seemed to benefit consumers.

1953   *United States* v. *United Shoe Machinery,* 110 F. Supp. 295 (U.S. District Court for Massachusetts). District court judge applied doctrine of Alcoa case to practices such as insistence on lease and service contracts for shoe machines which had been held legal in three previous cases against the company.

1955   FTC published guides for staff use in evaluating cigarette advertising after conferences with producers concerning standards.

1956   Six major consent decrees were announced in four weeks in January and February. Sherman Act (Section 2) cases included *United States* v. *Western Electric and A. T. & T.* (U.S. District Court for New Jersey, January 25, 1956); *United States* v. *International Business Machines Corp.* (U.S. District Court for Southern New York, January 25, 1956).

In both cases, compulsory licensing was required on substantially all patents. The first two settlements under Section 7 of Clayton Act were consent decrees: *United States* v. *Hilton Hotels Corp. and Statler Hotels (Del.) Corp.* (U.S. District Court for Northern Illinois, February 6, 1956); *United States* v. *General Shoe Corp.* (U.S. District Court for Middle Tennessee, February 17, 1956). Hilton was requested to sell three hotels; both accepted limitations on future acquisitions.

1956 *United States* v. *E. I. du Pont de Nemours & Co.,* 351 U.S. 377. Government lost Sherman Act (Section 2) case when Supreme Court, by four-to-three decision, upheld district court opinion that du Pont did not monopolize relevant market for "flexible wrapping materials."

1956 *Standard Oil Co.* v. *Federal Trade Commission,* 233 F. (2d) 649. Circuit court judge ruled that Standard had valid "good faith meeting of competition" defense for price discrimination in the late 1930's. This leading case under Section 2 (*b*) of Robinson-Patman Amendment to Clayton Act had been under litigation since 1940.

1957 *United States* v. *E. I. du Pont de Nemours et al.,* 353 U.S. 586. Government won split decision against 23 per cent acquisition of General Motors stock by du Pont in 1917 under Section 7 of Clayton Act, on the ground that competition may be substantially lessened in the automobile finishes and fabric market.

1958 *United States* v. *District Court* permanently enjoined proposed merger between Bethlehem Steel and Youngstown Sheet & Tube (U.S. District Court for Southern District of New York, November 21, 1958). Companies announced no appeal early in 1959.

1961 Government won criminal price conspiracy case against twenty-nine electrical equipment manufacturers. Seven executives served jail sentences. Consent decrees were reached in accompanying civil cases in 1961 and 1962.

1962 *United States* v. *Brown Shoe Co.,* 370 U.S. 294. First Supreme Court ruling on amended Section 7 of Clayton Act, required Brown Shoe Company to divest itself of stock and assets of G. R. Kinney Company, principally a shoe retailer.

QUESTIONS

1. What are the major antitrust laws, and what is barred under each? Which are concerned with corporate power?

2. What procedures are available under the antitrust laws? What advantage is there in a civil suit under the Sherman Act? What is a consent decree?

CASE 16–1: THE CELLOPHANE CASE

E. I. du Pont de Nemours & Co., in 1956, ranked as the leading domestic producer of commercial explosives, dyes, cellophane and nylon, and was one of the leaders in the production of rayon, finishes, pigments, plastics, heavy chemicals, and refrigerants. The company earned a net income of $431,555,884 with sales of $1,909,197,444 in 1955. (Dividends on du Pont's holdings of General Motors stock were about 20 per cent of before-tax income.) Du Pont was the defendant in a suit charging monopolization of cellophane manufacture and sale which was heard by the Supreme Court in October, 1955. Decision for the company was announced in June, 1956.

In 1923, du Pont and La Cellophane, a subsidiary of a French company which was the sole manufacturer of cellophane, organized an American company for the manufacture of cellophane. Du Pont received the exclusive rights to make and sell cellophane under the patents and secret processes of the French company in North and Central America. Du Pont bought the minority 48 per cent stock interest of La Cellophane in the subsidiary in 1929 in exchange for stock valued at $90 million.

Du Pont embarked on a program of product improvement, price reduction, and output expansion in which the 1924 production of 361,249 pounds sold at an average price of $2.508 increased to 202,826,066 pounds sold at an average price of $0.490 in 1950. The most important product improvement was through a basic patent covering moisture-proof cellophane developed by 1927. Substantial expenditures on technical activities, including process and quality improvement, continued and amounted to $2,782,706 in 1950.

From 1925 to 1928, imports from a new Belgian plant of Societe Industrielle de la Cellulose (SIDAC) amounted to as much as 24 per cent of the market, but a rise in tariffs in which du Pont was influential prevented imports from again being an important factor. SIDAC, however, established an American competitor, the Sylvania Industrial Corporation, which completed a plant in Virginia in 1930. Du Pont regarded Sylvania's process for producing moistureproof cellophane as an infringement and brought suit. The settlement agreed upon gave Sylvania a nonexclusive license on basic patents for a royalty of 2 per cent of net cellophane sales under the patents. Provision for the cross-licensing of future patents was made. But the settlement also provided that Sylvania should pay a penalty royalty of 20 cents a pound if its production exceeded 20 per cent of total moistureproof cellophane sales. This percentage was to rise by a per cent a year until it reached 29 per cent in 1942. Sylvania never reached the quota and averaged about 23 per cent of the market from 1933 to 1945. This share increased only by 1 per cent after the expiration of the agreement in 1945 and the sale of Sylvania to American Viscose in 1946.

After the antitrust suit was filed in 1947, du Pont actively sought out another firm to enter the field with its technical assistance and found a willing entrant in Olin Industries. After Olin's plant went into production in 1951, du Pont's share of celophane capacity was reduced to about 68 per cent.

The Antitrust Suit

The United States filed a complaint against du Pont in December, 1947, charging du Pont with monopolizing, attempting to monopolize, and conspiracy to monopolize interstate commerce in cellophane, all violations of Section 2 of the Sherman Act. The suit, a civil one, sought relief by injunction and by actions such as divestiture to dissipate the effect of monopolization. On du Pont's motion the case was transferred from the District of Columbia to the District of Delaware.

Judge Leahy's decision for the District Court was a lengthy one, winnowing out some 854 findings of fact out of 7,500 pages of testimony and 7,000 exhibits. He found for the defendants, and the government appealed the decision to the Supreme Court. After hearing the case in October, 1955, the Supreme Court, in a four-to-three decision, sustained the District Court in an opinion handed down on June 11, 1956.

The Strategies of the Two Contenders

The government's basic strategy was a simple one. It sought to show that du Pont had a dominant enough position in cellophane to constitute a monopoly with the power to control prices and exclude competitors. It counted on the 75 per cent plus share of the market plus the restrictions on the only other producer to establish this dominance. It felt amply prepared to demonstrate that this dominance was not "thrust upon du Pont" but was actively enough sought to constitute "monopolizing." The latter step could be well documented by du Pont's maneuvers in getting and protecting exclusive rights in the U.S. market.

Du Pont's strategy was to swamp the government's case in market facts and to "demonstrate that du Pont cellophane is sold under such competitive conditions that acquisition of market control or monopoly power is a practical impossibility." It aimed at showing that du Pont was competing in a broader market, "the flexible packaging materials market." Under the able legal leadership of Gerhard A. Gesell, it made an all-out effort to gather market evidence, spending in excess of $1 million for information on the customers of packaging converters.

How well du Pont's approach worked is shown by the District Court's opinion:

"Market setting" in which cellophane is sold was fully developed at trial. Evidence was of a most practical type. Defendant did not rely on economic theory but rested its proof on testimony of independent businessmen engaged in various aspects of the flexible packaging business. Not a single market witness was called by the Government. Defendant presented testimony of competing manufacturers, from large and small converters, and from users of packaging materials located in different parts of the country and engaged in different lines of business. This evidence was supplemented by a market survey, by studies from trade associations, by reports of du Pont's own salesmen, by physical samples of materials and wraps, by testimony of company officials concerned with competitive problems, and by reference to extensive documentation in reliable trade journals and authoritative texts. I attended in Atlantic City together with counsel for both sides the Annual Packaging Show in April, 1952 to see the manner in which these materials are offered to the trade.

Market evidence is complete. Defendant has showed a detailed development of evidence to bring before me an appreciation of the intense competition existing in the flexible packaging markets, and an understanding of the business considerations which motivated du Pont in the various steps it took to develop cellophane. . . .

Much of the flavor of du Pont's case is caught in the findings cited in the majority opinion of the Supreme Court reproduced below, but it is worth noting other evidence at this point. For example, other packaging manufacturers testified along these lines:

Vice President of Rhinelander, a large glassine manufacturer: "Cellophane is the product with which Rhinelander's products compete most directly and is Rhinelander's most annoying competitor."

Frederick S. Leinbach, Riegel Paper Corporation:

There is a terrific competition now going on in bread and in the bake field, cakes, and I mentioned before, potato chips; the snack specialty field, of which Fritos [indicating] are an example. It is all the time in a state of flux; we lose them, we get them back. The same thing happens with cellophane. Frankly, almost any one of these barrier jobs here is a competing point, as you see. Even in cereal we have to compete with cellophane because a fellow can put his stuff up in a duplex cellophane bag or a waxed paper barrier of some sort. It is a choice he has to make.

The theme that paper and glassine manufacturers were able to strike back was also developed in an analysis of the candy market. Curtiss had gone to cellophane for its "Baby Ruth" bars in the early 1930's. "Within one to two years Curtiss shifted back to a glassine outer wrapper at the insistence of the Sales Division, because the wrapper, particularly in the case of the Baby Ruth bars, had become so well associated with the bar that customers and retailers complained of the change." And later: "The improvements in wax paper and glassine have affected their acceptability to Curtiss as packaging mediums and caused Curtiss to continue using them."

The case was finally decided upon du Pont's contention that the relevant market was that for "flexible packaging materials" rather than that for cellophane alone. The Supreme Court's opinion conceded that "if cellophane is the 'market' that du Pont is found to dominate, it may be assumed that it does have monopoly power over that market" but that "there is no cellophane market separate and distinct from the market for flexible packaging materials."

The Opinion of the Court[25]

. . . If cellophane is the "market" that du Pont is found to dominate, it may be assumed it does have monopoly power over that "market." Monopoly power is the power to control prices or exclude competition. It seems apparent that du Pont's power to set the price of cellophane has been limited only by the competition afforded by other flexible packaging materials. Moreover, it may be practically impossible for anyone to commence manufacturing cellophane without full access to du Pont's technique. However, du Pont has no power to prevent competition from other wrapping materials. The trial court consequently had to determine whether competition from the other wrappings prevented du Pont from possessing monopoly power in violation of Section 2. Price and competition are so initimately entwined that any discussion of theory must treat them as one. It is inconceivable that price could be controlled without power over competition or vice versa. This approach to the determination of monopoly power is strengthened by this Court's conclusion in prior cases that, when an alleged monopolist has power over price and competition, an intention to monopolize in a proper case may be assumed.

If a large number of buyers and sellers deal freely in a standardized product, such as salt or wheat, we have complete or pure competition. Patents, on the other hand, furnish the most familiar type of classic monopoly. As the producers of a standardized product bring about significant differentiations of quality, design, or packaging in the product that permit differences of use, competition becomes to a greater or less degree incomplete and the producer's power over price and competition greater over his article and its use, according to the differentiation he is able to create and maintain. A retail seller may have in one sense a monopoly on certain trade because of location, as an isolated country

---

[25]*United States* v. *E. I. du Pont de Nemours & Co.,* 351 U.S. 377 (1956). Mr. Justice Reed, with whom Mr. Justice Minton and Mr. Justice Burton joined, gave the opinion. Mr. Justice Frankfurter concurred in "the conclusion that cellophane . . . was a part of the relevant market for flexible packaging materials." The opinion is reproduced in full, except for deletions of introductory material, some references, footnotes, and part of the Appendix.

store or filling station, or because no one else makes a product of just the quality or attractiveness of his product, as for example in cigarettes. Thus one can theorize that we have monopolistic competition in every nonstandardized commodity with each manufacturer having power over the price and production of his own product. However, this power that, let us say, automobile or soft-drink manufacturers have over their trademarked products is not the power that makes an illegal monopoly. Illegal power must be appraised in terms of the competitive market for the product.

Determination of the competitive market for commodities depends on how different from one another are the offered commodities in character or use, how far buyers will go to substitute one commodity for another. For example, one can think of building materials as in commodity competition but one could hardly say that brick competed with steel or wood or cement or stone in the meaning of Sherman Act litigation; the products are too different. This is the interindustry competition emphasized by some economists. On the other hand, there are certain differences in the formulae for soft drinks but one can hardly say that each one is an illegal monopoly. Whatever the market may be, we hold that control of price or competition establishes the existence of monopoly power under Section 2. Section 2 requires the application of a reasonable approach in determining the existence of monopoly power just as surely as did Section 1. This of course does not mean that there can be a reasonable monopoly. Our next step is to determine whether du Pont has monopoly power over cellophane: that is, power over its price in relation to or competition with other commodities. The charge was monopolization of cellophane. The defense, that cellophane was merely a part of the relevant market for flexible packaging materials.

When a product is controlled by one interest, without substitutes available in the market, there is monopoly power. Because most products have possible substitutes, we cannot, as we said in *Time-Picayune Co.* v. *United States,* 345 U.S. 594, 612, give "that infinite range" to the definition of substitutes. Nor is it a proper interpretation of the Sherman Act to require that products be fungible to be considered in the relevant market.

The Government argues:

"We do not here urge that in *no* circumstances may competition of substitutes negate possession of monopolistic power over trade in a product. The decisions make it clear at the least that the courts will not consider substitutes other than those which are substantially fungible with the monopolized product and sell at substantially the same price."

But where there are market alternatives that buyers may readily use for their purposes, illegal monopoly does not exist merely because the product said to be monopolized differs from others. If it were not so, only physically identical products would be a part of the market. To accept the Government's argument, we would have to conclude that the manufacturers of plain as well as moisture-proof cellophane were monopolists, and so with films such as Pliofilm, foil, glassine, polyethylene, and Saran, for each of these wrapping materials is distinguishable. These were all exhibits in the case. New wrappings appear, generally similar to cellophane: is each a monopoly? What is called for is an appraisal of the "cross-elasticity" of demand in the trade. The varying circumstances of each case determine the result. In considering what is the relevant market for determining the control of price and competition, no more definite rule can be declared than that commodities reasonably interchangeable by consumers for the same purposes make up that "part of the trade or commerce," monopolization of which may be illegal. As respects flexible packaging materials, the market geographically is nationwide.

Industrial activities cannot be confined to trim categories. Illegal monopolies under Section 2 may well exist over limited products in narrow fields where competition is eliminated. That does not settle the issue here. In determining the market under the Sherman Act, it is the use or uses to which the commodity is put that control. The selling price between commodities with similar uses and different characteristics may vary, so that the cheaper product can drive out the more expensive. Or, the superior quality of higher priced articles may make dominant the more desirable. Cellophane costs more than many competing products and less than a few. But whatever the price, there are various flexible wrapping materials that are bought by manufacturers for packaging their goods in their own plants or are sold to converters who shape and print them for use in the packaging of the commodities to be wrapped.

Cellophane differs from other flexible packaging materials. From some it differs more than from others. The basic materials from which the wrappings are made and the advantages and disadvantages of the products to the packaging industry are summarized in Findings 62 and 63. They are aluminum, cellulose acetate, chlorides, wood pulp, rubber hydrochloride, and ethylene gas. It will adequate illustrate the similarity in characteristics of the various products by noting here Finding 63 as to glassine. Its use is almost as extensive as cellophane, and many of its characteristics equally or more satisfactory to users.[26]

It may be admitted that cellophane combines the desirable elements of transparency, strength and cheapness more definitely than any of the others. Comparative characteristics have been noted thus:

"Moistureproof cellophane is highly transparent, tears readily but has high bursting strength, is highly impervious to moisture and gasses, and is resistant to grease and oils. Heat sealable, printable, and adapted to use on wrapping machines, it makes an excellent packaging material for both display and protection of commodities.

---

[26]"63.   There are respects in which other flexible packaging materials are as satisfactory as cellophane:

Glassine.

"Glassine is, in some types, about 90% transparent, so printing is legible through it.

"Glassine affords low cost transparency.

"Moisture protection afforded by waxed or lacquered glassine is as good as that of moistureproof cellophane.

"Glassine has greater resistance to tearing and breaking than cellophane.

"Glassine can be printed faster than cellophane, and can be run faster than moistureproof cellophane on bag machines.

"Glassine has greater resistance than cellophane to rancidity-introducing ultraviolet rays.

"Glassine has dimensional stability superior to cellophane.

"Glassine is more durable in cold weather than cellophane.

"Printed glassine can be sold against cellophane on the basis of appearance.

"Glassine may be more easily laminated than cellophane.

"Glassine is cheaper than cellophane in some types, comparable in others.

"Glassine runs on packaging machinery with ease equal to that of cellophane."

"Other flexible wrapping materials fall into four major categories: (1) Opaque nonmoistureproof wrapping *paper* designed primarily for convenience and protection in handling packages; (2) moistureproof *films* of varying degrees of transparency designed primarily either to protect, or to display and protect, the products they encompass; (3) nonmoistureproof transparent *films* designed primarily to display and to some extent protect, but which obviously do a poor protecting job where exclusion or retention of moisture is important; and (4) moistureproof *materials* other than films of varying degrees of transparency (foils and paper products) designed to protect and display."[27]

An examination of Finding 59, Appendix B, will make this clear.

But despite cellophane's advantage, it has to meet competition from other materials in every one of its uses. Cellophane's principal uses are analyzed in Appendix A. Food products are the chief outlet, with cigarettes next. The Government makes no challenge to Finding 283 that cellophane furnishes less than 7% of wrappings for bakery products, 25% for candy, 32% for snacks, 35% for meats and poultry, 27% for crackers and biscuits, 47% for fresh produce, and 24% for frozen foods. Seventy-five to eighty per cent of cigarettes are wrapped in cellophane. Thus, cellophane shares the packaging market with others. The over-all result is that cellophane accounts for 17.9% of flexible wrapping materials, measured by the wrapping surface. Finding 280. Appendix A.

Moreover a very considerable degree of functional interchangeability exists between these products, as is shown by the tables of Appendix A and Findings 150–278. It will be noted, Appendix B, that except as to permeability to gases, cellophane has no qualities that are not possessed by a number of other materials. Meat will do as an example of interchangeability. Although du Pont's sales to the meat industry have reached 19,000,000 pounds annually, nearly 35%, this volume is attributed "to the rise of self-service retailing of fresh meat." Findings 212 and 283. In fact, since the popularity of self-service meats, du Pont has lost "a considerable proportion" of this packaging business to Pliofilm. Pliofilm is more expensive than cellophane, but its superior physical characteristics apparently offset cellophane's price advantage. While retailers shift continually between the two, the trial court found that Pliofilm is increasing its share of the business. One further example is worth noting. Before World War II, du Pont cellophane wrapped between 5 and 10% of baked and smoked meats. The peak year was 1933. Thereafter du Pont was unable to meet the competition of Sylvania and of greaseproof paper. Its sales declined and the 1933 volume was not reached again until 1947. It will be noted that greaseproof paper, glassine, waxed paper, foil and Pliofilm are used as well as cellophane. Findings 209–210 show the competition and 215–216 the advantages that have caused the more expensive Pliofilm to increase its proportion of the business.

An element for consideration as to cross-elasticity of demand between products is the responsiveness of the sales of one product to price changes of the other. If a slight decrease in the price of cellophane causes a considerable number of customers of other flexible wrappings to switch to cellophane, it would be an indication that a high cross-elasticity of demand exists between them; that the products compete in the same market. The court below held that the "great

---

[27] [George W. Stocking and Willard F. Mueller, "The Cellophane Case and the New Competition," *American Economic Review*, March, 1955, pp. 48–49.]

sensitivity of customers in the flexible packaging markets to price or quality changes" prevented du Pont from possessing monopoly control over price. The record sustains these findings. See references made by the trial court in Findings 123–149.

We conclude that cellophane's interchangeability with the other materials mentioned suffices to make it a part of this flexible packaging material market.

The Government stresses the fact that the variation in price between cellophane and other materials demonstrates they are noncompetitive. As these products are all flexible wrapping materials, it seems reasonable to consider, as was done at the trial, their comparative cost to the consumer in terms of square area. This can be seen in Finding 130, Appendix C. Findings as to price competition are set out in the margin.[28] Cellophane costs two or three times as much, surface measure, as its chief competitors for the flexible wrapping market, glassine and greaseproof papers. Other forms of cellulose wrappings and those from other chemical or mineral substances, with the exception of aluminum foil, are more expensive. The uses of these materials, as can be observed by Finding 283 in Appendix A, are largely to wrap small packages for retail distribution. The wrapping is a relatively small proportion of the entire cost of the article. Different producers need different qualities in wrappings and their need may vary from time to time as their products undergo change. But the necessity for flexible wrappings is the central and unchanging demand. We cannot say that these differences in cost gave du Pont monopoly power over prices in view of the findings of fact on that subject.

It is the variable characteristics of the different flexible wrappings and the energy and ability with which the manufacturers push their wares that determine choice. A glance at "Modern Packaging," a trade journal, will give, by its various advertisements, examples of the competition among manufacturers for the flexible packaging market. The trial judge visited the 1952 Annual Packaging Show at Atlantic City, with the consent of counsel. He observed exhibits offered by "machinery manufacturers, converters and manufacturers of flexible packaging materials." He states that these personal observations confirmed his esti-

---

[28]Among these were:

133. Cellophane has always been higher priced than the two largest selling flexible packaging materials, wax paper and glassine, and this has represented a disadvantage to sales of cellophane.

135. Du Pont, in reducing its prices, intended to narrow price differential between cellophane and packaging papers, particularly glassine and waxed paper. The objective of this effort has been to increase the use of cellophane. Each price reduction was intended to open up new uses for cellophane, and to attract new customers who had not used cellophane because of its price.

140. Some users are sensitive to the cost of flexible packaging materials; others are not. Users to whom cost is important include substantial business: for example, General Foods, Armour, Curtiss Candy Co., and smaller users in the bread industry, cracker industry, and frozen food industry. These customers are unwilling to use more cellophane because of its relatively high price, would use more if the price were reduced, and have increased their use as the price of cellophane has been reduced.

141. The cost factor slips accounts away from cellophane. This hits at the precarious users, whose profit margins on their products are low, and has been put in motion by competitive developments in the user's trade. Examples include the losses of business to glassine in candy bar wraps in the 30's, frozen food business to waxed paper in the late 40's, and recent losses to glassine in cracker packaging.

mate of the competition between cellophane and other packaging materials. From this wide variety of evidence, the Court reached the conclusion expressed in Finding 838:

"The record establishes that plain cellophane and moistureproof cellophane are each flexible packaging materials which are functionally interchangeable with other flexible packaging materials and sold at the same time to the same customers for the same purpose at competitive prices; there is no distinct and separate cellophane market; the market for flexible packaging materials is the relevant market for determining the nature and extent of du Pont's market control; and du Pont has at all times competed with other cellophane producers and manufacturers of other flexible packaging materials in all aspects of its cellophane business."

The facts above considered dispose also of any contention that competitors have been excluded by du Pont from the packaging material market. That market has many producers and there is no proof du Pont ever has possessed power to exclude any of them from the rapidly expanding flexible packaging market. The Government apparently concedes as much, for it states that "lack of power to inhibit entry into this so-called market [i.e., flexible packaging materials] comprising widely disparate products, is no indicium of absence of power to exclude competition in the manufacture and sale of cellophane." The record shows the multiplicity of competitors and the financial strength of some with individual assets running to the hundreds of millions. Findings 66–72.[29] Indeed, the trial court found that du Pont could not exclude competitors even from the manufacture of cellophane. Nor can we say that du Pont's profits, while liberal (according to the Government 15.9% net after taxes on the 1937–1947 average), demonstrate the existence of a monopoly without proof of lack of comparable profits during those years in other prosperous industries. Cellophane was a leader, over 17%, in the flexible packaging materials market. There is no showing that du Pont's rate of return was greater or less than that of other producers of flexible packaging materials. Finding 719.

The "market" which one must study to determine when a producer has monopoly power will vary with the part of commerce under consideration. The tests are constant. That market is composed of products that have reasonable

---

[29]These findings may be summarized as follows (the figures in parentheses are total assets in 1949 in thousands of dollars which were given for selected companies):

Glassine and greaseproof papers—10 companies including Riegel Paper Company ($15,285) and Rhinelander Paper Co. ($14,720).

Waxed papers and other packaging papers—number not estimated but included was Marathon Corp. ($61,888).

Cellulose acetate film—Three companies including Celanese Corp. ($254,886) and du Pont with less than 20% of market.

Aluminum foil—Nine companies including Alcoa ($525,870).

Polyethylene film—Three hundred companies including du Pont with less than 10% of market.

Pliofilm—Goodyear Tire and Rubber Co. ($424,126).

Saran—Dow Chemical Company.

Cry-O-Rap—Dewey and Almy Chemical Co.

All of these materials are sold direct to packager and indirectly through converters, none of whom converts cellophane exclusively.

interchangeability for the purposes for which they are produced—price, use and qualities considered. While the application of the tests remains uncertain, it seems to us that du Pont should not be found to monopolize cellophane when that product has the competition and interchangeability with other wrappings that this record shows.

On the findings of the District Court, its judgment is

Affirmed.

APPENDIX A TO OPINION OF THE COURT

VIII. Results of du Pont's Competition With Other Materials.

(Findings 279–292)

279. . . .

280. Of the production and imports of flexible packaging materials in 1949 measured in wrapping surface, du Pont cellophane accounted for less than 20% of flexible packaging materials consumed in the United States in that year. The figures on this are [shown in Exhibit 1].

[*Exhibit 1*]

Thousands of Sq. Yds.

Glassine, Greaseproof and Vegetable Parchment Papers	3,125,826
Waxing Papers (18 Pounds and over)	4,614,685
Sulphite Bag and Wrapping Papers	1,788,615
Aluminum Foil	1,317,807
Cellophane	3,366,068
Cellulose Acetate	133,982
Pliofilm, Polyethylene, Saran and Cry-O-Rap	373,871
Total	14,720,854
Total du Pont Cellophane Production	2,629,747
Du Pont Cellophane Per Cent of Total United States Production and Imports of These Flexible Packaging Materials	17.9%

281. Eighty per cent of cellophane made by du Pont is sold for packaging in the food industry. Of this quantity, 80% is sold for packaging baked goods, meat, candy, crackers and biscuits, frozen foods, fresh vegetables and produce, potato chips, and "snacks," such as peanut butter sandwiches, popcorn, etc. Largest nonfood use of cellophane is the overwrapping of cigarette packages.

The breakdown of du Pont cellophane sales for the year 1949 was [as shown in Exhibit 2].

[*Exhibit 2*]

Use	Sales (M Pounds)	Per Cent of Total Sales	Use	Sales (M Pounds)	Per Cent of Total Sales
Tobacco:			Food Products (cont.):		
Cigarettes	20,584	11.6	Popcorn & Potato		
Cigars	3,195	1.8	Chips	6,929	3.9
Other Tobacco	1,657	0.9	Dairy Products	3,808	2.1
			Fresh Produce	4,564	2.6
Total	25,436	14.3	Unclassified Foods	8,750	4.9
			Total	120,478	67.7
Food Products:			Miscellaneous:		
Candy & Gum	17,054	9.6	Hosiery	1,370	0.7
Bread & Cake	40,081	22.5	Textiles	3,141	1.8
Crackers &			Drugs	1,031	0.6
Biscuits	12,614	7.1	Rubber	317	0.2
Meat	11,596	6.5	Paper	2,736	1.5
Noodles &			Unclassified	18,602	10.5
Macaroni	2,602	1.5			
Tea & Coffee	1,380	0.8	Total	27,197	15.3
Cereals	2,487	1.4			
Frozen Foods	5,234	2.9	Domestic Total	173,011	97.3
Dried Fruit	333	0.2	Export	4,820	2.7
Nuts	2,946	1.7	Grand Total	177,831	100.0

283. 1949 sales of 19 major representative converters whose business covered a substantial segment of the total converting of flexible packaging materials for that year . . . as to their sales of flexible packaging materials, classified by end use [are shown in Exhibit 3].

[*Exhibit 3*]

	Bakery Products	Candy	Snacks	Poultry	Biscuits	Produce	Frozen Food Excluding Dairy Products
Cellophane	6.8	24.4	34.9	34.9	26.6	47.2	33.6
Foil	.2	32.5	.8	.1	.2	.1	.7
Glassine	4.4	21.4	62.8	2.7	10.0	.1	2.1
Papers	88.6	21.6	4.4	57.5	63.2	45.6	60.3
Films	.0	.1	.1	4.8	.0	7.0	3.3
	100.0	100.0	100.0	100.0	100.0	100.0	100.0
Quantity in Billion Sq. Inches.	1,625	550	192	169	113	112	94

APPENDIX B

59. [Exhibit 4] compares, descriptively, physical properties of cellophane and other flexible packaging materials.

[*Exhibit 4*]

PHYSICAL PROPERTIES

Packaging Materials	Heat Seal-ability	Print-ability	Clarity	Tear Strength (Elmen-dorf)	Bursting Strength	Water Absorption in 24 Hrs. Immersion	Moisture Permeability	Perme-ability to Gases (2)	Dimens. Change with Humid Diff.	Resist-ance to Grease and Oils	Wrapping Machine Running Qualities
Cellophane (plain)	Yes (if coated)	Yes	Highly Transparent	Low	High	High	High	Very Low	Large	Excellent	O.K.
Cellophane (Moisture-proof)	Yes (if coated)	Yes	Highly Transparent	Low	High	High	Low-Medium	Very Low	Large	Excellent	O.K.
Plain greaseproof paper	No	Yes	Opaque	Good	Low	High	High	Medium	Moderate	Good	O.K.
Plain Glassine	No	Yes	Commercially Transparent to Opaque	Good	Low	High	High	Low	Moderate	Good	O.K.
Lacquered Glassine	Yes	Yes	Commercially Transparent to Translucent	Good	Low	Low	Low-Medium	Low	Moderate	Good	O.K.
Waxed Glassine	Yes	(1)	Commercially Transparent to Translucent	Good	Low	Low	Low	Low	Moderate	Good	O.K.
Vegetable Parchment	No	Yes	Tends to be Opaque	Good	Good	High	High	Low	Moderate	Good	O.K.
Waxed Paper (18 lbs. or over)	Yes	(1)	Commercially Transparent	High	Good	Low	Low-Medium	High	Moderate	None	O.K.
Aluminum Foil	No	Yes	Opaque	Low	Low	Nil	Very Low	Very Low	None	Excellent	O.K.
Aluminum Foil (Heat Sealing)	Yes	Yes	Opaque	Low	Low	Nil	Nearly Nil	Very Low	None	Excellent	O.K.
Cellulose Acetate	Yes	Yes	Highly Transparent	Low	High	Low	High	Variable	Very Small	Excellent	O.K.
Pliofilm (rubber hydro-chloride)	Yes (3)	Yes (3)	Highly Transparent with Slight Haze	Medium	High	Low	Medium	Low	Very Small	Excellent	Good (3)
Saran (Vinylidene Chloride)	Yes (3)	Yes (3)	Highly Transparent	High	High	Low	Very Low	Very Low	None	Excellent	Poor (3)
Polyethylene	Yes (3)	Yes (3)	Transparent with Slight Haze	High	High	Low	Medium	High	None	(4)	Poor (3)
Cry-O-Rap	Yes (3)	Yes (3)	Transparent with Slight Haze	High	High	Low	Medium	Low	None	Excellent	Poor (3)
Sulphite (high finish wrapper and label paper)	No	Yes	Opaque	High	Medium	High	Very High	High	Moderate	None	O.K.

References:

(1) Normally printed before waxing.

(2) The permeability to gases can vary greatly depending upon the gas and the humidity conditions. The levels indicated in this chart apply particularly to flavor type volatiles as found in many food products.

(3) Plastic films may require special heat sealing techniques, and printing processes or special machines.

(4) Not affected by greases but penetrated by some oils.

(5) The information on this chart is based upon the generally accepted properties of the materials listed; however, materials produced by different processes, formulations, coatings, raw materials. surface treatments, and thicknesses can show considerable variation from the properties indicated.

APPENDIX C

Average wholesale prices of flexible packaging materials in the United States were (1949) [as shown in Exhibit 5].

[*Exhibit 5*]

	Price per 1,000 Sq. In. (Cents)	Price per Lb. (Cents)	Yield per Lb. (Sq. In.)
Saran (100 Gauge #517)	6.1	99.0	16,300
Cellulose Acetate (.00088")	3.3	82.0	25,000
Polyethylene (.002"–18" Flat Width)	5.4	81.0	15,000
Pliofilm (120 Gauge N 2)	3.8	80.8	21,000
Aluminum Foil (.00035")	1.8	52.2	29,200
Moistureproof Cellophane (300 MST–51)	2.3	47.8	21,000
Plain Cellophane (300 PT)	2.1	44.8	21,500
Vegetable Parchment (27#)	1.4	22.3	16,000
Bleached Glassine (25#)	1.0	17.8	17,280
Bleached Greaseproof (25#)	.9	15.8	17,280
Plain Waxed Sulphite (25# Self-Sealing)	1.1	15.2	14,400
Plain Waxed Sulphite (25# Coated Opaque)	.7	11.9	17,280
Cry-O-Rap	Sold only in converted form. No unconverted quotations		

The Dissenting Opinion[30]

MR. CHIEF JUSTICE WARREN, with whom MR. JUSTICE BLACK and MR. JUSTICE DOUGLAS join, dissenting.

This case, like many under the Sherman Act, turns upon the proper definition of the market. In defining the market in which du Pont's economic power is to be measured, the majority virtually emasculate Section 2 of the Sherman Act. They admit that "cellophane combines the desirable elements of transparency, strength and cheapness more definitely than any of" a host of other packaging materials. Yet they hold that all of those materials are so indistinguishable from cellophane as to warrant their inclusion in the market. We cannot agree that cellophane, in the language of *Times-Picayune Publishing Co.* v. *United States,* 345 U.S. 594, 613, is "the selfsame product" as glassine, greaseproof and vegetable parchment papers, waxed papers, sulphite papers, aluminum foil, cellulose acetate, and Pliofilm and other films.[31]

The majority opinion states that "[I]t will adequately illustrate the similarity in characteristics of the various products by noting here Finding 62 as to glassine." But Finding 62 merely states the respects in which the selected flexible

---

[30]The dissent is included in its entirety except for the omission of some footnotes.

[31]In *Times-Picayune Publishing Co.* v. *United States,* 345 U.S. 594, 612, note 31, the Court said:

"For every product, substitutes exist. But a relevant market cannot meaningfully encompass that infinite range. The circle must be drawn narrowly to exclude any other product to which, within reasonable variations in price, only a limited number of buyers will turn; in technical terms, products whose 'cross-elasticities of demand' are small."

packaging materials are as satisfactory as cellophane; it does not compare all the physical properties of cellophane and other materials. The Table [Exhibit 4] incorporated in Finding 59 (Appendix B) does make such a comparison, and enables us to note cellophane's unique combination of qualities lacking among less expensive materials in varying degrees.[32] A glance at this Table reveals that cellophane has a high bursting strength while glassine's is low; that cellophane's permeability to gases is lower than that of glassine; and that both its transparency and its resistance to grease and oils are greater than glassine's. Similarly, we see that waxed paper's bursting strength is less than cellophane's and that it is highly permeable to gases and offers no resistance whatsoever to grease and oils. With respect to the other major products held to be close substitutes for cellophane, Finding 59 makes the majority's market definition more dubious. In contrast to cellophane, aluminum foil is actually opaque and has a low bursting strength. And sulphite papers, in addition to being opaque, are highly permeable to both moisture and gases, have no resistance to grease and oils, have a lower bursting strength than cellophane, and are not even heat sealable. Indeed, the majority go further than placing cellophane in the same market with such products. They also include the transparent films, which are more expensive than cellophane. These bear even less resemblance to the lower priced packaging materials than does cellophane. The juxtaposition of one of these films, Cry-O-Rap, with sulphite in the Table facilitates a comparison which shows that Cry-O-Rap is markedly different and far superior.

If the conduct of buyers indicated that glassine, waxed and sulphite papers and aluminum foil were actually "the selfsame products" as cellophane, the qualitative differences demonstrated by the comparison of physical properties in Finding 59 would not be conclusive. But the record provides convincing proof that businessmen did not so regard these products. During the period covered by the complaint (1923–1947) cellophane enjoyed phenomenal growth. Du Pont's 1924 production was 361,249 pounds, which sold for $1,306,662. Its 1947 production was 133,502,858 pounds which sold for $55,339,626. Yet throughout this period the price of cellophane was far greater than that of glassine, waxed paper or sulphite paper. Finding 136 states that in 1929 cellophane's price was seven times that of glassine; in 1934, four times, and in 1949 still more than twice glassine's price. Reference to DX-994, the graph upon which Finding 136 is based, shows that cellophane had a similar price relation to waxed paper and that sulphite paper sold at even less than glassine and waxed paper. We cannot believe that buyers, practical businessmen, would have bought cellophane in increasing amounts over a quarter of a century if close substitutes were available at from one-seventh to one-half cellophane's price. That they did so is testimony to cellophane's distinctiveness.

The inference yielded by the conduct of cellophane buyers is reinforced by

---

[32]The majority opinion quotes at length from Stocking and Mueller, [*op. cit.,* pp.] 48–49, in noting the comparative characteristics of cellophane and other products. Unfortunately, the opinion fails to quote the conclusion reached by these economists. They state: "The [trial] court to the contrary notwithstanding, the market in which cellophane meets the 'competition' of other wrappers is narrower than the market for all flexible packaging materials." And they conclude that ". . . cellophane is so differentiated from other flexible wrapping materials that its cross elasticity of demand gives du Pont significant and continuing monopoly power."

the conduct of sellers other than du Pont. Finding 587 states that Sylvania, the only other cellophane producer, absolutely and immediately followed every du Pont price change, even dating back its price list to the effective date of du Pont's change. Producers of glassine and waxed paper, on the other hand, displayed apparent indifference to du Pont's repeated and substantial price cuts. DX–994 shows that from 1924 to 1932 du Pont dropped the price of plain cellophane 84%, while the price of glassine remained constant. And during the period 1933–1946 the prices for glassine and waxed paper actually increased in the face of a further 21% decline in the price of cellophane. If "shifts of business" due to "price sensitivity" had been substantial, glassine and waxed paper producers who wanted to stay in business would have been compelled by market forces to meet du Pont's price challenge just as Sylvania was. The majority correctly point out that:

> "An element for consideration as to cross-elasticity of demand between products is the responsiveness of the sales of one product to price changes of the other. If a slight decrease in the price of cellophane causes a considerable number of customers of other flexible wrappings to switch to cellophane, it would be an indication that a high cross-elasticity of demand exists between them; that the products compete in the same market."

Surely there was more than "a slight decrease in the price of cellophane" during the period covered by the complaint. That producers of glassine and waxed paper remained dominant in the flexible packaging materials market without meeting cellophane's tremendous price cuts convinces us that cellophane was not in effective competition with their products.

Certainly du Pont itself shared our view. From the first, du Pont recognized that it need not concern itself with competition from other packaging materials. For example, when du Pont was contemplating entry into cellophane production, its Development Department reported that glassine "is so inferior that it belongs in an entirely different class and has hardly to be considered as a competitor of cellophane."[33] This was still du Pont's view in 1950 when its survey of competitive prospects wholly omitted references to glassine, waxed paper or sulphite paper and stated that "Competition for du Pont cellophane will come from competitive cellophane and from non-cellophane films made by us or by others."[34]

Du Pont's every action was directed toward maintaining dominance over cellophane. Its 1923 agreement with La Cellophane, the French concern which first produced commercial cellophane, gave du Pont exclusive North and Central American rights to cellophane's technology, manufacture and sale, and provided, without any limitation in time, that all existing and future information pertaining to the cellophane process be considered "secret and confidential," and be held in an exclusive common pool. In its subsequent agreements with foreign licensees, du Pont was careful to preserve its continental market inviolate. In 1929, while it was still the sole domestic producer of cellophane,

---

[33]R. 3549, GX–392. The record contains many reports prepared by du Pont from 1928 to 1947. They virtually ignore the possibility of competition from other packaging materials.

[34]R. 4070. It is interesting to note that du Pont had almost 70% of the market which this report considered relevant.

du Pont won its long struggle to raise the tariff from 25% to 60%, ad valorem, on cellophane imports, substantially foreclosing foreign competition. When Sylvania became the second American cellophane producer the following year and du Point filed suit claiming infringement of its moistureproof patents, they settled the suit by entering into a cross-licensing agreement. Under this agreement, du Pont obtained the right to exclude third persons from use of any patentable moistureproof invention made during the next 15 years by the sole other domestic cellophane producer, and, by a prohibitive royalty provision, it limited Sylvania's moistureproof production to approximately 20% of the industry's moistureproof sales. The record shows that du Pont and Sylvania were aware that, by settling the infringement suit, they avoided the possibility that the courts might hold the patent claims invalid and thereby open cellophane manufacture to additional competition. If close substitutes for cellophane had been commercially available, du Pont, an enlightened enterprise, would not have gone to such lengths to control cellophane.

As predicted by its 1923 market analysis, du Pont's dominance in cellophane proved enormously profitable from the outset. After only five years of production, when du Pont bought out the minority stock interests in its cellophane subsidiary, it had to pay more than fifteen times the original price of the stock. But such success was not limited to the period of innovation, limited sales and complete domestic monopoly. A confidential du Pont report shows that during the period 1937–1947, despite great expansion of sales, du Pont's "operative return" (before taxes) averaged 31%, while its average "net return" (after deduction of taxes, bonuses, and fundamental research expenditure) was 15.9%. Such profits provide a powerful incentive for the entry of competitors.[35] Yet from 1924 to 1951 only one new firm, Sylvania, was able to begin cellophane production. And Sylvania could not have entered if La Cellophane's secret process had not been stolen. It is significant that for 15 years Olin Industries, a substantial firm, was unsuccessful in its attempt to produce cellophane, finally abandoning the project in 1944 after having spent about $1,000,000. When the Government brought this suit, du Pont, "To reduce the hazard of being judged to have a monopoly of the U.S. cellophane business," decided to let Olin enter the industry. Despite this demonstration of the control achieved by du Pont through its exclusive dominion over the cellophane process, the District Court found that du Pont could not exclude competitors from the manufacture of cellophane. Finding 727. This finding is "clearly erroneous." The majority avoid passing upon Finding 727 by stating that it is "immaterial . . . if the market is flexible packaging material." They do not appear to disagree with our conclusion, however, since they concede that. . . it may be practically impossible

---

[35]See Stocking and Mueller [*op. cit.* pp. 60–63], where the authors compare the domestitic economic history of rayon with that of cellophane. The first American rayon producer earned 64.2% on its investment in 1920, thereby attracting du Pont. After a loss in 1921, du Pont's average return for the next four years was roughly 32%. As more firms began rayon production, du Pont's and the industry's return on investment began to drop. When 6 new firms entered the industry in 1930, bringing the number of producers to 20, average industry earnings for that year declined to 5%, and du Pont suffered a net loss. "From the beginning of the depression in 1929 through the succeeding recovery and the 1938 recession du Pont averaged 29.6 per cent before taxes on its cellophane investment. On its rayon investment it averaged only 6.3 per cent."

for anyone to commence manufacturing cellophane without full access to du Pont's technique.

The trial court found that:

> "Du Pont has no power to set cellophane prices arbitrarily. If prices for cellophane increase in relation to prices of other flexible packaging materials it will lose business to manufacturers of such materials in varying amounts for each of du Pont cellophane's major end uses."

This further reveals its misconception of the antitrust laws. A monopolist seeking to maximize profits cannot raise prices "arbitrarily." Higher prices of course mean smaller sales, but they also mean higher per-unit profit. Lower prices will increase sales but reduce per-unit profit. Within these limits a monopolist has a considerable degree of latitude in determining which course to pursue in attempting to maximize profits. The trial judge thought that, if du Pont raised its price, the market would "penalize" it with smaller profits as well as lower sales. Du Pont proved him wrong. When 1947 operating earnings dropped below 26% for the first time in 10 years, it increased cellophane's price 7% and boosted its earnings in 1948. Du Pont's division manager then reported that "If an operative return of 31% is considered inadequate then an upward revision in prices will be necessary to improve the return." It is this latitude with respect to price, this broad power of choice, that the antitrust laws forbid. Du Pont's independent pricing policy and the great profits consistently yielded by that policy leave no room for doubt that it had power to control the price of cellophane. The findings of fact cited by the majority cannot affect this conclusion. For they merely demonstrate that, during the period covered by the complaint, du Pont was a "good monopolist," i.e., that it did not engage in predatory practices and that it chose to maximize profits by lowering price and expanding sales. Proof of enlightened exercise of monopoly power certainly does not refute the existence of that power.

The majority opinion purports to reject the theory of "interindustry competition." Brick, steel, wood, cement and stone, it says, are "too different" to be placed in the same market. But cellophane, glassine, wax papers, sulphite papers, greaseproof and vegetable parchment papers, aluminum foil, cellulose acetate, Pliofilm and other films are not "too different," the opinion concludes. The majority approach would apparently enable a monopolist of motion picture exhibition to avoid Sherman Act consequences by showing that motion pictures compete in substantial measure with legitimate theater, television, radio, sporting events and other forms of entertainment. Here, too, "shifts of business" undoubtedly accompany fluctuations in price and "there are market alternatives that buyers may readily use for their purposes." Yet, in *United States* v. *Paramount Pictures,* 334 U.S. 131, where the District Court had confined the relevant market to that for nationwide movie exhibition, this Court remanded the case to the District Court with directions to determine whether there was a monopoly on the part of the five major distributors "in the *first-run* field for the entire country, in the *first-run* field in the 92 largest cities of the country, or in the *first-run* field in separate localities." Similarly, it is difficult to square the majority view with *United States* v. *Aluminum Co. of America,* 148 F. 2d 416, a landmark Section 2 case. There Judge Learned Hand, reversing a district court, held that the close competition which "secondary" (used) aluminum offered to "virgin" aluminus did not justify including the former within the relevant market for measuring Alcoa's economic power. Against these and other precedents, which the Court's opinion approves but does not follow, the formula of "reasonable interchangeability," as applied by the majority, appears indistinguishable from the theory of "interindustry competition." The danger in it is that, as demonstrated in this case, it is "perfectly compatible with a fully monopolized economy."[36]

The majority hold in effect that, because cellophane meets competition for many end uses, those buyers for other uses who need or want only cellophane are not entitled to the benefits of competition within the cellophane industry. For example, Finding 282 shows that the largest single use of cellophane in 1951 was for wrapping cigarettes, and Finding 292 shows that 75 to 80% of all cigarettes are wrapped with cellophane. As the recent report of the Attorney General's National Committee to Study the Antitrust Laws states: "In the interest of rivalry that extends to *all* buyers and *all* uses, competition among rivals within the industry is always important." (Emphasis added.) Furthermore, those buyers who have "reasonable alternatives" between cellophane and other products are also entitled to competition within the cellophane industry, for such competition may lead to lower prices and improved quality.

The foregoing analysis of the record shows conclusively that cellophane is the relevant market. Since du Pont has the lion's share of that market, it must have monopoly power, as the majority concede. This being so, we think it clear that, in the circumstances of this case, du Pont is guilty of "monopolization." The briefest sketch of du Pont's business history precludes it from falling within the "exception to the Sherman Act prohibitions of monopoly power" (majority opinion, pp. 390–391) by successfully asserting that monopoly was "thrust upon" it. Du Pont was not "the passive beneficiary of a monopoly" within the meaning of *United States* v. *Aluminum Co. of America.* It sought and maintained dominance through illegal agreements dividing the world market, concealing and suppressing technological information, and restricting its licensee's production by prohibitive royalties, and through numerous maneuvers which might have been "honestly industrial" but whose necessary effect was nevertheless exclusionary. Du Pont cannot bear "the burden of proving that it owes its monopoly *solely* to superior skill. . . ."[37]

Nor can du Pont rely upon its moistureproof patents as a defense to the charge of monopolization. Once du Pont acquired the basic cellophane process as a result of its illegal 1923 agreements with La Cellophane, development of moistureproofing was relatively easy. Du Pont's moistureproof patents were fully subject to the exclusive pooling arrangements and territorial restrictions established by those agreements. And they were the subject of the illicit and exclusionary du Pont–Sylvania agreement. Hence, these patents became tainted as part and parcel of du Pont's illegal monopoly.[38] Any other result would permit

---

[36] [Adams, "The 'Rule of Reason': Workable Competition or Workable Monopoly?" *Yale Law Journal,* January, 1954, pp. 348, 364.]

[37] (Emphasis supplied.) *United States* v. *United Shoe Machinery Corp.,* 110 F. Supp. 295, 342, aff'd per curiam," 347 U.S. 521.

[38] Cf. *Mercoid Corp.* v. *Mid-Continent Co.,* 320 U.S. 661, 670.

one who monopolizes a market to escape the statutory liability by patenting a simple improvement on his product.

If competition is at the core of the Sherman Act, we cannot agree that it was consistent with that Act for the enormously lucrative cellophane industry to have no more than two sellers from 1924 to 1951. The conduct of du Pont and Sylvania illustrates that a few sellers tend to act like one and that an industry which does not have a competitive structure will not have competitive behavior. The public should not be left to rely upon the dispensations of management in order to obtain the benefits which normally accompany competition. Such beneficience is of uncertain tenure. Only actual competition can assure long-run enjoyment of the goals of a free economy.

We would reverse the decision below and remand the cause to the District Court with directions to determine the relief which should be granted against du Pont.

Concluding Notes

The Cellophane case has two unusual features. The first was the emphasis by both opinions on the cross elasticity of demand, an economic concept not typically pushed into the foreground in legal opinions. The second was the considerable citation by both sides from the same article published in a professional economists' journal, "The Cellophane Case and the New Competition," by George W. Stocking and Willard F. Mueller.

Cross Elasticity of Demand.   Cross elasticity can be defined as the ratio between the percentage change of A's quantity in response to a certain percentage change in B's price (or of B's quantity to A's price). If the ratio is negative, the demands for the two goods are complementary. For example, a lower price for beer (negative) might increase the sale of pretzels (positive), giving a ratio which is negative. Were competitive conditions in an industry a close approximation to those of the economic model for pure competition (many small firms producing an identical product), the ratios would be very large and positive. For example, a small cotton gray-goods manufacturer could expect to lose close to 100 per cent of sales if it failed to follow a 5 per cent decline in the price of other gray-goods producers.

In the product group embracing all flexible packaging materials, a whole series of cross elasticities become relevant between cellophane and glassine, cellophane and aluminum foil, etc. The contention of the majority seems to be that these are positive and large, so that aggregate gains of other producers at du Pont's expense if cellophane prices should be raised would be great enough that du Pont's power to control price would be very limited. The dissenting opinion concedes some shifts of business in marginal uses with shifts in relative prices, i.e., the cross elasticities are positive but small, with du Pont thus having considerable discretion over cellophane prices.

The Stocking and Mueller Article. The fundamental arguments of this article are repeated in the dissenting opinion: that in much of its business strategy, du Pont acted as though it were protecting a valuable near-monopoly position; that in many uses, cellophane's rivals were not close substitutes; that cellophane profits were an indication of monopoly power.

The article concluded:

. . . cellophane is so differentiated from other flexible wrapping materials that its cross elasticity of demand gives du Pont significant and continuing monopoly power.

Du Pont has used its power with foresight and wisdom. It has apparently recognized that it could increase its earnings by decreasing its costs and prices, by educating its potential customers to the benefits of wrapping their products in cellophane, by improving machinery for packaging, by helping converters and packagers solve their technical problems.[39] It has built a better mousetrap and taught people how to use it.

But du Pont has not surrendered its monopoly power. Its strategy, cellophane's distinctive qualities, and the course of its prices and earnings indicate this. Du Pont's strategy was designed to protect a monopoly in the sale of a product it regarded as unique, and its pricing policies reflected the judgment of its executives on how best to maximize earnings. We think its earnings illustrate Knight's distinction between justifiable profits to the innovator and unjustifiable monopoly gains. They have been "too large" and have lasted "too long."[40]

---

[39]President Yerkes of the Du Pont Cellophane Company, Inc., concluded as early as 1924 that to maximize earnings, du Pont should reduce cellophane prices. On this issue, he said: "I am in favor of lowering the price. . . . [I] think it will undoubtedly increase sales and widen distribution. . . . Our price I think is too high based purely on manufacturing cost and too high in comparison with other wrapping papers on the market, and while we cannot approach the price of glassine or other oil papers, if we make a substantial reduction we will in some cases get somewhere near there." (DX 337.)

Walter S. Carpenter, Jr., chairman of du Pont's board of directors, expressed a similar idea when he testified in the Cellophane case: ". . . the purpose of reducing our price and also improving our quality was to broaden our market. . . . As a general philosophy I was always in favor of the reduction of the price as we were able to do so by the reduced costs, and I think that I consistently urged that on the management." (Transcript, pp. 6278–79).

The article expressed the opinion that "the Yerkes-Carpenter philosophy apparently prevailed."

[40]Stocking and Mueller, *op. cit.*, p. 63.

QUESTIONS

1. Why might the government think it had a strong case against du Pont? What was du Pont's strategy in meeting the case?

2. Was du Pont a "good monopolist," a "workable competitor," or neither? What was the fundamental objection of the minority to a "good monopolist"?

3. What "area of discretion" or "power" did du Pont have in pricing? What were its limits? What picture does the case give of du Pont's business policy in developing cellophane?

4. Appraise the use of the concept of "cross-elasticity of demand" both in the minority and in the majority opinions.

5. Have developments in packaging since 1956 strengthened or weakened the government's contention of monopoly?

CASE 16–2:   THE PROPOSED MERGER OF BETHLEHEM
AND YOUNGSTOWN

The merger proposal of the Bethlehem Steel Corporation and the Youngstown Sheet and Tube Company in 1954 stirred up considerable excitement on the good American grounds of being big and of promising not only one but possibly two major struggles, one between the government and the companies, and the second between Bethlehem and United States Steel.

The merger promised to be the biggest yet in terms of dollar assets— $2.3 billion. Such are the mathematics of growth and inflation that this figure is 50 per cent greater than the $1.5 billion (including "water") of the merger creating U.S. Steel in 1901. While 1954 had a bumper crop of big merger proposals, such as Olin Industries–Mathieson Chemicals ($584 million), W. R. Grace & Company–Davidson Chemical ($384 million), Nash-Kelvinator–Hudson ($341 million), and Burlington Mills–Pacific Mills–Goodall-Sanford ($428 million), all of them involved less than one quarter of the assets of the steel merger proposal.

Antitrust and Steel Mergers.   The Antitrust Division opened fire by getting a temporary injunction against the merger under the amended Section 7 of the Clayton Act. Its previous record against mergers in the steel industry had not been successful, although it had lost some close decisions. In 1920, nine years after litigation began, its attempt to break up the U.S. Steel combination in a Sherman Act case failed by a four-to-three decision in the Supreme Court. The Federal Trade Commission dropped its Clayton Act case against Bethlehem's acquisition of the Lackawanna Steel Company and of the Midvale Steel and Ordnance Company in the 1920's. After more than doubling its capacity in these mergers, Bethlehem was blocked from taking over Youngstown in 1930 not by the Antitrust Division but by minority stockholders in Youngstown. The government's most recent defeat on the steel merger front had been in the Columbia Steel case, when it charged U.S. Steel with attempting to monopolize when its subsidiary Columbia acquired Consolidated Steel, a West Coast fabricator. The five-to-four setback in the Supreme Court, however, proved helpful in getting Congress to close the loophole in Section 7 of the Clayton Act which, while barring stock acquisitions which may substantially lessen competition or tend to monopoly, permitted the merger of assets.

The second potential struggle which added interest to the Bethlehem-Youngstown proposal was the prospect of Bethlehem invading the Chicago area market and challenging U.S. Steel. Since U.S. Steel had recently opened its Fairless Mills in the eastern seaboard area where Bethlehem had been the leader, the situation had elements of "tit for tat." In its antitrust case, Bethlehem was to lay considerable emphasis on the increase in competition which might follow from its invasion of steel production in the Chicago area.

The Industry and Concentration in Steel Ingot Capacity

The steel industry is usually defined as consisting of the integrated companies which produce pig iron, steel ingots, and rolled steel (of the 24 such companies in 1956, the 15 largest had 86 per cent of the total ingot capacity); of the semi-integrated companies (56) that do not produce pig iron; of the nonintegrated companies (128) that buy crude and semifinished steel for rolling; and of the merchant pig iron producers (12) that sell to foundaries and steel makers. There were also about 3,000 iron and steel foundaries in 1956.

The "Big Eight." A picture of considerable stability in concentration is obtained by examining the share of the largest eight producers in steel ingot capacity, which rose from 71 per cent in 1904 to 79 per cent in 1940 and then declined to 76 per cent in 1956 (see Exhibit 1). Actually, since U.S. Steel, with only 48 per cent of the capacity, was producing 63 per cent of the ingots in 1904 (much of the independent capacity was apparently obsolescent), the indicated rise in concentration after its formation should be discounted.

This statistical stability in concentration has been produced by oppos-
ing tendencies. Paramount in the reduction of the share of the largest
eight has been the decline in the share of U.S. Steel, a decline that may
be coming to an end. Moderate-sized firms have been able to expand
vigorously, though no firm through internal growth has been able to
add over 4 per cent to its share of the market (the size of Inland Steel,
which has been the least dependent of the "Big Eight" on mergers).
Under the pressure of wartime and regional needs, four firms were able
to hurdle the substantial investment requirements and join the ranks
of integrated producers since 1940 (Kaiser, Detroit, McLouth and
Lone Star).

Exhibit 1

STEEL: SHARE OF LEADING COMPANIES IN STEEL INGOT CAPACITY,
1904–56

(Per Cent)

	1904	1916	1928	1940	1948	1956
Largest firm...	48.0	47.3	39.7	34.1	33.1	30.6
Next two......	8.8	9.1	18.7	23.6	23.8	23.6
Next five......	13.9	15.0	14.3	21.3	20.8	22.0
Largest eight..	70.8	71.3	72.8	79.0	77.7	76.1

Sources: American Iron and Steel Institute, *Directory of Iron and Steel Works of the United States and
Canada* for earlier years, and *Annual Capacities of Coke Ovens, Blast Furnaces and Steelmaking Furnaces
as of January 1, 1955, by Companies, States and Districts (United States and Canada)*, pp. 13–15 (as compiled in Simon N. Whitney, *Antitrust Policies* [New York: Twentieth Century Fund, 1958], p. 290).

Forces working to increase concentration have been those behind
the decline in the number of companies making steel or pig iron from
500 in 1904 to 220 in 1956. Associated with the needs of advancing
technology, integration and larger plant size has been substantial merger activity. For example, Bethlehem which was not in the first ten in
1904 absorbed the third, fourth, sixth, and eighth largest firms of that
year. Thirteen acquisitions of Republic Steel during the 1915 to 1945
period accounted for 64% of its additions to assets.

The Companies' Case for the Merger: (a) The Affidavit of Arthur B. Homer, President of Bethlehem Steel[41]

[*Growth of Chicago Market.*]   Bethlehem's reasons for desiring the merger
are simple. They are legitimate business reasons, completely devoid of any anticompetitive or monopolistic intent.

[41]This and the following section are excerpts from "Affidavits on Behalf of the Defendants in Opposition to the Plaintiffs Motion for Summary Judgment," September 26,
1957. The government sought and lost the motion.

The greatest growth in demand for steel products over the next 15 or 20 years is expected to take place in the Mid-Continent Area, particularly in the region in and around Chicago. For many years the demand for steel products in that region has substantially exceeded the capacity of the plants located there, and it is anticipated that such demand will increase materially with the opening of the St. Lawrence Seaway. The products which are in the shortest supply in that region are heavy structural shapes and plates—products which Bethlehem has had wide experience in producing and selling and which are produced in the Mid-Continent Area in a complete range of sizes by only one producer—United States Steel Corporation (U.S. Steel).[42] There also have been recurring shortages in the entire Mid-Continent Area for other products such as tin plate and hot rolled sheets.

Bethlehem, as a major steel producer, has a ligitemate desire to serve the Mid-Continent Area, particularly the region of which Chicago is the center, and to be a substantial participant in its growth. It cannot do so effectively from its existing plants in the East and far West because of the freight disadvantages involved in shipments from those plants to destinations in the Mid-Continent Area. The tonnages that Bethlehem now ships into the Mid-Continent Area constitute a relatively small percentage of the steel products consumed in that Area, and the competition in that Area is dominated by the companies with plants located there. The market in and around the whole Chicago region is virtually out of reach of Bethlehem's Eastern plants as an area of effective competition.

[Acquisition Only Feasible Approach.] For sound business reasons, the acquisition by Bethlehem of the Youngstown plants is the only feasible way in which Bethlehem in the foreseeable future can become an effective and substantial competitor in the Mid-Continent Area and help carry out the expansion in that Area which it believes necessary to satisfy the needs of the steel consumers there. Neither Bethlehem nor Youngstown, alone, will be able to provide the expansion that is envisioned as a result of the merger. Under the expansion program as presently projected by Bethlehem, if the merger is carried out, the steel-making capacity of the Youngstown plants would be expanded by 2,588,000 ingot tons annually (602,000 at the Youngstown Plant and 1,986,000 tons at the Chicago Plant).

The existing area of the Chicago Plant is inadequate to accommodate the full expansion scheduled for that plant. Bethlehem has, however, acquired additional property on Lake Michigan which will provide adequate space for the continued expansion of the Chicago Plant. In order to take advantage of the lower cost of expanding existing capacity, finishing facilities will be erected on the new property, which will be supplied with semi-finished steel from the expanded facilities on the existing plant area.

[Expansion Costs.] It is estimated that the cost of such expansion of the existing Youngstown plants would be approximately $358,000,000. Because the

---

[42]Of the total, 2,225,000 tons of industry capacity in the Chicago region for plates, U.S. Steel has 54.7% and Inland Steel Company (Inland) has 29.7% and of the total 1,890,-000 tons of industry capacity in that region for structural shapes, U.S. Steel has 55.7% and Inland has 24.9%. Both U.S. Steel and Inland are in the process of expanding their capacities in the Chicago region for structural shapes and U.S. Steel is also expanding its capacity there for plates.

new capacity would be obtained by expanding existing plants, the cost per ingot ton of such expansion would be approximately $135, and such expansion could be carried out by the merged companies within the present price structure of the industry and within their available financial resources.

The reason why Bethlehem, or any other steel producer, cannot under present conditions build a large new integrated steel plant in the Chicago region is that the tremendous cost of such a plant would prohibit profitable operations for many years to come. Such a plant, including capacity for the production of raw steel and finishing facilities for a normal range of products, would cost about $300 per ingot ton at today's prices. The average net profits earned in 1956 by the producers with more than 93% of the steel-making capacity in the United States (including Bethlehem and Youngstown) were $8.64 per ingot ton of capacity, after average charges per ingot ton of capacity of $5.87 for depreciation and $0.58 for interest. On the basis of capital costs of $300 per ton of ingot capacity for a new plant, depreciation charges on a 4% basis would be $12 per ton of ingot capacity and, assuming 60% debt financing at a 5% rate, interest charges would be $9 per ton of ingot capacity. Depreciation and interest charges for a new plant would thus be $14.65 more than the average of such charges for existing facilities. A new plant would also require a substantial addition to working capital and would entail large nonrecurring expenses customarily incurred in starting up new facilities.[43]

It is easy to see, therefore, why the one feasible way to accomplish large-scale increases in capacity is through the expansion of existing plants. That is the only way in which in the last ten years companies other than U.S. Steel have been able to keep the cost of their expansion within manageable bounds. That is the only way in which it will be possible in the future for Bethlehem, and companies smaller than Bethlehem, to create significant new capacity without completely distorting the cost of capital facilities. It is, of course, in the public interest that new capacity required to supply the demand for steel be provided at the lowest possible cost, because, in the end, the cost of facilities must be repaid by the public through the prices paid for steel products or otherwise.

U.S. Steel several years ago was able to build a new integrated plant at Fairless Hills, Pennsylvania, which has a present ingot capacity of 2,200,000 tons and is estimated to have cost upwards of $600,000,000. But the cost of that plant was much smaller in relation to the total physical and financial assets of U.S. Steel than the cost of such a plant would be in relation to Bethlehem or any other steel producer; hence it did not distort U.S. Steel's financial situation to the same degree as it would in the case of any other producer. Furthermore, U.S. Steel received Government aid (not now available to the rest of the industry) in constructing the Fairless Hills Plant, in the form of rapid tax amortization for approximately $468,000,000 of the total cost of that plant.

A smaller, less costly plant is not the answer. The necessity for both size and diversity of finishing capacity indicates a sizeable plant. There are substantial economic obstacles to building a small plant for the production of such basic items as structurals, plates, sheets, and bars.

---

[43]"Financial Analysis of the Steel Industry for 1956," *Steel Magazine,* April 1, 1957.

[*Inability of Youngstown to Carry Out Expansion.*] As appears in Mr. McCuskey's affidavit, Youngstown is not in a position alone to carry out the above outlined expansion program of its plants projected by Bethlehem. The total book value of Youngstown's existing plants, buildings, machinery, and equipment (including construction in progress) is less than $200,000,000, or about $32 per ingot ton of capacity.

Furthermore, Youngstown has not had any previous experience in the heavy structural and plate businesses.

[*Strengthening of Competition.*] Far from having a tendency to lessen competition or to create a monopoly, the merger appears to be the only feasible way in which in the near future necessary substantial additional capacity for the production of steel products in the Mid-Continent Area can be made available *as a new competitive force in the hands of a steel producer other than the existing strongly entrenched companies already dominant in that Area.*

The steel industry today has only one nation-wide steel company—U.S. Steel—which is larger than the next three companies combined, which has important steel production and finishing facilities in all parts of the country and which is in a position to exert strong competitive force in every market area. The merger will result in another company capable of waging effective competition in many of the markets of U.S. Steel, to the benefit of suppliers, customers and the public alike.

The merger will result in salutary strengthening of the forces of competition in the steel industry, and do so without impairing, or even tending to impair, the vigor of competition in any market area and without tending to create a monopoly.

The Companies' Case for the Merger: (b) The Affidavit of George McCuskey, Vice President for Finance, Youngstown Steel

Youngstown desires to consummate the merger with Bethlehem for sound business reasons which are in the public interest and are the complete antithesis of any anticompetitive or monopolistic purpose, objective or result.

[*Geographic Expansion.*] In the first place, the consummation of the merger would enable stockholders of Youngstown to participate in the geographic markets located in the Eastern and Western Areas and also to obtain the benefits of the broad diversification of products now enjoyed by Bethlehem. Bethlehem produces some 35 classes of steel products which Youngstown does not produce.

. . . The complementary aspects of the locations of the Youngstown plants in the Mid-Continent Area and the Bethlehem plants in the Eastern and Western Areas (as well as the locations of their respective geographic areas of effective competition) and of their respective product lines, are unique in the entire steel industry. No two other major steel companies complement each other so completely.

Unless the proposed merger is carried out, Youngstown will not be able to compete effectively in the Eastern and Western Areas without the construction of new basic integrated steel facilities at new locations in those Areas. It is estimated that the cost of constructing such facilities would be approximately $300 per ton of ingot capacity. These facilities would have to compete with existing steel plants which were constructed at a much lower relative cost. It is clear that, under the steel price structure now prevailing and foreseeable, the broadening of the geographic areas in which Youngstown can effectively compete, by the construction of new basic steel plants in new locations, would be unprofitable for many years. It is also clear that the construction of such plants is beyond Youngstown's ability to finance.

Youngstown's other major interest in the merger is that it will provide the greatly increased financial resources necessary to permit the full and prompt development of Youngstown's strategically located properties in the Mid-Continent Area.

[*Diversification Sought, Particularly into Heavy Structurals.*]   For many years Youngstown's management has recognized that it would be desirable and beneficial to increase Youngstown's capacity substantially so as to meet deficits in the local supply of various products in the respective natural markets of Youngstown's Chicago and Ohio plants. Not only would this increased capacity, as such, be of obvious public benefit, but the diversification of products contemplated would have many advantages. Diversification of the product line of a steel plant, such as the Youngstown plant at Chicago or in Ohio, substantially increases (1) the efficiency and economy of plant operation, (2) the stability of plant earnings and employment and (3) the ability of the plant to serve consumers. A broadening of the product line of a steel plant makes it possible more fully and continuously to utilize its steel making or ingot capacity by increasing its production of some, and decreasing its production of other, finished products as the relative volume of the requirements of consumers from time to time shifts among the various finished steel products. . . .

Indicative of this fact, Youngstown's Chicago plant operated at a rate of only 83.0% of capacity during the first six months of 1957, whereas its neighbor, Inland Steel Company, was able to operate at 102.5% of capacity due primarily to its facilities for the manufacture of heavy plates, structurals, and other items in short supply. For the same reasons the Lackawanna and Sparrows Point plants of Bethlehem were able to operate at 97.6% and 102.8% of capacity, respectively, during the same period.

Nothwithstanding temporary periods of adequate supply, the demand for important steel products in the home market of Youngstown's Chicago plant has in many years substantially exceeded the capacity of the plants located in the Chicago area. It is estimated that in the next 15 or 20 years the largest growth in the demand for steel products in the United States will be in the Mid-Continent Area and particularly in the Chicago region. This growth will be greatly accelerated and increased by the opening of the St. Lawrence Seaway. . . .

Heavy structural shapes and plates, which Youngstown does not and cannot now make, have been and are in especially short supply in the Chicago region. In that region these products are made by only two large producers—U.S. Steel and Inland Steel—and U.S. Steel alone produces a complete range of sizes. . . .

[*Youngstown's Limited Ability for Financing.*]   To enlarge the facilities of

Youngstown's Chicago and Ohio plants so as to provide the needed increase in capacities and diversification of product lines will require very large capital expenditures. Recent studies indicate that the cost of expanding Youngstown's present facilities to the extent necessary to provide such product diversification and increased capacities would be approximately $350 million.

At the present time Youngstown has a net worth of approximately $400 million. Its present funded debt totals $98 million, in addition to which it has an indirect obligation with respect to 35% of the $308 million funded debt of Erie Mining Company incurred to finance the development of a tremendous taconite project in Minnesota. Even though Youngstown has maintained a strong financial position, it would be manifestly impossible for it alone to secure the necessary financing for a project of the magnitude to be undertaken if the merger is consummated. . . .

[*Contributions to National Defense and Efficiency.*]   In my opinion the proposed merger will also result in a substantial increase in the capacity of this country to carry on our national program. Bethlehem has had considerable experience over a period of years in providing our Government with different lines of necessary defense materials and products. This know-how, coupled with the existing and expanded production facilities of Youngstown, will constitute a combination of experience, manpower and plant which will greatly enhance the capabilities of this country to produce materials necessary either for national defense or war.

Another substantial, although less important, result of the proposed merger will be to effect savings in operating costs and to promote efficiency. For example, the merger will eliminate or reduce cross-hauling of iron ore by making it possible to divert Bethlehem's ore production at the head of the Great Lakes to the Youngstown plants in the Mid-Continent Area and to divert Youngstown's ore production in Labrador and Quebec to Bethlehem's plants in the Eastern Area.

[*The Effect of the Merger in Increasing Competition and Serving the Public Interest.*]   Contrary to Plaintiff's claims, the merger will increase competition and guard against monopoly in the steel industry and will promote the interests of the public and of the companies involved, in the following ways:

First: The merger will make economically feasible the diversification of the product lines and the increase of the capacities of the Chicago and Ohio plants of Youngstown through expansion of their respective facilities, as shown above. The immediate program for expansion of Youngstown's plants upon consummation of the merger is designed to relieve at least in part the present and prospective undersupply of important steel products in the respective home territories of those plants. . . .

Second: In the Chicago region, heavy structural shapes and plates are made by only two producers, of which only one produces a complete range of sizes. Their combined capacities do not nearly meet the local demand for such products. The merger will provide additional effective competition in those products in the Chicago region and is the most feasible means by which a new competitor can enter this market in the near future.

Third: The program for expansion of facilities at the Chicago and Ohio plants of Youngstown which is projected upon consummation of the merger, will provide permanent employment for a large number of persons. . . .

Fourth: Consummation of the merger will not result in the closing of any plant or in curtailing the capacity or production of any plant. . . .

Fifth: Consummation of the merger will enable Youngstown stockholders to share in important markets in the Eastern and Western Areas (in which Youngstown plants cannot effectively compete) and in the benefits of much wider product diversification. It will enable Bethlehem stockholders to share in important markets in the Mid-Continent Area (in which Bethlehem plants cannot effectively compete) and in the benefits of a somewhat broader diversification of products.

The merger will also strengthen the national defense capabilities of this country and will make possible saving in operating costs, illustrated by elimination or reduction of cross-hauling of iron ore. . . .

The Government's Case

The government's brief was a simple one. It had to show that "in any line of commerce" and "in any section of the country" the merger "may substantially lessen competition" or "tend to monopoly." The amended Clayton Act made it clear that the phrase "in any line of commerce" applied to the lessening of competition rather than only to the phrase "tend to monopoly" as in the original act.

Market Share of Shipments of Common Products. The government concentrated on market shares in terms of common finished steel product shipments. It contended that "market shares are the ultimate results of all competitive forces" and that "actual shipments are more significant than plant locations inasmuch as sales achieved represent an ability to overcome 'natural barriers.' "

Since Bethlehem's and Youngstown's production were primarily of common products, although Bethlehem was in heavy structurals and Youngstown was not, and Youngstown emphasized pipe more than Bethlehem, and since both companies shipped to several common areas (this overlap was largely due to Bethlehem's Lackawanna plant at Buffalo and Youngstown's mills at Youngstown), the government was able to present the data shown in Exhibit 2. Figures are percentages of industry total for products produced by both companies.

The government then went on to present evidence that for particular product categories, such as cold-rolled sheets, both Bethlehem and Youngstown were shipping substantial amounts to common customers in common county locations. The government concluded that 7 per cent of Bethlehem's sales of all finished steel products and about 8 per cent of Youngstown's were of the same products to the same customers in the same states (these percentages take in only the shipments to Michigan and Ohio of sheets and bars, although the denominators are all United States shipments of the respective companies).

The basic government case, then, was simply that if a firm buys out another firm which is making a substantial proportion of its shipments in the same products to the same customers in the same places, it follows that the probability of substantial lessening of competition has been established within the meaning of the Clayton Act. The buyer has one less independent source of supply competing for his trade.

Exhibit 2

	Bethlehem	Youngstown	B-Y
United States	15	5	20
Northeastern states (plus Chicago)	15	5	20
Northeastern states (including Michigan and Ohio)	20–21	3–4	20–25
Michigan, Ohio, Pennsylvania, New York	16–17	4	20–22
Michigan–Ohio	7–9	6	13–15
Michigan	12	3	15
Ohio	5	9–10	15

Other Government Arguments. The Antitrust Division supplemented this basic argument based on market shares and numbers with several other points. It pointed out vertical dangers of the merger in such products as wire rope. Bethlehem was integrated to produce and sell wire rope, Youngstown produced rope wire for sale to nonintegrated rope companies and bought wire rope for sale from such companies. The merger could wipe out an independent source of supply for them. It stressed the fact that Bethlehem and always maintained or increased its market share after previous mergers, so that the increase in concentration could be expected to be permanent. No new entrant of Youngstown's size could reasonably be expected in the steel industry.

Antitrust emphasized the irrelevance of the defendants' expansion plans. They might change them unless the court sat in as "an administrative supervisor of the projected expansion," a procedure "foreign to legislative intent." An inquiry into the motives for the merger would mean "no limit to the number of interesting and highly speculative lines of inquiry" which conceivably belong in a Sherman Act proceeding but have no place in a Clayton Act case if the act is to have any meaning. "Finally, insofar as heavy structurals are concerned, why should Youngstown be sacrificed as an important independent competitor in light steel products for the purpose of further entrenching the duopoly of Bethlehem and U.S. Steel in heavy structurals that now exists in the United States (the two had over 75 per cent of structural capacity)?"

The Rebuttal of the Companies

Bethlehem and Youngstown sought to combat the government's case not only by stressing the possibilities of meeting U.S. Steel more effectively in Chicago but by suggesting that the government's use of market shares and regional breakdowns exaggerated any negative effects on competition. Their case concentrated on plant locations in three broad regions, the Eastern (15 Atlantic seaboard states), the Mid-Continent, and the Western (seven Far Western states). Bethlehem operated only in the Eastern and Western; Youngstown only in the Mid-Continent, which included Michigan and Ohio. They argued that mills were effective competitors only near the plant because of the high ratios of transportation cost. "In their own territories, the mills set the standards (including price) which distant producers must meet; in serving distant territories, on the other hand . . . to a much greater extent, they merely supply deficiencies in production in those territories rather than fix or influence the setting of standards of competitive performance."[44] The Pittsburgh producing center, with its excess of capacity over local demand, was held to ward off the Eastern and Mid-Continent producers from effective competition with each other.

While the Pittsburgh barrier was not much of a factor for the Lackawanna plant at Buffalo, Lackawanna's advantage was held to be in the Detroit area, while the mills at Youngstown competed effectively in western Michigan.

In dealing with the government's shipment data, the companies emphasized the large shares of other companies in Michigan and Ohio, used years other than 1955, when the overlap in sales had been somewhat higher than usual because of the booming automobile demand, and stressed the Mid-Continent area rather than the government's choice of the Northeastern states. Their conclusion was that "the merger will not materially reduce effective alternative sources of supply" because of a "sufficient number of other producers in a strong competitive position."

---

[44]This quotation and much of the argument of this section is from the affidavit of C. H. H. Wikel, September 16, 1957 (Civil Action 115–328 before U.S. District Court, Southern District of New York).

United States v. Bethlehem Steel Corporation and Youngstown Sheet Tube Company[45]

To sum up the court's conclusions as to the impact of the merger, it is clear that the acquisition of Youngstown, by Bethlehem, would violate Section 7 in that in each of the relevant markets considered the effect may be substantially to lessen competition or to tend to create a monopoly.

[*Substantial Competition Eliminated.*] The proposed merger would eliminate the present substantial competition between Bethlehem and Youngstown in substantial relevant markets. If would eliminate substantial potential competition between them. It would eliminate a substantial independent alternative source of supply for all steel consumers. It would eliminate Youngstown as a vital source of supply for independent fabricators who are in competition with Bethlehem in the sale of certain fabricated steel products. It would eliminate Youngstown as a substantial buyer of certain fabricated steel products.

[*The Argument as to Beneficial Aspects of the Merger.*] One final matter remains to be considered. The defendants urge earnestly that in considering the impact on competition of the proposed merger the court take into account what they point to as its beneficial aspects. Any lessening of competition resulting from the merger should be balanced, they say, against the benefits which would accrue from Bethlehem's plants thus creating new steel capacity in an existing deficit area and enhancing the power of the merged company to give United States Steel more effective and vigorous competition than Bethlehem and Youngstown can now give separately.

We pass for the moment the question of whether or not this contention is anything more than an expression of good intention and high purpose.

[*The Shortage of Steel in Chicago Area.*] The substance of their argument is: the steel mills in and around the Chicago area lack sufficient plant capacity to satisfy demand in that area, especially for heavy structural shapes and plates; these have been in critical short supply for years and the lag has been supplied by distant steel producers at excessive freight costs and premium prices. The defendants contend that the situation will become more acute in the years ahead and that the shortage has already resulted in new steel-consuming industries locating their plants in other regions of the country—a "kind of chain reaction [which] is a wasteful drag on the country's economic resources." The defendants say a remedy is sorely needed "and that the merger will unquestionably provide that remedy." In essence this summarizes their justification for the merger.

[*The Proposal for Expansion in Chicago.*] What is planned under the proposed merger is an expansion of the ingot capacity of Youngstown's two existing plants, one at Chicago and the other at Youngstown, by 2,588,000 tons, and a new plate mill and a new structural shape mill at Youngstown's Chicago plant with combined capacity of 1,176,000 tons. The plan also provides for a modernization program which would increase capacity to roll certain products

---

[45]U.S. District Court, Southern District of New York, Civil Action No. 115-328, reproduced as the conclusion of Judge Weinfeld's opinion enjoining the proposed merger of the two companies. Opinion delivered on November 21, 1958.

at the Chicago and Youngstown plants. This part of the plan is unrelated to the structural shape and plate program.

It is undoubtedly easier and cheaper to acquire and develop existing plant capacity than to build entirely anew. Each defendant in urging the merger takes a dim view of its ability to undertake, on its own, a program to meet the existing and anticipated demand for heavy structural shapes and plates in the Chicago area.

Youngstown claims it is without the know-how, the experienced personnel or the requisite capital to enter into the structural shape and plate business. Bethlehem, acknowledging it has the know-how and the experience in that field, contends that the construction of an entirely new fully integrated plant in the Chicago area of 2,500,000 tons of ingot capacity is not economically feasible. It estimates that such a new plant would cost $750,000,000 (or $300 per ton of ingot capacity) as compared to $358,000,000 (or $135 per ton ingot capacity) for expansion of Youngstown's existing plants under the plan outlined above. Bethlehem also rules out as uneconomical the construction of a new plant in the Chicago area limited to structural shape and plate mills.

The defendants' apprehensions, which, of course, involve matters of business judgment and, in a sense, matters of preference, are not persuasive in the light of their prior activities and history, their financial resources, their growth and demonstrated capacity through the years to meet the challenge of a constantly growing economy.

[*The Expansion Record of Bethlehem.*]   Over the decades Bethlehem has grown internally; it has not only maintained but bettered its position in a highly concentrated industry; it has never lacked the financial resources or the effective means required to expand and keep pace with the increased demands of our national economy.

From an ingot capacity of 212,800 tons in 1905 Bethlehem's capacity reached 23,000,000 by January 1, 1958. During the nine-year period from January 1, 1948, to January 1, 1957, it expanded its ingot capacity from 13,800,000 tons to 20,500,000 tons, an increase of 6,700,000 tons or 48.6 per cent. Over the five-year period from 1953 to 1958 the percentage increase was 30.7 per cent.

The fact is that within one year of the commencement of this action to enjoin the merger, Bethlehem increased its steel capacity by 2,500,000 tons. The significance of this increase is apparent when it is noted that as of January 1, 1957, there were in the United States eighty-four companies with steel ingot capacity, of which seventy-five had a total capacity of less than 2,500,000 tons.

[*The Expansion Record of Youngstown.*]   Youngstown no less than Bethlehem has demonstrated ability to keep pace with the demands of our growing economy. Youngstown expanded from an ingot capacity of 806,400 tons in 1906 to 6,500,000 tons by January 1, 1958. During the nine-year period from January 1, 1948, to January 1, 1957, it expanded its ingot capacity from 4,002,000 tons to 6,240,000—an increase of 2,238,000 or 55.9 per cent. Over the five-year period from 1953 to 1958 its ingot capacity grew 31.4 per cent.

Youngstown, too, has been a vigorous factor in the steel industry. Its position as No. 6 casts it in the role of one of the giants of that mammoth industry. Through the years it has carried on a regular expansion program. In 1955, without regard to the merger, it projected a comprehensive future development plan, part of which has already been put into effect. During the 10-year period, 1947–56, Youngstown made capital expenditures of $530,000,000.

[*Youngstown as a Successful Firm.*] A fact not to be overlooked—indeed one to be underscored—is that no adverse factor justifies Youngstown's participation in the proposed merger. Indeed for a number of years the return on its invested capital was greater than that earned by either United States Steel or Bethlehem. No financial stringency, present or threatened, justifies its absorption by Bethlehem.

[*Alternatives for Meeting Chicago Demand.*] The Court is not persuaded that the proposed merger is the only way in which the supply of plates and shapes in the Chicago area can be expanded. Other steel producers are capable of meeting the challenge. In fact both United States Steel and Inland are in the process of expanding their capacities in the Chicago area for structural shapes and United States Steel is also expanding its capacity for plates in that area.

[*The Failure of the Defendants' Argument.*] In essence, the defendants are maintaining that a proposed capacity increase of 1,176,000 tons in the Chicago area for plates and structural shapes counterbalances a merger between companies which produced over 24,000,000 tons of ingots and shipped almost 15,000,-000 tons of a great variety of finished steel products in 1955. It has already been noted that hot rolled sheets, cold rolled sheets and hot rolled bars are the three most important products of the iron and steel industry and that Bethlehem and Youngstown are substantial and important factors in the production of these key products.

Plates and structural shapes are substantially less important in terms of tonnage than hot and cold rolled sheets and hot rolled bars. Assuming the relevance of the argument, the defendants have failed to establish counterbalancing benefits to offset the substantial lessening of competition which would result from the merger.

Not only do the facts fail to support the defendants' contention, but the argument does not hold up as a matter of law. If the merger offends the statute in any relevant market then good motives and even demonstrable benefits are irrelevant and afford no defense. Section 7 "is violated whether or not actual restraints or monopolies, or the substantial lessening of competition, have occurred or are intended."

[*The Objectives and Application of the Clayton Act.*] The antitrust laws articulate the policy formulated by Congress. The significance and objectives of the Clayton Act and the 1950 amendment are well documented. In approving the policy embodied in these acts, Congress rejected the alleged advantages of size in favor of the preservation of a competitive system. The consideration to be accorded to benefits of one kind or another in one section or another of the country which may flow from a merger involving a substantial lessening of competition is a matter properly to be urged upon Congress. It is outside the province of the Court. The simple test under Section 7 is whether or not the merger may substantially lessen competition "in any line of commerce in any section of the country."

Any alleged benefit to the steel consumer in the Chicago district because of reduced freight charges and an increased supply cannot, under the law, be bought at the expense of other consumers of numerous other steel products where the effects of the merger violate the act. A merger may have a different impact in different markets—but if the prescribed effect is visited on one or more relevant markets then it matters not what the claimed benefits may be elsewhere.

And for that matter, with respect to oil field equipment and supplies, as separate lines of commerce, the contention itself is by its own terms unavailing. Amended Section 7 as stated in the committee reports ". . . is intended [to prohibit] acquisitions which substantially lessen competition, as well as those which tend to create a monopoly . . . if they have the specified effect in any line of commerce, whether or not that line of commerce is a large part of the business of any of the corporations involved in the acquisition. . . . The purpose of the bill is to protect competition in each line of commerce in each section of the country."

[*Dangers of Chain Reaction.*]   The merger offers an incipient threat of setting into motion a chain of reaction of further mergers by the other but less powerful companies in the steel industry. If there is logic to the defendants' contention that their joinder is justified to enable them, in their own language, to offer "challenging competition to United States Steel . . . which exercises dominant influence over competitive conditions in the steel industry . . ." then the remaining large producers in the "Big Twelve" could with equal logic urge that they, too, be permitted to join forces and to concentrate their economic resources in order to give more effective competition to the enhanced "Big Two"; and so we reach a point of more intense concentration in an industry already highly concentrated—indeed we head in the direction of triopoly.

[*Congressional Purpose—No Distinction between Good Mergers and Bad Mergers.*]   Congress in seeking to halt the growing tendency to increased concentration of power in various industries was fully aware of the arguments in support of the supposed advantages of size and the claim of greater efficiency and lower cost to the ultimate consumer. It made no distinction between good mergers and bad mergers. It condemned all which came within the reach of the prohibition of Section 7. The function of the Court is to carry out declared Congressional policy. "Though our preference were for monopoly and against competition, we should 'guard against the danger of sliding unconsciously from the narrow confines of law into the more spacious domain of policy.'" The Court must take the statute as written.

The proposed merger runs afoul of the prohibition of the statute in so many directions that to permit it, is to render Section 7 sterile. To say that the elimination of Youngstown would not result in "a significant reduction in the vigor of competition" in the steel industry is, in the light of its history, to disregard experience.

[*Lines of Commerce with Reasonable Probability of Substantially Lessened Competition.*]   The Court concludes that there is a reasonable probability that the merger of Bethlehem and Youngstown would, in violation of Section 7, substantially lessen competition and tend to create a monopoly in:

(1) the iron and steel industry,

(2) hot rolled sheets,

(3) cold rolled sheets and
(4) hot rolled bars, in
    (*a*) the United States as a whole,
    (*b*) the northeast quadrant of the United States,
    (*c*) Michigan, Ohio, Pennsylvania and New York,
    (*d*) Michigan and Ohio,
    (*e*) Michigan, and
    (*f*) Ohio,
(5) buttweld pipe,
(6) electricweld pipe,
(7) seamless pipe,
(8) oil field equipment,
(9) oil field equipment and supplies,
(10) tin plate,
(11) track spikes, and
(12) wire rope.

[*Court Instructions.*] Submit decree within ten days, in accordance with the foregoing and the further enumerated findings of fact and conclusions of law filed herewith, enjoining the proposed merger as violative of Section 7 of the Clayton Act.

Shortly afterwards the companies announced that there would be no appeal and that the merger proposal had been dropped.

Addendum

Despite reduced profits from 1958 through 1961 as shown in Exhibit 3, the Bethlehem Steel Corporation did not abandon its goal of a location in the important midwestern market. In December, 1962, it formally announced plans to spend $250 million over three years in building a steel-rolling and -finishing plant at Burns Harbor, Indiana. Its capacity was announced as 592,000 tons of plate a year, 284,000 tons of tin plate, 720,000 tons of cold-rolled sheet, and 354,000 tons of hot-rolled sheet.

This finishing plant, which would first utilize raw steel from other Bethlehem plants, was contemplated as the first stage of an integrated plant that would produce raw steel.

Arthur B. Homer, Chairman of the Board of Bethlehem, stated that "all indications are that the Midwest market is going to be growing in the future at a more rapid rate than at the present" and also that "in the last four or five years, we've shipped very little into the Midwest." The company estimated that the Midwest constituted almost one third of the total steel industry market but accounted for nearly 50 per cent of the plate, 75 per cent of the cold-rolled sheets (used extensively in automobiles), and about 40 per cent of the tin plate used in tin cans.[46]

Exhibit 3

BILLINGS, ASSETS, AND INCOME OF BETHLEHEM STEEL CORPORATION
AND YOUNGSTOWN SHEET & TUBE COMPANY, 1951–61
(Millions of Dollars)

Year	Net Billings	Net Assets	Net Worth	Net Income after Taxes	Net Income/ Net Worth
BETHLEHEM STEEL CORPORATION					
1951	$1,793.1	$1,541.7	$ 919.1	$106.5	12.19%
1952	1,691.7	1,610.1	966.8	90.9	9.88
1953	2,082.0	1,783.0	1,017.9	133.9	13.28
1954	1,656.8	1,613.4	1,133.5	132.8	12.30
1955	2,096.6	1,998.7	1,243.8	180.2	15.19
1956	2,326.7	2,090.0	1,389.6	161.4	12.14
1957	2,603.7	2,260.3	1,616.7	191.0	11.81
1958	2,005.9	2,195.0	1,656.6	137.7	8.47
1959	2,055.7	2,269.4	1,672.3	117.2	7.14
1960	2,178.1	2,275.0	1,679.2	121.2	7.35
1961	2,033.9	2,302.9	1,686.7	124.5	7.39
YOUNGSTOWN SHEET & TUBE COMPANY					
1951	$483.7	$439.1	$303.8	$30.6	10.43%
1952	434.2	479.2	317.4	22.9	7.47
1953	548.1	514.0	336.0	30.8	9.49
1954	428.2	500.5	343.4	20.2	6.06
1955	617.4	573.5	375.8	41.7	11.49
1956	676.3	620.6	416.2	43.2	10.80
1957	679.9	636.0	449.3	42.5	9.74
1958	499.6	660.2	464.7	21.5	4.87
1959	608.1	715.9	485.9	31.0	6.79
1960	574.2	755.3	501.5	25.7	5.53
1961	545.8	765.4	516.3	24.7	4.77

Source: *Moody's Industrial Manual.*

QUESTIONS

1. Were there strong business reasons for the Bethlehem-Youngstown merger? What did each company have to gain? Why may the companies have decided not to appeal the decision?

2. What was the government's case? What meaning did it seek for such key phrases of the Clayton Act amendment as "in any line of commerce" and

[46]*Wall Street Journal,* December 4, 1962, and January 10, 1963.

"may substantially lessen competition"? Did it prove that the "net competitive effects" of the merger would be adverse?

3. Why was the government so confident and the companies so modest about the companies' capabilities for expansion in the Chicago area? Does Bethlehem's announcement in late 1962 of expansion tend to support the government's contention?

4. Do you think the decision was or was not in the economic interest of the United States? What criteria would enter into such an assessment?

CASE 16–3:   THE 1956 CONSENT DECREE OF AMERICAN TELEPHONE & TELEGRAPH COMPANY

Introduction

The consent decree (a court order issued without trial with the consent of all parties) has become the method of settling the majority of the recent civil suits brought under the antitrust laws, and several leading firms, including American Can Company and International Business Machines, have agreed to the compulsory licensing of long lists of patents. The American Telephone & Telegraph consent decree of 1956 falls into this category, in which part of the government's contention is that the sheer aggregation of patents in a field of technology adds up to more monopoly power than the individual patents were designed to grant. Both the government and management face interesting decisions in their willingness to accept such decrees. The government must weigh economy and quicker, surer relief against the possibilities of losing an effective precedent for subsequent cases, of failing to develop a record that would provide a basis for private treble-damage suits, and of settling for limited remedies. Management may gain from the avoidance of more severe penalties from public or private litigation, from better public relations, and from a friendlier climate for establishing standards of conduct in the "gray" areas left by the uncertainties in the meaning and application of antitrust laws. These gains must be weighed against the stringency of the remedies it accepts.

The Concentration of Patents and Compulsory Licensing.   Action to monopolize patents through agreement between separate companies has been long considered illegal. The Hartford-Empire case in 1945 was the first that called for compulsory licensing of the patents by decree of the Supreme Court. Even more recently has the undue concentration of patents by one firm in an industry been found illegal. The government charged the United Shoe Machinery Company, in a case decided in 1953, with being "engaged in a program of engrossing all patents and inventions of importance relating to shoe machinery for the purpose of blanketing the shoe machinery industry with patents under the control of United and thereby suppressing competition in the industry." It was required to grant patents at reasonable royalties.

Several consent decrees have been concluded since the war with leading firms in various industries with compulsory licensing provisions. The typical decree has required royalty-free licensing of past patents and licensing at a reasonable royalty of future patents. The trend has been toward provisions that require the furnishing of the necessary know-how as well, through manuals, drawings, and technical personnel.

The Complaint. The consent decree signed in *United States* v. *Western Electric & A. T. & T.* (1956) involved 8,600 patents of the Bell System. The original complaint, issued in 1949, had charged violations of Sections 1 and 2 of the Sherman Act. Among other specific charges, it maintained that Western Electric had monopolized the production of telephonic apparatus and equipment "by acquiring substantially all basic patents in the field of wire telephony." The Justice Department sought the remedy of dissolution of Western Electric into three companies, to be followed by competitive bidding in the purchase of telephonic equipment. One effect of such dissolution might be to alleviate a regulatory problem brought out in the FCC investigation. Western Electric had been alleged to manufacture about 90 per cent of the telephonic equipment in the FCC report. The FCC had concluded that excessive charges made by Western Electric for equipment entered into the operating expenses and property valuations of the regional telephone companies. Rates were then set that yielded somewhat more than a fair return.[47]

Provisions of the Consent Decree[48]

IV. *A.* The defendants are each enjoined . . . from commencing and after three years . . . continuing . . . to manufacture . . . any equipment which is of a type not sold or leased or intended to be sold or leased to companies of the Bell System. . . .

V. The defendant A. T. & T. is enjoined . . . from engaging . . . in any business other than furnishing common carrier communications service . . . [except where made for government contracts, experiments on new communication devices]. . . .

---

[47]Federal Communications Commission, *Investigation of the Telephone Industry in the United States,* House Document 340 (Washington, D.C.: U.S. Government Printing Office, 1939), particularly chap. xviii.

[48]*United States* v. *Western Electric and A. T. & T.* (U.S. District Court for New Jersey, January 25, 1956).

IX. Western is ordered . . . to maintain cost accounting methods . . . that affords a valid basis . . . for determining the cost to Western of equipment sold to A. T. & T. and Bell operating companies. . . .

X. The defendants are each ordered . . . to grant . . . to any applicant . . . nonexclusive licenses under . . . all existing and future Bell System patents. . . . Such licenses . . . shall be royalty free under all patents prior to date of the Final Judgment [about 8,000 patents were involved] and to be at reasonable royalties to persons under all other existing and future Bell System patents [but on the condition that such persons will grant licenses to defendants on all patents over which they have control at reasonable royalties]. . . .

XIV. The defendants are each ordered . . . to furnish . . . technical information [relating to use of patents]. . . .

What the Antitrust Suit Consent Decree Means[49]

These questions and answers were prepared as being of interest to the Bell System managers.

1. *What was the government's reason for starting the Antitrust Suit?* When the Federal Government in January 1949 filed its Civil Antitrust Suit under the Sherman Act against AT&T and Western Electric, it alleged that the two companies have unreasonably restrained and monopolized commerce in telephone equipment and supplies.

   The complaint asked that AT&T sell Western and that Western be broken up into three separate companies, that the Bell Companies be restricted to buying their equipment and supplies by competitive bidding, that working relationships between AT&T and the associated companies provided under the license contract be discontinued, that it be made compulsory for AT&T, Western and the Labs to license all patents to all applicants on a nondiscriminatory basis, and that they be required to furnish technical information to licensees under such patents.

2. *What was our answer to this complaint?* AT&T and Western filed an answer asking that the complaint be dismissed. The companies stated that they believe the charges are without foundation. Furthermore, the companies pointed out, the existing relationships and arrangements between the associated companies have been and are of the highest value to the users of the telephone service and to the public generally. We maintained at that time—and we still maintain—that we have done nothing illegal. Entry of this decree does not constitute any evidence or admission to the allegations in the complaint.

3. *What developed after this complaint was filed and we answered it?* This case never actually came to trial. Since 1949 the Bell System has furnished the Justice Department with thousands of pages of documents and exhibits. Discussions over an extended period of time among rep-

[49]*Management Topics No. 6*, public relations brochure of Northern California area of Pacific Telephone, February 6, 1956 (San Francisco). Some deletions and rearrangements have been made.

resentatives of AT&T, Western and the Federal Government resulted in the consent decree, or final judgment, of January 24, 1956.

4. *Does this decree settle this antitrust matter once and for all?* Yes. In the absence of changed conditions, the issues from the point of view of both the Government and the Bell System are settled.

5. *What effect does the decree have on the organization of the Bell System?* The decree does not affect the general relationship among AT&T, Western Electric, Bell Telephone Laboratories and the associated companies that has been successfully serving the communications needs of our nation and the National Defense for almost 80 years.

   The decree does confine the activities of the System to common carrier communications services. This means those services which are subject to public regulation, with certain specified exceptions.

6. *Does the decree affect our relationships with the Bell Telephone Laboratories or limit in any way the research activities of the Bell Labs?* No, it has no effect at all on our relationships with the Labs—and does not in any way curtail the Labs' activities.

7. *Can Western Electric continue to work on defense jobs, such as NIKE, SAGE, the DEW Line, etc.?* Yes, the decree specifically excludes from the regulation requirement any and all services performed by any unit of the Bell System for the U.S. government and its agencies.

8. *Will the decree adversely affect Bell System revenues?* Revenue losses will not be great in relation to total revenues.

9. *What does the decree specify on Bell System patents?* The decree specifies that W. E. and AT&T are to license all their present and future U.S. patents to all applicants, "with no limit as to time or the use to which they may be put." This makes mandatory our present licensing policy.

   United States patents issued prior to January 24, 1956—and there are about 8,600 of them—are in almost all cases to be licensed royalty-free to all applicants. Any patents issued subsequent to January 24, 1956, are to be licensed to any applicant at reasonable royalties.

10. *Can the Bell System continue to obtain needed licenses under the patents of others?* Yes, applicants for licenses under Bell System patents can be required to grant to the Bell System any licenses the latter wants for use in its common carrier communications business, subject to reasonable royalties.

11. *What important patents are covered by the royalty-free provisions?* A number of basic patents including patents covering such items as transistors, microwave systems, vacuum tubes, carrier systems, coaxial cables and special tubes used in electronic "brains."

12. *What does the decree say about making "technical information" available?* It states that W. E. and AT&T must, in addition to patents, make available to their licensees at reasonable cost certain technical information associated with patents that have been licensed. This information includes Western's manufacturing drawings and specifications relating to equipment that it makes for the Bell System.

13. *How does Bell System management feel about this final judgment?* In commenting on the decree, C. F. Craig, President of the American Telephone and Telegraph Company, said:

"During the seven years since this suit was brought, the Bell System has furnished the Government with extensive information. While the terms of this decree are stringent they do recognize the position we have held from the beginning that supervision by Federal and State regulatory bodies safeguards the public interest.

"We believe the long-standing relationships among the manufacturing, research and operating functions of the Bell System are in the public interest and under the decree they remain intact.

"To a very large extent, it is the unique combination and teamwork of the operating companies, the Bell Telephone Laboratories and the Western Electric Company that, over the years, has produced for the people of this country the finest, most widely used and progressive telephone service in the world."

QUESTIONS

1. From the admittedly limited presentation available, why were the managements of A. T. & T. and Western Electric willing to accept a consent decree?

2. Has the government a legitimate objection to the mere aggregation of many legal patents by one firm?

Index

Index of Cases

This book has been set on the Linotype in 12 point Garamond Light, leaded 1 point. Chapter numbers are in 18 point Radiant Extra Condensed Bold and chapter titles are in 24 point Radiant Medium. The size of the type page is 27 by 46½ picas.

The paper is 50# Tone-O-Paque.